Early Modern China and Northeast Asia

In this revisionist history of early modern China, Evelyn Rawski challenges the notion of Chinese history as a linear narrative of dynasties dominated by the Central Plains and Han Chinese culture from a unique, peripheral perspective. Rawski argues that China has been shaped by its relations with Japan, Korea, and the Jurchen/Manchu and Mongol States, and must therefore be viewed both within the context of a regional framework, and as part of a global maritime network of trade. Drawing on a rich variety of Japanese, Korean, Manchu, and Chinese archival sources, Rawski analyses the conflicts and regime changes that accompanied the region's integration into the world economy during the sixteenth and seventeenth centuries. *Early Modern China and Northeast Asia* places Sino-Korean and Sino-Japanese relations within the context of Northeast Asian geopolitics, surveying the complex connections which continue to this day.

EVELYN S. RAWSKI is Distinguished University Professor of History at the University of Pittsburgh.

ASIAN CONNECTIONS

Series editors

Sunil Amrith, Birkbeck College, University of London
Tim Harper, University of Cambridge
Engseng Ho, Duke University

Asian Connections is a major series of ambitious works that look beyond the traditional templates of area, regional or national studies to consider the trans-regional phenomena which have connected and influenced various parts of Asia through time. The series will focus on empirically grounded work exploring circulations, connections, convergences and comparisons within and beyond Asia. Themes of particular interest include transport and communication, mercantile networks and trade, migration, religious connections, urban history, environmental history, oceanic history, the spread of language and ideas, and political alliances. The series aims to build new ways of understanding fundamental concepts, such as modernity, pluralism or capitalism, from the experience of Asian societies. It is hoped that this conceptual framework will facilitate connections across fields of knowledge and bridge historical perspectives with contemporary concerns.

Early Modern China and Northeast Asia

and Northeast Asia

Cross-Border Perspectives

Evelyn S. Rawski

University of Pittsburgh

CAMBRIDGE
UNIVERSITY PRESS

University Printing House, Cambridge CB2 8BS, United Kingdom

Cambridge University Press is part of the University of Cambridge.

It furthers the University's mission by disseminating knowledge in the pursuit of education, learning and research at the highest international levels of excellence.

www.cambridge.org
Information on this title: www.cambridge.org/9781107471528

© Evelyn S. Rawski 2015

First published 2015

Printed in the United States of America by Sheridan Books, Inc.

A catalogue record for this publication is available from the British Library

ISBN 978-1-107-09308-9 Hardback
ISBN 978-1-107-47152-8 Paperback

Contents

Maps and tables

Maps

Tables

Acknowledgements

The inspiration for this book came from the Reischauer lectures that I delivered at Harvard University in April 1994. In order to pursue my interest in cross-border interactions, I realized I needed to add Korean to my research tools. My study and research in the years that followed were generously supported by research grants and research leave from the Dietrich School of Arts and Sciences and the University Center for International Studies at my home institution, the University of Pittsburgh. The Institute for Advanced Study, Princeton, awarded me a fellowship for four months in 2007, where I benefited from my intellectual exchanges with Nicola Di Cosmo, Lucille Chia, Sue Naquin, and Christopher Atwood, among many others. I spent three weeks working on revising the book manuscript as an "accompanying spouse" at the Rockefeller Institute at Bellagio in August 2013; I am extremely grateful for the hospitality I received there.

Many other scholars and librarians have materially supported my research. I must first express my deep appreciation for the extraordinary support provided by former and current librarians at the East Asia Collection, Hillman Library, University of Pittsburgh. My requests for Japanese-language books, articles, and reference tools elicited immediate responses from Sachie Noguchi and Hiroyuki Good; Zhang Haihui was enormously helpful with bibliographic suggestions and my requests for book acquisitions; and Zou Xiuying patiently helped me out with my requests for Korean-language materials. Thanks, too, to librarians at Harvard-Yenching Library and Princeton's Gest Library who allowed me to explore their wonderful collections. Stephanie Casey prepared the maps that appear in this book, and Hea-jin Kim helped correct my Korean romanization. Most of all, I must thank my husband, Tom Rawski, for acting as a sympathetic soundboard and rigorous critic throughout the process of writing this book.

Note on transcription and other conventions

Citations of English-language materials reproduce titles and authors' names as published. For Asian-language books and articles, I observe the following conventions: the pinyin system of Romanization for Chinese, modified Hepburn system employed by the Library of Congress for Japanese, and McCune-Reischauer romanization system for Korean. Manchu words and names are transcribed according to the Mollendorff system. Chinese, Japanese, and Korean names are transcribed in the traditional order: surname first. Terms rendered in their Chinese, Japanese, Korean, or Manchu forms in the text are marked C, J, K, or M respectively.

Citations from the *Chosŏn wangjo sillok* give the date (presented in terms of reign year, lunar month, and day), and the number of the document in the online database (see Bibliography for web address). Interlinear lunar months are indicated by an italicized "i" preceding the lunar month. The same dating system is used for citations from the *Ming shilu* and *Qing shilu*.

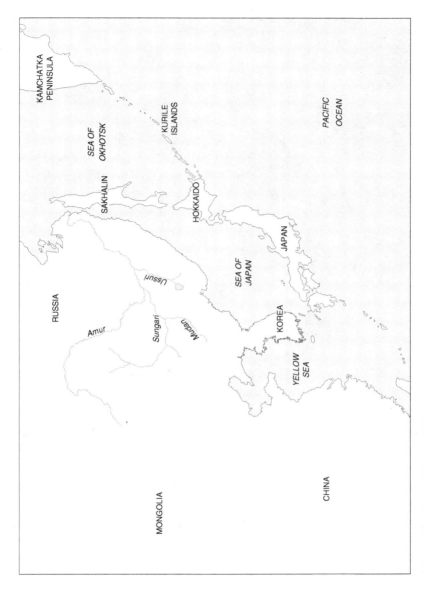

Map 1. Northeast Asia, *c.* 1700

Map 2. Centers of trade in the early modern period

Introduction

This book explores what we might gain by looking at Chinese history from the periphery rather than from the core. The project of "de-centering China" is intended to counter the tradition of conceiving of Chinese history in terms of an unbroken sequence of dynasties, an organizational structure that emphasizes long-term historical continuity at the expense of downplaying the significance of ruling houses and dynastic policies. This book questions the dominant theme in modern historiography, which treats Chinese history as a linear narrative centered on the culture of the Central Plain and its original inhabitants, the Han Chinese.[1] I argue that while what others have described as the "history of the nation" serves the interests of the modern nation-state that is the People's Republic of China (hereafter PRC), its emphasis on China as the history of the Han Chinese creates new problems for the state as it tries to create a tighter bond with its ethnic minorities.

De-centering China

The primary task in de-centering Chinese history is to examine it from the perspective of the periphery, and not the core. There is no lack of evidence from ancient times onward of intensive interactions between frontier and indigenous peoples (presently identified as the "Han Chinese") in the Central Plain (*zhongyuan*), which is widely considered to be the "cradle" or core region of Chinese civilization.[2] Migrants from its northern and

---

[1] See, for example, Ping-ti Ho's *Cradle of the East: An Inquiry into the Indigenous Origins of Techniques and Ideas of Neolithic and Early Historic China, 5000–1000 BC* (Chicago: University of Chicago Press, 1975), and his Chinese-language book, *Huang tu yu Zhongguo nongye de qiyuan* (The yellow earth and the origins of Chinese agriculture) (Kowloon: Chinese University of Hong Kong, 1969). The dominant view of Han identity as a historical concept is presented by Xu Jieshun, "Understanding the Snowball Theory of the Han Nationality," in *Critical Han Studies: The History, Representation, and Identity of China's Majority*, ed. Thomas S. Mullaney, James Leibold, Stéphane Gros, and Eric Vanden Bussche (Berkeley: University of California Press, 2012), pp. 113–27.

[2] For the purposes of discussion, "Central Plain" will also be designated as "China."

1

western frontiers moved into the Central Plain, and their descendants eventually established states that ruled north China from the third to the seventh century. Later, conquest regimes from the northeast occupied first parts then all of north China and, in the thirteenth century, the Mongols successfully conquered the south and incorporated it into their empire. Yet we know relatively little about the peoples who headed the "sixteen barbarian states" who ruled north China in the third to fifth centuries, or the Khitan Liao, Jurchen Jin, and even the Mongol Yuan, because they left few written records, leaving most ordinary people to believe that the militarily superior frontier peoples eventually succumbed to the culturally superior Han Chinese; that is, that Central Plain culture triumphed over the culture of the frontier.

This thesis is rarely subjected to critical scrutiny, with the exception of an essay by Victor Mair. Scrutinizing the states ruling over the Central Plain, Mair declares that "both the institution and the periodic reinstitution of dominant political entities in the territory ... have inordinately been the result of initiatives taken by north(west)ern steppe peoples and agro-pastoralists."[3] Mair proposes that the *locus* or dynamic center of Chinese history was not north-central China (the Central Plain) but the Ordos, "the zone of consummate interface between the settled and the steppe."[4] Recognition of the importance of this interaction has led others to analyze Chinese history in term of its relations with the "Turko-Mongolian" or "Central Eurasian" world.[5]

Victor Lieberman expands on this point. Tracing the long-term political evolution of Eurasian states, Lieberman places China in the "exposed zone," which was vulnerable to Inner Asian invasions and conquests. Inner Asian regimes such as the Sui successfully unified the north and south after the fall of Han, while the Mongols and Manchus reversed political atomization, incorporated China into large empires, and brought Chinese administration to "unprecedented levels of efficiency."[6] For Lieberman, the frequency and intensity of Inner Asian influence is the critical factor that distinguishes China's historical

---

[3] Victor Mair, "The Northwestern Peoples and the Recurrent Origins of the 'Chinese State,'" in *The Teleology of the Modern Nation-State: Japan and China*, ed. Joshua A. Fogel (Philadelphia: University of Pennsylvania Press, 2005), p. 83.

[4] *Ibid.*, p. 81.

[5] Christopher Beckwith, for example, places China on the fringes of his history, *Empires of the Silk Road: A History of Central Eurasia from the Bronze Age to the Present* (Princeton: Princeton University Press, 2009). See also Jonathan Karam Skaff, *Sui-Tang China and Its Turko-Mongol Neighbors: Culture, Power, and Connections, 580–800* (Oxford: Oxford University Press, 2012).

[6] Victor Lieberman, *Strange Parallels: Southeast Asia in Global Context, c. 800–1830* (Cambridge: Cambridge University Press, 2009), vol. II, p. 103.

evolution from the major Eurasian patterns. From the perspective of the sixteenth and seventeenth centuries, the focus of this book, the primary Inner Asian influences come from northeast Asia.

One of the primary obstacles to studying China from the periphery is the paucity of records that are not written in Chinese (and hence from a Chinese perspective). The Chinese possessed what Peter Perdue called the "hegemony of inscriptions."[7] As Endymion Wilkinson has observed, the treatment accorded non-Han peoples in many of the standard dynastic *Histories* was "prejudicial." Terms for these peoples were "written with animal and other significs to underline their bestial nature," and it was assumed that those resisting acculturation needed "further education."[8]

Chinese texts dominate the existing historical record of northeast Asia through the first millennium CE, making it difficult for scholars to directly access the voice of frontier peoples. The scarcity of documents in the language of the conquerors also hampers study of the tenth- to fourteenth-century conquest regimes. Because "few specimens of the Khitan and Jurchen scripts have survived," and the texts written in Tangut and Mongol rarely outlived the empires that commissioned their invention, there are vast gaps in the historical documentation of these empires.[9]

The project of "de-centering China" requires documents. This book makes extensive use of Japanese, Korean, and Manchu-language texts, all of which present non-Chinese perspectives, and draw upon the divergent interpretations presented in the abundant secondary historical literature in Japanese and Korean. De-centering also entails analyzing the cultural engagement of Japanese and Korean elites with ritual and ideological elements originating in China. The term "sinicization" encapsulates the underlying issue. The borrowing of institutions, a system of law, and bureaucratic practices was also historically important in the parts of Europe encompassed by the Roman empire, yet acknowledgment of this historical legacy does not prevent historians from studying European nations as separate entities, each with its distinctive evolutionary path. Japanese and Korean state rituals, succession practices, and discourse distinguishing themselves from their neighbors evolved along separate paths. The same was true of the Manchu Qing.

---

[7] Peter Perdue, "Military Mobilization in Seventeenth- and Eighteenth-Century China, Russia, and Mongolia," *Modern Asian Studies* 30.4 (1996): 782.

[8] Endymion Wilkinson, *Chinese History: A New Manual* (Cambridge, MA: Harvard University Asia Center, 2012), p. 643.

[9] Quotation from Herbert Franke and Denis Twitchett, "Introduction," in *The Cambridge History of China*, vol. VI: *Alien Regimes and Border States, 907–1368*, ed. Herbert Franke and Denis Twitchett (Cambridge: Cambridge University Press, 1994), p. 31.

Japan and Korea as northeast Asia

The dominant consensus separates Korea and Japan from the Manchurian plain that nurtured the Khitan Liao (907–1125), Jurchen Jin (1126–1234) and Qing (1644–1911) dynastic houses that ruled China for over half of the millennium before the Republican Revolution. As part of East Asia, Korea and Japan are usually seen as culturally if not politically subordinate to China, in contrast to the Khitan, Jurchen, and Manchu conquest regimes. "East Asia," a term popularized in the 1960s in the United States by John K. Fairbank and Edwin Reischauer, included China, Japan, Korea, and "to a lesser extent, Vietnam." It was defined, most importantly, by a shared culture and "primary system of writing" derived from "ancient China."[10] The National Defense Education Act (1958), which funded "regional studies" in American universities, institutionalized "East Asia" (defined as China, Japan, and Korea) as a major academic field.[11] Although the concept of "East Asia" has been critiqued for its Sinocentric biases and essentialization of historically fluid relationships, it retains a considerable presence in the scholarly literature.[12] The notion that adopting/adapting Chinese practices and institutions makes the borrower "Sinicized" has come under sustained scholarly attack, but not yet in the PRC. I argue instead that Korea and Japan are better understood by classifying them with the Manchurian states which constituted China's northeast frontier.

From the tenth to fourteenth century, much if not all of the Chinese-speaking world was actually situated at the periphery of empires based not in the Central Plain but in the northeast.[13] Yet virtually all studies of the Khitan, Jurchen Jin, and Mongol empires view them only within a

[10] Edwin O. Reischauer and John K. Fairbank, *East Asia: The Great Tradition* (Boston: Houghton Mifflin Company, 1960), p. 3.

[11] See the discussion of the historical antecedents in Martin W. Lewis and Kären E. Wigen, *The Myth of Continents: A Critique of Metageography* (Berkeley: University of California Press, 1997), pp. 124–25, 128–29, 132–33, and on the federal funding of the field, pp. 166–67. US government funding of secondary education focusing on strategically important languages has caused the teaching and research on Vietnam to be shifted from "East Asia" to "Southeast Asia."

[12] Recent examples of works include Charles Holcombe, *The Genesis of East Asia, 221 BC–AD 907* (Honolulu: University of Hawai'i Press, 2001), and David C. Kang, *East Asia Before the West: Five Centuries of Trade and Tribute* (New York: Columbia University Press, 2010).

[13] Kiyohiko Sugiyama, "The Qing Empire in the Central Eurasian Context: Its Structure of Rule as Seen from the Eight Banner System," in *Comparative Imperiology*, ed. Kimitaka Matsuzato (Sapporo: Slavic Research Center, Hokkaido University, 2009), pp. 87–108, argues in favor of calling Qing a "Central Eurasian state." For maps of the Liao, Jin, and Mongol empires, see Maps 7, 17, and 50, pp. 118–19, 236–37, and 425 in *The Cambridge History of China*, vol. VI.

Chinese framework.[14] One exception to this observation is David M. Robinson's study of the fourteenth-century Korean Koryŏ kingdom during the last days of the Mongol empire, when the Korean peninsula was subjected to Mongol overlordship.[15] Robinson focuses on a major event, the Red Turban movement, which disrupted law and order beyond north China and spread into the northeast. Robinson also underlines the degree to which Mongol–Koryŏ relations – which included significant inter-marriage between the ruling houses – epitomized the Mongol success in incorporating the elites of different subject peoples.[16] Here and elsewhere, the Mongol achievement in unifying the steppe and sown regions introduced "a matrix of political, economic, military, cultural, technological and ethnic connections that differed qualitatively from earlier periods."[17] Mongol policies were a harbinger of developments under the Qing.

Robinson's monograph depicts a region with multiple state players. His statement that "In Northeast Asia, Jurchen, Mongol, Chinese, Korean, and Japanese interests intersected (and would continue to intersect until the last days of imperial East Asia)" is the starting point for my research on a period several centuries after the fall of the Yuan empire. This multi-state framework demands analysis of materials produced by the different state actors. Kenneth M. Swope's thought-provoking survey of the Japanese, Korean, and Chinese accounts of the events following Toyotomi Hideyoshi's 1592 invasion of Korea nicely illustrates the benefit of taking this point seriously. Swope uses these different records to illuminate many aspects of Chinese, Japanese, and Korean interaction that would otherwise remain hidden from view, such as the autonomy enjoyed by the Chinese and Japanese negotiators, whose misrepresentations to their superiors brought on a diplomatic debacle in 1595 that prompted Hideyoshi to launch a second massive Korean campaign.[18] The episode reminds us of the perpetual need to

---

[14] For example, the most influential body of essays on these empires was published as vol. VI in *The Cambridge History of China*.

[15] David M. Robinson, *Empire's Twilight: Northeast Asia Under the Mongols* (Cambridge, MA: Harvard Asia Center, 2009).

[16] Remco Breuker, "Within or Without? Ambiguity of Borders and Koryŏ Koreans' Travels during the Liao, Jin, Song and Yuan," *East Asian History* 38 (2014): 56, argues that Koryŏ elites re-oriented themselves to Yuan as the "new wellspring of civilization."

[17] D. Robinson, *Empire's Twilight*, p. 289.

[18] Kenneth M. Swope, *A Dragon's Head and a Serpent's Tail: Ming China and the First Great East Asian War, 1592–1598* (Norman: University of Oklahoma Press, 2009), chapter 5; Kenneth M. Swope, "Deceit, Disguise, and Dependence: China, Japan, and the Future of the Tributary System, 1592–1596," *The International History Review* 24.4 (2002): 757–82.

interrogate official documents, which have their biases and are edited with internal political agendas.

What Swope calls the "First Great East Asian War" set off a sequence of events that was to alter the geopolitical balance of the region and batter the Korean peninsula, which occupied a strategic position between the Ming and the rising Jurchen/Manchu regime. Korean historians treat the period from Hideyoshi's invasion to the second Manchu invasion of Korea (1637) as one of national disaster and humiliation. Japanese specialists view this failed invasion as a minor episode in the events that led to the establishment of the Tokugawa shogunate. The same events are all but ignored in histories of China, yet had the outcome been different, the Japanese might have made a lasting impact on Korea and thus eroded the foundations of what became the Qing empire.

Japan and Korea shared many attributes with the northeast conquest regimes. Both were populated by groups that originated in northeast Asia.[19] By virtue of its geographical position, the northeast was linked to the steppe and responsive to shifts in the political fortunes of the steppe nomads. Operating in a multi-state political arena which included the Central Plain regimes along with other entities in the region, ambitious leaders of northeast Asian states viewed China as a source of cultural and political capital that would support their own political aspirations. They were happy to do whatever was required to obtain the books, commodities, and customary symbols of legitimation that they sought, while preserving their political independence and cultural identity. Over time, this region's relations with China ran the whole gamut from petitioning for investiture to using military superiority to extract tribute from China, and, in some cases, capturing and governing former Chinese territories.

Japan and Korea were no different. Like the Chinese states, they also waged military campaigns (with varying success) against the northeast states. There were instances (in the fifth and seventh centuries) when the Yamato court sent troops to the Korean peninsula to aid its ally in intra-Korean conflict, others (in the seventh century) when Korean states allied with Chinese states against their internal rivals, and still others (in the tenth and eleventh centuries) when the Korean regime was forced to choose sides in conflicts between Chinese and northeast frontier states. Even though its insular status helped to shield Japan, the Mongol invasions of 1274 and 1281 reinforced elite fears that Japan's security from continental military threats could not be guaranteed. For Korea, the

---

[19] Although specialists talk about Southeast Asia as a possible place of origin for the Japanese people, there seems to be consensus concerning the northeast Asian origin of many Japanese.

geopolitical situation from the tenth century onward was merely an exaggerated version of earlier circumstances which obliged peninsular states to exercise nimble diplomacy to survive pressures from powerful neighbors.

Beyond national history

Chinese national histories treat Hideyoshi's invasion of Korea as part of the Wanli reign, when the emperor's refusal to attend to affairs of state, increasing military campaigns to repress unrest along the empire's borders, growing factional struggles within the Ming court, and deepening fiscal deficits presaged dynastic decline.[20] Written with the assumption that history is the record of the rise and fall of dynasties, this traditional understanding of the sixteenth century fails to capture historic transformations occurring within China's economy and society stimulated by the boom in maritime trade.

This book analyzes the events of the late sixteenth and early seventeenth centuries, the period of the Wanli reign, within a dynamic regional and global context that spurred China's advance toward early modernity. Unlike Lieberman, I link Tokugawa Japan and Chosŏn Korea (part of his "protected zone") with Ming China and the Jurchen Later Jin state, to consider how the actions of one affected the others. *Contra* Lieberman, who argued that the Inner Asian factor simultaneously functioned as a creative stimulus to innovations in state formation and as a hindrance to military modernization and long-term fiscal and administrative centralization,[21] I argue that the entire region advanced along these lines in response to innovations introduced by European traders, and that abandoning the constricting limits of national history clarifies the chronology of stimulus-response.

Cultural borrowing and sinicization

Like the northeast Asian conquest regimes, Korea and Japan avidly imported political and religious concepts and institutions from the Central Plain society. Many scholars (including Fairbank and Reischauer) cite the use of Chinese writing as a sign of Chinese cultural hegemony. In recent scholarly debates within the PRC, use of Chinese writing is also frequently taken to indicate that a state was under the spell

[20] See Ray Huang, *1587: A Year of No Significance* (New Haven: Yale University Press, 1981).
[21] Lieberman, *Strange Parallels*, pp. 622–27.

of Chinese culture.[22] Rulers wishing to establish diplomatic relations with Central Plain states communicated in Chinese, using forms that were dictated by the Central Plain states to ensure that superior–inferior status hierarchies were observed. The borrowers, however, seem to have understood and subverted the complicated protocol governing written communications in fairly short order.

Japanese and Korean belong to a different language group from Chinese. The process of accommodating their own languages to Chinese writing took several centuries. Substantial numbers of texts indicating that Koreans had successfully adapted Chinese writing to their own language appear only in the sixth and seventh centuries, even though Chinese writing must have entered the Korean peninsula soon after 108 BCE.[23] Similarly, although the earliest texts inscribed with Chinese characters discovered in the Japanese archipelago date from the first century BCE, evidence of a substantive upsurge in literacy comes only in the seventh century.[24]

The task of translating (both literally and figuratively) Chinese-language texts and adapting the Chinese writing system to their own spoken languages was accomplished through a complex of practices that Japanese called *kundoku*, "reading by gloss," which "involved preserving the visual *kanbun* (Chinese) text while arranging it into Japanese word order during the reading process." Borrowed from the Korean peninsula and brought to Japan in the seventh century by Paekche scribes and refugees,[25] *kundoku* allowed Japanese to develop their own interpretive traditions of Chinese texts.

Awareness of the gap between Chinese and their own spoken languages probably stimulated the Japanese and Koreans to innovate. Like the other northeast states, the Japanese and Koreans eventually created their own

---

[22] See the Epilogue for concrete arguments concerning historical "ownership" of Gaogouli/Koguryŏ based on precisely this criterion.

[23] David B. Lurie, *Realms of Literacy: Early Japan and the History of Writing* (Cambridge, MA: Harvard University Asia Center, 2011), pp. 199–201; a notable exception, p. 197, is the Kwanggaet'o stele inscription, dated 414 CE, which shows "extensive command of writing by Koguryŏ affiliates by the early fifth century." See Ju Bo Don, "Problems Concerning the Basic Historical Documents Related to the Samhan," in *Early Korea*, vol. II: *The Samhan Period in Korean History*, ed. Mark E. Byington (Cambridge, MA: Korea Institute, Harvard University, 2009), pp. 95–122, on the Chinese texts which form the major sources for early Korean history.

[24] Lurie, *Realms of Literacy*, p. 3. Lurie focuses on the existence of individuals who could read and write, i.e. communicate, in Japanese using the Chinese writing system, which is an intellectual activity that is separate from writing a Chinese text in accordance with diplomatic protocols set by the Chinese state, as will be discussed in what follows.

[25] See Lurie's detailed examination of *kundoku* in chapter 4 of his *Realms of Literacy*.

writing systems.[26] In Japan, gradual processes of graphic simplification, expansion of literacy, and development of printing supported the creation of new syllabaries, *katakana* and *hiragana*, which appear in written documents beginning in the tenth century.[27] The Korean alphabet, *Han'gŭl*, was commissioned in the fifteenth century by the king, Sejong, to enable commoners to express themselves in writing without mastering Chinese characters.[28]

Rather than promoting acculturation, adopting and reading Chinese texts may paradoxically have reinforced recipients' determination to assert their own identities. Recent studies show that culture recipients such as the Koreans and Japanese used Chinese forms to contradict or challenge the Sinic position. An example is a letter sent in 600 CE to the Sui in which the Yamato ruler flouted Chinese rules and used his native title, rendered phonetically. His break with the protocol of the time signified his wish to display his "independent authority and dignity," i.e. to challenge the Sinocentric world order.[29] Similarly, although *Nihon shoki*, one of the earliest histories produced in Japan (720), was written in "classical Chinese," one of its main themes was to portray Japan as "an equal of China," "an empire, like China, worthy of respect."[30] Similar assertions of self-identity appear in Manchu-language and Korean documents. It is for precisely this reason that, I argue, we should examine both sides of exchanges between the Central Plain and the northeast.

An abundance of documentary materials allows us to pursue this research agenda. Korean and Japanese elites responded to political, economic, and cultural exchanges with Chinese regimes in ways that parallel the actions of northeast conquest regimes, and reinforce recent work on the dynamic impact on China of groups originating along its northern frontiers. Moreover, the extensive secondary literature produced by Korean and Japanese historians presents scholarly interpretations that

[26] On the commissioning of a writing system by the northeast conquest regimes, see Franke and Twitchett, "Introduction," pp. 30–33.

[27] Yoshihiko Amino provides a social history of these syllabaries and *kanji* in his "On Writing," pp. 123–43 in Amino, trans. Alan S. Christy, *Rethinking Japanese History* (Ann Arbor: Center for Japanese Studies, University of Michigan, 2012).

[28] See the "Introduction," pp. 2–3, and other essays in Young-Key Kim-Renaud, ed., *The Korean Alphabet: Its History and Structure* (Honolulu: University of Hawai'i Press, 1997).

[29] Zhenping Wang, "Speaking with a Forked Tongue: Diplomatic Correspondence between China and Japan, 238–608 AD," *Journal of the American Oriental Society* 114.1 (1994): 28–29. Wang notes that the Sui court mistook the phonetic rendering of the title as the Yamato ruler's personal name, and accepted a missive that they would have rejected had they properly understood the text.

[30] John R. Bentley, "The Birth and Flowering of Japanese Historiography from Chronicles to Tales to Historical Interpretation," in *The Oxford History of Historical Writing*, vol. II: *400–1400*, ed. Sarah Foot and Chase F. Robinson (Oxford: Oxford University Press, 2012), p. 62.

differ not only from those of Chinese authors but also of modern China specialists. This book synthesizes information from secondary literature in Japanese, Korean, Chinese, and English.

Primary and secondary sources

Views of long-term historical shifts in Chinese, Korean, and Japanese history are drawn from a number of sources and the work of many scholars. There is an abundance of scholarship on the late sixteenth and early seventeenth centuries. Primary sources and secondary literature in Japanese provide detailed information on Hideyoshi's invasions of Korea. Compilations of excerpts from Ming and Chosŏn official documents relating to the Hideyoshi invasion and to Sino-Korean relations ease the scholar's task.[31] Contemporary historiography written in English, Japanese, and Korean also gives divergent views concerning events.

The primary sources tracing Nurhaci's emergence as a regional leader, the relations between his Later Jin state, the Chosŏn dynasty, and the Ming are also multi-lingual and multi-national. Chinese records include the *Ming shilu* (Veritable Records for the Ming dynasty) and *Da Qing shilu* (Veritable Records for the Qing dynasty), chronologies of each reign that summarize key state deliberations and decisions.[32] For at least the period before 1644, the official record was initially written in Manchu, a script invented in 1599 and revised in the 1630s. Manchu writing, referred to after 1644 as *Qing wen* 清文, became one of the two documentary languages of the Qing state.

Voluminous Manchu-language documents for the period after 1644 are scattered in library collections in Taiwan, China, Japan, Europe, and the United States.[33] The pre-1644 records are fewer in number but have

---

[31] Li Guangtao, comp., *Chaoxian renzhen wohuo shiliao* (Historical materials on the Japanese invasion of Chosŏn), 5 vols. (Taipei: Institute of History and Philology, 1970); Wu Fengpei et al., comp., *Renzhen zhi yi shiliao huiji* (Collected historical materials on the Japanese invasion) 2 vols. (Beijing: Quanguo tushugan wenxian suowei fuzhi zhongxin chubanshe, 1990); Wang Qiju, comp, *Ming shilu: Lingguo Chaoxian pian ziliao* (Materials in the *Ming shilu* relating to Chosŏn) (Beijing: Zhongguo bianjiang shidi yanjiu, 1983) and Wang Qiju, comp., *Qing shilu: Lingguo Chaoxian pian ziliao* (Materials in the *Qing shilu* relating to Chosŏn) (Beijing: Zhongguo bianjiang shidi yanjiu, 1987); Li Guangtao, comp., *Ji Mingji Chaoxian zhi [Dingmao lühuo] yu [Bingzi lühuo]* (Ming and Chosŏn records on the 1627 and 1636 invasions of Chosŏn) (Taipei: Institute of History and Philology, 1972).

[32] The *Ming shilu* is also available in the Scripta Sinica full-text database online.

[33] For an overview of the scholarly repercussions, see Mark C. Elliott, "Manshūgo bunsho shiryō to atarashii Shinchōshi" (Manchu language archives and the New Qing History), in *Shinchōshi kenkyū no aratanaru chihei* (New perspectives on Qing history), ed. Hoyosa Yoshio (Tokyo: Yamakawa shuppansha, 2008), pp. 124–39.

been intensively studied.[34] They were taken to Peking[35] after the Manchu take-over in 1644, and formed the basis for compiling the Veritable Records of the first two reigns (*Taizu Gao huangdi shilu, Taizong Wen huangdi shilu*). These Veritable Records underwent a series of revisions that were driven by disputes about the legitimacy of Hongtaiji's accession, the desire to edit out occurrences and practices that deviated from the Chinese model of rulership, and to smooth out discrepancies between different accounts. For example, the writing of events during Nurhaci's lifetime began in 1635, but went through multiple revisions during the Shunzhi reign (1644–61) and again in the Kangxi (1662–1722) and Yongzheng reigns (1723–35).[36]

The rediscovery of the original Manchu-language archives is an amazing story. In the eighteenth century, when thirty-seven volumes of Manchu documents from the pre-1644 period were found in Peking, they were "damaged and spoiled by age."[37] After the texts were transcribed into "new Manchu," the originals were returned to storage. Housed after 1644 in the Grand Secretariat and recopied in the second half of the eighteenth century, the originals were carefully guarded from scrutiny by Han Chinese high ministers and Hanlin scholars.[38]

[34] The development of Manchu studies based on these archival materials is described in Nobuo Kanda, "Present State of Preservation of Manchu Literature," *Memoirs of the Research Department of the Toyo Bunko* No. 26 (1968): 63–95 and "From *Man Wen Lao Tang* to *Chiu Man-chou Tang*," *Memoirs of the Research Department of the Toyo Bunko* 38 (1980): 71–94; Zhou Yuanlian, "'Manwen laodang' yu Qingchao kaiguoshi yanjiu" (The old Manchu archive and research on the founding of the Qing dynasty), in *Ming Qing dang'an yu lishi yanjiu, Zhongguo diyi lishi dang'anguan liushi zhounian jinian lunwenji* (Historical research in the Ming-Qing archives: collected writings on the 60th anniversary of the First Historical Archives), ed. Zhongguo diyi lishi dang'anguan, I: 322–41 (Beijing: Zhongguo diyi lishidang'anguan, 1988); and Liu Housheng, *Jiu Manzhoudang yanjiu* (Research on the old Manchu archives) (Changchun: Jilin wenshi chubanshe, 1993).
[35] Throughout this book I use "Peking" to denote the pre-1911 city that was the Ming and Qing capital, and "Beijing" to denote the same city from 1912 onward, recognizing the anachronism involved (under the Guomindang, the city was renamed "Beiping," then renamed "Beijing" from 1949 onward).
[36] Mitamura Taisuke, "Shin Taiso jitsuroku no sanshū ni tsuite" (On the editing of the veritable records of Qing Taizu), *Tōhōgaku* 19 (1959): 1–12; Matsumura Jun, *Shin Taiso jitsuroku no kenkyū* (Research on the Qing veritable records for Nurhaci) (Tokyo: Ajia bunken kenkyūkai, 2001); Tōyō Bunko Tōhoku Ajia kenkyūshitsu, comp., *Naikokushiento Tensō gonen* (Archival Manchu-language records from the Imperial Historiography office for Tiancong 5, 1631), (Tokyo: Toyo Bunko, 2011), xi–xv; Chen Jiexian, "Jiu Manzhou dang shulüe" (Brief overview of the old Manchu archive), in Guoli gugong bowuyuan, comp., *Jiu Manzhou dang* (Old Manchu-language archive) (Taipei: National Palace Museum, 1969), pp. 9–10.
[37] Chieh-hsien Chen, "The Value of the Chiu Man-chou Tang (*The Early Manchu Archives*), in his *Manchu Archival Materials* (Taipei: Linking Publishing, 1988), pp. 14–15.
[38] Mitamura, "Shin Taiso jitsuroku." On "new Manchu," see Pamela K. Crossley and Evelyn S. Rawski, "A Profile of the Manchu Language in Ch'ing History," *Harvard Journal of Asiatic Studies* 58.1 (1993): 66.

Several copies of the new Manchu version were made, one for the emperor's reference in the Forbidden City and another to be kept in Mukden, where in 1905, Naitō Torajirō was to discover them (see below). The original text came to light again in 1930 when the Palace Museum began inventorying the Grand Secretariat archives; an additional three volumes were also discovered at that time. Altogether there were twenty volumes on Nurhaci's rule and the same number covering Hongtaiji's reign: the earliest document was dated to 1607 and the last to 1636. These documents were moved to Taiwan in 1949 and reprinted in 1969.[39]

Japanese scholars began to translate and collate Manchu-language texts early in the twentieth century. When the well-known Sinologist Naitō Torajirō found the *Manwen laodang* in the imperial palace at Mukden in 1905, he photographed the collection and took it to Japan. Its discovery and translation was hailed as "an epochal event" in Qing historical circles.[40] More recently, additional documents in Manchu dating from before 1644 were found in the State Historical Office (Guoshi guan) in Beijing and in the northeast.[41] Translations of

---

[39] The chronology of the redactions is presented in Matsumura, *Shin Taiso jitsuroku*. The 1969 reprint, compiled by the Palace Museum, was entitled *Jiu Manzhoudang*.

[40] Kanda Nobuo, "Japanese Studies in Ch'ing History, Particularly Those Based on Manchu Source Materials," *Acta Asiatica* 53 (1988): 84; Kanda Nobuo et al., comp. and trans., *Manbun rōtō*, 10 vols. (Tokyo: Toyo Bunko, 1955–63).

[41] Bilingual editions of Manchu-language texts housed in the First Historical Archive, Beijing, include *Naikokushientō: Tensō shichinen* (Early Manchu Archives of the Qing Historiography Academy, The Seventh Year of Tiancong, 1633/34), comp. Kanda Nobuo et al. (Tokyo: Seminar on Manchu History, Toyo Bunko, 2003), and Kawachi Yoshihiro's *Chūgoku daiichi rekishitōankansō Naikokushien Manbun tōan yakuchū: Sūtoku ni, san nenbun* (Translation and annotation of Manchu-language archives in the Qing Historiography Academy, the second and third years of the Chongde reign, 1637, 1638) (Kyoto: Shōkōdo, 2010), hereafter Kawachi 2010. A volume entitled *Naikokushientō: Tensōhachinen* (The early Manchu archives of the Imperial Historiographical Office, the eighth year of Tiancong, 1634), by the Toyo Bunko's Seminar on Manchu History in 2 vols. (Tokyo, 2009), includes photographic reproductions of the original text and indices of personal and place names. The Japanese publications listed above differentiate themselves from Chinese publications in providing the original text alongside the translation, which is very useful in pursuing research on early Jurchen political and social history. Chinese publications include *Qingchu Neiguoshiyuan Manwen dang'an yibian* (Chinese translation of early Manchu archives in the Nei Guoshiyuan), comp. Zhongguo Diyi lishi dang'an guan (Beijing: Guangming ribao chubanshe, 1989); *Manwen laodang* (Old Manchu-language archives), trans. Zhongguo Diyi lishi dang'an guang and Zhongguo shehui kexueyuan, Lishi yanjiusuo (Beijing: Zhonghua shuju, 1990). For surveys of the development of studies focused on the Manchu archives, see Guan Jialu and Tong Yonggong, "Zhongguo Manwen jiqi wenxian zhengli yanjiu" (On the organization of China's Manchu-language texts and their contribution), *Qingshi yanjiu* 4 (1991): 29–36.

the texts, in bilingual and Chinese editions, have filled in many gaps in the *Manwen laodang*, including those for the 1636–37 period.[42]

The Manchu archival records begin in 1607. Mongolian language archives, housed at the First Historical Archives, Beijing, include important documents that highlight Manchu relations with the Mongol tribes before 1644, illuminating a hitherto neglected subject in pre-1644 Manchu studies.[43] And then there are the Korean records. Japanese and Chinese scholars studying the history of the Jurchen before that date have long been aware of the Chosŏn Veritable Records, *Chosŏn wangjo sillok* (hereafter *sillok*), and compiled multi-volume works presenting excerpted passages relating to specific events or to Sino-Korean relations.[44]

The South Korean National Institute of History has posted the entire contents of the Veritable Records of the Chosŏn dynasty as an online database, with both the original text and a modern Korean rendering.[45] The *sillok* provides detailed information on the activities of the Jianzhou Jurchen ancestors of Nurhaci from the fourteenth century onward. The *sillok* texts show that although the Chosŏn court was aware of Nurhaci, their attention was episodic and unfocused for a long time; their inattention may be ascribed to the Japanese invasion, which dominated state deliberations in the 1590s. Perhaps it was also due to King Sejo's success at bringing the Jurchen under control through military means. What is recorded are the court's responses to border infractions by Jurchen crossing to trade or to raid Chosŏn villages.[46] Repatriation of individuals who

---

[42] The *Manwen laodang* ends with the onset of the second invasion (twelfth lunar month, first day) in 1636; the new archival records found in the Historiographical Institute and published in a bilingual edition (Kawachi 2010), picks the chronological account in the first lunar month of 1637.

[43] Nicola DiCosmo and Dalizhabu Bao, *Manchu–Mongol Relations on the Eve of Qing Conquest: A Documentary History* (Leiden: E. J. Brill, 2003).

[44] *Chaoxian [Li chao shilu] zhong de Zhongguo shiliao* (Historical materials about China in the *Chosŏn wangjo sillok*), ed. Wu Han (Beijing: Zhonghua shuju, 1980); *Chaoxian [Lichao shilu] zhong de Nüzhen shiliao xuanbian* (Jurchen historical materials from the Korean *Yichao shilu*), ed. Wang Zhonghan (Shenyang: Liaoning daxue lishixi, 1979); *Mindai Man Mō shiryō: Richō jitsuroku shō* (Historical materials excerpted from the Yi Dynasty Veritable Records pertaining to Manchu and Mongolian matters during the Ming), comp., Tokyo Daigaku, Bungaku Bu (Tokyo: Tokyo Daigaku Bungaku Bu, 1949–59).

[45] http://sillok.history.go.kr. An English translation of the *T'aejo sillok* has been published: *The Annals of King T'aejo, Founder of Korea's Chosŏn Dynasty*, trans. and annotated by Byonghyon Choi (Cambridge, MA: Harvard University Press, 2014).

[46] Kenneth R. Robinson, "Shaping Interactions with Jurchens in the Early Chosŏn Period," in *Embracing the Other: The Interaction of Korean and Foreign Cultures* (Songnam: Academy of Korean Studies, 2002), pp. 1443–50 also mentions Jurchen who settled within Chosŏn and others who paid tribute to Chosŏn in the fifteenth and early sixteenth centuries.

wandered across the border to pick ginseng was the primary item of business between the two countries.[47]

Reading and comparing documentation produced by different states vividly exposes their biases. Elisions and omission are not confined to the Chinese record alone. The documents from multiple sources provide valuable information that was censored or edited out of Chinese texts, and reveal other views that are absent from the diplomatic correspondence between states. Each of these documentary sources displays a particular political perspective. The Ming Veritable Records portray Chosŏn as a faithful vassal which was honor-bound to "repay the imperial favor" of Ming military aid that helped expel Japanese armies from the peninsula in the 1590s. The Chosŏn Veritable Records for King Kwanghae's reign (1608–23) seek to justify the coup d'état which deposed him in favor of Injo. The *sillok* of Injo's reign expresses deep hostility toward the Jurchen/ Manchus, which the invasions only intensified.

The structure of this book

This book is divided into two parts. Part I surveys northeast Asia's role in Chinese history. Chapter 1 locates the Central Plain with respect to the northeast frontier. The northeast region had its own historical dynamic, yet interacted closely with the cultures emanating from the Central Plain. The historical eastward movement of the capitals of successive Chinese states reflects the pull of the frontier as northeast Asia developed its own culture, society, and economy, producing states that resisted incorporation by Central Plain regimes. By the tenth century, these frontier states were powerful enough to dominate areas previously ruled by Chinese regimes.

Historical exchanges between the Central Plain and Japan and Korea were of long standing. Maritime routes connected Japan, Korea, and Shandong province from early times, with evidence of extensive contact in the northeastern edge of the North China Plain, where the present-day city of Beijing is located. The chapter describes the tribute trade system that structured Japanese and Korean relations with Ming before the sixteenth century, when the advent of European traders to Asian shores caused trade to slip out of official control.

Chapter 2 explores historical explanations for the political transitions that occurred in Japan and China in the 1550–1650 period, when the

---

[47] The situation continued into the Qing: see Seonmin Kim, "Borders and Crossings: Trade, Diplomacy and Ginseng Between Qing China and Chosŏn Korea," PhD thesis, Duke University, 2006.

Chinese court was forced to operate in a multi-state geopolitical system.[48] Toyotomi Hideyoshi's invasion of Korea (1592), the failed Ming–Chosŏn military campaign against Nurhaci's Jianzhou Jurchen forces (1619), and Hongtaiji's 1627 and 1636–37 invasions of Korea, were key events dictated by strategic concerns springing from the regional power configuration, which had itself been altered by the boom in maritime commerce.

The Edo shogunate in 1600 and the Qing court in 1644 inaugurated periods of political stability that endured until the middle of the nineteenth century. Both regimes exhibited many of the characteristics of states in early modern Europe. Cartographic projects became a means of collecting demographic and other information in order to better control subjects. Interstate rivalry, particularly the explorations and mapping efforts of European and rival states, spurred the shogunate and Qing court to order exploratory expeditions into the north Pacific. Beginning in the late seventeenth century, both governments began to view their realms in territorial rather than metaphorical or cosmological terms.

Part II turns to issues of culture and identity, in an age, the seventeenth and eighteenth centuries, when states across Eurasia were creating "politicized ethnicity," "a discrete secular culture" that differentiated its adherents from neighboring peoples.[49] Chapters 3 and 4 examine Japanese and Korean adaptations of Chinese models. Japanese and Korean state rituals, the subject of Chapter 3, are performances aimed at political legitimation. State rites both affirmed notions imported from the continent and created distance in order to claim uniqueness. Despite the commonalities in their initial inspiration, what eventually emerged as the dominant state rituals could not be more differentiated, not only from each other but from the Chinese rites that had inspired their creation.

Indigenous elements fused with cultic practices imported from the mainland to create the Sun Goddess (Amaterasu) cult that legitimated the imperial house in Japan. Early modern Japan saw Confucian scholars grapple with others who rejected their values as inferior to Japan's native belief systems. In Korea, officials who created a state ritual system were preoccupied with the gaps between their own rites and the Chinese precedents on which they were based. To further complicate matters,

---

[48] Evelyn Rawski, "Chinese Strategy and Security Issues in Historical Perspective," in *China's Rise in Historical Perspective*, ed. Brantley Womack (Lanham, MD: Rowman & Littlefield, 2010), pp. 63–87.

[49] Victor Lieberman, "What *Strange Parallels* Sought to Accomplish," *Journal of Asian Studies* 70.4 (2011): 932.

the same ritual repertoire allowed Koreans to challenge Qing claims to the "Mandate of Heaven" and rulership in a Sinocentric world order.

Chapter 4 examines the tension between indigenous kinship structures and the patrilineal kinship embedded in Chinese codes that were taken over by Japan and Korea. Even though the elites of both countries eventually adopted patrilineality, their kinship systems retained important elements of indigenous practices, notably in royal succession, which were distinctly irregular from the Chinese perspective. Japanese elites ignored the Chinese norms, but Korean officials, who were engaged in the Ming tribute system, did not have the luxury of doing so. Instead, they had to request investiture for distantly related collateral kinsmen who were installed on the throne. Ming approval would strengthen the legitimacy of what was essentially an illegitimate political act. Documents from both the Ming and Chosŏn courts illustrate the gap between normative and actual diplomatic exchanges, not only over politically sensitive episodes of succession, but also over statements in Chinese documents that threatened the legitimacy of the Chosŏn throne.

Chapter 5 analyzes the discourse of "civilized" (C. *Hua*) and "barbarian" (C. *Yi*) in order to explore how elites in the seventeenth and eighteenth centuries resolved identity issues. Recent studies suggest that Chinese attitudes toward the frontier peoples were initially much more tolerant, with anecdotal evidence that some frontier elites intermarried with Hua and Xia elites and even occupied high office in Central Plain regimes during the Warring States period (fifth to third centuries BCE).[50] First appearing in Chinese writings distinguishing themselves from their non-Chinese neighbors, the *Hua–Yi* binome acquired international currency. Japanese elites used *Hua* and *Yi* (*Ka-I* in Japanese) not only in discourse contrasting themselves to the Chinese, but as a perjorative term to distinguish the imperial court from the shogunal court, the elites in the imperial capital from the provincials residing elsewhere in the country. Korean elites, too, used *Yi* to designate the groups at the peripheries of their own kingdom whom they regarded as culturally inferior. Both the Japanese and the Koreans turned the *Hua–Yi* discourse against the Manchu rulers of the Qing in order to assert their own visions of the Asian world order. Moreover, Chinese intellectuals in the

---

[50] Yuri Pines, "Beasts or Humans: Pre-Imperial Origins of the 'Sino-Barbarian' Dichotomy," in *Mongols, Turks, and Others: Eurasian Nomads and the Sedentary World,* ed. Reuven Amitai and Michal Biran (Leiden: Brill, 2005), pp. 59–102; Shao-yun Yang, "Becoming *Zhongguo*, Becoming Han: Tracing and Reconceptualizing Ethnicity in Ancient North China, 770 BC–AD 581," MA thesis, National University of Singapore, 2007. See Cho-yun Hsu, trans. Timothy D. Baker, Jr. and Michael S. Duke, *China: A New Cultural History* (New York: Columbia University Press, 2012) for a multi-cultural approach to Chinese history.

seventeenth century used the same line of attack to challenge the legitimacy of Qing emperors. In each case, elite manipulation showed the extreme flexibility of the Chinese symbolic code and its adaptability to diverse situations.

Like Japan and Korea, the Manchu Qing also engaged in a process of cultural negotiation that encompassed but was not subsumed by Ming precedent. Qing state rituals were compartmentalized and designed to address the belief systems of its major Inner Asian subjects, as represented in the state rituals, the shamanic *tangzi,* and the Tibetan Buddhist chapels within the Forbidden City. Qing succession practices boldly departed from the Ming eldest-son principle. Countering challenges to its legitimacy with rhetoric borrowed from earlier regimes, the Qing upheld its separate identity as a conquest regime into the last decade of its rule.

The specter of histories written from the perspective of the nation-state hangs over all of the subjects treated in this book. This attempt to revise long-standing generalizations is not an esoteric or merely academic enterprise. The Epilogue surveys historical understandings that complicate contemporary China's relations not only with Korea and Japan, but also with the minority peoples living within its territorial boundaries. If China's current government aims to win the allegiance of its minority citizens and encourage their loyalty to the Chinese nation, the first step toward achieving this goal may be to reassess the ways in which its history is written, by acknowledging the multi-ethnic nature of Chinese history and the complexity of the human interactions that produced the marvel we call Chinese civilization.

Part I

China in regional and world history

1   The northeast frontier in Chinese history

Frontiers, or borderlands, can connote a boundary line which separates two states from one another, but refers here to a broader, more diffuse zone or place where different cultures mingle and meet. Like virtually all states before the eighteenth and nineteenth centuries, China's borders were not fixed in the modern sense, but much more fluid sites where different peoples commingled. Claims to sovereignty did not match actual administrative control, which peaked in the political center and weakened as one moved toward the peripheries. In this chapter, we view frontiers/borderlands as "permeable ... and interpenetrable" spaces, zones of transition which also engendered societal transformation.[1]

This chapter has several aims. First, it situates the northeast with respect to China's core region, the Central Plain, as a borderland which gave birth to states that borrowed from yet were not subsumed by the precocious polities of the Central Plain. In addition, it situates states in the Korean peninsula and the Japanese archipelago within the geopolitical boundary of China's northeast Asian frontier. Korean and Japanese states were created through intense interaction with other entities on the steppe and the Central Plain. The periodic crises that swept across the steppe initiated political reverberations through the northeast and the Central Plain. When these political forces collided, they sparked military clashes among China, Korea, and Japan. A brief survey demonstrates that China's historical interactions with Japan and Korea replicated every dimension of its interaction with northeast Asia. The chapter ends with the arrival of Europeans in maritime Asia, an event which disrupted and eventually shifted the power balance among these states and lifted Chinese restrictions on the movement of goods and people.

---

[1] Diana Lary, "Introduction," in *The Chinese State at the Borders*, ed. Diana Lary (Vancouver: University of British Columbia Press, 2007), pp. 5–6.

The Central Plain

The earliest historical records locate Chinese states emerging in the Yellow River drainage as it flows south and turns eastward on the borders of present-day Shaanxi, the area that historians denote as the Central Plain (*zhongyuan*). According to a popular contemporary encyclopedia, the capitals of these early states were clustered in the present-day province of Henan.[2] To its north were the deserts and steppes of Mongolia; to its west, tall mountain ranges and high plateaus. The middle and lower reaches of the Yellow River consist of plains formed by yellow loess, which can be farmed, though only with concentrated labor. The Central Plain itself comprises the southwestern part of the larger North China Plain, which extends from the Yanshan mountains on the north, the Taihang mountains on the west, and the Yangzi plain on the south. The Yellow River flows through this loess plain and into the Yellow Sea. From the Shandong peninsula, a coastal plain encompasses Beijing and stretches northeastward to connect north China with the Liao River valley, forming a transitional zone between the Central Plain and northeast Asia.

From ancient times, the Hua and Xia people whom scholars identify as the ancestors of the Chinese/Han Chinese people were surrounded by others. According to Diana Lary, over seven hundred ethnonyms are found in Chinese texts covering the span of China's history, which suggests that multi-cultural contact formed an integral component of China's long-term evolution.[3] The Han-oriented discourse of Chinese elites writing in the sixteenth and seventeenth centuries should not blind us to evidence in early texts that reveals the mixed, multi-ethnic nature of early Central Plain society in what is regarded as the homeland of "Chinese" civilization.[4] The cultural intermingling and the political instability that inheres to frontier zones perhaps inspired Chinese elites

---

[2] "Zhongyuan diqu," http//baike.baidu.com/view/47532.htm. The description of China's primary geographical features is drawn from Hsu, *China*, pp. 11–14.

[3] Lary, "Introduction," p. 5.

[4] Hsu, *China*, chapters 1–2. Yuri Pines, "Beasts or Humans: Pre-Imperial Origins of the 'Sino-Barbarian' Dichotomy," in *Mongols, Turks, and Others: Eurasian Nomads and the Sedentary World*, ed. Reuven Amitai and Michal Biran (Leiden: E. J. Brill, 2005), cites many passages which talk about *Rong* and *Di* peoples who intermarried with the Hua and Xia elites and even occupied government posts in the Warring States period. Charles Holcombe, "Re-Imagining China: The Chinese Identity Crisis at the Start of the Southern Dynasties Period," *Journal of the American Oriental Society* 115.1 (1995): 1–14 comments on both the ability of early Chinese society to accept through intermarriage leaders of non-Han ancestry and the emphasis on ritual conformity stimulated by legitimacy crises, causing (p. 9) Confucian ritual to become "a cornerstone of *shih* (literati) identification" by the second century CE.

to create the notion of "an eternal civilizing political centre, committed to the unification of ever-widening areas and the peoples around it."[5]

Chinese rhetoric belied the inability of the Chinese state to control the vast territories that it claimed.[6] Actual control of the territories ruled by various Han empires varied enormously. Terms such as *jimi* (羈縻loose reins, or indirect rule) implied power over regional non-Han rulers that was rarely borne out by reality.[7] Efforts to shore up imperial power at the frontiers were costly endeavors, which the early imperial Chinese state was often unable to sustain.

The Chinese notion of an imperial center endured, despite (perhaps because of) its divergence from the historical reality of political fragmentation and challenges emanating from the borderlands. The political atomization of north China and its conquest by rulers descended from frontier peoples between the third and sixth centuries (known as the Six Dynasties period), the eventual unification by the (non-Han) Tuoba Wei, and the alienation of the area around present-day Beijing from the ninth through the middle of the fourteenth centuries were political realities that shattered the fiction of a Sinocentric world order.[8]

Northeast Asia and the Central Plain

Northeast Asia

While historians frequently present northeast Asia as peripheral to the Central Plain (*zhongyuan*), archaeologists find that this region (C. *dongbei*), which is "virtually identical" to the contemporary provinces of Liaoning, Jilin, and Heilongjiang in the PRC, had its own prehistoric developmental arc and cultural characteristics.[9]

Seen from the Central Plain, northeast Asia was a "frontier zone." The region was bounded on the south by the Gulf of Bohai, stretched westward to the Greater Xing'an range and the Yan mountains

---

[5] Alexander Woodside, "The Centre and the Borderlands in Chinese Political Theory," in *Chinese State at the Borders*, ed. Lary, p. 11.

[6] See Peter C. Perdue, "Embracing Victory, Effacing Defeat: Rewriting the Qing Frontier Campaigns," in *Chinese State at the Borders*, ed. Lary, pp. 106–25.

[7] Rawski, "Chinese Strategy and Security Issues," pp. 66, 71, 80.

[8] Holcombe, "Re-Imagining China," p. 1 calls the fourth-century sweep of north China by non-Chinese rulers China's "most serious national crisis, prior to the onslaught of the industrialized West in modern times." The political atomization of north China is linked to the collapse of the Xiongnu empire by some scholars: see the "Introduction," p. 5, in Scott Pearce, Audrey Spiro, and Patricia Ebrey, eds., *Culture and Power in the Reconstitution of the Chinese Realm, 200–600* (Cambridge, MA: Harvard University Asia Center, 2001).

[9] Sarah M. Nelson, "Introduction," in *The Archaeology of Northeast China: Beyond the Great Wall*, ed. Sarah M. Nelson (London: Routledge, 1995), pp. 1–18.

(thus abutting the Central Plain) and eastward to the Changbaishan mountain range at the northeastern edge of the Korean peninsula. The Liao River plain, where intensive agriculture emerged approximately 7000 BCE, extends northward to the so-called Manchurian plain which meets the Lesser Xing'an mountains, which run from northwest to southeast. Although a narrow coastal plain links it to the North China Plain,[10] the northeast was sufficiently guarded by natural barriers to develop its own regional culture in prehistoric times. Intraregional transport and communications were facilitated by two river systems. The Liao River, which flows eastward, permits goods to be shipped downriver to the Gulf of Bohai, but the Sungari River and Ussuri River flow northward into the Amur River, which enters the ocean in the north Pacific, carrying goods in the opposite direction.[11] With over two hundred tributaries flowing into it from Mongolia, Russia, and (today) the PRC, the Amur was navigable and served as a major highway for northeast peoples from early times.[12]

The Liao River plain supplied the northeast region with the resources for early development of agriculture. Archaeological excavations have uncovered early human settlements dating from *c.* 4700 BCE, which produced ceramic and worked jade objects.[13] The diversity of ecological systems in the region created an environment that supported sedentary agriculturalists, nomadic pastoralists, and hunting-fishing peoples. According to Thomas Barfield, it was this environment of mixed cultures that produced historically significant empires of conquest that impacted Chinese regimes.[14]

[10] While European and North American geographies talk about the North China Plain, there is a large Chinese-language literature which focuses instead on the "Central Plain" (*zhongyuan*), the middle and lower reaches of the Yellow River in north China, which is identified as the birthplace of Chinese civilization, the core area of the Hua and Xia peoples, who are regarded as the ancestors of modern Chinese. The North China Plain, which is defined as the lower reaches of the Yellow River, would therefore be a sub-region of the Central Plain. It stretches from the Taihang mountain range in the west to the Yellow Sea in the east.

[11] See chapters 4 and 5 in Owen Lattimore, *Inner Asian Frontiers of China* (Hong Kong: Oxford University Press, 1988); also Institute of Geography, USSR Academy of Sciences, *The Physical Geography of China* (New York: Frederick A. Praeger, 1969), I: 129–34, II: 89–114; Gina L. Barnes, *The Rise of Civilization in East Asia: The Archeology of China, Korea and Japan* (London: Thames and Hudson, 1999), chapter 6.

[12] Victor Zatsepine, "The Amur: As River, as Border," in *Chinese State at the Borders*, pp. 152–54, notes that seasonal floods regularly flooded the valleys and discouraged agriculture.

[13] See the essays in Nelson, ed., *Archaeology of Northeast China*. Nelson observes in her "Conclusion" in this volume (pp. 251–52) that recent findings suggest early indigenous domestication of millet, buckwheat, and even rice.

[14] Thomas J. Barfield, *The Perilous Frontier: Nomadic Empires and China* (Oxford: Blackwell, 1989); see Lattimore, *Inner Asian Frontiers*, pp. 108–15 for analysis of the geographical features of the region, and Barnes, *Rise of Civilization*, chapter 1.

Japan and Korea in northeast Asia

The Korean peninsula and the Japanese archipelago were at the periphery of the northeast region. Regimes established in the Korean peninsula enjoyed significant communication and contact with the Liao River basin. Despite the Changbai mountain range, which creates the hilly terrain of Liaodong, and the Tumen and Yalu (K. Amnok) Rivers, which mark the contemporary northeast and northwest boundaries of the two Koreas, persistent border incursions in the historical record demonstrate that these natural boundaries were easy to cross. At the same time, by virtue of its geographical location, the Korean peninsula was influenced by both northeast and Central Plain cultures.[15]

In addition to overland routes skirting its coastal plain, boats could sail across the Gulf of Bohai to the Shandong peninsula in China, which was located in a frontier zone between the Central Plain and Dongbei. Artifacts discovered in archaeological excavations in Shandong and the Korean peninsula suggest that this maritime route was already in use during China's Warring States period (fifth to third centuries BCE). Refugees fleeing Shandong after the Qin conquest (221 BCE) used the sea route to migrate to present-day Chŏlla province in the southwest tip of the Korean peninsula.[16]

Archaeologists have also determined that the Japanese archipelago was initially linked to the Asian continent through land bridges.[17] After being separated from the continent by the Japan Sea (K. East Sea, *Tonghae*), Japanese maintained contact with the continent through the island of Tsushima, 50 kilometers from Korea, and visible on clear days.[18] Indeed, Amino Yoshihiko cites specialized studies to argue that the region

[15] See Barnes, *Rise of Civilization*, pp. 50–52 on debates concerning early human settlements in Korea and Japan, and pp. 26–27 on cultural influences: according to Barnes, iron technology and perhaps rice cultivation technology entered Korea from "the China Mainland," i.e. the Central Plain. For reports summarizing recent Korean archaeological studies, see *Early Korea*, vol. I: "Reconsidering Early Korean History Through Archaeology," ed. Mark E. Byington (Cambridge, MA: Korea Institute, Harvard University, 2008).

[16] Li Huizhu, "Handai yiqian Shandong yu Chaoxian bandao nanbu de jiaowang" (Contact between Shandong and the southern part of the Korean peninsula before the Han dynasty), *Beifang wenwu* 1 (2004): 16–23.

[17] Barnes, *Rise of Civilization*, Box 4, pp. 64–65.

[18] Bruce L. Batten, *Gateway to Japan: Hakata in War and Peace, 500–1300* (Honolulu: University of Hawai'i Press, 2006), p. 6. J. Edward Kidder, Jr., *Himiko and Japan's Elusive Chiefdom of Yamatai: Archaeology, History, and Mythology* (Honolulu: University of Hawai'i Press, 2007), p. 39 comments on the seasonality of seaborne travel between Japan and the continent.

encompassing Tsushima, northern Kyushu, and the eastern and southern Korean coast shared a common fishing culture in prehistoric times.[19]

Although the distance between the peninsula and northern Kyushu was only 805 kilometers, strong ocean currents and the frequency of typhoons and seasonal storms limited travel. The ships constructed by Japanese seafarers enabled them to navigate along the sheltered coast of the Korean peninsula. Once they reached the Gulf of Bohai, sailing to ports on the Shandong peninsula was an easy matter. After being defeated in a naval battle off the western coast of Korea in 660, Japanese travelers elected the more dangerous open ocean voyage from Hakata to Ningbo and other ports in the Yangzi delta. The Japanese also ventured further south via the Ryukyus to the Canton delta.[20] Ships sailing in the open ocean were constrained by the prevailing winds to limit voyages to the spring and autumn. Unlike visual sailing between western Japan and Korea, ocean sailing required more skillful navigators. Until the twelfth century, most Japanese who sailed to the continent did so on ships piloted by Koreans and Chinese.[21]

Archaeological excavations suggest that ceramics, agriculture, and bronze technology originating in the northeast moved southward into the Korean peninsula and across the Japan Sea to Japan, ushering in the Yayoi period (300 BCE – 300 CE).[22] During the Yayoi period, wet-rice farming and other new cultural elements such as bronze and iron tools, domesticated pigs, and megalithic tombs flowed through the Korean peninsula into Japan.[23]

An alternative route from the northeast to Japan went from southern Sakhalin island to northern Hokkaido. It was "one of the overland bridges over which migrations of the Paleolithic and Neolithic peoples of Northeast Asia crossed," and a route that migrants belonging to a north

---

[19] Yoshihiko Amino, trans. Alan S. Christy, "The Maritime View of the Japanese Archipelago," in his *Rethinking Japanese History* (Ann Arbor: Center for Japanese Studies, 2012), pp. 32–33.

[20] On archaeological evidence regarding Japanese boat-building, see Kidder, *Himiko and Japan's Elusive Chiefdom*, pp. 39, 1–45; also p. 47 on coastal navigation.

[21] Marcia Yonemoto, "Maps and Metaphors of the 'Small Eastern Sea' in Tokugawa Japan (1603–1868)," *The Geographical Review* 89.2 (1999): 172. She argues that the difficulty of the voyage, which depended on favorable winds, caused Japanese to think of the ocean as "unpredictable."

[22] Keiji Imamura, *Prehistoric Japan: New Perspectives on Insular East Asia* (Honolulu: University of Hawai'i Press, 1996), chapter 11; Mark J. Hudson, *Ruins of Identity: Ethnogenesis in the Japanese Islands* (Honolulu: University of Hawai'i Press, 1999), analyzes the contemporary academic debates about Japanese origins.

[23] Hudson, *Ruins*, chapter 5. Wet-rice agriculture could also have entered Japan directly from the Shanghai delta; see Barnes, *Rise of Civilization*, pp. 169–70, and Ki-baik Lee, trans. Edward W. Wagner with Edward J. Shultz, *A New History of Korea* (Cambridge, MA: Harvard University Press, 1984), p. 14.

Asian "Okhotsk culture" used to enter Hokkaido.[24] These "Northeast Asian Vikings," known as the Satsumon people, were skilled sailors, whale hunters, and traders.[25] The recent discovery of a hunting-fishing settlement dating to 3500–2000 BCE in Aomori prefecture, northern Honshu, underlines the importance of this historic migration route into Japan, and has stimulated some intellectuals to identify the Jomon (and not the Yayoi) as the epoch which laid down the "roots" of Japanese culture.[26]

Northeast Asian peoples and states

The northeast housed a multitude of tribal peoples, whose many names continue to confuse historians. Northeast Asians belong to a language group that extends westward from the North Pacific coast to Turkey.[27] According to modern linguistic analysis, the region was populated by speakers of the Altaic languages, primarily forms of Tungus (for example, Jurchen/Manchu), Mongolian, and Korean, which, like Japanese, is classified by many specialists as Altaic. Their native language separates them from the Chinese speakers who form the vast majority of peoples living in China Proper.[28]

Despite significant cultural contact, their language and lifestyle distinguished northeast Asians from the Hua and Xia peoples of the Central Plain. Northeast Asia experienced its own period of state formation, which was stimulated by the expansion of Central Plain regimes into the eastern portion of the North China Plain. Recent archaeological

---

[24] Anatolii Trekhsviatskyi, "At the Far Edge of the Chinese Oikoumene: Mutual Relations of the Indigenous Population of Sakhalin with the Yuan and Ming Dynasties," *Journal of Asian History* 41.2 (2007): 131–55; Imamura, *Prehistoric Japan*, p. 1; Toshihiko Kikuchi, "Continental Culture and Hokkaido," in *Windows on the Japanese Past: Studies in Archaeology and Prehistory*, ed. Richard J. Pearson (Ann Arbor: Center for Japanese Studies, University of Michigan, 1986), p. 158. Kikuchi notes that the Okhotsk culture was "closely related" to the Mohe/Jurchin (Jurchen) cultures. On the Sakhalin trade route during the Qing, see Wu Ling and Li Xiaokang, "Cong Shandan maoyi de bianqian kan Qingdai dui Dongbei diqu tongzhi de ruohua" (The weakening of Qing control over the northeast localities from the perspective of the changes in the Shandan trade), *Beifang wenwu* 2007 #1: 91–98.

[25] Amino, "Maritime View," pp. 51–2.

[26] Junko Habu and Clare Fawcett, "Jomon Archaeology and the Representation of Japanese Origins," *Antiquity* 73 (1999): 591; Amino, "Maritime View," p. 41.

[27] See S. Robert Ramsay, *The Languages of China* (Princeton: Princeton University Press, 1987), figure 4, "The Languages of China Grouped by Family," and pp. 171, 173. Also see Mark Byington, "A History of the Puyŏ State, Its People, and Its Legacy," PhD thesis, East Asian Languages and Civilizations, Harvard University, May 2003, pp. 55–57.

[28] "China Proper" refers to the eighteen provinces administered by the Ming empire, i.e. the population living south of the Great Wall, and excludes the Inner Asian territories added to the Qing empire, whose majority populations before 1911 were non-Han.

discoveries indicate that while the elites of Yan, one of the last Warring States kingdoms to be subjugated by the unifier Qin Shihuangdi, followed Shang and Zhou burial practices, Yan also ruled a subject population indigenous to the Beijing environs.[29] Here, Central Plain customs mingled with what archaeologists call the local Zhangjiayuan culture, making Yan a state that "differed in many ways from the states closer to the Zhou core in the Central Plains."[30]

In ancient times the Central Plain states were not able to penetrate the northeast easily. "Formidable indigenous groups who seem to have remained beyond the sphere of Yan control"stalled Yan's expansion northward beyond the Tangshan, Tianjin, and Beijing area.[31] The individual names of these peoples: the Rong, Guzhu, Lingzhi, and others, appear in Yan chronicles. By the middle of the fourth century BCE, Yan had advanced into the coastal corridor of western Liaoning.[32] Later, the Han fixed their border at the Liao River, which divides Liaoxi from Liaodong. Han attempts to penetrate further east culminated in the establishment of four Han commanderies (108–107 BCE), although only one, Lelang (K. Nangnang), was to survive for very long.[33] Lelang was a source of Chinese political and cultural models that influenced state formation in the peninsula.[34] State formation appears in the peninsula during the long interregnum separating the Han and Sui, a period of Chinese political atomization. A number of small city states arose, to be followed by confederated kingdoms, then through a process of conquest, four and finally three states emerged in the middle of the sixth century CE.

Despite their emulation of Chinese political models, the northeast Asian states actively resisted and were mostly successful in preventing their political incorporation into the Chinese body politic. Control of Xuantu (K. Hyŏndo), a commandery established in the area between the Yalu and Tongjia Rivers, became an object of struggle between Han and the first northeast Asian state, the kingdom of Puyŏ (C. Fuyu). Established about the third century BCE in the Songhua River region in present-day Jilin province, Puyŏ survived until the late fifth century CE, outlasting the Han state. Puyŏ acted as an independent agent for most of

[29] Byington, "History of the Puyŏ State," p. 39, also figure 2.3, pp. 40, 41.
[30] *Ibid.*, pp. 42–43. Pines, "Beasts or Human," writes, p. 87, that Yan was regarded as "beyond the immediate boundaries" of the "Chinese cultural realm" in writings of the fifth to third centuries BCE.
[31] *Ibid.*, p. 43.   [32] *Ibid.*, p. 70.
[33] Lee, *New History*, pp. 19–21; Barnes, *Rise of Civilization*, pp. 208–21.
[34] See Hyung Il Pai, *Constructing "Korean" Origins: A Critical Review of Archaeology, Historiography, and Racial Myth in Korean State-Formation Theories* (Cambridge, MA: Harvard University Asia Center, 2000), chapters 5 and 6.

its existence, making and abandoning alliances in response to the shifting balance of power within the region.

Confronting the Han state in northeast Liaodong, Puyŏ was "a powerful non-Chinese state playing a decisive role in the interregional politics of northeast Asia."[35] Like the Han, Puyŏ faced security threats from the nomadic groups to their west, the Xiongnu, then the Xianbei. They had a major rival in Koguryŏ, another northeast Asian state which established itself in the first century BCE. Puyŏ was in touch with Chinese polities from its inception, but free from their direct control. Texts of Puyŏ's exchanges with Yan and with the Han regime document successful military rebuffs of several Han efforts to strengthen its presence in the Liaodong area, particularly with respect to Xuantu, which had become a Puyŏ buffer state.[36]

The Koguryŏ kingdom which arose in the first century BCE was situated in the Han River drainage in present-day Jilin province. During the reign of King Kwanggaet'o (r. 391–413), its territory extended over Liaodong to the west, the Sungari River on the northeast, the Han and Naktong Rivers to the south, up to the borders of the Korean states of Paekche and Silla. At this point, Koguryŏ bordered territory claimed by Han.[37] Like Puyŏ, this northeast Asian state responded to shifting power configurations in the region, at times allying with and at other times militarily opposing the Han state. In 75 BCE, for example, Koguryŏ expelled the Han from Xuantu.[38] After the demise of the Han empire, Koguryŏ and Paekche, which was established in the third century CE, captured the Han commanderies of Lelang and Daifang. In the fourth century, Koguryŏ annexed both Puyŏ and Liaodong.

In the late sixth century, Koguryŏ engaged in a new round of geopolitical maneuvering as the emergent Sui regime in China confronted a powerful Turk empire on its northern frontier. By this period, the states responding to the shifting balance of power included the peninsular states of Paekche and Silla, as well as the emerging Yamato regime in Japan. A chain of events was set off when Koguryŏ sought an alliance with the

---

[35] Byington, "History of the Puyŏ State," p. 232. Puyŏ was subjugated by Koguryŏ following a Xianbei attack in 346 CE. Its government was finally expelled from the region at the end of the fifth century.

[36] *Ibid.*

[37] Richard D. McBride II, "Introduction," in *State and Society in Middle and Late Silla*, ed. Richard D. McBride II (Cambridge, MA: Korea Institute, Harvard University, 2010), p. 6.

[38] Song Nai Rhee, "Secondary State Formation: The Case of Koguryŏ State," in *Pacific Northeast Asia in Prehistory: Hunter-Fisher-Gatherers, Farmers, and Sociopolitical Elites*, ed. C. Melvin Aikens and Song Nai Rhee (Pullman: Washington State University Press, 1992), p.195; Lee, *New History*, pp. 23–24, 38–40.

Turks against Sui. Because its primary rival, Paekche, was allied with Koguryŏ, Silla allied with the Sui. Sui military campaigns against Koguryŏ in 612, 613, and 614, were unsuccessful. China's new Tang rulers ignored a 626 embassy from Paekche and Silla seeking a joint military campaign against Koguryŏ; they were otherwise occupied with campaigns against the Eastern Turks. Sporadic attacks on Koguryŏ in the 640s by Tang, Silla, Paekche, and other Tang allies failed.

The final round of hostilities was sparked by Koguryŏ's attack on the Khitan, who had become clients of the Tang, in 654.[39] The following year, Koguryŏ joined Paekche to capture over thirty Silla towns, causing Silla to turn to its ally Tang, which launched new campaigns against Koguryŏ (655, 658, 659, 661). Paekche, which was allied with the Japanese Yamato court, was defeated by Silla in 663. Silla then cooperated with Tang in the final military expedition that defeated Koguryŏ. Having eliminated its major rivals and "unified" the peninsula, Silla then did a radical *volte-face* to resist Chinese military expansion into the Korean peninsula. The Tang court, beset by its problems with Tibet, withdrew its troops and did not attempt to consolidate its hold on the former Koguryŏ territories.

Japan in northeast Asia

Korean specialists agree that the Han commanderies, especially Lelang, helped stimulate the establishment of the early northeast Asian states, not only in the peninsula, but also through Lelang's role in advancing Korean iron production to western Kyushu. In the fourth century, Japan became "the new focus of trade for the peninsular polities."[40]

Japanese demand for iron heightened contact between the archipelago and the peninsula. Competition spurred tribal chieftains in Kyushu and the Kin'ai district in Honshu to increase their ties with the peninsula, importing iron tools and also the metalworkers who produced them (Japan did not smelt its own iron until the late fifth century).[41] According to Joan Piggott, "control of trade in iron and production of

---

[39] Lee, *New History*, pp. 47–48, 66–71. For a recent reappraisal of Koguryŏ's place in Korean history, see Kyung Moon Hwang, *A History of Korea* (New York: Palgrave Macmillan, 2010), chapter 1.

[40] Cheun Soo Park, "Kaya and Silla in Archaeological Perspective," in *Early Korea*, vol. I: *Reconsidering Early Korean History Through Archaeology*, ed. Mark E. Byington (Cambridge, MA: Korea Institute, Harvard University, 2008), p. 116.

[41] Barnes, *Rise of Civilization*, chapters 11, 13; William Wayne Farris, *Sacred Texts and Buried Treasures: Issues in the Historical Archaeology of Ancient Japan* (Honolulu: University of Hawai'i Press, 1998), chapter 1. See also Li Huizhu, "Handai yiqian Shandong yu Chaoxian bandao nanbu."

iron goods were key factors contributing to the preeminent influence of Wa paramounts (regional chieftains)."[42] Improved techniques in salt and ceramic production were also imported, as was the fashion of chiefly burial in round key-hole shaped tombs.

The flows were not in one direction only. Having discovered several settlements in northern Kyushu that "are known for certain to have been populated by immigrants from the Korean peninsula," archaeologists hypothesize that the new technologies signal a "new wave" of human migration from the continent.[43] Japanese also migrated to Korea. Funerary objects in excavated early fourth-century tombs in Kimhae, a major transport center on Korea's southeast coast directly opposite western Honshu and northwest Kyushu, include stone ornaments and shields with bronze spiral-shaped motifs originating in Japan's Kinai region. Body armor uncovered in Japan and in cemeteries in south Korea include Mongolian helmets, suits in the Koguryŏ style, and Yamato-style helmets and cuirasses.[44] Silla products in Yamato tombs and Japanese products in Silla tombs in Kyŏngju dating from the middle of the fifth century attest to the mutuality of these exchanges.[45] By the middle of the fourth century CE, Silla, Paekche, and Koguryŏ had established themselves as "centralized aristocratic states" on the Korean peninsula. Their elites had adopted a writing system based on Chinese characters and were familiar with Confucian texts. In 372 Koguryŏ established a National Confucian Academy (K. T'aehak 太學) with a curriculum that included the Five Classics. All three kingdoms promulgated Chinese-style legal codes.[46]

---

[42] Joan R. Piggott, *The Emergence of Japanese Kingship* (Stanford: Stanford University Press, 1997), p. 52. The Japanese were able to smelt their own iron in the late sixth century.

[43] Imamura, *Prehistoric Japan*, p. 149.

[44] Gina Barnes, "Discoveries of Iron Armour on the Korean Peninsula," in her *State Formation in Korea: Historical and Archaeological Perspectives* (Richmond: Curzon, 2001), pp. 125–51. Park, "Kaya and Silla," pp. 144–45, speculates that "those interred in the Wa-style tombs throughout the Kaya territories were Wa people transplanted by Tae Kaya and So Kaya in order to keep a check on the diplomatic and military activities in support of Paekche of those buried in the keyhole-shaped tombs on the Yŏngsan River." Oh Young Kwŏn, "The Influence of Recent Archaeological Discoveries on the Research of Paekche History," in *Early Korea*, vol. I: *Reconsidering Early Korean History Through Archaeology*, ed. Byington, pp. 96–102, also cites the discovery of keyhole-shaped tombs on the "Wa" model in the Yŏngsan River region in the southern peninsula, which date from the first half of the sixth century but are modeled on Japanese keyhole-shaped tombs dated to the third century CE. A tomb in Kohŭng featured a man wearing a Paekche-style gilt bronze crown and shoes, but "what appears to be Wa-style armor," p. 102.

[45] Park, "Kaya and Silla," describes the internal political shifts on the Korean peninsula, including the rise of Tae Kaya as the "new central power in Kaya" (p. 140) and the central trading power with Japan; and its rivalry with Paekche, pp. 143–45.

[46] Lee, *New History*, pp. 58–59.

Stimulated by the trade boom of the fourth century, Japan's state-building effort was further enhanced by Korean elites who emigrated in the fourth and fifth centuries. Recent studies indicate that the majority of Yamato scribes and accountants were descendants of Korean immigrants. They served on the committee that compiled the three Chinese-style penal and administrative codes (*ritsuryō*) during 668–701, which ushered in an emperor-led governmental structure based on the Chinese model.[47]

Korean unification

The mid-seventh century power configuration that led Silla to ally with Tang in order to counter the Paekche alliance with Koguryŏ and Yamato marked what would be a historic turning point in the consolidation of power. In this instance, Silla and Tang emerged victorious, defeating first Paekche (663) and then destroying Koguryŏ, the first major northeast Asian state. These defeats affected Japan: many aristocrats fled Paekche and sought refuge in Japan, where some obtained court posts and intermarried with Japanese elite families.[48] Emperor Kanmu's mother was descended from such an immigrant family. She was a member of the Yamato lineage, who were descended from a king of Paekche.[49] The size of this migration is evident from the finding that one-third of the 1,182 elite lineages recorded in the ninth-century genealogy *Shinsen shōjiroku* 新撰姓氏錄 were of foreign origin.[50] The contribution of Paekche immigrants to the compilation/adoption of Chinese-style administrative codes is well recognized. Japanese motivation for the promulgation of the Taihō civil and criminal codes (701) and the revised Yōrō civil and criminal codes in 718 was both defensive – because of anxiety about the possibility of invasion from the Asian mainland – and

---

[47] Farris, *Sacred Texts and Buried Treasures*, pp. 104–5. See his chapter 2 for an overview of the scholarship on Japanese–Korean interactions during the ancient period; also Hudson, *Ruins of Identity*, chapter 7.

[48] Hirano Kunio, *Kikajin to kodai kokka* (Immigrants and the ancient state) (Tokyo: Yoshikawa kōbunkan, 1993). According to Charlotte von Verschuer, trans. Kristen Lee Hunter, *Across the Perilous Sea: Japanese Trade with China and Korea from the Seventh to the Sixteenth Centuries* (Ithaca: Center for East Asian Studies, 2006), p. 6, the incomers included about a hundred Chinese prisoners of war, who were settled in Mino province (present-day Gifu).

[49] Ellen van Goethem, *Nagaoka: Japan's Forgotten Capital* (Leiden: E. J. Brill, 2008), pp. 11, 17–19.

[50] Michael Como, *Weaving and Binding: Immigrant Gods and Female Immortals in Ancient Japan* (Honolulu: University of Hawai'i Press, 2009), p. 9.

positive – reflecting the desire of the Yamato rulers to strengthen their control within Japan.[51]

Koguryŏ's demise did not mark the end of powerful northeast Asian challenges to the Central Plain states. Except for brief intervals, northeast Asia from the third to the thirteenth century was dominated by locally based states such as Koguryŏ and its successor, Parhae (C. Bohai, 719–926), that operated outside the control of regimes based on the Central Plain. Parhae accepted investiture from Tang in 726 to strengthen its legitimacy, but dealt with groups on its own frontier by adopting the Chinese "loose reins" (jimi 羈縻) policy of indirect rule. Parhae used the jimi policy to deal with the Mohe, ancestors of the Jurchen, who had established the state of Da Zuo in present-day Jilin province's Dunhua region. In 738 Parhae created a network of administrative units and invested Mohe tribal chieftains with Parhae titles of office.[52] Simultaneously, to defend against encroachment from Tang and Silla on its western and southern borders, Parhae sought an alliance with the Japanese court, which received embassies from Parhae during the eighth and ninth centuries.[53]

The northeast also produced the Murong Xianbei and Tuoba Xianbei, the Khitan and Jurchen, whose empires extended into north China. By 750 the Uighur empire, Parhae, Silla, and Japan which confronted Tang on its northern and northeastern frontiers were stable polities, each with documentary capacities and literate elites, using Chinese or a writing system of their own for state affairs, who used the "common language and formalities derived from the T'ang system" to form diplomatic coalitions with each other, irrespective of the Tang.[54] Parhae, Silla, and Japan were diplomatically allied in this way.

---

[51] Delmer M. Brown, "Introduction," in *The Cambridge History of Japan*, vol. I: *Ancient Japan*, ed. Delmer M. Brown (Cambridge: Cambridge University Press, 1993), pp. 32–33; Herman Ooms, *Imperial Politics and Symbolics in Ancient Japan: The Tenmu Dynasty, 650–800* (Honolulu: University of Hawai'i Press, 2009). For an appreciation of the impact of current scholarship on received understandings of ancient Japanese history, see the review of Como's monograph by Lori Meeks in *The Journal of Japanese Studies* 37.2 (2011): 397–401.

[52] Sakayori Masashi, "Tōhoku Ajia no dōō to kodai Nihon – Botsukai no shiten kara" (Trends in northeast Asia and ancient Japan – the view from Parhae), in *Shinpan kodai no Nihon*, vol. II: *Ajia kara mita Nihon*, ed. Tsuboi Kiyotari and Hirano Kunio (Tokyo: Kadokawa shoten, 1992), pp. 305–7. On the Mohe/Malgal/Jurchen connection, see Herbert Franke, "The Chin Dynasty," in *The Cambridge History of China*, vol. VI: *Alien Regimes and Border States, 907–1368*, ed. Herbert Franke and Denis Twitchett (Cambridge: Cambridge University Press, 1994), pp. 217–18.

[53] Batten, *Gateway to Japan*, pp 18–33; Teng Hongyan, "Bohai zhi Riben liwu tanzhe" (Inquiry into the gifts presented by Bohai to Japan), *Zhongguo bianjiang shidi yanjiu* 16.2 (2006): 69–76.

[54] See Franke and Twitchett, "Introduction," in *The Cambridge History of China*, vol. VI, pp. 2–4.

The northeast Asian conquest regimes

Northeast Asian regimes came into their own in the tenth to fourteenth centuries. Their rise was partly a response to the waning of Tang power after the An Lushan rebellion of 755. Shifting to a defensive posture on its borders, Tang ceded power to provincial governors who gradually acquired autonomy during the late ninth century, a period of crisis which featured the collapse of the Tibetan kingdom and the Uighur empire, as well as the Tang. Following the Tang downfall, Turks, Uighurs, Xianbei, Tanguts, and other peoples came to occupy most of the North China Plain. A succession of short-lived regimes, led by former Tang generals of non-Han origin, ruled north China.[55] This region, from Beijing to the Great Wall, called the "Sixteen Prefectures," was controlled by the Khitan Liao, then the Jurchen Jin, and finally the Mongols.[56] The Song not only failed to win back the Sixteen Prefectures but were forced to flee north China in 1127. Finally, in 1279, the Mongol ruler Khubilai succeeded in defeating the Southern Song regime and incorporated all of China into the Mongol empire. This was the northeastern heritage claimed by Nurhaci and Hongtaiji, the foundational leaders of the Jurchen/Manchu regime that incorporated China into the Qing empire.

The Khitan, Jurchen, and Mongol empires mark the apogee of northeast Asian geopolitics. Each ruled territory that extended beyond China Proper, to encompass nomadic peoples. Their conquest moved the "frontier" northward to encompass Inner Asian peoples who would also be subjected by the last northeast Asian empire, the Qing. Whereas the Khitan had been in touch with Chinese officials since at least the sixth century, appearing in various guises as bearers of tribute and as soldiers in Chinese armies, the Jurchen learned about Chinese bureaucratic practices from their experience as subordinates to the Khitan Liao. Similarly, the Mongols learned from their service as vassals to the Jurchen Jin.[57]

The conquest regimes of the tenth to fourteenth century synthesized elements derived from Inner Asia and the Central Plain. Unlike the Central Plain states, they used different sets of rules, framed in multiple

---

[55] The pragmatism of political alliances in the early tenth century, which reflected the fluid geopolitical situation of the time, is analyzed by Naomi Standen, *Unbounded Loyalty: Frontier Crossing in Liao China* (Honolulu: University of Hawai'i Press, 2007). Standen underlines the permeability of self-identities in this transitional era.

[56] Robert M. Somers, "The End of the T'ang," in *The Cambridge History of China*, vol. III: *Sui and T'ang China, 589–906*, part 1, ed. Denis Twitchett (Cambridge: Cambridge University Press, 1979), pp. 762–63.

[57] Franke and Twitchett, "Introduction," pp. 10–14; Naomi Standen, "(Re)Constructing the Frontiers of Tenth-Century China," in *Frontiers in Question: Eurasian Borderlands, 700–1700*, ed. Daniel Power and Naomi Standen (New York: St. Martin's Press, 1999), p. 62.

languages to rule subjects from nomadic and sedentary societies. They used institutions adapted to their comparative military advantage, the possession of mobile cavalry. Scholars have observed that these regimes created power centers around the ruler and his close kinsmen that bypassed the formal bureaucracies inherited from the Central Plain.[58] Each used the practice of companionship to create bonds that "transcended tribal and national barriers."[59] Confucian norms concerning the privileged role of educated officials did not protect them from court beatings. To counter their absolute power, rulers were constrained by strong traditions of collective decision-making by deliberative bodies for kinsmen and peers.

Korea's responses to its neighbors

Modern depictions of Korea as "the Hermit Kingdom" belie the historical reality that Korean states enjoyed extensive trading and diplomatic contacts with their East Asian neighbors as early as the Three Kingdoms period.[60] Korea's geographical situation made it vulnerable to military pressures from Manchurian regimes. As Peter Yun notes, Korea often confronted not just one but two regional powers, located in northeast Asia and in the North China Plain. Korean foreign policy "can best be characterized as continual realignments of military alliances to maintain equilibrium," with a preference for alliance with more distant regimes to enhance its security vis-à-vis states sharing common borders. Silla's political unification of the Korean peninsula in the seventh century probably could not have taken place without its alliance with Tang. Silla's deft use of the alliance to defeat its rival Koguryŏ and subsequently to counter the emergent power of Parhae exemplifies its ability to maneuver in a multistate context. There were many instances, however, when later Korean states could not withstand the military pressures. The history of Korean interactions with other northeast Asian tribes illustrates the complexity of the situation.[61]

The ancestors of the Jurchen, "a semi-nomadic Tungusic people scattered in many tribes over a wide expanse of Manchuria, southern Siberia,

---

[58] Franke and Twitchett, "Introduction," pp. 29–36.   [59] *Ibid.*, pp. 21–22.

[60] Peter Yun, "Foreigners in Korea during the Period of Mongol Interference," in *Embracing the Other: The Interaction of Korean and Foreign Cultures, Proceedings of the First World Congress of Korean Studies 2002* (Songnam: Academy of Korean Studies, 2002) vol. 3, pp. 1221–28.

[61] See, for example, the complicated maneuvers triangulating Song, Khitan, and Koryŏ relations described in Peter Yun, "Koryŏ–Khitan Relations and Khitan Cultural Influence in the Eleventh and Twelfth Centuries," *Journal of Central Eurasian Studies* 3 (2012): 69–83.

and northeast Korea" called Malgal (in Chinese, Mohe 靺鞨),[62] were subjects of Koguryŏ, Parhae, and Liao. Although some Malgal succeeded in joining the Parhae elite, "the bulk of the Malgal constituted a subject people, some of whom at times were reduced to forced labor or slave status and so became an unfree class serving masters who belonged to the ruling class of Koguryŏ origins."[63]

Before the eleventh century, Korea treated the Malgal/Jurchen as clients. According to Ki-baek Lee, the Jurchen "looked upon Koryŏ ... as their 'parent country' and as the source of the trappings of civilization they so desired to acquire."[64] There was brisk trade, with the Jurchen exchanging horses and furs for Korean grain, cloth, and iron weapons and tools. Some Jurchen moved into the Koryŏ lands; others went as emissaries to the Northern Song capital at Kaifeng. When the Khitan managed to seal off the land route, the Jurchen went by sea, and after the Koryŏ defeat of the Khitan, as members of Korean embassies to Song.[65]

Relations between Koryŏ and the Jurchen shifted in tone and intensity during the rise of the Wanyan clan under Wugunai (1021–74), who extended Jurchen domination from the Changbaishan northward. Wugunai's brother Aguda united the Jurchen and founded the Jin state (1115). He subjugated the Khitan Liao (1125), and captured the Song capital, Kaifeng (1127). Koryŏ's King Injong (r. 1122–46) declared himself a vassal of Jin in 1126, even though "There were many in Koryŏ who were outraged" at the demand that Koryŏ acknowledge Jin's dominant status in the tributary relationship.[66]

Multi-state alliances were made in an effort to defend Korea against the Jurchen Jin. In a situation that would be repeated during the late sixteenth century, the Khitan Liao and the Song sent envoys to ensure that Koryŏ would remain neutral in a Liao–Song conflict. The Koryŏ king initially sent missions to the Song court, hoping for a military alliance against the Khitan, but he reluctantly accepted the Liao calendar in 994, and in 1022 again subordinated himself as a tributary vassal. Although it also resumed diplomatic relations with Song, Koryŏ was forced to become a Jin vassal in 1130, after the Jin conquest of north China.[67] Later, Koryŏ allied with

---

[62] Lee, *New History of Korea*, p. 72. For a longer description of the early Jurchen history, see Franke, "Chin Dynasty," pp. 216–18.

[63] Lee, *New History of Korea*, p. 89.   [64] *Ibid.*, p. 126.

[65] Franke, "Chin Dynasty," p. 219.

[66] *Ibid.*, p. 229, quotation from Lee, *New History of Korea*, p. 128.

[67] Michael C. Rogers, "Sukchong of Koryŏ: His Accession and His Relations with Liao," *T'oung Pao* 47.1–2 (1959): 30–42; also his "The Regularization of Koryŏ–Chin Relations (1116–1131)," *Central Asiatic Journal* 6.2 (1961): 51–84 and "National Consciousness in Medieval Korea: The Impact of Liao and Chin on Koryŏ," in *China Among Equals: The*

the Mongols to defeat Khitan remnants fleeing south of the Yalu River
(1219). Subjected to Mongol attacks beginning in 1231, Koryŏ surrendered in 1259.

Like Song China, Koryŏ was incorporated into a Mongol multi-
ethnic empire. The *pax Mongolorum* blurred the social and geographical
boundaries separating Koreans from their north Asian neighbors.[68]
The Mongols reorganized the Koryŏ military on the model of their
tumen system, and stimulated the economic development of present-
day Liaodong through the relocation of Koryŏ households and the
creation of a network of overland relay stations linking the peninsula
to the rest of their empire. Politically favored families joined Uighur
and Turkestani merchants in long-distance trade. Intermarriage
between the Koryŏ and Mongol ruling houses began in 1269; over
1500 daughters of the Koryŏ elite became Mongol wives and consorts,
while Korean women of lower status were seized as war booty and
enslaved or married off to Mongol soldiers.[69] Many Mongols and
Central Asians accompanied Mongol princesses to reside at the Koryŏ
court, while Koryŏ royal sons lived in the Mongol capital, Daidu, as
hostages. From the late thirteenth century, Koryŏ kings adopted
Mongol clothing and hairstyle to "reflect their subordinate status
within the empire."[70]

Japan's relations with the continent

While continuing to exhibit a strong interest in Chinese cultural objects,
Japan strongly resisted subordination within a Sinocentric world order
after the state building period. Official relations between Japan and the
continent dropped off significantly, although aristocratic adherence to
Buddhism and the appearance of Buddhist monasteries ensured a continuing demand for scriptures and visits to mother temples in China by
monks.

Elite interest in and demand for Chinese cultural goods never faltered.
They were obtained mainly through private channels, via Korea or other
entities in northeast Asia, for example, Parhae. Particularly intense in the
early ninth century – nine missions were sent in the period 809–827
alone – these Parhae missions brought Chinese books as well as ginseng

---

Middle Kingdom and Its Neighbors, 10th–14th Centuries, ed. Morris Rossabi (Berkeley:
  University of California Press, 1983), pp. 151–72.
[68] Yun, "Foreigners in Korea," pp. 1221–28; D. Robinson, *Empire's Twilight*; Breuker,
  "Within or Without?"
[69] D. Robinson, *Empire's Twilight*, pp. 53, 100–4.
[70] *Ibid.*, p. 59. Daidu was a Mongol rendering of Dadu.

and furs to Japan.[71] According to the diary of Jōjin, a monk-courtier who was well received by the eleventh-century Northern Song court, travel to China aboard a Chinese merchant ship, though not routine, was not a pioneering venture.[72] Japanese Buddhist temples engaged in the China trade as a means of funding temple renovation, and realized high profits from filling the demand for Chinese goods. Aristocratic interest in *karamono* (literally, Tang objects) grew during the Song–Yuan transition.[73] A ship, wrecked off the coast of southwest Korea in 1323, carried 28 tons of goods: Chinese pottery, coins, sandalwood, and drugs such as pepper, betel nut, and jasmine.[74] Among some 20,500 pieces of pottery, the majority were celadon and white ware pieces produced in Zhejiang and Jiangxi provinces, including vases destined to grace the new tea ceremony that was being taken up by upwardly mobile regional military figures.[75]

Buddhist monks played a key role in three "waves" of continent–archipelago transmission in the late eighth and early ninth centuries, the late twelfth and early thirteenth centuries, and the middle of the thirteenth century, during the Song–Yuan interregnum. Buddhism created a transnational network which allowed Japanese monks to visit Chinese monasteries and acquire religious instruction, and some Chinese monks to seek refuge in Japan during periods of dynastic change. By virtue of their literacy in written Chinese (monks based their Japanese translations of the sutras on Chinese texts), Japanese monks performed multiple roles as intermediaries in dealings with the continent. Japanese elites demanded Chinese books, which were often imported into Japan by monks. Until about 1600, Japanese printing was religious in nature: there were fewer than five hundred domestic imprints, most from Buddhist monasteries serving a clerical readership.[76] Texts moved in both directions. Jōjin actually brought sutras and other religious texts with him to

---

[71] According to Sakayori, "Tōhoku Ajia," p. 313, Japanese sources mention trade with Mohe people living along the coast across the Japan Sea from Hokkaido and artifacts from archaeological excavations support these texts.

[72] Robert Borgen, "Jōjin's Travels from Center to Center (with Some Periphery in Between)," in *Heian Japan: Centers and Peripheries*, ed. Mikael Adophson, Edward Kamens, and Stacie Matsumoto (Honolulu: University of Hawai'i Press, 2006), pp. 384–413.

[73] Kōji Saeki, trans. Peter Shapinsky, "Chinese Trade Ceramics in Medieval Japan," in *Tools of Culture: Japan's Cultural, Intellectual, Medical, and Technological Contacts in East Asia, 1000–1500s*, ed. Andrew Edmund Goble, Kenneth R. Robinson, and Haruko Wakabayashi (Ann Arbor: Association for Asian Studies, 2009), pp. 163–82.

[74] Andrew Edmund Goble, Kenneth R. Robinson, and Haruko Wakabayashi, "Introduction," in *Tools of Culture*, ed. Goble, Robinson, and Wakabayashi, p. 8.

[75] Saeki, "Chinese Trade Ceramics," p. 166. Saeki identifies the late twelfth century through the thirteenth century as the period when Japanese imports of Chinese pottery peaked, p. 175.

[76] Peter Kornicki, *The Book in Japan: A Cultural History from the Beginnings to the Nineteenth Century* (Honolulu: University of Hawai'i Press, 2001), p. 20.

show his Chinese counterparts, but he also purchased an equivalent number of Chinese books to send home with his disciples.[77] By request, the books he acquired included works on Chinese administration and Chinese medicine.[78]

Insular Japan was not isolated from the major political transitions on the continent. Ignoring repeated attempts by Khubilai to initiate diplomatic relations, the shogunate prepared its defenses. Though torn by internal divisions, the Kamakura shogunate mobilized warriors to repel Mongol invasions in 1274 and again in 1281, in both cases with the aid of "divine winds" (*kamikaze*), emerging from the crisis stronger than before.[79] Upheavals on the continent also brought refugees to Japan. Twenty-five Chinese monks from west China and the Yangzi delta became tutors to the Hōjō at the Kamakura shogunal court. The ensuing expansion of Rinzai Zen suggests that these foreign migrants, though small in number, nonetheless exercised significant influence.[80] Along with their religion, these monks introduced Japan to "models of institutional organization, new forms of architecture, new styles of painting and portraiture, and new forms of aesthetic appreciation" such as the ceremonial consumption of tea.[81]

Japanese also obtained Chinese products, including printed editions of the Buddhist canon, from Korea. The Ashikaga shoguns patronized Zen Buddhism in order to strengthen their rule.[82] Especially during the Koryŏ dynasty (918–1392), Korea was also an active participant in the dissemination of Buddhist scriptures. Shortly after the Northern Song printing of the Tripitaka (983), the Koryŏ court requested and received a copy

[77] Robert Borgen, "Jōjin's Discoveries in Song China," in *Tools of Culture*, ed. Goble, Robinson, and Wakabayashi, pp. 42–43.

[78] *Ibid.*

[79] Ishii Susumu, trans. Jeffrey P. Mass and Hitomi Tonomura, "The Decline of the Kamakura Bakufu," in *Warrior Rule in Japan*, ed. Marius B. Jansen (Cambridge: Cambridge University Press, 1995), pp. 47–64, suggests that the shogunate may have been influenced by Buddhist monks from south China, fleeing the Mongol conquest; also, since the Mongol letter was addressed to the "king" of Japan, decisions on a response rested with the emperor, not the shogun. The actual text of the Mongol letter is discussed by Kenneth W. Chase, "Mongol Intentions towards Japan in 1266: Evidence from a Mongol Letter to the Sung," *Sino-Japanese Studies* 9.2 (1997): 13–28.

[80] Martin Collcutt, "Lanxi Daolong (1213–1278) at Kenchōji: Chinese Contributions to the Making of Medieval Japanese Rinzai Zen," in *Tools of Culture*, ed. Goble, Robinson, and Wakabayashi, pp. 135–59.

[81] Andrew Edmund Goble, "Kajiwara Shōzen (1265–1337) and the Medical Silk Road: Chinese and Arabic Influences on Early Medieval Japanese Medicine," in *Tools of Culture*, ed. Goble, Robinson, and Wakabayashi, p. 231. Goble's essay focuses on the importation of medical texts from China to Japan.

[82] Kenneth R. Robinson, "Treated as Treasures: The Circulation of Sutras in Maritime Northeast Asia from 1388 to the Mid-Sixteenth Century," *East Asian History* 21 (2001): 42.

(991). The Northern Song Tripitaka inspired Koryŏ, the Liao, and Jin rulers to order their own imprints of the Buddhist canon.[83] The Koryŏ court commissioned two printings, based on a late tenth-century Chinese edition, in the late eleventh and mid-twelfth centuries. Japanese (and Ryukyuans) found it easier to acquire the Tripitaka from Korea than from China, but the Korean court favored recipients who could assist them in suppressing the Japanese pirates such as the Ōuchi, governors in western Honshu and northern Kyushu, and the Sō, who controlled Tsushima. Requests from Ashikaga shoguns were also granted.[84]

Confucian texts and Chinese administrative codes also entered Japan from an early period. We have a list of 125 books that the Japanese courtier and Sinophile Fujiwara no Yorinaga (1120–56) wished a Chinese merchant to acquire on his behalf. Most were commentaries on the Confucian canon, but his library also included dynastic histories.[85] His contemporary, Fujiwara no Michinori (1106–59), also left a sizable personal library.

Success in warding off threatened Mongol naval attacks seems to have hardened elite attitudes toward subsequent attempts by Chinese rulers to draw Japan into the Sinocentric world order. Henceforth, with the sole exception of the period 1398–1408, when the Ashikaga shogun Yoshimitsu (1358–1408) accepted investiture from the Ming dynasty, Japanese authorities rejected incorporation into the Chinese tribute system, despite desiring trading relations with China.[86] Thus in 1394, when Yoshimitsu thought about adopting an era name based on the reign

---

[83] Lewis R. Lancaster, "The Buddhist Canon in the Koryŏ Period," in *Buddhism in Koryŏ: A Royal Religion*, ed. Lewis R. Lancaster, Kikun Suh, and Chai-shin Yu (Berkeley: University of California Institute of East Asian Studies, 1996), pp. 174–75.

[84] K. Robinson, "Treated as Treasures," writes that the Koryŏ and Chosŏn courts received "approximately one hundred" requests for Buddhist sutras between 1388 and the middle of the sixteenth century. On the publication work of Korean Buddhist monks, see Boudewijn Walraven, "Reader's Etiquette, and Other Aspects of Book Culture in Chosŏn Korea," in *Books in Numbers: Conference Papers*, ed. Wilt L. Idema (Cambridge, MA: Harvard-Yenching Library, 2007), p. 247.

[85] Ivo Smits, "China as Classic Text: Chinese Books and Twelfth-Century Japanese Collectors," in *Tools of Culture*, ed. Goble, Robinson, and Wakabayashi, p. 190.

[86] Charlotte von Verschuer, "Ashikaga Yoshimitsu's Foreign Policy 1398 to 1408 AD: A Translation from *Zenrin Kokuhōki*, the Cambridge Manuscript," *Monumenta Nipponica* 62.3 (2007): 261–97. The motivation for Yoshimitsu's break with tradition may have been his desire to supplant the imperial lineage: see Akira Imatani, trans. Kozo Yamamura, "Not for Lack of Will or Wile: Yoshimitsu's Failure to Supplant the Imperial Lineage," *Journal of Japanese Studies* 18.1 (1992): 45–78; Shalmit Bejarano, "Picturing Rice Agriculture and Silk Production: Appropriation and Ideology in Early Modern Japanese Painting," PhD thesis, University of Pittsburgh, 2010, p. 63 suggests that the Ashikaga shoguns may have collected Chinese paintings as a "conscious denial of traditional Japanese themes, which were associated with the imperial court."

name (Hongwu) of the Ming founder, his minister of the left, Ichijō Tsunetsugu, objected "on the grounds that borrowing a character already used as part of an era name in China would be 'a shame to our nation.'"[87]

Private cultural and commercial exchanges kept the Japanese in touch with continental culture. Amino Yoshihiko reminds us of the centrality of trade in medieval Japan: records locate Chinese and Korean traders in Japanese ports from the early ninth century. Japanese documents at Dazaifu, the Kyushu office handling foreign trade, show sales of perfumes, medicines, silks, Chinese books, and Chinese ceramics to aristocrats at the imperial court in return for gold, sulfur, pearls, swords, fans, and paper.[88] In addition to the important maritime ports located along the Inland Sea and Kyushu, archaeological evidence suggests that from the seventh century onward, Japanese also obtained products from the continent via trade between the residents living along the Amur River, the Mohe on the northeast Asian coast, and the Ezo in Hokkaido.[89]

Shandong's trade with Korea produced special Korean settlements called "Silla Quarters," where the residents were permitted to select one of their number to lead their communities and handle their own internal affairs.[90] Merchant settlements at major inter-Asian ports spurred marriages whose progeny acquired multiple or mixed identities. When, for example, Ningbo officials intervened in an 1191 dispute between two ship captains, they discovered that one, named Chen Qitai, had been born in China (and hence was a Song subject) but the other, Yang Rong, had been born in Japan.[91] Several decades earlier, records of Ningbo temple donations by three individuals from Hakata show that two, named Ding and Zhang Ning, were Chinese traders residing in Hakata, while the third, Zhang Gongyuan, was a Hakata trader who hailed from Fujian. The Chinese residing in Hakata had families – shrine records there show women bearing Chinese surnames who married Japanese and were incorporated into Japanese society.[92] Similar cases appear in Korean annals: for example, in 1441 the governor of Kyŏngsang province petitioned on behalf of a wae'in (Japanese) named Saemonkurō 左衛門九郎 who petitioned to become a Koryŏ subject because his parents were

---

[87] Imatani, "Not for Lack of Will or Wile," pp. 66–67.

[88] von Verschuer, *Across the Perilous Sea*, chapters 2 and 3.

[89] Sakayori Masashi, trans. Han Kyuch'ŏl, "Ilbon kwa Parhae, Malgal ŭi kyoryu – Tonghae, Ohoch'ŭk'ŭ [Okhotsk] haeyŏkkwŏn kwa sŏn – " (Japan's exchanges with Parhae and Malgal – the East Sea Okhotsk maritime zone and ships), *Kuksakwŏn nonch'ong* 85 (1999): 263–77; Kojima Yoshitaka, "Kōkurei, Botsukai to no kōryu" (The exchanges with Koguryŏ and Parhae), in *Nihonkai to hokkoku bunka: Umi to rettō bunka*, ed. Amino Yoshihiko et al. (Tokyo: Shūgakkan, 1990), I: 195–230.

[90] Hwang, *History of Korea*, pp. 24–26.

[91] Goble, Robinson, and Wakabayashi, "Introduction," p. 8. [92] *Ibid.*, p. 9.

both "subjects of our country."[93] In 1455, a priest named Saburōzaemon 三郎左衛門, sent to Tsushima as an envoy, declared that both of his parents were Korean and he wished to be repatriated.[94]

The Japanese force sent by Yamato to succor Paekche in the seventh century and the failed Mongol invasions of Japan six centuries later mark the two instances when Japan militarily engaged armies of regimes controlling the Central Plain. Both clashes were embedded in broader geopolitical movements. In the first, the internal struggle among peninsular states for hegemony coincided with a Tang surge to eliminate a potential challenger on its northeast frontier. In the second, the Mongol pursuit of world conquest failed, thanks to determined Japanese defenders, aided by what Japanese called the *kamikaze*, which destroyed a significant part of the Mongol fleet. Larger forces also provided the conditions that enabled a Koryŏ general, Yi Sŏnggye, to found a new dynasty.

Korea under the Mongols

The Yuan–Ming dynastic transition coincided with and was a background factor in the Red Turban rebellion, which began in Jiangnan but moved northward into Shandong, southern Liaodong, and twice invaded the Korean peninsula. The twenty-year effort to put down the Red Turbans provided career opportunities for military leaders. Zhu Yuanzhang, who would go on to found the Ming dynasty, was a participant in the Red Turban movement in the Yangzi delta. In 1368, after Zhu's forces captured the Mongol capital, Dadu (modern-day Beijing), the Koryŏ King Kongmin (r. 1351–74) attempted to establish friendly relations with both the newly proclaimed Ming dynasty and the commanders of the surviving Yuan force that had fled into the northeast. In 1388, fearing that the Ming were about to annex territory south of the Tumen River, King U, Kongmin's successor, ordered General Yi Sŏnggye to mount a counter-expedition into Liaodong. Yi instead orchestrated a coup and proclaimed the founding of a new dynasty.[95]

---

[93] Murai Shōsuke, "Wakō to wa dareka – juyon, jugo seiki no Chōsen hantō wo chūshin ni – " (The identity of the Wakō – focusing on the Korean peninsula in the fourteenth and fifteenth centuries), *Tōhōgaku* 119 (2010): 2.

[94] *Ibid.*

[95] Peter Yun, "Rethinking the Tribute System: Korean States and Northeast Asia Relations, 600–1600," PhD thesis, University of California at Los Angeles, 1998, pp. 167–86.

Little in the Korean historical record before the sixteenth century supports scholarly characterizations of the Chosŏn dynasty (1392–1907) as a "model tributary state."[96] It is true that the founder of the new ruling house, T'aejo (Yi Sŏnggye) sought legal recognition and legitimation of his new regime from the Ming founder Zhu Yuanzhang (Ming Taizu) but what was established was far from the ideal overlord–vassal relationship.[97] Early relations were cool and marked by mutual suspicion sparked by Taizu's concern with suppressing Mongol resistance in the northeast and demands that Chosŏn repatriate Jurchen who had fled across the border.[98] State-to-state relations relaxed after Taizu's death in 1398, and were reinforced by the Korean court's efforts to revive Confucian studies in the following decades.

The court deliberations recorded in the *Chosŏn wangjo sillok* (Veritable records of the Chosŏn dynasty) reveal complex Korean attitudes toward the Ming. Both Ming and Chosŏn made systematic efforts to penetrate and win over tribal peoples living within their mutual frontiers, in particular the Jurchen tribes inhabiting the region between Shanhaiguan and the Yalu and Tumen Rivers.[99] Both invested tribal leaders who submitted to their rule with military titles in commandery units designed to hold off "barbarians."[100] These competitive efforts allowed the Jurchen to play off one side against the other, maneuvering to obtain goods and yet retain autonomy.

The Ming court won over Mŏngke Temür, leader of the Odori Jurchen, who had previously allied himself to the Chosŏn: he was installed as leader of the Left Jianzhou guard in 1410. Both he and Li Manzhu 李滿住, another Jianzhou leader, existed in a buffer zone between the Ming

---

[96] Quote taken from Hae-jong Chun, "Sino-Korean Tributary Relations in the Ch'ing Period," in *The Chinese World Order*, ed. John K. Fairbank (Cambridge, MA: Harvard University Press, 1968), p. 90.

[97] Recorded in the *Hongwu shilu*, dated Hongwu 25/11/17, announcing the death of the Koryŏ crown prince; Hongwu 25/i12/9, in which Hongwu responded to Yi Sŏnggye's request by selecting Chosŏn as the name of the new dynasty: Wang Qiju, comp. *Ming shilu: Lingguo Chaoxian pian ziliao* (Beijing: Zhongguo bianjiang shidi yanjiu zhongxin, 1983), p. 36.

[98] A Korean historian surmises that these "Jurchen" probably included Koryŏ subjects who had been relocated into Liaodong by the Yuan: see Yun, "Rethinking the Tribute System," p. 192.

[99] Kenneth R. Robinson, "Residence and Foreign Relations in the Peninsular Northeast during the Fifteenth and Sixteenth Centuries," in *The Northern Region of Korea: History, Identity and Culture*, ed. Sun Joo Kim (Seattle: University of Washington Press, 2010), pp. 18–36.

[100] See Morris Rossabi, "The Ming and Inner Asia," in *The Cambridge History of China, 1368–1633*, vol. VIII, part 2: *The Ming Dynasty, 1368–1644*, ed. Denis Twitchett and Frederick W. Mote (Cambridge: Cambridge University Press, 1998), pp. 258–71.

and Korean authorities, as both countries sought to strengthen their respective positions by winning over tribal leaders and giving them official posts.[101] While they were subjected to pressures from both sides, the recurrent Mongol threat to Ming power enabled Jurchen leaders and their followers to exercise considerable autonomy. After Li Manzhu's requests in the 1420s and 1436 to relocate into Ming territory were rejected, he moved near the Pozhu 婆豬 River, north of the Yalu, where he came into conflict with the Chosŏn court.

Even though at least one major supporter of Yi Sŏnggye, the Chosŏn founder, was a Jurchen, early Chosŏn accounts of the Jurchen refer to tribes of "Yain" (野人), "barbarians" who lived on the southern banks of the Tumen and Yalu Rivers.[102] The Veritable Records of the Sejong reign (1426–50) record numerous instances of Yain raids for food, clothing, and tools, and attempts to recapture escaped slaves or kidnapped concubines.[103] In 1425, for example, the Korean records show that Jurchen Jin Fujie's wife was kidnapped and taken across the border into Chosŏn territory. A battalion commander in the Jianzhou guard appealed to the Chosŏn authorities for her return, to no avail. Friction arose when Jurchen slaves fled to Chosŏn. Li Manzhu had ten slaves abscond to Chosŏn in 1428.[104] A 1432 raid that captured 77 Koreans incited a Chosŏn expedition against the Jurchen. Concluding that the Jianzhou guard were the primary instigators, the Chosŏn warned Mŏngke Temŭr against interference and successfully attacked Li Manzhu's followers, killing 260 Jurchen, seizing 248 men, 62 horses, and 118 head of cattle.[105]

Border incursions in both directions were a major and persistent issue between Chosŏn and the Ming. By the middle of the fifteenth century, Choson had erected six garrison forts and four outposts on the Yalu River

[101] Kenneth R. Robinson, "From Raiders to Traders: Border Security and Border Control in Early Chosŏn, 1392–1450," *Korean Studies* 16 (1992): 98. In a later article, "Chōsen ō-chō – jushoku Joshinjin no kankei to 'Chōsen'" (The Chosŏn dynasty – the relationship of Jurchen holding office and 'Chosŏn'), *Rekishi hyoron* 592 (1999): 29–42, Kenneth Robinson talks about the incorporation of at least part of the Jurchen population into Korean society in the fifteenth and sixteenth centuries.

[102] Pamela K. Crossley, *The Manchus* (Oxford: Blackwell, 1997), p. 39, cites "the Jurchen Li Douran (Yi Tu-ran)." Li Doulan 李豆蘭 is identified as "Yi Chiran" 李之蘭, who was a Chosŏn Consolidated Army Command Official in 1398: see John B. Duncan, *The Origins of the Chosŏn Dynasty* (Seattle: University of Washington Press, 2000), Table 5.1, p. 227, p. 354.

[103] K. Robinson, "From Raiders to Traders," pp. 97–99.

[104] Xie Zhaohua, "Pingzhe Chaoxian dui Jianzhouwei Nüzhen de diyici yongbing" (The first use of troops by Chosŏn against the Jianzhou Jurchen guard), *Zhongyang minzu daxue xuebao* 4 (2000): 54–58.

[105] Xie, "Pingzhe Chaoxian," pp. 56–7; Xie notes differences in the dating of the incident, and Rossabi, pp. 41–42, dates the Korean campaign to 1434.

to demarcate its boundary with the Ming. While strengthening border defenses, Chosŏn also tried to create incentives for Jurchen leaders to trade rather than conduct raids.[106] According to Ki-baek Lee, the campaigns against the Jurchen stimulated Korean improvements in the casting of cannon, which then became effective offensive weapons. Yain uprisings persisted, however, into the late sixteenth century.[107]

In the early seventeenth century, the *Chosŏn wangjo sillok* records many requests from the emerging northeastern power that became the Later Jin state for the return of refugees who had fled Jurchen control by crossing the Yalu or Tumen Rivers. Many Korean subjects crossed into Liaodong in order to gather ginseng; during the Japanese invasion, slaves sought to escape their servile status by fleeing north. The handling of individuals who were caught on the wrong side of the border continued to plague both governments in later periods.[108]

Dealing with Japanese pirates and traders

Chosŏn's policies toward Japan and other states on its periphery paralleled actions of Central Plain regimes toward their own neighbors. When the fourteenth-century Korean court failed to obtain cooperation from the Japanese central authority in stamping out Japanese pirates (*waegu, waejŏk*), it began to deal directly with regional lords in Japan.[109] The same Ōuchi family who sent embassies to Ming also sent missions to the Chosŏn court. From 1396, the Ōuchi and the Sō lords of Tsushima, along with the Ōtomo and the Munakata, cooperated with the Koreans in suppressing pirate raids on the peninsula and repatriating Koreans captured by pirates.[110] In 1419, Chosŏn forces attacked and wiped out pirate bases in Tsushima.[111] The Chosŏn court regarded Tsushima "as part of the royal realm" during the fifteenth and sixteenth centuries and the Sō daimyo the primary agents representing Japan.[112]

[106] K. Robinson, "From Raiders to Traders," pp. 97–101; Lee, *New History*, pp. 190–91.

[107] Lee, *New History*, pp. 197, 191.

[108] Seonmin Kim, "Borders and Crossings;" also Yi Hwa, "Ch'ŏng ŭi Chungwŏn ipkwan chŏnhu Chosŏn'in ŭi wŏlgyŏng munje rŭl tolrŏssan Cho-Ch'ŏng kyosŏp" (Chosŏn-Qing negotiations concerning the problem of Koreans crossing the border illegally around the time of the Qing entry into the Central Plain [1644]), *Han'guk hakpo* 112 (2003): 103–37.

[109] K. Robinson, "From Raiders to Traders," pp. 94–115.

[110] K. Robinson, "Treated as Treasures."

[111] According to K. Robinson, "Treated as Treasures," p. 35, "Japanese pirates" (the group included Koreans) raided the Korean peninsula 387 times between 1350 and 1392.

[112] Kenneth R. Robinson, "An Island's Place in History: Tsushima in Japan and in Chosŏn, 1392–1592," *Korean Studies* 30 (2006): 39. See also Tanaka Takeo with Robert Sakai, "Japan's Relations with Overseas Countries," in *Japan in the Muromachi Age*, ed. John W. Hall and Toyoda Takeshi (Berkeley: University of California Press,

Japanese regional lords in Hakata and elsewhere in northern Kyushu sent ships to trade in Korean and Chinese ports. The breakdown of centralized authority in Japan after 1467 allowed regional barons to fraudulently participate in Japanese–Ming "tributary trade." Ming documents show that embassies from Japan continued to arrive in China until the early sixteenth century. The Hosokawa and Ōuchi, regional lords situated on the Inland Sea and northern Kyushu, presented tallies collected during the 1401–5 period to pass as the envoys of various Ashikaga shoguns.[113] Once in Peking,[114] they would request and receive further tallies, thus perpetuating the system.

Since these regional lords also engaged in piracy, it is not surprising that such "tribute missions" occasionally became violent. After members of the 1496 embassy "killed people with their swords" en route from Peking, the number of embassy personnel permitted to appear in Peking was reduced. The false tribute missions were exposed in 1523, when the Hosokawa and Ōuchi both sent embassies to Ningbo, where an Office of Overseas Trade supervised the maritime tribute missions from Korea and Japan. The two envoys quarreled over which was the legitimate tributary embassy. Although the Ōuchi envoy, Shusetsu Gendo, had arrived first, the Ming eunuch official gave priority to the Hosokawa envoy, So Sokyo, in the customs inspection and seated him above his rival at the banquet. The enraged Shusetsu attacked his rival, who sought refuge inside the city walls of Shaoxing. Shusetsu killed some of So Sokyo's men in the affray and set fire to So's ship, while his men plundered and burned buildings before setting sail in captured boats, killing some Ming naval personnel who attempted to arrest them.[115]

1977), pp. 173–74; Etsuko Hae-Jin Kang, *Diplomacy and Ideology in Japanese–Korean Relations from the Fifteenth to the Eighteenth Century* (New York: St. Martin's Press, 1997), chapter 2.

[113] Kwan-wai So, *Japanese Piracy in Ming China During the 16th* Century (Dearborn: Michigan State University Press, 1975), p. 4; the details are presented in So's translation of the section on Japan in the *Mingshi*, pp. 161–202.

[114] Throughout this book, "Peking" is used instead of "Beijing" to refer to the capital city in Ming and Qing times, when it was called by various names; see the explanation in Susan Naquin, *Peking: Temples and City Life, 1400–1900* (Berkeley: University of California Press, 2000), pp. xxxiii–xxxiv.

[115] The incident is described in So, *Japanese Piracy*, pp. 4–5. Also Jurgis Elisonas, "The Inseparable Trinity: Japan's Relations with China and Korea," in *The Cambridge History of Japan*, vol. IV: *Early Modern Japan*, ed. John Whitney Hall (Cambridge: Cambridge University Press, 1991), pp. 235–39; James Geiss, "The Chia-ching Reign, 1522–1566," in *The Cambridge History of China*, vol. VII, part 1: *The Ming Dynasty, 1368–1644*, ed. Frederick W. Mote and Denis Twitchett (Cambridge: Cambridge University Press, 1988), pp. 491–92. On Ningbo and tributary administration, see Yoshinobu Shiba, "Ningpo and Its Hinterland," in *The City in Late Imperial China*, ed. G. William Skinner (Stanford: Stanford University Press, 1977), pp. 391–439.

The 1523 incident prompted a Ming investigation.[116] After questioning So Sokyo, the Ministry of Rites recommended that he be permitted to return home, but before that occurred, the Chosŏn authorities turned over two of Shusetsu's followers, who were captured when their ship was blown off course to Korea. A request in 1530 from the Hosokawa (sent via the Ryukyuan embassy) to pardon So Sokyo and issue new tallies was denied; missions arriving in 1545 and 1547 were sent back because they did not comply with the schedule for embassies.[117] The Ōuchi missions in 1539–40 and 1548–49 were allowed to travel to Peking for the court audience, but their requests for new tallies were denied. The 1549 mission marked the end of "official" relations between the Ming dynasty and the "King of Japan."

The Ming attempt to confine trade within the tribute framework failed. Ignoring an edict from Ming Emperor Yingzong (1459) that the rulers of vassal states should not receive envoys from states outside the tribute system, Chosŏn imposed trade regulations that mirrored the Ming system. First, Japanese wishing to trade in Korea had to present themselves at court with their official diplomatic credentials from the Japanese ruler.[118] Beginning in 1418, Japanese had to obtain seals or stamps from the Chosŏn government before they were permitted to enter the kingdom. The Chosŏn also stipulated the number of envoys permitted to come to the capital, the number of ships allowed, and the ports at which they could dock.[119] The number of ports open to Japanese ships was limited to one after 1544.[120] Yet in 1500 about two hundred ships sailed annually from Japanese ports to Pusan, Naeip'o, and Yomp'o. A 1494 census counted over 3,200 Japanese living around the three ports.[121]

Chosŏn also received embassies from other countries. The Ryukyus, which began sending embassies to Ming in 1372, sent their first mission to Chosŏn in 1389, returning captured Koreans. Other embassies followed, totaling "more than two dozen" in the period

---

[116] Translation of the section on Japan in *Mingshi*, translated by So, *Japanese Piracy*, pp. 173–77.

[117] Tribute tallies were issued by the Ming court to a vassal state for presentation by ambassadors coming to the court at stipulated intervals to present tribute. See Chun, "Sino-Korean Tributary Relations," for details on the tribute system.

[118] Kenneth R. Robinson, "The Jiubian and Ezogachishima Embassies to Chosŏn, 1478–1482," *Chōsenshi kenkyūkai ronbunshū* 35 (1997): 55–86; also his "The Imposter Branch of the Hatakeyama Family and Japanese–Chosŏn Korea Court Relations, 1455–1580s," *Asian Cultural Studies* 25 (1999): 67–87.

[119] Elisonas, "Inseparable Trinity," pp. 240–46.

[120] Etsuko Hae-Jin Kang, *Diplomacy and Ideology*, pp. 66–68.

[121] Elisonas, "Inseparable Trinity," p. 246.

1392–1592.[122] Even though the Ryukyus were conquered by Satsuma in 1609, Ryukyuan embassies continued to appear at both the Qing and the Chosŏn courts. In fact, from the fifteenth century, many of the so-called Ryukyuan embassies were headed by Japanese from Tsushima and Hakata who took on false Ryukyuan identities in order to trade.[123] Genealogies were falsified, and state documents were forged with abandon: why, Korean officials wondered, was the calligraphy on the "state letters" purportedly written by the ruler of "Jiubian" (actually Japanese from Satsuma domain) written in a Japanese style? After the imposter embassies from Jiubian in 1478, 1482, and 1483 were quizzed about their country, native customs, and ruling house, Chosŏn officials concluded that these envoys were Japanese and rejected them.[124]

The expansion of the maritime frontier

The last phase in the breakdown of the tribute system began in the early sixteenth century, with the advent of European traders to Asian shores. The number of European ships sailing into Asian waters was at first small, and waiting for the right monsoon winds made for lengthy voyages. For example, it might take three years for a Portuguese vessel to sail from Goa to Macao to Nagasaki and back. Before 1634, fewer than four ships a year, on average, made the voyage. Before 1680, Nagasaki was "the only port in the East China Sea ever to become of any significance to European trade."[125]

Europeans initially played a minor role in what was essentially an intra-Asian trade which already reached from Southeast Asia up the China coast to Korea and the Japanese archipelago.[126] The Europeans found Japanese alongside Chinese and Ryukyuan traders in all of the major ports in Southeast Asia, from the Philippines in the east to Malacca in the west. Chinese traders formed expatriate communities in Naha, an international trading center in the Ryukyus, as well as in Manila, where the Spanish

---

[122] Shunzō Sakamaki, "Ryukyu and Southeast Asia," *Journal of Asian Studies* 23.3 (1964): 384; Kenneth R. Robinson, "Centering the King of Chosŏn: Aspects of Korean Maritime Diplomacy, 1392–1592," *Journal of Asian Studies* 59.1 (2000): 109.

[123] K. Robinson, "Imposter Branch of the Hatakeyama Family," and "Jiubian and Ezogachishima Embassies."

[124] K. Robinson, "Jiubian and Ezogachishima Embassies," "Centering the King of Chosŏn," and "Imposter Branch of the Hatakeyama Family."

[125] Peter W. Klein, "The China Seas and the World Economy between the Sixteenth and Nineteenth Centuries: The Changing Structures of Trade," in *Interactions in the World Economy: Perspectives from International Economic History*, ed. Carl-Ludwig Holtfrerich (New York: New York University Press, 1989), p. 74, quote from p. 66.

[126] For an excellent overview, see Klein, "China Seas and the World Economy," pp. 61–89.

found them when they established their colony there in 1571.[127] Chinese merchants figured prominently in the bustling inter-Asian trade between Korean ports, Zhejiang ports such as Hangzhou and Ningbo, the Fujian port of Quanzhou, and the northern Kyushu port of Hakata.

The first to arrive were the Portuguese, who established trading posts in the Indian Ocean (Goa, 1510) and on the Malay peninsula (Malacca, 1511). Portuguese ships first reached the Pearl River delta in south China in 1517, but their request for formal relations was rejected by the Ming, who thought they were pirates.[128] Expelled from the Pearl River delta (1522), Portuguese ships conducted an illicit trade with Chinese along the China coast until the 1550s, when the Ming authorities permitted them to settle in Macao. Portuguese ships first came to Shuangyu, a harbor on an island near the Zhejiang city of Ningbo in 1539, but Shuangyu's growth as a center for international trade in the East China Sea seems to date from the appearance of Japanese traders in 1545.[129] Like the Portuguese, the Dutch East India Company tried but failed to obtain direct access to Chinese markets, where they hoped to buy silk. Turned away from Macao, they established a trading post on Taiwan in 1624, which they held until 1662.[130] They took Chinese silk to Nagasaki, where it was exchanged for silver.

The introduction of European traders into Asian ports in the sixteenth century marked the beginning of a global world trading system. Chinese and Japanese traders took advantage of governmental decline in their respective countries to bypass the Ming tribute framework to engage in private trade.[131] The expansion of this trade in the sixteenth century, sparked by European demand for Asian textiles and Chinese demand for Japanese and New World silver, affected not just the economies of Asian ports but their hinterlands, including southeast China and northeast Asia.

---

[127] *Ibid.*, pp. 70–72; Uezato Takashi, "Ko Ryūkyū, Naha no [Wajin] kyoryūchi to kan Shinakai sekai" (The Japanese settlement in Naha, old Ryukyu and the world of the China Sea), *Shigaku zasshi* 114.7 (2005): 1–33; Maehira Fusaaki, "Taigai kankei ni okeru Kakyō to kokka – Ryūkyū no Minjin sanjuroku shō o megutte" (The Overseas Chinese merchants and the state in foreign relations – the thirty-six Fujianese surnames in the Ryūkyūs), in *Ajia no naka no Nihonshi*, vol. III, ed. Arano Yasunori, Ishii Masatoshi, and Murai Shōsuke (Tokyo: University of Tokyo Press, 1992), pp. 245–64.

[128] James Geiss, "The Cheng-te Reign, 1506–1521," *The Cambridge History of China*, vol. VII, part 1, pp. 433–34.

[129] The division of maritime space into the East China Sea (northern half) and South China Sea is taken from Klein, "China Seas and the World Economy," pp. 66–67, 70–73. On Ningbo, see Shiba, "Ningpo and Its Hinterland," p. 399.

[130] Tonio Andrade, *How Taiwan Became Chinese: Dutch, Spanish, and Han Colonization in the Seventeenth Century* (New York: Columbia University Press, 2008).

[131] So, *Japanese Piracy*, pp. 5, 41.

The illicit trade provoked an official response from the Ming government. After Chu Wan's campaigns in 1548–49 against Shuangyu made conditions there untenable, the Portuguese ships and their Asian partners moved further south to sites off the Fujian coast. Although Ningbo's trade revived with the lifting of the ban on maritime trade in 1567, Fujian remained a major trade center through the 1550s, and merchants from Fujian and Guangdong occupied leading roles in markets.[132] To keep a closer watch on their greatly increased presence in Zhangzhou waters, the government established a new county, Haicheng, in 1567, and legalized the overseas trade.

Haicheng also benefitted from the Spanish founding of Manila in 1571, a half-century after Ferdinand Magellan's voyage to the Philippines (1520). Beginning in 1565, annual Spanish shipments of New World silver from Acapulco to Manila laid the foundations for an economic boom that linked China to the world economy. The Fujian coastal prefectures of Zhangzhou and Quanzhou were active in a maritime network that spanned the East and South China Seas. Dyestuffs, spices, and medicinal herbs from Southeast Asia flowed north from the Ryukyus through Hakata and other ports; Japanese copper and iron, then silver, flowed westward toward China; Korean ginseng moved to Japan; and Chinese cotton and silk flowed to other Asian markets. Official prohibitions on trade were meaningless: Japanese purchased lead, saltpeter, and other officially banned military imports indirectly through third countries, or directly from Southeast Asia.[133]

Trading relations between China and northeast Asia

The seventeenth century reveals a new international landscape for trade, in which a newly reunified Japanese state created its own system of governmentally controlled foreign trade. While nominally adhering to the protocol governing tribute missions to China, Chosŏn regulated its own trade with Japan and the Ryukyus. The Qing, whose pre-1644 experience inclined them to a pro-trade stance, abandoned the official tribute framework of the Ming.

---

[132] See Chu Wan's biography in *Dictionary of Ming Biography, 1368–1644*, ed. L. Carrington Goodrich and Chaoying Fang (New York: Columbia University Press, 1976), I: 372–75.
[133] Nakajima Gakusho, "Jūroku seikimatsu no Kyūshu – Tōnan Ajia bōeki – Katō Kiyomasa no Luzon bōeki wo megutte" (Kyushu and the Southeast Asian trade in the sixteenth century: Examining Katō Kiyomasa's trade). *Shigaku zasshi* 118.8 (2009): 1–36.

Japan followed the precedent set by Ming China and Chosŏn Korea in banning unauthorized maritime voyages abroad.[134] As Japan emerged from its sixteenth-century civil wars, its new leaders quickly moved to assert control over trade. Even as he deliberated on requesting permits (勘合, J. *kangō*) for trade from the Ming, Tokugawa Ieyasu himself sent trading ships to ports in the East and South China Seas with his own licenses to trade, called *shuin* (朱印 literally, "red seals"). Moreover, he sent letters to Southeast Asian rulers requesting them to trade only with Japanese vessels bearing these documents.[135] From 1604 until 1635, when the *shuin* system functioned, the Tokugawa shogunate issued 356 *shuin* to vessels sailing to Cochin China, Siam, Luzon (including Manila), Annam, and Cambodia.[136]

In 1640 the Tokugawa shogunate, having consolidated its control over a unified Japan, expelled the Portuguese and Spanish traders, conferred a trading monopoly on the Dutch East India Company, and confined Dutch and Chinese traders to Nagasaki. Recent Japanese scholarship has refuted the notion that the Nagasaki trading system signaled Japan's retreat from contact with the outside world.[137] Beginning with Asao Naohiro's critique of the *sakoku* (closed country) policy in the 1970s and continuing through the 1990s writings of Arano Yasunori, scholars rebutted the generalization that the Edo shogunate (1600–1868) adopted *sakoku*.[138] *Sakoku* refers to a sequence of shogunal decrees, issued between 1633 and 1639, which banned Japanese and Japanese ships from sailing abroad, persecuted Japanese Christians and foreign missionaries, expelled Spaniards, Englishmen, and Portuguese from Japan, and permitted only the Dutch and the Chinese to trade under shogunal supervision at Nagasaki.

According to Arano, the term *sakoku* did not appear in contemporary Japanese documents until the early nineteenth century, and its widespread acceptance as a generalization about Edo foreign relations

[134] See Arano Yasunori's argument in "Kaikin to sakoku" (Maritime ban and closed country), in *Ajia no naka no Nihonshi*, vol. II, ed. Arano Yasunori, Ishii Masatoshi, and Murai Shōsuke (Tokyo: University of Tokyo Press, 1992), pp. 191–222.

[135] See fn20, p. 61 in Ronald P. Toby, *State and Diplomacy in Early Modern Japan: Asia in the Development of the Tokugawa Bakufu* (Princeton: Princeton University Press, 1984).

[136] Wai-ming Ng, "Overseas Chinese in the Japan–Southeast Asia Maritime Trade during the Tokugawa Period," in *Maritime China in Transition, 1750–1850*, ed. Wang Gungwu and Ng Chin-keong (Wiesbaden: Harrassowitz, 2004), pp. 214–15.

[137] Tashiro Kazui, trans. Susan Downing Videen, "Foreign Relations during the Edo Period: Sakoku Reexamined," *Journal of Japanese Studies* 8.2 (1982): 283–306.

[138] Arano Yasunori, "Preface," in his *Kinsei Nihon no Higashi Ajia* (Tokyo: Tokyo University Press, 1988), pp. i–xviii; Brett L. Walker, "Reappraising the *Sakoku* Paradigm: The Ezo Trade and the Extension of Tokugawa Political Space into Hokkaidō," *Journal of Asian History* 30.2 (1996): 169–92; Toby, *State and Diplomacy*.

dates only to the period after the Meiji Restoration in 1868. Arano argued that the shogunate's restriction of foreign trade to Nagasaki, rather than being unique to early modern Japan, was modeled on the maritime prohibitions enacted by Ming China and Chosŏn Korea.[139] Chinese private traders could sail into one port, Nagasaki, if they had the proper tallies issued by shogunal authorities. The same rules applied to the Dutch. Governments in all three East Asian countries adopted policies persecuting native Christians and Christian missionaries during the early modern period.

Arano also noted that Japan was never completely closed to foreign trade or diplomacy: instead the shogunate chose to delegate the conduct of these matters to selected fiefs while directly supervising the Nagasaki trade. Relations with foreign countries were institutionalized into the "four gates," *yottsu no kuchi*: the Matsumae domain in northern Honshu was delegated to supervise relations with the Ezo, ancestors of the present-day Ainu peoples of Hokkaido; the Shimazu of Satsuma domain, in southern Kyushu, managed relations with Ryukyu, which was subjugated by Satsuma in 1609; relations with Chosŏn were handled by the Sō daimyo of Tsushima.[140] Only in the case of the Chinese and Dutch trading communities in Nagasaki was a shogunal official, the Nagasaki magistrate (長崎奉行 *bugyo*), directly involved.[141] Despite the absence of official (tributary) relations between the Qing dynasty and the Tokugawa

---

[139] Arano, "Preface," pp. iv–vii; see Table 1, p. v, comparing Chinese, Korean, and Japanese maritime prohibitions.

[140] Arano, "Preface," p. xiii; on the Ryukyuan trade, see Sakamaki, "Ryukyu and Southeast Asia," pp. 383–89; on the Ainu trade, see Emori Susumu, *Hokkaidō kinseishi no kenkyū – Bakuhan taisei to Ezochi* (The early modern history of Hokkaidō – the bakuhan system and Ezochi) (Sapporo: Hokkaidō shuppan kikaku sentā, 1982), pp. 159–62; Matsuura Shigeru, *Shinchō no Amūru seisaku to shōsū minzoku* (Qing policy toward the Amur district and minorities) (Kyoto: Kyoto University Press, 2006), chapter 4; on the Korean trade, Tashiro Kazui, "Jūshichi seiki goki-jūhachi seiki Nihon kin no kaigai yushutsu – toku ni Tsushima, Chōsen ru-to wo chūshin ni" (The export of silver from Japan in the seventeenth and eighteenth centuries, especially focusing on the Tsushima and Korea route), in *Atarashii Edo jidai shizo wo motomete – sono shakai keizai shiteki sekkin*, ed. Shakai keizai shigakkai (Tokyo: Tōyō keizai shinpōsha, 1977), pp. 47–68 and her "Exports of Japan's Silver to China via Korea and Changes in the Tokugawa Monetary System During the Seventeenth and Eighteenth Centuries," in *Precious Metals, Coinage and the Changes of Monetary Structures in Latin-America, Europe and Asia (Later Middle Ages – Early Modern Times)*, ed. Eddy H. G. Van Cauwenburghe (Leuven: Leuven University Press, 1989), pp. 99–116.

[141] Kei Tsuruta, "The Establishment and Characteristic of the 'Tsushima Gate,'" *Acta Asiatica* 6.7 (1994): 30–48; David Howell, "Territoriality and Collective Identity in Tokugawa Japan," *Daedalus*, special issue on "Early Modernities," 127.3(1998): 119–21. According to Naohiro Asao, these arrangements were initiated by Hideyoshi: see his "The Sixteenth-Century Unification," in *The Cambridge History of Japan*, vol. IV: *Early Modern Japan*, pp. 68–69.

shogunate, Chinese goods continued to flow into Japan through Korea, the Ryukyus, and on Chinese junks to Nagasaki.[142]

During the late sixteenth to early seventeenth century, copper replaced silver as the dominant Japanese export to China.[143] Concerned with the steady outflow of monetary metals, the shogunate issued the "New Regulations of the Shōtoku Era" in 1715, which reduced the number of Chinese junks allowed in Nagasaki and limited the amount of money metals that could be shipped out of the country. To curb smuggling, they also required Chinese traders to present tallies issued by the Nagasaki magistrate. Those obeying Japanese law would be permitted to trade, while violators would be sent back to China. Because these tallies resembled Ming chits issued to Japanese trading vessels entering Chinese ports, the Chinese merchants of the time (and contemporary scholars) interpreted them as an ideologically inspired challenge to the Sinocentric tributary order – one that the Qing court eventually chose to ignore.[144]

The Chosŏn dynasty also moved to institutionalize trading relations with Japan after 1598. Acting on the recommendations of Kang Hang, a Confucian scholar who was taken to Japan as a prisoner of war during the Japanese invasion, the court adopted a policy of containment.[145] New

---

[142] The pursuit of trade as a primary motive is suggested in the Satsuma willingness to conceal its dominance over the Ryukyus because of the fear that its changed status might reduce Ryukyu's tributary ranking and the frequency of its tribute missions, and hence reduce opportunities for importation of Chinese goods: see Robert L. Hellyer, *Defining Engagement: Japan and Global Contexts, 1640–1868* (Cambridge, MA: Harvard University Asia Center, 2009), pp. 38–39.

[143] John Hall, "Notes on the Early Ch'ing Copper Trade with Japan," *Harvard Journal of Asiatic Studies*, 12.3/4 (1949): 444–61. Von Glahn, *Fountain of Fortune: Money and Monetary Policy in China, 1000–1700* (Berkeley: University of California Press, 1996), pp. 229–30 takes a revisionist view of Hall's argument that the copper went directly into government mints; also Yi Huili, "Qing Kangxi chao houqi zhengzhi yu Zhong Ri changqi maoyi" (On the politics of the late Kangxi reign and Sino-Japanese Nagasaki trade), *Shehui kexue* 2004 #1: 96–103.

[144] Kate Wildman Nakai, *Shogunal Politics: Arai Hakuseki and the Premises of Tokugawa Rule* (Cambridge, MA: Council on East Asian Studies, Harvard University, 1988), p. 110, observes that the tally system was "doubtlessly inspired by the methods traditionally used by Chinese rulers to regulate foreign access to Chinese wealth;" Toby, *State and Diplomacy*, pp. 198–200 cites the "split seal" that mimicked the Ming tally, the use of Japanese (instead of Chinese) reign dates and naming China as "Tang" instead of "Da Qing" as expressions of the new Japanese-centered world order. See also Yi Huili, "Qing Kangxi chao houqi zhengzhi," who cites the two-year stoppage of trade in direct response to the 1715 Japanese regulations. For a milder interpretation of Japanese actions, see Norihito Mizuno, "China in Tokugawa Foreign Relations: The Tokugawa Bakufu's Perception of and Attitudes toward Ming-Qing China," *Sino-Japanese Studies* 15 (2003): 142–44.

[145] Etsuko Hae-Jin Kang, *Diplomacy and Ideology*, pp. 111–23. See also Suzuki Nobuaki, "Richō Ninsoki o torimaku taigai kankei – tai Min, tai Shin, tai Nichi seisaku o megutte" (Foreign relations surrounding the Injo reign in the Yi dynasty: Policy towards the Ming,

rules restricted the number and size of Japanese trading ships and confined trade to Pusan, where officially licensed Korean merchants met Japanese traders at a market near "Japan House," *Waegwan* 倭館. The authorized agents were Tsushima on the Japanese side and the Tongnae magistrate on the Chosŏn side. Before 1592, Japanese envoys had traveled to the capital along routes by which the invading armies advanced to capture Hansŏng. This privilege the court now withdrew. Pusan's "Japan House" became "Korea's sole base for diplomacy and trade in Japanese relations."[146] This system for handling Japanese trade, which was implemented from 1609 to 1876, predated the Tokugawa shogunate's Nagasaki system: "Japan House" was "analogous to the Dutch trading factory that would later be established at Nagasaki."[147]

Chosŏn's numerous tribute missions to the Qing capital included substantial components of traders and goods. In addition to its tributary trade, Chosŏn conducted exchanges with Qing at several markets along the banks of the Amnŏk River, which marked the boundary between the two states. According to Anders Karlsson, trade at official markets was a small fraction of the illegal trade that took place elsewhere in the border area.[148]

In contrast to earlier scholarship which posited Qing indifference to the economic potential of maritime trade, Gang Zhao argues that the Kangxi emperor drew on a legacy of pro-trade attitudes to end the ban on maritime trade in 1684, permitting Chinese to travel abroad and ushering in a new age of flourishing private trade.[149] Kangxi showed himself to be flexible in determining policy, ignoring the flagrant challenge of the Tokugawa shogunate because the imports of Japanese copper helped to increase the coinage. The court also ignored Chosŏn's actions, which mimicked the Ming order.[150] The Chinese diaspora,

Qing, and Japan), in *Zenkindai no Nihon to Higashi Ajia*, ed. Tanaka Takeo (Tokyo: Yoshikawa kōbunkan, 1995), pp. 421–50.

[146] Etsuko Hae-Jin Kang, *Diplomacy and Ideology*, pp. 66–68; Elisonas, "Inseparable Trinity," pp. 246, 296.

[147] Toby, *State and Diplomacy*, p. 40; see James B. Lewis, "Late Chosŏn-Era Korean Interaction with Japanese in Pusan: Defining Boundaries," in *Embracing the Other: The Interaction of Korean and Foreign Culture, Proceedings of the First World Congress of Korean Studies, 2002*, Sponsored by the Academy of Korean Studies, International Society for Korean Studies, Association for Korean Studies in Europe, and Korean Studies Association of Australasia (Songnam: Korean Academy, 2002), III: 1275–88.

[148] Anders Karlsson, "A Hermit Nation Not for Everyone: First-hand Contacts with Qing and Their Consequences in Late Chosŏn P'yŏngan Province," in *Embracing the Other*, III: 1289–300.

[149] Gang Zhao, *The Qing Opening to the Ocean: Chinese Maritime Policies, 1684–1757* (Honolulu: University of Hawai'i Press, 2013).

[150] Liu Wei, "Qingdai Chaoxian shituan maoyi zhidu shulüe – Zhong Chao chaogong maoyi yanjiu zhiyi" (A brief outline of the system of Chosŏn tributary trade in the

running throughout the course of Qing history, created broad networks of economic exchange that extended far beyond the tribute system.[151] The court made exceptions for Russia because it wished to obtain the tsar's neutrality in a Qing–Zunghar confrontation. The Treaty of Kiakhta (1727) allowed the Russians to supplement tributary trade with markets at two border towns; they also had the unique privilege of stationing their own subjects in Peking to staff a language school and an ecclesiastical mission.[152] Until at least the 1790s, Qing relations with Tibet proceeded along multiple lines, at least some of which transcended the vassal–overlord framework.

Challenging a Sinocentric world order

The system of inter-Asian trade that emerged from changes in state regulations during the seventeenth century reflected shifts in the regional power balance as well as the expansion of the geopolitical arena. Like the founder of a Chinese dynasty, Hideyoshi and his successor, Tokugawa Ieyasu, both sent letters to rulers in Southeast Asia (including the Spanish viceroy in the Philippines) informing them of a new regime in Japan that would seek new relations with them.[153] Such efforts were not confined to national leaders – even lesser lords sought advantage in new places. The daimyo of Hirado, hearing of a Spanish scheme to assemble an army of European and Japanese soldiers to invade China, quickly sent an emissary to Manila, promising "to send as many people and soldiers as should be requested . . . without asking

Qing period: research into Sino-Korean tributary trade), *Zhongguo bianjiang shidi yanjiu* 12.4 (2002): 36–47; Tao Mian, "Qing Han Zhongjiang maoyi shulüe" (A brief outline of the Qing trade at Zhonggang in Korea), *Zhongguo bianjiang shidi yanjiu* 1997 #1: 46–54; Chul-sung Lee, "Re-evaluation of the Chosŏn Dynasty's Trade Relationship with the Ch'ing Dynasty," *International Journal of Korean History* 3 (2002): 95–122, argues that both civilian and official trade must be quantitatively measured.

[151] See John K. Fairbank, "A Preliminary Framework," in *The Chinese World Order*, table 2, p. 13.

[152] S. C. M. Paine, *Imperial Rivals: China, Russia, and Their Disputed Frontier* (Armonk: M. E. Sharpe, 1996), p. 30.

[153] Shōsaku Takagi, "Hideyoshi's and Ieyasu's Views of Japan as a Land of the Gods and Its Antecedents: With Reference to the 'Writ for the Expulsion of Missionaries' of 1614," *Acta Asiatica* 87 (2004): 60–63. Earlier Chinese parallels include the letter sent by Khubilai to Japan and Ming Taizu's missive; see Kawazoe Shōji, trans. G. Cameron Hurst III, "Japan and East Asia," in *The Cambridge History of Japan*, vol. III: *Medieval Japan*, ed. Kōzō Yamamura (Cambridge: Cambridge University Press, 1990), p. 414. On Zhu's embassies to Korea, Japan, Annam, Champa, and Tibet, see John D. Langlois, Jr., "The Hung-wu Reign," in *The Cambridge History of China*, vol. VII, part 1, pp. 140–42, 165–67; Donald N. Clark, "Sino-Korean Tributary Relations Under the Ming," in *The Cambridge History of China*, vol. VIII, part 2, p. 274.

anything in return," and was rewarded with permission to trade directly with the Spanish colony.[154]

In the seventeenth century, the Tokugawa shogunate attempted to create a Japan-centered world order which directly challenged the Chinese claim to regional hegemony. Japan might proclaim itself as the center of the Asian world order, but in actuality it acquiesced in trading relations with Korea on terms dictated by the Korean court.[155] During the fifteenth and sixteenth centuries, the Chosŏn court's dealings with Tsushima, reinforced by the absence of a strong central authority that could control Japanese maritime activity along the Korean coast, took the form of a *jimi* (K. *kimi*) policy: the court distinguished between diplomatic exchanges with the shogun, which were conducted on the basis of titular equality, and relations with the lord of Tsushima, who accepted an official title from Chosŏn. There are many passages in the Chosŏn *sillok* that indicate the court's belief that by doing so, Tsushima had joined the Korean political order.[156] Chosŏn officials treated T'aema-do (J. Tsushima) as part of their own territory in documents and maps, which depicted the island as administratively subordinate to Kyŏngsang province. From 1418 to 1496, the Chosŏn court dispatched civil and military officials to T'aema/Tsushima, and regarded its governor as "an adjunct official of the king of Chosŏn" who was instrumental in regulating Japanese ships bound for the peninsula.[157]

There was a diplomatic stand-off over embassies. The shogunate invited Korean and Ryukyuan embassies to its capital, Edo, and to the shrine of the shogunal founder at Nikkō, using illustrated booklets on the ambassadorial processions to support its claims to primacy in an Asian world order.[158] Twelve Chosŏn "embassies" were sent to Japan between 1607 and 1811, but the Chosŏn court refused to accept Japanese attempts to portray these as tributary missions. The motivation on the Korean side

[154] Adam Clulow, "From Global Entrepot to Early Modern Domain: Hirado, 1609–1641," *Monumenta Nipponica* 65.1 (2010): 6.

[155] That Korea held the upper hand before 1600 was perhaps inevitable, given the collapse of a centralized authority in Japan. The continuation of a Korean-imposed trade system during the Edo period was probably supported by the decentralized allocation of responsibility for managing the trade to Tsushima.

[156] Kenneth R. Robinson, "The Tsushima Governor and Regulation of Japanese Access to Chosŏn in the Fifteenth and Sixteenth Centuries," *Korean Studies* 20 (1996): 25. On the Chosŏn use of *kimi* policy, see also Son Sŭngch'ŏl, "Chosŏn t'ongsinsa wa 21 segi Han-Il kwan'gye" (The Chosŏn envoys and Korean–Japanese relations in the twenty-first century), *Toedola pon Han -Il kwan'gyesa* (Revisiting the Korean–Japanese relationship) (Seoul: Kyŏn-in munhwa sa, 2005),147–47; Min Tokki, "Chosŏn sidae kyorin ŭi inyŏm kwa kukje sahoe ŭi kyorin" (The concept of 'kyorin'in the Chosŏn period and international social relations with neighbors), *Minjok munhwa* 21 (1998):28.

[157] K. Robinson, "The Tsushima Governor," pp. 42, 55.

[158] Toby, *State and Diplomacy*, chapter 5.

was initially to repatriate prisoners of war captured during the Japanese invasion; later, it was to promote *kyorin*, or the normative friendly relations between neighboring states, and to collect intelligence on the domestic situation within Japan.[159]

The two countries could not agree on protocol. Chosŏn asserted its diplomatic equality but insisted on using Chinese reign dates in interstate communications as befitted its status within first the Ming then the Qing tributary system. The Japanese balked at adopting the Korean suggestion that they identify themselves in writing as "king of Japan" (*Nihon koku ō*) and initially compromised by adopting dates in the sexagenary cycle.[160] Even as the bakufu directed personnel receiving the Chosŏn envoys to treat them "as a tributary mission of a subordinate state," it cautioned them to keep this designation from the envoys themselves. According to Norihito Mizuno, despite its "desire to treat Korea as an inferior," the shogunate tacitly "restored diplomatic relations with Korea on the basis of parity between the shogun and the Korean king."[161] The reality of the Japan–Chosŏn relationship was concealed from the public, which could view the Korean embassies as tributary missions.

In the seventeenth century Tokugawa Japan and Chosŏn Korea entered a significant new stage in their relations with the outside world and with each other. Despite their undiminished interest in Chinese goods and Chinese books,[162] both of which enjoyed high prestige value, neither state adhered to the traditional strictures of a China-centered Asian order. The highly selective Japanese and Korean elite reception of Chinese culture is revealed in the language issue.[163]

---

[159] Elisonas, "Inseparable Trinity," p. 299; Toby, *State and Diplomacy*, chapter 3. On the Japanese reception of the embassies, see Fumio Tamamuro, "The Korean Embassy to Tokugawa Japan in 1748: Protocol and Reception by the Tokugawa Bakufu," in *Korea Between Tradition and Modernity: Selected Papers from the Fourth Pacific and Asian Conference on Korean Studies*, ed. Chang Yun-shik, Donald L. Baker, Hur Nam-lin, and Ross King (Vancouver: University of British Columbia Press, 2000), pp. 139–46.

[160] Since the Tokugawa shogun nominally accepted his position from the emperor, he could not accept the title of "king." The sexagenary cycle is a system of dating that first appeared in Chinese oracle bone texts from the Shang dynasty, which Japan and Korea later adopted. The virtue of this system is that it was not based on imperial era names. See Wilkinson, *Chinese History: A New Manual*, pp. 496–98.

[161] Norihito Mizuno, "Japan and its East Asian Neighbors: Japan's Perception of China and Korea and the Making of Foreign Policy from the Seventeenth to the Nineteenth Century," PhD thesis, Ohio State University, 2004, p. 23, also pp. 66, 72–73.

[162] A great deal of information on the Chinese books imported into Nagasaki during the Edo period is presented in the essays by Ōba Osamu, trans. Joshua A. Fogel, *Books and Boats: Sino-Japanese Relations in the Seventeenth and Eighteenth Centuries* (Portland: MerwinAsia, 2012), chapters 3, 4, and 5.

[163] Oral fluency was probably more common among traders living in mixed communities in Japanese, Korean, and Chinese ports.

After receding in popularity in the second half of the ninth century, *Kangaku*, the Japanese study of Chinese texts, was perpetuated as the "house tradition" of a small group of specialists who transmitted their own traditions of reading and interpretation.[164] The eighteenth-century Confucian scholar Ogyū Sorai (1666–1728), complained that the tradition of Japanese readings of the canon, which dominated Confucian studies in the country, had obscured the original Confucian teachings. He argued that his disciples should learn spoken Chinese in order to approach the canon "with an internal awareness of its linguistic contours and pronunciation."[165] Increasing imports of Chinese books, especially vernacular texts, fueled interest in *Tōwagaku* 唐話學, the study of spoken Chinese. Literary Chinese, which Japanese scholars had been reading for centuries, became *Kajin gengo* 華人言語, the "speech of the Chinese," and a separate language from *bun* 文, "writing" (with Chinese characters), which was universal in its connotations.[166]

Despite a long continuous tradition of cultural exchange, few educated Koreans were actually able to speak Chinese. In order to facilitate diplomatic exchanges, the Chosŏn government established a translation office (Sayŏgwŏn 司譯院) to train interpreters in Mongolian, Chinese, Japanese, and Jurchen (later Manchu), who could help prepare official documents in foreign relations.[167] Chinese speaking interpreters were posted along the route taken by Chinese embassies to Hansŏng and assigned to accompany Korean embassies to Peking. Approximately twenty interpreters would be assigned to an embassy, which would number over 200 persons.[168] Korean envoys to Peking conducted "conversations" with Chinese (and Manchu) scholars through writing – or rather, through poetry, which became the customary mode of communication for diplomatic exchanges.[169] Just as Chosŏn trained interpreters to deal

[164] The importance of *Kangaku* in the Edo period is emphasized by Ōba, *Books and Boats*.
[165] Emanuel Pastreich, "Grappling with Chinese Writing as a Material Language: Ogyū Sorai's *Yakubunsentei*," *Harvard Journal of Asiatic Studies* 61.1 (2001): 120.
[166] Emmanuel Pastreich, *The Observable Mundane: Vernacular Chinese and the Emergence of a Literary Discourse on Popular Narrative in Edo Japan* (Seoul: Seoul National University Press, 2011), pp. 135–36, 146–47; see Pastreich's chapter 5 on how vernacular Chinese fiction stimulated Japanese fiction.
[167] Ki-joong Song, *The Study of Foreign Languages in the Chosŏn Dynasty (1392–1910)* (Seoul: Chimmundang, 2001).
[168] Song, *Study of Foreign Languages*, p. 43.
[169] Shōsuke Murai, trans. and adapted by Haruko Wakabayashi, "Poetry in Chinese as a Diplomatic Art in Premodern East Asia," in *Tools of Culture*, ed. Goble, Robinson, and Wakabayashi, pp. 49–69. But having to communicate through writing did not deter Pak Chiwŏn, who was on the 1780 embassy to congratulate the Qianlong emperor on his seventieth birthday, from engaging in convivial drinking bouts with Qing subjects encountered en route: see Pak Chiwŏn, trans. Yang Hi Choe-Wall, *The Jehol Diary: Yŏrha ilgi of Pak Chi-wŏn, 1737–1805* (Leiden: E. J. Brill, 2010), pp. 100–2.

with the Japanese in Pusan's *Waegwan*, so Tsushima employed Korean interpreters who mediated between the traders and Chosŏn officials. In addition, the interpreters were also ordered to compile intelligence about contemporary events, which was reported to the shogunal officials.[170] One can be sure that intelligence collection was a regular activity, conducted by all of the countries.

Conclusion

In this chapter, I have presented northeast Asia as a region with a historical evolution that is separate from, though affected by, the Central Plain culture, and pressed the case for treating Korea's and Japan's dealings with China as part of China's relations with her northeast Asian frontier. China's northeast frontier was both a landed and a maritime frontier, meeting the Central Plain in the North China Plain's northeast segment and at ports in Shandong and Zhejiang provinces.

In an early phase, which lasted until the seventh century, groups on China's northeast frontier formed autochthonous states by adapting Chinese political models and practices, obtained through contact with the Central Plain state of Yan, which had pushed into present-day Shandong and northern Hebei, and the Han commandery at Lelang. This intensive economic and cultural interaction among the northeast Asian groups produced a succession of northeastern states: Puyŏ, Koguryŏ, Paekche, Silla, and Yamato.

This period of northeastern state formation coincided with political atomization in China, marked by the fall of Han (220 CE), which lasted until the unification by Sui (589), then Tang (618). During these centuries, there was intense interaction among states at the periphery rather than direct contact with Central Plain polities, in part because at this time north China was ruled by descendants of northern frontier peoples who had settled in the *zhongyuan* during the Han. Peninsular state formation built on knowledge disseminated by the Han commandery at Lelang. During this period, Korea was divided into a number of states, each seeking advantage over its rivals through alliances with states on the North China Plain, south China and Japan. Silla's alliance with Tang finally allowed it to defeat its rivals and unify the peninsula under its rule. Meanwhile, in the late seventh and early eighth centuries the Yamato

---

[170] Ho Ch'i'ŭn, "Kŭnsei ch'yosyu (Chōshu) ŭi Sach'ŭma (Satsuma) ŭi Chosŏn'ŏ t'ongsa wa Chosŏn chŏngbu sujip" (Choshu and Satsuma's Korean interpreters and the collection of information by the Chosŏn government), *Tongyang sahak yŏn'gu* 109 (2009): 311–58.

state's adaptation of Chinese legal codes capped Japan's process of state building.

During the ninth and tenth centuries, following an interval of strong unified Tang rule, power shifted to Northeast Asian states that used their comparative military advantage to defeat regimes based in the Central Plain. In contrast to their predecessors, these states, whose empires encompassed nomadic as well as agrarian subjects, chose to administer the Chinese-speaking population from Peking, which was situated in an area where the Central Plain and the northeast region overlapped, an area that was controlled by northeast groups during the third to sixth centuries and again from the ninth century to the fourteenth.

That the political fortunes of Korea and Japan were affected by events occurring in the Central Plain and northeast Asia is a point well illustrated by scrutiny of the tenth to fourteenth centuries, when the power vacuum resulting from Tang decline caused north China to fragment. Non-Han provincial governors with military backgrounds exercised increasing autonomy and eventually ceded the northeastern edge of north China to the Khitan. Attempts by the Song government to retrieve the Sixteen Prefectures and simultaneously defend the northeastern border led them to counter the Khitan by allying with Koryŏ and the Khitan vassals. But the Jurchen succeeded instead in turning the old Chinese strategy of "using barbarians to control barbarians" (*yi Yi zhi Yi*) against Song, who lost north China to them in 1127. The stalemate that ensued – the Southern Song was unable to militarily take back the north, but the Jurchen failed in their attempts to conquer the south – was eventually broken by the Mongols, who overran China, subjugated Koryŏ, and threatened to invade Japan. Mongol rule ended when popular uprisings swept from north China into the northeast, laying the ground for the founding of new regimes in China and Korea. Meanwhile, the nominal presence of a centralized polity in Japan was belied by the explosion of Japanese "pirate" raids on the Korean and Chinese coasts.

A third phase of interaction began in the sixteenth century, when the arrival of European traders in Asian waters stimulated new activity in what was already a well-established intra-Asian trade. Spanish colonization of the Philippines and Japanese innovation in metallurgy coupled with the collapse of shogunal authority spurred regional lords in Kyushu to send ships abroad. Chinese merchants and Japanese traders engaged with Portuguese adventurers. This unprecedented maritime expansion was founded on mercantile activity outside the bureaucratic-military confines dictated by the Ming government. The period of official control over maritime commerce was over when the Ming tacitly gave up the struggle in 1571.

The expansion of the maritime economy led an increasingly confident Japan and Korea, each with its own self-centered notion of the Asian world order, to challenge Qing. Already, long before the sixteenth century, Chosŏn had attempted to impose its own restrictions on the trade with Japan. Its actions in dealing with neighboring states in matters of trade and diplomacy were at odds with its many protestations of loyalty to a Sinocentric world order. Especially in the seventeenth century, both Japan and Korea behaved as players, not subordinates, in an Asia that was now part of a much larger global world.

2 Transformations in early modern northeast Asia

The second half of the sixteenth century found the Portuguese cruising in waters off the coasts of Asia, the Spanish colonizing the Philippines, and Jesuit and Dominican missionaries evangelizing in Japan and China. How did these newcomers affect the maritime and coastal frontiers discussed in the last chapter? More specifically, was the European advent linked to regime change in Japan and China? In contrast to earlier accounts, which place the Tokugawa shogunate and the Qing conquest within separate national histories, this chapter demonstrates the importance of regional interaction in shaping these seemingly independent events. Additionally, it shows how introduction of a world history context that the national histories ignore advances our understanding of the dynastic transition in China, the reunification of Japan, and Korea's traumatic experience of three invasions.

We begin with the 1592 invasion of Korea by Toyotomi Hideyoshi, the culminating event of his successful military career, and the Ming military intervention that stymied Hideyoshi's initiative. Several decades later, another tripartite confrontation of forces involved the Ming, Chosŏn, and a new northeast regional power who would go on to conquer and rule China as the Qing empire. The chapter surveys the Jurchen origins of the Qing ruling house, traces its expanding influence, and chronicles its shifting relations with the Ming and the Chosŏn state. Initially regarded by the Ming and Koreans as mobile marauders on the northeast Asian frontier, the Jianzhou Jurchen successfully created a military force that eventually bested both regimes. Their story presents many elements familiar from the history of earlier conquest dynasties, but with a twist – the new opportunities for wealth accumulation provided by the expanding maritime frontier.

Activities on the maritime frontier and the land frontier in Siberia stimulated political, cultural, and economic transformations in China, Japan and Korea that make the 1550–1650 period "early modern." The European impact extended far beyond the introduction of improved firearms. Serving as cartographers, architects, craftsmen, translators, and interpreters, Jesuits introduced new technologies to Ming and Qing rulers. The Qing then used their knowledge of European practices in negotiating with the Russians who had moved into northeast Asia.

European expansion into Asia involved not just western Europe but also Russia. More than the overseas empires of Portugal, Spain, or the Netherlands, Russia's presence on its Inner Asian borders commanded the Qing court's attention and produced a flexible foreign policy during the late seventeenth and early eighteenth centuries. While ingratiating itself with the Tsarist court in St. Petersburg in order to ensure Russian neutrality in its campaigns to subjugate the Zunghar empire, the Qing took military action to curb Russia's expansion into Siberia. Russian exploration in North Asia and the North Pacific impelled both the Tokugawa and Qing to exploration and mapping efforts of their own. Cartography provided each state with fresh perspectives on a suddenly enlarged world, even as the collection of more and more detailed information on minority peoples living in the periphery strengthened the state's ability to directly rule its subjects. The heightening of cultural exchange and the growth of commercial publishing advanced the dissemination of knowledge to a broader segment of urban society, requiring the state to create more sophisticated mechanisms to monitor state-society relations. In their policy responses to geopolitical competition, economic development, and urbanization, the Japanese and Qing authorities behaved much like early modern European states.

Hideyoshi's invasion, *Imjin waeran*

The events at the core of this narrative began on May 23, 1592, when a flotilla of four hundred Japanese ships appeared at the Korean port of Pusan and demanded entry for an expedition aimed at subjugating the Ming dynasty.[1] Despite hints of Hideyoshi's intentions, gleaned during the Chosŏn envoy's visit to Japan in 1591, the Koreans were caught by surprise.[2] When the Koreans rejected the fleet's demands, the Japanese

---

[1] A full account of the Japanese invasions (1592–98) and the Ming military response is provided in Swope, *Dragon's Head*. See also Samuel Hawley, *The Imjin War: Japan's Sixteenth-Century Invasion of Korea and Attempt to Conquer China* (Berkeley: Institute of East Asian Studies, University of California, 2005). Many accounts of the invasion exist in Japanese: see Kitajima Manji, *Toyotomi Hideyoshi no Chōsen shiryaku* (Toyotomi Hideyoshi's Korean invasions) (Tokyo: University of Tokyo Press, 1995) for a sample. For the Korean perspective, see the essays in Chŏng Tuhŭi and Yi Kyŏngsun, eds. *Imjin waeran, Tong Asia samguk chŏnjaeng* (A transnational history of the Japanese invasions, 1592–1598: the East Asian dimension) (Seoul: Hyumonisut'ŭ, 2007).

[2] On the factional infighting that divided the Chosŏn court, which not only could not agree on a course of action but also on whether Hideyoshi's plans should be reported to the Ming, see Kitajima Manji, "Jinshin waranki no Chōsen to Min" (Chosŏn and Ming during

easily captured Pusan. The force, totaling 150,000 men, was at first highly successful, advancing northward along the west coast of the Korean peninsula to occupy the capital, Hansŏng, then P'yŏngyang, and to threaten the border town of Ŭiju, on the Amnŏk (Yalu) River. King Sŏnjo fled northward in disarray. He contemplated seeking refuge with the Ming, but ultimately remained on the Korean side of the Yalu River and called on the Ming for rescue. After some hesitation, and despite the near-annihilation of the first Ming relief force, Ming troops helped push the Japanese troops southward down the peninsula in 1593.[3]

A military stalemate ensued (1593–95); negotiations between the Japanese commander, Konishi Yukinaga, and the Ming negotiator, Shen Weijing (sidelining the Koreans, who watched the proceedings with anxiety and distrust) involved "deceit perpetrated on all sides in the interests of reaching a peace settlement."[4] The Japanese generals on the ground hoped to appease Hideyoshi by offering access to trade with Ming as a tributary vassal; Shen accepted their assurances and hoped that Hideyoshi's true goal, to conquer the Ming, could be concealed from his superiors. The two parties negotiated a peace treaty that had Hideyoshi accepting Ming investiture as king of Japan and withdrawing his troops from Korea and Tsushima in return for the restoration of tributary trade. When Hideyoshi learned that the Ming embassy he had entertained was offering investiture instead of complete capitulation, he flew into a rage and was with difficulty dissuaded from killing the Chinese officials.[5] The second invasion, begun in 1597, finally ended with the withdrawal of Japanese forces after Hideyoshi's death (1598).

Hideyoshi's invasion), in Arano Yasunori, Ishii Masatoshi, and Murai Shōsuke, eds., *Ajia no naka no Nihon shi* (Japanese history within an Asian context), vol. II: *Gaikō to sensō* (Diplomacy and war) (Tokyo: University of Tokyo Press, 1992), pp. 129–30.

[3] The deliberations within both courts are analyzed in Ryu Pojŏn, "Imjin waeran si pabyŏng ŭ silsang e taehan ilgo – kŭ konggi wa sigi rŭl chungsim ŭro" (An investigation of the Ming dynasty's dispatch of troops in the Japanese invasion – focused on the motives and timing), *Han'guksa hakpo* 14 (2003): 151–84. The Ming suspected that Chosŏn had collaborated with Japan in the invasion. According to Gari Ledyard, "Confucianism and War: The Korean Security Crisis of 1598," *Journal of Korean Studies* 6 (1988–89): 84, fn2, the Ming dispatched troops only after an official visited Ŭiju in August, 1592 and examined all of the documents, including letters from the Japanese commander, relating to the invasion. See also Kitajima, "Jinshin waranki," p. 131. On the destruction of the first Ming force sent in July 1592, see Swope, *Dragon's Head*, pp. 123–24.

[4] Swope, "Deceit, Disguise, and Dependence," p. 758.

[5] *Ibid.*, pp. 772–79. Since Hideyoshi did not speak or read Chinese, he learned about the investiture after he had fêted the Ming envoys.

Northeast Asian regional power: the Jianzhou Jurchen

Several scholars have noted that the Japanese invasion and Ming response strengthened the ability of Nurhaci, the founder of the Jurchen Later Jin state, to expand his sway among neighboring northeast Asian tribes.[6] His rise to power in the northeast has to be put within the framework of Ming policies toward tribesmen in the northern and northeastern borderlands. Nurhaci's ancestors lived on the southern banks of the Tumen and Yalu Rivers in Chosŏn territory in the early fifteenth century (see Chapter 1). They relocated, moving north in 1410 to accept Ming appointments as leaders of the Left Commandery of the Jianzhou Jurchen. As a commandery official, Nurhaci and his immediate forebears became well-versed in Chinese bureaucratic modes, not only through contact with Ming military officials but also through the Ming requirement that commandery leaders periodically present themselves at court in the capital, Peking. In his capacity as a Ming vassal, Nurhaci visited Peking seven times (1589, 1590, 1593, 1597, 1601, 1608, 1611) to present tribute.[7]

Nurhaci succeeded to the Ming office of *duzhihuishi* (都指揮使, Regional Military Commissioner) in 1583, after his father and grandfather were killed in a Ming raid on the headquarters of a rival leader, Wang Gao. Shortly thereafter, in 1584, with a "vendetta" against the Hada chieftain Nikan Wailan, Nurhaci began a series of military campaigns against neighboring tribes. His success in using a blend of marriage diplomacy and coercive force to expand his power base earned him promotion to *dudu qianshi* (都督僉使, Assistant Commander-in-Chief) of the Jianzhou Left Commandery in 1589 and then to "Dragon Tiger General" (龍虎將軍) in 1594.[8]

Nurhaci was still regarded as a minor tribal chieftain in the 1590s, when he first appears in the Korean records.[9] The occasion was the Hideyoshi invasion of 1592. The first Ming force sent in August 1592 to respond to

---

[6] Kye Sŭngbŏm, "Imjin waeran Nurŭhach'i: Tong Asia ŭi saeroun p'aeja, Nurŭhach'i sigak esŏ pon chŏnjaeng" (The Japanese invasion and Nurhaci: The new winner in East Asia, the battle from Nurhaci's perspective), in *Imjin waeran: Tong Asia samguk chŏnjaeng* (The Japanese invasion of Korea: a three-country war), ed. Chŏng Tuhwi and Yi Kyŏngsun (Seoul: Humanities Press, 2007), pp. 355–84.

[7] Nurhaci's biography appears in Arthur W. Hummel, ed., *Eminent Chinese of the Ch'ing Period* (Washington, DC: US Government Printing Office, 1943), I: 594–99. See also Frederic Wakeman, Jr., *The Great Enterprise: The Manchu Reconstruction of Imperial Order in Seventeenth-Century China* (Berkeley: University of California Press, 1985), I: 49–58.

[8] Information taken from the chronicle compiled by Yan Chongnian, *Nuerhachi zhuan* (Biography of Nurhaci) (Beijing: Beijing chubanshe, 1983), pp. 307–26 and Teng Shaozhen, *Nuerhachi pingzhuan* (Biography of Nurhaci) (Shenyang: Liaoning renmin chubanshe, 1985), pp. 382–402.

[9] *Sŏnjo sillok* 25/9/17, #4 (October 21, 1592), 22/7/12, #1 (August 22, 1589), 28/7/25, #2 (August 30, 1595) refer to Nurhaci as Noahapche (the Korean pronunciation of 女兒哈赤),

King Sŏnjo's appeal for aid was slaughtered. In October, when Nurhaci offered to cross the Yalu to assist Chosŏn, the Ming military commander in the northeast apparently contemplated accepting the offer, which was opposed by the Chosŏn court.[10] The Koreans also rejected Nurhaci's bid for a compact of friendship in 1596, and his hints that he might accept a Chosŏn official title.[11]

While the Ming and Chosŏn courts expelled the Japanese invaders, Nurhaci continued to subjugate other Jurchen tribes, including the Hada (1599), the Hoifa (1607), the Ula (1613) and the Yehe (1619). In 1616, Nurhaci declared himself Khan of the Later Jin state, and in 1618 he directly challenged the Ming by issuing the "Seven Great Grievances" against the Ming, and taking the garrison of Fushun.[12]

In 1618, Nurhaci's success in repulsing several attempts to retake Fushun attracted the attention of the Ming court, which prepared a massive expeditionary force against him. The Chosŏn king, Kwanghae (r. 1608–1623), found himself in a delicate position, sandwiched between the Jurchen and the Ming. Studies of the Ming and Jurchen communications, drawing on the *Kwanghaegun ilgi* 光海君日記 in the *Chosŏn wangjo sillok* provide remarkable insight into the geopolitical calculations that shaped Kwanghae's actions.

Korean historians have noted that Kwanghae's hold on the throne was not completely secure. Although he was the oldest surviving son of King Sŏnjo at the time of the *Imjin waeran*, when he was made Crown Prince, Kwanghae should, strictly speaking, have given way to the son of Sŏnjo's second queen, Yongch'ang, who was a two-year old infant when Sŏnjo died. The Koreans adhered to the Ming succession principle which privileged the eldest surviving son of the queen over other sons. During Sŏnjo's final illness, there had been a debate about the succession in which the "Daebuk" or Great Northern faction had prevailed. Although Kwanghae became king when Sŏnjo died, factional conflicts continued, leading to the execution of Dowager Queen Inmok's father, Kim Chenam, the exile of Prince Yongch'ang in 1613, and the "internal exile" of Inmok herself in 1618.[13] These

Noŭlgaje 老乙可赤, and Nogaje 老可恥. *Sŏnjo sillok 28/7/1*, #1 (August 6, 1595) calls Nurhaci the "Jianzhou Ho leader, Noahabche."

[10] *Sŏnjo sillok* 25/9/14, #2 (October 18, 1592) and 14/9/17, #4 (October 21, 1592).

[11] *Sŏnjo sillok* 29/2/1, #3 (February 28, 1596), 29/1/30, #3 (February 27, 1596).

[12] Teng Shaozhen, "Shilun Ming yu Hou Jin zhanzheng de yuanyin ji qi xingzhi" (On the causes and the nature of the war between Ming and Later Jin), *Minzu yanjiu* 1980 #5: 11–20.

[13] Seung B. Kye, "In the Shadow of the Father: Court Opposition and the Reign of King Kwanghae in Early Seventeenth-Century Chosŏn Korea," PhD thesis, University of Washington, 2006.

factional tensions influenced the court's response to Nurhaci's advances in 1618 and early 1619.[14]

The battle of Sarhū

As the Ming assembled their expeditionary force in 1618 and early 1619, Ming officials managing the anti-Jurchen campaign sent notices to Chosŏn requesting military supplies and troops. Nurhaci also made overtures to the Kwanghae court. In March 1618, as Nurhaci attacked the Ming, he sent envoys to persuade Chosŏn to remain neutral.[15] If Chosŏn sent troops into Liaodong to help the Ming, the Jurchen threatened to retaliate with raids on Korean settlements.

How should the king respond? High officials split along factional lines. Perhaps because of his earlier experience with the Japanese invasion, Kwanghae was reluctant to be drawn into the Ming–Jurchen confrontation. Intelligence available to the court underlined the strength of the Jurchen forces and pointed to the military vulnerabilities of the Ming. The Border Defense Council (Pibyŏnsa) noted that Chosŏn was militarily weak and already bore the burden of defending against the Japanese as well as the Jurchen. "Moreover, these Jurchen are thoroughly familiar with our country; on the day of the Ming expedition, they will seize the opportunity to enter our country."[16] The Pibyŏnsa recommended that Chosŏn remain neutral.

The Ming applied moral pressure, reminding Chosŏn of its obligations as a vassal state and of the Wanli emperor's magnanimity in ridding the country of Japanese invaders. The Vice-Minister of the Ming Board of War, Wang Keshou, wrote, "When your country had difficulties with the Japanese 倭奴, we immediately dispatched 100,000 troops [the actual number sent was much smaller]."[17] Sending troops to participate in a joint attack on the Jurchen would allow the king to "recompense the Ming" 報效本朝.[18]

---

[14] *Chŏnju Yi si taegwan* (Genealogy of the Chŏju Yi), comp. Chŏnju Yi si taedong ch'ong yagwŏn (Seoul: Chŏnju Yi si taedong ch'ong yagwŏn, 2002), pp. 451, 463. Also Bai Xinliang, "Saerhu zhi zhan yu Chaoxian chubing" (The battle of Sarhu and the Chosŏn dispatch of troops), *Qingshi yanjiu* 3 (1997): 9–15; Diao Shuren, "Lun Saerhu zhi zhan qianhou Hou Jin yu Chaoxian de guanxi" (On the relations between the Later Jin and Korea before and after the battle of Sarhu), *Qingshi yanjiu* 4 (2001): 43–50.

[15] Bai Xinliang, "Saerhu zhi zhan"; Diao Shuren, "Lun Saerhu."

[16] *Kwanghaegun ilgi* dated Kwanghae 10/i4/20#4 (June 12, 1618); also cited by Bai, "Saerhu zhi zhan," p. 10.

[17] *Kwanghaegun ilgi*, Kwanghae 10/i4/27#6=June 19, 1618.

[18] *Kwanghaegun ilgi*, Kwanghae 10/i4/27#6=June 19, 1618; also cited in Bai, "Saerhu zhi zhan," p. 45 and Diao, "Lun Saerhu," p. 45.

Baoxiao (K. *bohyo*), "rendering service to repay kindness," has deep resonances in Chinese Confucian thought.[19] Yi Yich'ŏm (1560–1623) spoke eloquently about Chosŏn's duty as a vassal state to go to the aid of its overlord, lamenting the present situation, in which people "do not know what it is to *bo*."[20] Even proponents of caution such as Im Yŏn argued that "the grace bestowed on the country at the time of the Imjin debacle has to be reciprocated, even if it leads to the death of the country," revealing the power of this sentiment among Kwanghae's officials.[21]

Caught between pleas for caution and demands that Chosŏn repay the Wanli emperor's "imperial grace," the king finally acquiesced to an imperial order 勅書 from Wanli requiring Chosŏn to participate in a joint campaign against the Jurchen. On April 3–7, 1619, General Kang Hong'ip led a force of 13,000 men across the Yalu River into Liaodong. The Korean accounts express dissatisfaction over the troops' state of readiness, their poor equipment and low morale. Doubts about whether the joint forces could actually defeat Nurhaci lingered. Reports from the field complained that the Ming army with whom the Koreans liaised was far smaller than promised. In any case, Nurhaci's decisive victory over the combined Ming and Chosŏn army at Sarhū (1619) quickly gave rise to rumors in Chosŏn that the king had secretly communicated with Nurhaci in order to forestall retribution in the event of a Ming defeat.[22]

In 1618, *realpolitik* battled against pro-Ming loyalism in the Chosŏn court deliberations. By virtue of its strategic location, Korea was caught between opposing forces, the Ming pressing for a joint campaign and Nurhaci for neutrality in the coming confrontation. Korean intelligence on the relative strengths of the two sides, their long experience with Jurchen military prowess, and their fear of Jurchen attack initially inclined King Kwanghae to favor neutrality. The pressure put on him from Peking and pro-Ming loyalists at court, however, proved to be overwhelming.

Nurhaci's decisive victory at Sarhū was a turning point in the fortunes of the Later Jin state. In a series of military triumphs, his troops quickly captured major Ming garrisons, thus securing control of Liaodong.

---

[19] See Lien-sheng Yang, "The Concept of 'Pao' as a Basis for Social Relations in China," in *Chinese Thought and Institutions*, ed. John K. Fairbank (Chicago: University of Chicago Press, 1957), pp. 291–309.

[20] *Kwanghaegun ilgi*, Kwanghae 10/5/5#2=June 26, 1618; also cited in Diao, "Lun Saerhu," p. 45.

[21] *Kwanghaegun ilgi*, Kwanghae 10/5/5#5=June 26, 1618, also cited in Diao, "Lun Saerhu."

[22] Bai, "Saerhu zhi zhan," p. 11; Diao, "Lun Saerhu," pp. 46–7. See Wakeman, *Great Enterprise*, I: 62–63 on the separate battles at Sarhū that killed approximately 45,000 Ming troops, about half the number mustered.

Nurhaci then turned his attention to the region to the west of the Liao River, but held back his forces, partly to avoid conflict with the Mongols on his northwestern flank and partly to secure his southern flank (the border with Korea) and avoid a two-front war as he confronted the Ming.[23]

The 1627 invasion

The two Jurchen/Manchu invasions of Korea took place under Nurhaci's son and successor, Hongtaiji (r. 1627–43). By 1627 the leadership among the Jurchen and the Koreans had changed. Following a coup d'état in 1623 that installed a new king, Injo (1595–1649), a pro-Ming faction dominated the Chosŏn court.[24] Since an important justification for removing Kwanghae had been his disloyalty to Ming, Injo's administration conducted a "blatantly pro-Ming anti-Manchu policy."[25]

Nurhaci's death may also have made a difference. The Jurchen had accumulated grievances against Chosŏn. Chosŏn officials referred to the Jurchen and their leader with perjoratives such as "barbarian" and "bandit." Chosŏn's repeated evasions of diplomatic offers of alliance had led some *beile* (banner lords) to propose attacking Chosŏn, but Nurhaci had ignored these slights to pursue a wider political and diplomatic agenda.

The Later Jin invasion in 1627 listed multiple grievances against Chosŏn: troop incursions across their mutual border; Chosŏn's refusal to repatriate political and economic refugees from Liaodong; its participation in the 1619 Ming offensive against the Later Jin, and especially the harboring of a former Ming military officer, Mao Wenlong, who built a regional base within Chosŏn territory from which to launch attacks on Liaodong; and Chosŏn's failure to send condolences upon Nurhaci's death in 1626. Scholars agree that the primary motives were to terminate Mao's activities and intimidate Chosŏn into refusing aid to

---

[23] Nicola Di Cosmo and Dalizhabu Bao, "Introduction: A Brief Survey of Manchu–Mongol Relations Before the Qing Conquest," in *Manchu–Mongol Relations on the Eve of the Manchu Conquest: A Documentary History*, ed. Nicola Di Cosmo and Dalizhabu Bao (Leiden: E. J. Brill, 2003), pp. 1–14. Nurhaci also had to consolidate his hold over the rapidly expanding banner forces that were created as a result of his victories; see Gertraude Roth Li, "The Manchu–Chinese Relationship," in *From Ming to Ch'ing: Conquest, Region, and Continuity in Seventeenth-Century China*, ed. Jonathan D. Spence and John E. Wills, Jr. (New Haven: Yale University Press, 1979), pp. 1–38.

[24] Yi Yŏngch'un, *Chosŏn hugi wangwi gyesŭng yŏn'gu* (Royal succession in the late Chosŏn) (Seoul: Chimmundang, 1998), c. 2, 3; also Kye, "In the Shadow of the Father."

[25] Quotation from Lee, *New History*, p. 215.

the Ming.[26] The invasion took place during a period of severe food shortages in Liaodong, so obtaining grain supplies may have been another (though unstated) factor.[27]

In his study of the 1627 invasion, Ki-baek Lee also cites the rebellion of Yi Kwal, a participant in the Injo coup who subsequently turned against it in 1624. After the suppression of this uprising, some of Yi Kwal's followers crossed into Liaodong and appealed to the Jurchen to "redress the injustice of Kwanghaegun's removal from the throne."[28]

The 1627 invasion of Chosŏn was led by Amin, Nurhaci's nephew and one of the four senior *beile* ruling collectively after Nurhaci's death. After capturing Ŭiju, on the Korean bank of the Yalu River, the Jurchen attacked and drove Mao Wenlong out of his stronghold at Ch'ŏlsan (C. Tieshan). P'yŏngyang fell on March 13. The Chosŏn court apparently received word of the Later Jin army's approach at Ŭiju, which had occurred on February 29, only on March 4. Plans for guarding the king, determined at a court conference, were not implemented; some officials hoped that the Ming would send troops to help them repulse the Jurchen forces, but no such aid materialized.

Injo's hopes of resistance faded as his officials and troops fled. His ministers were divided, with a majority who counseled negotiating with Amin for peace while a minority advocated fighting to the death. Negotiations faltered in the face of Chosŏn's refusal to break off its tribute relationship with the Ming and recognize Later Jin overlordship by adopting its calendar. Eventually Amin agreed to a compromise: Chosŏn could use either calendar in its communications with the Later Jin. An "elder and younger brother" alliance was ritually sealed. Chosŏn agreed to send tribute three times a year and to open markets on the Yalu.[29] Soon thereafter, Amin's forces withdrew from the peninsula, leaving only a garrison at Ŭiju.

---

[26] According to Wakeman, *Great Enterprise*, pp. 127–30, the Ming were actually ambivalent about Mao's activities and suspected him of harboring ambitions to become a regional warlord. Mao was forced to leave Chosŏn in March 1627, during the Manchu invasion. He was executed in 1629 by the Ming official in charge of the northeast forces, Yuan Chonghuan. See also Li Shanhong, "Hou Jin Chaoxian [Ding mao zhi yi] yuanyin qianzhe" (A preliminary analysis of the causes of the 1627 invasion of Chosŏn by the Later Jin), in *Zhong Han guanxishi lunwenji* (Collected essays on the history of Sino-Korean relations), ed. Diao Shuren and Yi Xingguo (Changchun: Jilin wenshi chubanshe, 1995), pp. 322–28.

[27] Li, "Manchu–Chinese Relationship," p. 27.

[28] Lee, *New History*, pp. 215–16; Kim Han'gyu, *Han Chung kwan'gye sa* (History of Korean–Chinese relations) (Seoul: Arche, 1999), p. 716. There seems to be no mention of Yi Kwal in the Chinese historians' accounts.

[29] Kim Han'gyu, *Han Chung kwan'gye sa*, p. 717; Chen Jiexian, "Luelun Tiancong nianjiang Hou Jin yu Chaoxian de guanxi" (Relations between Later Jin and Chosŏn in the Tiancong era), in *Zhong Chao guanxishi lunwenji*, ed. Diao and Yi, pp. 299–321.

Although Chinese accounts emphasize the crushing of Chosŏn forces by Amin's troops, the Korean studies raise questions about why, if Chosŏn were so weak, the Jurchen did not press for unconditional surrender. The 1627 invasion did not achieve its goals, which were finally attained a decade later in the second invasion. Perhaps their overall strategic situation vis-à-vis the Ming influenced the Later Jin willingness to compromise. The 1627 invasion of Chosŏn took place during a truce between Hongtaiji and Yuan Chonghuan, at that point the Ming governor of Liaodong.[30] In order to send 30,000 men (with later reinforcements) to Ŭiju, the Jurchen lifted their military pressure on Ming defenses in Liaoxi. The hasty withdrawal of Jurchen troops from the Korean peninsula shortly after a successful two-week campaign (March 1 to March 19, 1627) may have reflected Hongtaiji's desire to prevent Yuan from altering the military balance on the Liaoxi front lines.

The 1637 invasion

Hongtaiji announced the causes of the 1636–37 Manchu invasion (called the *Pyŏngja horan* in Korean) on December 21, 1636, eight days before the beginning of the campaign. Hongtaiji complained that the Chosŏn had skimped on tribute payments that were specified in the 1627 peace accord (since they regarded the tribute as involuntary, Chosŏn presented excuses for delays in shipment). Injo had failed to honor the terms of the peace agreement. His court continued to communicate with the Ming and clung to the Ming calendar. Injo also failed to meet Hongtaiji's demands for troops and boats. The immediate cause of the invasion, however, was the Chosŏn refusal to acknowledge Hongtaiji's adoption of the title of emperor and his creation of the Qing state.[31]

In 1635, Hongtaiji achieved two important milestones in his life. After many years of struggle, he defeated the Caqar Mongol confederation led by Ligdan Khan, a significant step toward subjugating the Eastern Mongols. The year 1635 also marked the posthumous purge of Manggūltai, the last of the eight banner lords whom Nurhaci had entrusted with collegial rule, leaving Hongtaiji as the sole ruler of the

---

[30] Hummel, *Eminent Chinese*, II: 954.
[31] Kim Han'gyu, *Han Chung kwan'gye sa*, pp. 719–20, 724. But the biography of Inggūldai (1596–1648) in Hummel, *Eminent Chinese*, I: 394, records that Inggūldai visited Chosŏn twice "to arrange for levies of grain," and after 1637 he continued to obtain grain supplies there. Before 1644, Manchu alternative sources for scarce food and other supplies were relatively limited, so there was strong pressure on Chosŏn.

Later Jin state. His proclamation establishing the Qing state and pro-claiming his emperorship followed shortly thereafter.

Hongtaiji's actions directly challenged the Ming dynasty (Manchu documents referred to Ming as the "southern dynasty") and were certain to anger the pro-Ming faction dominating the Injo court. Chosŏn envoys who happened to be in the Later Jin/Qing capital at the time refused to perform the ritual of submission after the dynastic proclamation. Fearing punishment from their superiors, they abandoned a letter for Injo that was entrusted to them and hastened home.

Hongtaiji next dispatched a delegation, led by Inggŭldai, to invite the Chosŏn king to send a royal kinsman to the official ceremonies that would celebrate Hongtaiji as emperor. Hongtaiji's acquisition of the Yuan state seal from Ligdan Khan held enormous political weight in the Mongol world, which was probably why he sent Mongol nobles to accompany Inggŭldai. The envoys explained this to the Korean official who met the group at the border town of Ŭiju, but the court ignored this information.

The arrival of the delegation threw the Chosŏn court into an uproar. Many high officials opposed any concessions to the Qing. Declaring that "Since the time I was born, I have only known the Great Ming Son of Heaven," Hong Ikhan (1586–1637) argued that Chosŏn's glory lay in its Confucian commitment to ritual (C. *li*) and principle (C. *yi*). The "Western Tartars" (meaning the Mongols) who accompanied the embassy were ignorant of proper rites and principles. Hongtaiji was pressing the issue because he wanted to tell the rest of the world that "Chosŏn respects us as the son of Heaven."[32] Hong proposed that the Qing envoy be decapitated and his head sent along with Hongtaiji's letter to the Ming, and 138 officials collectively petitioned in support of his advice.[33] Another group of more cautious officials urged restraint.[34] Injo decided he would not accept Hongtaiji's letter and refused to meet Inggŭldai, who departed without meeting the king.

On December 27, 1636, Hongtaiji led an army of 100,000 men from his capital, Shenyang. He captured Ŭiju on January 4, 1637, and moved south, entering P'yŏngyang on the 9th. Despite preparing from October 1636 in anticipation of the Manchu invasion, the Chosŏn troops could not hold their ground. As the Manchu vanguard approached the capital, Injo fled Hansŏng for the mountain fortress, Nam Hansansŏng. The king's hopes for a rescue by the Ming were disappointed, and he was

---

[32] *Injo sillok* 14/2/21 #1.
[33] *Injo sillok* 14/2/25#1; Sun Wenliang and Li Zhiting, *Tiancong han, Chongde di* (Biography of Hongtaiji)(Changchun: Jilin wenshi chubanshe, 1993), pp. 202–3.
[34] *Injo sillok* 14/2/26 #2.

forced to surrender despite fierce opposition from many of his high ministers.[35] Chosŏn was forced to accept Qing overlordship.

From the Manchu perspective, the second invasion provided the necessary assurance that their long-anticipated attack on the Ming could take place without worrying about a Chosŏn attack to their rear.[36] Until 1644, when the Qing occupation of Peking gave them access to the resources of the Central Plain, the second invasion was also important in wresting weapons, gold and silver, and grain resources from Chosŏn. Its decisive victory in the second invasion also demonstrated the Qing ability to impose its will on neighbors who were reluctant to acknowledge its legitimacy, at a crucial moment in its transition from regional to dynastic power.

Chosŏn's importance for the Manchus faded after 1644, as Dorgon and other members of the ruling elite focused their attention on the conquest of the Ming. Korean scholars note that the earlier "harsh attitude" toward Chosŏn was gradually replaced by a more relaxed posture; the quantity of goods demanded in tribute declined; as did the number and size of embassies (and the corresponding cost).[37] This easing of tensions did not alter the Chosŏn court's hostility toward the Qing, which lingered into the early eighteenth century, as will become evident in Chapters 3 and 5.

Ming defense strategies

None of the national histories comprehends the larger currents underlying the sequence of events that brought Japan, Korea, and China into close engagement. Some of these were domestically induced: border unrest was the product of the Ming court's practice of appointing individuals with strong local ties to semi-autonomous regional military commands. This placed major frontier commanderies under the control of families with deep local roots, whose loyalty to the dynasty wavered when asked to choose between their personal interest and the

[35] For a Korean perspective, see Hŏ T'aegu, "Pyŏngja horan kanghwa hyŏpsang ŭi ch'u'i wa Chosŏn ŭi tae'ŭng" (Changes in the peace negotiations during the 1636–37 Manchu invasion and the response of Chosŏn), *Chosŏn sidaesa hakpo* 52 (2010): 51–88.

[36] Li, "Manchu–Chinese Relationship," pp. 32–33, suggests that the pause in military action between 1637 and 1644 was due to a weakening of the Manchu forces. She underlines the importance of Li Zicheng's attack on Peking and Wu Sangui's subsequent change of loyalties in the crucial 1644 entry of the banner forces into China Proper.

[37] Kim Han'gyu, *Han Chung kwan'gye sa*, p. 724; see Chun, "Sino-Korean Tributary Relations," tables 5 and 6, pp. 103–5 for details on the tributary goods and local products.

state's.[38] Pübei, implicated in the Ningxia uprising (1592), Yang Yinglong, leader of an uprising in southwest China during the 1590s, and Mao Wenlong, a Ming officer who eventually became a regional warlord on the Ming–Chosŏn–Jurchen border, are outstanding examples of such persons.[39] The same generalization could, of course, be applied to Nurhaci, who followed his father and grandfather in first accepting titles from the Ming before turning against them in 1616, and to his patron, Li Chengliang.

Li Chengliang (1526–1618), a Ming military official, was the *de facto* regional hegemon in Liaodong.[40] Li belonged to a group of hereditary military officials who played a prominent role in Ming border operations in the Wanli reign, and many of his sons headed major military operations in the last decades of Ming rule. Li Rusong, who commanded the Ming forces sent to expel the Japanese from the Korean peninsula, was Chengliang's son.[41] A fifth-generation descendant of a Korean military family[42] who had served the Ming for several generations, Li Chengliang became the general charged with defending Liaodong against Mongols and Jurchen. His twenty-two-year tenure allowed him to construct a formidable local power base in Liaodong, by staffing military positions throughout the region with real and fictive kinsmen.

The story of Li Chengliang's regional power reads remarkably like descriptions of the non-Han provincial governors who dominated the North China Plain in the ninth century. Iwai Shigeki calls him a leading Liaodong "warlord."[43] He used his official status to not only wipe out opponents of the Ming but also to consolidate his own regional power and tap into the profits of the economic boom. According to Wada Masahiro,

---

[38] Kenneth M. Swope, "A Few Good Men: The Li Family and China's Northern Frontier in the Late Ming," *Ming Studies* 49 (2004): 41, has an alternative explanation: that the Wanli emperor and Zhang Juzheng held these commanders in check through their personal patron–client ties. When the patron was no longer on the scene, the court "lost its ability to properly check the arrogation of authority by these powerful hereditary military families."

[39] On Pübei and Yang Yinglong, see Ray Huang, "The Lung-ch'ing and Wan-li reigns, 1567–1620," in *The Cambridge History of China*, vol. VII, part 1, pp. 566–67, 564–65. See Yang Ying long's biography *Dictionary of Ming Biography*, ed. Goodrich and Fang, pp. 1553–56; on Mao Wen-long, see Wakeman, *Great Enterprise*, I: 127–30.

[40] Swope, "A Few Good Men;" see Li's biography in Hummel, *Eminent Chinese*, I: 450–52.

[41] According to Swope, "A Few Good Men," p. 38, "Members of the Li family were involved in virtually every military action conducted by the Ming from the 1560s through 1620." See also pp. 36–37 and 40–41.

[42] Pamela K. Crossley, *A Translucent Mirror: History and Identity in Qing Imperial Ideology* (Berkeley: University of California Press, 1999), p. 87, suggests that Li's ancestor was Jurchen and not Korean.

[43] Iwai Shigeki, "China's Frontier Society in the Sixteenth and Seventeenth Centuries," *Acta Asiatica* 88 (2005): 14.

the reason troop readiness in Liaodong was so poor in the 1570s was because half of the state allocations were being diverted by Liang to support his private army.[44] With the wealth and power gleaned from official and unofficial activities, Li was able to create a large patronage network in Liaodong. Nurhaci's father and grandfather had been part of this network, and it was Li who confirmed Nurhaci as successor following their deaths in 1583.

In sharp contrast to the early fifteenth century, when Ming armies advanced into the empire's frontiers, the middle of the sixteenth century marked a low point in dynastic fortunes, when the frontier pressed upon the political center.[45] Mongol tribes mobilized on the northern frontier under Dayan Khan, then Altan Khan, to challenge Ming military power. Revolts at the Ming garrison at Datong in 1524–25, 1533, and 1545, and annual Mongol raids on the capital, Peking, from 1520–1566, indicate the persistence and depth of the Mongol problem.[46]

The border defense issue was exacerbated by the Ming fiscal crisis of the 1550s and 1560s. The state failed to reap revenues from the commercial boom and could not even collect agrarian taxes at levels previously achieved.[47] Output from the military farms (*tuntian*), established by the Hongwu emperor to enable garrison troops to produce their own food, had steadily declined, and the central government was forced to ship increasing quantities of grain from China proper to its frontier outposts.[48] The monetization of the tax system during the sixteenth century had failed to redress the annual deficits even as frontier rebellions and the Korean campaign caused military expenditures to soar. Beset internally by peasant rebellions and by military attacks on its northeast frontier, the

---

[44] Wada Masahiro, "Ri Seiryō kenryoku ni okeru zaiseiteki kiban" (The fiscal foundation of Li Chengliang's authority), part 1, *Seinan gakuin daigaku bunri ronshū* 25.2 (1984): 101–6.

[45] See Geiss, "Cheng-te Reign," pp. 403–39 and "Chia-ching Reign," pp. 440–510.

[46] See Morris Rossabi, *China and Inner Asia from 1368 to the Present Day* (New York: Pica Press, 1975); Dayan Khan and Altan Khan are discussed in Christopher P. Atwood, *Encyclopedia of Mongolia and the Mongol Empire* (New York: Facts on File, 2004), pp. 138, 9–10.

[47] The fiscal dilemma is summarized in Jack A. Goldstone, *Revolution and Rebellion in the Early Modern World* (Berkeley: University of California Press, 1991), pp. 368–75; he concludes, p. 374, that "The critical fiscal problem in Ming China was that rising military costs collided with a decreasingly effective tax system."

[48] On the establishment of *tuntian*, see Edward L. Dreyer, "Military Origins of Ming China," in *The Cambridge History of China*, vol. VII, part 1, pp. 104–5, also Edward L. Farmer, *Early Ming Government: The Evolution of Dual Capitals* (Cambridge, MA: Harvard University East Asian Center, 1976), pp. 154–55, 161; on *tuntian* problems in late Ming Liaodong, see Li Jiancai, *Mingdai dongbei* (The northeast during the Ming) (Shenyang: Liaoning renmin chubanshe, 1986), pp. 192–93.

Ming succumbed first to the peasant rebel Li Zicheng. His occupation of the Ming capital and the death of the emperor (a suicide) created an opportunity that the Manchu banner forces were quick to seize.[49] The story of the conquest, beginning with Qing entry into Peking and concluding with the suppression of the Sanfan rebellions in 1683, is well known and beyond the scope of this book.

The problems that the Ming encountered on the northern and northeastern frontiers also stemmed from their practice of co-opting frontier groups by providing opportunities to trade at official horse markets. An important element of the Ming policy to "pacify by welcoming" (*zhaofu* 招撫) the tribes, horse markets, opened in 1406, were a way to provide the Ming cavalry with mounts while satisfying the desire of frontier peoples to acquire iron cooking pots, iron plows, and Chinese textiles.[50] Situated on important postal routes, the markets were supervised by officials who inspected and paid for horses presented as tribute. Over time, however, official exchanges were overshadowed by the private trade between tribal leaders and Han Chinese merchants, who came from outside the region to buy ginseng, freshwater pearls, medicinal herbs, and sable pelts.

The proliferation of markets, together with the increasing frequency of market days, was especially marked in the Jianzhou Jurchen territory. In 1576, responding to Jianzhou Jurchen requests, the Ming increased the number of markets from the initial five (three held at Kaiyuan 開元) to eight. The additional markets were located at Qinghe 清河, Aiyang 靉陽, and Kuandian 寬甸, south of Fushun along the Liao River. In 1595 a market for wood was also opened at Yizhou 義州.[51] Nurhaci was certainly involved with trade. In 1587, he took ginseng and sable pelts to market at Fushun, Qinghe, Kuandian, and Aiyang.[52] He is credited with disseminating an improved method of preserving ginseng among the Jurchen.[53]

[49] On Li Zicheng's occupation of Peking, see Frederic Wakeman, Jr., "The Shun Interregnum of 1644," in *From Ming to Ch'ing*, ed. Spence and Wills, Jr., pp. 39–87.

[50] Wang Dongfang and Ji Mingming, *Nüzhen – Manzu jian'guo yanjiu* (Jurchen: the Manchu establishment of a state) (Beijing: Xueyuan chubanshe, 2009), p. 278. This thirst for trade was shared by the Mongols: see M. Sanjdorj, trans. Urgunge Onon, *Manchu Colonial Rule in Northern Mongolia* (New York: St. Martin's Press, 1980), p. 5. See also Hou Jen-chih, "Frontier Horse Markets in the Ming Dynasty," in *Chinese Social History: Translations of Selected Studies*, comp. E-tu Zen Sun and John De Francis (Reprint of 1966 edn.) (Taipei: Rainbow Bridge Book Co., 1972), pp. 299–332.

[51] Yan Chongnian, *Tianming han* (Biography of Nurhaci) (Changchun: Jilin wenshi chubanshe, 1993), p. 420.

[52] *Ibid.*, p. 418.   [53] *Ibid.*, p. 423 (1605).

Regime change in regional and world historical context

Frontiers and market expansion

The Ming crisis grew out of larger historical movements stemming from Asia's sixteenth-century integration into a maritime world economy. Following Iwai Shigeki, this narrative focuses on the region's maritime and landed peripheries. It expands Iwai's work to incorporate Japan as well as China into an overview of just how the arrival of the Portuguese and the Spanish into Asian waters (described in Chapter 1) and the simultaneous appearance of Russians along the Amur River in north Asia impacted East Asia.

In a 2005 article, Iwai explained how the late sixteenth- and seventeenth-century trade expansion influenced the Ming–Qing transition.[54] Profits from trade stimulated the "emergence of composite groups of frontier raiders transcending differences of language and ethnicity" on China's northern frontier in Liaodong and in the East and South China Seas. "Deeply dependent" on profits from the northern trade in sable and ginseng, Nurhaci's regional power grew with the influx of silver flowing into the frontier economy. Iwai argued that "the political upheavals of the Ming–Ch'ing transition in the mid-seventeenth century could be regarded as one outcome of the growth of interregional trade and the mobilization of frontier society that occurred concurrently in the north and south of East Asia."[55]

By the late sixteenth century the Jurchen and other frontier tribes were participating in an expanding commerce in ginseng and sable. Ginseng, an important medicinal root, was shipped to Chinese, Korean, and Japanese consumers.[56] According to one study, 80 to 90 percent of the ginseng marketed in China during the Ming period came from the

---

[54] Iwai, "China's Frontier Society"; "Jūroku, jūshichi seiki no Chūgoku henkyō shakai (Chinese frontier society in the sixteenth and seventeenth centuries), in *Minmatsu Shinsho no shakai to bunka* (Chinese society and culture in late Ming and early Qing), ed. Ono Kazuko (Kyoto: Kyoto daigaku Jinbun kagaku kenkyūjo, 1996), pp. 625–59; "Jūroku seiki Chūgoku ni okeru bōeki chitsujō no mosaku – goshi no genjitsu to sono ninshiki" (The pattern of the trading order in sixteenth-century China – the realization of mutual trade marts and their acknowledgement), in *Chūgoku kinsei shakai no chitsujo keisei* (The formation of early modern Chinese society), ed. Iwai Shigeki (Kyoto: Kyoto University Press, 2004), pp. 97–142. The connection between world economic trends, ginseng exports, and the emergence of the Later Jin/Qing state is also made by Seonmin Kim, "Borders and Crossings."

[55] Iwai, "China's Frontier Society," p. 18. See also Gang Zhao, *Qing Opening to the Ocean*, chapter 3.

[56] In 1694, ginseng constituted over 36 percent of total imports from Korea via Tsushima: see table 1, pp. 88–89 in Tashiro Kazui, "Tsushima Han's Korean Trade, 1684–1710," *Acta Asiatica* 30 (1976): 85–105; but this ginseng was mostly produced in Korea itself (p. 102), as opposed to the ginseng of inferior quality from the northeast.

northeast.[57] By the early seventeenth century, income from ginseng sales was estimated at 0.8 to 2.5 million taels a year.[58] The profitability of these trade ventures produced ever-increasing requests by Jurchen tribes to be permitted to "present tribute," arousing complaints from Ming officials that the size of the annual tribute missions far exceeded the space allotted in the official hostels.[59]

Of course, the Jianzhou Jurchen were not the only group to enrich themselves from trade. The prospect of profit also attracted Mongol and other Jurchen leaders, who obtained patents in exchange for maintaining law and order and formally submitting to Ming rule.[60] Altan Khan (1508–82) of the Right Flank Mongols, for example, demanded in 1571 that new markets be opened along the northern frontier to accommodate Chinese–Mongol trade, and sought to obtain the patents (chishu 敕書, ejehe in Manchu), documents conferring military titles, which carried with them the privilege of presenting tribute, i.e. of trading in the official markets.[61] By seizing the patents of other tribes, a leader could increase his marketing opportunities. Although the Haixi Jurchen patents authorized approximately 1,000 and the Jianzhou Jurchen approximately 500 missions a year, there were times when the Hada (a Haixi Jurchen tribe) held all 1,500 patents.[62]

This competition for the expanding trade revenues adds an important dimension to our understanding of the conditions that supported Nurhaci's rise to power. It may also explain the decision by Nurhaci's father and grandfather to cooperate secretly with Li Chengliang against Wang Gao, nominal head of the Jianzhou Right Commandery.[63] Wang was a newcomer who had risen to a leadership position as a result of wealth acquired through trade and through raids on Liaodong settlements in a competition to obtain the Ming patents that provided a legitimate source of commercial income.

When Nurhaci subjugated a tribe, he also acquired its Ming patents, adding to the number of trade missions to China under his aegis. Feng Yuan, who served on the Liaodong–Kaiyuan Military Defense Circuit, wrote in the early seventeenth century about the struggle among Jurchen in the southern tier to seize such profits by acting as middlemen and interpreters for other Jurchen bearing ginseng and furs from the Sungari

---

[57] Van Jay Symons, Ch'ing Ginseng Management: Ch'ing Monopolies in Microcosm (Tempe: Arizona State University Press, 1981), p. 72.
[58] Ibid., p. 10.
[59] Wang Dongfang and Ji Mingming, Nüzhen, reported date 1447, p. 284.
[60] Iwai, "China's Frontier Society," p. 13.
[61] Di Cosmo and Bao, "Introduction," p. 4.   [62] Ibid.
[63] Kawachi Yoshihiro, Mindai Joshinshi no kenkyū (Studies in Jurchen history during the Ming period) (Kyoto: Dōhōsha, 1992), pp. 718–21.

and Amur River drainage, many of whom lacked the official documents (patents) that provided access to official Ming markets. After the chieftain of the Hada built a mountain fortress at an important pass to monopolize profits along this route, the Yehe did likewise; but now "the profits have all fallen into the hands of Nurhaci. The reason that disputes break out every year among the Jurchens is that they are fighting over patents, but in actual fact they are fighting over commercial profits."[64]

By 1596, Nurhaci "had already amassed a great fortune by monopolizing the trade in pearls, ginseng, fur, etc.; by mining; by taking silver in return for his yearly tribute to the Ming; and by pillaging weaker tribes."[65] As he unified first the Jianzhou, then the Haixi Jurchen tribes, Nurhaci collected ginseng as tribute from tribesmen, seized the ginseng gathered by Chinese and Koreans who illegally entered his territory to gather the root, and dispatched private slaves to collect ginseng in the Changbai mountains. After Nurhaci extended his power to Fushun, he supplanted the Haixi Jurchen and monopolized the profit from sales of sable and ginseng, amounting to 100,000 taels a year.[66]

After 1599, when Nurhaci received the submission of some of the tribes living in the middle reaches of the Amur River, he gained access to the black sable pelts that they paid in tribute.[67] Iron, essential in producing military weaponry, was a strategic commodity that the Jurchen had initially imported. Chosŏn and Ming banned sales of iron implements to the Jurchen. In the 1590s, Nurhaci recruited skilled ironworkers, opened mines, and was able to produce his own iron barbs for arrows and iron plated armor.[68] With Nurhaci's capture of the Ming cities of Kaiyuan and Tieling after his victory at Sarhū (1619), key segments of the main

[64] Quote cited in Iwai, "China's Frontier Society," p. 11. The actual term for "patent" in the Japanese-language text of this article (Iwai, "Jūroku, jūshichi seiki," p. 637) is *chishu*, "letters patent," as translated by John K. Fairbank and Ssŭ-yu Teng, *Ch'ing Administration: Three Studies* (Cambridge, MA: Harvard University Press, 1960), p. 48. For a description of the author of *Kaiyuan tushuo*, written c. 1601–1619, see Lynn A. Struve, *The Ming–Qing Conflict, 1619–1683: A Historiography and Source Guide* (Ann Arbor: Association for Asian Studies, 1998), pp. 191–92.

[65] Hummel, *Eminent Chinese*, p. 596. Wakeman, *Great Enterprise*, p. 48, n. 59, writes that, "The revenues from the ginseng trade must have been substantial, because by the 1620s there was abundant silver among the Manchus."

[66] Li Jiancai, *Mingdai dongbei*, p. 209.

[67] Matsuura Shigeru, "Jūshichi seiki igo no Tōhoku Ajia ni okeru keizai kōryū-" (Economic exchange in northeast Asia from the seventeenth century onward), in *Matsumura Jun sensei kōki kinen Shindai shi ronsō* (Collected articles on Qing history, Festschrift in honor of Professor Matsumura Jun's seventieth birthday) (Tokyo: Kyuko shoin, 1994), p. 37; also his *Shinchō no Amuru seisaku*, c. 4; Wu and Li, "Cong Shandan maoyi."

[68] Zhang Deyu, *Manzhu fayuandi lishi yanjiu* (Historical research on the Manchu homeland) (Shenyang: Liaoning minzu chubanshe, 2001), p. 370, quotes the report of a Chosŏn envoy who visited Fei Ala in 1594. Apparently Nurhaci recruited skilled artisans and treated them very well: see pp. 370–71.

north–south trade route linking the northeast to China Proper came under his control.

Waging war requires resources. For a tribal leader like Nurhaci, these resources were at least partially acquired through raids that netted booty and slaves. As his forces grew in size, he faced the problems of feeding a growing population and acquiring the weapons and horses that gave the Jurchen cavalry its competitive advantage. We can infer the scale of the cost involved in military action by looking at the Ming, who expended 800,000 taels of silver in mobilizing troops and sending 180–200,000 men to Liaodong after Nurhaci defeated them at Sarhū. Ming military expenditures on Liaodong for less than three years (1622–25) totaled over 20 million taels, an enormous sum when compared to annual tax revenue estimated at 27 million taels.[69] In their attempts to militarily contain Nurhaci, the Ming also paid several hundred thousand taels of silver to the Caqar and Qalqa Mongol tribes for "protection against Manchu attacks."[70]

Surging demand for products of the wilderness, market expansion, and silver: these elements form a recurrent motif in the narrative of Nurhaci's rise to power and link his state-building efforts to a broader global context. The Chinese economic boom of 1550–1650 was spurred by injections of silver from the Americas and Japan. Japanese mining, stimulated by the introduction of a more efficient technique for separating silver from copper, delivered significant quantities of silver into the international market via the legal trade with Korea and the "pirate" trade discussed in Chapter 1.[71] To this was added the American silver mined in the colonies of Spain, at least one-third of which ended up in China.[72] Monetary historians interpret the worldwide net flow of silver into China in this period as the effect of arbitrage: Chinese demand created

---

[69] Teng Shaozhen, "Shilun Ming yu Hou Jin," p. 19. On the estimate of annual tax revenues, see Ray Huang, *Taxation and Governmental Finance in Sixteenth-Century Ming China* (Cambridge: Cambridge University Press, 1974), p. 46. Huang comments, p. 35, that despite contemporary writers who complained about high taxes, the major problem for Ming was "that the projected state income was too small and its level not readjustable."

[70] Di Cosmo and Bao, *Manchu–Mongol Relations*, p. 10, report that 300,000 taels of silver were paid to the two Mongol groups in 1621 and 360,000 taels in 1622–23.

[71] On the Japan–Korea trade, see Tashiro, "Jūshichi seiki goki – jūhachi seiki Nihon gin no kaigai yushutsu," pp. 47–68; on a downward revision of her estimates, see the discussion in James B. Lewis, *Frontier Contact Between Chosŏn Korea and Tokugawa Japan* (London: Routledge Curzon, 2003), pp. 97–98. See also Doo-hwan Oh, "The Silver Trade and Silver Currency in Chosŏn Korea," *Acta Koreana* 7.1 (2004): 89–92.

[72] Von Glahn, *Fountain of Fortune*, p. 113. For a recent reappraisal of the role of world silver movements in the Ming–Qing transition, see Dennis O. Flynn and Marie A. Lee, "East Asian Trade Before/After 1590s Occupation of Korea: Modeling Imports and Exports in Global Context," *Asian Review of World Histories* 1.1 (2013): 117–49.

the highest world prices for silver, offering opportunities to earn large profits by shipping silver to China in exchange for silk textiles, which were in high demand in other markets.[73]

Estimates of silver flows into China during the 1550–1650 period are varied and contested.[74] Comparisons suggest that the silver output from domestic mining was only 9 to 13% of the imported silver during 1550–1600, and 4 to 5% of the quantities of imported silver during 1600–1650.[75] Put another way, "about half of the silver production accounted for in the world between 1500 and 1800" ended up in China.[76] There was a massive inflow of silver from abroad, which must have supported, even if it did not cause, the silver monetization of the Ming economy.

The rise of maritime mercantile empires in the East and South China Seas followed a similar trajectory. One of the earliest maritime entrepreneurs, credited with bringing Portuguese and Japanese traders to Shuangyu, a harbor on an island near the Zhejiang city of Ningbo in 1639, was Wang Zhi, a Chinese who traded with Hirado and based himself in the Goto Islands west of this Japanese port.[77] Like the Lower Yangzi merchants *cum* pirates from Zhejiang/Jiangsu/Anhui who first dominated the trade, Wang Zhi was a native of She xian, an important commercial center in Anhui province. He and many other Chinese were part of the polyglot group of Japanese, Koreans, and Chinese who ignored the ban on maritime trade, leading the Ming to call them "Japanese pirates" (倭寇 C. *wokou*, J. *wakō*, K. *waegu*).[78]

Although the Ming could still bring their power to bear on individuals such as Wang Zhi, whom they executed in 1549, they could not prevent the devolution of wealth and power into the hands of Chinese merchants

---

[73] Pioneering estimates of the silver flows were made in two articles by Dennis Flynn and Arturo Giraldez, "China and the Manila Galleons," in *Japanese Industrialization and the Asian Economy*, ed. A. J. H. Latham and Heita Kawakatsu (London: Routledge, 1994), pp. 71–90 and "Arbitrage, China, and World Trade in the Early Modern Period," *Journal of the Economic and Social History of the Orient* 38.4 (1995): 429–48.

[74] Richard von Glahn, "Myth and Reality of China's Seventeenth-Century Monetary Crisis," *Journal of Economic History* 56.2 (1996): 429–54. See Andre Gunder Frank, *ReOrient: Global Economy in the Asian Age* (Berkeley: University of California Press, 1998), pp. 146–49.

[75] Figures for the calculations are taken from von Glahn, *Fountain of Fortune*, pp. 139–40.

[76] *Ibid.*, p. 146.

[77] John E. Wills, Jr., "Maritime China from Wang Chih to Shih Lang: Themes in Peripheral History," in *From Ming to Ch'ing*, ed. Jonathan D. Spence and John E. Wills Jr. (New Haven: Yale University Press, 1979), pp. 212–13. According to Ng, "Overseas Chinese," p. 214, the peak of the Japan–Southeast Asia trade was from 1600 to 1670.

[78] The problem of "Japanese pirates" plagued governments in Korea and China from the thirteenth through the sixteenth century. For the period before 1500 see Murai Shōsuke, "Wakō to wa dareka;" So, *Japanese Piracy in Ming China*, chapter 1.

such as Li Dan (d. 1625) and Zheng Zhilong (1604–61). Both men were natives of Quanzhou, Fujian, who flourished in the early seventeenth century.[79] Li began his trading career in Manila, then moved to Japan in 1607–8, after the Spanish massacre of Chinese settlers in that city (1603). Becoming the "head" of the Chinese merchants in Hirado, Japan, an important international trade center, Li presided over an extensive network stretching into Vietnam, the Philippines, Taiwan, and his native Fujian. In Chinese records, Li Dan only appears as a pirate who redeemed himself (in the eyes of Ming officials) by assisting them in their efforts to expel the Dutch from the Pescadores. The rest of the information about him appears in English, Dutch, and Japanese accounts.[80]

Zheng Zhilong, the father of the better-known Zheng Chenggong (Koxingga)[81] began his career working for Europeans in Macao, Manila, and perhaps Taiwan. By the age of twenty he was in Hirado. He preyed on Dutch and Chinese shipping before being pardoned by the Ming in 1628. The Ming put him in charge of suppressing piracy: this enabled Zhilong to eliminate his competitors and consolidate a maritime empire which had branches in Nagasaki, the Philippines, and Taiwan. After 1628, Zheng controlled a large portion of coastal Fujian. He managed overseas trade in Xiamen and Taiwan, collecting taxes and commissions on goods traded from these ports and on ships at sea.[82] In 1646, Zheng surrendered to the Qing, who had promised to appoint him governor-general of Fujian and Guangdong provinces, but instead held him hostage in Peking. The power of the Zheng organization moved into the hands of his son, Chenggong.

Although Zheng Chenggong's anti-Qing resistance inspired twentieth-century nationalist historians to hail him as a patriotic hero, his motives may have been somewhat more self-interested. Chenggong proclaimed loyalty to the Yongli emperor, whose court was situated in Guangdong, conveniently distant from his coastal Fujian headquarters, leaving him free to maximize personal advantage while cloaking himself in Ming loyalist legitimacy. In comparison with the Qing, Zheng Chenggong's organization in Fujian went down to the grassroots, which provided him

---

[79] A biography of Li Dan is in *Dictionary of Ming Biography*, ed. Goodrich and Fang, I: 871–74; Zheng Zhilong's biography is in Hummel, *Eminent Chinese*, I: 110–11.

[80] *Dictionary of Ming Biography*, ed. Goodrich and Fang, I: 871.

[81] Zheng Chenggong's biography is in Hummel, *Eminent Chinese*, I: 108–10.

[82] Patrizia Carioti, "The Zhengs' Maritime Power in the International Context of the 17th Century Far Eastern Seas: The Rise of a 'Centralised Piratical Organisation' and Its Gradual Development into an Informal 'State,'" *Ming Qing yanjiu* (1996): 29–67; also her *Cina e Giappone sui mari nei secoli XVI e XVII* (Naples: Edizioni Scientifiche Italiane, 2006), chapter 8.

with excellent military intelligence. His military confrontations with Qing forces were financed and equipped with resources (weapons, ships, and money) obtained through the organization's semi-piratical and semi-legitimate maritime activities.

Zheng Chenggong's empire withstood the best efforts of the Qing, surviving his death in 1662 and the death of his son, Zheng Jing, in 1681. Driven from Fujian by mounting Qing military pressure, Chenggong was able to shift his headquarters to Taiwan in 1661 and force the Dutch East India Company out of their trading post on the island's southwest coast. In contrast to how Wang Zhi worked, the Zheng trading enterprise "in many respects resembled the contemporary East India Companies of Europe, with an international viewpoint, very large financial resources, major military power, and well-coordinated commercial strategies."[83]

Wang Zhi, Li Dan, and Zheng Zhilong were products of what Iwai Shigeki has called China's maritime frontier. Using the concept of frontiers as dynamic regions where cultures mingle to produce new social forces, Iwai argued that the non-tributary trade of the 1550–1650 period facilitated the emergence of not only these maritime entrepreneurs but also their counterparts in northeast Asia. Nurhaci and Wang Zhi share similar characteristics: they were both military leaders and frontier entrepreneurs.[84]

War on the frontier

By definition, frontiers are dynamic localities where different cultures intersect. By the 1630s, military technologies imported from Europe appeared on Asian battlefields. Information about the new firearms came through several channels: a cannon produced in the Ottoman empire, Portuguese cannoneers in Maco, and a Dutch ship which sank off the Guangdong coast.[85] Here we discuss another source of

---

[83] Chuimei Ho, "The Ceramic Trade in Asia, 1602–82," in *Japanese Industrialization and the Asian Economy*, ed. Latham and Kawakatsu, p. 47.

[84] See Matsuura, "Jūshichi seiki," pp. 35–67, and his *Shinchō Amūru seisaku*.

[85] See Joseph Needham et al., *Science and Civilization in China*, vol. V: *Chemistry and Chemical Technology*, part 7: *Military Technology: The Gunpowder Epic* (Cambridge: Cambridge University Press, 1986), pp. 365–424. Also Huang Yi-long, trans. Peter Engelfriet, "Sun Yuanhua (1581–1632): A Christian Convert Who Put Xu Guangqi's Military Reform Policy into Practice," in *Statecraft and Intellectual Renewal in Late Ming China: The Cross-Cultural Synthesis of Xu Guangqi (1562–1633)*, ed. Catherine Jami, Peter Engelfriet, and Gregory Blue (Leiden: E. J. Brill, 2001), pp. 225–59; Shin Tōkei (Sin Tonggyu), "Orandajin hōryūmin to Chōsen no Seiyōshiki buki no kaihatsu" (Dutch castaways and the development of western weapons in Korea), *Shien* 61.1 (2000): 54–70; Zhu Yafei, "Lun Ming Qing shiqi Shandong bandao yu Chaoxian de jiaowang" (On exchanges

transmission, the adoption of muskets by the Japanese, who used them to reunify the archipelago.

The European arquebus introduced into Japan in 1543 was an improvement on Chinese guns.[86] Domestic production of muskets quickly followed; regional lords could also import guns from abroad and used them in the civil wars of the second half of the sixteenth century. Oda Nobunaga organized special military units equipped with muskets and demonstrated their effectiveness in battle, the most famous being his victory over rival Takeda forces at Nagashino (1575). Equipped with guns, Japanese generals with artillery units enjoyed a competitive advantage that proved decisive: "firearms created a snowball effect that helped make unification possible."[87]

Hideyoshi's 1592 invasion of Korea featured Japanese artillery units, whose superiority over Korean troops marked the first phase of the campaign. Japanese guns captured in battle were taken and studied; Japanese prisoners were recruited to instruct Korean and Chinese troops in the manufacture and handling of the new weapons.[88] Some Japanese captives accompanied the Ming troops who were deployed to suppress the Yang Yinglong uprising in southwest China in 1599; their superior firepower helped to defeat the rebels, who were armed with only bows and

between the Shandong peninsula and Chosŏn during the Ming and Qing), *Shandong shifan daxue xuebao Renwen shehui kexue ban* 49.5 (2004): 81–85.

[86] On the dissemination of earlier Chinese firearms, see Sun Laichen, "Military Technology Transfers from Ming China and the Emergence of Northern Mainland Southeast Asia (*c.* 1390–1527)," *Journal of Southeast Asian Studies* 34.3 (2003): 495–517. Udagawa Takehisa, *Teppō no denrai: Heiki ga kataru kinsei no tanjō* (The transmission of firearms: what military weapons say about the birth of the early modern era) (Tokyo: Chūō Kōron, 1990); Kenneth Chase, *Firearms: A Global History to 1700* (Cambridge: Cambridge University Press, 2003), pp. 178–88.

[87] Chase, *Firearms*, p. 184. On the nature of the musket itself, see pp. 23–27 and chapters 6–7 on developments in East Asia. Geoffrey Parker discusses Japan's sixteenth-century adaptation of firearms in *The Military Revolution: Military Innovation and the Rise of the West, 1500–1800* (Cambridge: Cambridge University Press, 1988), pp. 136–45. See also Udagawa, *Teppō no denrai*, and Peter A. Lorge, *The Asian Military Revolution: From Gunpowder to the Bomb* (Cambridge: Cambridge University Press, 2008), pp. 53–59.

[88] Udagawa, *Teppō no denrai*, pp. 103–16; Kuba Takashi, "Chōsen no eki ni okeru Nihon heihoryo – Minchō ni okeru renkō to shochi" (Japanese prisoners of war in the Korea campaign: their treatment at the hands of the Ming), *Tōhōgaku* 105 (2003): 106–20. According to Yonetani Hitoshi, "Jūshichi seiki zenki Nitchō kankei ni okeru buki yūshutsu" (The export of weapons in Japanese–Korean relations in the first half of the seventeenth century), in *Jūshichi seiki no Nihon to Higashi Ajia* (Japan and East Asia in the seventeenth century), ed. Fujita Satoru (Tokyo: Yamakawa shuppansha, 2000), pp. 39–67, Korean envoys to Japan in 1607 and thereafter purchased firearms from the Japanese. The trade continued despite the Tokugawa shogunate's 1621 ban on weapons exports.

arrows.[89] At the same time, the Ming–Japanese military engagement at P'yŏngyang was won by heavy Ming cannon (themselves adapted from sixteenth-century Portuguese models). The invasion also demonstrated the superiority of armored Korean ships mounted with cannon: Korean navies had profited from their long campaigns to suppress "Japanese pirates."[90]

Although cannon did not play an important role in Japan's sixteenth-century battles, the Manchu campaign against Ming needed them to penetrate the pounded-earth walls enclosing Chinese administrative and economic centers. The Ming employed Portuguese cannoneers to manufacture cannon and train troops in their use for campaigns in the northeast.[91] Ming garrisons west of the Liao River, equipped with "red barbarian cannon" (hongyi pao, introduced by the Dutch in 1604), resisted Manchu cavalry onslaughts. It was not until they learned to cast cannon and formed their own special artillery units (hanjun) that the Manchus turned the tide of battle in their favor.[92] One military resource that the Ming and Manchus sought were Chosŏn's special artillery units 精銳鐵砲隊, formed after 1598,[93] which participated in the 1654 and 1658 Qing expeditions into the Amur River region.[94]

Beyond muskets, the Japanese reunification also reflected the effect of the sixteenth-century market expansion. While Nobunaga, Hideyoshi, and Ieyasu fought for dominance in eastern Japan, regional warlords in Kyushu actively participated in the profitable maritime trade during

[89] Kuba Takashi, "Jūroku seiki matsu, Nihonshiki teppō no Minchō e no dempa – Manreki Chōsen no eki kara Banshū Yō Ōryū no ran e" (On the dissemination of Japanese-type muskets to the Ming in the sixteenth century: from the Wanli Chosŏn campaign to the Bozhou Yang Yinglong rebellion), Tōyōgakuhō 84.1 (2002): 33–54; Peter Lorge, War, Politics, and Society in Early Modern China, 900–1795 (New York: Routledge, 2005), pp. 136–37.

[90] Kenneth M. Swope, "Crouching Tigers, Secret Weapons: Military Technology Employed during the Sino-Japanese-Korean War, 1592–1598," Journal of Military History 69.1 (2004): 11–41.

[91] Nicola Di Cosmo, "Did Guns Matter? Firearms and the Qing Formation," in The Qing Formation in World Historical Time, ed. Lynn Struve (Cambridge: Harvard University Asia Center, 2004), pp. 121–66; Lorge, Asian Military Revolution, p. 56.

[92] The use of the term hanjun, translated as "Chinese-martial," suggests that their artillery skills were what caused the Manchus to recruit Chinese into the banners. See Nicola Di Cosmo, "European Technology and Manchu Power: Reflections on the 'Military Revolution' in Seventeenth-Century China," in Making Sense of Global History: The Nineteenth International Congress of the Historical Sciences, ed. Sølvi Sogner (Oslo: Universitetsforlaget, 2000), pp. 119–39.

[93] Shin Tōkei, "Orandajin hōryūmin."

[94] Kye Sŭng-bŏm, Chosŏn sidae haeoe p'abyŏng kwa Han Chung kwan'gye (Foreign dispatch of troops in the Chosŏn period and Korean-Chinese relations) (Seoul: P'urŭn yŏksa, 2009); the musket units were presumably effective in terrain too hilly to deploy Ming heavy cannon.

Japan's "Warring States" period (1467–1588). This was especially true of Kyushu's prominent warrior families, which supplemented their agrarian tax revenues by financing and sponsoring trading voyages. These trading ventures were frequently coordinated with Chinese merchants who worked out of ports such as Hirado and Hakata.

The Japanese army enjoyed a comparative advantage with its superior muskets, but retaining that advantage necessitated a constant re-supply of muskets and of ammunition. The letters of Katō Kiyomasa, one of three generals commanding the Korean invasion force, sound this theme constantly.[95] The Kyushu daimyo who commanded the bulk of the invasion forces were required to each mobilize a stipulated number of soldiers for the campaign, equip them using their own resources, and pay for a certain amount of the military supplies from their own pockets. How could they accomplish this task?

In order to support troops under his command in the field, Katō Kiyomasa, like the other daimyo engaged in the Korea campaign, was forced to engage in trade. Before the 1580s, saltpeter was not produced in Japan but obtained from China through the Portuguese, Chinese offshore traders, and Southeast Asian ports. Even a decade later, Katō was trying to obtain saltpeter from abroad, suggesting that domestic output was still small. Using funds from the coffers of his own domain, Katō put particular emphasis on obtaining the raw materials needed to make guns and ammunition: iron, lead, sulphur, and saltpeter. Katō's trading schemes involved collecting wheat flour (produced in his domain), shipping it on a chartered Chinese junk to Luzon in exchange for gold, which was brought back to Japan in order to profit from the arbitrage. According to the Jesuit financial accounts of that time, a 25-percent profit could be realized in shipping gold from Macao to Nagasaki, while in Manila the gold price (calculated in silver) was roughly half that in Japan.[96]

Trade was the element common to militarists on the maritime and northeast frontiers. Nurhaci and Hongtaiji were able to build their followers into a regional power capable of challenging the Ming empire thanks to several major factors. First, they were tutored by the Ming, who appointed them to man frontier commanderies, and nurtured by the Ming practice of allowing oversight of these frontier regions to lapse into personal baronies. In their turn, these leaders adopted inclusive policies to swell their armies while at the same time maintaining control through the invention of the banner system. Second, unlike the Ming government, the Jianzhou Jurchen were extremely attentive to gleaning the profits attained through the sale of products gathered in the wilderness such as

[95] Nakajima, "Jūroku seikimatsu no Kyūshū – Tōnan Ajia bōeki."   [96] Ibid., p. 17.

ginseng and fur. They collected these goods as tribute from subjugated northeast tribes and imposed transit taxes on commercial traffic. Finally, following the lead of the Japanese regional lords, the Koreans, and the Ming, the Manchus appropriated the new European weaponry to defeat Chinese walled garrisons.

Exploration and mapping on the Japanese and Qing periphery

The engagement with Europe that began in the sixteenth century extended beyond trade and guns. Much has been written about Qing and Tokugawa dealings with British, Dutch, and other western European powers seeking access to ports in Japan and off China's southern coast. Less well known is the narrative concerning both countries' scrutiny of Russian intentions and actions in north Asia. The Qing responded to Russian exploration and mapping with projects of their own. Security concerns drove Japanese officials, who asked whether the archipelago was linked at its northern extremity to the Asian continent by a land bridge, to explore the uncharted waters off Hokkaido and to worry about Russian incursions on the Kurile Islands. Defense of its northern border was the primary stimulus for Chosŏn's cartographic projects during the early fifteenth and late sixteenth centuries.

Tightly linked to the security of the realm, maps were state secrets and prohibited from export.[97] In 1712, King Sukchong (1674–1720) denied the Qing official Mukedeng's request for a general map of Chosŏn, and eventually fobbed him off with as imprecise a map as he dared.[98] The Tokugawa shogunate prohibited the export of maps of Japan, and expelled Philipp Franz von Siebold, who served at Deshima as a physician to the Dutch East India Company (1823–29), for attempting to smuggle out a new (and more accurate) map of Japan in his luggage. The Japanese authorities also imprisoned the shogunal astronomer in charge of the mapping project and many of von Siebold's students.[99]

[97] Cordell D. K. Yee, "Chinese Maps in Political Culture," in *The History of Cartography*, vol. II: *Cartography in the Traditional East and Southeast Asian Societies*, ed. J. B. Harley and David Woodward (Chicago: University of Chicago Press, 1994), pp. 73, 83–84. On the early modern use of maps as a vital component of statecraft, see Peter Perdue, "Boundaries, Maps, and Movement: Chinese, Russian, and Mongolian Empires in Early Modern Central Eurasia," *International History Review* 20.2 (1998): 253–304.

[98] Gari Ledyard, "Cartography in Korea," in *Cartography in the Traditional East and Southeast Asian Societies*, ed. Hartley and Woodward, pp. 301–3.

[99] Kazutaka Unno, "Cartography in Japan," in *Cartography in the Traditional East and Southeast Asian Societies*, ed. Harley and Woodward, pp. 439–40.

Russian tsars dispatched entrepreneurs to explore and colonize central Eurasia, in a search for sable that culminated in the seventeenth-century Russian acquisition of Siberia.[100] The vast territory was held together by a chain of fortified settlements that sent sable pelts, collected as tributary payments from native tribes, westward to European markets.[101] In the eighteenth century, Russian fur exports turned to Asian markets. First sable, then sea-otter fur became Russia's "chief export" to China.[102]

The Russians moved into Siberia to secure a grain-producing area that could supply their dispersed outposts, erecting forts along the Amur River in the second half of the sixteenth century. Here they came into contact with China's market network, which brought ginseng, furs, and Chinese textiles down through the tributaries of the Amur River. The region had a long history of interaction with Central Plain and northeast Asian regimes. The Tang dynasty, followed by the states of Parhae, Liao, and Jin, had collected tribute from Amur River tribes. Under the Mongols, garrisons were also built on the Sungari and Amur Rivers. In the early fourteenth century, Mongol power extended to the Amur River delta and beyond to Sakhalin Island.

The Ming dynasty revived this tribute system along the Amur and Ussuri Rivers and dispatched several expeditions to secure its control over the territory surrounding the river and Sakhalin.[103] Three Ming commanderies were established on Sakhalin by 1410. By the middle of the fifteenth century, various groups living along the lower reaches of the Amur and Sakhalin were "paying tribute" in the form of fur pelts at Chinese outposts and receiving "textiles and other goods" in exchange.[104] In this fashion, a

[100] Mark Bassin, "Expansion and Colonialism on the Eastern Frontier: Views of Siberia and the Far East in Pre-Petrine Russia," *Journal of Historical Geography* 14.1 (1988): 3–21; Kikuchi Toshihiko, "Hoppō sekai to Roshia no shinshutsu" (The northern world and Russia's advance), in *Sekai rekishi*, vol. XIII: *Higashi Ajia, Tōnan Ajia dentō shakai no keisei, 16–18 seiki* (World history: The formation of traditional East and Southeast Asian society, 16th–18th centuries), ed. Kishimoto Mio et al. (Tokyo: Iwanami, 1998), pp. 121–48.

[101] Fred W. Bergholz, *The Partition of the Steppe: The Struggle of the Russians, Manchus, and the Zunghar Mongols for Empire in Central Asia, 1619–1758: A Study in Power Politics* (New York: Peter Lang, 1993), chapter 1; Mark Mancall, *Russia and China: Their Diplomatic Relations to 1728* (Cambridge, MA: Harvard University Press, 1971).

[102] Chikashi Takahashi, "Inter-Asian Competition in the Fur Market in the Eighteenth and Nineteenth Centuries," in *Intra-Asian Trade and the World Market*, ed. A. J. H. Latham and Heita Kawakatsu (London: Routledge, 2006), pp. 37–45; Bassin, "Expansion and Colonialism," pp. 8, 11–12.

[103] John H. Stephan, *The Russian Far East: A History* (Stanford: Stanford University Press, 1994), pp. 14–17.

[104] Brett L. Walker, *The Conquest of Ainu Lands: Ecology and Culture in Japanese Expansion, 1590–1800* (Berkeley: University of California Press, 2001), p. 133; Emori Susumu, "Jūsan-jūkyu seiki no Nihon ni okeru Hoppō chiiki no kyōkai ninshiki" (Perceptions of

trade network linked the residents of north Asia, including Sakhalin Island, to the Ming capital, Peking. What the Chinese might not have known, however, was that the same trading network also moved in a southeasterly direction, via Ainu traders on Sakhalin, to Hokkaido Ainu and thence into Japan's urban markets.

The northernmost island of Hokkaido is strategically located between the fortieth and forty-fifth parallel, with only a narrow strait separating it from the southern tip of Sakhalin Island, known to the Japanese as Karafuto. The Kurile Island chain stretches from Hokkaido's northeast shore to the southern tip of the Kamchatka peninsula. The inhabitants of sixteenth-century Hokkaido, ancestors of the present-day Ainu, participated in a cultural and economic sphere that encompassed the north Asian mainland and the Kuriles.[105] Although trade with the continent had a long history, the entry of Russia into the north Pacific caused Japan's leaders to pay special attention to this region in the late sixteenth century.

For sixteenth-century Japanese, Hokkaido was a largely unknown territory called "Ezo" or "Ezochi." In 1558, a Ming silk brocade coat worn by Kakizaki Suehiro, a daimyo from northern Honshu, attracted Tokugawa Ieyasu's attention. When pressed to explain its origins, Kakizaki said the silk came from "an island called Karafuto" which was in "deep northern Ezo."[106] Uncertainty about the precise geography of "Ezochi," which some believed to be on the Asian mainland, caused Hideyoshi to fear the possibility of an overland invasion from the Jurchen, who resided in "Orankai" (*Orank'ae* in Korean).[107] During his 1592 invasion of the Korean peninsula, Hideyoshi ordered Katō Kiyomasa to explore the region north of the Tumen River in search of more precise geographic information.[108]

---

northern boundaries in thirteenth to nineteenth century Japan), *Rekishigaku kenkyū* 613 (1990): 6.

[105] On the prehistorical cultural sphere, see Toshihiko Kikuchi, "Continental Culture and Hokkaido and his "Hoppō sekai to Roshia no shinshutsu." Also Kikuchi Isao, *Ainu minzoku to Nihonjin: Higashi Ajia no naka no Ezochi* (The Ainu people and Japanese: Ezochi within East Asia) (Tokyo: Asahi shinbunsha, 1994), chapter 4.

[106] Walker, *Conquest*, p. 138.

[107] The idea of a land bridge to Hokkaido was also entertained by the Mongols. According to Walker, *Conquest*, p. 133, the Mongol push into the lower Amur "not only stemmed from a desire to find a passageway into Japan but was also a military response to Ainu attempts at expansion and fighting with other groups on Sakhalin." See Nobuyuki Kamiya, "Japanese Control of Ezochi and the Role of Northern Koryŏ," *Acta Asiatica* 67 (1994): 53 on Hideyoshi's 1591 attempts to collect information on Orankai.

[108] Kamiya, "Japanese Control"; Emori, *Hokkaidō kinseishi no kenkyū*, pp. 159–62.

Katō's investigations, although not definitive, enabled the Japanese to hypothesize that the people of Orankai were the same group identified by Ming officials as Tartars 韃靼 (C. Dada) and known in Japan as "Ezo." According to Kamiya Nobuyuki, the tribes whom Katō found were "wild" Jurchen, and the political instability that he observed reflected Nurhaci's drive to unify all of the Jurchen tribes in the region (he had already unified the Jianzhou Jurchen in 1588).[109] Katō's ten-day foray into the region lying north of the Tumen River informed Hideyoshi that a process of state-building was taking place there. Kamiya suggests that Hideyoshi's decision to consolidate Japanese control over Ezochi by awarding monopoly control over the Ezo trade to the Kakizaki (later, Matsumae) was at least partially prompted by continuing concerns over the potential repercussions of Jurchen unification.[110]

What remained unresolved was whether Orankai was linked by a land bridge to the Japanese archipelago. The Jesuit Jeronimo de Angelis, who visited Hokkaido in 1620 and 1622, reported to his superiors that "Yezo" was an island, but the map he appended to his report revealed many gaps in his knowledge of the geography of Hokkaido and its location with respect to the Asian continent.[111] According to Engelbert Kaempfer (1651–1716), the Dutch polymath who resided in Japan in the early 1690s, Andrei Andreeivich Vinius (1641–1717), the head of the Russian embassy to Peking from 1675 to 1678, "did everything possible" to learn about "Great Tartary" on his journeys to and from the Qing capital, but "the Siberian shores and the neighboring country of Ezo have not been indicated" on the map Vinius produced. Kaempfer added,

Also unknown to the Japanese is the nature of the country beyond Ezo ga shima, which they call Oku Ezō, except that it is supposed to be 300 Japanese miles long. A ship's captain who was cast up there a few years ago, reported that among the rough natives he had seen a few people dressed in fine China cloth, which led him to believe there was a connection with Datsu, or Tartary.[112]

---

[109] Kamiya Nobuyuki, "Nihon kinsei no tōitsu to Tattan" (The unification of early modern Japan and the Tartars), in *Nihon zenkindai no kokka to taigai kankei* (The state and foreign relations in Japan's premodern era), ed. Tanaka Takeo (Tokyo: Yoshikawa kōbunkan, 1987), pp. 155–58.

[110] *Ibid.*, pp. 161–62; Walker, *Conquest*, pp. 31–33. Hideyoshi possessed maps that showed that Ezo was linked to the continent, and he knew that Ezo traded with Orankai. Walker argues, p. 33, that Hideyoshi's conferral of rank and privilege on Kakizaki was "to strengthen the family as a bulwark against Jurchen and Tatar unification wars in Orankai that might spill over in Ezo."

[111] Takao Abé, "The Seventeenth Century Jesuit Missionary Reports on Hokkaido," *Journal of Asian History* 39.2 (2005): 121–24.

[112] Engelbert Kaempfer, trans. and annotated by Beatrice M. Bodart-Bailey, *Kaempfer's Japan: Tokugawa Culture Observed* (Honolulu: University of Hawai'i Press, 1999), quoted passage pp. 45–46, fn36, fn37, p. 459. See p. 44, where Kaempfer wrote,

The Russian quest for more precise geographical knowledge of the north Pacific coast continued into the early nineteenth century. Gerhard Friedrich Müller, a geographer at the St. Petersburg Academy of Sciences, joined the Second Kamchatka Expedition (1733–43) that travelled in Siberia. In a 1741 memorandum to the tsar, he complained of "insufficient geographical knowledge" of the area where the Amur River flowed into the Pacific Ocean, which impeded the mapping that would settle outstanding border issues between Russia and the Qing.[113] The mapping issue would not be settled for Japan until the early nineteenth-century explorations of Mamiya Rinzō. Through surveys of Sakhalin conducted in 1785 and 1792, the shogunate learned that the Qing had re-established tribute relations with local groups. Its decision to move to direct control over "Eastern Ezochi"/south Sakhalin was prompted as much by the Qing as by the Russian presence.[114]

Commercial and geopolitical competition drove the Russians and Japanese to explore the north Pacific. Both countries competed with the Qing to claim Sakhalin. Russian interest in Sakhalin, and their exploration of the north Pacific in the eighteenth century, alarmed Tokugawa authorities, who held a proprietary interest in the Sakhalin Ainu and the people inhabiting the Kurile Islands. After the suppression of an Ainu uprising (1669), Japanese ships were allowed to trade in southern Sakhalin, and Japanese trading posts were established there. The Japanese called this the "Santan" trade: the Chinese brocades acquired through this marketing network were known as "Santan nishiki" 山丹錦.[115] Japan also exported sea-otter furs, obtained through the Ainu from the Kuriles, to China.[116]

Like Japan, China attempted to map new regions with potential commercial value, especially the lands in the "Small Eastern Sea," the portion of the Pacific Ocean closest to Asia and the Japanese archipelago.[117] Dutch ships had made exploratory voyages into the north Pacific in the

"Behind this island [Ezo/Ezogashima], toward the north, lies the mainland Oku Ezo ... This is the country our geographers know exists but do not know whether it is connected to Tartary or America."

[113] Lothar Maier, "Gerhard Friedrich Müller's Memoranda on Russian Relations with China and the Reconquest of the Amur," *The Slavonic and East European Review* 59.2 (1981): 222–23.

[114] Wu and Li, "Cong Shandan maoyi," pp. 94–95. On Qing exploration and penetration of the Amur drainage, see Matsuura, *Shinchō no Amuru seisaku*.

[115] Emori, *Hokkaidō kinseishi*, p. 160. According to Wu Ling and Li Xiaokang, p. 91, the Japanese alternatively wrote "Santan" as 山旦.

[116] Takahashi, "Inter-Asian Competition," pp. 40–43, observes that the Japanese also purchased seal skins, fish oil, and tree fiber cloth from the Ainu. Walker, *Conquest*, pp. 139–44; also see his "Reappraising the *Sakoku* Paradigm," pp. 176, 187.

[117] Yonemoto, "Maps and Metaphors of the 'Small Eastern Sea,'" p. 177. According to Yonemoto, this was the Japanese response to Ricci's world map and its depiction of the Pacific Ocean.

second half of the sixteenth century. Russian entrance into Siberia raised new geopolitical concerns for the Qing state, which mobilized forces after 1683 to block the Russian access to lands south of the Amur River.

Qing cartography

Russian colonization enhanced Qing territorial consciousness and prompted attempts to strengthen defenses against potential invasion.[118] In response to information from Daur Mongols of a foreign presence along the Amur River region, the Qing sent exploratory expeditions in 1654 and 1658, in which Chosŏn troops participated.[119] A defeat of Russian forces near the junction of the Sungari and Amur Rivers (1658) checked their initial advance; there would be further military clashes before the 1680s, when a concerted Qing attack on the Russian fort at Albazin forced a negotiated border in the Treaty of Nerchinsk (1689).[120]

Jesuits serving at the Qing court introduced European cartography to China. The Kangxi emperor was quickly convinced of the value of precise geographical information about different regions, not only for the fixing of borders with other states, but also for use in military campaigns. He employed Jesuits to mark the boundaries with Russia after the Treaty of Nerchinsk (1689), which for the first time set up stone markers on the boundary line.[121] When fifteen French missionaries with cartographic skills came to China in 1698, the emperor asked them to make a trial map of the capital city, Peking. Later, in 1708, Jesuits mapped the Great Wall and, in 1709, the drainage of the Liao, Hun, and Suifen Rivers in the northeast.[122] Jesuit efforts later produced an empire-wide atlas, the *Huangyu quanlan tu* (Complete map of the empire, 1717). The Jesuit maps were incorporated into the atlases of the empire, but may not have been widely disseminated.[123]

In addition to the work done by the Jesuits themselves, Manchus and Chinese trained in European cartographic techniques were sent to survey and map northeast Asia. The survey team explored the many tributaries of the Amur to their headwaters, and set up stone monuments at the

---

[118] Perdue, "Boundaries," pp. 263–86; also pp. 442–60 in his *China Marches West: The Qing Conquest of Central Eurasia* (Cambridge, MA: Belknap Press, 2005).

[119] Kye, *Chosŏn sidae hae'oe*, pp. 248–51, 251–55.

[120] Mancall, *Russia and China*, chapters 1 and 3.

[121] Perdue, *China Marches West*, pp. 168–69 and his "Boundaries," p. 274.

[122] Cordell D. K. Yee, "Traditional Chinese Cartography and the Myth of Westernization," in *The History of Cartography*, ed. Hartley and Woodward, II.2: 170–202; Yang Zhaoquan and Sun Yumei, *Zhong Chao bianjie shi* (History of Sino-Korean borders) (Changchun: Jilin wenshi chubanshe, 1993), pp. 168–70.

[123] Yee, "Traditional Chinese Cartography."

source of the Tugur River and the mouths of the Argun and Gorbitsa Rivers. This survey became the official Qing record of the Sino-Russian border.[124] Later, in 1709, a survey team led by Jean-Baptiste Règis explored the lower reaches of the Amur River in a quest to locate "Yezo"; Règis concluded that Yezo was an island near Japan.[125] In meetings with Russian diplomats in 1726 and 1727, the Russian claim that Yezo was part of Russian territory caused the Qing to explore central and south Sakhalin (1727, 1729, 1732), then send forces to gain control of parts of the island.[126]

Mapping also became a way to reify Manchu cultural symbols. In 1677 the Kangxi emperor ordered the exploration of the mountain sacred to the Manchus, Changbaishan (Paektusan in Korean). According to the Veritable Records compiled in the seventeenth century, Changbaishan, a mountain range on the border of present-day Jilin province and Korea, was the birthplace of the progenitor of the Manchus, Bukuri Yongson.[127] Teams were sent to survey and map the Qing northeast homeland in 1679, 1684, and 1691–92.

Diplomatic brouhahas over repeated incursions across the Qing–Chosŏn border at the Yalu and Tumen Rivers drove the Kangxi emperor to map the exact location of the boundary between the two countries, a project that entailed surveying the various streams originating in the mountains clustered around Changbaishan in order to discover the origins of the Yalu and Tumen Rivers. By 1679, when the Manchus requested that the Chosŏn supply maps and compass bearings of the area of Changbaishan, Chosŏn officials were horrified to see the detail of the information that they had acquired.[128]

In attempting to fix its boundary with Chosŏn and to obtain accurate maps of the Korean peninsula, the Qing followed an early modern trend toward conceiving of state boundaries in geographical space.[129] In 1709

[124] Matsuura, *Shinchō no Amuru*, chapter 1.
[125] Matsuura, *Shinchō no Amuru*, chapter 2.
[126] Matsuura, *Shinchō no Amuru*, chapter 3.
[127] Pamela K. Crossley, "*Manzhou yuanliu kao* and the Formalization of the Manchu Heritage," *Journal of Asian Studies* 46.4 (1987): 761–90; Liu Housheng, "Changbaishan yu Manzu de zuxian chongbai" (Changbaishan and Manchu ancestor worship), *Qingshi yanjiu* 3 (1996): 93–96.
[128] Ledyard, "Cartography in Korea," p. 298.
[129] Yang and Sun, *Zhong Chao bianjie shi*; Diao Shuren, "Kangxi nianjian Mukedeng chabian dingjie kaobian" (Analyzing Mukedeng's frontier survey and fixing of the border in the Kangxi period), *Zhongguo bianjiang shidi yanjiu* 13.3 (2003): 45–56; Ren Xijun, "Changbaishan 'Ding jie pei' shimo – jiankao Tumenjiang bianjie wenti" (On the stele marking the border at Changbaishan – and an examination of the Tumen river border issue), in *Zhong Han guanxi shi lunwenji* (Collected essays on the history of Sino-Korean relations), ed. Diao Shuren and Yi Xingguo (Changchun: Jilin wenshi chubanshe, 1995), pp. 234–52. See Ledyard, "Cartography in Korea," pp. 298–305,

and 1710, Jesuit cartographers Jean-Baptiste Règis, Pierre Hartoux, and Ehrenbert Xavier Fridelli mapped the Manchu–Korean frontier. When the Jesuits were forbidden from entering Chosŏn, the bannerman Mukedeng, who led Qing expeditions to map Changbaishan in 1711 and 1712, took a team with a Chinese mathematician and Jesuit-trained surveyors into Chosŏn in 1713. He made observations and took rope measurements from the Qing town of Fenghuang to the Korean border town of Ŭiju on the Yalu River and thence to the capital, Hansŏng. Using the latitude at the capital and the distance from Fenghuang on the Chinese side, the team was able to calculate the distance from Hansŏng to the tip of the peninsula.[130]

New maps for Korea

The Chosŏn court's mapping activities clustered in two historical periods. During the first half of the fifteenth century, as the state expanded northward, maps such as the *Sinch'an pa'ldo chiriji* 新產八道地理志 (New edition of the geography of the right provinces, 1432) and the *Tongguk chido* 東國地圖 (Maps of Korea, 1463), supplied more detailed and specific information about the country's territory.[131] A second wave of mapmaking responded to perceived military crises in the second half of the sixteenth century. Although many maps copied earlier works, this period produced the first map of the capital city, Hansŏng, and detailed maps of the Yalu and Tumen Rivers, which served as Chosŏn's northern borders. During the 1590s, the campaign to repel the Japanese invaders elicited new military maps. A map of approaches to P'yŏngyang (which the Japanese had occupied) and a map of the city itself helped the Ming/Chosŏn force retake this central place. Preparations for eventualities prompted maps of Kanghwa Island and a map of the mountain fortress Nam Hansansŏng, which became Injo's refuge in 1637.[132] Maps of Jurchen territory in 1610, of critical sites on the Yalu River (1618), and of the northernmost provinces signaled Chosŏn's apprehension of Nurhaci's growing power. Military maps continued to be produced

with respect to Mukedeng's mapping activities in Chosŏn. Ledyard notes that the Koreans quickly acquired the "observational and calculating devices" that the Qing mapping team brought with them, p. 305.

[130] Ledyard, "Cartography in Korea," p. 299.

[131] Young-woo Han, trans. Byonghyon Choi, "The Historical Development of Korean Cartography," in *The Artistry of Early Korean Cartography*, ed. Young-woo Han, Hwi-Joon Ahn, and Bae Woo Sung (Larkspur, CA: Tamal Vista Publications, 1999), pp. 12–13.

[132] *Ibid.*, pp. 18–26.

during the late seventeenth century as Chosŏn officials contemplated possible actions in the event of a failed Qing conquest.[133]

Dissemination of Western maps

Maps moved across political borders despite legal restrictions on their export. Western cartography moved quickly into Korea via China. Matteo Ricci's 1602 *mappa mundi*, *Kunyu wanguo quantu* (Complete terrestrial map of all countries) reached Korea in 1603, to be followed by Ricci's 1603 *Liangyi xuanlan tu* (Map of the Heavens and the Earth as seen from obscurity). Matteo Ricci's *mappa mundi*, which was a "flattened sphere projection with parallel latitudes and curving longitudes," caused many scholars to re-evaluate not only the relative position of China but also the shape of the world and the other lands within it.[134] Ricci's world maps, followed by those of Aleni and Ferdinand Verbiest, all found their way to Korea.[135] The Chosŏn court learned of the new cartographic techniques through its contact with Qing projects, most particularly the 1709 Jesuit mapping of the northeast and the borders of Korea, the 1710 mapping of the Amur drainage, and the 1713 mapping of Korea by Mukedeng. A Chosŏn official accompanied Mukedeng's surveying team and by the time it departed from the Korean capital (July 29, 1713), the Koreans had observed the new instruments and working methods "of probably the most advanced mapmaking operation in the world at that time" (they quickly acquired the instruments).[136]

European cartographic concepts and technologies were brought to Japan during the sixteenth century by Portuguese and Spanish missionaries and traders. A terrestrial globe was imported into Japan by 1580, when Oda Nobunaga brought it to a meeting with two Jesuits.[137] Portuguese maritime route maps influenced the creation of Japanese marine charts, which were used to guide ships at sea.[138] Matteo Ricci's world maps also moved quickly from China to Japan, where they were

---

[133] *Ibid.*, pp. 27–34.
[134] Benjamin A. Elman, "Geographical Research in the Ming–Ch'ing Period," *Monumenta Serica* 35 (1981–83): 8–9. The Korean reaction to Ricci's *mappa mundi* is also recorded in Bae Woo Sung, trans. Byonghyon Choi, "Worldviews and Early Cartography," in *Artistry of Early Korean Cartography*, p. 96.
[135] Sung, "Worldviews and Early Cartography," pp. 101, 105–6.
[136] Ledyard, "Cartography in Korea," pp. 298–304.
[137] Unno, "Cartography in Japan," p. 377.
[138] Ryōichi Aihara, "Ignacio Moreira's Cartographical Activities in Japan (1590–2), with Special Reference to Hessel Gerritsz's Hemispheric World Map," *Memoirs of the Research Department of the Toyo Bunko* 34 (1976): 240–41. Aihara also traces the erasure of inaccuracies in the early European maps through comparison, demonstrating that Japanese policies to keep maps a state secret were ineffective.

used to teach geography at the Jesuit academy in Kyoto from 1605.[139] Jesuit maps commissioned by the Kangxi emperor also made their way in the eighteenth century to Japan, where the portions depicting north Asia attracted interest.[140]

Ricci's 1602 map exerted great influence in Japan on world-maps printed commercially from the middle of the seventeenth century and designed partly to be hung in the *tokonoma* (alcove) of houses. These "Nanban-style world maps" may have been primarily decorative, but they revealed "that the Japanese at this date were keenly aware of their country as part of a larger world."[141] Despite the ban on travel abroad, Japanese obtained information about the outside world from shipwrecked sailors, Chinese political refugees, the Korean and Ryukyuan embassies, the Dutch resident at Deshima (Nagasaki), and from books brought to Japan by the Dutch and Chinese.[142] In the eighteenth century, specialists in "Dutch Learning" (*Rangaku*) translated Dutch world atlases, terrestrial and celestial globes into Japanese. Information in Russian maps, presented to the *bakufu* by Adam K. Laxman (1792), made their way into Japanese, but these were not widely circulated.[143] Although the Japanese initially simply reproduced Chinese maps and adopted a European-style map of China only in the second half of the nineteenth

[139] Yonemoto, *Mapping Early Modern Japan*, p. 16; Unno, "Cartography in Japan," pp. 404–5; see pp. 409–10 on the different versions of the Ricci map that were produced in Japan. Also Ōji Toshiaki, *Echizu no sekaizō* (World images of maps) (Tokyo: Iwanami shoten, 1996), chapter 4, on the impact of early modern European world maps on Japan.

[140] Funakoshi Akio, *Sakoku Nihon ni kita [Kōkizu] no chirigaku shiteki kenkyū* (Research on the geographical history of the Kangxi map which entered Japan in the era of seclusion) (Tokyo: Hōsei daigaku shuppankyoku, 1986); Sawa Miki, "Tō'an shiryō kara mita [Kōyo zenranto] to Yoroppa gijutsu" (The archival *Huangyu quanlantu* and European technology), *Shikan* 121 (1989): 53–64.

[141] Unno, "Cartography in Japan," p. 379.

[142] Torii Yumiko, "Kinsei Nihon no Ajia ninshiki" (Asian consciousness in early modern Japan), in *Ajia kara kangaeru* 1: *Kōsaku suru Ajia* (From the Asian perspective: diverse Asia), ed. Mizoguchi Yūzō et al. (Tokyo: Tokyo University Press, 1993), pp. 219–52; Arano Yasunori, "Edo bakufu to Higashi Ajia – aru josei no tegami kara, jō ni kaete" (The Edo shogunate and East Asia from a woman's letter, in place of a preface) in *Edo bakufu to Higashi Ajia* (Tokyo: Yoshikawa kōbunkan, 2003), pp. 7–181; and Ba Zhaoxiang, "17–19 shiji zhongye Zhong Ri shuji jiaoliu shi de jingjixue fenzhe: yi difangzhi wei li" (An economic analysis of the history of Sino-Japanese book exchange from the seventeenth to the middle of the nineteenth century: a case study of Chinese local gazeteers), *Qingshi yanjiu* 2 (2008): 37–48. On Ming refugees in Japan, see Baoping Wang, "Chinese Scholars in Japan in the Late Qing: How They Lived and Whom They Knew," in *Sagacious Monks and Bloodthirsty Warriors: Chinese Views of Japan in the Ming–Qing Period*, ed. Joshua A. Fogel (Norwalk: EastBridge, 2002), pp. 185–99.

[143] Unno, "Cartography in Japan," pp. 432–36.

century, *Shina* and *Ajia*, cited in these European geographies, appeared in early nineteenth-century Japanese world geographies.[144]

Like other early modern states (including the Qing), Korea and Japan also moved from mapping frontiers to mapping the realm. King Yŏngjo (r. 1724–76) ordered maps of the provinces of Korea and ushered in an era of "remarkable development in the field of cartography."[145] Japan's Tokugawa shogunate also fully appreciated the intelligence potential of maps. The government ordered daimyo to map and collect detailed information about the lands within their domains, and produced the first maps of Japan.[146] These maps flowed into the public realm through reproduction in popular commercial imprints. During the second half of the seventeenth century, popular books depicting *honcho* (our empire) or *zenkoku* (all the provinces) provided ordinary Japanese with a new spatialized vision of their country.[147]

Conclusion

This chapter constructs a regional narrative against the background of global events usually treated within national histories. Hideyoshi's Korean invasion is treated as a sideshow in the Japanese national narrative of reunification. His death in 1598 allowed one of his generals, Tokugawa Ieyasu, to seize power and in 1600 to prevail over his opponents on the battlefield of Sekigahara. The shogunate that Ieyasu founded was to provide Japan with peace and stability until 1868. Edo-period historians have focused not on the individuals who led the unification, but rather on "a major transformation in social and political organization, military and economic capacity, and cultural style" that took place in the last half of the sixteenth century.[148]

---

[144] According to Torii, "Kinsei Nihon," p. 221, Ricci's *Kunyu wanguo quantu* (1602), Aleni's *Zhi fangwai ji* (1623), the *Algemeene Geographie* (1769), and *Kouranten-tolk* (1748) were among the sources for world geographies such as Nishikawa Jōken's [*Zōho*] *Ka'I tsūshō kō* (Supplementary thoughts on trade and communication with the civilized and barbarian) (1708). *Ajia* appeared in Arai Hakuseki's *Sairan igen* (1713), which was not published until 1874, but a revised version by Yamamura Shōei was published in 1803. The term also appeared in a geography by Sugita Gentan, published in 1856 (pp. 232–33).

[145] Young-woo Han, "Historical Development of Korean Cartography," p. 52.

[146] Kawamura Hirotada, *Edo bakufu sen kuni-ezu no kenkyū* (Study of domain maps compiled by the Tokugawa shogunate) (Tokyo: Kojin shoin, 1984); Yonemoto, *Mapping*, pp. 9, 12–13. According to Yonemoto, p. 13, the first map of Japan omitted Hokkaido (Ezo), including only Honshu, Kyushu, and Shikoku.

[147] Yonemoto, *Mapping*, chapter 1.

[148] John Whitney Hall, "Introduction," *The Cambridge History of Japan*, vol. IV: *Early Modern Japan*, ed. John Whitney Hall (Cambridge: Cambridge University Press, 1991), p. 6.

Between 1550 and 1650, the balance of forces tilted against the Korean state. Unable to match the power of Japan or China, its role as a buffer between two regional powers made it the object of their unwelcome attentions. In his influential history of Korea, Ki-baik Lee devotes two pages to the national crises induced by the Manchus, noting that although the physical damage was slight, the invasions stimulated "an intense hostility toward Ch'ing."[149] Kim Han'gyu's survey of Sino-Korean relations details the intense surveillance and harsh exactions of the Manchus from 1637 to 1644.[150] Others have talked about the political repercussions of the two invasions on internal power struggles within the Injo court.[151]

By contrast, Chinese historians in the PRC have not completely broken with the dynastic tradition, which organizes the narrative in terms of the rise and fall of a ruling house. The national narrative for the late sixteenth and early seventeenth centuries focuses on the demise of the Ming empire and the Qing conquest. Research on the pre-1644 history of the Jianzhou Jurchen/Manchu Qing state is institutionally separated from what followed after the Qing banners passed through the Great Wall and commenced the formal takeover of Ming territory. The first topic was classified as the history of ethnic minorities, the second was Qing history, an addition to and continuation of the earlier dynastic narratives that comprise the official traditional history of China.[152] Putting these events, normally studied in isolation from one another, creates a different picture, one of the interregional reverberations that ushered in a period of intense interaction between China and its northeast frontier. In the moves and counter-moves encompassing the Japanese invasion, Chinese intervention, and the increasing rivalry between the Jurchen Jin and Ming to which Chosŏn fell victim, we see at play the force of events beyond the control of any individual state. That these events were also affected by large global historical movements is the second theme of the chapter.

The 1550–1650 period saw Japan and China join a worldwide maritime economy. Japanese access to foreign knowledge and foreign

---

[149] Lee, *New History*, p. 216.   [150] Kim Han'gyu, *Han Chung kwan'gye*, pp. 714–24.

[151] Han Myŏnggi, "Pyŏngja Horan p'aejŏn ŭi chŏngch'ijŏk p'ajang – Ch'ŏng ŭi Chosŏn ap'pak kwa Injo ŭi tae'ŭng ŭl chungsim ŭro" (The second Manchu invasion surrender's political effects: focusing on the Qing pressure on Chosŏn and Injo's response), *Tongbang hakji* 119 (2003): 53–93.

[152] For a fascinating analysis of the late seventeenth-century intellectual milieu that helped produce this bifurcation of historical subjects, see Struve, *Ming–Qing Conflict*, pp. 25–47.

goods peaked in this century. In 1550, Japan was in the middle of a civil war, better known as the "Warring States" period (*sengoku jidai*). Central authority had collapsed. Japanese regional lords in pursuit of comparative advantage took on European advisers. Some converted to Catholicism and others organized artillery units to incorporate European firearms into their military repertoire. European muskets, which were reproduced in Japan within a decade of their introduction, tipped the scale. Artillery units, organized by Oda Nobunaga, then Toyotomi Hideyoshi, allowed Hideyoshi to unify Japan by military means. The successful adoption of the gun sharply raised the demand for weapons but also for saltpeter, an essential component in the production of gunpowder. Seeking military supplies and funds to support their military operations, regional lords tapped far-flung mercantile networks, which extended from Japan to Manila and Southeast Asia.

Through contact with Spanish and Portuguese missionaries and traders, Hideyoshi became aware of the Spanish colonization of the Philippines signaling the extension of Europe's territorial control into Asia. The boundaries of his world expanded. His 1592 invasion of Korea was the first stage in a declared campaign to conquer the biggest political entity in his world, Ming China.

From 1550 to 1650, China's insatiable demand for silver drove its trade with Europe, Japan, and Southeast Asia. Silver from Japan and the Americas flowed into China, causing the economic boom of the sixteenth century. China's monetization of silver and commutation of many corvée taxes into silver payments transformed the Chinese economy. The benefits of maritime trade were most visible in the economies of the southeast coast and the Yangzi delta, where they stimulated an efflorescence of urban culture that is one of the highlights of Chinese history. From 1571 onward, Ming officials no longer tried to contain trade with Southeast Asia within official channels. The flow of Chinese emigrants to Southeast Asia (despite imperial prohibitions) also began in the sixteenth century and was to substantially affect the later history of that region. In this chapter, however, we focused instead on how the trading boom affected the fortunes of northeast Asia.

A juxtaposition of domestic and exogenous factors caused the fall of the Ming imperial house. Some have pointed to the stultifying effects of a palace upbringing on emperors and the intense factionalism that debilitated the sixteenth-century Ming literati. Others have suggested that the sixteenth century economic boom produced negative consequences that weakened the Ming government, notably the inflation created by a monetary policy that clung to paper money, and the government's vulnerability to abrupt shifts in silver imports occasioned by external crises.[153] Here, we focus on the frontiers of the Ming to query the narrative of domestically induced dynastic decline.

Weak state control allowed Japanese and Chinese traders to easily participate in the dynamic maritime trade, and provided essential resources to men with political ambitions. The path to Japan's reunification is crammed with local militarists who profited from the commodities and new knowledge brought to them through Europeans. The story of the Zheng family, Chinese trader/pirates who built large maritime empires and controlled large fleets that could militarily resist Qing troops and expel the Dutch from Taiwan, substantiates the thesis that the frontier, not the core region, was the source of the greatest challenges to confront the Ming and Qing forces.

Nurhaci was the northeast frontier's counterpart to Zheng Chenggong. The expansive sixteenth century economic boom caused demand for goods gleaned from the wilderness such as sable and ginseng to rise, inducing groups like the Jurchen to enter the export trade. The Jianzhou Jurchen were able to seize the opportunities for political expansion by virtue of their long political and economic tutelage at the hands of Korean and Chinese regimes. Trade funded their military campaigns, which in turn, through the acquisition of patents, commercial levies, and collection of export goods as tribute increased the revenues to support further military campaigns. Similarly, the Manchu subjugation of Korea supplied resources to the Qing state at a critical juncture in its military campaign against the Ming.

The three military episodes recounted in this chapter vividly exemplify the inter-connectedness of these states. Hideyoshi's invasion was sparked by his dream of Asian hegemony as the capstone to a steller military career. It was foiled by the Wanli emperor's military intervention, in a campaign in which the Chinese big cannon defeated Japanese musket units. That the weapons brought to war by both sides were initially acquired from the Portuguese, underlines the European connection to these events.

In contrast to the 1592–98 Korean–Ming–Japanese confrontation, the 1627 and 1637 Manchu invasions of Korea reveal the growing weakness of the Ming. The primary issue of the time was the Ming government's need to squash the challenge posed by the new northeast power. The Later Jin defeat of a joint Ming–Chosŏn force in 1619 significantly shifted

---

[153] On the controversies regarding drops in silver inflows as a cause of Ming decline, see William Atwell, "Another Look at Silver Imports into China, ca. 1635–1644," *Journal of World History* 16.4 (2006): 467–89.

the regional balance of power to favor the Later Jin. The two Manchu invasions forced the Korean court to switch its allegiance to the Jurchen state. In both instances, Korea's appeals for military aid went unanswered by Ming.

The actions of the Tokugawa shogunate and the Qing court after 1650 show that the transformations taking place in the preceding century were irreversible. Both regimes continued trading with Europe. China's prosperous eighteenth century was fuelled by the growing export trade. Although banned in Japan, Jesuits served Qing emperors, whose interest in European-derived knowledge, from calculus to music, has been revealed by recent studies.[154] The conduit for European knowledge in Japan was *Rangaku* (Dutch learning), based on books and goods imported by the Dutch traders at Nagasaki.

This chapter argues that one consequence of the exchanges initiated with Europe was that Qing and Japan adopted the perspectives of early modern European states. Japanese, Chinese, and Manchu leaders responded to the Russian exploration and colonization of Siberia with efforts of their own. Their borders, increasingly, were territorially defined and fixed by treaty. Exploration and mapping projects on the fringes of the polity were followed by mapping projects of the lands within the borders. The Jesuit mapping of northeast Asia and of the sacred home-land of the Jurchen/Manchu, Changbaishan, was followed by an imperial commission to compile maps for a gazetteer that would cover the eighteen provinces of the former Ming empire. As in Europe, the cartographic project entailed collecting detailed economic, demographic, and cultural information on subject peoples under Qing rule. Later imperial commissions would focus on the newly acquired western regions. Mapping became a normal mode for the state to symbolically stake its claims of sovereignty and for Qing to compare itself favorably with the achievements of its predecessors.

Japan's early modern order also included mapmaking. For the first time, the shogunate commissioned maps that standardized cartographic information for all of the domains in Japan, and commercial imprints of these maps were eventually available to a broad readership, changing the way in which ordinary Japanese conceived of their relationship not only to their local domain (*kuni* in its pre-1868 meaning), but also to the

---

[154] For a sampling, see Benjamin Elman, "Jesuit *Scientia* and Natural Studies in Late Imperial China, 1600–1800," *Journal of Early Modern History* 6.3 (2002): 209–31; Catherine Jami, "Imperial Control and Western Learning: The Kangxi Emperor's Performance," *Late Imperial China* 23.1 (2002): 28–49; and Joanna Waley-Cohen, "China and Western Technology in the Late Eighteenth Century," *American Historical Review* 98.5 (1993): 1525–44.

nation-in-the making, and finally to the larger world in which Japan found itself. Not coincidentally, the Edo period was one in which intellectuals were increasingly prone to articulating a distinctive Japanese identity. This, and other cultural ramifications of the China–Korea–Japan zone, are treated in the chapters of Part II.

The close parallels in Japanese and Chinese responses to the European presence in Asia and their interactions reaffirm our contention that China, Korea, and Japan constitute a meaningful socio-geopolitical region. In this chapter we have presented a case for embedding the region into a world historical context, arguing that cross-border exchanges, new state technologies, and multi-state competition drove Japan and Qing to adopt new practices that were transformative. Although the 1550–1650 events did not create replicas of the European nation-state in Asia, the regimes that emerged in the post-1650 period were significantly different from their pre-1550 counterparts. The Tokugawa, Chosŏn, and Qing all pursued cultural agendas based on shared symbolic repertoires to elaborate on their differences. As global forces advanced regional integration, the cultural boundaries delineating national self-image rose. That is the topic of Part II.

Part II

Cultural negotiations

3   Unity and diversity in state rituals

The three chapters in Part II examine what Lieberman calls "politicized ethnicity," the cultural practices created by elites that simultaneously affirmed their shared civilizational roots and their uniqueness. This chapter looks at state rituals. A large body of secondary literature attests that rituals, "symbolic behavior that is socially standardized and repetitive," shape our perception of reality and the world.[1] State rituals are an important instrument by which rulers and ritual specialists fuse potent cultural symbols into emotion-stirring choreographed sequences of gesture, music, and voiced utterance in an attempt to legitimate political systems and create symbolic communities. Rituals are multi-media vehicles for the expression of collective sentiments about one's own community and the community's view of itself. Rather than being fixed and stable, they are evolving and fluid. They provide a rich source for insights about the self-images of East Asian states at different points in their long entangled history.

Surveying its ritual repertoire, we argue that calling China's state rituals "Confucian" ignores the diversity of religious practice and the persistence of indigenous "religious orientations" such as ancestor worship, an "omnipresent" orientation that, Benjamin Schwartz noted, was "central to the entire development of Chinese civilization."[2] Ancestor worship, dating from long before the life of Confucius (541–479 BCE), and the ancillary idea that human beings could become gods, featured in Chinese state rites to 1911. By the Ming and Qing period, the state supported Daoist, Buddhist, and shamanic rites; it sacrificed at altars to nature deities originating in pre-Confucian times, and to others that marked the Manchu identity of the Qing regime.

Before the second half of the seventh century, when Japan imported elements of proto-Daoist and other religious and ritual practices from the

---

[1] David Kertzer, *Ritual, Politics, and Power* (New Haven: Yale University Press, 1988), p. 9.
[2] Benjamin I. Schwartz, *The World of Thought in Ancient China* (Cambridge, MA: Belknap Press, 1985), pp. 20–21.

continent, shamanism was the dominant religious orientation. Striving to advance political centralization and consolidate the power of the imperial line, rulers seized upon the continental imports to position Amaterasu as the focal ancestress of the imperial family. In this process, they transformed and systematized the indigenous belief system, which evolved until its grand metamorphosis into State Shinto during the second half of the nineteenth century.

Shamanism was the native religious system of north and northeast Asia. Shamans were present in Japanese, Korean, Mongol, and Manchu society. In addition, Buddhism rivaled Confucianism in providing a cohesive structure for state rites in many Central Plain states, including Tang China and the conquest dynasties of the tenth to fourteenth centuries. Buddhism also dominated Korean courts from the sixth to the fifteenth century, and Japan from the eighth century onward. Here, too, the commonalities shared by co-religionists often gave way to unique adaptations that emerged over time. In Japan, Shinto deities were incorporated into the Buddhist pantheon. Shinto–Buddhist doctrinal developments in the sixteenth century allowed men vying for national leadership to bolster their status through self-enshrinement, a phenomenon that was quite different from the Chinese practice of posthumous deification.

In addition to their legitimating functions, rituals voiced the desires of ordinary people for good harvests and peace, or for protection against natural calamity. Since the Confucians posited a positive correlation between benevolent rule and nature, drought, locusts, and other natural disasters posed a direct challenge to a ruler's legitimacy. This was especially true in the case of rituals performed to pray for rain in the increasingly arid North China Plain. On this subject, Confucian orthodoxy gave way to pragmatism: rulers resorted to a "shotgun" approach, sacrificing at a wide array of altars sited in popular as well as official religion.

Because they mirror politics, the rituals and associated court deliberations reflect inter-state tensions as well as each state's desire to assert its identity. Rejecting incorporation into a Sinocentric tribute system, Japan used state-sponsored rituals that blended Shinto and Buddhist elements to express its uniqueness. As officials in fifteenth-century Korea began to study the Chinese ritual code, Confucian proponents complained that the rites being performed deviated significantly from those outlined in Chinese ritual codes. Attacking the Korean king's performance of the sacrifice to Heaven, a ritual that China reserved for the Ming emperor, as *lèse majesté*, Confucian officials argued that *sadae* ("serving the great") required absolute conformity to the Sino-centered hierarchical world order. Against this, the king and his supporters reiterated the ruler's preeminent obligation to serve his own subjects (and assert Korea's distinctive identity). The ritual debate was not only about the obligation to conform to the hierarchy embedded in the Chinese ritual code, but obliquely involved the assertion of *yangban*-based scholarship over royal prerogative. The triumph of Confucian norms in this instance provides added piquancy to the seventeenth-century turn, when Korean officials used state rituals to proclaim their adherence to the Confucian norms associated with Ming, in defiance of Qing overlordship.

Chinese state rituals: not simply Confucian

Although the traditional Chinese state is often described as Confucian, studies of state patronage and ritual calendars show that imperial courts accommodated the entire range of religions and religious practices found in the society. Certain distinctive orientations predate the emergence of Confucianism. One was a predilection for "ancestor worship," an "emphasis on the continuity of kinship links between the living and the dead, the belief that ancestors could intercede with deities on behalf of their living descendants."[3] The earliest state rituals, performed in honor of the royal ancestors, were shamanic in nature. The founders of the Xia, Shang, and Zhou dynasties were healers, rainmakers, exorcists, and prophets, shamans who claimed the ability to communicate with the deities through the intermediation of their royal ancestors to obtain foreknowledge of important events. Even after the Zhou conquerors introduced the concept of the Mandate of Heaven to legitimate their own rule, myths of the ancestors lingered in stories of the founding ancestors of the ruling houses, which retained ancestor worship as a tool of power.[4] Later, after the Tang raised the sacrifice to Heaven to the supreme act legitimating a dynasty, the rituals performed at the dynasty's Ancestral Temple (*Taimiao*) were ranked only below the sacrifices at the altars of Heaven and Earth.[5]

The Mandate of Heaven concept was adopted by subsequent rulers to explain dynastic change. The appearance of multiple states ruled by peoples of non-Han origin spurred another innovation, the notion of an

[3] Evelyn S. Rawski, "A Historian's Approach to Chinese Death Ritual," in *Death Ritual in Late Imperial and Modern China*, ed. James L. Watson and Evelyn S. Rawski (Berkeley: University of California Press, 1988), p. 23.
[4] K. C. Chang, *Art, Myth, and Ritual: The Path to Political Authority in Ancient China* (Cambridge, MA: Harvard University Press, 1983).
[5] Howard J. Wechsler, *Offerings of Jade and Silk: Ritual and Symbol in the Legitimation of the T'ang Dynasty* (New Haven: Yale University Press, 1985).

"orthodox succession" that recast dynastic succession into a unilinear narrative. *Zhengtong* (orthodox succession) developed out of the Han synthesis of Confucianism with cosmological theories. In Han times, it referred to the orthodox or legitimate line of succession within a ruling house or family. In the Tang and Song dynasties, the term was generalized to mean a legitimate line of rulership extending from antiquity to the present. Legitimacy crossed over descent lines and could be transmitted from one ruling house to another. Ritual reflected what Howard Wechsler called a shift from worship of "lineal ancestors" to "political ancestors," as the state supported sacrifices at the tombs and at the Temple to Rulers of Successive Dynasties (*Lidai di wang miao*).[6] By incorporating their predecessors into state ritual, a ruling house expanded the foundations of imperial legitimacy by asserting "the hallowed notion that the empire was not the perpetual monopoly of one house only."[7]

The worship of nature deities, gods of the sky, mountains, and streams, also predates the advent of Confucianism. These deities were incorporated into state rituals after Confucianism was adopted as state doctrine in the second century BC. Many new cosmological ideas such as the Five Elements and *yinyang* theory entered Han Confucianism. Emperor Wu, who is credited with endorsing a Confucian curriculum at the National Academy, is famous for travelling to Mount Tai in Shandong to perform the *feng* and *shan* sacrifices to Heaven and Earth. These rituals, which are recognized as "one of the central events" in the history of the Former Han dynasty (202 BCE – CE 9), were "a fundamental element" in Emperor Wu's drive to strengthen the dynasty's legitimacy. They constituted a creative synthesis of earlier rituals of power, combining sacrifices to mountain deities and ancient shamanic rites, performed at the mountain sacred to an immortality cult. The heterodox and diverse origins of the *feng* and *shan* rites were masked by later scholars, who incorporated them into Confucian rites.[8] Much the same could be said for many of the state rituals of the Ming and Qing dynasties.

Historical records outline a long and ultimately successful series of attempts by officials in the sixth to eighth centuries to bring local religious cults under bureaucratic control, a process exemplified in the creation of city gods that became a permanent fixture in the state religious hierarchy

---

[6] Evelyn S. Rawski, *The Last Emperors: A Social History of Qing Imperial Institutions* (Berkeley: University of California Press, 1998), p. 202. This was a second-rank state ritual.
[7] Wechsler, *Offerings of Jade and Silk*, p. 136.
[8] Mark Edward Lewis, "The *feng* and *shan* sacrifices of Emperor Wu of the Han," in *State and Court Ritual in China*, ed. Joseph P. McDermott (Cambridge: Cambridge University Press, 1999), pp. 50–80.

and the spiritual counterpart to the district magistrate. The forebears of the city god were animal spirits, dragon gods, or even demons worshipped in rural-based local cults that flourished in the lower reaches of the Yangzi River drainage and along the southeast coast. The process by which local officials and educated clergy transformed former officials or locally prominent men into religious functionaries is linked with urbanization and the "domestication" of autonomous, thus potentially dangerous deities. Anecdotes, like the one about the officials in a prefecture in northern Zhejiang who had to oust the deity, Xiang Yu, before they could occupy the prefectural office, suggest that the suppression of local deities did not go uncontested.[9]

Daoism also found its way into the state ritual system. Some emperors explicitly employed Daoist specialists,[10] but many others commissioned calendrical and exorcist rituals that fell under the rubric of popular Daoism.[11] An example is the prayer for rain, which did not originate as a Confucian ritual.[12] During the Warring States period, shamanic rites for rain featured the Yellow Emperor and a mythical figure, Chi You. Later, Daoist masters were called in to invoke rain, a tradition that persisted into the Qing period.[13] Qing state-sponsored rituals to relieve drought not only included imperial acts of penitence but also the invocation of local rain-making deities by district magistrates. As Jeffrey Snyder-Reinke argues, these rituals were by no means confined to the Confucian order: officials regularly performed sacrifices to Buddhist and Daoist deities, employing techniques drawn from

[9] David Johnson, "The City-God Cults in T'ang and Sung China," *Harvard Journal of Asiatic Studies* 45.2 (1985): 363–457.

[10] Song Huizong (r. 1100–26) was criticized by Confucian scholars for his promotion of Daoism; see Ari Daniel Levine, "The Reigns of Hui-tsung and Ch'in-tsung," in *The Cambridge History of China*, Vol. V: *The Sung Dynasty and Its Precursors, 907–1279*, part 1, ed. Denis Twitchett and Paul Jakov Smith (Cambridge: Cambridge University Press, 2009), pp. 616–14. On the Zhengde emperor's patronage of Daoism, see James Geiss, "The Leopard Quarter During the Cheng-te Reign," *Ming Studies* 24 (1987): 1–38; his successor, the Jiajing emperor, alarmed officials by his intense interest in Daoist techniques of fertility and longevity. See Geiss, "Chia-ching reign," pp. 479–82.

[11] Throughout this chapter, references to "Daoism" are confined to religious Daoism and not its philosophic strand.

[12] See Jeffrey Snyder-Reinke, *Dry Spells: State Rainmaking and Local Governance in Late Imperial China* (Cambridge, MA: Harvard University Asia Center, 2009), chapter 7 for a discussion challenging the received wisdom, based on a detailed survey of the recent secondary literature, in particular the assumption that Confucianism triumphed over other religious systems from the Song dynasty onward, and that the prescriptive regulations issued by the state were actually implemented on the ground.

[13] Sarah Allen, "Drought, Human Sacrifice and the Mandate of Heaven in a Lost Text from the *Shang Shu*," *Bulletin, School of Oriental and African Studies, London University* 47 (1984): 523–39; Kenneth Pomeranz, "Water to Iron, Widows to Warlords: The Handan Rain Shrine in Modern Chinese History," *Late Imperial China* 12.1 (1991): 62–99.

popular religion, even if these practices were forbidden by official regulations.[14]

Imperial patronage of Buddhism was initially intended to support the longevity of the state as well as the ruler. Throughout Asia, rulers responded to "the concept that Buddhist deities, vast in number and limitless in power, will protect a kingdom and its ruling families" if these families supported the religious community and the church.[15] Buddhism also supplied political legitimacy in the idea of the "wheel-turning" monarch, the *cakravartin*, who is a universal ruler. The first to pattern himself on the *cakravartin* ideal was Emperor Wu of the Liao dynasty (502–557 CE),[16] but others, such as the founder of the Sui dynasty, Sui Wendi (r. 581–604) and Empress Wu (r. 690–705) of the Tang dynasty, followed.[17]

Buddhism also attracted non-Han rulers. It was "the preeminent state religion" for the Tangut state (*c.* 982–1227) and its emperor.[18] The octagonal pagoda, massive Buddhist halls, and elaborate tombs that they built present abundant evidence of the Buddhist beliefs of the Khitan Liao rulers (907–1122).[19] The Jurchen Jin (1115–1234) also patronized Buddhism, while the founder of the Mongol Yuan (1279–1368) dynasty drew upon Mongolian, Chinese, and Buddhist ideas to create a model of legitimation that would bind together a vast multi-cultural empire.[20]

[14] Snyder-Reinke, *Dry Spells*, p. 186.

[15] John M. Rosenfield, "Introduction: Tōdai-ji in Japanese History and Art," in *The Great Eastern Temple: Treasures of Japanese Buddhist Art from Tōdai-ji*, ed. Yutaka Mino et al. (Bloomington: Art Institute of Chicago and Indiana University Press, 1986), p. 19.

[16] Arthur F. Wright, *Buddhism in Chinese History* (Stanford: Stanford University Press, 1957), pp. 50–51 and Arthur F. Wright, "The Sui Dynasty (581–617)," in *The Cambridge History of China*, vol. III, part 1: *Sui and T'ang China, 589–906*, ed. Denis Twitchett (Cambridge: Cambridge University Press, 1979), pp. 75–77.

[17] Ruth W. Dunnell, *The Great State of White and High: Buddhism and State Formation in Eleventh-Century Xia* (Honolulu: University of Hawai'i Press, 1996), pp. 18–26, discusses the historical links between Buddhism and rulership in Chinese history.

[18] Ruth W. Dunnell, "The Hsi Hsia," in *The Cambridge History of China*, vol. VI: *Alien Regimes and Border States, 907–1368*, ed. Herbert Franke and Denis Twitchett (Cambridge: Cambridge University Press, 1994), pp. 154–55.

[19] Nancy Shatzman Steinhardt, *Liao Architecture* (Honolulu: University of Hawai'i Press, 1997), chapter 14. The Liao court patronage of Buddhism did not exclude similar support of Daoism: see Franke, "The Chin Dynasty," pp. 314, 316–18 for Jin patronage of Buddhism and Daoism. Also Taochung Yao, "Buddhism and Taoism under the Chin," in *China Under Jurchen Rule*, ed. Hoyt Cleveland Tillman and Stephen H. West (Albany: State University of New York Press, 1995), pp. 145–80.

[20] Herbert Franke, *From Tribal Chieftain to Universal Emperor and God: The Legitimation of the Yuan Dynasty* (Munich: Verlag der Bayerischen Akademie der Wissenschaften, 1978).

The idea of reincarnation enhanced the appeal of Buddhism as a source for political legitimacy. The notion that a reincarnate being will be reborn in the person of his successor, and has the power to select and foretell the circumstances of his rebirth first appeared in the Tibetan Karma pa lineage in the late thirteenth to early fourteenth centuries. Mongol Yuan rulers adopted the reincarnate model to insert Khorichar-mergen, an ancestor of Chinggis, into a Buddhist framework by claiming that Khorichar-mergen was the reincarnation of Padmasambhava, the Indian monk who introduced Buddhism into Tibet. Chinggis became a protective deity of Tibetan Buddhism.[21]

Imperial patronage of Tibetan Buddhism was heavily influenced by the geopolitical situation in Asia. Mongol, Ming, and Qing rulers established sustained relationships not only with Chinese Buddhist temples but also with Tibetan Buddhist prelates, up to and including the Dalai Lama.[22] A Tibetan Buddhist monk filled the post of State Preceptor at the court of Möngke Khan in Karakorum. In 1260 Khubilai Khan appointed the head of the 'Pags pa sect as State Preceptor, and gave him overall religious authority over the Yuan empire.[23] The Yuan adopted the "lama-patron" model whereby the Khan was protector of the faith and acknowledged the spiritual leadership of the lama. For their part, Tibetan monastic orders competing for dominance within a weak and decentralized Tibetan polity sought external patrons who could tip the military balance in their favor. Until 1720, these foreign patrons were unable or unwilling to muster the logistics to conquer Tibet's forbidding terrain in order to physically incorporate Tibet into their empires.[24]

---

[21] Turrell Wylie, "Reincarnation: A Political Innovation in Tibetan Buddhism," in *Proceedings of the Csoma de Kőrős Memorial Symposium Held at Mátrafüred, Hungary, September 1976*, ed. Louis Ligeti (Budapest: Akádemiao Kiadó, 1978), pp. 579–86.

[22] Xiangyun Wang, "The Qing Court's Tibet Connection: Lcang skya Rol pa'i rdo rje and the Qianlong Emperor," *Harvard Journal of Asiatic Studies* 60.1 (2000): 125–63; Xiangyun Wang, "Tibetan Buddhism at the Court of Qing: The Life and Work of lCang-skya Rol-pa'i-rdo-rje (1717–86)," PhD thesis, Harvard University, 1995. But some Tibetan Buddhist deities were introduced into China as early as the Tang dynasty: see Wang Yao, "The Cult of Mahakala and a Temple in Beijing," *Journal of Chinese Religions* 22 (1994): 117–26.

[23] See Morris Rossabi, *Khubilai Khan: His Life and Times* (Berkeley: University of California Press, 1988), pp. 37–43 for a discussion of Khubilai's interest in Daoism as well as Tibetan Buddhism.

[24] Elliot Sperling, "The Fifth Karma-pa and Some Aspects of the Relationship Between Tibet and the Early Ming," *Tibetan Studies in Honour of Hugh Richardson*, ed. Michael Aris and Aung San Suu Kyi (Warminster: Aris and Phillips, 1980), 280–89; Elliot H. Sperling, "Early Ming Policy Toward Tibet: An Examination of the Proposition that the Early Ming Emperors Adopted a 'Divide and Rule' Policy toward Tibet," PhD thesis, Indiana University, 1983; Zhang Weiguang, "Mingchao zhengfu zai Hehuang diqu de Zangzhuan Fojiao zhengce shulun" (The Ming government policy on Tibetan

Ming Tibetan policy continued the Yuan tradition. The Yongle emperor (r. 1403–1424) invited the head of the Karma pa order to visit his capital, Nanjing, and conferred the title of State Preceptor on him in 1406. There were further exchanges with Tibetan prelates, which helped the Ming protect the trade routes that supplied Ming armies with horses from Inner Asia. This active exchange with Tibet ended in the early sixteenth century, when the Mongols replaced the Ming as the dominant power in the Amdo region.[25] In 1578, when the eastern Mongol leader Altan Khan met with bSod nams rgya mtsho (1543–88), head of the dGe lugs pa, a Tibetan Buddhist order founded in the fourteenth century, Mongol leaders were ready to expand their political authority by using the Tibetan Buddhist lama-patron relationship. Altan Khan accepted bSod nams rgya mtsho as his "spiritual guide and refuge" and in return conferred the title "Dalai Lama" on him (bSod nams rgya mtsho is traditionally identified as the third Dalai). The rise of the dGe lugs pa order to preeminence within Tibet began with this event. The possibility of "finding" future rebirths among the Mongolian elite – the fourth Dalai Lama was a fourth-generation descendant of Altan Khan – allowed the Mongol chieftains to fully utilize the symbolic capital acquired by conversion to Tibetan Buddhism.

A great wave of conversion swept through Mongolia in the late six-teenth and early seventeenth centuries, and the Dalai Lama, who had been put on the throne of Tibet in 1642, held enormous authority among the Mongols. The Manchus also felt the attraction: Nurhaci appointed a lama as the state preceptor of the Manchu *gurun* (tribe, i.e. nation) in 1621. Manchu rulers maintained relations with several competing Tibetan Buddhist orders until the eighteenth century. Qing emperors commissioned printings of the Tibetan Tripitaka, subsidized monas-teries, and asserted the power to confer recognition on reincarnate prelates in a new religious hierarchy created after 1691.[26] Manchu patronage of Tibetan Buddhism was politically expedient in dealings with Mongols and Tibetans, but also personal: some members of the imperial family, including the Qianlong emperor (r. 1736–95) were devout Tibetan Buddhists.[27]

Buddhism in the region where the Yellow River bends), *Qinghai shehui kexue* #2 (1989): 93–96.

[25] Pu Wencheng, "Zang zhuan Fojiao zhupai zai Qinghai de zaoqi zhuangbo ji qi gaizong" (The early propagation and reform of Tibetan Buddhist sects in Qinghai), *Xizang yanjiu* 2 (1990): 107–12, 125; T. Wylie, "Lama Tribute in the Ming Dynasty," in *Tibetan Studies in Honour of Hugh Richardson*, ed. Aris and Kyi, pp. 335–40.

[26] Rawski, *Last Emperors*, pp. 260–63.   [27] *Ibid.*, chapter 7.

Chinese state rituals were codified. Ming and Qing state rites were outlined in the collected regulations of the dynasty, the *huidian*, and placed under the jurisdiction of the Board of Rites. They were divided into five groups, defined by the nature of the occasion: 129 "auspicious rites" (*jili*), beginning with the sacrifices to Heaven and Earth; 74 "joyous rites" (*jiali*) such as the accession ceremony, the imperial audience, and reception of embassies; 18 "military rites" (*junli*), which included the rites performed when troops were led on campaign by the emperor; 20 "guest rites" (*binli*), detailing the submission of tribute by vassal states; and 15 "rites of misfortune" (*xiongli*), funeral rituals for persons of different status.[28] Many state rituals such as the reception of embassies and guest rituals were secular in nature. The others were centered on sacrifice. These rites were organized hierarchically into three classes, and ranked within each class, affirming the minute attention to status differentiation that is a persistent element in Chinese ritual culture. The perspective provided by the Qing *huidian* is somewhat misleading in its blurring of the large and significant gaps in ritual practice and ritual doctrines that existed among the rites themselves. Rather than an integrated and comprehensive ritual system, the *huidian* rites were a congeries of diverse elements drawn from different cultural traditions.

Qing court rituals reflected the emperors' vision of themselves as the pivotal figures of a multi-ethnic empire. The Qing quickly adopted but did not confine themselves to the elaborately structured state rituals of the Ming dynasty. They also privately patronized Chinese and Tibetan Buddhism as a matter of personal belief and state policy. Emperors also attempted to woo their Muslim subjects with donations to saints' shrines in the far west, while seeking to preserve their own cultural identity through supporting shamanic altars. The banner lords brought with them from the northeast their own shamanic rituals and established ritual centers, the *tangzi*, in Peking and Mukden (Shenyang), where members of the conquest elite worshipped Heaven (M. *abka*) in rites that paralleled but did not intersect with the sacrifices performed at the Round Altar.[29]

If emperors inserted a Manchu element into the state rituals, the Han Chinese bureaucratic culture also affected Manchu shamanism. The imperially commissioned *hesei toktobuha manju wecere metere kooli bithe*, compiled in 1747 and later translated into Chinese (*Qinding Manzhou jishen jitian dianli*) for incorporation into the Four Treasuries (*Siku quanshu*), far from carrying out the Qianlong emperor's desire to preserve Manchu shamanistic rituals, in actuality significantly altered ritual

[28] *Ibid.*, chapter 6.   [29] *Ibid.*, pp. 236–40.

practice, replacing diverse rituals performed by kinship groups in the northeast with the Aisin Gioro (imperial family) rituals, and replacing the classic shaman with hereditary clan practitioners.[30]

Chinese state rituals included worship of nature deities, headed by Heaven, and the ancestral cult, as well as shamanic rituals and Daoist rites. Nothing about these practices, or the idea that human beings of exceptional qualities could become deities after their demise, is innately Confucian. Whether the elaborate and hierarchically structured ritual order and the detailed regulations intended to control religious practices that are characteristic of the Chinese state ritual system should be called Confucian is also open to question. One could argue that the *huidian* should not be seen as constituting the entirety of the state's ritual activities, if by that one means all of the activities of the rulers and their relatives that are partially recorded in the voluminous Veritable Records (*shilu*) of a dynasty, the Diaries of Rest and Repose (*qiju zhu*), and even more fully (for the Qing dynasty) in the First Historical Archives materials of the Imperial Household Department (Neiwufu).[31]

That state rituals were highly eclectic is an observation that probably holds true for all Chinese dynasties. Few rulers were primarily concerned with drawing boundaries and differentiating between religious practices and "isms" as scholars are wont to do. Deities were highly mobile, moving from one altar to another, sometimes bewilderingly so. Consider that during the Yuan dynasty, Chinggis was one of four Kaghan who were worshipped in shamanic rites in the imperial ancestral temple, as a result of his placement in the Buddhist reincarnate lineage created long after his death. Ming and Qing emperors were committed to the state rites included in the *huidian*, but their mothers and wives, and sometimes even they, continued to patronize Buddhist temples with donations, the translation, compilation, and publication of Buddhist sutras, the subsidizing of temple construction, and the award of imperial plaques.[32]

This complex pastiche of religious affiliation is exemplified in the Qing imperial worship of a Daoist deity, Guandi, the god of war (but also of wealth). The Jiaqing emperor credited Guandi with repulsing rebels who stormed the imperial palace in the 1813 Eight Trigrams uprising, and his successors prayed to him during the troubled nineteenth century. Worship took place not only in Guandi's official city temple but also

---

[30] *Ibid.*, pp. 240–42.   [31] *Ibid.*, chapter 8.

[32] Thomas Shiyu Li and Susan Naquin, "The Baoming Temple: Religion and the Throne in Ming and Qing China," *Harvard Journal of Asiatic Studies* 48 (1988): 131–88; Naquin, *Peking: Temples and City Life*, pp. 167–70, 324–53 on the impact of imperial patronage in Ming and Qing Peking.

within the *tangzi*, the structure inside the Forbidden City that was dedicated to Manchu shamanism. Regular worship on *tangzi* altars directed to Sakyamuni Buddha, Guanyin, and Guandi underlines the danger of drawing hard lines between the different religions or accepting the stereotype of a Confucian-dominated ritual order.[33]

The cosmopolitan and polymorphous nature of Chinese state rituals as they developed over the course of recorded history reflected China's intense and sustained cultural interaction with Inner Asian peoples living at its peripheries who sometimes invaded and conquered the Chinese-speaking population. Chinese state rituals crossing into the Korean peninsula and into the Japanese archipelago encountered quite different social–cultural realities. How did the political conditions of these places affect and shape the state rituals that emerged? We turn first to Japan.

Japan: deconstructing "native" origins

Historians tracing Japan's pursuit of primacy in the East Asian world order of the seventeenth century focus on the concept of *shinkoku* (神國, literally country of the gods), enunciated by Toyotomi Hideyoshi and his successors. Elaborated in the late nineteenth century as *tennōsei* 天皇制 or emperor-centered ideology, the concept was closely associated with Shinto, the indigenous religious system. To underline the native origin of these beliefs, modernizing reformers purged Japan's shrines of Buddhist influence, and created a state Shinto system which was implemented throughout the home islands and symbolically planted into territories colonized by the expanding Japanese empire.[34] Recent investigations of ancient Japanese ritual, however, stress that Shinto did not exist as a coherent religious system until much later; and that it was produced through a synthesis of indigenous cults with practices and beliefs imported from continental Asia.[35]

---

[33] Guo Songyi, "Lun Ming Qing shiqi de Guan Yu chongbai" (On the worship of Guan Yu in Ming and Qing times), *Zhongguo shi yanjiu* 3 (1990): 127–39; Rawski, *Last Emperors*, pp. 236–38; Naquin, *Peking*, pp. 327–38 on the Guandi temple outside the palace. Also see Prasenjit Duara, "Superscribing Symbols: The Myth of Guandi, Chinese God of War," *Journal of Asian Studies* 47.4 (1988): 778–95.

[34] For a historiographical survey of the secondary literature on Shinto, see John Breen and Mark Teeuwen, "Introduction: Shinto Past and Present," in *Shinto in History: Ways of the Kami*, ed. John Breen and Mark Teeuwen (Honolulu: University of Hawai'i Press, 2000), pp. 1–12. On the purge of Buddhism in the Meiji era, see James E. Ketelaar, *Of Heretics and Martyrs in Meiji Japan: Buddhism and its Persecution* (Princeton: Princeton University Press, 1990). On the Meiji development of state Shinto, see Helen Hardacre, *Shinto and the State, 1868–1988* (Princeton: Princeton University Press, 1989).

[35] Toshio Kuroda, trans. James C. Dobbins and Suzanne Gay, "Shinto in the History of Japanese Religion," *Journal of Japanese Studies* 7.1 (1988): 1–21 argued that Shintō did

Ancient Japan

Japanese historians have detected a wide range of Daoist elements in the institutional evolution of the Japanese state during 650–800 CE.[36] The breadth and depth of borrowing, from the invention of a new type of ruler, the *tennō* (天皇, emperor), during the Tenmu reign (673–686), to the creation of an imperial cult dedicated to the ancestress Amaterasu, lead some scholars to conclude that "'Shinto,' in its earliest known usage, was . . . nothing but a Chinese cultural import."[37] Written to refute earlier claims of autochthonous origins, this statement exaggerates in downplaying the role of indigenous elements in the development of Shinto, but correctly points to the selective adaptation of Chinese models.

Chinese models stimulated the centralization and systematization of local cults under the Jingikan (神祇官, Office for Deity Affairs) in the last decades of the seventh century and spurred the Tenmu emperor to compile the *Kojiki*, which, borrowing Chinese cosmological ideas of the Han dynasty, placed the ruler in an astral order centered on the pole star, the abode of Tianhuang Dadi 天皇大帝, the penultimate Daoist deity (whose name is the source for the Japanese term for emperor, *tennō*).[38] Daoist elements, incorporated into Song Buddhist rituals, also appear in

not become a separate, self-contained religious doctrine and institution until the nineteenth century. Hitomi Maeda, "Imperial Authority and Local Shrines: The Yoshida House and the Creation of a Countrywide Shinto Institution in Early Modern Japan," PhD thesis, Harvard University, 2003, moves the date for the creation of a systemic Shinto to the Edo period, in particular the middle of the seventeenth century. Kazuhiko Yoshida, "Revisioning Religion in Ancient Japan," *Japanese Journal of Religious Studies* 30.1–2 (2003): 2 states that "The view that 'Shinto' existed as an independent entity before the introduction of Buddhism in the sixth century is untenable today."

[36] It would, however, be anachronistic to assume that Daoism and the other doctrinal systems were cohesive integrated thought systems in their contemporary Chinese setting; see Tim Barrett, "Shinto and Taoism in Early Japan," in *Shinto in History: Ways of the Kami*, ed. John Breen and Mark Teeuwen (Honolulu: University of Hawai'i Press, 2000), pp. 18–23.

[37] Quote from Breen and Teeuwen, "Introduction," p. 5; Kuroda, "Shinto in the History of Japanese Religion"; Ooms, *Imperial Politics*. See also Nelly Naumann, "The State Cult of the Nara and Early Heian Periods," in *Shinto in History*, ed. Breen and Teeuwen, pp. 47–67; Barrett, "Shinto and Taoism in Early Japan"; Senda Minoru, *Ise jingū – Higashi Ajia no Amaterasu* (The Ise shrine: East Asia's Amaterasu) (Tokyo: Chūōkōronshinsha, 2005), chapter 2. Matsumae Takeshi, "Early Kami Worship," in *The Cambridge History of Japan*, vol. I: *Ancient Japan*, ed. Delmer M. Brown (Cambridge: Cambridge University Press, 1993), pp. 317–58, represents an older approach which does not recognize Daoist influences on the development of Shinto.

[38] Naumann, "State Cult," p. 48. The idea that the Japanese emperor was a "living god" (*kami*) dates from the Tenmu reign. See D. C. Holtom, *The Japanese Enthronement Ceremonies* (Tokyo: Sophia University Press, 1972), who observes (p. 60) that despite nineteenth-century efforts to rid the *sokui-rei* from Chinese influences, "this part of the enthronement ceremonies is more Chinese in its historical affiliations than it is Japanese."

medieval Japanese Zen Buddhist services designed to protect the emperor by "invoking the sages" (*shukushin* 祝聖).[39]

The state that emerged during the late seventh to late eighth century used rituals to extend its political grasp into localities.[40] According to Ooms, there were thirteen state festivals in ancient Japan, four of which were observed throughout the country and centered on the mainstay of the economy, agriculture. Prayers for the harvest were conducted at the Toshigoi festival, on the fourth day of the second lunar month, the Tsukinami festival, on the eleventh day of the sixth and twelfth months, and the Niiname festival, held during the eleventh month, to give thanks for the harvest. These rituals were supervised by the Jingikan, one of two major state agencies. Other state rituals sought to ward off contagious diseases, to protect the capital city from fire and evil spirits, and to "strengthen" the "emperor's spirit."[41]

The court appointed specialists from Korea to the Yin-yang Bureau (陰陽寮 Onmyōryō) and the Jingikan.[42] The Nakatomi originally served as diviners and the Inbe prepared the offerings for the sacrifices presented at *matsuri* 祭 (festivals). These calendrical sacrifices were performed in order to exorcise evil spirits, including those causing epidemics and fires; to ask the gods for good crops and long life for the ruler; and to give thanks to deities for abundant harvests. Eighth-century rulers also patronized Buddhism, erecting great temples in the capital and commissioning "protect the nation" rituals in them.[43]

Other late seventh-century ritual innovations accompanied the strengthening of the state. The indigenous accession ritual, which had consisted of "stepping onto a raised platform to be acclaimed by Yamato magnates," was made more elaborate to reflect the new cosmology of the Yamato state. Rituals marking the transfer of the imperial regalia to the

---

[39] Michel Mohr, "Invocation of the Sage: The Ritual to Glorify the Emperor," in *Zen Ritual: Studies of Zen Buddhist Theory in Practice*, ed. Steven Heine and Dale S. Wright (Oxford: Oxford University Press, 2008), pp. 205–22.

[40] Matsumae, "Early Kami Worship," pp. 342–43.

[41] Ooms, *Imperial Politics*, table 2, p. 107 and pp. 106–9. The Jingikan and the Daijōkan (Council of State) were of roughly equal status (p. 82). On Oom's vision of ancient Japan's "liturgical state," see pp. 109–12.

[42] On the role of immigrants from the Korean peninsula, see Michael Como, "Silla Immigrants and the Early Shōtoku Cult: Ritual and the Poetics of Power in Early Yamato," PhD thesis, Stanford University, 2000. Reviewing Como's later monograph, *Ethnicity, Ritual and Violence in the Japanese Buddhist Tradition*, in *Journal of Japanese Studies* 36.1 (2010): 190, Donald McCallum observes that Paekche immigrants also played a "fundamentally important role in early Japanese political and religious history."

[43] Kōyū Sonoda with Delmer M. Brown, "Early Buddha Worship," in *The Cambridge History of Japan*, vol. I: *Ancient Japan*, pp. 359–414; Piggott, *The Emergence of Japanese Kingship*, pp. 255–57.

new ruler were accompanied by the appearance of ritual specialist lineages, whose primary role was to safeguard and transmit the regalia.[44] Of the three objects that make up the modern imperial regalia, the sword seems to have been the earliest to appear as part of the transmission of rulership. Its significance stemmed from the *Kojiki*, which describes it as the sword used by Susanoo. After Susanoo gave the sword to his sister Amaterasu, it passed down through her descendants and was eventually housed in the Atsuta shrine in Owari. The mirror, said to be given by Amaterasu to her descendants, appeared in the sixth century alongside a sword in records of kingly accession; the original was kept in the shrine to the goddess at Ise. According to the Taihō Code, these two insignia were handed to the new ruler by a ritual specialist. The jewel (*magatama*), cited as part of the imperial regalia in the *Kojiki*, did not appear in the Taihō Code, perhaps because of opposition by the Inbe, a ritual specialist *uji*, or descent group. Added to the accession ritual after the Nakatomi became the dominant ritual specialists at court, the jewel was the only object of the three used in the accession rite that was not a duplicate.

The imperial ancestral cult centered on Amaterasu no mikami was itself a creation of the formative state-building period. Some scholars attribute the process by which the original ancestral (male) deity of the Yamato house, Takamimusubi, was replaced by the female sun goddess to influence from the Korean peninsula, where sun worship was common. Others suggest that Daoist ideas identifying a region to the east of the continent, Penglai, as the abode of the immortals influenced the relocation of the deity from the interior to Ise.[45] The division of Ise worship into rituals at inner and outer shrines, and the designation of women in the imperial descent line as priestesses at Ise, took place in the last three decades of the seventh century.

At the same time, older rites were "reformulated and staged as a celebration of the emperor's privileged relationship with the Sun Goddess, Amaterasu."[46] The transfer of imperial regalia was followed by the *Daijōsai* (大嘗祭, literally "great feast"), which reflected a merger of a celebration of first fruits with a ceremony of submission. A new ceremony sacrificed to the *kami* of Heaven and Earth.[47] During the thirteenth century, Buddhist esoteric rites entered imperial accession

[44] Ooms, *Imperial Politics*, p. 124. See p. 123, where Ooms observes that none of the imperial regalia are mentioned in the *Nihon shoki*.
[45] Matsumae, "Early Kami Worship," pp. 348–49; see Senda, *Ise jingū*, chapter 2.
[46] Breen and Teeuwen, "Introduction," p. 6.
[47] Ooms, *Imperial Politics*, pp. 55–58. According to Ooms, p. 128, the *magatama* (jewel) was first mentioned only in the ninth century. He ascribes the dispute on whether there were two or three imperial regalia to a competition between two rival lineages of ritual specialists: see pp. 127–29.

ceremonies.[48] The rituals tying the imperial family to the Amaterasu cult were not performed in the fifteenth century, when civil war devastated the imperial capital, Kyoto, and the Jingikan buildings and shrines were destroyed by fire. During the sixteenth and seventeenth centuries, Shinto shrines were highly localized, and state rituals were not continuously performed by the court.[49] The accession rites became prominent again in the second half of the nineteenth century, after the Meiji Restoration.

The accession ritual as performed after 1868 continued to be divided into several parts. The *sokui no rei* 即位之禮, in which the new emperor ascends the throne to receive the acclamation (and implicit submission) of his officials and subjects, features many elements borrowed from the Chinese model. The name of the hall in which the event takes place, for example, the Shishinden 紫宸殿, refers to the cosmic symbolism, centered on the pole star, which produced the Chinese name for Peking's imperial palace compound, *Zijincheng* 紫禁城 (literally, "purple forbidden city").[50] Even though the primary origins of the other major ritual, the *Daijōsai*, are resolutely indigenous, the one-year interval between the two rituals marked by national mourning, seems to have been a seventh-century adaptation to Chinese practice.[51]

Japan continued to incorporate elements from continental Asia into its distinctive religious practice. Medieval Japanese patronage of Buddhism focused on rituals to protect the ruler and the country commenced in the middle of the eighth century with the construction of the massive Tōdaiji in Nara. The court commissioned Tendai, Shingon, and even Zen Buddhist rites invoking the Buddhas to bring long life to emperors, ensure victory in battle, and alleviate natural disasters and drought. Annual performances of esoteric Buddhist rituals aimed at protecting the emperor, and by extension the country, continue even today.[52] During

---

[48] Allan G. Grapard, "Of Emperors and Foxy Ladies," *Cahiers d'Extrême-Asie* 13 (2002–3): 134–43.

[49] See Maeda, "Imperial Authority and Local Shrines."

[50] Holtom, *Japanese Enthronement*, p. 59. For a discussion of the Chinese symbolic system, see Jeffrey F. Meyer, *The Dragons of Tiananmen: Beijing as a Sacred City* (Columbia, S.C: University of South Carolina Press, 1991), p. 36.

[51] Holtom, *Japanese Enthronement*, p. 48; on the *daijōsai*, see Robert S. Ellwood, *The Feast of Kingship: Accession Ceremonies in Ancient Japan* (Tokyo: Sophia University Press, 1973).

[52] Naoki Kōjirō, trans. Felicia G. Bock, "The Nara State," in *The Cambridge History of Japan*, vol. I, pp. 254–58; Fabio Rambelli, "The Emperor's New Robes: Processes of Resignification in Shingon Imperial Rituals," *Cahiers d'Extrême-Asie* 13 (2002–3): 427–53, focuses on the Second Week Imperial Ritual (*goshichinichi no mishuhō*), a standard court ritual of imperial empowerment performed from 835 until the fourteenth century, which was revived by the Tokugawa in 1625, abolished in the 1870s, revived in 1883 and performed until 1945, then revived again in 1968 and performed to this day. Another

the period of internal dissension within the ruling house known as the Northern and Southern dynasties (1336–92), the *daijōsai* rituals were replaced with a Buddhist accession ritual, the *sokui kanjō* 即位灌頂; this Buddhist rite continued to be performed at Japanese accessions until 1847.[53]

Self-deification in Japan

From the eighth century onward, imperial and aristocratic patronage of Buddhism produced a Shinto–Buddhist syncretism that incorporated *kami* as emanations of Buddhist deities in *mandalas* and other religious objects at Kasuga and other cultic centers.[54] The imperial court brought shrines dedicated to *ujigami*, the tutelary deities of aristocratic lineages, under its aegis and standardized the ritual code. In the Kamakura period (1183–1333), new salvationist schools of Buddhism gained a mass following, gradually supplanting older esoteric Buddhist sects. By the early modern period, Japanese Buddhist temples served believers in an evolving ancestral cult, acting as religious specialists in funerary rites in a cultural specialization that persists to the present.

According to Bitō Masahide, doctrinal developments in Buddhist (Ryōbu) Shinto and Yoshida Shinto promoted the notion that *hotoke* 佛 (literally, Buddhas; the state attained by individuals after death) and *kami* (神, gods) were fundamentally the same, and led to acceptance of the possibility that humans with "extraordinary ability and accomplishments" could become *kami*.[55] This was the doctrinal basis on which Oda Nobunaga established himself as a deity. After fighting his way to Kyoto, Nobunaga did not attempt to become shogun. Instead, he "restored" Ashikaga Yoshiaki to the shogunal post, but set up mechanisms to bypass Yoshiaki in decision-making. In 1578, he resigned the court titles awarded by the emperor, and before his death in 1582, he ordered that he be worshipped above all Buddhas in a special temple at his

esoteric protective ritual, the *Daigensui no mishuhō*, followed the same performance history until 1945, when it was abolished.

[53] Michio Kamikawa, "Accession Rituals and Buddhism in Medieval Japan," *Japanese Journal of Religious Studies* 17.3/4 (1990): 243–80.

[54] For a sample list of the equivalences between Buddhist and Shinto deities, see Elizabeth ten Grotenhuis, *Japanese Mandalas: Representations of Sacred Geography* (Honolulu: University of Hawai'i Press, 1999), pp. 146–47; see Allan G. Grapard, *The Protocol of the Gods: A Study of the Kasuga Cult in Japanese History* (Berkeley: University of California Press, 1992).

[55] Bitō Masahide, "Thought and Religion: 1550–1700," in *The Cambridge History of Japan*, vol. IV: *Early Modern Japan*, ed. John Whitney Hall (Cambridge: Cambridge University Press, 1991), p. 394. On *hotoke* and *kami*, see Robert J. Smith, *Ancestor Worship in Contemporary Japan* (Stanford: Stanford University Press, 1974), chapter 2.

new castle of Azuchi, where worshippers would receive wealth, descendants, long life, and health.[56]

Nobunaga's posthumous deification was replicated by Hideyoshi in 1599. A self-made man, Hideyoshi was enshrined as Toyokuni daimyōjin 豐國大明神 (Great august deity of the east); Bitō interprets his deification as the equivalent of creating "an *ujigami* (氏神) protector of his house."[57] Hideyoshi thus became the tutelary deity of his own descent line, the Japanese equivalent of the focal ancestor of a descent line. In the same vein, Ieyasu was enshrined as Tōshō Daigongen 東照大觀現 (Great incarnation shining over the east) and enshrined at Nikkō.[58] Tōshōgū shrines were also erected at the shogun's palace in Edo, and in the residences of the three main collateral branches of the Tokugawa descent line.[59] The observances on the twenty-first, twenty-fifth, and thirty-third anniversaries of Ieyasu's death were especially elaborate, building, according to Sonehara Satoshi, a ritual edifice for the idea that shogun and emperor together form a public authority 公武正權 which transcends private interest.[60]

In the 1630s to 1660s, the Tokugawa shogunate developed a system of temple registration that favored Buddhist rituals and de-legitimized self-deification, but the precedent set by Nobunaga, Hideyoshi, and Ieyasu prompted at least fifteen daimyo to follow suit with Shinto burials and *kami* titles obtained from Yoshida Shinto.[61] Scholars have argued over whether such attempts to expand their own symbolic capital created "personality cults" around still living leaders.[62] The prime example is

---

[56] Smith, *Ancestor Worship*, pp. 29–39. William Coaldrake, *Architecture and Authority in Japan* (London: Routledge, 1996), pp. 106–19, analyzes Azuchi Castle as "the embodiment of Nobunaga's personal power" and "the revelation of the inner workings of his ambition" (p. 106). Azuchi was the prototype of the castles built later by Hideyoshi and Tokugawa Ieyasu.

[57] Bitō, "Thought and Religion," p. 395. *Ujigami* were deities who watched over a particular clan or descent group.

[58] Bitō, "Thought and Religion," pp. 393–95; Herman Ooms, *Tokugawa Ideology: Early Constructs, 1570–1680* (Princeton: Princeton University Press, 1985), pp. 49–50, 58–62. W. J. Boot, "The Death of a Shogun: Deification in Early Modern Japan," in *Shinto in History*, ed. Breen and Teeuwen, pp. 144–66.

[59] Boot, "Death of a Shogun," p. 160. Luke S. Roberts, *Performing the Great Peace: Political Space and Open Secrets in Tokugawa Japan* (Honolulu: University of Hawai'i Press, 2012), p. 143, notes that Ieyasu's successors Hidetada and Iemitsu were also enshrined at Nikkō.

[60] Sonehara Satoshi, "Tokugawa Ieyasu nenki kōji ni arawareta shinkoku isshiki – Iemitsu ki wo taisō to shite" (The divine country consciousness revealed in commemoration of Tokugawa Ieyasu's death day – focusing on the Iemitsu period), *Nihonshi kenkyū* 510 (2004): 92–119.

[61] Roberts, *Performing the Great Peace*, chapter 5.

[62] Herman Ooms, *Charismatic Bureaucrat: A Political Biography of Matsudaira Sadanobu, 1758–1829* (Chicago: University of Chicago Press, 1975), pp. 43–45, 60–61. For a critique of Ooms' position, which is based on the scholarship of Asao Naohiro,

Matsudaira Sadanobu (1758–1829) senior councillor to shogun Ienari (1787–1837). Born into a collateral shogunal house, Sadanobu was appointed the daimyo of Shirakawa in 1783. At that point the domain "was on the brink of famine: cash and food reserves were extremely low; two months earlier, the peasants had staged a destructive riot in the castle town, protesting high rice prices; and retainers' stipends had been reduced to help meet the crisis situation."[63] In autumn 1784, despite food shortages, Sadanobu installed "a wooden image" and objects that had belonged to the founder of his house, Sadatsuna, in a shrine in the castle, together with a copy of the house rules and his pledge to fulfill his obligations as adoptive heir. Granted the title *Chinkoku daimyōjin* (Great Deity of the Pacified Land) in 1792 by the Yoshida house, which headed the Shinto establishment, he later performed daily rituals to a wooden effigy of himself.[64] Sadanobu declared himself to be a follower of "the Way of *Shinbu* 神武, an amalgam of Shinto and the martial arts.[65] The Japanese religious culture of the time held out the possibility that humans, through mental techniques of self-cultivation, could achieve the transformation of the "human spirit" that constituted divinity. Ooms concludes, "This particular blend of the profane and the sacred must be understood within the context of Japan's indigenous religious mode of construing reality and human experience."[66]

Self-deification in one's lifetime was highly unusual, but not absent in continental traditions, which used Tibetan Buddhism's belief in emanations of bodhisattvas to the same purpose. The most notable artifacts that document this practice are the Qianlong era *tankas* (religious paintings) depicting the emperor himself as Manjusri, the Bodhisattva of Wisdom and Compassion.[67] These tankas were, however, not publicly distributed

see Boot, "Death of a Shogun," pp. 145–46. Boot challenges the veracity of the Portuguese source for Oda's deification, but goes back to the deification of Fujiwara no Kamatari (614–69), indicating a much longer historical span in which the practice occurred. The motivation, Boot insists, is not "to render absolute one's own authority over one's vassals" but rather to protect one's descendants (p. 158).

[63] Ooms, *Charismatic Bureaucrat*, p. 16.

[64] *Ibid.*, pp. 43–45. On the Yoshida house's integration of the Shinto establishment in the Edo period, see Hiromi Maeda, "Imperial Authority and Local Shrines," chapters 2 and 3.

[65] Fukaya Kentarō, *Matsudaira Sadanobu kō to keishin sonnō no kyōiku* (Matsudaira Sadanobu and education in revering the gods, respecting the emperor) (Tokyo: Hokkai shuppansha, 1931), with thanks to Naoko Gunji for sharing her research on Sadanobu and this specific reference. Fukaya also stresses Sadanobu's deep knowledge of and commitment to Shingon Buddhism.

[66] Ooms, *Charismatic Bureaucrat*, p. 44.

[67] Rawski, *Last Emperors*, pp 262–63; Patricia Berger, *Empire of Emptiness: Buddhist Art and Political Authority in Qing China* (Honolulu: University of Hawai'i Press, 2003), pp. 58–61; David Farquhar "Emperor as Bodhisattva in the Governance of the Qing Empire," *Harvard Journal of Asiatic Studies* 38 (1978): 5–34.

but probably viewed by a select few who had access to chapels in the Dalai Lama's palace in Lhasa or the emperor's private chapels in the Forbidden City.

Rhetoric linking the leader to cosmic forces was another practice that the sixteenth-century unifiers of Japan adopted for themselves. Alongside *kōgi* 公儀 (literally, "public affairs"), Oda Nobunaga and Hideyoshi appealed to *tenka* 天下 (all under Heaven, C. *tianxia*).[68] After capturing Kyoto, Nobunaga changed his official seal to read *tenka fubu* 天下布武 (covering all under Heaven with military might). His successor, Hideyoshi, talked of himself as the instrument of *tendō* (天道, literally the Way of Heaven). Adopting the language of Chinese dynastic founders, he wrote that "the sun had entered his breast when he was born, thus predestining him to rule East and West."[69] *Tōshōgū goikun* (東照宮御遺訓, Venerable testament of Ieyasu), published during the rule of the third shogun, Iemitsu, also presented the Tokugawa shogunate as "an embodiment of *tendō*, the Way of Heaven."[70] Heaven entrusted Ieyasu with the administration of the realm and would continue to support him only as long as he ruled in accordance with *tendō*, i.e. Ieyasu had received the Mandate from Heaven, not from the emperor. Vassals who had sworn loyalty to Ieyasu were thus obeying "*tenmei*, Heaven's Mandate."[71]

Korean state ritual: discourse on identity

The first rituals practiced in the Korean peninsula were to ancestors and nature deities.[72] Like their Japanese counterparts, the rulers of Silla were simultaneously shamanic priests; the gold crowns found in Silla royal tombs "were worn ... as the sign of the chief shaman of the kingdom."[73] Buddhism was introduced in the late fourth century into Koguryŏ and Paekche from regimes ruling north China, including the Northern Wei (386–534), founded by the Tuoba, a Turkic group descended from the Xianbei. In the Northern Wei and its successor states, Buddhist clerics worked closely with the rulers on state affairs. It was this tradition, rather

---

[68] Ooms, *Tokugawa Ideology*, p. 27. According to Roberts, *Performing the Great Peace*, p. 11, the most common term for the shogunate in the Edo period was *kogi* 公儀, 公義, and the shogun often referred to himself as *kubō*, 公方. Roberts also notes, p. 13, that *kuni* could refer to domains, all of which were subsumed under *tenka*, which denoted all of Japan.

[69] Ooms, *Tokugawa Ideology*, p. 45.   [70] *Ibid.*, p. 65.   [71] *Ibid.*, p. 67.

[72] Chu-kun Chang, "An Introduction to Korean Shamanism," and "Some Correlations between the Ancient Religions of Japan and Korea," in *Shamanism: The Spirit World of Korea*, ed. Richard W. I. Guisso and Chai-shin Yu (Berkeley: Asian Humanities Press, 1988), pp. 30–51, 52–59. Also Na Hwira, "Kodae Han'guk ŭi syamanichŭmjŏk segegwan kwa pulkyojŏk isang sege" (The ancient Korean shamanistic worldview and the Buddhist ideal world), *Han'guk kodaesa yŏn'gu* 20 (2000): 197–249.

[73] Chang, "Introduction to Korean Shamanism," p. 31.

than the philosophically oriented Buddhism of south China, that was taken up by the Koreans.[74]

Silla was the first to appoint a Buddhist National Patriarch (*kukt'ong* 國統), in the late sixth century. This was the forerunner of the State Preceptor (國師, K. *kuksa*), a post established in the late seventh century.[75] The blending of Buddhist and indigenous beliefs that characterized the period is documented in the will of King Munmu (r. 661–681), who broke with tradition when he asked to be cremated in the "Indian style" after he died.[76] Instead of being interred in a tumulus, as was customary, Munmu's ashes were scattered in the East Sea to facilitate his promise that "in the next life he would become a dragon that would protect and serve the Buddhadharma."[77]

Buddhism in medieval Korea depended on royal patronage which peaked in the Koryŏ period, when "more Buddhist rituals were held ... than at any other time in Korean history."[78] The most frequently scheduled ritual from the eleventh to the early fourteenth century was the *sojae toryang* 消災道場, which sought Buddha's intercession in natural calamities: earthquakes, strong winds, and floods as well as protection from foreign invasion and the long life of the king.[79] It was held almost once a year in the Kojong reign (1213–1259), and twice in 1254, during the Mongol invasions which brought Koryŏ into the Mongol empire.[80] The next most frequently performed rite was the Humane Kings Assembly, *Inwang toryang* 仁王道場, based on the *Scripture for Humane Kings*, a ritual first held at the Silla court in the middle of the sixth century

---

[74] Lewis R. Lancaster, "Introduction," in *Buddhism in Koryŏ: A Royal Religion*, ed. Lewis R. Lancaster, Kikun Suh and Chai-shin Yu (Berkeley: University of California Institute of East Asian Studies, 1996), pp. xi–xv. On the northern and southern Buddhist traditions that developed after the fall of the Han dynasty, see Kenneth Ch'en, *Buddhism in China: A Historical Survey* (Princeton: Princeton University Press, 1964), chapters 5, 6, and 7.

[75] Hŭng-sik Hŏ, "Buddhism and Koryŏ Society," in *Buddhism in Koryŏ*, pp. 4–6; Sang-hyun Kim, "Buddhism and the State in Middle and Late Silla," in *State and Society in Middle and Late Silla*, ed. Richard D. McBride II (Cambridge, MA: Harvard University Korea Institute, 2010), p. 129.

[76] Sang-hyun Kim, "Buddhism and the State," p. 135.   [77] *Ibid.*, pp. 134–35.

[78] Jongmyung Kim, "Buddhist Rituals in Medieval Korea (918–1392)," PhD thesis, UCLA, 1994, p. xiii. Kim Ch'ŏl'ung, "Koryŏ kukka chesa ŭi cheje wa kŭ t'ŭkching" (The organization and characteristics of Koryŏ state rites), *Han'guksa yŏn'gu* 118 (2002): 135–60. Buddhist death rituals continued to be performed by families in early Chosŏn: see Ch'oe Chaebok, "Chosŏn ch'ogi kuksan esŏ 49chae sŏlhaeng kwa pyŏnhwa" (The forty-nine days of abstinence and changes in state mourning in early Chosŏn), *Chosŏn sidaesa hakpo* 19 (2001): 5–28.

[79] Jongmyung Kim, "Buddhist Rituals in Medieval Korea," table 5, p. 88 and pp. 89–94.

[80] *Ibid.*, p. 95. Kim's table 5, p. 88 and table 6, p. 105, however, show that neither the *sojae toryang* nor the *Inwang toryang* was performed in 990 during the Liao invasion which forced Koryŏ into vassalage.

and probably also performed in Koguryŏ.[81] In Korea as in Japan, the ritual sought to protect the state and to respond to comets and other astronomical phenomena. After the kingdom joined the Mongol empire between the thirteenth and fourteenth centuries, Korean Buddhism was also influenced by the tantric/esoteric schools favored by the Mongols.[82]

Confucianism in Korea

Knowledge of Confucian doctrines came relatively early to the Korean peninsula.[83] By the middle of the fourth century AD, when Silla, Paekche, and Koguryŏ emerged as "centralized aristocratic states" on the Korean peninsula, the elites of these societies already had a writing system based on Chinese characters and were acquainted with Chinese Confucian texts. Conflict with Chinese regimes "did not diminish the ardor of the Korean states for the introduction of Chinese culture."[84] Koguryŏ established a National Confucian Academy 太學 in 372 with a curriculum that included the Five Classics. Despite the promulgation of Chinese-style legal codes in the three kingdoms,[85] Buddhism overshadowed interest in Confucian doctrines for a long period. Not until the fifteenth century did the royal court consciously adopt a policy that favored Confucian studies. The long delay in elite commitment to Confucian principles – specialists argue that the Confucianization of Korean society was not completed until the seventeenth century – may help to explain the prominence of ritual controversies throughout the seventeenth and eighteenth centuries.[86]

Nonetheless, some state rituals built on the Chinese model were performed during the Koryŏ period.[87] In 1114 and 1116, as the Jurchen leader Aguda defeated Liao forces and declared himself master of the northeast, Song Huizong (r. 1000–1125) sent 167 musical instruments

---

[81] *Ibid.*, pp. 101–2.

[82] D. Robinson, *Empire's Twilight*, pp. 65–66, 121–22; Henrik H. Sørensen, "Lamaism in Korea during the Late Koryŏ Dynasty," *Korea Journal* 33.3 (1993): 67–81.

[83] In this section, we take the perspective of the Korean historical actors in using "Confucian" to denote the complex of ritual practices embodied in Chinese ritual handbooks, regardless of their origin, a problem discussed earlier in this chapter.

[84] Lee, *New History*, p. 46.   [85] *Ibid.*, pp. 58–59.

[86] Martina Deuchler, *The Confucian Transformation of Korea: A Study of Society and Ideology* (Cambridge, MA: Council on East Asian Studies, Harvard University, 1992). See also her essay, "The Practice of Confucianism: Ritual and Order in Chosŏn Dynasty Korea," in *Rethinking Confucianism: Past and Present in China, Japan, Korea, and Vietnam*, ed. Benjamin A. Elman, John B. Duncan, and Herman Ooms (Los Angeles: UCLA International Institute, 2002), pp. 292–334 on the efforts to extend Confucian norms to the villagers.

[87] Kim Ch'ŏl'ung, "Koryŏ kukka chesa."

and music books to the Koryŏ court, seeking allies against the Liao, who had forced Song to agree to the Treaty of Shanyuan (1005).[88] Chinese ritual music is said to have been performed in the Royal Ancestral Shrine, one of the major state altars, but the instruments and ritual paraphernalia were largely destroyed when the Red Turbans sacked the central capital, Kaesŏng, in 1361. Despite the arrival of new instruments sent in 1370 by the Ming Hongwu emperor, ritual music (and probably the rituals themselves) were in "a sorry state" at the start of the Chosŏn dynasty: "the original music had been ... mixed with native *hyang'ak* (Korean music), the ensembles had been altered, the instruments had been destroyed, and the performance tradition interrupted."[89]

Chosŏn Confucianists focused on ritual issues at the beginning of the dynasty, citing different texts for their positions. When Chŏng Tojŏn (1342–1398), a major advisor to the Chosŏn founder, Yi Sŏnggye, attacked the Buddhist establishment and outlined the structure of a new government that incorporated principles from the Confucian classic, the *Rituals of Zhou* (*Zhou li*),[90] he began a tradition in which proponents of governmental reform drew directly for inspiration on the ancient canonical text. Zhu Xi's commentaries, however, dominated Chosŏn Confucian studies through the sixteenth century.[91] Doctrinal differences separating individuals often cleaved along kinship and regional lines.[92]

Standardizing the rites: debating the sacrifice to Heaven

Codification and systematization of the state rituals began in the reign of King Sejong (1418–1450), who commissioned scholars to consult

---

[88] Denis Twitchett and Klaus-Peter Tietze, "The Liao," in *The Cambridge History of China*, vol. VI, pp. 100–11; Robert C. Provine, *Essays on Sino-Korean Musicology: Early Sources for Korean Ritual Music* (Seoul: Il Ji Sa, 1988), pp. 8–9.

[89] Provine, *Essays on Sino-Korean Musicology*, p. 11. The move toward Chinese-type state rituals is described in Han Ugŭn, "Chosŏn wangjo ch'ogi e issŏsŏ ŭi Yugyo inyŏm ŭi silch'ŏn kwa sin'ang, chonggyo chesa munje rŭl chungsim ŭro" (The implementation of Confucian concepts, beliefs and religion in the early Chosŏn – focusing on ritual issues) *Han'guk saron* 3 (1976): 147–228.

[90] Chai-sik Chung, "Chŏng Tojon: 'Architect' of Yi Dynasty Government and Ideology," in *The Rise of Neo-Confucianism in Korea*, ed. William T. de Bary and JaHyun Kim Haboush (New York: Columbia University Press, 1985), pp. 59–88.

[91] William T. de Bary, "Introduction," in *Rise of Neo-Confucianism in Korea*, pp. 1–53; JaHyun Kim Haboush, "Yun Hyu and the Search for Dominance: a Seventeenth-Century Korean Reading of the *Offices of Zhou* and the *Rituals of Zhou*," in *Statecraft and Classical Learning: The "Rituals of Zhou" in East Asian History*, ed. Benjamin A. Elman and Martin Kern (Leiden: E. J. Brill, 2010), pp. 309–29.

[92] Lee, *New History*, pp. 221–22; for a parallel analysis of Chinese Confucian schools, see Benjamin A. Elman, *Classicism, Politics, and Kinship: The Ch'ang-chou School of New Text Confucianism in Late Imperial China* (Berkeley: University of California Press, 1990).

Chinese ritual books in order to compile an authoritative and comprehensive ritual code for the kingdom. The code was organized according to the Chinese five-fold categories by officials appointed to the Chiphyŏnjŏn (集賢殿, Hall of Worthies) by virtue of their examination success and superior literary skills. Rites Minister Hŏ Cho (1369–1429) consulted the *Zhou li* (Rites of Zhou), the Tang period ritual code, (*Da Tang*) *Kaiyuan li* (Rites of the Tang Kaiyuan reign, 732) and the *Hongwu lizhi* (洪武禮制, Ritual code of the Hongwu reign) in compiling the first section of the *Orye ŭiju* 五禮儀注 (Five rites) in 1415, which outlined the "auspicious rites," those comprising the most important state sacrifices.[93] The second section covering the other four kinds of state rituals was not completed until 1444–51. A revision of this new ritual code, entitled *Kukcho orye ŭi* (The dynastic five rites), appeared in 1474.[94]

In keeping with the Confucian emphasis on the construction of a cosmic order through ritual enactment, the *Kukcho orye ŭi* presented only those rituals which the ruler of a vassal state could perform. As in China, the highest order of "grand sacrifice" 大祀, was "auspicious rites" 吉禮, but the Korean ritual handbook omitted the sacrifice to Heaven during the winter solstice and the sacrifice to Earth during the summer solstice, rituals that were monopolized by the emperor.[95]

The compilation of a state ritual code was intended to unify and systematize the various rituals that had been performed during the Koryŏ and into the first decades of the Chosŏn dynasty. Almost immediately, fifteenth-century ritual specialists drew attention to a major problem: how could Chosŏn (and indeed Koryŏ) profess to be tribute vassals, yet perform the sacrifices on the "Round Altar" (圓丘 K. Wŏn'gu, C. Yuanqiu), i.e. the sacrifice to Heaven, which only the "Son of Heaven," the Chinese emperor, could perform?

---

[93] Kim Haeyŏng, *Chosŏn ch'ogi chesa chŏllye yŏn'gu* (Research on the sacrificial rituals in early Chosŏn) (Seoul: Chimmundang, 2003), chapter 1, discusses the sources for the *Orye ŭiju;* see chapter 3 for a detailed discussion of the contents of this work. Yi Wŏnjae and Kim Songhŭi, "Chosŏn ch'ogi ŭi Yugyo chŏk kukka ŭirye taehan yŏn'gu – oryeŭi ŭiryegwan ŭl chungsim ŭro – " (Research on Confucian state rites in early Chosŏn, focusing on the ritual officials of the 'Five Rites'), *Han'guk sasang sahak* 10 (1998): 31–63.

[94] Yi Wŏnjae and Kim Songhŭi, "Chosŏn ch'ogi ŭi Yugyo," pp. 34–37; Yi Pŏmjik, "Kukjo orye'ŭi ŭi songnip e taehan il koch'al" (An investigation of the establishment of the *Gukjo orye'ŭi*), *Yŏksa hakpo* 122 (1989): 1–27; Yi Yŏngch'un, "Chosŏn hugi ŭi sajŏn ŭi chaepyŏn kwa kukka chesa" (The revision of the ritual code and state sacrifices in late Chosŏn), *Han'guksa yŏn'gu* 118 (2002): 195–219 studies the eighteenth century further revision of the ritual code.

[95] *Kukcho oryeŭi* (The dynastic five rites), 1474. Reprint edn. (Seoul: Muchang munhwasa, 1994), *juan* 卷 1, can be compared with *Qinding Da Qing huidian*, 26.6b.

Chinese precedents and Koryŏ state rituals

The Round Altar is first cited in the *Rites of Zhou* as the site of a sacrifice to Heaven during the winter solstice. Balancing the sacrifice to Heaven was the square altar, *Fangqiu*, which was dedicated to a sacrifice to Earth, performed at the summer solstice. What came to be known as the suburban sacrifices became important in the Han dynasty, after Confucianism was adopted as state doctrine. Altars were established in the Former Han capital, Chang'an, but the sacrifices were not regularly performed. In the Later Han (25–220 AD), however, it became customary for the emperor to personally sacrifice to Heaven.[96]

Many states that rose and fell in the period after the fall of the Han dynasty and before the reunification by Sui performed the sacrifice to Heaven at a round altar. The specific ritual practices carried out by Sui and later Tang were those of the regimes located in north China, but ritual reforms enacted in the middle of the seventh century broke with the northern ritual tradition in dispensing with the multiple deities worshipped at the round altar and reinstalling Haotian shangdi 昊天上帝 as the object of the sacrifice. Haotian shangdi also became the deity to whom prayers for good harvests were directed.

The *(Da Tang) Kaiyuan li*, the source consulted by the Korean officials who compiled the Chosŏn ritual code, outlined a ritual system which had substantively changed from the one in place when the Tang state was first established. Worship of Haotian shangdi stood at the pinnacle of the state rites, above the formerly preeminent ancestral rites.[97] Ideologically, a new emperor, "to express fully the legitimate nature of his power," had to personally perform the sacrifices to Heaven and Earth at the suburban altars shortly after ascending the throne. The emperor's sacrifices symbolically linked Heaven, Earth, and Man, while they also proved his "fitness to rule as the man who could ... show the unity of Heaven and Earth."[98]

Performing the sacrifice to Heaven was from ancient times associated with kingship. Popular acceptance of the Mandate of Heaven concept reinforced the connection, such that the founder of the Ming dynasty made it a test of his legitimacy:[99]

[96] Wechsler, *Offerings of Jade and Silk*, chapter 5, "The Suburban Sacrifices and the Cult of Heaven."

[97] Wechsler, *Offerings of Jade and Silk*, pp. 40–54.

[98] Quote from Angela R. Zito, "Re-Presenting Sacrifice: Cosmology and the Editing of Texts," *Ch'ing-shih wen-t'i* 5.2 (1984): 52. See also Angela Zito, *Of Body and Brush: Grand Sacrifice as Text/Performance in Eighteenth-Century China* (Chicago: University of Chicago Press, 1997), chapter 5, "Sacrificial Spaces: Contextualizing the City."

[99] Passages taken from Romeyn Taylor, "Official and Popular Religion and the Political Organization of Chinese Society in the Ming," in *Orthodoxy in Late Imperial China*, ed. Kwang-ching Liu (Berkeley: University of California Press, 1990), pp. 137–38.

On 12 January, eleven days after his enthronement, T'ai-tsu told his officials that on the twenty-third he would offer a sacrifice and make an announcement to *Shang-ti* and *Hou-t'u* (Empress Earth). If the gods accepted his assumption of imperial rule, they would draw near and cause the heaven to be clear and the *ch'i* to be pure, but if they opposed it, they would show their displeasure by fierce winds and unnatural darkness. From the tenth of January to the twentieth, it was raining and snowing under dark skies, but beginning at daybreak of the twentieth the snow let up for three days . . . Early on the twenty-third at the moment of the sacrifice, the heavens were untroubled and the stars and planets were clearly seen. All those present were filled with joy.

Even though the Veritable Records, the source for this passage, cites only Hongwu's sacrifice to Heaven in 1368, the ritual was embedded in a balanced cosmological framework that is outlined in the following passage:[100]

The Sacrifices to Heaven and Earth were a matched pair of ceremonies, one occurring at the Round Mound . . . the other at the Square Pool to the north. These shapes reflected the traditional belief that the Heavens were round and the Earth Square . . . the two sacrifices divided the year in two: at the winter solstice, when yin influence had maximized, the Sacrifice to Heaven was performed to boost the cosmos into its yang phase. At mid-summer, at the summer solstice, the cosmos was again eased into its yin phase with the performance of the Sacrifice to Earth. This pair of Grand Sacrifices explicitly maintained the cosmic social order.

In 1377, the altars to Heaven and Earth were merged, and sacrifice took place within a Great Sacrificial Hall in a combined early spring rite. That innovation was rejected by the Jiajing emperor (r. 1522–66), who ordered that the earlier open-air round and square altars be rebuilt for separate seasonal sacrifice.[101] The Qing continued to sacrifice at the Altar to Heaven, renamed Tiantan 天壇, until it was enlarged in the Qianlong reign (1736–95).

The *Kaiyuan li* presented the sacrifice to Heaven and Earth as the prerogative of the emperor who was *primus inter pares* in a Sinocentric world order: sacrifice at the winter and summer solstices fulfilled the emperor's cosmic role as Son of Heaven. Koryŏ's enactment of rites at the Round Altar expressed its position outside that order. Although Koryŏ engaged in the tribute–trade system with Song, the geopolitical circumstances of the time hindered the cultivation of close relations.

See Marcel Granet, trans. Maurice Freedman *The Religion of the Chinese People* (Oxford: Blackwell, 1975), p. 112, on the worship of Heaven: "Its cult was reserved to the suzerain."

[100] Zito, *Of Body and Brush*, pp. 125, 126–27.

[101] Taylor, "Official and Popular Religion," pp. 138–40; also Meyer, *Dragons of Tiananmen*, chapter 3.

When the Koryŏ state was established in 918, China was still divided into regional states, a political situation that is best described by the period's designation as the Five Dynasties and Ten Kingdoms.[102] During this period, Koryŏ allied with the regimes that had come to power in north China. It adopted the Song calendar, symbolizing its acceptance of status as a tribute vassal and exchanged embassies from 968 to 1020.[103] Embassies were exchanged in the second half of the eleventh century, but the envoys had to take the maritime route to coastal ports in Zhejiang because the overland route was controlled by the Khitan Liao, who subjugated Koryŏ through a series of invasions in the 990s.[104] From the twelfth to the fourteenth century, Koryŏ was effectively under Jurchen Jin, then Mongol hegemony.

The unstable geopolitical conditions confronting Koryŏ and its neighbors may account for its relatively late participation in Chinese state rites. The "Rituals" section of the *Koryŏ sa* lists four altars receiving "Grand Sacrifice" 大祀: the Round Altar, Square Pool, Altar to Land and Grain, and the Ancestral Temple. The deity worshipped at the Round Altar was Haotian shangdi; the Koryŏ dynastic founder, T'aejo, and the emperors of the five directions (they had been part of the Chinese worship of Heaven until the middle of the seventh century ritual reforms) were also ancillary objects of sacrifice.[105]

Unlike the Tang or Song, the Koryŏ sacrifice to Haotian shangdi was not performed at the winter solstice. Sacrifices at the Round Altar were conducted by the king, who would pray for a good harvest in the first month of spring, and for rain in the first month of summer. The first sacrifice at the Round Altar took place in 983, but a government agency to supervise the rites was not instituted until the reign of Yejong (1105–1122), and a ritual code was not compiled until the production of the *Sangjŏng kogŭm yemun* (詳定古今禮文, Codified ancient and contemporary rites) in the 1160s.[106]

---

[102] See map 2, "The Five Dynasties and the Ten Kingdoms, 906–960," pp. 2–3 in *The Cambridge History of China*, vol. V, part 1: *The Sung Dynasty and Its Precursors, 907–1279*, ed. Denis Twitchett and Paul Jakov Smith (Cambridge: Cambridge University Press, 2009), pp. 2–3.

[103] Rogers, "National Consciousness in Medieval Korea," pp. 154–55, and his "Regularization of Koryŏ–Chin Relations," p. 51.

[104] Michael C. Rogers, "Sung–Koryŏ Relations: Some Inhibiting Factors," *Oriens* 11.1–2 (1958): 194–202.

[105] Kim Haeyŏng, *Chosŏn ch'ogi*, pp. 36–39.

[106] Kim Haeyŏng, *Chosŏn ch'ogi*, pp. 23–24, citing the *Koryŏ sa*; see also Provine, *Essays*, pp. 22–25 on this code, which is no longer extant.

Chosŏn: Confucianization of rites

In contrast to the Koryŏ, who had favored Buddhism and Buddhist rituals above all others, the men surrounding Yi Sŏnggye, the founder of the Chosŏn dynasty, proposed to replace the eclectic mixture of state rituals with a systematized ritual code based on the Chinese model.[107] Almost immediately, there were challenges to the Altars of Heaven and Earth that Koryŏ rulers had installed in the capital. A 1392 memorial by Chosŏn Minister of Rites Cho Bak stated, "The altar of Heaven ritual is where the Son of Heaven sacrifices to heaven; this should be abolished." A new dynasty, he said, should issue new regulations for the ordering of the state rites, which were an eclectic mix of shamanism, Daoist halls and exorcistic rituals, esoteric Buddhist rites, and sacrifices to city gods of different administrative units. The "erroneous" customs of the Koryŏ must be corrected; rulers might conduct non-Confucian rituals in their private sphere, but the state ritual system should be Confucian.[108]

Cho Bak's memorial strongly suggests that he thought the sacrifices to Heaven and to Earth directly contravened the regulations governing tribute vassals, since both Chosŏn and Koryŏ had submitted to the authority of Ming Taizu. T'aejo did not approve Cho Bak's request to abolish the Round Altar. In 1394, when he moved his capital from Kaesŏng to Hanyang, his new state altars conformed to Chinese spatial models, the Ancestral Temple being placed to the east of the Altar to Grain and the Harvest, south of the palace. A Round Altar must have been part of the new capital plan, since a 1394 memorial from the Rites Ministry requests that the name of the altar be changed to Wŏndan 圓壇, and later that the sacrificial music be reformed.[109]

---

[107] Even so, Daoist rites to pray for rain and in response to comets and unusual astral events were performed until the Sŏngjong reign (1469–94) and Buddhism continued to flourish, even though official control over monasteries and monastic power increased: See the table in fn 12, p. 167, in Yi Uk, "Chosŏn chŏngi Yugyo kukka ŭi sŏngnip kwa kukka chesa ŭi pyŏnhwa" (The establishment of a Confucian state in early Chosŏn and changes of the state sacrifices), *Han'guksa yŏn'gu* 118 (2002): 167. On Buddhism, see Ugŭn Han, "Policies Toward Buddhism in Late Koryŏ and Early Chosŏn," in *Buddhism in the Early Chosŏn*, pp. 1–58. Ch'oe Sŏnhye, "Chosŏn ch'ogi T'aejo, T'aejongdae ch'oje ŭi sihaeng wa wang kwŏn kanghwa" (The implementation of the *jiao* ritual during the T'aejo and T'aejong reigns in early Chosŏ and the strengthening of the royal prerogative), *Han'guk sasang sahak* 17 (2001): 359–93 argues that the Daoist rite allowed the king to perform rituals that his subordinate status as a tribute vassal otherwise prohibited; see also Kim Ch'ŏl'ung, "Chosŏn ch'o ŭi Togyo wa cho'rye" (Early Chosŏn Daoism and the ch'o rite), *Han'guk sasang sahak* 15 (2000): 359–93.

[108] Yi Uk, "Chosŏn chŏngi," p. 165. Han Hyŏngju, *Chosŏn ch'ogi kukka cherye yŏn'gu* (Research on state rites in early Chosŏn) (Seoul: Ilchogak, 2002), p. 22, records approval of the name change, but *sillok* records from the Sejong reign (1418–50) also refer to the Round Altar as the Wŏn'gu; see table 4, pp. 32–33.

[109] Han Hyŏngju, *Chosŏn ch'ogi*, table 3, p. 25; Yi Uk, "Chosŏn chŏngi," pp. 168–69.

Scholars who defended sacrifices at the Round Altar pointed to their use in prayers for rain. The *Veritable Records* for the T'aejo (1392–98) and T'aejong (1400–18) reigns show that prayers for rain were performed at the Wŏndan. A drought in 1398 elicited sacrifices for rain at the Ancestral Temple (Chongmyo 宗廟), the Altar for Grain and the Harvest (Sajik 社祭) and the Round Altar, listed in that order (Chinese records would have put the Round Altar first).[110] A prolonged drought in August 1406 shows that the king accepted the Confucian idea that his misdeeds had caused the problem. T'aejong cut down on royal meals, wine, and music and declared an amnesty. He consulted his officials: "Heaven's withholding of rain must be my fault." The king wept and asked the censors to point out imbalances in rewards and punishments, mistakes in personnel appointments, extravagance in dress and other royal misdeeds that might account for Heaven's displeasure.[111]

The prayers for rain at the Wŏndan followed the Chinese tradition practiced by Ming and Qing emperors. Confucians viewed drought as a clear sign of Heaven's displeasure with secular rule that called for acts of contrition, the exact opposite of what was required at the sacrifice to Heaven during the winter solstice, when the emperor and officials donned *chaofu* 朝服 (court dress), music was played, and sacrifices of oxen were burned, along with prayers at the altar of Heaven. Rites of penitence began with three days of abstinence by the emperor, princes, and ritual officials preceding the actual day of prayer; during this period it was forbidden for butchers to slaughter livestock. The emperor, wearing "plain clothes" (素服 *sufu*; also worn during mourning rituals) walked to the altar instead of being carried in a sedan chair. Such rituals eschewed display of imperial regalia, musical performance, and worship of ancillary objects.[112]

Prolonged droughts drove Qing emperors to abandon Confucian orthodoxy for whatever worked.[113] A similarly eclectic policy seems to have prevailed in early Chosŏn, which saw the king's performance at the Wŏndan as the last resort. From 1398 to 1418 officials were sent at least thirteen times to the Wŏndan to pray for rain, and on several other occasions to pray for a good harvest.[114]

---

[110] *T'aejo sillok*, T'aejo 7/4/21 #1; *T'aejong sillok*, T'aejong 5/5/8 #1.

[111] *T'aejong sillok*, T'aejong 6/7/23 #1.   [112] Rawski, *Last Emperors*, pp. 220–21.

[113] *Ibid.*, pp. 220–3. Rituals to bring rain were also carried out in localities; see Snyder-Reinke, *Dry Spells*.

[114] On prayers for rain at the Wŏndan, see *T'aejo sillok*, T'aejo 7/4/21#1, 7/4/27#1, *T'aejong sillok*, T'aejong 1/4/30#4, 5/5/8#1, 6/7/27#2, 7/5/26#2, 7/6/28#1,10/6/25#1, 12/4/7#1, 16/6/7#1, 17/i5/5#2, 17/i5/12#2, 18/7/1#1. On prayers at the Wŏndan for a good harvest, see *T'aejong sillok*, T'aejong 1/1/20#1, 4/1/9#2, and 6/1/10#1.

Some droughts elicited prayers for rain only at the altars to mountains and rivers. On other occasions, officials sacrificed at the Ancestral Temple and the Altar of Grain and Harvest.[115] The 1406 drought cited above inspired T'aejong to additionally summon shamans to pray for rain on August 11.[116] On August 13 the king not only sent an official to the Wŏndan to conduct the summer prayer for rain, but also ordered that Daoist altars be set up and dispatched provincial officials to pray at the local altars to mountains and rivers.[117] Two days later T'aejong broached the idea of going to the Wŏndan himself to conduct the prayer, but was persuaded to let his officials make one last attempt with a Daoist rite for rain. On August 20, with no relief in sight, the prayers for rain were again conducted at the Ancestral Temple, the altar for Land and Grain, the northern suburban altar, and the altar for mountains and rivers. Much to the king's relief, a "great rain" fell three days later, on August 23.[118]

Even so, no one could be certain exactly what divinity had actually brought the rain. Some believed it was due to the spiritual merit of a Buddhist priest named Chang Wŏnsim, who had acquired a widespread reputation for charitable works. The belief was that rain came in response to Chang's prayers at the Ch'ŏnhŭng temple; T'aejong responded with delight and rewarded Chang with gifts of cloth, rice, and beans.[119]

Sejong (r. 1418–50) followed the precedents set by T'aejong. During the three weeks from July 2 to July 23, 1425, Sejong focused on how to end a drought that was said to be the worst in twenty years.[120] Sejong publicly stated that the drought was a sign of Heaven's displeasure with his rule, and invited his ministers to suggest reforms.[121] He stopped the serving of wine in the palaces, cut down on his meals, curtailed his ordinary routines, and suspended large public works projects.[122] Daoist practitioners, shamans, and Buddhist priests of the Meditation (Sŏn) and Doctrine (Kyo) sects were summoned to pray for rain, and eventually the

---

[115] On sacrifices for rain at altars for mountains and rivers, see *T'aejo sillok*, T'aejo 7/4/19#1, 7/4/27#1; *T'aejong sillok*, T'aejong 6/7/25#1, 6/17/3#1. On sacrifices for rain at the Chongmyo and Sajik, *T'aejo sillok*, T'aejo 7/4/21 #1, 5/5/8#1, 6/7/25#1, 6/17/3#1.

[116] *T'aejong sillok*, T'aejong 6/7/25.   [117] *T'aejong sillok*, T'aejong 6/7/27#2.

[118] *T'aejong sillok*, T'aejong 6/7/29#3, 6/i7/3, 6/i7/6.

[119] *T'aejong sillok*, T'aejong 6/i7/6#4.

[120] *Sejong sillok*, Sejong 7/7/7#1. Han Hyŏngju, *Chosŏn ch'ogi*, table 4, pp. 32–33, lists entries in the *sillok* pertaining to the sacrifice to Heaven in 1419, 1423, 1425, 1426, 1427, 1430, 1431, 1439, 1443, and 1449. Of course, there are many entries pertaining to the ritual responses to the drought at other altars, as exemplified in the case of the 1425 drought.

[121] *Sejong sillok*, Sejong 7/6/17#4, 7/6/20#1, 7/6/23#4, and 7/7/7#1.

[122] On food restrictions, *Sejong sillok*, Sejong 7/6/18#4, 7/6/20#2. On restricting his normal schedule, *Sejong sillok*, Sejong 7/6/19#1. On halting public works, *Sejong sillok*, Sejong 7/6/21#1.

king himself performed the sacrifice at the Wŏndan.[123] Prayers were also offered at local altars of river and mountain deities and altars at Buddhist temples. Ordinary citizens were asked to gather at the village shrine 里社 to pray. Officials cited the Chinese work *Munhŏn tonggo* (文獻通考, C. *Wenxian tongkao*) which arrived in Chosŏn in 1419, as an authority to recommend closing the south gate (the *yang* direction) and opening the north gate to permit the *yin* influence to enter the capital city.[124] Rain fell in the southern provinces of Chŏlla and Kangwŏn on July 20, but the capital got no relief until the 22nd. When officials tried to congratulate Sejong for having persuaded Heaven to bring rain, the king answered that on the contrary, the rain was the result of the officials' concentrated efforts at contrition. He also rewarded the Daoists and all of the officials who had sacrificed at the state and local altars.

Each drought caused kings to ask their officials for remonstrance and instruction on how to correct the misrule that had incurred Heaven's wrath. Officials and kings drew from a wide and varied ritual repertoire with the sacrifice to Heaven often deployed as the last resort. One might argue that the prayer for rain at the Wŏndan did not therefore really constitute a symbolic challenge to the Chinese sacrifice to Heaven, since it was not performed at the winter solstice, nor at the beginning of a reign, much less the founding of a dynasty. The only exception to this generalization are the sacrifices at the Wŏndan from 1457 to 1462 by Sejo (r. 1455–68).

Sejo's performances of the sacrifice to Heaven helped him legitimize his usurpation of the throne. Acting as regent, Prince Suyang (the future Sejo) had dethroned his nephew Tanjong (1455) with the help of "disaffected elements among the literati."[125] Ruthlessly suppressing officials opposing the coup d'état, he applied for and obtained investiture from the Ming in 1456. In the interval between the coup d'état and the Ming investiture, Sejo sacrificed at the Royal Ancestral Temple (Chongmyo) to report his accession, after which he proceeded to the Kŭnjŏngjŏn 勤政殿, the hall where the Chosŏn kings were enthroned, to

---

[123] On Daoists, see *Sejong sillok*, Sejong 7/6/22#3, 7/6/25#1, 7/7/6#2, 7/7/8#1. On Buddhist clerics, see *Sejong sillok*, Sejong 7/7/2#4, 7/7/6#4. On shamans and female shamanesses, see *Sejong sillok*, Sejong 7/6/20#3, 7/6/21#2, 7/7/6#4. *Sejong sillok*, Sejong 7/6/19#3 notes that prayers for rain were regularly performed at the Chongmyo and the Sajik but should also be conducted at all of the other sites where prayers of rain were appropriate. The prayers at the Wŏndan are specifically cited in *Sejong sillok*, Sejong 7/6/19#4 which orders preparations for a ritual to be held on the first day of the seventh month (July 15, 1425). Sejong's personal participation in the prayer for rain at the Wŏndan occurred on the fourth day of the seventh lunar month (July 18): see *Sejong sillok*, Sejong 7/7/4#1=July 18, 1425; the text of the prayers to Haotian shangdi and the Five emperors is recorded in an entry dated Sejong 7/7/5#4.

[124] *Sejong sillok*, Sejong 7/6/20#3.   [125] Lee, *New History*, p. 173.

receive the congratulations of assembled officials. He sacrificed at the Sajik (Altar of Land and Grain) the next day.

Sejo first sacrificed to Heaven in 1457. On the fifteenth day of the first month (February 9 by the Western calendar), the king ascended the Wŏndan and performed the sacrifices to Heaven, Earth, and to the tablet of his ancestor, dynastic founder T'aejo. Sejo performed the three offerings; his crown prince performed the offerings for the deities of Great Ming and the Wind, Clouds, Thunder, and Rain, while Deliberative Councillor Chŏng Inji made the offerings to the tablets of the moon, the seas, mountain peaks, mountains, and rivers.[126]

That Sejo modeled his sacrifice on Chinese precedents is evident from the Chosŏn Veritable Records, which note the king's queries to and responses from the officials at the Ministry of Rites, beginning in May 1456, when specific details about the measurements of the Altar to Heaven, the layout, and the ritual performance were reported to the king.[127] Nonetheless, the ritual was not identical to the one performed by the Chinese emperor. For example, it was not performed at the winter solstice, and the ancillary sacrifices included many more tablets. Sejo generally sacrificed to Heaven on the fifteenth day of the first lunar month in 1458, 1460, 1461, 1462, and 1463; in 1459 the sacrifice was held on the thirteenth day.[128] The sacrifice was stopped because of Sejo's illness in 1463; he refused the suggestion by the Ministry of Rites officials that someone else could be delegated to perform the sacrifice in his stead, siding with the Sŭngjŏngwŏn (Royal Secretariat) against the Ministry. In 1464 he reiterated the ban on performing the sacrifice.[129]

After Sejo abolished the sacrifice to Heaven, it dropped out of the state ritual repertoire. The Kukcho orye ŭi (1474) did not include this ritual, showing that its opponents had won the internal debate. The arguments of the proponents, however, provide fascinating glimpses into the ever-present political-cultural issue: how to fit into a China-centered world order and yet simultaneously assert a distinctive identity. The Koryŏ, for example, submitted to the Liao, Song, and Jin regimes during their first thirty years of rule, but continued to describe their territories by the term "all under heaven" (天下 K. ch'ŏnha, C. tianxia). Records refer to King Munjong (r. 1046–83) as "emperor" (K. hwangje, C. huangdi), and in direct address, officials

[126] Sejo sillok, Sejo 3/1/15#1 has a very detailed description of the ritual.
[127] Sejo sillok, Sejo 2/12/12#1; 2/12/19#2, 2/12/22#5, 2/12/23#5, 2/12/24#4, 2/12/27#1, 2/12/30#2, 3/1/10#1, 3/1/11#4, 3/1/11#8, 3/1/14#2, 3/1/16#3, 4/1/15#1.
[128] Sejo sillok, Sejo 4/1/15#1; 5/1/13#1, 6/1/15#1, 7/1/15#1, 8/1/15#1.
[129] Sejo sillok, Sejo 9/1/6#1, 9/1/7#1, 10/12/8#1.

used the term *p'yeha* 陛下 (C. *bixia*). The Koryŏ king wore yellow robes, a color traditionally reserved for the Chinese emperor. The posthumous names of kings used the suffixes traditionally given to Chinese imperial temple names (宗 K. *–chong,* 祖 K. *–cho,*), his communications to officials were called by the same terms as the emperor's communications (詔 K. *cho,* 制 K. *che*). The Koryŏ kings sacrificed to Heaven, they had a Korea-centered tribute relationship of their own with neighboring states and tribes, and occasionally they referred to the king as "Son of Heaven of East of the Sea (東海天子)."[130]

Those who defended retention of the Altar to Heaven sacrifices for rain and for a good harvest argued that the rites should not be abolished since they predated relations with China, going back to the Three Kingdoms (Sam Han) era of Korean history. Besides, Heaven was the ultimate deity to grant relief when all other prayers had failed. The altar should be retained, but its name changed so that it did not replicate the name of China's altar to Heaven. Another line of argument was that *hanul* (the native Korean word for heaven) was different from the Chinese *tian*. Still another suggested that since Chosŏn was located to the east of China, the object of worship at the Wŏndan should not be Hoch'ŏn shangje (昊天上帝, C. Haotian shangdi) but the Black Emperor of the East 東方青帝, one of the Five Emperors who were worshipped by Chinese rulers at the Altar to Heaven before the middle of the seventh century.[131]

Both before and after the Sejo reign, the ritual controversy over the Wŏndan focused on prayers for rain. Officials argued that an absolute ban of the ritual would make it very difficult to respond to times of extreme drought. The circumstances surrounding Sejo's decision to worship at the Wŏndan were quite different. Ascending the throne by ousting his nephew, Sejo deployed rituals alongside military and political policies designed to strengthen his control over the bureaucracy and court. While successfully seeking recognition from the Ming and investiture for himself, his wife, and his heir as the legitimate rulers, Sejo made sacrificing to Heaven, Earth, and the founding ancestor of his dynasty the culminating symbolic act that completed his takeover of power. This sacrifice would not be revived until the late nineteenth

---

[130] Remco E. Breuker, "Koryŏ as an Independent Realm: The Emperor's Clothes?" *Korean Studies* 27 (2003): 69. An alternative translation might be "Son of Heaven of the East Sea."

[131] Han Hyŏngju, "Chosŏn Sejodae ŭi chech'ŏn ye e taehan yŏn'gu – T'aejo, Sejongdae chech'ŏn ye wa ŭi pigyo – kŏmt'o rŭl chungsim uro – " (Research on the sacrifice to Heaven ritual in Chosŏn during the Sejo reign, focusing on an examination and comparison with the sacrifice to Heaven rite from the T'aejo to Sejong reigns), *Chindan hakpo* 81 (1996): 107–33.

century, when King Kojong sacrificed to Heaven as ruler of the Great Han Empire.[132]

The 1474 edition of the *Kukjo oryeŭ* was later revised and published in 1744.[133] As elite knowledge of the Chinese ritual code deepened, Korean deviations from Confucian norms made their way into debates at court. The ritual controversy that arose following the death of Hyojong (r. 1649–59) and resurfaced after the death of his successor, Hyŏnjong in 1674, dealt with fundamental issues concerning the eldest-son succession principle, and whether "private" obligations (such as filiality) trumped "public" ones (the preeminent status of the king).[134] These debates, conducted against a backdrop of factional strife at court, focused on issues of legitimacy.

Confucian scholars also worried about the other areas in which Chosŏn practices deviated from the normative behavior of a vassal state. As early as the sixth and seventh centuries, Korean rulers had followed the Chinese custom of conferring the temple name, T'aejo 太祖 (C. Taizu) on dynastic founders, and naming subsequent kings with the temple suffix –jong.[135] Except for a brief interval in the late thirteenth and fourteenth centuries, successive Korean dynasties had independently selected the temple and posthumous names of deceased kings, a matter that abrogated the overlord–vassal relationship. Worried that it was "presumption" for a vassal to append the suffixes –cho and –chong in the Chinese mode, the Confucian Chŏng Tojŏn (1342–98) retroactively altered the temple names of the Koryŏ rulers to –wang 王.[136]

Debates on the stance expected of a vassal state continued at the early Chosŏn court. When a king died, his successor should report his death to the Chinese emperor and request a posthumous name (諡 K. *si*), which would stand alongside a temple name as the deceased ruler's historical identity.[137] Highlighted during the compilation and

---

[132] Hiraki Makoto, "Chōsen kōki ni okeru Enkudō sairei ni tsuite (2)" (The Altar to Heaven sacrifice in late Chosŏn, 2), *Chōsen gakuhō* 176/77 (2000): 283–310. Hiraki also traces the historical changes in the names assigned to the Altar of Heaven in this article.

[133] Yi Yŏngch'un, "Chosŏn hugi ŭi sajŏn."

[134] JaHyun Kim Haboush, "Constructing the Center: The Ritual Controversy and the Search for a New Identity in Seventeenth-Century Korea," in *Culture and the State in Late Chosŏn Korea*, ed. JaHyun Kim Haboush and Martina Deuchler (Cambridge, MA: Harvard University Asia Center, 1999), pp. 46–90; Yi Wŏntaek, "Sukchong ch'o ŭlmyo pokje nonjaeng ŭi sasangsajŏk ham'ŭi" (The ideological content of the debates in the early Sukchong reign on the ŭlmyo dress code), *Han'guk sasang sahak* 14 (2000): 25–52.

[135] The Chinese customarily bestowed a temple name on a ruler after his death; this was the name inscribed on the ruler's tablet in the Ancestral Temple (Taimiao) and the one by which he was thereafter known.

[136] Im Minhyŏk, "Chosŏn sidae ŭi myoho wa sadae ŭisik" (Temple names in Chosŏn and the consciousness of "serving the great"), *Chosŏn sidaesa hakpo* 19 (2001): 147–68.

[137] *Ibid.*

subsequent revision of the official dynastic history of Koryŏ, this issue was never fully resolved. Alternating policies produced two versions of kings' names: one with the suffix –*wang*, and another with the "presumptuous" suffixes still attached.

Controversy concerning the propriety of performing rituals forbidden to vassals revealed the anxiety of Confucian intellectuals who identified with the policy of *sadae* and believed that Chosŏn should serve as a Confucian exemplar. These scholars prized their commitment to Confucianism above their commitment to the Chosŏn royal house, but they viewed Confucian values as universal and not necessarily tied to the Central Plain. The ritual debates over two mythical founders of the Korean people, Kija 箕子 and Tangun 壇君, expressed the ambivalence many elites felt about Korea's relationship to China.

According to early Chinese records, Kija was a refugee from Shang who fled east and established the first Chosŏn state.[138] He appears in the *Samguk sagi* 三國史記 as a Chinese vassal who created the first Korean state, thereby connecting the peninsula with the Central Plain culture. By contrast, Tan'gun, the offspring of a she-bear and the sun god, who was also regarded as a progenitor of the Korean people, had no connection with China. In the late thirteenth to fourteenth century Kija was depicted as a historical figure who lived after Tan'gun. The early Chosŏn state offered national-level sacrifices to both founders.

In later periods, Kija appeared in several guises. During the Sejong and Sŏngjong reigns of the fifteenth century when they wished to stress their independence from China, officials pointed out that Kija had refused to serve the Zhou Court. Others stressed that Korea was in no way inferior to the Central Plain. In the *Real Records of Kija* (箕子實紀 *Kija silgi*, 1580), the noted Confucian Yi Yulgok presented a Kija who "transformed Korea into a state equivalent to Lu . . . and Ch'i," the native places of Confucius and Mencius; he was a sage that could stand comparison with the Chinese sages.[139]

The Confucianization of Korean state ritual produced somewhat contradictory responses. While some Korean scholar-officials zealously sought to bring state rites into compliance with the status order (*mingfen* 名分) of the Sinocentric world, others defended the historical precedent that revealed that earlier Korean states had used rites to assert autonomy. These ritual debates deeply divided Chosŏn officialdom until the two Manchu invasions. When forced by the Qing to break off their tribute relationship with Ming, humiliated Chosŏn intellectuals challenged Manchu legitimacy with rituals deliberately emphasizing their fidelity to

---

[138] Young-woo Han, "Kija Worship."   [139] *Ibid.*, p. 370.

Ming. At the same time, they attempted to construct a new Chosŏn-centered order that would preserve a civilization which had departed from the Central Plain.

Anti-Qing rituals

Chosŏn officials were unified in resisting their forced submission to the Manchus in 1637. The Qing demanded that Chosŏn excise the Ming reign name from its official documents, discard the Ming seals of investiture, and break relations with the Ming. Chosŏn was instead to accept the Qing calendar and with it the obligations of a vassal state. The diplomatic language used in corresponding with the Ming emperor was now to be adopted when petitioning Hongtaiji. In addition, the king was forced to turn over three anti-Qing officials for execution by the victors. Injo's eldest son, Crown Prince Sohyŏn, his second son, Prince Pongnim, and the sons of some high ministers were taken to Shenyang as hostages.

The measures taken by the victors to ensure compliance with a Manchu-imposed peace settlement inflamed anti-Manchu sentiments at the Korean court. Chosŏn fulfilled the nominal requirements – regular embassies to the Qing court, presentation of tribute, and "requests" for investiture of royal successors – but also established counter-hegemonic rituals which portrayed Qing as an illegitimate regime and embraced a rhetorical loyalty to the fallen Ming.

The easing of tensions after 1644 did not lessen the Chosŏn court's hostility. Chosŏn did agree that "before the 30th day of the first month (1637) we were the servants of the Ming; after the 30th day of the first month, we have become the vassals of the Qing."[140] But the court continued to use the Ming calendar and reign names on its internal documents. This came to light in 1730, when Ming Tianqi reign dates were discovered on the "identification plaques" (馬牌 *map'ae*) of a Korean vessel driven into Chinese waters by a storm. The Qing inquiry into this matter forced King Yŏngjo (r. 1724–76) to apologize to the Qing and order new plaques using the Qing dates.[141] The clause in the treaty that obliged Chosŏn to supply troops to Qing was not honored in 1638 and 1639; on the latter occasion, Kim Sanghŏn (1570–1652), an anti-Qing proponent who opposed fulfilling this Qing demand, was taken

---

[140] Kim Han'gyu, *Han-Chung kwan'gye sa*, p. 721: the source is the *Qing Taizong shilu*.

[141] JaHyun Kim Haboush, *A Heritage of Kings: One Man's Monarchy in the Confucian World* (New York: Columbia University Press, 1988), pp. 45–46; *Chosŏn wangjo sillok*, Yŏngjo 6/6/12 #1 (July 26, 1730), 6/7/12#4 (August 25, 1730) and 6/7/14 #1 (August 27, 1730). The matter does not appear in the *Qing shilu's* record for 1730.

by the Qing and held for six years.[142] Even Ch'oe Myŏnggil (1586–1647), the minister who successfully argued for peace negotiations with the Qing in 1637 and participated in drawing up the peace treaty, secretly passed information on Qing conditions to Ming officials.[143]

A pro-Ming faction continued to dominate the Injo court. In 1645, Crown Prince Sohyŏn was released from Qing custody and returned to Chosŏn, only to die under questionable circumstances two months later. There are suggestions that he was poisoned because of his pro-Qing stance: he had accompanied the Qing to Peking, and upon his return to Hansŏng suggested that aspects of Qing institutions could be emulated.[144] Interpretations of the death as politically motivated are supported by the banishment of his four brothers-in-law (they were accused of treason), and the execution of his wife in 1646. Sohyŏn's three sons were passed over and his younger brother, Prince Pongnim, was made Crown Prince.[145]

When Pongnim ascended the throne as Hyojong (r. 1649–59), he was a strong proponent of military reform, hoping to strengthen the troops in order to carry out a "northern expedition" against the Qing.[146] Officials gathered intelligence on the progress of the Manchu conquest during the Hyŏnjong (r. 1659–74) and Sukchong (r. 1674–1720) reigns, hoping for an opportunity to invade the Manchu homeland. The Rebellion of the Three Feudatories (Sanfan) in 1673 and news of the anti-Qing resistance of Koxingga's successor, Zheng Jing, aroused Chosŏn hopes for a northern expedition: there were proposals that Chosŏn should send emissaries to ally with Zheng and break off relations with Qing. Discussions stalled with the death of Hyŏnjong and the accession of a new king, Sukchong. Meanwhile, the Qing strengthened their troop dispositions along the border with Chosŏn, and signified that

---

[142] Hanguk sajŏn p'yŏnch'anhoe, comp. *Han'guk kojung sesa sajŏn* (Dictionary of matters in Korea during ancient and medieval times) (Seoul: Kalam kihoek, 1995), p. 434.

[143] *Ibid.*; Kim Han'gyu, *Han-Chung kwan'gye*, p. 722.

[144] Liu Jiaju, *Qingdai chuqi de Zhong Han guanxi* (Sino-Korean relations in early Qing) (Taipei: Wenshizhe chubanshe, 1986), pp. 158–62.

[145] The legitimacy of putting Injo's second son on the throne became the focus of a major controversy over mourning ritual after Hyojong's death. See Haboush, "Constructing the Center," pp. 62–64.

[146] Kim Seyŏng, "Chosŏn Hyojongjo pukpŏllon yon'gu" (Research on discussions of a northern expedition in the Chosŏn Hyojong reign), *Paeksan hakpo* 51 (1998): 121–53. The strength of anti-Qing sentiments at the Chosŏn court and its impact on the court's foreign relations is also stated in Han Myŏnggi, "Sipch'il, p'al Han-Chung kwan'gye wa Injo panjŏng – Chosŏn hugi ŭi 'Injo panjŏng pyŏnmu' munje" (Korean–Chinese relations in the seventeenth and eighteenth centuries and the Injo coup – The late Chosŏn problem of revising the charge of "usurpation"), *Han'guksa hakpo* 13 (2002): 9–14.

Chosŏn's actions were under severe scrutiny, so a "wait and see" attitude was adopted.[147]

As hope for a Ming restoration faded in the 1670s, the Chosŏn court intensified its symbolic defiance of the Manchu overlords by creating altars to Ming emperors. Acting on a proposal from the Confucian stalwart Song Siyŏl (1607–89), a shrine for the Wanli and Chongzhen emperors was erected at Hwayangdong, Song's birthplace, to "symbolize repaying the kindness of the Ming and for implanting . . . the spirit of *ch'unch'u taeŭi*" (春秋大義, the principle of loyalty even when the state was collapsing).[148] King Sukchong proposed 1704, the sixtieth anniversary of the Chongzhen emperor's death, for the first sacrifice at this shrine.[149] In the eulogy accompanying the first-rank offerings (*taesa* 大祀), he voiced laments "for the collapse of civilization in China, the deep shame Koreans felt at their continued existence without having avenged the Ming, and their resolve to carry out their mission to perpetuate civilization."[150]

King Sukchong's 1704 sacrifice to the Chongzhen emperor was a one-time rite. When he prepared to create a permanent altar dedicated to the Wanli emperor, who had rescued Chosŏn from the Japanese invaders, officials objected that such an altar had no precedent in the Chinese ritual code. Moreover, sacrifices to the Wanli emperor as Chosŏn's overlord would rank above those for the king's own royal ancestors, creating an unthinkable dilemma. However, support from students at the Royal Confucian Academy enabled the king to go ahead with the building of the shrine, which was called the Taebodan (大報壇, Altar of gratitude) and to determine that sacrifices would be performed there in the third month each year. His successor, King Yŏngjo, expanded the Taebodan to include the tablets of the Ming founder (because Ming Taizu had formally recognized the Chosŏn dynasty and bestowed this name upon the ruling house), and the Chongzhen emperor (because, like the Wanli emperor, he had helped Chosŏn).

Through these ritual acts, Yŏngjo affirmed Chosŏn as the heir to Ming civilization. His officials objected. They noted that sacrificing to the dynastic founder was a privilege reserved for lineal descendants and

[147] Kim Han'gyu, *Han Chung kwan'gye*, pp. 722–23.
[148] Quote from David A. Mason, "The *Sam Hwangje Paehyang* (Sacrificial Ceremony for Three Emperors): Korea's Link to the Ming Dynasty," *Korea Journal* (Autumn 1991): 125. Haboush, "Constructing the Center," pp. 39–40.
[149] JaHyun Kim Haboush, "Contesting Chinese Time, Nationalizing Temporal Space: Temporal Inscription in Late Chosŏn Korea," in *Time, Temporality, and Imperial Transition: East Asia from Ming to Qing*, ed. Lynn A. Struve (Honolulu: University of Hawai'i Press, 2005) p. 124.
[150] *Ibid.*

taboo for others. Nonetheless, Yŏngjo performed the first sacrifice to the three Ming emperors at the Taebodan on May 26, 1749.[151] The king proposed sacrificing to the Ming Hongwu emperor, arguing that Hongwu's choice of Chosŏn as the dynastic name was a direct allusion to Kija Chosŏn. With the demise of Ming, "the Central Plains exude the stenches of barbarians and our Green Hills are alone."[152]

Conclusion

Nominally Confucian, China's state rituals as practiced by the Qing were an eclectic mixture of Ming conventions interspersed with a heavy commitment to shamanic rites derived from the northeast Asian tradition inherited by the Jurchen/Manchus. Imperial patronage of Tibetan Buddhism and Chinese popular religious cults of rain deities reflected the multi-cultural policies that the emperors used to govern their multi-ethnic empire. The Qing state ritual order represents an example of "politicized ethnicity," claiming the Central Plain cultural heritage of emperorship, even as it incorporated Mongol and Manchu ritual practices. Compartmentalization of the cultural patronage appealing to different subjects in the empire was a hallmark of the Qing ritual system.

Japan's state ritual system evolved along a different path. Japanese elites successfully merged elements of indigenous and continental cults to create an imperial cult with a divine ancestress, the sun goddess, Amaterasu. Local religious observances were systematized and organized into a state ritual calendar, and new accession rituals accompanied the establishment of a stable polity. Changes in Buddhist–Shinto doctrine in the sixteenth century allowed militarists to use self-deification as a mode of acquiring the symbolic capital to claim nationwide leadership. This religious innovation sprang from Japanese soil, resuscitating the ancient idea of *ujigami* in a new form. Matsudaira Sadanobu's self-deification, built on ideas springing from Shinto's merger with the martial arts, represents an extension of continental practice that was not replicated in China, where the Tibetan Buddhist notion of the multiple embodiment of bodhisattva framed the *tankas* depicting the Qianlong emperor as Manjusri.

Korea took a somewhat different evolutionary path. Shamanism and Buddhism continued to play primary roles in state rites until the

---

[151] Haboush, "Constructing the Center," pp. 42, 44. Yŏngjo also performed the sacrifice to the Chongzhen emperor on the second sixtieth year anniversary of his death.
[152] Quotation from Haboush, *Heritage of Kings*, p. 41.

fifteenth century, when Chinese ritual codes inspired the compilation of the Chosŏn ritual handbook. "Confucianization" of the state rites brought issues of Korea's role in a Sinocentric world order to the fore, and highlighted (even if it did not eliminate) the divergence of Korean practices from the Confucian order. Korean elite attitudes toward China shifted over time. The Wanli emperor's military intervention during Hideyoshi's invasion intensified the internal pressure on Korean scholar-officials to ritually express their subordination to Ming, while Injo's forced submission to Qing authority had a liberating effect. Korean elites were severed from their vassalage to Ming. Humiliated, their intense hatred for the Qing, and rejection of Qing claims to universal emperorship freed them to posit an idealized order in which they, not Qing, played the central role.

4   Kinship and succession in China, Japan, and Korea

The last chapter examined how northeast conquest regimes and nearby states shaped a ritual vocabulary imported from the Central Plain to meet their specific situations. By exploring issues surrounding the legitimacy of royal succession that arose when newly emergent states in Korea and Japan adopted Chinese-style legal codes, this chapter aims to provide a fresh perspective on the idiosyncrasies of Chinese Confucian practices.[1] The native legacy of rulership and succession which constrained the exportability of Confucian practices helps explain how, despite commonalities in their initial kinship systems, Japanese and Korean regimes ended up with strikingly different resolutions in their attempts to implement Chinese-style political structures.

The fundamental problem was the Chinese legal code that was introduced into the emerging states of the Korean peninsula and thence into the Japanese archipelago during the state-building era. The normative ideas of political legitimacy embedded in the codes were generally regarded as Confucian, referring to a set of principles which were incorporated into the education of elites and rulers.[2] Assumed to be universally applicable, these norms were in actuality predicated on the Chinese patrilineal kinship system rather than the very different indigenous kinship and succession systems practiced in early Korea and Japan. Ancient Japanese and Korean kingship was based on bilateral kinship, which emphasized the blood lines of mothers as well as fathers. Rulership was dominated by a royal lineage, which practiced brother–sister marriage. Chinese legal principles denied inheritance rights to daughters and wives and dictated that only sons could ascend the throne. They proved difficult

---

[1] The chapter will focus on the contrast between Chinese patrilineality and Japanese/Korean bilateral kinship, leaving aside the issue of Qing adaptation to the Chinese model. See Rawski, *The Last Emperors*, which discusses Manchu policies of group endogamy for daughters (chapter 4), rejection of eldest-son succession (chapter 3), and the special role of widows as regents (chapter 2).

[2] See Chapter 3 for the argument that the term "Confucian" covered a wide range of ritual practices that extended far beyond what Confucius and his followers would have supported.

to implement, especially because they threatened the legitimacy of native rulers. Although Japan and Korea eventually adopted patrilineal principles, the end results deviated from the Chinese system and from each other in significant respects.

This chapter begins with a brief survey of the Chinese patrilineal kinship system, which marked status differences by gender, generation, and birth order within the descent group or lineage. Chinese custom favored males, causing women's status and property rights to decline during the first millennium of Chinese history. Only males could rule, and succession adhered to the eldest-son principle.

When Japan adopted a Chinese-style law code, it was a society with starkly different traditions of inheritance and succession. Rulership was monopolized by the Yamato or imperial lineage, and brother–sister marriage was considered optimal. The historical shifts in Japanese inheritance and kinship practices from the eighth to the seventeenth century reveal both the deep-rootedness of certain traditions within the imperial house and the profound accommodations to patrilineality reflected in shogunal and commoner circles.

The Korean response to the introduction of Confucian norms concerning inheritance and succession took yet a different path. As in Japan, the throne was monopolized by one royal lineage in ancient Korea, women could rule, and they could inherit equally with sons. By the seventeenth century, patrilineal kinship had restructured elite family organization and removed women's rights to property, but older social dynamics allowing wife-givers to influence the royal family colored court politics and royal succession, creating tensions in Sino-Korean relations. As a vassal state, Chosŏn Korea had to inform the Ming of each change of rulership in order to obtain the investiture documents that legitimized the new king. Chosŏn officials sought to conceal the realities of coups d'état, lest Ming officials and emperors view instances of usurpation as violations of the normative order. Because the king's legitimacy was based on adherence to Confucian norms, Ming records labeling his succession as usurpation posed a direct political challenge that could not be ignored. Chosŏn responses to external judgments on the royal succession expose the venal realities lying beneath the diplomatic exchanges between the two countries.

Confucianism and Chinese patrilineality

Although the Chinese presented Confucianism as a universal thought system, one essential component, the ritual regulations, was predicated on China's own patrilineal or "agnatic kinship" practices. Chinese traced family relationships through the male line and differentiated their relations with kinsmen, males who shared descent from a common male ancestor, from relations with outsiders. Daughters received dowries, but only sons held inheritance rights to family estates. From at least the Han dynasty (202 BCE – 220 CE), Chinese prohibited marriage within the descent group.[3] When elite men without an heir adopted a successor, the adoptive son should be born into the descent group and belong to the junior generation.[4]

In Song times, the ritual practices of ancestor worship, degrees of mourning, and mortuary rites once confined to the elite were disseminated among commoners through works such as Zhu Xi's ritual manual.[5] As social mobility rose when the civil service examinations became the gateway to official appointment (and elite status), the power of aristocratic families declined, and women's status and property rights, significant in Han China, dwindled. Ming and Qing women continued to receive dowries from their natal families and widows might temporarily serve as heads of households for under-age sons upon the death of their husbands, but the deceased husband's brothers often overrode these latter rights.

Patrilineality shaped Chinese traditions of rulership, which was confined to males, preferably sons, in the descent line.[6] Throughout recorded history, Chinese viewed female rulers as usurpers, and successive dynasties devised policies to avoid the problem of maternal affines (*waiqi*) subverting the imperial authority upon a ruler's death.[7] In the *Ancestral Injunctions* issued in 1381 and revised in 1395, which were "to serve as the

---

[3] For variations in conceptions of the lineage stemming from the perspectives of anthropology and history, see James L. Watson, "Introduction," in *Kinship Organization in Late Imperial China, 1000–1940*, ed. Patricia Buckley Ebrey and James L. Watson (Berkeley: University of California Press, 1986), pp. 1–15, and Ebrey's essay, "The Early Stages in the Development of Descent Group Organization," pp. 16–61 in the same volume. The definition of "lineage" in the text is actually what Watson defines as "descent group"; the inclusion of corporate estates that marks Watson's "lineage" is regionally confined to south and southeast China.

[4] Ebrey, "Early Stages."

[5] See Patricia Buckley Ebrey, *Confucianism and Family Rituals in Imperial China: A Social History of Writing about Rites* (Princeton: Princeton University Press, 1991), and Zhu Xi, trans. and annotated by Patricia Buckley Ebrey, *Chu Hsi's Family Rituals: A Twelfth-Century Chinese Manual for the Performance of Cappings, Weddings, Funerals, and Ancestral Rites* (Princeton: Princeton University Press, 1991) (hereafter, *Chu Hsi's Family Rituals*).

[6] These generalizations refer to Han Chinese norms, which were frequently ignored by conquest dynasties.

[7] Jennifer Holmgren, "Imperial Marriage in the Native Chinese and Non-Han State, Han to Ming," in *Marriage and Inequality in Chinese Society*, ed. Rubie S. Watson and Patricia Buckley Ebrey (Berkeley: University of California Press, 1991), pp. 58–96; also Patricia Buckley Ebrey, "Introduction," pp. 1–24 in the same volume.

unchanging constitution of the state,"[8] the Ming founder, Zhu Yuanzhang, specified that succession in the hereditary princedoms of his sons (and the emperorship) would favor the eldest son of the wife; sons of "secondary consorts" (concubines) were ineligible to succeed.

The *Ancestral Injunctions* followed a long Confucian tradition, first expressed in the *Zhou li*: "succession passed from the eldest son by the official wife to the eldest grandson, or, if he were not living, to other sons by the same mother, and then to sons by lesser wives."[9] An alternative model underlined the importance of "succession by generation," *beifen* 輩分; "if there were no eldest son by the wife, then select a younger brother; failing that, appoint a grandson."[10]

Table 4.1, which provides information on the sixteen men who ascended the Ming throne (twice in the case of the Zhengtong emperor), suggests that Ming imperial succession generally adhered to the eldest-son rule.[11] The exceptions in this table can be explained in terms of their historical context. When Zhu Yuanzhang formally ascended the throne in 1368, he proclaimed Zhu Biao (1355–92), his eldest son by Empress Ma, his Heir Apparent. After Zhu Biao died, his eldest son, Zhu Yunwen, was named Heir Apparent.[12] Zhu Di, Yunwen's uncle, was ineligible not only because of birth order (he was Yuanzhang's fourth son), but primarily because his mother was a "secondary consort." After he dethroned Yunwen and ascended the throne as the Yongle emperor, Zhu Di attempted to alter the historical record to claim that he was a son of Empress Ma who should have been named Heir Apparent in 1392 by virtue of then being the eldest surviving son.[13]

In 1449 Zhu Qizhen, the Zhengtong emperor, was captured by the Oirat Mongols, creating a military and political crisis. Officials passed

[8] John D. Langlois, Jr., "The Hung-wu reign, 1368–1398," in *The Cambridge History of China*, vol. VII: *The Ming Dynasty, 1368–1644*, part 1, ed. Frederick W. Mote and Denis Twitchett (Cambridge: Cambridge University Press, 1988), p. 177.

[9] See *Chu Hsi's Family Rituals*, text on p. 9 and fn23, p. 9; also, pp. xx–xxi and descent line chart, p. xxii.

[10] Tatsuo Chikusa, "Succession to Ancestral Sacrifices and Adoption of Heirs to the Sacrifices: As Seen from an Inquiry into Customary Institutions in Manchuria," in *Chinese Family Law and Social Change in Historical and Comparative Perspective*, ed. David C. Buxbaum (Seattle: University of Washington Press, 1978), pp. 153–54.

[11] Denis Twitchett and Tilemann Grimm, "The Cheng-t'ung, Ching-t'ai, and T'ien-shun Reigns, 1436–1464," in *The Cambridge History of China*, vol. VII, part 1, pp. 326–7, 330, and 337–38; see Chu Ch'i-chen's biography in *Dictionary of Ming Biography*, ed. Goodrich and Fang, I: 289–94.

[12] John D. Langlois, Jr., "The Hung-wu Reign, 1368–1398," in *The Cambridge History of China*, vol. VII, part 1, pp. 108, 164, 177, 178.

[13] Hok-lam Chan, "The Chien-wen, Yung-lo, Hung-hsi, and Hsüan-te reigns, 1399, 1435," in *The Cambridge History of China*, vol. VII, part 1, pp. 214–18; the imperial genealogy and the Veritable Records were altered to insert this claim.

Table 4.1. *Ming imperial succession*

Emperor	Life dates	Reign dates	Relation to predecessor	Age when invested as crown prince
Hongwu	1328–1398	1368–1398		
Jianwen	1377–1402	1399–1402	eldest son of crown prince	1392, after father's death
Yongle	1360–1424	1403–1424	uncle (Hongwu's 4th son)	usurper
Hongxi	1378–1425	1425	#1 son by wife	26 (1404)
Xuande	1399–1435	1426–1435	#1 son by wife	25 (1424)
Zhengtong	1427–1464	1436–1449	#1 son by wife	3 months (1428)
Jingtai	1428–1457	1450–1456	younger brother by consort	put on throne when brother is kidnapped
Tianshun	1427–1464	1457–1464	elder brother	released by captors
Chenghua	1447–1487	1465–1487	#1 son by wife	2 (1449–52), 1457–64
Hongzhi	1470–1505	1488–1505	eldest surviving son by maid	5 (1475)
Zhengde	1491–1521	1506–1521	#1 son by wife	1 (1492)
Jiajing	1507–1567	1522–1566	cousin (collateral branch)	14
Longqing	1537–1572	1567–1572	eldest surviving son by consort	not in father's lifetime
Wanli	1563–1620	1573–1620	eldest surviving son by consort	5 (1568)
Taichang	1582–1620	1620	eldest son by consort	19 (1601)
Tianqi	1605–1627	1621–1627	eldest son	
Chongzhen	1611–1644	1628–1644	younger brother	

Sources: Compiled from data in "Genealogy of the Ming Imperial Family," in *The Cambridge History of China*, vol. VII, part 1, ed. Frederick W. Mote and Denis Twitchett (Cambridge: Cambridge University Press, 1988), p. xiii, and biographies of emperors in *Dictionary of Ming Biography, 1368–1644*, ed. L. Carrington Goodrich and Chaoying Fang (New York: Columbia University Press, 1976).

over the infant Heir Apparent and replaced Zhu Qizhen with a half-brother, Qiyu, an adult who could "provide stability and give courage to army and population alike." Zhu Qiyu, Prince Cheng, had been appointed "Protector of the State" when the emperor departed from Peking at the head of the Ming army. Three weeks after the emperor's capture at Tumu, Prince Cheng was enthroned as the Jingtai emperor.[14]

[14] Twitchett and Grimm, "Cheng-t'ung, Ching-t'ai, and T'ien-shun reigns," pp. 330–31; see Zhu Qiyu's biography in *Dictionary of Ming Biography*, ed. Goodrich and Fang, I: 294–98. On the Jingtai reign, see Philip de Heer, *The Caretaker Emperor: Aspects of the Imperial Institution in Fifteenth-Century China as Reflected in the Political History of the Reign of Chu Ch'i-yü* (Leiden: E. J. Brill, 1986).

When the Ming rejected Oirat overtures to return the kidnapped ruler in exchange for concessions, Zhu Qizhen was released (September 1450), but he had to renounce his claim to the throne before being permitted back into the palace. The Jingtai emperor excluded Qizhen from court activities, and attempted at one point to replace Qizhen's Heir Apparent with his own son. Zhu Qizhen was eventually restored to the throne by a military coup, and ruled for another seven years as the Tianshun emperor.[15]

From the middle of the fifteenth century, sons of secondary consorts mounted the throne as the pool of prospective heirs dwindled, but in conformity with the general principle, the Hongzhi, Longqing, Wanli, and Taichang emperors were their father's eldest surviving sons.[16] Jennifer Holmgren's analysis of earlier Chinese dynasties suggests that the Ming case actually conforms to a broader pattern of infertility among empresses.[17] There were two instances when a dying emperor left no son. Because Zhu Houzhao, the Zhengde emperor, also had no brothers, his successor had to be selected from the previous generation, the sons of Xianzong, the Chenghua emperor (see Table 4.1). When Zhu Youjiao, the Tianqi emperor, died without issue in 1627, his younger brother Youjian succeeded him as the Chongzhen emperor.[18]

Bilateral kinship in Japan

The Taihō civil and criminal codes promulgated in 701 AD and the revised Yōrō civil and criminal codes of 718 introduced Chinese patrilineal principles into Yamato Japan and sparked the first of two major shifts in Japanese inheritance and succession practices.[19] While the

---

[15] Details of the events immediately following Esen's capture of the Zhengtong emperor are presented in de Heer, *Caretaker Emperor*, pp. 18–28.

[16] Traditional historical accounts of the domestic affairs of rulers frequently couch issues of succession within a conspiratorial framework. A typical example is the identification of the cause of the Chenghua emperor's misfortunes concerning an heir, which blames his consort Lady Wan for ensuring that no sons born in his harem would survive. The exception was the Hongzhi emperor, born to a very low-status aboriginal palace maid, who escaped death by being raised in hiding. See Frederick Mote, "The Ch'eng-hua and Hung-chih Reigns, 1465–1505," in *The Cambridge History of China*, VII.1: 344–47.

[17] Holmgren, "Imperial Marriage," fn 10, p. 91 notes that eleven of sixteen wives in the Former Han failed to produce an heir and that "very few" of the nine rulers of the Northern Song dynasty (979–1126) were sons of an empress.

[18] See the biography of Zhu Yijun, the Wanli emperor, in *Dictionary of Ming Biography*, ed. Goodrich and Fang, I: 324–28. The biography of Zhu Changle, the Taichang emperor, is in Hummel, *Eminent Chinese*, I: 176; for biographies of Zhu Youjiao and Zhu Youjian, see I: 190 and 191–92.

[19] See Jeffrey P. Mass, *Lordship and Inheritance in Early Medieval Japan: A Study of the Kamakura Sōryō System* (Stanford: Stanford University Press, 1989), chapter 1.

exclusion of women from inheritance, a Chinese-style regulation included in the Taihō Code, was revised in the Yōrō Code, other major Chinese principles such as "lineal primogeniture in the matter of house succession, and divided inheritance in the matter of property,"[20] were retained. Even though these clauses were implemented unevenly, they gradually affected the course of political development.

The Taihō Code established a normative framework for imperial succession that excluded women from rulership, in opposition to the ancient Japanese practice of brother–sister ruling pairs.[21] Women occupied important religious and ritual roles that are frequently identified as constituting the core of Japanese kingship.[22] Both men and women were eligible to rule by virtue of their birth in the descent group, which held a monopoly on the right to rule. In stark contrast to Chinese patrilineality, endogamy was not only accepted but welcomed. What Herman Ooms calls "double royal succession," inheriting royal blood through both parents, was the optimal qualification for rule.[23] Women ascending the throne did so on the basis of their own royal birth: they were blood descendants of the imperial line.[24]

Royal endogamy was gradually abandoned after adoption of the Taihō code, giving way to a system in which emperors and their sons took wives from aristocratic families. Until 729, however, the highest rank for an imperial consort, kōgō 皇后 (empress) could only be held by an imperial kinswoman.[25] Even when the emperor's sons were allowed to marry into other descent lines, not until 792 could daughters of the emperor marry men of Fujiwara descent; sons of other noble houses could only marry imperial granddaughters. The first actual marriage of

---

[20] Mass, *Lordship and Inheritance*, p. 11.

[21] Joan R. Piggott, "Chieftain Pairs and Corulers: Female Sovereignty in Early Japan," in *Women and Class in Japanese History*, ed. Hitomi Tonomura, Anne Walthall, and Wakita Haruko (Ann Arbor: Center for Japanese Studies, University of Michigan, 1999), p. 17. Inoue Mitsusada's opposing interpretation, that women were put on the throne as "stand-ins" for men, is discussed and evaluated in G. Cameron Hurst, III, "Insei," in *The Cambridge History of Japan*, vol. II: *Heian Japan*, ed. Donald H. Shively and William H. McCullough (New York and Cambridge: Cambridge University Press, 1999), pp. 578–79. While Hurst agrees with Inoue that female rulers appeared at times of dynastic crisis, he concludes (fn5, p. 578) that they were not figureheads: "they could and did rule in precisely the same way as male sovereigns." For the most recent analysis see Ooms, *Imperial Politics*.

[22] See Brown, "Introduction," p. 29.   [23] Ooms, *Imperial Politics*, pp. 14–15.

[24] On the genealogical ties of the six women who ascended the Japanese throne between 592 and 765, see their brief biographies in R. A. B. Posonby-Fane, *The Imperial House of Japan* (Kyoto: Posonby Memorial Society, 1959), pp. 48, 49, 51–52, 54–55, 56, 58, 59–60. Each was a member of the imperial family; some were also the widows of emperors.

[25] Naoki, "Nara State," fn25, p. 249 and text on that page.

an emperor's daughter outside the imperial line took place about a century later.[26]

Basic changes in the conceptualization and organization of kin-based groups accompanied the development of the state. In ancient Japan, the dominant elite kinship group, the *uji* 氏, were "lineal groups or clans ... that dominated the lands and people of entire regions."[27] Before the middle of the seventh century Japan consisted of "a loosely united federation of *uji*," each "bound together by descent from a common ancestor, the clan deity (氏神 *ujigami*)."[28] The Soga and the Nakatomi (Nakatomi no Kamatari, 614–69, would found the Fujiwara lineage) were prominent *uji* during the period of state formation, but the most powerful of all was the imperial *uji*.[29]

In the Heian period (794–1185), the *uji* lost most of its former political importance. It became "a loosely knit, patrilineal kin group of nobles whose members shared an ancestral or guardian deity, bore a common patronymic ... and hereditary title of status, acknowledged a common clan chieftain (氏長子 *uji no chōja*), and were usually buried together in a clan cemetery."[30] Headship was no longer established by birth order, but rather by rank, the *uji no chōja* being the *uji* member holding the highest court office who had his headship confirmed by the emperor.[31]

The Heian imperial family shared many (but not all) of the characteristics of a Chinese lineage. By law (until 798), the Japanese imperial family included all male and female descendants of emperors down to the fifth generation. Amaterasu, the Sun Goddess, was the *ujigami* or "focal ancestor" of the imperial line who was the object of worship at the Ise Grand Shrine. The state provided financial support and honors to imperial descendants within the stipulated five generations of descent, although an effort to reduce the cost of state stipends removed imperial descendants in the fifth generation from the rolls in 798.[32] Further shrinkages of the imperial family took place under Emperor Kammu (805), Emperor Saga (r. 809–23), and their successors.[33] The children of lower-ranking consorts and more distant imperial kinsmen demoted

[26] William H. McCullough, "The Capital and Its Society," in *Cambridge History of Japan*, II: 48, 125.

[27] Brown, "Introduction," p. 28.

[28] G. Cameron Hurst III, *Insei: Abdicated Sovereigns in the Politics of Late Heian Japan, 1086–1185* (New York: Columbia University Press, 1976), p. 11; Donald H. Shively and William H. McCullough, "Introduction," *The Cambridge History of Japan*, II: 3.

[29] Delmer M. Brown, "Introduction," and "The Yamato Kingdom," in *The Cambridge History of Japan*, I: 18, 134–35.

[30] *Ibid.*, p. 128.   [31] Hurst, *Insei*, pp. 14–15.

[32] McCullough, "Capital and Its Society," p. 124.

[33] *Ibid.*, pp. 125–26; also Shively and McCullough, "Introduction," p. 7.

into the nobility were granted clan names such as Minamoto (Genji), Taira, and Ariwara. The shogunal governments established after 1185 were led by imperial descendants, especially the Minamoto.[34]

The dynamic kinship unit during the Heian period was not the *uji* but rather what McCullough calls "the clan sublineage." In emphasizing a descent line rather than a broader kinship group, the elite noble houses of the Heian period resembled their Chinese counterparts during the Northern Song. Both groups directed their attention to achieving national rather than local prominence.[35] Succession to the headship of the Heian house (with preference for the eldest son) was linked with possession of *shiki* (職, offices with rights to propertied income). Although there was a tendency to link inter-generational transmission of *shiki* with the headship, property was dispersed rather than concentrated through the practice of partible inheritance. Both husband and wife possessed estates and were able to pass them on to their sons and daughters. Partible inheritance equalized siblings (at least potentially); "siblings and collaterals normally sought to avoid subordinate status,"[36] and weakened the organizational potential of lineages and lineage branches. Members sharing a common surname were atomized: the Minamoto, for example, were not only internally divided into branches but also regionally dispersed in the provinces and at court. Within a branch, partible inheritance created dissension among brothers, so that the heads of the branches had "little real authority."[37] What McCullough calls "the coresidential family of household" and not the larger *kado* was the important center of loyalty and affection for individuals belonging to the Heian elite. Alternatively called the *ie* (家, "house"), the Heian-period *ie* should not be confused with the institution bearing the same name which flourished centuries later in the Tokugawa period.[38]

Court politics centered on the imperial succession, and within it, on imperial prerogatives. Uxorilocal marriage enabled imperial wife-givers to

---

[34] William H. McCullough, "The Heian Court, 794–1070," in *The Cambridge History of Japan*, II: 39; McCullough, "Capital and Its Society," p. 129 states that the Minamoto were "a single clan despite the diverse imperial origins of its various lineages," whereas Takeuchi Rizō, "The Rise of the Warriors," *The Cambridge History of Japan*, II: 650, places more emphasis on the different descent lines existing under this surname.

[35] Robert P. Hymes, "Marriage, Descent Groups, and the Localist Strategy in Sung and Yuan Fu-chou," in *Kinship Organization in Late Imperial China*, ed. Ebrey and Watson, p. 128.

[36] Mass, *Lordship and Inheritance*, p. 128, see also pp. 122, 124.

[37] Mass notes, in *Lordship and Inheritance*, p. 143, that the Taira under Kiyomori "exhibited greater internal house cohesion than the more visibly fragmented Minamoto."

[38] *Ibid.*, p. 134; see Jeffrey P. Mass, *Antiquity and Anachronism in Japanese History* (Stanford: Stanford University Press, 1992), pp. 191–92, for a critique of the anachronistic attempt by Murakami Yasusuke to discern the Tokugawa type of *ie* in the medieval period.

dominate the throne. Through the twelfth century, the newly wed husband either moved to his wife's house or continued to reside with his own mother. If the couple moved to a residence of their own, it was likely to be supplied by the wife's family, and pass through the female line. This contrasted with the practice in China, where a wife generally moved to reside in a house belonging to her husband or parents-in-law.[39] Hurst notes that uxorilocality strengthened the ability of the Fujiwara to perpetuate their monopoly on the regency during the Heian period: "an imperial prince born of a Fujiwara woman was reared in the residence of his grandfather or uncle. Strong ties of affection developed. When the child became emperor, it was natural that he would be dominated by his Fujiwara kin."[40]

From the period of state formation to at least the onset of civil war in the sixteenth century, Japanese history is replete with efforts by a few elite non-imperial descent groups to confine emperors to a symbolic role and control administrative functions. The Fujiwara emerged as the leading noble clan in the central government after the Soga fell from power in 645. In 858, Fujiwara no Yoshifusa became the regent for his eight-year-old grandson, Emperor Seiwa (r. 858–76). He was the first man from outside the imperial line to hold this position, attained by virtue of his status as (simultaneously) maternal uncle and father-in-law to Emperor Montoku.[41] Seiwa and his successor, Yōzei (r. 876–84), were also the first "child-emperors" to ascend the throne.[42] Beginning with Emperor Seiwa, Fujiwara men held the highest offices at court for approximately three centuries.

According to Ooms, the lack of a legal rule of succession until the Imperial Household Acts of 1889 and 1947 created a political instability that runs throughout Japanese history from the Nara period onward.[43] Fierce succession struggles punctuated the period of Fujiwara hegemony and the subsequent era of the powerful retired emperors (*insei*)

---

[39] For a succinct summary of the Chinese system, see Ebrey, "Introduction," in *Kinship Organization*, ed. Ebrey and Watson, pp. 1–15.

[40] Hurst, "Insei," pp. 582–83. After Emperor Seiwa abdicated, he first resided in Yoshifusa's mansion before he became a lay priest; Hurst, *Insei*, pp. 69–70.

[41] Hurst, *Insei*, pp. 583–85 describes Yorimichi's twenty-three-year search for an alternative Fujiwara heir; see also his pp. 67–68. McCullough, "Heian Court," pp. 45, 48–49; the relationship of Yorimichi to Montoku is clarified by Fig. 1.1, "Genealogy of Heian emperors," pp. 22–23.

[42] McCullough, "Heian Court," p. 45; G. Cameron Hurst III, "The Structure of the Heian Court: Some Thoughts on the Nature of 'Familial Authority' in Heian Japan," in *Medieval Japan: Essays in Institutional History*, ed. John W. Hall and Jeffrey P. Mass (New Haven: Yale University Press, 1974), pp. 43–53 on the Fujiwara in Heian court society, pp. 56–57 on the imperial lineage and marriage ties with the Fujiwara.

[43] Ooms, *Imperial Politics*, chapter 1.

(see Table 4.2). Slightly over half (fourteen) of the twenty-seven emperors from Seiwa (r. 858–76) to Go-Toba (r. 1183–98) inherited the throne from their fathers; about a quarter (seven) of the successions were from brother to brother; 15 percent (four) were cases of "zig-zag" succession, alternating between the descent lines of two brothers: father–son succession was important but older forms of fraternal succession continued. Imperial reigns were short, abdication was common, and ex-emperors competed with their own successors to determine the next heir.[44]

Emperor Shirakawa (r. 1072–86), for example, opposed his father's efforts to place three sons on the throne and established his own son as crown prince. As retired emperor, Shirakawa tried to control affairs at court through the reigns of his son, grandson, and great-grandson. It was only after his death that his grandson Emperor Toba captured the leadership of the imperial lineage and the court.[45] These customs persisted in the imperial line during the Edo period (1600–1868), when emperors resorted to abdication (ten out of fifteen cases) and mixed father–son (eight out of fifteen cases) with fraternal succession (see Table 4.3). Two women (Meishō, Sakuramachi) were brought in to reign for an infant half-brother and a nephew.

Succession struggles also troubled the shogunate.[46] A succession dispute in the Ashikaga shogunal line was the direct cause of the Ōnin War (1467–77), which devastated Kyoto, the imperial and shogunal capital, and initiated over a century of political atomization that Japanese historians term the Sengoku or Warring States period. Ashikaga Yoshimasa wished to retire from his shogunal responsibilities. Lacking a son, in 1464 he persuaded his younger brother to succeed him, but this plan failed when his wife, Hino Tomiko, gave birth to a son in 1465. The warrior elite split, one group supporting the brother and

---

[44] An example from the Nara period concerns Empress Gemmei's rejection of Shōmu as her successor when she abdicated (715): see Naoki, "Nara State," p. 245. For examples of Fujiwara manipulations of succession, see Hurst, *Insei*, on the accession of Kōkō (p. 72), on the accession of Kōkō's son Prince Sadami who had already been excised from the imperial house (p. 73), the selection of Emperor Suzaku (p. 80). Hurst, *Insei*, also cites the conflict between Fujiwara no Saneyori and Minamoto no Takaakira over the succession to Emperor Murakami (pp. 83–84).

[45] Hurst, "Insei," pp. 608–10, 617–18 on Shirakawa and Toba, Toba and Sutoku.

[46] See Hurst, *Insei: Abdicated Sovereigns*, chapter 3, especially pp. 47–48; on alternating succession between the descent lines of two brothers, see his "The Koobu Polity: Court–Bakufu Relations in Kamakura Japan," in *Court and Bakufu in Japan: Essays in Kamakura History*, ed. Jeffrey P. Mass (New Haven: Yale University Press, 1982), pp. 24–25. On the institution of "cloister government" or *insei* featuring an abdicated ruler, see his "The Development of the *Insei*: A Problem in Japanese History and Historiography," in *Medieval Japan: Essays*, ed. Hall and Mass, pp. 60–90.

Table 4.2. *Japanese imperial succession, 858–1198*

Emperor	Reign Dates	Relationship to predecessor	Maternal grandfather	Sessho (Regent for a minor)	Kampaku (Regent)
Seiwa	858–876	son	Fujiwara Yoshifusa	Fujiwara Yoshifusa, 857–872	
Yōzei	876–884	son	Fujiwara Nagara	Fujiwara Mototsune, 873–880	
Kōkō	884–887	great-grandfather's son	Fujiwara Fusatsugu		Fujiwara Mototsune, 880–891
Uda	887–897	son	Prince Nakano		
Daigo	897–930	son	Fujiwara Takafuji		
Suzaku	930–946	son	Fujiwara Mototsune	Fujiwara Tadahira, 930–941	Fujiwara Tadahira, 941–949
Murakami	946–967	younger brother	Fujiwara Mototsune		
Reizei	967–969	son	Fujiwara Morosuke		Fujiwara Saneyori, 967–969
En'yu	969–984	younger brother	Fujiwara Morosuke	Fujiwara Saneyori, 969–970	
				Fujiwara Koretada, 970–972	Fujiwara Kanemichi, 972–977
					Fujiwara Yoritada, 977–986
Kazan	984–986	son of brother Reizei	Fujiwara Koretada		
Ichijō	986–1011	son of father's brother En'yu	Fujiwara Kaneie	Fujiwara Kaneie, 986–990	Fujiwara Kaneie, 990
				Fujiwara Michitaka, 990–993	Fujiwara Michitaka, 993–995
					Fujiwara Michikane, 995
Sanjō	1011–1016	son of father's brother Reizei	Fujiwara Kaneie	Fujiwara Michinaga, 1016–1017	Fujiwara Michinaga, 995–1017*
Go-Ichijō	1016–1036	son of father's brother En'yu	Fujiwara Michinaga	Fujiwara Yorimichi, 1017–1019	Fujiwara Yorimichi, 1019–1068
Go-Suzaku	1036–1045	older brother	Fujiwara Michinaga		
Go-Reizei	1045–1068	son	Fujiwara Michinaga		Fujiwara Norimichi, 1068–1075
Go-Sanjō	1068–1072	half-brother	Prince Sanjō		
Shirakawa	1072–1086	son	Fujiwara Yoshinobu		Fujiwara Morozane, 1075–1086

Emperor	Reign	Relationship	Maternal grandfather	Sesshō	Kampaku
Horikawa	1086–1107	son	Fujiwara Morozane	Fujiwara Morozane, 1088–1090	Fujiwara Morozane, 1090–1094; Fujiwara Moromichi, 1094–1099
Toba	1107–1123	son	Fujiwara Sanesue	Fujiwara Tadazane, 1107–1113	Fujiwara Tadazane, 1105–1107; Fujiwara Tadazane, 1113–1121
Sutoku	1123–1141	son	Fujiwara Kinzane	Fujiwara Tadamichi, 1123–1129	Fujiwara Tadamichi, 1121–1123; Fujiwara Tadamichi, 1129–1141
Konoe	1141–1155	half-brother	Fujiwara Nagazane	Fujiwara Tadamichi, 1141–1150	Fujiwara Tadamichi, 1150–1158
Go-Shirakawa	1155–1158	half-brother	Fujiwara Kinzane		
Nijō	1158–1165	son	Fujiwara Tsunezane	Fujiwara Motozane, 1165–1166	Fujiwara Motozane, 1158–1165
Rokujō	1165–1168	son	non-Fujiwara	Fujiwara Motofusa, 1166–1172	
Takakura	1168–1180	son of grandfather Go-Shirakawa	Taira Tokinobu	Fujiwara Motomichi, 1180–1183	Fujiwara Motomichi, 1179–1180
Antoku	1180–1183	son	Taira Kiyomori	Fujiwara Motomichi, 1184–1186	
Go-Toba	1183–1198	half-brother	Fujiwara	Fujiwara Moroiye, 1183–1184	

Sources: Compiled from data in William H. McCullough, "The Heian Court," in *The Cambridge History of Japan*, vol. II, ed. Donald H. Shively and William H. McCullough (Cambridge: Cambridge University Press, 1999), Fig. 1.1, pp. 22–23.

Table 4.3. *Japanese imperial succession, 1586–1867*

Emperor	Reign dates	Relationship to predecessor	Comments
Goyōzei	1586–1611	grandson (father dead)	forced to abdicate
GoMizunoō	1611–1629	son by consort	abdicated
Meishō	1629–1643	daughter by Tokugawa consort	father did have sons; abdicated
GoKōmyō	1643–1654	half-brother	son of Gomizunoō
Gosai	1654–1663	half-brother	son of Gomizunoō; forced to abdicate
Reigen	1663–1687	half-brother	son of Gomizunoō; abdicated
Higashiyama	1687–1709	son	abdicated
Nakamikado	1709–1735	son	abdicated
Sakuramachi	1735–1747	son	abdicated
Momozono	1747–1762	son	
GoSakuramachi	1762–1770	aunt	daughter of Sakuramachi; abdicated
GoMomozono	1770–1779	nephew	son of Sakuramachi; left one daughter
Kōkaku	1779–1817	collateral line	married GoMomozono's daughter; abdicated
Ninkō	1817–1846	son	
Kōmei	1846–1867	son	died of smallpox

Source: R. A. B. Posonby Fane, *The Imperial House of Japan.* Kyoto: Posonby Memorial Society, 1959.

the other the son; other factors, especially struggles over succession within the Hatakeyama clan and the competition between two powerful military clans, the Hatakeyama and the Hosokawa, contributed to the military escalation.[47]

By the late Heian period, "Blood kin ties were an inadequate basis for political allegiance."[48] From the tenth century onward, patron–client networks were created via the custom of wet-nursing. Court nobles and elite warrior families sent their children to be reared by a wet-nurse's family (i.e., men could be appointed as wet-nurses). The custom provided an opportunity for an elite family to establish emotional bonds with a young child that were later translated into political access. The Taira, who competed for national leadership against the Minamoto during the second half of the twelfth century, first became prominent at court on

[47] See Mary Elizabeth Berry, *The Culture of Civil War in Kyoto* (Berkeley: University of California Press, 1994), pp. 14–34.

[48] Thomas D. Conlan, "Thicker than Blood: The Social and Political Significance of Wet Nurses in Japan, 950–1330," *Harvard Journal of Asiatic Studies* 65.1 (2005): 160.

the basis of their wet-nurse relationships to Emperor Go-Shirakawa; Taira Kiyomori's wife had been Emperor Nijō's wet-nurse.[49] Yoshida Sadafusa, who served as *omenoto* ("wet-nurse" 御乳母) to Emperor Go-Daigo, saw his career and those of his sons and kinsmen rise sharply when Go-Daigo ascended the throne.[50] From the ruler's perspective, wet-nurses' families, who had no alternative base of power, were often more reliable allies than kinsmen: the children of the wet-nurse (*menotogo* 乳母子, *chi-kyōdai*) were his intimate friends and firm supporters in political-military alliances.[51]

Wet-nursing duplicated the conditions of Heian uxorilocal marriage. Rather than developing strong bonds of affection with his birth parents and siblings, the child became an adult whose loyalties were to his wet-nurse's family.[52] The actions of Hōjō Masako (1157–1225), wife of the founder of the Kamakura shogunate, illustrate the political fallout from this practice.

Hōjō Masako was born on the Izu peninsula into a warrior family which was allied to the Taira. After the victory of the Taira over the Minamoto in the Heiji Uprising (1159), her future husband, Minamoto no Yoritomo, was entrusted to her father, Hōjō Takimasa, as a hostage. Against her father's (initial) wishes, Masako married Yoritomo, cementing an alliance between the Hōjō and the Minamoto which benefited both families. Hōjō fortunes rose after Yoritomo established the Kamakura bakufu (1185).

Masako behaved in the tradition of the Heian-era Fujiwara daughters, "putting the interests of her natal family above those of her husband's lineage." Not only did she select her husband's successors, she "guaranteed that a Hōjō would always be regent to puppet shoguns imported from Kyoto as Yoritomo's adopted successors."[53] Masako and Yoritomo's two sons and two daughters were sent out to be wet-nursed. Yoritomo's first-born son, Yoriie, was raised in the family of his wet-nurse, Hiki no

---

[49] *Ibid.*, pp. 184–86.

[50] Andrew E. Goble, *Kenmu: Go-Daigo's Revolution* (Cambridge, MA: Council on East Asian Studies, Harvard University, 1996), pp. 11, 31, and 85.

[51] Conlan, "Thicker than Blood," pp. 159–205; Hurst, *Insei: Abdicated Sovereigns*, pp. 243–44.

[52] Noted in Conlan, "Thicker than Blood," p. 175.

[53] Hitomi Tonomura and Anne Walthall, "Introduction," in *Women and Class in Japanese History*, ed. Hitomi Tonomura, Anne Walthall, and Haruko Wakita (Ann Arbor: Center for Japanese Studies, University of Michigan, 1999), p. 6. There was a parallel between Masako's actions and those of her father's second wife, Makiko. After Sanetomo's death, Makiko plotted to have her own daughter's husband, a collateral member of the Minamoto clan, made shogun; this would presumably have given Makiko the upper hand at the shogunal court, but Masako managed to foil the scheme. See Kenneth D. Butler, "Woman of Power Behind the Kamakura Bakufu: Hōjō Masako," in *Great Historical Figures of Japan*, ed. Hyōe Murakami (Tokyo: Japan Cultural Institute, 1978), pp. 92–93.

Zen, and married his "breast sister." When he succeeded his father as shogun in 1202, he sided with his in-laws, the Hiki, who attempted to replace the Hōjō as the dominant power at the shogunal court. The struggle ended with Yoriie's forced abdication, exile, and eventual assassination at the hands of the Hōjō.[54]

Yoriie's younger brother, Sanetomo, succeeded him as shogun in 1203 (Masako rejected attempts to make Yoriie's sons the heirs). Sanetomo's loyalties (from Masako's perspective) were, unlike Yoriie's, unproblematic, because his nurse was Masako's younger sister, and thus his networks were securely Hōjō.[55] Aged eleven when he became shogun, he was guided by "his uncle (Hōjō) Yoshitoki and (his mother) Masako." After Sanetomo's assassination in 1219, a new shogun was not appointed until 1226, when a two-year old child was installed in the position. In the interim, administrative matters were handled by Hōjō Masako, who was thus a powerful figure in her own right.

Over the thirteenth to fifteenth centuries, Japanese elite inheritance and succession customs were transformed, even as provincial warrior houses clashed in disputes over inheritance and succession.[56] There was a "shift from a divided to a unitary inheritance practice," accompanied by the concentration of authority in the hands of a male head (sōryō).[57] Women's claims to property were eventually ceded to their husbands and sons, while the claims of secondary sons were relinquished to the one son (generally the eldest) who now possessed the consolidated estate. Unigeniture (one-person inheritance) took place not only among the elite but also gradually penetrated into village society. By the seventeenth century, marriage had become patrilocal.[58]

[54] Martin Collcutt, "'Nun-Shogun': Politics and Religion in the Life of Hōjō Masako (1157–1225)," in *Engendering Faith: Women and Buddhism in Premodern Japan*, ed. Barbara Ruch (Ann Arbor: Center for Japanese Studies, University of Michigan, 2002), pp. 170–75; Pierre François Souyri, *The World Turned Upside Down: Medieval Japanese Society* (New York: Columbia University Press, 2001), p. 50, states that Masako and her father killed Yoriie's young son, while Yoriie himself was assassinated somewhat later, perhaps by a "hit man hired by the Hōjō." See also Butler, "Woman of Power," pp. 91–101. According to Conlan, "Thicker than Blood," pp. 192–93, the Hōjō destroyed not only the Hiki but the wet-nurse families of all of Yoritomo's sons and grandsons, including the Nitta, the Wada, and the Miura. In the end, however, because they continued to send their children out to be raised by wet-nurses, the real leadership in shogunal affairs moved to the husband of Hōjō Sadatoki's wet-nurse, Taira Yoshitsuna, and his brother (p. 196).
[55] Collcutt, "Nun-Shogun," pp. 92–93; Souyri, *World Turned Upside Down*, p. 50.
[56] Souyri, *World Turned Upside Down*, pp. 124, 168.
[57] Hitomi Tonomura, "Women and Inheritance in Japan's Early Warrior Society," *Comparative Studies in Society and History* 32.3 (1990): 592.
[58] Haruko Wakita, "Marriage and Property in Premodern Japan from the Perspective of Women's History," *Journal of Japanese Studies* 10.1 (1984): 73–99; Lee Butler, *Emperor and Aristocracy in Japan, 1467–1680: Resilience and Renewal* (Cambridge, MA: Harvard

These changes in inheritance and marriage patterns supported the consolidation of power that accompanied the reemergence of a unified political authority in sixteenth-century Japan. But "the problem with kinsmen was that because they were eligible for family succession, they were potential rivals to the existing family head."[59] The appearance of powerful regional military leaders during the sixteenth century was based on vassalage rather than kinship: families like the Matsudaira created a more stable military organization with centralized authority by making vassals of their collateral kinsmen and installing non-kin warriors in key military positions. These hereditary vassals (*fudai*) occupied important administrative posts after 1600.

Edo-period kinship

Unitary patrilineal inheritance provided the foundation for the *ie* (家, household), the kin-linked organization that dominated Tokugawa society. "A concept which penetrates every nook and cranny of Japanese society,"[60] the *ie* grew out of the co-residential family group but transcended it.[61] As a "corporate residential group" consisting, ideally (at a minimum), of the *iemoto* (家元, head of household) and his wife and children, the *ie* resembled the Chinese *chia* or family/household, which is "the basic unit of production, consumption, and political authority, whose members normally reside together and share a common budget for everyday expenses."[62] Like the *jiazhang*, the *iemoto*, as the steward of corporate property, coordinated the labor power of household members. In both countries, membership in the *ie* could include servants and other non-kin members of the household. Yet, despite its structural similarity, the *ie* displayed characteristics that were unique to Japan. The *ie*'s claims to loyalty superseded blood ties, meritocratic performance became a

University Asia Center, 2002), pp. 181–82. Akira Hayami, "The Myth of Primogeniture and Impartible Inheritance in Tokugawa Japan," *Journal of Family History* 8 (1983): 3–29 uses household registers to argue that many exceptions to the general rules existed in villages into the late eighteenth and nineteenth centuries; he finds instances of partible inheritance, female headed households, and similar adaptations to specific domestic circumstances that contradict the general historical trend.

59 John W. Hall, "The *Bakuhan* System," in *The Cambridge History of Japan*, vol. IV: *Early Modern Japan*, ed. John W. Hall (Cambridge: Cambridge University Press, 1991), p. 162; Conrad Totman, *Politics in the Tokugawa Bakufu, 1600–1843* (Berkeley: University of California Press, 1988), chapter 8.

60 Chie Nakane, *Japanese Society* (Berkeley: University of California Press, 1970), p. 4.

61 Takie Sugiyama Lebra, *Above the Clouds: Status Culture of the Modern Japanese Nobility* (Berkeley: University of California Press, 1993), p. 108.

62 The Chinese kinship terms are taken from Ebrey and Watson, "Introduction," in *Kinship Organization in Late Imperial China*, pp. 4–6.

Table 4.4. *Tokugawa shogunal succession*

Shogun	In characters	Reign dates	Life dates	Age at investiture	Relation to previous shogun
Ieyasu	家康	1603–1605	1542–1616		
Hidetada	秀忠	1605–1623	1579–1632	26	3rd son
Iemitsu	家光	1623–1651	1604–1651	19	1st son
Ietsuna	家綱	1651–1680	1641–1680	10	1st son
Tsunayoshi	綱吉	1680–1709	1646–1709	34	younger brother
Ienobu	家宣	1709–1713	1662–1712	47	nephew
Ietsugu	家繼	1713–1716	1709–1716	4	only surviving son
Yoshimune	吉宗	1716–1745	1684–1751	32	Kii branch, Go Sanke
Ieshige	家重	1745–1760	1711–1761	34	1st son
Ieharu	家治	1760–1786	1737–1786	23	3rd son; other two adopted out
Ienari	家齋	1787–1837	1773–1841	14	Hitotsubashi branch
Ieyoshi	家慶	1837–1853	1793–1853	44	only son
Iesada	家定	1853–1858	1824–1858	29	son
Iemochi	家茂	1858–1866	1846–1866	12	
Yoshinobu	慶喜	1866–1867	1837–1913	29	

Sources: Compiled from data in *Tokugawa shoka keifu*; Hall, "*Bakuhan* System," table 4.1, p. 132; and Jansen, *The Making of Modern Japan*, p. 44.

major criterion for the selection of an heir, and parents frequently adopted heirs from outside even when their own sons were still alive.[63]

By 1600, when Ieyasu (1542–1616) founded the Tokugawa shogunal house, the custom among warrior families was for the eldest son to succeed to the headship.[64] As Table 4.4 shows, only a minority of the fifteen men who became shogun in the Edo period were actually first sons. Decisions concerning succession were made by a council which included the heads of the main Tokugawa collateral branches: the *Sanke* 三家 of Owari, Kii, and Mito, descended from Ieyasu's ninth, tenth, and eleventh sons, and, after Yoshimune (1684–1751), the *Sankyō* 三卿, the

[63] Susan B. Hanley, "Family and Fertility in Four Tokugawa Villages," in *Family and Population in East Asian History*, ed. Susan B. Hanley and Arthur P. Wolf (Stanford: Stanford University Press, 1985), p. 220; Susan B. Hanley and Kozo Yamamura, *Economic and Demographic Change in Preindustrial Japan, 1600–1868* (Princeton: Princeton University Press, 1977), pp. 227–32.

[64] Marius B. Jansen, *The Making of Modern Japan* (Cambridge, MA: Belknap Press, 2000), p. 45; Beatrice M. Bodart-Bailey, *The Dog Shogun: The Personality and Politics of Tokugawa Tsunayoshi* (Honolulu: University of Hawai'i Press, 2006), p. 12. The primary source for information on the Tokugawa shogunal succession is *Tokugawa shoka keifu*, comp. Saiki Kazuma, revised Iwasawa Toshihiko (4 vols., Tokyo: Zokugunsho ruijū kanseikai, 1970–84).

Hitotsubashi, Tayasu, and Shimizu branches descended from Yoshimune and his son Ieshige.[65]

In four instances, two in the eighteenth century, the shogunal title was given to a kinsman from a collateral house. A group of officials, together with the heads of the Owari and Mito collateral branches, selected Yoshimune (1684–1751), the third son of the head of the Kii collateral branch, as Ietsugu's successor. Low in the birth order, Yoshimune would ordinarily have faced life as a minor *daimyō*, but he unexpectedly succeeded his father upon the deaths of two elder brothers. By 1716, when Ietsugu died, Yoshimune had achieved notice as an effective administrator; he went on to lead the first major reform of Tokugawa governance in the Kyōhō era (1716–1735).[66]

When shogun Ieharu (1737–86) died, he was succeeded by Ienari (1773–1841), of the Hitotsubashi branch descended from Yoshimune's fourth son, Munetada. Ienari, installed as the shogunal heir in 1781, seems to have been the choice of Ieharu's influential Senior Councillor, Tanuma Okitsugu.[67] In the event, it was not he but Matsudaira Sadanobu who emerged as the most powerful official in the shogunate, the man who implemented the second major shogunal reforms during the Kansei era (1789–99).[68]

Ieyasu's decision to make primogeniture the succession principle of the shogunal house was no doubt prompted by his personal experience of the political havoc wrought by disputes over succession. Adherence to the eldest son principle promotes political stability: the heir can be identified at a very young age and trained for his future duties. The cost of adopting the eldest son principle is that ability may not follow birth order. Noting that "youth and adolescence in the pampered interior of the Chiyoda Castle" did not promote effective leadership, Jansen comments, "It is notable that in almost every case in which the shogun really counted he proved to have come to the top through irregular, 'outside' channels through adoption."[69]

---

[65] Hall, "*Bakuhan* System," pp. 154, 165.

[66] On the succession deliberations, see Totman, *Politics in the Tokugawa Bakufu*, p. 217, who notes the other candidate was Ienobu's brother. On Yoshimune's personal background, see Jansen, *Making of Modern Japan*, p. 46; and Tsuji Tatsuya, "Politics in the Eighteenth Century," in *The Cambridge History of Japan*, IV: 441–44. On the Kyōhō Reforms, see Totman, *Politics in the Tokugawa Bakufu*, chapter 14 and Tsuji, "Politics in the Eighteenth Century," pp. 445–56.

[67] Totman, *Politics in the Tokugawa Bakufu*, p. 223; Ooms, *Charismatic Bureaucrat*, pp. 21–22, notes that Sadanobu himself might have become shogun had it not been for his adoption out of the Tayasu house into the Shirakawa Matsudaira house.

[68] Tsuji, "Politics in the Eighteenth Century," pp. 467–77, notes that Sadanobu's patron was Ienari's birth father, Hitotsubashi Harusada.

[69] Jansen, *Making of Modern Japan*, p. 45.

Korea: from bilateral kinship to patrilineality

The introduction of Chinese legal codes also stimulated a major social transformation of kinship practices in Korea. Although the first Confucian academy appeared as early as 372 AD,[70] Confucian ideas on kinship had little effect on Korean society until the fourteenth century. Legislation to formalize the principle of eldest-son succession to the throne was passed in 1046, but was not implemented. Further legislation followed the establishment of the Chosŏn dynasty (1392), but as Martina Deuchler and Mark Peterson have demonstrated, the Confucianization of Korea took place only gradually and was not completed until the end of the seventeenth century.[71]

Like Japan, Korean elite kinship was initially bilateral. Migration and cultural diffusion in the fourth and the fifth centuries, when many Koreans from Paekche and Kaya emigrated to Japan and served the emerging Yamato court, may have reinforced the similarities between the two societies.[72] Descendants of Korean immigrants constituted the majority of the Yamato scribes and accountants, and also served on the committee that compiled three Chinese-style penal and administrative codes (*ritsuryō*) during the 668–701 period.[73]

In Korea, too, royal succession initially embraced a much wider range of alternatives than in China.[74] Father–son succession was the dominant pattern in Paekche and Koguryŏ, but there were also instances of fraternal and "zig-zag" fraternal succession.[75] This was also the case in the state of Silla. Although a third of the Silla kings mounted the throne through father–son succession, there were also many instances of brother–brother or the type of "zig-zag" fraternal succession (son of elder brother, succeeded by son of younger brother) found in late Heian Japan.[76] In addition, three Silla queens are listed

---

[70] In Koguryŏ; see Deuchler, *Confucian Transformation*, p. 14.

[71] *Ibid.*; Mark A. Peterson, *Korean Adoption and Inheritance: Case Studies in the Creation of a Classic Confucian Society* (Ithaca: East Asia Program, Cornell University, 1996).

[72] Ooms, *Imperial Politics*, chapter 4.

[73] Farris, *Sacred Texts and Buried Treasures*, pp. 104–5; see his chapter 2 for an overview of the scholarship on Japanese–Korean interactions during the ancient period. Also Hudson, *Ruins of Identity*, chapter 7.

[74] Cautions about the primary sources, the *Samguk sagi* (1145) and *Samguk yusa* of the thirteenth century, are articulately presented in Werner Sasse, "Trying to Figure Out How Kings Became Kings in Silla," in *Mélanges offerts à Li Ogg et Daniel Bouchez, Cahiers d'Études, Coréenes* No. 7 (Paris: Centre d'Études Coréenes, 2001), pp. 229–30.

[75] J. H. Grayson, "Some Structural Patterns of the Royal Families of Ancient Korea," *Korea Journal* 16.6 (1976): pp. 28–29.

[76] *Ibid.*, pp. 29–30.

in the *Samguk sagi* and *Samguk yusa*: Sŏndŏk (r. 632–47), Chindŏk (r. 648–54) and Chinsŏng (r. 887–94).[77]

As in ancient Japan, Silla kingship rested on birth, not gender. Silla rulers had to be born into the *sŏnggol* (聖骨 Holy Bone) status group: "Neither primogeniture nor patriliny was a necessary category in selection of the ruler, but *sŏnggol* status was *sine qua non* ... given *sŏnggol* birth, 'the holders of the highest status ... were eligible for the throne regardless of sex.'"[78] Since membership in the *sŏnggol* was limited to a few families with the surnames Pak, Sŏk, and Kim, attempts to remain "pure" produced endogamous marriages crossing generational lines (for example, between a niece and an uncle) that were forbidden in Chinese kinship regulations. Preference for marriage between half-sisters and half-brothers within the royal lineage continued into the Koryŏ dynasty.[79] Succession did not follow "simple linearity"; descent was "reckoned bilaterally," and a man could become king through his mother or wife as well as through his father. Werner Sasse hypothesizes that in Silla,[80]

if there was a boy qualified enough, he would become king. If there was "only" a daughter with the proper legitimation available, she would pass on the kingship to her husband ... in case neither was at hand, but there was a daughter of a former king, who had a son, this boy also was qualified to become king ... succession was not restricted to the next generation; it could pass within the same generation, as well as jump over a number of generations.

The bone rank (*kolp'um* 骨品) system which defined the Silla aristocracy eventually gave way to elite surname groups who identified themselves with a locality. Many *pon'gwan ssijok* 本貫氏族, the Korean version of the "great medieval clans" of Tang China, were descendants of Silla aristocrats who had moved to the provinces after 668 AD.[81] For most of the

[77] Sarah M. Nelson, "The Queens of Silla: Power and Connections to the Spirit World," in *Ancient Queens: Archaeological Explorations*, ed. Sarah M. Nelson (Walnut Creek, CA: Altamira Press, 2003), pp. 77–92, cites seven cases of kings whose qualification for rule rested on the lineage of their queens.

[78] Sarah M. Nelson, "Gender Hierarchy and the Queens of Silla," in *Sex and Gender Hierarchies*, ed. Barbara D. Miller (Cambridge: Cambridge University Press, 1993), p. 301, citing Chong-sun Kim. There is also a suggestion that there may have been joint rule by a man and woman: see Sarah M. Nelson, "The Statuses of Women in Ko-Shilla: Evidence from Archaeology and Historic Documents," *Korea Journal* 31.2 (1991): 106.

[79] Deuchler, *Confucian Transformation*, pp. 57–60; Koryŏ royal marriage practice incurred criticism from the Mongols, see p. 60.

[80] Sasse, "Trying to Figure Out," p. 231.

[81] John B. Duncan, "The Formation of the Central Aristocracy in Early Koryŏ," *Korean Studies* 12 (1988): 39–58; see also James B. Palais, "Confucianism and the Aristocratic/Bureaucratic Balance in Korea," *Harvard Journal of Asiatic Studies* 44.2 (1984): 427–68.

Koryŏ period, the *pon'gwan ssijok* dominated their localities. As late as the middle of the twelfth century, the central government was able to place its own officials in only about a third of the country's prefectures and counties.[82]

The establishment of a civil service examination system in 958 AD introduced a new mode of recruitment for government office that continued through the Chosŏn dynasty (1392–1910). During the eleventh and twelfth centuries, ambitious men from the *pon'gwan ssijok* moved to the capital to take up the newly created high-ranking offices.[83] The major new social development of the late Koryŏ period was the segmentation of the *pon'gwan ssijok*, as the descendants of men who achieved high official rank and moved permanently to the capital formed a new "central aristocracy," although the formal establishment of independent clan branches often occurred only in the fifteenth and sixteenth centuries.[84]

The transformation of the Korean *chok* 族 into patrilineages dates from the seventeenth century onward. Henceforth, the term *chok* specifically designates patrilineal groups. The *chok* of eighteenth-century Chosŏn *yangban* society, described as "one of the most rigidly patrilineal descent systems known to ethnography," most resembled an extreme form of the lineage found in modern south China.[85] Daughters lost their inheritance rights but in return received dowries. Their brothers, too, were now sharply differentiated into the sons of the wife, who inherited *yangban* status, and sons of concubines, who were excluded.

Members of a *yangban* 兩班 lineage traced their ancestry back to a focal ancestor whose surname they shared.[86] They identified themselves with

For exposition of the Tang model, see David G. Johnson, *The Medieval Chinese Oligarchy* (Boulder: Westview Press, 1977).

[82] Duncan, "Formation of the Central Aristocracy."   [83] *Ibid.*, pp. 46–47.

[84] John Duncan, "The Social Background of the Founding of the Chosŏn Dynasty: Change or Continuity?" *Journal of Korean Studies* 6 (1988–89): 66–75.

[85] The quotation is from Mutsuhiko Shima, "In Quest of Social Recognition: A Retrospective View on the Development of Korean Lineage Organization," *Harvard Journal of Asiatic Studies* 50.1 (1990): 87. On the use of the south/southeast China model, see Deuchler, *Confucian Transformation*, pp. 6–9 and especially fn 2 and 3, pp. 307–8, which cite essays by James L. Watson and Maurice Freedman as sources for technical kinship terms: both scholars specialized in research on south and southeast Chinese lineages, which tended to be the most androcentric lineages with large corporate landholdings and local power. On the different types of lineages in China, see the essays in Ebrey and Watson, *Kinship Organization in Late Imperial China* and Patricia B. Ebrey, "Types of Lineages in Ch'ing China: A Reexamination of the Chang Lineage of T'ung-ch'eng," *Ch'ing-shih wen-t'i* 4.9 (1983): 1–20.

[86] Although Shima, "In Quest of Social Recognition," equates *chok* with the "clan," and calls segmented branches (*munjung*) "lineages" or "sub-lineages," the phenomena he describes are two to three centuries after the period treated in this text, when kinship organization in Korea had developed to levels that were not achieved in earlier periods.

"a common ancestral seat" (本貫 *pon'gwan*).[87] Beginning in the seventeenth century, prominent lineages compiled and published genealogies which included information on the main line (the line descending from the eldest son of the wife, in each generation) and branches. Sacrifices to the ancestors were conducted by male kinsmen, often with revenues acquired from corporately owned lands, at ancestral halls (司堂 *sadang*) and at the lineage graveyards.

The Chosŏn patrilineage differed from its Chinese counterpart in several important respects. This kind of organization was limited to a select number of elite Korean descent groups. Unlike Chinese lineages, membership was confined to the sons of the wife; sons by concubines were excluded. By definition, a *yangban* wife had to be born of *yangban* parents on both the father's and the mother's side. Deuchler notes that it is ironic that in such a deeply androcentric society, a man's *yangban* status hinged on the social status of his mother.[88]

Chosŏn royal succession

Korean historians of the Chosŏn dynasty (1392–1907) tend to cast royal succession in Confucian terms. The proper heir to the throne is the eldest son of the wife.[89] The heir should be invested as Crown Prince, *seja* 世子, while other royal sons receive princely titles but leave the palace at age eighteen.[90] Table 4.5, however, shows that this ideal was realized by only ten of the twenty-seven Chosŏn kings and was never observed during the first half-century after the establishment of the state.[91] Seven of thirteen Crown Princes failed to achieve kingship, three through their premature

---

[87] The *pon'gwan* continued to feature in Korean kinship in the twentieth century, but members of the *chok* were frequently distributed across the entire country: see Shima, "In Quest of Social Recognition," p. 89.

[88] Martina Deuchler, "'Heaven Does Not Discriminate': A Study of Secondary Sons in Chosŏn Korea," *Journal of Korean Studies* 6 (1988–89): 125: "women were key figures in transmitting the right to membership in the husbands' descent group. Only *yangban* women could bestow *yangban* qualification upon their children, and this limitation made the *yangban* a practically endogamous status group."

[89] See, for example, Yi Pŏmjik, "Chosŏn hugi wangsil kujo yŏngu – Injodae rŭl chungsim ŭro," *Kuksagwan nonch'ong* 80 (1998): 279–316; Yi Yŏngch'un, *Chosŏn hugi wangwi*, p. 87: "The principle of lineage law regarding royal succession, that is, the idea that the eldest son of the wife should be the successor, can be thought to have been settled since the Three Kingdoms era in our country."

[90] JaHyun Kim Haboush, *The Confucian Kingship in Korea: Yŏngjo and the Politics of Sagacity* (New York: Columbia University Press, 2001), pp. 104–5; Oh Chongnok, "Chosŏn sidae ŭi wang" (Kings of the Chosŏn period), *Yŏksa pip'yŏng* 54 (2001): 292, 300.

[91] Yi Yŏngch'un, *Chosŏn hugi wang'wi*, table 3, p. 90 lists fourteen royals who were designated as heir but never ascended the throne; of these, only Yangnyŏng taegun, the first son of T'aejong's queen, was appointed before the middle of the fifteenth century.

Table 4.5. *Chosŏn royal succession*

Ruler	Name	Life dates	Reign dates	Relationship to predecessor
T'aejo	太祖	1335–1408	1392–1398	
Chŏngjong	定宗	1357–1419	1398–1400	#2 son of Queen Sin'ŭi 神懿, 韓氏
T'aejong	太宗	1367–1422	1400–1418	younger bro, #5 son of Queen Sin'ŭi
Sejong	世宗	1397–1450	1418–1450	#3 son of Queen Wŏn'gyŏng 元敬, 閔氏
Munjong	文宗	1414–1452	1450–1452	#1 son of Queen Sohŏn 昭憲, 沈氏
Tanjong	端宗	1441–1457	1452–1455	#1 son of Queen Hyŏndŏk, 顯德, 權氏
Sejo	世祖	1417–1468	1455–1468	uncle, #2 son of Queen Sohŏn & Sejong
Yejong	睿宗	1450–1469	1468–1469	#2 son of Queen Chŏnghŭi 貞熹, 尹氏
Sŏngjong	成宗	1457–1494	1469–1494	Yejong's eldest brother's second son
Yonsangun	燕山君	1476–1506	1494–1506	#2 son from a concubine, 尹氏
Chungjong	中宗	1488–1544	1506–1544	older half-brother, son of Queen Chŏnghyŏn 貞顯, 尹氏
Injong	仁宗	1515–1545	1544–1545	#1 son of Queen Changgyŏng 章敬, 尹氏
Myŏngjong	明宗	1534–1567	1545–1567	half-brother, son of Queen Munjŏng 文定, 尹氏
Sŏnjo	宣祖	1552–1608	1567–1608	generation below Myongjong, his father was #9 son of Chungjong from Ch'angbin 昌嬪, 安氏
Kwanghaegun	光海君	1575–1641	1608–1623	#3 son of Kongbin 恭嬪, 金氏
Injo	仁祖	1595–1649	1623–1649	nephew, through younger half-brother
Hyojong	孝宗	1619–1659	1649–1659	#2 son of Queen Inyŏl 仁烈, 韓氏
Hyŏnjong	顯宗	1641–1674	1659–1674	#1 son of Queen Insŏn 仁宣, 張氏
Sukchong	肅宗	1661–1720	1674–1720	only son of Queen Myŏngsŏng 明聖, 金氏
Kyŏngjong	景宗	1688–1724	1720–1724	#1 son of Hŭi bin 禧嬪, 張氏
Yŏngjo	英祖	1694–1776	1724–1776	younger brother, #2 son of Sukchong by Sukbin 淑嬪, 崔氏
Chŏngjo	正祖	1752–1800	1776–1800	grandson, through Prince Sado
Sunjo	純祖	1790–1834	1800–1834	eldest (only) surviving son of Subin 綏嬪, 朴氏
Hŏnjong	憲宗	1827–1849	1834–1849	grandson through only son and consort Mme 趙氏
Ch'ŏljong	哲宗	1831–1863	1849–1863	different segment; predecessor had no sons. Same generation as Honjong, great-grandson of Yŏngjo
Kojong	高宗	1852–1919	1863–1907	Ch'ŏljong without sons; fifth generation descendant of Yŏngjo

Sources: Compiled from data in *Chŏnju Yi ssi taegwan* 全州李氏大觀, comp. Chonju Yi ssi taedong ch'ongyagwŏn. Seoul: Chonju Yi ssi taedong ch'ongyagwŏn, 2002.

demise and two others when their fathers were dethroned. In two instances the eldest son was passed over in favor of the second son: this was how Yejong (r. 1468–69) and Sŏngjong (r. 1469–94) attained the throne.

When Yejong died in 1469, fourteen months after being enthroned, decisions concerning his successor were the prerogative of the senior widow, his mother Dowager Queen Chŏnghŭi, from the famous P'ap'yŏng Yun lineage. Yejong had a son by Queen Changsun, Mme Han, but the dowager queen passed over this son and a son by his consort, another Mme Han, selecting instead her grandson through Yejong's elder brother, Prince Ŭigyŏng. By selecting a thirteen-year-old king, Dowager Queen Chŏnghŭi established herself as regent. Hers was the first of seven female regencies during the Chosŏn period.[92] As we shall see below, female regencies were the Korean equivalent of the Fujiwara regents. The senior woman wielded her prerogative to place an immature ruler on the throne, allowing her natal kinsmen to occupy major offices at court under her regency.[93]

Female regencies were a distinctive feature of the late Chosŏn period. By far the most dramatic political events at court were those known as *panjŏng* 反正, or coups d'état, because they initiated a series of events which had to be explained to the Ming court, occasioning a flurry of deliberations on both the Chinese and Korean sides that help us visualize the texture of diplomatic relations as they actually existed. We begin by focusing on one of the most famous, the overthrow of King Kwanghae, known as the Injo panjŏng.

Korean coups d'état: exchanges with Ming

The palace coup that dethroned the Chosŏn King Kwanghae on April 13, 1623 was preceded by a period of mounting tension within the capital,

[92] Kim Ugi, "Chosŏn Sŏngjongdae Chŏnghŭi wanghu ŭi suryŏm ch'ŏngjŏng" (The regency of Queen Chŏnghŭi during the Sŏngjong reign in the Chosŏn dynasty). *Chosŏnsa yŏn'gu* 10 (2001): 169–212. Im Hyeryŏn, "Sunjo ch'oban Chŏngsun wanghu ŭi suryom ch'ŏngjŏng kwa ch'ŏngguk pyŏnhwa" (The female regency of Queen Chŏngsun during the first half of the Sunjo reign and political change). *Chosŏn sidaesa hakpo* 15 (2000): 153–79, notes that the Koreans justified female regency by citing the example of Song Empress Dowager Xuanren (1032–93) who served as "temporary regent" upon the death of Shenzong in 1085. On the political impact of her regency, which reversed the New Policies enacted under Shenzong, see Ari Daniel Levine, "Che-tsung's Reign (1085–1100) and the Age of Faction," in *The Cambridge History of China*, vol. V, part 1: *The Sung Dynasty and Its Precursors, 907–1279*, ed. Denis Twitchett and Paul Jakov Smith (Cambridge: Cambridge University Press, 2009), pp. 484–531.
[93] Empresses Dowager could also play an important role during moments of crisis in Ming China; see de Heer, *Caretaker Emperor*, pp. 10–11, 21–23.

Hansŏng. Two days earlier, the Minister of Military Affairs, Kwŏn Chin, had reported that four days had gone by since troops from Kyŏnggi and Chŏlla had gathered at the Muhwa palace. A resolution of the tense situation was needed.[94] That same day there was a secret report that the "bandit general" had been captured. Yi Yiban had met a friend on the street who invited him to join in the coup d'état, so the two men proceeded to the palace. That night, the inner quarters of the palace caught fire. Yi Hŭng'nip, commander of the Military Training Agency, supported Kim Ryu, Yi Kui, and the other coup leaders, who entered the palace and occupied the audience hall of the Ch'angdŏk palace (Injŏngjŏn) while Kwanghae climbed a ladder to escape and sought refuge at the house of a doctor, An Kuksin. The Crown Prince also went into hiding.[95]

On the next day, April 12, the insurgents captured the Privy Seal and announced the coup d'état to the officials at the Kyŏng'un palace, hunting down and in some cases killing *Taebuk* factional leaders and other officials who had played prominent roles in the Kwanghae administration.[96] With the aid of an informant, Kwanghae was discovered; he was escorted to the palace, where he "presented" the Privy Seal to the Dowager Queen.[97] Kwanghae and his son, the Crown Prince, were then reduced to commoner status.[98]

A proclamation, issued in the name of the Dowager Queen, Inmok taebi (Sŏnjo's second queen), laid out the justification for the coup.[99] First, as the son of a concubine, Kwanghae was not the proper heir. In 1608, when Sŏnjo died, Inmok taebi's own son, Prince Yŏngch'ang, born in 1606, should have become king according to the eldest son principle. Second, even before becoming king, Kwanghae's "lack of virtue" dismayed his father, who "deeply regretted" his decision to declare Kwanghae his heir. Although Kwanghae should have treated Inmok taebi as his mother, he was misled by "the slanders of deceitful and cunning ministers" into murdering Inmok's parents, taking Prince

[94] *Kwanghaegun ilgi, Taebaek sansa*, ed. Kwanghae 15/3/12 #1.
[95] *Kwanghaegun ilgi*, ed. Kwanghae 15/3/12 #6. On the Injŏngjŏn, see Edward B. Adams, *Palaces of Seoul: Yi Dynasty Palaces in Korea's Capital City* (Seoul: Taewon Publishing Co., 1972), pp. 83–85.
[96] According to Adams, *Palaces of Seoul*, p. 158, the Kyŏng'ungong was a royal villa on the site of today's Tŏksu kung. The Taebuk faction dominated the Kwanghae court.
[97] On the major events of April 12, see *Kwanghaegun* ilgi, ed. Kwanghae 15/3/13, #1, 2, 3, 4, 7, 8, 9 (see the variant texts in the Chŏngjongsansa edition, which is also available on the database.)
[98] *Kwanghaegun ilgi*, ed. Kwanghae 15/3/14 (April 13, 1623), #1.
[99] The entire text from *Injo sillok* is translated by JaHyun Kim Haboush in her *Epistolary Korea: Letters in the Communicative Space of the Chosŏn, 1392–1910* (New York: Columbia University Press, 2009), pp. 34–36.

Yŏngch'ang into custody (and killing him); putting Inmok under house arrest; murdering other members of the royal family; and initiating purges which harmed many innocent people. Kwanghae was also guilty of lavish expenditures on "two enormous palaces." He expelled trusted old ministers from office and favored palace women, eunuchs, and his in-laws. Favoritism and corruption were rampant at court, corvée and other tax burdens caused misery among the populace.

The enumeration of Kwanghae's crimes culminated in his rejection of the behavior proper to a vassal state. Instead of exerting himself to *sadae*, i.e. to serve his overlord, as had his ancestors, he forgot the indebtedness due Ming for coming to Chosŏn's aid during the Japanese invasion. He "displayed undue friendship" with the Jurchen barbarians.[100] In 1619 "he confidentially ordered a general (who led the Korean contingent) to move with caution." This led to the surrender at the battle of Sarhū, in which the Ming experienced a major military setback. As a result, "an ugly and humiliating rumor" that he ordered the Koreans to surrender to the Jurchen spread "far and wide within the four seas." Ming requests for military aid were repeatedly rejected. "Kwanghae betrayed the principle of Heaven and destroyed human relationships, sinning against the dynasty ... and causing resentment among the people ... Now that his crimes have reached this degree, how can he be permitted to govern the state, reign over the people, occupy the Heaven-given throne, and worship the spirits at the Altar of Land and Grain?"

Inmok taebi replaced Kwanghae with a grandson of Sŏnjo, Prince Nŭngyang. Favored by Sŏnjo and reared in the palace, the future King Injo had received the childhood name "Heaven-Appointed Heir." Freeing Inmok taebi and restoring her titles, the prince's "merit is so great and resplendent, causing gods and humans alike to turn to him, as to qualify him to take the throne and to inherit the mantle of King Sŏnjo."

What Korean historians call the "Injo panjŏng" (literally, the Injo "restoration to orthodoxy") was the last of four such events in the Chosŏn dynasty The first coup d'état was carried out by T'aejong (Yi Pangwŏn, r. 1400–18), whose situation was comparable to that of the Ming Yongle emperor (r. 1403–24). The dynastic founder Yi Sŏnggye had several sons who were important military commanders; the eldest, Pang'u, predeceased his father, who in 1398 designated Pangsŏk, a second son by his second wife, Mme Kang, as Crown Prince. Pangsŏk and his older brother Pangbŏn were killed for "crimes" by a half-brother,

[100] All quotations are from Yi Yŏngch'un, *Chosŏn hugi wangwi*, pp. 87–96.

Pangwŏn, who deposed his older brother, Yi Sŏnggye's second eldest son, Panggwa, and took the throne.[101]

As in the early Ming, the military prowess that allowed a man to overthrow the established authority and create a new ruling house also provided his sons with an independent power base with which to contest the succession. Coups could arise from tensions within the royal family or from conflicts between the king and Confucian scholar-officials. Court politics pitted the king against his royal kinsmen on the one hand, and his mother's and wife's relatives on the other. Kings had to find a way to balance these forces while struggling against an obstreperous officialdom, coalesced around factions, that was determined to fight for the decision-making prerogative.

Tanjong, the eldest son of the queen, was only eleven years old when he was enthroned in 1452. Normally his mother, Queen Hyŏndŏk, or grandmother, Dowager Queen Sohyŏn, would have served as regent until he reached adulthood, but neither was alive, so his father's younger brother Prince Suyang (Yi Yu) took charge of state affairs. The prince dealt decisively to eliminate high ministers who opposed him. In the sixth intercalary month of 1455, he banished Tanjong's full brother, Prince Kŭmsŏng, other royal kinsmen and officials, and took the throne with the support of "disaffected elements among the literati."[102] As Sejo, he ruled from 1455 to 1468, purging officials who attempted to restore Tanjong to the throne and exiling (then killing) his rival for power, his full brother, Prince Anp'yŏng.[103]

---

[101] On Pang'u, see his treatment in *Chŏnju Yi ssi taegwan*, comp. Chŏnju Yi ssi taedong chong yagwŏn (Seoul: Chŏnju Yi ssi taedong chong yagwŏn, 2000), p. 777. This modern compilation of the royal Yi genealogy shows that Pang'u left two sons, the eldest of whom also had two sons; but their life dates are not included. Both Yi Pangbŏn and Yi Panggwa are listed by Duncan, *Origins of the Chosŏn Dynasty*, table 5.1, p. 227 as "consolidated army command officials" in 1393. Duncan, p. 228, also describes Yi Pangwŏn's attacks on followers of Pangsŏk and brother Panggan during efforts to centralize control over military forces. Peterson, *Korean Adoption*, p. 81, calls the attack on Pangsŏk "a preemptive coup."

[102] *Sejo sillok*, Sejo 1/i6/11#1=July 25, 1455. See Han Chunghŭi, "Chosŏn Sejo dae (1455–1468) ŭi naejongch'in e taehayŏ" (On the royal kinsmen in the Chosŏn Sejo reign, 1455–1468), *Kyŏngbuk sahak* 21 (1998): 913–44, also Im Chung'ung, *Chosŏn wangjo wangbi yŏlchŏn* (Biographies of Chosŏn kings and queens) (Seoul: Sŏkch'ŏn midiŏ, 2002), pp. 69–72. For particulars on the coup politics, see Chi Tu-hwan, *Chosŏn chŏngi ŭirye yŏn'gu – sŏngnihak chŏngt'ongnon ŭl chungsim ŭro* (A study of early Chosŏn ritual – focusing on orthodox Neo-Confucianism) (Seoul: Seoul University Press, 1994), pp. 68–71 and Kim Ton, "Sejodae 'Tanjong pongnip undong' kwa wang'wi sŭnggye munje" (The movement to restore Tanjong during the Sejo reign, and succession issues), *Yŏksa kyoyuk* 98 (2006): 205–35.

[103] Quotation from Lee, *New History*, p. 173; Han Chunghŭi, "Chosŏn Sejo dae." Also Yi Yŏngch'un, *Chosŏn hugi wangwi*, p. 92; Pak Yŏnggyu, *Han kwŏn ŭro ingnŭn Chosŏn*

The timing of the coup raised some awkward diplomatic moments, since Ming envoys were actually in the country.[104] The Ming court initially hesitated to invest Yi Yu as king: if Tanjong were sickly, there was still a chance he would regain his health and be able to resume his royal duties.[105] Rumors about the coup d'état circulated despite the Korean court's efforts at concealment. Eventually, in the fourth lunar month of 1546 (May 24, 1546), Yi Yu received the Ming emperor's investiture.[106]

Different circumstances surrounded the dethronement of Yŏnsangun and the installation of his younger, half-brother Chungjong (r. 1506–44). Like Tanjong, Yŏnsangun was the eldest son of the queen, hence the legitimate heir. Moreover, he was eighteen when he became king and ruled in his own right. The explanations for the coup against him that are recorded in the *sillok* cite Yŏnsangun's violent and tyrannical behavior, exemplified in two major purges of the literati.[107] The *Muo sahwa* (literati

---

wangsil kyebo (A condensed genealogy of the Chosŏn royal house) (Seoul: Ŭngjin, 2008), pp. 78–84, 192–96. See the biography of Tanjong in Im Chung'ung, *Chosŏn wangjo wangbi yŏlchŏn*, pp. 69–72; Kim Ton, "Sejo dae 'Tanjong pongnip undong." The men who supported Tanjong's restoration and were executed are known as the Six Martyred Officials 死六臣. Sejo's removal of Munjong's queen's grave and tablet from the sacrifices accorded royal ancestors became an issue for Confucian scholars in the reign of Yŏnsangun (1494–1506): see Yi Hyŏnjin, "Chosŏn chŏngi Sorŭng pokwiron ŭi ch'u'i wa kŭ ŭimi" (Changes in the controversy over the restoration of Sorŭng in early Chosŏn and its meaning), *Chosŏn sidae sahakpo* 23 (2002): 49–83.

[104] *Sejo sillok*, Sejo 1/i6/13#9=July 27, 1455, which reports that "a Chinese envoy, Gao Fu, requests permission to report the news of the "joyful event" (the coup) to Ming so that the proper royal attire can be sent to Sejo. Also 1/i6/16#4=July 30, 1455, which records that Prince Nosan (the deposed Tanjong) and Sejo both fêted the Ming envoys. The envoys did not leave until August; see *Sejo sillok*, Sejo 1/7/6#1=August 18, 1455; Sejo 1/7/7#1=August 19, 1455; Sejo 1/7/8#1 and #2=August 20, 1455, and Sejo 1/7/9#1 and #2= August 21, 1455.

[105] See Wang Qiju, ed., *Ming shilu: Lingguo Chaoxian pian ziliao* (Beijing: Zhongguo bianjiang shidi yanjiu zhongxin, 1983) (hereafter MSLC), pp. 152–53, Jingtai 6/8/22=November 1, 1455, see Korean draft of this document, *Sejo sillok*, Sejo 1/i6/29#2=August 12, 1455 and the Ming response in the Korean record, *Sejo sillok*, Sejo 1/10/13#3=November 22, 1455. In *Sejo sillok*, Sejo 1/10/13#3=November 22, 1455, the Chumun Envoy, Kim Ha, returned from the Ming capital bearing the imperial *chi*. He reported that during his travels en route to Peking, on September 9, he had a conversation with a military officer in Songshanbao who said, "I hear that Prince Shouyang (Sejo) has taken the throne, and that everyone is delighted."

[106] The coup d'état was disguised as Tanjong's "retirement" for reasons of ill health; see *Sejo sillok*, Sejo 1/i6/29#2=August 12, 1455, 1/10/13#3=November 1, 1455, 1/10/24#1=November 12, 1455, and 2/4/20#2=May 24, 1456; for the Ming version of these communications, see MSLC, p. 152, entry dated Jingtai 6/8/22=October 3, 1455 and p. 153, entry dated Jingtai 7/1/5=February 20, 1456.

[107] Oh, Chongnok, "Chosŏn sidae ŭi wang;" Pak Yŏnggyu, *Han kwŏn ŭro ingnŭn*, pp. 92–94. See also JaHyun Kim Haboush, "The Education of the Yi Crown Prince: A Study in Confucian Pedagogy," in *The Rise of Neo-Confucianism in Korea*, ed. W. T. de Bary and JaHyun Kim Haboush (New York: Columbia University Press, 1985), pp. 210–12.

purge of 1498) was the first of its kind and has been interpreted as the result of a struggle between two elite groups at court, the "meritorious elite," many of whom derived high status from marital connections with the royal family, and Confucian scholars staffing the Censorate and the Office of Special Advisers. The direct stimulus was the inclusion of veiled critiques of the Sejo usurpation in the draft annals of Sŏngjong's reign. The second, the *Kapcha sahwa* (1504) targeted not only literati but palace ladies and royal kinsmen whom Yŏnsangun blamed for the dismissal and execution of his mother, Sŏngjong's second queen, Mme Yun.[108]

The Chosŏn usurpations perpetuated a tradition of irregularities in succession. In the Koryŏ dynasty, especially during the period of military rule (1170–1259), three kings were dethroned, but even earlier, there were occasions when the choice of potential successors seems to have been checked only by fear of the ensuing diplomatic repercussions.[109] T'aejong decreed that sons of concubines (*sŏja*) should not be allowed to serve in high office, but the rule was broken more than once.[110] Even after the "Confucianization" of inheritance practices in the seventeenth century created patrilineages among the *yangban* elite, royal succession remained idiosyncratic. Only one king in each of the eighteenth and nineteenth centuries was the natural son of his predecessor, and none was the eldest son of the queen.[111]

Informing the Ming

The different politico-cultural traditions of Chosŏn Korea and Ming China confronted each other most prominently in the implementation

---

[108] Lee, *New History*, pp. 204–5. The 1494 literati purge (*Mu'o sahwa*) and the 1504 purge (*Kapcha sahwa*) are extensively studied; recent studies analyzing them as struggles between the throne and the Confucian bureaucracy include Kim Pŏm, *Sahwa wa panchŏng ŭi sidae* (Eras of literati purges and coups d'états) (Seoul: Yŏksa pip'yŏnsa, 2007), chapter 2, and Kim Ton, *Chosŏn chŏngi kunsin kwŏllyŏk kwan'gye yŏn'gu* (Research on ruler–servant authority relations in early Chosŏn) (Seoul: Seoul University Press, 1997), pp. 59–97.

[109] As a vassal state, Koryŏ was expected to report on abdications and obtain approval of a new ruler to the overlord: see the long negotiations with the Liao court ensuing from Wang Ong's usurpation of the throne from his nephew King Hŏnjong (1095) in Rogers, "Sukchong of Koryŏ," pp. 33, 35. On similar negotiations between the military dictators and the Jin court, see Michael C. Rogers, "Koryŏ's Military Dictatorship and Its Relations with Chin," *T'oung Pao* 47.1–2 (1959): 43–62. On the domestic impact of coups d'états, see Remco E. Breuker, "Forging the Truth: Creative Deception and National Identity in Medieval Korea," *East Asian History* 35 (2008): 1–73, who argues that T'aejo's "Ten Injunctions" were forged during the reign of Hyŏnjong (1009–31) by high officials seeking to bolster his legitimacy (Hyŏnjong also ascended the throne through a coup d'état).

[110] Peterson, *Korean Adoption*, p. 81.

[111] Oh Chongnok, "Chosŏn sidae ŭi wang," p. 299.

of the tribute system. As a vassal state, Chosŏn had to inform its Ming overlord of any change of ruler in order to obtain the imperial patents, seals of office, and court clothing that legitimized each new king. Chosŏn officials worried about how to report the sudden replacement of one king by another. Their fabrications, designed to conceal the illegality of the irregular transfer of power, aroused Ming suspicions, which are recorded in the Veritable Records of the Ming (*Ming shilu*).

Although the coup d'état that dethroned Kwanghae occurred on the thirteenth day of the third month (April 12, 1623), the *Ming shilu* first mentions the event in the entry for May 27. The "promulgation" by Dowager Queen Inmok denouncing Kwanghae was transmitted to the court through Ming commander Mao Wenlong, who was garrisoned at Dengzhou.[112] Recounting Kwanghae's crimes, the document ends with the statement that Inmok named Prince Nŭngyang as the successor in response to the people's wishes.[113] Shortly before the Ming court's deliberations, the Chosŏn court dispatched Prince Hanp'yŏng, Yi Kyŏngjin, to lead a delegation to Peking to request investiture for the new king. It took over two years after the coup for official recognition: the Ming patent and regalia for investiture did not arrive in Hansŏng until July 6, 1625.[114]

The Korean missive was accompanied by a memorial from Yuan Keli, Ming governor of Dengzhou, who expressed his horror at the rupture of the status order that determined superior and inferior (*mingfen*). Noting that what Yi Chong (Injo) had done "would be called a crime which shakes up the guiding principle of kingship," Yuan did not favor bestowing legitimacy. Instead, he suggested that the seriousness of the matter warranted close investigation to determine the culprits and the sentiment of the people.[115]

Yuan Keli's comments reveal the most pressing objection confronting the Ming court and its high officials when they deliberated on the Chosŏn coup d'état. Openly acknowledging and legitimizing the dethronement of a king by his subjects challenged the hierarchical world order that was centered on the Ming emperor, and by implication, the stability of all rulers. It was one thing to recognize the founder of a new dynasty; the dynastic cycle could be ascribed to the Mandate of Heaven. But for subjects to overthrow their sovereign was not to be lightly condoned. After all, as one official noted, the Chosŏn people should have asked the Ming emperor for redress instead of taking matters into their own hands.

[112] The full text of Inmok's decree has been translated into English by Haboush, *Epistolary Korea*, pp. 34–36.
[113] MSLC, p. 556, memorial dated Tianqi 3/4/29.   [114] *Injo sillok*, Injo 3/6/3 #1.
[115] *Ibid.*

The Injo coup differed from its predecessors in openly declaring that Kwanghae had been deposed because of his crimes. T'aejong's coup in 1400 was presented to the Ming as a petition: "The Chosŏn king, Yi Tan, is aged and requests that his son Pangwŏn be made his successor."[116] Again, when Tanjong was overthrown in 1455 by his uncle, the petition to the Ming stated that because of his sickly and enfeebled condition, Tanjong was requesting that his uncle take charge of state affairs.[117] Approval of the petition, embodied in the dispatch of eunuchs bearing the imperial *chi*, patent, and royal regalia, came in less than a year.[118]

The ease with which the Ming court approved Tanjong's "petition" to pass the throne to his uncle may reflect the court's preoccupation during the 1450s with the Mongol Esen's raids on the capital following his capture of Yingzong, the Zhengtong emperor (1449). This event necessitated the hasty installation of the emperor's younger brother, Prince Cheng, first as regent, then as emperor. From 1450 to 1457, when Yingzong resumed rule, Ming officials were busy handling pressing military matters within the empire as well as on the frontier.[119]

The situation was rather different in the coup d'état of September 17, 1506, which dethroned Yŏnsan (known as Prince Yŏnsan, Yŏnsangun) and put Chungjong on the throne.[120] Whereas the *Chosŏn sillok*, edited after the coup, portrayed the former king "as an irresponsible and unstable tyrant who lashed out viciously against the upright Neo-Confucians who staffed Korea's Censorate,"[121] recent scholarship has placed Yŏnsan's actions within the broader context of the throne's effort to reduce the power and authority of the Confucian establishment, which had come to dominate court politics.[122]

The enumeration of Yŏnsan's crimes, intended for a domestic elite audience,[123] was not repeated in Chosŏn petitions to the overlord. According to the exchange of diplomatic correspondence recorded in the *Ming shilu*, the Chosŏn king, Yi Yung (King Yŏnsan), had "long been ill." Lacking an heir, he requested that his younger brother

---

[116] Tan Qian, *Guoque* 11.813, dated Jianwen 1/12/丁酉朔, in MSLC, p. 48.
[117] MSLC, pp. 152–3, document dated Jingtai 6/8/22.
[118] MSLC, p. 153, document dated Jingtai 7/2/4.
[119] Twitchett and Grimm, "Cheng-t'ung, Ching-t'ai, and T'ien-shun Reigns," pp. 322–39.
[120] See Yŏnsangun's biography in *Chŏnju Yi ssi taegwan*, pp. 388–404; also Pak Yŏnggyu, *Han kwŏn ŭro ingnŭn*, pp. 92–94.
[121] David M. Robinson, "Korean Lobbying at the Ming Court: King Chungjong's Usurpation of 1506: A Research Note," *Ming Studies* 41 (1999): 38.
[122] Kim Pŏm, *Sahwa wa panjŏng*, pp. 104–61.
[123] See for example Pak Yŏnggyu, *Han kwŏn ŭro ingnŭn*, pp. 92–94.

Yi Yŏk, Prince Chinsŏng, take over the management of state affairs. The Ming Board of Rites recommended investigation of the exact circumstances behind the transfer of authority, and worried about possible difficulties if Yung regained his health: wouldn't it be better for Yŏk to temporarily manage affairs and petition for investiture only after Yung died? When Chosŏn repeatedly sent envoys to apply for immediate investiture, the Ming court first demanded a formal petition from the senior consort to affirm Yung's illness, the virtue and abilities of Yŏk, and the unanimous support for Yŏk's enthronement among Chosŏn's officials and populace.[124] The Ming acknowledged Yi Yŏk as regent on December 30, 1507, and he was invested as king the following February.

Another Ming objection to Yi Yŏk's enthronement was that he was the brother, not the son, of his predecessor. The Chosŏn request falsely stated that Yi Yung had no sons: he actually had two sons by his wife, and two more by a consort. Unlike China, where fraternal succession was not normative, Korea had a long tradition of brother–brother succession. Similarly, Ming officials hesitated to approve Kwanghae's own investiture as crown prince because he was the son of Sŏnjo by a concubine. When his father fled before advancing Japanese troops in 1592, the court named Kwanghae crown prince at the age of eighteen, and Kwanghae went on to play an important role in mobilizing military resistance to the invaders. Obtaining the Ming emperor's consent, however, was a protracted process.

The *Ming shilu* records a petition from the Chosŏn king, Yi Yŏn (Sŏnjo), dated January 9, 1595. Having no son by his queen, he requested that Hon (the future Kwanghae), his second son by a concubine, be designated as Crown Prince. The Board of Rites replied that this request would be difficult to approve because the successor should really be the eldest son. Yi Yŏn's response explained that his eldest son, Yi Chin (1574–1609) was unfit to be king. Although he was no longer consorting with bandits (i.e., unfit to rule), he was not in good health and was easily agitated. By contrast Yi Hon was magnetic, had glorious achievements to his credit, and was gaining experience in military defense efforts. Ming officials at the Board of Rites were still unconvinced. Fan Qianzhi and Censor Xie Sancai emphasized the importance of the implementing of the Great Principle (*Da yi*) of retaining the proper distinction between elder and junior. To the emperor, the Board wondered just how it was supposed to ascertain the truth during chaotic times (the Japanese invasion would not be resolved until 1598),

[124] MSLC, pp. 230–32, memorials dated Zhengde 2/1/13, 2/1/27, 2/5/7, and 2/12/9.

and recommended postponing the decision until conditions were more stable.[125]

Further petitions for the investiture of Yi Hon arrived at the Ming court in April 1596 and March 1603. The Board of Rites officials were reluctant to alienate a "loyal and obedient" vassal state, but hesitated to override the eldest son succession principle. How, they asked, could a state which claimed to be a "country of ritual and principle (*li* and *yi*)" recklessly override the establishing principles by putting aside the eldest son in favor of his younger brother?

This hesitation continued even after Sŏnjo's death in 1608. In June 1608, shortly after it had received official notification of King Sŏnjo's death, the Ming Board of Rites bewailed the fact that Yi Hon was in charge of state affairs and that the senior consort had formally requested his investiture as king. Chosŏn should have petitioned and waited for a determination from their overlord instead of repudiating precedent. What was at stake was not simply Chosŏn's royal legitimacy, but the legitimacy of the Ming state, which rested on its adherence to Confucian "fixed principles." The Wanli emperor ordered that the elder statesmen in Chosŏn should be summoned to explain just why Kwanghae should become king in place of his elder brother.[126]

Other voices in the Ming court spoke in favor of approving the Chosŏn petitions. "The Chosŏn succession matter is in the hands of that country, it is difficult to make decisions from afar."[127] The Chosŏn documents praised Yi Hon's battle merit in the *Imjin waeran*; the Ming Board of War also pointed to the delicate geopolitical situation in the northeast, where the Jurchen chief, Nurhaci, was strengthening his position as a regional power: "what the Jurchen chief wants is to make ties with Chosŏn, spruce up his military, and improve border defences."[128] In the meantime, Sŏnjo's death had been reported to the Ming court, so approval of a successor was no academic matter. In December 1608, the Board of Rites obtained an imperial edict which stated the Ming preference for eldest-son succession, but acquiesced to the Chosŏn request for investiture of Yi Hon, because "this matter is in a barbarian country (*yi bang*), they should follow their preferences."[129]

[125] MSLC, pp. 364, 372, dated Wanli 22/11/29 (January 9, 1595) and Wanli 23/9/1 (October 3, 1595) respectively.
[126] MSLC, pp. 383, 500, 509–10, memorials dated Wanli 24/4/1 (April 27, 1596), 31/2/14 (March 26, 1603), 36/4/23 (June 5, 1608), 36/4/26 (June 8, 1608); p. 509, *Wanli dichao*, p. 1555, edict dated Wanli 36/3 (April 1608).
[127] MSLC, p. 510, memorial dated Wanli 36/5/1 (June 12, 1608).
[128] MSLC, p. 510, memorial dated Wanli 36/5/4 (June 15, 1608).
[129] MSLC, p. 512, memorial dated Wanli 36/10/26 (December 3, 1608).

The Chosŏn side of the story

That the negotiations with Ming for investiture, i.e. sanction, of the change of kings described above are presented very differently in the *Chosŏn wangjo sillok* should come as no surprise. Studying the Korean attempts to obtain Ming approval of the 1506 coup, David Robinson observes that both the Chinese and Korean official accounts of the diplomacy attending these political transitions were sanitized, but for different purposes: the *sillok* records produced justifications for coups d'état by blackening the former king's character, while the *Ming shi* provides only a very condensed summary of both the documentary exchange and the human interaction, omitting completely the "gifts" conferred by Chosŏn on Ming envoys and officials to grease the path to approval of the *fait accompli.*[130] Korean envoys, taking the favored over-land route to Peking, first presented gifts to the Regional Commander of Liaodong, then to the Ming palace eunuchs, then to officials in the Board of Rites who handled relations with vassal states. Palace eunuchs were particularly useful to the envoys, not only because they could provide useful advice concerning court practices but also because they sometimes served as Ming envoys to Korea.

The extensive preparations of funds for "gifts" and the collection of intelligence concerning Ming responses to Chosŏn representations that Robinson cites for 1506–7 also characterize the diplomatic activities after the 1623 coup. Envoys Prince Hanp'yŏng, Yi Kyŏngjon, Yun Hwŏn, and Yi Minsŏng were dispatched to Peking on May 25, 1623. When the entourage reached Dengzhou (the Manchu takeover of Liaodong forced abandonment of the old overland route) and handed over the petition and list of presents, the military official in charge asked Memorializing Official (奏聞使, *chumunsa*)Yi Kyŏngjon, "Do you have a deposed king?" And he told Yi that news about the coup had reached Dengzhou on April 17, just four days after the actual occurrence.[131]

During his stay in Peking, Yi and his deputy, Yun Hwŏn, encountered various bureaucratic obstacles. Reporting from the Ming capital eight and a half months later, Yi noted that he had obtained assurances from Board of Rites President Lin Yaoyu that on the seventeenth day of the twelfth month (January 23, 1624), after lengthy consultations with officials in the Six Boards, Grand Secretariat, and Censorate, the Tianqi emperor had approved the Korean petition to obtain investiture for Injo. Yi's request of investiture for Injo's queen elicited further delay. To his query about the schedule for sending an envoy to carry the imperial patent and seals

[130] David M. Robinson, "Korean Lobbying," p. 38.
[131] *Injo sillok*, Tianqi 3/4/27 #2 (May 25, 1623).

investing Injo as king of Korea, the Board of Rites blamed the "unsafe conditions of sea passage" and the difficulty of finding anyone willing to undertake the assignment.[132] The investiture matter remained unresolved by the time Yi returned home and became the responsibility of the next Chosŏn envoy, Yi Tŏkdong, who was appointed in May 1624. Yi blamed the laggard response of Ming officials to Chosŏn requests for investiture on "the Ming side, (who) knowing the importance of this matter, have a thousand pretexts to suddenly create obstacles in order to demand [bribes]."[133]

Bureaucratic obstacles and delay necessitated the "greasing" of wheels, so taking extra funds for bribes seems to have been standard procedure when making requests of the overlord. During the intensive drive for "correcting" the record (辯 誣 K. *pyŏnmu*, literally, disputing a falsity) during the Chungjong reign (1506–44) and the Yŏngjo reign (1724–76), envoys sent to the Ming and Qing courts went armed with special funds for this purpose.[134]

Correcting the record

What Korean historians identify as the "Dispute about the Royal Lineage" *Chonggye pyŏnmu* 宗系辨誣 first arose after 1511, when Koreans learned that the first edition of the *Da Ming huidian* (Collected Statutes of the Ming Dynasty)[135] mistakenly identified the Chosŏn founder, Yi Sŏnggye, as the son of a prominent late Koryŏ official Yi In'im (李仁人) a man who was Yi's political opponent.[136] Citing information gleaned from the *Huang Ming zuxun* (Precepts of the Ming founder), the Collected Statutes noted that between 1373 and 1395 Yi Sŏnggye had murdered four Koryŏ royal kinsmen, and thus attained the throne by killing off the previous ruling line.[137]

---

[132] *Injo sillok*, Tianqi 4/3/15 #2 (May 2, 1624); see also Yi's report upon his return, Tianqi 4/ 4/21 #2 (June 7, 1624).

[133] *Injo sillok*, Tianqi 4/3/25 #3 (May 12, 1624) and 4/4/1 #3 (May 17, 1624).

[134] In the Yŏngjo reign, see the king's discussion on funds in Yŏngjo 47/5/22#4 (July 4, 1771).

[135] See Wolfgang Franke, *An Introduction to the Sources of Ming History* (Kuala Lumpur: University of Malaya Press, 1968), 6.1.2, p. 178 for particulars on the two editions of the *Da Ming huidian*. Also Wilkinson, *Chinese History: A New Manual*, p. 797. On the *Chonggye pyŏnmu*, see Lee, *New History*, p. 189, and Hwang Wŏn'gu, "Ch'ŏngdae ch'iljong sŏ sojae Chosŏn kisa ŭi pyŏnjong" (Corrections of Chosŏn affairs recorded in seven Qing books), *Tongbang hakji* 30 (1982): 265–73.

[136] According to Lee, *New History*, p. 189, the Ming mistakenly identified Yi Sŏnggye as "the son of the notorious, and anti-Ming, Yi In-im." See the Chinese text in the Zhengde edition of the *Da Ming huidian* (j. 96, Libu 55, *chaogong* 1).

[137] See Franke, *Introduction to Sources*, 6.1.5 (#10), p. 180 on inclusion of the *Huang Ming zuxun* in Zhang Lu's 1579 work, *Huang Ming zhishu*, and *Huang Ming zuxun lu* (1373).

The information was partially true. Yi Sŏnggye was a general serving under Koryŏ King Kongyang (r. 1389–92) when he rebelled and founded the new Chosŏn state. In 1392, he applied to Ming Taizu for recognition as a tribute vassal to shore up the legitimacy of his regime. Since the Ming court had already established lord–vassal relations with the Koryŏ kings, Yi's petition explained the dynastic transition by claiming that the Koryŏ royal line had died out and that Yi was selected by popular and official acclamation to lead the country.

The Chosŏn application to Ming Taizu draws attention to a problem that arose when applying Confucian principles to an international order based on geopolitical realities. When was a new regime no longer accused of usurping the established order? Because Chosŏn's legitimacy depended on its status within the Sinocentric world order, it was extremely sensitive to Chinese records about Korean political events, petitioning the Ming and later the Qing court for corrections of the historical record.

The arrival of the Ming Collected Statutes in Hansŏng kicked off a furor among officials. After the 1514 destruction of the library attached to the National Academy (Sŏnggyun'gwan), a major repository of such books,[138] Chosŏn sought to acquire Chinese ritual codes from the Ming. In response to the Chosŏn court's orders, the Zhengde edition of the Da Ming huidian was brought back to Hansŏng in 1518 by the tribute envoy. Reading the "very alarming" statements about the Chosŏn dynastic founder (described earlier in this chapter) in the section on Chosŏn under "Tributaries," the officials of the Royal Secretariat (Sŭngjŏngwŏn) reported that, "These volumes cannot be picked up by ordinary people," but recognized that there was a major obstacle in attempting to alter statements included in the Ming founder's preface, which "the [Ming] court has selected through group deliberations."[139] The Chosŏn court decided to send envoys to petition for a correction of the statements, which it feared would circulate widely through the Da Ming huidian and affect the opinions of future generations.

Because Chinese models were critical in efforts to systematize the ritual order, the Da Ming huidian was reprinted in Korea in 1551 as Tae Myŏng

---

The entries in Ming shilu are somewhat different: see the first mention of Yi Sŏnggye's overthrow of the Koryŏ in Hongwu 25/5/30 and the next entry, dated Hongwu 25/9/12, in MSLC, pp. 34–35.

[138] Kuwano Eiji, "Chōsen han [Shōtoku Dai Min kaiten] no seiritsu to sono genson – Chōsen zenki taiMin gaikō kōshō to sono kanren kara" (The establishment of a Chosŏn edition of the Zhengde Da Ming huidian and its current whereabouts – relating to foreign negotiations with Ming in early Chosŏn), Chōsen bunka kenkyū 5 (1998): 15.

[139] Chosŏn wangjo sillok, Chungjong 13/4/26 #1 (June 3, 1518); the offending passage occurs in juan 96, under the Board of Rites section in the Zhengde Da Ming huidian.

hoejŏn, with the offending passage excised.[140] Repeated attempts made through the Chungjong reign failed, in large part because of delays in the revision of the *Da Ming huidian*. Success came only in 1587, when the new Wanli edition of the *Da Ming huidian* omitted the offending passages.[141]

The sixteenth-century Chosŏn court also worried about what the Ming official compilations might say about succession. By the eighteenth century, a dynamic book culture spanning East Asia made censorship efforts much more difficult and complex. In July 1771, King Yŏngjo (r. 1724–76) summoned his councilors to discuss a book that had recently been purchased in Peking, *Kanggam hoech'an* (C. *Gangjian huizuan* 綱鑑會纂, The complete outline and details and the Comprehensive Mirror, edited as one).[142] Compiled by Zhu Lin in 1696, this unofficial history (野史 K. *ya sa*, C. *ye shi*) drew upon the Zhengde *Da Ming huidian* to repeat the calumny about Yi Sŏnggye's ancestry, which, after repeated petitions to the Ming court, had been erased from the Wanli edition.

Some officials argued for focusing the court's efforts on the official Ming History, then in preparation. *Ya sa* were money-making ventures and beneath notice, but the king feared that Zhu Lin's status as a Grand Secretary and the preface by President of the Board of Rites Zhang Ying would lend credence to the book's assertions. Yŏngjo was determined to eradicate these stains on the memory of his ancestors. Envoys should be sent to Peking to request that copies of *Kanggam hoech'an* be destroyed along with the carved woodblocks, and the compiler should be punished. But first, Yŏngjo decided to identify and punish those responsible for importing the book into Korea, and collect and destroy all copies of the work in Korea. Individuals who owned and/or had read these works were arrested, interrogated, and punished.[143]

Through July 1771, Yŏngjo expanded the hunt to include the offending texts which appeared in other publications: Zhu Lin's *Ming ji jilüe*

---

[140] Franke, *Introduction to Sources*, 6.1.2, p. 178; Kuwano, "Chōsen han [*Shōtoku Dai Min kaiten*] no seiritsu," studies an extant copy of the Korean edition which is held by the Hōsa bunko in Japan.

[141] On the Wanli edition, see Franke, *Introduction to Sources*, 6.1.2, p. 178.

[142] Yŏngjo 47/5/20#2=July 2, 1771, Yŏngjo 47/5/21#1=July 3, 1771. See Franke, *Introduction to Sources*, 1.3.9, p. 40, under *Tongjian Mingji chuanzai jilüe* by Zhu Lin. Franke notes that the work was "written in a rather careless way," but appeared in many editions that enjoyed wide circulation in early Qing times.

[143] See the punishment of Pak P'ilsun, Yŏngjo 47/5/23#3 (July 5, 1771), 47/5/26#1 (July 8, 1771), 47/5/26#1 (July 8, 1771); Chŏng Dŭkhan and Chŏng Lin, 47/6/1#3 (July 12, 1771), 47/6/2#3 (July 13, 1771); arrests of interpreters, 47/6/5#1 (July 16, 1771). According to a note on the record for 47/6/11#1 (July 22, 1771), ten people died as a result of this inquisition.

明記輯略 (K. *Myŏnggi chibyak*, Ming annals abbreviated), a historical chronicle of the late seventeenth century covering the period 1368–1659, which circulated widely in the early Qing period, drew on the Ming work *Huang Ming tongji* 皇明通紀 (Comprehensive annals of the Ming) by Chen Jian (1495–1567).[144] *Myŏngsa kangmok* 明史綱目 (Outline and details of the Ming History), a work compiled by a high Chosŏn official, Yi Hyŏnsŏk (1647–1703), was found to have included passages by Zhu Lin. Yi was posthumously stripped of his rank, and libraries holding copies of his book were ordered to erase the offending passage.[145] The king expanded his inquiries to *Pongju kanggam* 鳳洲鋼鑑 (C. *Fengzhou gangjian*, Fengzhou Outline and Mirror) and *Ch'ŏng'am ki* 青菴集 (C. *Qing'an ji*, Collection of the Qing'an).[146] It became an offense not simply to have read the book, but to have bought or sold it. At the same time, Yŏngjo acknowledged that the banning of books increased the desire of many to read forbidden passages, resulting in their quick reprinting.[147]

Injo panjŏng

As noted earlier, the Ming court had debated at some length before tacitly acquiescing to the coup d'état against Kwanghae by investing the new king, Injo, in 1625. Imagine the horror of the Chosŏn envoy Ko Yŏnghu, when he opened the pages of a newly published book entitled *Yangjo chongsinnok* (C. *Liangchao congxinlu* 兩朝從信錄, Trustworthy records of two dynasties) that he had purchased in Peking and brought back to Korea, thinking to deposit it in the Office of Special Counsellors (*Hongmungwan*). Glancing at the section on 1623, he came across the record of the Injo coup, which was recorded as "usurpation" (篡, K. *ch'an*, C. *cuan*): "My eyes could not scan the lines ... my hair stood on end, and my liver and innards were rent with pain ... if high officials did not read this book it would be fine, but if they were to read it, it could not be kept secret for one minute; so I have put a marker on the *kwŏn* (卷 C. *juan*) and am submitting this 24 *kwŏn* work under seal."[148]

[144] On *Huang Ming tongji*, see Franke, *Introduction to Sources*, 1.2.1, p. 33: this unofficial history of the 1351–1521 period was "one of the most popular histories of the Ming dynasty" despite its historical inaccuracies. The book was banned in the Qing but Franke writes of the existence of "a large number of later editions and supplements."

[145] Yŏngjo 47/5/29#4 (July 11, 1771).

[146] Yŏngjo 47/6/1#3 (July 12, 1771), 47/6/2#1 (July 13, 1771), 47/6/2#2 (July 13, 1771), 47/6/2#3 (July 13, 1771), 47/6/3#2 (July 14, 1771).

[147] Yŏngjo 47/5/26 (July 8, 1771).

[148] The passage appeared in a Korean work by Ko Puch'on (1578–1636), *Wŏlbonggi* 越峰集, and is quoted by Han Myŏnggi, "Sipch'al, p'al segi Han-Chung kwan'gye wa Injo

The 1630s were not propitious for petitions to correct the written record. A second Manchu invasion of Korea in 1636–37 forced the king to swear submission to the newly created Qing emperor, and there was heavy pressure (and surveillance) of the Chosŏn court until the Manchu entry into China Proper in 1644. Concerted action on removing these statements from the Chinese book did not take place until the Qing period. In 1676, even as the Chosŏn court waited for news of the Sanfan uprising in southwest China, King Sukjong (r. 1674–1720) convened high officials to discuss the discovery that the Injo coup d'état was reported in the *Liangchao congxin lu* and the *Huang Ming tongji* 皇明通紀. The court feared that the forthcoming officially commissioned Ming History would record the Injo coup as a usurpation.[149] After debate, the court decided to send an envoy to petition the Qing emperor for correction.[150] It was not until September, however, that Prince Poksŏn, Yi Nam, and deputy envoy Chŏng Sŏk received their orders to embark on the mission.[151]

Unfortunately for the Chosŏn court, *Huang Ming tongji* appeared in many editions and supplements, to eventually "outnumber all other works" in the *biannian* or annalistic pattern. Privately compiled by Chen Jian, a native of Guangdong and a *juren* of 1528, it was the "first comprehensive history of the Ming dynasty" when it appeared in 1555, giving an account of the 1351–1521 period.[152] The section of *Huang Ming tongji* covering 1351–98 was reprinted in Korea under the title *Hwang Myŏng kye'unnok* 皇明啟運錄, and in Japan as well.[153]

A popular book, *Huang Ming tongji* was incorporated into subsequent works. For example, it occupied the first fifteen of twenty-seven *juan* in Chen Longke's *Huang Ming tongji jilu* 皇明通紀紀錄, an early seventeenth-century book which extended the historical coverage to 1627.[154] *Huang Ming shiliu chao guanghui ji* 皇明十六朝廣彙記

panjŏng – Chosŏn hugi ŭi 'Injo panjŏng pyŏnmu' munje" (Sino-Korean relations in the seventeenth and eighteenth centuries and the Injo coup – the issue of the "Injo coup controversy" in late Chosŏn), *Han'guksa hakpo* 13 (2002): 16 fn19. For the Chinese record, see the *Ming Tianqi shilu*, Tianqi 3/4/29 (May 27, 1623), in MSLC, pp. 556–57, which states, "The king of Chaoxian, Li Zong (Yi Hon) has been ousted from the throne by his nephew, Li Zong (Yi Jong)" 朝鮮王李琿為其侄李倧所篡.

[149] *Chosŏn wangjo sillok*, Sukjong 2/1/25#1 (March 9, 1676).

[150] *Chosŏn wangjo sillok*, Sukjong 2/1/28 #3 (March 12, 1676).

[151] *Chosŏn wangjo sillok*, Sukjong 2/8/6#1 (September 13, 1676).

[152] Franke *Introduction to Sources*, 1.2.1 and p. 6. Franke identifies the many editions and supplements of this work on pp. 33–36.

[153] *Ibid.*, 1.2.2., p. 33, and 1.2.12, p. 36: the first Japanese edition, printed in Kyoto, was dated 1696, a second edition 1829.

[154] *Ibid.*, 1.2.8, p. 35.

(Records of the sixteen dynasties), a 1632 work by Wang Xiang, actually incorporates *Huang Ming tongji* in its first eleven juan.[155]

The Chosŏn efforts to eradicate all mentions of "usurpation" stemmed from the challenge that this reference made to the legitimacy of the ruling house. If Injo had illegally seized the throne, not only Injo but all subsequent kings were illegitimate. Officials at the court conference blamed the former Ming official Mao Wenlong for the "scurrilous" words. Against those who emphasized the difficulty of getting the Qing emperor to alter the Ming record, officials cited the Song History compiled by the Yuan dynasty: regardless of whether it truthfully reported on Song events, later generations took what was written as true.

Aware that the Kangxi emperor had commissioned the Ming History, high officials worried that the offending passages would be copied into the official record. Others noted that it was "mentally unsettling" (心有所未安) to request the despised Qing to change "old matters from the Ming era." Those counseling a "wait and see" policy recalled that the Ming had sent officials, including the governor of Dengzhou, to investigate the rumors of usurpation when they were debating approval of the Injo enthronement. Furthermore, the offending works were privately compiled, not officially commissioned; it was much more difficult to halt their circulation and erase the usurpation passage.

In the end, the king's sentiment ("When I read *Hwang Myŏng kiryak* 皇明紀略 with its statements that are unbearable to read and hear, when 'force' is recorded in the historical chronicles, pain fills my heart") prevailed.[156] The court would petition the Qing emperor and the Board of Rites for confiscation of books containing these passages. The expansion of printing in this era was correlated with increases in the frequency with which printed books moved across political borders. Chosŏn pique at the Qing invasions could not override the need to purge the historical record of references that impugned its own legitimacy.

Conclusion

The bilateral kinship systems indigenous to Japan and Korea continued to color royal succession, long after patrilineal kinship had transformed social organization among other social groups. The fundamental

[155] *Ibid.*, 1.2.7, p. 35.
[156] *Chosŏn wangjo sillok*, Sukjong 2/1/28 #3 (March 12, 1676).

contrast between the weak kingship of these northeast Asian countries and China's centralized government headed by a strong ruler persisted despite the historical changes described in this chapter.

Japan and Korea's system of weak kings and strong maternal affines was rooted in inheritance practices that enabled prominent families to perpetuate their status over centuries and even (in the Korean case) across dynasties.[157] Intermarriage created strong bonds that enabled the elites to present a united front against the throne. Wife-giving families manipulated royal succession to further their own interests.

Familial relationships determined the flow of power in Japan. Rulership in ancient Japan was limited to a single descent line, but the longevity of the Yamato descent group masked an actual devolution of power to powerful regents whose authority was based on the kinship relationships formed when they supplied wives to the imperial princes. Military figures (the shogun) administered the country after 1185, but actual power was wielded by shogunal widows who retained power through the twelfth and early thirteenth centuries. The example of Hōjō Masako, whose loyalties remained with her natal family, typifies the politics of the period when wet-nursing, uxorilocal marriage, and women's property rights resisted patriarchal dominance.

Unlike Japan, Korea experienced a succession of ruling houses in its history. As in Japan, the throne was manipulated by the elite lineages that produced queens. This structure, and the succession struggles that arose from it, persisted through dynastic change. After the establishment of a civil service examination system in the tenth century caused ambitious men to take office and move their families to the capital, a new national elite appeared who were the progenitors of the Chosŏn-era *yangban*. Korea's *yangban* adopted patrilineality, but the royal family dynamics continued in the old pattern. The heir to the throne was chosen by the senior royal woman, and her natal kinsmen dominated her son's court.

Japanese and Korean ruling elites took concubines as well as a legal wife and confronted a complex and inherently unstable system of succession, which they resolved in two different ways. In Japan, each *tennō* negotiated with imperial kinsmen and affines on whether his son or brother would be next in line for the throne. Abdication became a way to ensure that the negotiated agreement was actually implemented.

---

[157] Duncan, "Formation of the Central Aristocracy." For Japan, see the discussion of the Tokikuni family in the Noto peninsula in Amino, *Rethinking Japanese History*, pp. 6–12.

This practice continued in the Edo period, when the Tokugawa shogunal line adopted the Chinese principle of father–son succession.

In Japan, loyalty to the unilineal descent line, the *ie*, became a transcendent principle, which overrode blood ties. Loyalty to the *ie* overrode blood descent, favoring meritocratic adoption continuity over the ties of blood. Monogamy was the general rule. Korea, on the other hand, developed an extreme form of patrilineage in which membership was limited to the elite (the *yangban*), and generationally transmitted only to the sons of the wife, excluding sons of concubines, who fell back into commoner status. These principles applied to *yangban* but not to the royal family, who were polygynous. The rules of inheritance/succession for commoners differed significantly from those for rulers.

Our study of the separate evolutionary paths taken by northeast Asian states illuminates the tension between Confucian claims to universality and the specificity of the Chinese patrilineal kinship system on which Chinese administrative legal codes were based. The profound changes in gender relations, inheritance, and succession that accompanied the appearance of patrilineal kinship groups in early modern Japan and Korea did not produce convergence to the Chinese model.

The bilateral kinship systems of Korea and Japan in ancient times persisted in ways that helped make each society in early modern times unique, but especially with Chosŏn. Korean attempts to mask successions that did not meet Chinese norms are revealed in the diplomatic exchanges between Chosŏn and Ming that commenced when political changes in Korea had to be communicated to the "overlord" for approval. The anxiety expressed in court deliberations concerning requests for investiture indicate that Chosŏn officials were keenly aware that coups d'état and manipulations of the succession violated the normative principles that they applied to their own family affairs, but this awareness did not translate into a movement to reform royal marriage and inheritance practices. Korean *yangban* ignored these realities to instead extol their adherence to Confucian orthodoxy. They compiled enormous genealogies of their own descent groups, and did their best to compete in the royal marriage sweepstakes that were so influential in determining the choice of heir and thus the *chok* that would dominate the court.

A final perspective on the issue comes from considering the Qing modification of Chinese succession practices. Its northeast Asian origins may explain the initial reliance on collegial rule and the somewhat bloody process by which the principle of father–son succession was eventually institutionalized.[158] Qing rulers chose merit over political stability in their succession policy. The Kangxi emperor initially installed the eldest son of the empress as crown prince, but rejected this practice when he discovered a faction forming around the heir. Instead the Qing chose to make all imperial sons eligible for the throne, thereby precluding the emergence of powerful wife-giving families. Rather than banish all sons except for the heir from the capital, as had been the Ming custom, imperial princes resided in the capital and were groomed by being appointed to perform various military, diplomatic, and administrative tasks. The final choice was the emperor's, to be revealed on his deathbed, and it was made on the basis of merit, not of birth order. Qing treatment of the conquest nobility also applied meritocratic principles in the approval of successors to hereditary titles and, unlike the Ming, reduced the number of princedoms that required imperial subsidies.[159]

Even though Han and Tang emperors also confronted the problem of politically ambitious maternal affines, later rulers resolved the problem by expanding the pool of potential wife-givers to individuals of undistinguished birth. The Qing imperial house recruited imperial consorts from a wide social range of banner households (intermarriage with the conquered Chinese was forbidden), and did not limit the succession to sons of the empress.[160] Empress Dowager Cixi, who dominated the late nineteenth and early twentieth century court, allied with her husband's brothers, not the men of her natal family. Like the Mongols, Manchu empress dowagers acted as fully incorporated members of the ruling house, "in the same manner as an imperial sister or brother."[161] Cixi's actions replicated those of Bumbutai, a Khochin Mongol princess who was Hongtaiji's widow. As Dowager Empress Xiaozhuang, Bumbutai allied with imperial kinsmen and banner nobles in regencies in the 1640s and 1650s during the minorities of her son and grandson, the Shunzhi and Kangxi emperors.[162] In this, as in other points raised previously, Qing practices diverged from Chinese norms.

---

[158] Rawski, *The Last Emperors*, pp. 98–103, 136–37.   [159] *Ibid.*, pp. 93–94.
[160] *Ibid.*, chapter 2.   [161] Holmgren, "Imperial Marriage," p. 86.
[162] Rawski, *Last Emperors*, pp. 128, 135–36.

5   Identity issues: the civilized–barbarian discourse

This chapter confronts a question that lurks beneath the surface of virtually all exchanges amongst the northeast Asian states, namely, how did awareness of a borrowed culture, and the status hierarchy in which it was embedded, affect self-identity? We begin by looking carefully at names. What were the terms used to designate each East Asian entity – not just self-selected names, but the formal and informal names applied by others? Were names merely geographic references, or did they express judgments concerning a country's place in an international order? How did names change over time? By comparing the names East Asian states used in diplomatic exchanges with others employed in internal foreign policy deliberations and texts aimed at domestic audiences, we consider the ways in which names – both for self and for neighbors – reflect not only the domestic and international environment but also each state's manipulation of a complex symbolic "mode of relating to the world."[1]

Names introduce the larger subject: the internal tension between a universalizing and a xenophobic element in Chinese Confucianism, namely the long-standing distinction between *Hua* 華 and *Yi* 夷, commonly known as the "civilized–barbarian" discourse. Historically sited within Chinese history, the *Hua–Yi* binome was adopted by Korean and Japanese elites for use within a domestic context and also, on occasion, in diplomatic communications with other states.

The *Hua–Yi* discourse challenges the exportability of Confucianism by suggesting that identity flows from birth rather than education. The implications, which contradict the idea that Confucian transformation (化) is accessible to all, were understood by Japanese and Korean Confucian scholars.[2] Could Korean Confucians become "civilized" by adhering to

---

[1] Harry D. Harootunian, "The Function of China in Tokugawa Thought," in *The Chinese and the Japanese: Essays in Political and Cultural Interactions*, ed. Akira Iriye (Princeton: Princeton University Press, 1980), pp. 9–10.

[2] This central Confucian tenet assumed that men were fundamentally educable, i.e. that they could be transformed into individuals who would act according to principle 義 and not from the pursuit of profit.

normative Confucian values, or were they forever constrained by the circumstances of their birth to be "Eastern barbarians"? This question was relevant not only for Japanese and Koreans but also for Chinese conquest regimes, as most pointedly illustrated in the case of the Qing rulers.

Hua–Yi and the civilized–barbarian discourse

Should *Yi* be translated as "barbarian"? In the nineteenth century, *yi* was a prefix commonly found in references to Englishmen in Qing documents. In negotiating the Anglo-Chinese Treaty of Tianjin (1858), the British insisted on the insertion of Article 51: "It is agreed that, henceforward, the character "I" 夷 [barbarian] shall not be applied to the Government or subjects of Her Britannic Majesty in any Chinese official document issued by the Chinese Authorities either in the Capital or in the Provinces." As Lydia Liu notes, the British were particularly sensitive to this term because "its enunciation issues forth from the language of a non-European society which is regarded as less than civilized by the British."[3]

Faced with the British demand, Qing officials were quick to deny the imputed slur. *Yi* was simply a reference to non-Chinese living to the east, part of the generalized naming of foreigners according to the four compass directions – *Yi* in the east, *Rong* 戎 in the west, *Di* 狄 in the north and *Man* 蠻 in the south – that had existed from ancient times. The British objected to *Yi* not because it carried pejorative connotations in Chinese, but because the British were at that point in the process of creating their own colonial discourse of the "civilizing mission" that projected barbarism on the subjects of the expanding British empire. Liu argues that *Yi* did not carry racial/racist connotations in early Qing times, nor in the commentaries surrounding the Confucian canon: "To isolate this and other related usages from the classical Chinese texts as if they were proto-racial concepts is to run the risk not only of distorting the sources themselves but also of misrepresenting the classical commentarial traditions."[4]

Tracing identity in China

Liu's point is well-taken: *Yi* should not automatically be read as a pejorative term for "others."[5] The *Hua–Yi* concept goes back to antiquity, but

---

[3] Lydia H. Liu, *The Clash of Empires: The Invention of China in Modern World Making* (Cambridge, MA: Harvard University Press, 2004), fig. 1, p. 32 for treaty clause and p. 34 for the quotation.

[4] *Ibid.*

[5] See Shao-yun Yang, "Becoming *Zhongguo*, Becoming Han," fn28, p. 37 in which Yang cites Lydia Liu's discussion of the "super-sign problem" but argues that "in the Eastern Zhou discursive context the super-sign *yi/barbarian* is entirely appropriate."

its meaning in various historical periods is highly debated. Some scholars assert that Confucius merely used a cultural standard to distinguish the *Xia* 夏 from the *Yi* and *Di*; these distinctions could therefore be overcome through "transformation."[6] Faith in the ability of the peoples on the geographic and cultural periphery to adopt Chinese ways was a hallmark of Chinese frontier policy from ancient times onward, reflected in official documents differentiating "raw" from "cooked" (i.e. "civilized") ethnic minorities on Qing frontiers such as Taiwan.[7]

Those holding the opposite position point to statements in the Confucian canon about the *Rong* and *Di* barbarians: "they do not govern their passions; they are like the birds and beasts." Since birds and beasts are uneducable animals, this implies an impermeable boundary between the culturally superior *Hua/Xia* and the barbarians of the four compass directions.[8]

Along with *Xia, Hua* is generally understood today as the self-referent of the people who invented the Chinese writing system and civilization. Early twentieth-century writers identified the *Hua* and *Xia* as the ancestors of the Han Chinese who constituted the vast majority of the population in what became the Republic of China. As a generic name for all of the groups bordering *Hua/Xia* territories, *Yi* forms half of the binome *Hua–Yi*. Some scholars emphasize its appearance in the extension of overlord–vassal relations from domestic to foreign entities in the Zhou feudal system, as rulers of the Chinese-speaking heartland incorporated

---

[6] This is the argument articulated in Wang Gungwu, "The Chinese Urge to Civilize: Reflections on Change," *Journal of Asian History* 18.1 (1984): 1–34. Tsung-I Dow, "The Confucian Concept of A Nation and Its Historical Practice, *Asian Profile* 10.4 (1982): 352 calls the ideal of "transformation" "Confucian cosmopolitanism." Q. Edward Wang, "History, Space, and Ethnicity: The Chinese Worldview," *Journal of World History* 10.2 (1999): 285–305 argues that this faith in a culture-centered world order characterized the Han period, but not later periods. Yuri Pines, "Beasts or Human: Pre-Imperial Origins of the 'Sino-Barbarian' Dichotomy," in *Mongols, Turks and Others: Eurasian Nomads and the Sedentary World*, ed. Reuven Amitai and Michal Biran (Leiden: E. J. Brill, 2005), pp. 59–102, surveys the views expressed in major early texts to conclude that statesmen before Qin unification (p. 62) "conceived of the differences with aliens as primarily cultural, and hence changeable."

[7] See John Robert Shepherd, *Statecraft and Political Economy on the Taiwan Frontier, 1600–1800* (Stanford: Stanford University Press, 1993), fn22, p. 452. Magnus Fiskesjö, "On the 'Raw' and the 'Cooked' Barbarians of Imperial China," *Inner Asia* 1 (1999): 142 notes that *sheng* and *shu* were applied to the southern barbarians but almost never to peoples on China's northern frontier, and suggests two explanations: the ecological boundaries on the southern frontier were not as stark, and the southern peoples may have seemed more amenable to cultural transformation than their northern brethren.

[8] See the critique of He Xiu's position and the quoted passage by Kung-chuan Hsiao, trans. F. W. Mote, *A History of Chinese Political Thought* (Princeton: Princeton University Press, 1978), I: 137–40. Hsiao argued that the theory of "the adoption of Chinese ways to transform the barbarians" (p. 25) was an enduring theme in Chinese history.

other states on their borders into the Sinocentric tribute system.[9] Still others, reflecting current historical interest in the construction of national identities, study the evolving meanings of *Yi*, and debate the degree to which *Yi* and other group names found in Chinese-language texts are ethnonyms, citing historical examples of non-*Zhongguo* regimes who adopted the *Hua–Yi* terminology in their own political rhetoric.

In contrast to early twentieth-century writings which stress the Han ethnic group as the core of the Chinese nation, scholars working in the PRC currently emphasize *minzu tuanjie* (unity of nationalities), thus downplaying the cultural and psychological distinctions implicit in the *Hua–Yi* binome. A recent essay by Li Dalong, for example, proclaims that "From ancient times, China was a multi-ethnic unified state," and emphasizes that the *Yi* (all of the ethnic groups, apart from the Hua and Xia peoples of the Central Plain) contributed in equal measure to the formation of what became China.[10] Li credits groups that traditional Chinese histories treated as enemies, such as the Xiongnu during Western Han, as "contributing to territorial formation." Nonetheless, the Hua and the Xia played "the primary role" in the first stage of Chinese development because it was they who unified the core region, the Central Plain. Later periods saw non-Han ethnic groups become the major contributors. This was especially true of the Manchu Qing rulers, who achieved China's ultimate territorial form, i.e. the form of the modern nation-state. Without the Mongol Yuan or the Qing, it would be "very difficult" to imagine the territory that constitutes the PRC.[11]

Li Dalong traces the historical origin of the *Hua–Yi* discourse to before 221 BCE. By that time, the Hua/Xia people not only distinguished themselves from neighboring groups, but also believed that the groups who lived among the Hua/Xia could become transformed: "those who live in Xia are Xia" (居夏而夏).[12] This optimism changed in

---

[9] Sakuma Shigeo, "Min Shin kara mita Higashi Ajia no Ka-I chitsujō" (The Civilized-Barbarian Order of East Asia as seen during the Ming and Qing), in his *Nichi Min kankeishi no kenkyū* (Studies of Japan–Ming relations) (Tokyo: Yoshikawa kōbunkan, 1992), pp. 349–50.

[10] Quotation from Li Dalong, "Chuantong YiXia guan yu Zhongguo jiangyu de xing-cheng – Zhongguo jiangyu xingcheng lilun tantao zhiyi" (The formation of Chinese territory and the traditional concept of Yi and Xia – an exploration of the formation of Chinese territorial theory), *Zhongguo bianjiang shidi yanjiu* 14.1 (2004): 1. See Nimrod Baranovitch, "Others No More: The Changing Representation of Non-Han Peoples in Chinese History Textbooks, 1951–2003," *Journal of Asian Studies* 69.1 (1020): 85–122.

[11] Li Dalong, "Chuantong YiXia," pp. 2, 6, incorrectly identifies the Tang dynasty as a Han Chinese ruling house.

[12] *Ibid.*, p. 6, citing the *Xunzi*.

the epoch following the fall of the Han ruling house, when men of Qiang, Xiongnu, and Xianbei origin established states in north China, migrated into the Central Plain, and established regimes. Close contact with these people created greater hostility among the literati. The term *Huaren* 華 人 (people of *Hua*, meaning the core group) appears for the first time in 299 CE.[13]

Li's interpretation stands alongside other scholarship which emphasizes the historicity of the models of sinicization and the PRC position known as *minzu ronghe* 民族融合 (ethnic amalgamation). Until at least the late sixth century, the term *Zhongguo* referred specifically to the lower alluvial plain of the Yellow River (Shanxi, Henan, Hebei and Shandong), also known as the Central Plain. *Zhongguo/Zhuxia* 諸夏 was the territory ruled by Eastern Zhou, which was bounded by regions inhabited by the Yi, Rong, Man, and Di, groups that could collectively be called the "four *Yi*" (*siyi* 四夷).[14] Later, during the Western Han (211 BCE – 23 CE) territorial expansion, *siyi* was applied to new groups who were situated at the borders, and the convention persisted in subsequent dynasties until the nineteenth century. *Hu* 胡, which initially designated steppe peoples like the Xiongnu, became a generic term for people residing north and west of the Chinese ecumene or *Tianxia* 天下 (literally, "all under Heaven").[15]

From the northern dynasties (220 CE–589 CE) onward, Chinese writings include more passages describing the Yi and Di as persons without culture, sometimes likening them to "jackals and wolves," "animals" rather than humans. The phrase *feiwo zulei* 非我族類, which initially meant "not our kinsmen" came to mean "not our kind."[16] *Feiwo zulei* represented one pole of the political discourse concerning the relations of Chinese speaking groups with their neighbors. The other pole, Shao-yun Yang argues, was represented by the concept of *Tianxia* 天下, a civilizing expansive process which could transform the *siyi* into *Huaren*.[17] As a counter-argument, many of the northern states on the Central Plain with *feiwo zulei* origins stressed moral transformation. Liu Yuan, the Xiongnu founder of the Han Zhao state (304–29), claimed that what mattered was not birth but virtue – "even though … Yu … was said to have come from the Rong and King Wen … was said to have come from the Eastern Yi, these sage rulers had derived their rule from

---

[13] *Ibid.*, p. 52.   [14] Shao-yun Yang, "Becoming *Zhongguo*," p. 25.

[15] *Ibid.*, p. 52. In the Han, the term "Hanren" of course simply referred to "people of Han," and was not an ethnonym.

[16] Li Dalong, "Chuantong YiXia," pp. 6–7.

[17] *Tianxia* in the Warring States era meant "the boundaries of the Zhou world." Pines, "Beasts or Human?" p. 82.

Virtue 德."[18] Xianbei Murong Wei (r. 360–70), last ruler of Former Yan, repeated this sentiment.[19]

Northern Wei rulers (of Tuoba descent) applied the term *Yi* to others outside their territory, while referring to themselves as *Huaren*. Occupation of the Central Plain, the heartland of Chinese civilization made them the "central kingdom." As Edward Wang observes, a significant shift had occurred: "the dynasty's spatial location, rather than its ethnic superiority, became the foundation for center-periphery relations."[20] The Chinese-speaking groups that moved south and established rival states were *Nanren* (people of the south), or *Wuren* (people of Wu), never *Zhongguoren* or *Huaren*.[21] Other northern regimes adopted the same strategy.

One could argue that the long occupation of the Central Plain by non-Han states might have sharpened rather than dulled the Han perception of this ethnic boundary. When attempting to persuade the Tang dynastic founder, Gaozu (r. 618–26), to order an expedition to subjugate Koguryŏ, Wen Yanbo, Vice-Director of the Secretariat, argued, "If we allow ourselves to be put on an equal footing with Gaoli (Koguryŏ), how will the barbarians of the four directions look up to us? ... the Middle Kingdom is, for the barbarians, like the sun to all the stars. There is no reason to descend from superiority to be on a level of equality with those in the barrier zone."[22]

Optimism about the possibility of morally transforming the *siyi* faded as frontier states conquered parts of the Chinese-speaking world.[23] There was no scholarly consensus in the early fourteenth century, when the official histories of the Liao, Jin, and Song dynasties were compiled by officials serving the Mongol Yuan court. By the fifteenth century, many Ming scholar-officials had decided that the distinction between *Hua* and *Yi* could not be breached. Responding to Esen's capture of the Zhengtong emperor in 1449, an official, Qiu Jun (1421–95), presented a proposal on

---

[18] Yihong Pan, *Son of Heaven and Heavenly Qaghan: Sui-Tang China and Its Neighbors* (Bellingham: Center for East Asian Studies, Western Washington University, 1997), p. 33; Mark Edward Lewis, *China Between Empires: The Northern and Southern Dynasties* (Cambridge, MA: Belknap Press, 2009), pp. 51, 145, 167, notes that Liu Yuan took on the Han rulers' surname because he claimed to be descended from them.

[19] Pan, *Son of Heaven*, p. 33. "Gaoli" here refers to Gaogouli/Koguryŏ.

[20] Q. E. Wang, "History, Space, and Ethnicity," p. 299.

[21] Shao-yun Yang, "Becoming *Zhongguo*," pp. 82–84.   [22] *Ibid.*, p. 208.

[23] The intensification of the *Hua–Yi* discourse may be dated to the fifteenth century; see the suggestion by John Langlois that the scholarship emphasizing hostility to Mongol rule on the part of the Chinese subjects may be a product of the nationalist sentiments held by twentieth-century Chinese scholars in his "Introduction," pp. 13–14, 16–17.

"defense of the boundaries between *hua* and *yi*" (華夷之防).[24] Arguing that the best defense was to reinforce the boundaries because the two groups should not mix, Qiu repudiated the universalist assumptions of early Confucianism.

This position also appears in an essay entitled "Discussion of legitimate rule in ancient and present times" (古今正統大倫) attributable to the late Ming period, which distinguishes *Zhongguo* as the land of humans, not the Yi and Di. Like "dogs and sheep," the Yi and Di do not belong to the human race. Their animal nature is a product of the pastoral environment from which they originated. Even if they acquire human language, dress in [Chinese] clothing, and wear shoes, they cannot change their fundamental nature but will "forever remain animals." When the Yi and Di conquer *Zhongguo*, their "inborn nature" is "perverted" because of their fundamental alienation from the environment of sedentary agriculture. Hence, "it is only in the barbarians' own interest to run their own affairs and follow their own inborn nature."[25] The author of this essay concludes that barbarian conquest dynasties can never be included in the orthodox line of legitimate rule (正統 *zhengtong*).

The *Luochong lu* 贏蟲錄 (Record of naked creatures), which was "the most popular, comprehensive, and widely circulating source of documentation about exotic lands and peoples" published during the Ming period,[26] reflects the hardening of the ethnic divide. Inserted into daily-use encyclopedias in the early seventeenth century, the preface to the work, which paired illustrations with textual descriptions of the "360 kinds of naked creatures," explained just why "humans are the leader of the naked creatures":[27]

Those born and residing in the middle kingdom, who receive the correct and proper *qi* of Heaven and Earth, are human; those born outside the sphere of transformation 生居化外, who do not receive the correct and proper *qi* of Heaven and Earth, are animals 不得天地之正氣者為禽獸, and are therefore called "naked creatures." Confucius says, "Governing the *yi* barbarians is like governing animals."

The illustrations of the various "naked creatures" identified in the *Luochong lu* emphasized the gap between them and "humans," i.e. those

---

[24] Leo K. Shin, *The Making of the Chinese State: Ethnicity and Expansion on the Ming Borderlands* (Cambridge: Cambridge University Press, 2006), p. 161, see also pp. 159–66.

[25] Quotations from Achim Mittag, "Scribe in the Wilderness: The Manchu Conquest and the Loyal-Hearted Historiographer's (*xinshi* 心史) Mission," *Oriens Extremus* 44 (2003/4): 36. The essay is part of a work entitled *Xinshi*, which has been attributed to Zheng Sixiao, 1241–1318 but, Mittag argues, is more likely a late Ming work.

[26] Yuming He, "The Book and the Barbarian in Ming China and Beyond: The *Luo chong lu*, or 'Record of Naked Creatures,'" *Asia Major* 24.1 (2011): 44–45.

[27] *Ibid.*, pp. 70–71. The author comments, p. 72, that "the word *yi* was continuously imbued with slighting connotations in popular books."

who were "born and residing in the middle kingdom" 中國. This work also circulated in Japan. What did readers who were "born outside the sphere of transformation" make of the binome? During the process of state formation, Japanese and Koreans used Chinese political terminology in discussing domestic affairs. Analysis of the ways in which Japanese, Korean, and Qing elites construed the binome *Hua–Yi* (J. *Ka–I*, K. *Hwa–I*) reveals a pattern of cultural negotiation that typifies the exchanges between China and its northeast Asian neighbors.

Naming Japan

Chinese records contain the earliest historical references to states in the Japanese archipelago. One of the earliest, dated to the third century CE, mentions a kingdom in the Japanese archipelago called "Wo" 倭 (J. Wa, K. Wae), now identified by scholars as the kingdom of Yamatai, located in northern Kyushu. This same character appears in one of the compounds for the Yamato (大倭, 大和) kingdom, centered in the Nara Basin of southern Honshu, which became the dominant political power in the Japanese archipelago from the fourth century onward.[28] Although the Yamato imperial line eventually identified itself as Nippon (Nihon, 日本, C. Riben, K. Ilbon), Wo/Wae persisted in informal Chinese and Korean writings about Japan until modern times.[29]

The hundreds of discussions about Japan recorded in the *Ming shilu* (Veritable Records of the Ming) during the Japanese invasion of Korea, 1592–8, include the Chosŏn court's communications with the Wanli emperor, but consist mostly of reports to the throne from Ming generals and provincial officials concerning the military and diplomatic problems arising from the Ming participation in the Korean resistance.[30] As Table 5.1 shows, *Wo* was the most frequently used term denoting the Japanese in the

---

[28] Brown, "Introduction," pp. 1–2; cf. Imamura, *Prehistoric Japan*, p. 185, on the 57 CE embassy from the Na kingdom (thought to be in northern Kyushu) to the Han court; also, p. 186, on the confusing fact that "'Yamatai' is the modern Japanese pronunciation of a name written in Chinese characters ... [which] is thought to have been pronounced like 'Yamato' by the Chinese of the period" but in Japanese academic usage "Yamatai" is used "to distinguish the kingdom mentioned in the *Wei-shu* from the 'Yamato' Kingship, which existed in the Nara Basin by the fourth century AD at the latest." For scholarship on Yamatai, see Walter Edwards, "In Pursuit of Himiko: Postwar Archaeology and the Location of Yamatai," *Monumenta Nipponica* 51.1 (1996): 53–79, and Kidder, *Himiko and Japan's Elusive Chiefdom*.

[29] Amino, "Deconstructing 'Japan'."

[30] On the Ming court's deliberations during the 1590s see MSLC, pp. 315–467; also Li Guangtao, *Wanli ershisan nian feng Riben guowang Fengchen Xiuji kao* (A study of the 1595 investiture of King of Japan Toyotomi Hideyoshi) (Taipei: Institute of History and Philology, Academia Sinica, 1967).

Table 5.1. *Terms for Japan in the* Ming shilu

Year	*Wo* 倭 (dwarf)	*Wonü* 倭奴 (dwarf slaves)	*Woyi* 倭夷 (dwarf barbarians)	*Riben* 日本 (Japan)	*Wokou* 倭寇 (dwarf pirates)	*Wozei* 倭賊 (dwarf bandits)	Other
1592	24	7	1	1	1	4	
1593	63	30	3	1	1	1	東倭
1594	43	30	3	1	1	1	
1595	15			18			夷,島夷
1596	87	15	1	23		1	
1597	97	9	1	26		1	
1598	30	6		2		1	

Source: Wang Qiju, comp. *Ming shilu: Lingguo Chaoxian pian ziliao* (Beijing: Zhongguo bianjiang shidi yanjiu zhongxin, 1983), pp. 315–467.

governmental transcripts. *Wo* was prefixed to references to the "dwarf slaves" (倭奴 *Wonu*), "dwarf bandits" (倭賊 *Wozei*), "dwarf barbarians" (倭夷 *Woyi*), and "dwarf pirates" (倭寇 *Wokou*). Riben, little used in the first military campaign against Japan, appears in the Veritable Records during 1594 and 1595, when the Ming court deliberated on whether it should invest Hideyoshi as "king of Japan" (日本王), and after the Ming envoys' audience with Hideyoshi (July 1596), when the Ming envoys and the Japanese general Konishi Yukinaga attempted to explain to the Wanli court why the *kanpaku* (Regent) repudiated the investiture.[31] The many memorials analyzing the diplomatic fiasco account for the increased frequency of "Riben" in the Ming records of 1597, but Wang Yong suggests that the appearance of Japanese pirates in "many plays and works of fiction" during the Ming and Qing periods shows the deep and lingering impression pirate raids made on the popular imagination.[32]

Koreans followed the Chinese usage in naming Japan (*Ilbon* 日本) and the Japanese (*Waein* 倭人). Japanese pirates raiding the Korean coast were

[31] On the Ming patent which invested Hideyoshi as "Riben guowang" 日本國王: see the text in Tan Qian, *Guoque*, V: 474–77. Major figures on the Ming side, Shen Weijing and Shi Xing, were closely interrogated and Shen was eventually executed for creating the situation of "grievous insult" to the Ming: Swope, *A Dragon's Head and a Serpent's Tail*, pp. 224, 232, 238, 286.

[32] Wang Yong, trans. Laura E. Hess, "Realistic and Fantastic Images of 'Dwarf Pirates': The Evolution of Ming Dynasty Perceptions of the Japanese," in *Sagacious Monks and Bloodthirsty Warriors: Chinese Views of Japan in the Ming–Qing Period*, ed. Joshua A. Fogel (Norwalk, CT: EastBridge, 2002), pp. 17–41. The same point is made by Yuming He, *Home and the World: Editing the 'Glorious Ming' in Woodblock-Printed Books of the Sixteenth and Seventeenth Centuries* (Cambridge, MA: Harvard University Asia Center, 2013), pp. 214, 216, and 251 on entries in Ming popular encyclopedia.

Waegu.[33] Legitimate trade with Japan was conducted at "Japan House" (倭館 *Waegwan*) in Pusan. *Wae* became a prefix for Japanese-style (倭式 *Waesik*), Japanese food (倭食 *Wae sik*), and Japanese customs (倭風 *Wae p'ung*). Both the Japanese and the Jurchen/Manchus (野人 *Yain*, literally, wild men) were classified in court deliberations as *Yi* 夷, while Ming China was the "sacred Ming" 聖明, or the "Heavenly dynasty" 天朝.[34]

Especially after the *Imjin waeran*, Korean references to Japanese were filtered through "deep feelings of revenge, animosity, and contempt."[35] Kang Hang (1567–1618), captured and taken to Japan as a prisoner of war, converted Fujiwara Seika (1561–1619) to Confucianism and introduced the thought of Yi T'oegye to Japan. Kang described the Japanese as "bandits," "like a herd of dogs and sheep or a herd of aliens with squint eyes."[36] Sin Yuhan, who visited Japan as part of the Korean embassy of 1719 after the resumption of diplomatic exchanges, echoed the Korean literati's feeling of cultural superiority. The beauty of the Japanese landscape caused Sin to comment, "How on earth can barbarians like the Japanese deserve a beautiful land like this?"[37] Sin was also impressed at the high quality of Japanese craftsmanship, the cleanliness of the accommodations, and the eclectic offerings (including Korean books that were "classified materials" in Korea) in Osaka bookstores; but he decried the low social morals and the inferior literary standard of the Japanese scholars whom he met, which confirmed his faith in the superiority of Chosŏn civilization.[38]

---

[33] Kenneth R. Robinson, "An Island's Place in History," pp. 42–43.

[34] See the court deliberations during the 1636/37 Jurchen/Manchu invasions of Korea in the *Chosŏn wangjo sillok*, discussed in Chapter 2.

[35] Nam-lin Hur, "Korean Officials in the Land of the Kami: Diplomacy and the Prestige Economy, 1607–1811," in *Embracing the Other: The Interactions of Korean and Foreign Cultures, Proceedings of the First World Congress of Korean Studies, 2002* (Songnam: Academy of Korean Studies, 2002), I: 83.

[36] *Ibid.*, p. 88; also Etsuko Hae-jin Kang, *Diplomacy and Ideology*, pp.110–25.

[37] Nam-lin Hur, "A Korean Envoy Encounters Tokugawa Japan: Sin Yu-han and the Korean Embassy of 1719," in *Korea Between Tradition and Modernity: Selected Papers from the Fourth Pacific and Asian Conference on Korean Studies*, ed. Chang Yun-shik, Donald L. Baker, Nam-lin Hur, and Ross King (Vancouver: Institute of Asian Research, University of British Columbia, 2000), p. 148.

[38] *Ibid.*; see pp. 153–54 on the eager interest of many Japanese in Korean calligraphy and versification, which probably helped reinforce Sin's attitude of cultural superiority. Ronald P. Toby, "Carnival of the Aliens: Korean Embassies in Edo-Period Art and Culture," *Monumenta Nipponica* 41.4 (1986): 416–56, presents evidence of how Japanese woodblock prints and guidebooks popularized images of the Korean embassies to Japan; these images became enshrined in votive offerings (*ema*) deposited in Buddhist and Shinto shrines and were displayed as floats in annual shrine festivals.

Naming Korea

Korean literati in the early Koryŏ dynasty used "samhan" 三韓, a term in early Chinese records which referred to polities that predated Silla, Paekche, and Koguryŏ, to designate the three states that existed between the fall of Unified Silla (後三韓) and Wang Kŏn's reunification of 918. "Samhan" also came to denote the Korean peninsula. While it "represented Koryŏ's past in its historical quality," it also transcended the dynasty in its broader connotations.[39]

Chinese texts were also the first to cite a kingdom named Chosŏn (C. Chaoxian, J. Chōsen), which seems to have existed by the second century BCE. The same sources are also the *locus classicus* for the two primary myths, one attributing the origin of Koguryŏ from an egg which hatched to become the progenitor Chumong 朱蒙/Tongmyŏng 東明, and the other identifying a Chinese, Kija (箕子 C. Jizi), as the founder of the first Chosŏn state.[40] Tongmyŏng cults existed in Koguryŏ and Paekche and thrived during the Koryŏ dynasty. Tan'gun 檀君, the son of a she-bear and a sun god, emerged in the thirteenth century as the most important origin myth and was the object of state sacrifice in the Koryŏ and Chosŏn dynasties. Scholars have argued that the dual founding ancestors of Korea, Tan'gun and Kija, represent the ambivalence among Korean elites about asserting Korea's own cultural identity vs. identifying with the Chinese model of civilization.[41] This internal tension is not reflected in entries in Ming popular encyclopedia, which referred to Korea as "Gaoli" (Koryŏ) and commented, "Of all four

---

[39] Remco E. Breuker, *Establishing a Pluralist Society in Medieval Korea, 918–1170: History, Ideology and Identity in the Koryŏ Dynasty* (Leiden: E. J. Brill, 2010), quote p. 35, also pp. 30–36. Breuker observes, p. 39, that *Haedong* frequently included the Liaodong area in these Chinese sources.

[40] Young-woo Han, "Kija Worship in the Koryŏ and Early Yi Dynasties: A Cultural Symbol in the Relationship Between Korea and China," in *The Rise of Neo-Confucianism in Korea*, ed. William T. de Bary and JaHyun Kim Haboush (New York: Columbia University Press, 1985), 349–71. See Bert Hinsch, "Myth and the Construction of Foreign Ethnic Identity in Early and Medieval China," *Asian Ethnicity* 5.1 (2004): 81–103, who argues that Chinese texts frequently present a "Sinicised" version identifying a Chinese ancestor for a foreign people: this kind of myth supported the "Chinese expansionist project." Issues of Korean identity sharpened during the Chosŏn period deliberations concerning Tangun and Kija (see chapter 5). On a contemporary comment linking Tangun worship to Korean prejudice against foreigners, see Kyung Koo Han, "The Archaeology of the Ethnically Homogeneous Nation-State and Multiculturalism in Korea," *Korea Journal* 47.4 (2007): 8–31.

[41] Breuker, *Establishing a Pluralist Society*, pp. 98–110 and "Introduction," pp. 16–17; Jae-hoon Shim, "A New Understanding of Kija Chosŏn as a Historical Anachronism," *Harvard Journal of Asiatic Studies* 62.2 (2002): 271–305; Young-woo Han, "Kija Worship in the Koryŏ and Early Yi Dynasties."

barbarians outside the sphere of transformation, Gaoli is the most civilized."[42]

The *Nihon shoki* refers to the states of the Korean peninsula as "Kan" (韓C. and K. Han). In the early seventeenth century, Hayashi Razan would assert that the "Kan" states sent tribute to Japan and were hence Japanese vassals in ancient times.[43] In view of Japan's long diplomatic contact with Korean states, it is not surprising that some Edo-period maps referred to the peninsula as "Kōrai" 高麗, the name of the Koryŏ dynasty.[44] "Chōsen"朝鮮, the Japanese reading of the characters for the Chosŏn dynasty, alternated with "Yi chō," (李朝), the surname of the Chosŏn ruling house.[45] Like "Shina" 支那 (see below), Chōsen became associated with Japan's annexation of Korea (1910–45).

Although Koreans also applied the *Hwa-I* terminology in a Korea-centered framework that placed themselves at the civilized core, they were always conscious of the Sinocentric context in which they, along with the Japanese, belonged to the group of "eastern barbarians" (東夷).[46] Both the *Jiu Tang shu* (compiled in the tenth century) and *Xin Tang shu* classify Paekche and Silla biographies under the heading "eastern barbarians."[47] Koreans tacitly acknowledged the Chinese naming practice by using terms like *Haedong* 海東 (lit., "east of the sea"), *Tongbang* 東邦/*Tongguk* 東國 ("eastern country") and *Ch'ŏnggu* 青丘 ("azure hills") to designate their own country.[48] The *Xin Tang shu*, completed *c.* 1060, refers to Parhae (Bohai) as *Haedong shengguo* 海東盛國 (Flourishing country east of the sea). During the Koryŏ period, *Haedong*'s appearance in Korean inscriptions, poems, histories, and religious writings overshadowed "Koryŏ" or "Samhan."[49] Whereas "Samhan" was used by Korean writers as a "domestic reference," increasingly one that acquired the overtones of "our country," *Haedong, Tongguk, Tongbang,* and *Ch'ŏnggu* "were positioned in contrast with China," a strategy which the writers used to

---

[42] He, *Home and the World*, p. 212; this was because of Gaoli's adoption of Chinese institutions and dress.

[43] Toby, *State and Diplomacy in Early Modern Japan*, p. 215.

[44] Yonemoto, *Mapping Early Modern Japan*, p. 33.   [45] *Ibid.*

[46] Korean scholars were familiar with the Chinese classical references: see Kim Sihwang, "Ku-I wa Tong I" (The Nine I and the Eastern I), *Tongbang hanmunhak* 17.1 (1990): 71–90. On Chinese use of the term to "refer to foreign groups newly recognized by the Han but probably entirely unknown to the more ancient Chinese," see Byington, "History of the Puyŏ State."

[47] Ch'u Myŏng'op, "Koryŏ sigi [haedong] insik kwa haedong ch'ŏnha" (The consciousness of the terms *Haedong* [east of the sea] and *haedong ch'ŏnha* (all under heaven east of the sea) during the Koryŏ period), *Han'guksa yŏn'gu* 129 (2004): fn 5, 6, p. 31.

[48] Breuker, *Establishing a Pluralist Society*, pp. 36–44; azure was the color associated with the east, see fn 51, p. 41.

[49] *Ibid.*, p. 37.

"strengthen their claims of individuality and their equality with China."[50] The Koryŏ dynasty pursued a strategy of *Haedong ch'ŏnha* 海東天下, which implicitly assumed a China-centered world order, even if Wang Kŏn, the dynastic founder, styled himself "Son of Heaven" (*chŏnja*).[51] Nonetheless, the term also denoted Korea, so that a copper coin, minted in 1102, was called a *Haedong t'ongbo* 海東通寶.[52]

Titles of works such as *Tongguk t'onggam* (東國通鑑Comprehensive mirror of the Eastern kingdom, 1485), Yi Chonghwi's (1731–97) *Tongsa* (東史Korean history), the *Haedong yŏksa* (海東歷史History of Korea) by Han Ch'iyun (1765–1814) or the *Haedong yuju* (海東遺珠Pearls of Korean poetry) compiled by Hong Set'ae all show the self-identification of Korean elites with terms initially derived from Chinese texts.[53] These designations also appear in maps: the *Tongguk yŏji sŭngnam* 東國輿地勝覽 (Augmented survey of Korean geography), compiled in 1481 and published in 1487; its predecessor, the *Tongguk chido* 東國地圖, completed in 1463; and the *Haedong chido* (海東地圖 Map of Korea), dating from the middle of the eighteenth century.[54]

Koreans also used Haedong to refer to Japan. Although a collection of maps entitled *Haedong chido* (Map of Korea), produced in the middle of the eighteenth century, included *Waeguk chŏndo* 倭國全圖 (General map of Japan), Sin Sukju's *Haedong chegukki* 海東諸國記, completed in 1471, compiled regulations on Japanese trade issued by the Chosŏn government since 1400.[55]

Naming China

How did the Japanese refer to China? In the medieval period they used its name within a Buddhist cosmology: Shintan 震旦 and Japan (本朝) were part of the "three realms" – India, China, and Japan – which made up the world.[56] Japanese diplomatic correspondence often adopted the Chinese custom of using the dynastic name. At the same time, the Japanese were well acquainted with the concept of a Sinocentric world

[50] *Ibid.*, p. 44.
[51] Ch'u, "Koryŏ shigi [Haedong] insik kwa [Haedong chŏnha]." According to Ch'u, the Koryŏ founder also called himself "Son of Heaven east of the sea," *Haedong chŏnja*. Haedong was also an appellation for a school of Korean Buddhism: Sem Vermeersch, *The Power of the Buddhas: The Politics of Buddhism During the Koryŏ Dynasty (918–1392)* (Cambridge, MA: Harvard University Asia Center, 2008), p. 132.
[52] Lee, *A New History of Korea*, p. 122.   [53] *Ibid.*, pp. 194, 237, 244.
[54] Young-woo Han, "Historical Development of Korean Cartography," pp. 13, 20, 55–58; and Sung, "Worldviews and Early Cartography," in the same volume.
[55] Lewis, *Frontier Contact*, pp. 18, 229.
[56] On how this view changed after the failed Mongol invasions, see Souyri, *World Turned Upside Down*, p. 148.

order which lay behind the use of the term *Zhongguo* 中國.[57] Even though Japan ceased to send embassies (with one exception) from the eighth century onward, regional lords and traders seeking Chinese copper cash, silks, and Buddhist sutras dispatched many envoys to the Korean and Chinese courts asking for investiture as "king of Japan."

When Edo-period Confucian scholars referred to China as Chūka (中華C. Zhonghua) or Chūgoku (C. Zhongguo), the "China" being invoked was "a China removed from any real historicity."[58] Asami Keisai (1652–1711), reacting to the implied Sinocentrism, wrote, "The appellations of 'central kingdom' and 'barbarian' are names developed by the Chinese. If we refer to our country in the same manner we will simply be imitating the Chinese."[59] Those who rejected use of Chūka/Chūgoku were supported by new knowledge acquired from contact with Europeans. Arai Hakuseki (1663–1713) observed that European maps showed Chūka and Japan, like Korea, among the eastern barbarians, at the fringe and not the center of the world. Furthermore, quoting Sidotti, an Italian priest, Hakuseki argued that "The worth of a country should not be seen as depending on its size or whether its location is near or far."[60]

"Kan" (漢) and "Tō" (唐, alternatively read "kara") appear through the Edo period and into modern times to designate Chinese (唐人*Karajin, Karabito*),[61] Chinese-style gates (唐門*karamon*), Chinese textiles (唐綾

---

[57] Joshua A. Fogel, "On Japanese Expressions for 'China'," *Sino-Japanese Studies* 2.1 (1989): 5–16; Borgen, "Jōjin's Travels," pp. 404–10. Recently China specialists have paid considerable attention to the historical shifts in meaning and usage of Zhongguo: see Gang Zhao, "Reinventing China: Imperial Qing Ideology and the Rise of Modern Chinese National Identity in the Early Twentieth Century," *Modern China* 21.1 (2006): 3–30, and, for the early Ming, Yonglin Jiang, *The Mandate of Heaven and the Great Ming Code* (Seattle: University of Washington Press, 2011), pp. 103–5, also Jiang's "Thinking About 'Ming China' Anew: The Ethnocultural Space in a Diverse Empire – With Special Reference to the 'Miao Territory'," draft ms. My special thanks to Professor Jiang for allowing me to read and cite his draft article.

[58] Quoting Harootunian, "Function of China," p. 10. Contrast this statement with the description of the earlier period in Borgen, "Jōjin's Travels," pp. 406–8. On the "false embassies," see Kenneth R. Robinson, "Jiubian and Ezogachishima Embassies," his "Imposter Branch of the Hatakeyama Family," and his "Treated as Treasures."

[59] Kate Wildman Nakai, "The Naturalization of Confucianism in Tokugawa Japan: The Problem of Sinocentrism," *Harvard Journal of Asiatic Studies* 40.1 (1980): 184; in *Seiken igen narabi ni kōgi*, Asami himself used "Tang" to designate China (fn 54, p. 184).

[60] Nakai, *Shogunal Politics*, pp. 328–29; Harootunian, "Function of China," pp. 12–13.

[61] *Karabito* could also be used more generically to include Koreans; see Hur, "Korean Envoy," p. 153. Similarly, *Tōjin* could be applied generically to mean "foreigner," as in *Tōjin gyōretsu* (唐人行列'foreigners' parades'; see Toby, "Carnival of the Aliens," p. 445). Although Olof G. Lidin, in *Tanegashima: The Arrival of Europe in Japan* (Copenhagen: Nordic Institute of Asian Studies, 2002), p. 26, states that the term did not include European foreigners such as the Portuguese, who were called (adopting the Chinese

kara aya, 唐衣 *karagoromo*, 唐錦*karanishiki*), Confucian learning (漢學 *Kangaku*), Chinese words (漢語*kango*), characters (漢字*kanji*), literary Chinese (漢文*Kanbun*), vernacular Chinese (唐話*Tōwa*), and Chinese herbs (漢藥*Kanyaku*), among others. In Edo Japan, "Chinese imports came to mean 'elegant products.'"[62]

That was assuredly not the case with *Shina*, a term with roots going back to the Kamakura period which was not widely used until the nineteenth century. Okuni Takamasa (1792–1871), seems to have used *Shina* deliberately in order to "de-center China" by abandoning *Chūka* and *Chūgoku*'s Sinocentric connotations in order to assert Japan's superiority against the challenge of both European and Chinese concepts of world order.[63] In the early twentieth century, as growing Japanese power threatened Chinese security, many Chinese construed *Shina* as a demeaning term. The linkage between *Shina* and Japanese imperialism probably was the reason it disappeared after 1945, to be replaced by Chūgoku.[64]

Koreans also called Chinese characters and Chinese writing style *Hanja* 漢字 and *Hanmun* 漢文. *Hwa* 華, the first half of the binome "Civilized–Barbarian" could be used as a prefix to denote Chinese merchants (華商 *Hwasang*).[65] Korean *yangban* in the Chosŏn period referred to Ming Chinese by a variety of names, reflecting their historical and cultural history. Like the Japanese, Ming Chinese were called "men of Han" 漢人(K. *Han'in*), "men of Tang" 唐人 (K. *Tang'in*), or "men of Hwa" 華人 (literally, "civilized men"), or "men of the Heavenly dynasty" 天朝人, using a common referent to the Ming.[66]

---

usage) 'southern barbarians' (*nanban* 南蠻), the misidentification of an English group passing through Hakata in 1613 as Korean (Toby, "Carnival of the Aliens," p. 425) suggests that we should not underestimate the degree of ignorance in Japan about foreigners. As Toby notes, Hakata, a bustling port for foreign trade, should have been one of the locales where European and East Asian foreigners were "a relatively common sight."

[62] Harootunian, "Function of China," p. 11.

[63] *Ibid.*, pp. 26–27; but note the argument of Bob Tadashi Wakabayashi, "Rival States on a Loose Rein: The Neglected Tradition of Appeasement in Late Tokugawa Japan," in *The Ambivalence of Nationalism: Modern Japan between East and West*, ed. James W. White, Michio Umegaki, and Thomas R. H. Havens (Lanham: University Press of America, 1990), pp. 11–37, on the continued importance of China as a source of information on world affairs and foreign policy for some Japanese thinkers into the 1850s.

[64] Fogel, "On Japanese Expressions for 'China'"; Matsui Yōko, "Nagasaki Deshima to Karajin yashiki" (The Chinese residences in Deshima, Nagasaki), in *Edo bakufu to Higashi Ajia*, ed. Arano Yasunori (Tokyo: Yoshikawa kōbunkan, 2003), pp. 363–88.

[65] Ki-joong Song, *The Study of Foreign Languages in the Chosŏn Dynasty (1392–1910)* (Seoul: Chimmundang, 2001), pp. 54–84.

[66] Kye Sŭng-bŏm, "Chosŏn hugi Chunghwaron ŭi imyŏn kwa kŭ yusan – Myŏng, Ch'ŏng kwallyŏn hoch'ing ŭi pyŏnhwa rŭl chungsim ŭro" (On the inner face and legacy of the late Chosŏn discourse on civilized center – focusing on the changes in the naming of the connection with Ming and Qing). *Han'guk sahaksa hakpo* 19 (2009): 61.

The Manchu conquest and *Hua–Yi* discourse

The Manchu conquest of the Ming elicited strong responses from elites in China, Japan, and Korea. Ming loyalist sentiments infused an entire generation of individuals who experienced the Manchu conquest at first hand.[67] They expressed their grief for the fallen Ming and anger at the Manchu conquerors in historical fiction, poetry, and private histories of the Ming dynasty. Some, like Wang Duanshu, the daughter of Wang Siren (1575–1646), a famous poet, wrote poems in which she referred to the Manchus as "bandits" 寇; others veiled their meaning by alluding to Qin Shihuangdi, whose coercive unification of 221 BCE was reviled by Confucians.[68] Ming loyalist scholars such as Gu Yanwu (1613–82) and Wang Fuzhi (1619–92) expressed similar sentiments even more forcefully. For Gu, "there were virtually no historical forces capable of turning barbarians into civilized people."[69] Wang recognized the potential for moral transformation, but saw this as a very gradual, long-term process. Because the *Yi* and *Di* had a nomadic lifestyle and "values that were different from ours," "the extermination of them can not be considered as inhuman."[70] Wang argued that forced coexistence imposed by the Manchu conquest merely produced mutual suffering: injury to Chinese and their civilization, and suffering on the part of the conquerors as their native society and culture crumbled.[71]

The Manchu conquest of the Ming empire aroused both the Chosŏn court and the Tokugawa shogunate to declare that the Sinocentric world order had been overturned. Japanese and Korean observers used the term *Yi* (夷, I in Japanese and Korean) to refer to the Manchus: how, they argued, could "barbarians" vanquish the civilized 華 Ming, and claim to be the Sons of Heaven?

---

[67] For a sampling, see Lynn A. Struve, ed. and trans., *Voices from the Ming–Qing Cataclysm: China in Tigers' Jaws* (New Haven: Yale University Press, 1993).

[68] Kang-i Sun Chang, "Women's Poetic Witnessing: Late Ming and Late Qing Examples," in *Dynastic Crisis and Cultural Innovation: From the Late Ming to the Late Qing and Beyond*, ed. David Der-wei Wang and Shang Wei (Cambridge, MA: Harvard University Press, 2005), p. 508; Feng Menglong's *Xin lieguo zhi* (New chronicles of the warring states) is discussed in Robert E. Hegel, "Conclusions: Judgments on the Ends of Times," pp. 529–32 in the same volume.

[69] Crossley, *Translucent Mirror*, p. 248.

[70] Quotations from Wang's *Du tong jian lun*, see Dow, "Confucian Concept," p. 355. But Wang also concluded on the basis of these arguments that China should not expand beyond its "natural" boundaries, i.e. the area of an agrarian society: Mittag, "Scribe in the Wilderness," p. 37.

[71] Crossley, *Translucent Mirror*, pp. 249–51. Wang's experiences as a Ming loyalist are described in Ian McMorran, "The Patriot and the Partisans: Wang Fu-chih's Involvement in the Politics of the Yung-li Court," in *From Ming to Ch'ing: Conquest, Region, and Continuity in Seventeenth-Century China*, ed. Jonathan D. Spence and John E. Wills, Jr. (New Haven: Yale University Press, 1979), pp. 133–66.

As noted previously, Japanese leaders, who had collected information about the Jurchen since the 1590s, were keen observers of the Manchu conquest. News of the Qing capture of the Ming capital, Peking, in June 1644, was brought to Nagasaki by Chinese merchants arriving in October of that year. Requests for military assistance from Zheng Chenggong and other Ming loyalists quickly followed.[72] Hayashi Razan prepared a list of all official communications from China for shogun Iemitsu, who eventually decided to reject all such requests. Razan's son Hayashi Gahō (1618–80) was later ordered to compile information about these events. The title of his work, *Ka-I hentai* 華夷變態 (Metamorphosis from civilized to barbarian), summarizes the dominant Japanese interpretation of the Manchu conquest: the Qing were "upstarts from a small territory known even there as the land of the northern barbarians."[73]

The conquest also reflected badly on the Ming, whose military weakness stimulated unfavorable comparisons with Japan.[74] The northeast Asian origins of the Qing ruling house helped shape the Tokugawa foreign policy (and self-image) in the seventeenth century. For Yamaga Sokō (1622–85), a leading Confucian proponent, the conquest served to further weaken China's "ethical superiority;" its frequent takeover by "barbarians" was proof that it "lacked integrity."[75]

The Chosŏn attitude toward the Jurchen/Manchus is clearly visible during the diplomatic exchanges that preceded the 1636–37 Manchu invasion of Korea. Chosŏn representations to Hongtaiji stressed the distinction between *sadae*, duty to overlord, and *kyorin* 交鄰, relations with neighboring states which should be conducted on terms of equality. In 1636, in rejecting Hongtaiji's declaration of the Qing dynasty and assumption of the title of emperor (*huangdi*), the Chosŏn court pointed out that since both he and they were Ming vassals, *kyorin* was the only proper model for Korean–Manchu bilateral relations. Moreover, Hongtaiji's actions constituted an illegitimate rebellion of a vassal against his overlord; how could Chosŏn appear to acquiesce in them?[76] Anti-Manchu attitudes hardened after the humiliation of being forced to

---

[72] Toby, *State and Diplomacy*, pp. 118–40; also Mizuno, "China in Tokugawa Foreign Relations."

[73] Arai Hakuseki, quoted in Nakai, "Naturalization of Confucianism," p. 196.

[74] Mizuno, "China in Tokugawa Foreign Relations," quoting Yamaga Sokō, p. 137.

[75] Toby, *State and Diplomacy*, p. 223. For Toby's argument about the creation of a Japan-centered world order, see his "Contesting the Centre: International Sources of Japanese National Identity," *The International History Review* 7.3 (1985): 347–63.

[76] Diplomatic exchanges during the 1636/37 invasion are discussed in Evelyn Rawski, "War Letters: Hongtaiji and Injo during the Second Invasion of Korea," in *Political Strategies of Identity-Building in Non-Han Empires in China*, ed. Francesca Fiaschetti and Julia Schneider (Wiesbaden: Otto Harrassowitz, 2014), pp. 171–84.

declare fealty to the Qing. While nominally complying with the requirements of a tribute vassal, Confucianists at the Korean court repudiated
Manchu claims to the Heavenly Mandate and created a discourse of
Chosŏn as the repository of civilization (小華, *soHwa*, a small civilizational center).[77]

Ka-I discourse in Japan

Imported from the continent via the Korean peninsula in the seventh
century, the *Hua–Yi* binome was initially used to distinguish the core polity
in Kinai 近畿 from the "foreign lands" (外國, *gekoku, gaikoku*) outside
(Kigai 畿外). In the early eighth century, 'Nihon' referred to Kinai, the
core of Yamato power, and not the entire archipelago, and 'barbarian'
(*yi*, J. *ebisu*) to peoples dwelling outside Kinai.[78] This distinction – between
the civilized core and the primitive periphery – persisted through much of
Japanese history, emerging in distinctions between "civilized and barbarian
realms within the Japanese archipelago itself" during the Edo period
and beyond.[79] Among the most prominent *I* were the Emishi/Ezo 蝦夷,
the ancestors of today's Ainu people: Yamato campaigns against "local
chieftains" in Honshu accompanied the state-building effort.[80] This
ancient history is reflected in the full title of the shogun, *Sei-I tai-shōgun*
征夷大將軍 (literally, barbarian-quelling generalissimo), which the
Japanese emperor conferred on Minamoto Yoritomo in 1192.[81]

In a broader sense, people residing outside the capital were also liable
to be regarded as uncivilized (*I*).[82] Members of the Yamato elite

---

[77] Haboush, "Contesting Chinese Time."

[78] Amino, "Deconstructing 'Japan'," pp. 128–29. But also see Borgen, "Jōjin's Travels,"
p. 405, who notes that the Japanese applied the distinctions in Chinese administrative law
to their own institutions: thus, the office in charge of Buddhists and foreign guests was the
Genbaryō 玄蕃寮 (literally, Office for Barbarian Affairs). This office also handled visitors
from the Tang dynasty.

[79] David Howell, "Territoriality and Collective Identity," p. 121. See also
Sakayori Masashi, "Ka-I shisō no shosō (Aspects of civilized–barbarian thought), in
Ajia no naka no Nihonshi (Japanese history from within Asia), vol. V: *Jiishiki to sōgo
rikai* (An unauthorized Japanese history in Asia context: Reflection and Reciprocity),
ed. Arano Yasunori, Ishii Masatoshi, and Murai Shōsuke (Tokyo: University of Tokyo
Press, 1993), pp. 40–48.

[80] George Sansom, *A History of Japan* (Stanford: Stanford University Press, 1958), III: 19.
Sansom assumes that the "Emishi" were the ancestors of the Ainu; for a survey of the
scholarly debates, see Bruce L. Batten, *To the Ends of Japan: Premodern Frontiers,
Boundaries, and Interactions* (Honolulu: University of Hawai'i Press, 2003), pp. 101–6.

[81] Sansom, *History of Japan*, III: 331; Souyri, *World Turned Upside Down*, p. 46. "Barbarian-
quelling generalissimo" remained part of the shogunal title in the Edo period, see
Sonehara, "Tokugawa Ieyasu nenki," p.104.

[82] Yamato efforts to tame the Ezo/Emishi were presumably the reason for the inclusion of
"subjugating barbarians" in the shogun's title, "Sei-I taishōgun" 征夷大將軍;" see

conceptualized the world as a series of concentric circles drawn around the person of the emperor; the further the distance from the imperial palace and court, the greater the pollution, and the lower the cultural level of the inhabitants.[83] Because appointment to provincial office was tantamount to exile, many appointees remained in the capital, delegating their official responsibilities to subordinates. In the midst of a heated dispute over his pending retirement, Emperor Godaigo wrote a letter in 1324 referring to the shogunal officials at Kamakura as "eastern barbarians" 東夷. Andrew Goble calls this letter "one of the most extraordinary documents in Japanese history."[84] Written in the style "of a Chinese rather than a Japanese emperor," a contemporary considered it to be "equivalent to a declaration of war upon the bakufu."[85] In this instance, "eastern barbarians" was certainly used in a pejorative sense.

The expanding power of warrior households based in the provinces disrupted the medieval framework, in which Buddhist temples, the court aristocracy, and the imperial court dominated political power. The transition to shogunal government after 1185 initiated the gradual concentration of power achieved in the late sixteenth century by Toyotomi Hideyoshi and consolidated under the Tokugawa shogunate.

Tokugawa Japan was "by Western standards" "a nation without absolutely fixed borders or clearly defined sovereignty."[86] There was no centralized state with fiscal authority over the entire country but rather a splintering of authority, not just between emperor and shogun but between the shogunate and the fiefs. The very term used for "nation" in modern Japan, *kuni*, referred to the feudal domains.[87] The identities of individuals living before the second half of the nineteenth century were fixed by the status distinctions of a feudal order and their membership in a

---

"Glossary," p. 172 in John A. Ferejohn and Frances McCall Rosenbluth, eds., *War and State Building in Medieval Japan* (Stanford: Stanford University Press, 2010).

[83] Shōsuke Murai, "The Boundaries of Medieval Japan," *Acta Asiatica* 81 (2001): 72–73, 75.

[84] Goble, *Kenmu*, p. 67; an English translation of the letter appears on pp. 68–9. Go-Daigo later precipitated the period of divided imperial courts known in Japanese history as the Nanbokuchō (southern and northern courts), 1337–1392. See also Paul Varley, *Imperial Restoration in Medieval Japan* (New York: Columbia University Press, 1971).

[85] Goble, *Kenmu*, p. 67.

[86] Osamu Wakita, "The Emergence of the State in Sixteenth-Century Japan: From Oda to Tokugawa," *Journal of Japanese Studies* 8.2 (1982): 343–67; Howell, "Territoriality and Collective Identity."

[87] Mark Ravina, "State-building and Political Economy in Early-Modern Japan," *Journal of Asian Studies* 54.4 (1995): 997–1022; Roberts, *Performing the Great Peace*, pp. 13–15. Mary Elizabeth Berry, *Japan in Print: Information and Nation in the Early Modern Period* (Berkeley: University of California Press, 2006), p. 229, comments on the "obscure center" of the state during the Edo period. On the role of the emperor, see Wakabayashi, "In Name Only."

local community.[88] Foreign relations, normally a prerogative of centralized states, were farmed out to the daimyo of Tsushima, who dealt with Korea, and the Shimazu lords of Satsuma, who managed relations with the Ryukyus.[89]

Studies depicting the seventeenth century as "early modern" (*kinsei*) emphasize the dynamic aspects of Tokugawa history – the construction of a new status system, the "information revolution" that accompanied the mid-seventeenth-century expansion of printing, an increased awareness of territorial boundaries through the maps commissioned by the shogunate, and the development of new political ideologies outlining the relationship of Japan to the East Asian and world order.[90]

Common elements unified the discourse among Edo period thinkers concerning Japan's place in the world order.[91] Nishikawa Jōken, compiler of *Ka-I tsūshō kō* (An inquiry into trade and communication with the civilized and barbarian), a compendium of visual and textual information about the Qing and other realms beyond Japan, highlighted Edo, the shogunal capital, as the "civilized" core region in his geography, then organized countries in terms of their distance from Edo and the trade/diplomatic privileges granted them by the shogunate. Even though this displaced the Qing empire from its central position, the Qing still occupied a higher place in the pecking order than did the "outside countries" that lay beyond. Nishikawa distinguished sharply between China (*Chūka*) and the foreigners who wrote "from left to right," who, despite the artfulness of their exports, remained "foreign barbarians" (外夷).[92]

---

[88] David Howell, *Geographies of Identity in Nineteenth-Century Japan* (Berkeley: University of California Press, 2005), "Introduction."

[89] Toby, *State and Diplomacy*.

[90] Howell, "Territoriality and Collective Identity;" Richard Rubinger, *Popular Literacy in Early Modern Japan* (Honolulu: University of Hawai'i Press, 2007); Eiko Ikegami, *Bonds of Civility: Aesthetic Networks and the Political Origins of Japanese Culture* (Cambridge: Cambridge University Press, 2005); Marcia Yonemoto, *Mapping Early Modern Japan*; Berry, *Japan in Print*. The widespread acceptance of "early modern" is apparent in John Whitney Hall, ed., *The Cambridge History of Japan*, vol. IV (Cambridge: Cambridge University Press, 1991), which is entitled *Early Modern Japan*. On Japanese scholarship, see Yoshihiko Amino, "Deconstructing 'Japan.'" See also Batten, "Introduction," *To the Ends of Japan*, on the paradigm shift in Japanese history.

[91] See Peter Nosco, "Confucianism and Nativism in Tokugawa Japan," in *Meeting of Minds: Intellectual and Religious Interaction in East Asian Traditions of Thought*, ed. Irene Bloom and Joshua A. Fogel (New York: Columbia University Press, 1997), pp. 278–90, who notes that the separation of Confucian from *Kokugaku* thinkers was really a phenomenon of the eighteenth century.

[92] Fujita Yūji, "Kinsei Nihon ni okeru jinminzoku chūshinteki shikō – 'senmin' ishiki to shite no Nihon chūshin shugi" (An analysis of the core of ethnocentrism in Japan: the concept of a 'chosen people' and Japan-centered ideology), *Shisō* 832 (1993): 118; Yonemoto, "Maps and Metaphors of the 'Small Eastern Sea.'" Strangely enough, the British in

Even Confucianists who revered China as the source of the Confucian canon rejected the idea that China was therefore superior to Japan. Ogyū Sōrai (1666–1728), who once signed himself as "the Eastern barbarian of the country of Japan 日本國夷人," was criticized for his "slavish adulation of China."[93] Attacking scholars who, "seeing that Chinese books speak of Japan as barbaric, think 'Oh, how regrettable, how shameful! I was born a barbarian!'" Asami Keisai wrote that accepting the Sinocentric view "is like being spit upon and crying that one cannot wipe it off." Arai Hakuseki, a prominent Confucian serving the shogun Ienobu, wrote that it was completely natural for Chinese to regard their own country as superior, but "for us to adopt the viewpoint of those who regard us as barbarians and themselves as civilized is to turn against the Way of the Sages of antiquity."[94]

Ogyū Sōrai's commentary on the Ming code echoes the sentiment that the Japanese should regard their own country as the "central kingdom."[95] Whereas the Ming styled themselves as "great Ming" (大明), it was not necessary for Japanese, who had not been vassals to Ming, to use that prefix. As a Japanese, however, Sōrai would affix "great" to Japan.[96] Other scholars tried to bypass the issue by using "honchō" (本朝) to refer to Japan, and "ihō" 異邦 or "ikoku" 異國 (foreign country) to denote China.[97]

During the seventeenth and eighteenth centuries many Chinese books entered Japan. Most educated Japanese read these books by annotating them in a system known as *wakun* 和訓 (Japanese reading), changing the original word order in order to comply with Japanese grammar and syntax and thus obscuring its full meaning. When Ogyū Sōrai advocated studying spoken Chinese (*Kajin gengo* 華人言語) in order to read the Confucian canon more accurately, he was derided by Arai Hakuseki. How could

protesting the Qing use of "Yi" also used (unwittingly?) a hierarchical term, saying "Great Britain is not a *yi* state but a *wai* (outside) state": see Lydia Liu, *Clash of Empires*, p. 43.

[93] Nakai, "Naturalization of Confucianism," p. 16; Japanese text in *Ōgyū Sorai*, v. 36, p. 495 in *Nihon shisō taikei*, ed. Yoshikawa Kōjirō et al (Tokyo: Iwanami shoten, 1973). On Confucian thought during the Edo period, see Yoshio Abe, "Development of Neo-Confucianism in Japan, Korea and China: A Comparative Study," *Acta Asiatica* 19 (1970): 16–39; Samuel Hideo Yamashita, "Reading the New Tokugawa Intellectual Histories," *Journal of Japanese Studies* 22.1 (1996): 1–48; James McMullen, "Tokugawa Intellectual History: State of the Field," *Early Modern Japan* 10.1 (2002): 22–85.

[94] Nakai, "Naturalization of Confucianism"; quotation from her *Shogunal Politics*, p. 374.

[95] Nakai, "Naturalization of Confucianism," p. 184.   [96] *Ibid.*, pp. 182, 183.

[97] *Honchō suikoden* 本朝水滸傳 (1773); but this practice existed in the Heian period, cf. *Honchō kokushi mokuroku*, said to be a catalogue dating from the Heian period: Kornicki, *Book in Japan*, pp. 299, 424.

studying lower class colloquial Chinese be effective in "mastering the language of the ancients"?[98]

Several scholars argued that the Confucian Way (道) was the same as the Way in Shintō 神道:

To say, "It is the way of the Chinese sages," or, "It is the way of the kami rulers of Japan, is like arguing over whose sun and moon it is ... the way of the kami (*shintō*) of Japan ... at the same time ... is the way of the sages (*seidō* 聖道) of China."[99]

Equating the Confucian Way to Shintō meant that neither was superior to the other. Even those who rejected this claim, like Arai Hakuseki, asserted the potential for Japan to produce its own Way:

Where is the place that a sage cannot be born? How could it be that it was only in the so-called "flowery kingdom" that sages were born?[100]

As Asami Keisai wrote, "if one studies the Way through works in which it is elucidated, it becomes one's own Way of Heaven and Earth."[101] Japanese Confucianism did not entail slavish imitation of Chinese ways: rather, it would be created on Japanese soil.

When an idealized China was the standard of "creativity and civilization," Japan might seem small (and inferior) to the "great country," but for Yamaga Sokō (1622–85), precisely the opposite was true. Its "unbroken continuity of *taigi meibun*" (大義明分, the great principle of the unity of names and functions) made Japan the true "middle kingdom" (*chūchō* 中朝).[102] Asami Keisai asserted in *Seiken igen* (靖献遺言) that Japanese scholars should discard the *Ka–I* binome: the distinction it invoked had nothing to do with the values that mattered, "loyalty, duties and designations, legitimacy, or the master–retainer principle."[103] Alternatively, scholars might cite the Zhu Xi interpretation of a passage in the *Analects* which credited Confucius as stating, "The barbarians of the East and North have retained their princes. They are not in such a state of decay as we in China."[104]

---

[98] Kornicki, *Book in Japan*, p. 171. On Ogyū Sōrai's advocacy, see Pastreich, "Grappling with Chinese Writing."

[99] Kumazawa Banzan, *Miwa monogatari*, quotation from Nakai, "Naturalization of Confucianism," p. 163.

[100] Arai Hakuseki, *Koshitsū*, quoted in Nakai, "Naturalization of Confucianism," p. 166.

[101] Asami Keisai, *Seiken igen*, quoted in Nakai, "Naturalization of Confucianism," p. 164.

[102] Harootunian, "Function of China," p. 14, also pp. 13, 15. On the importance of *taigi meibun* in the development of the restorationist movement, see Wai-ming Ng, "Political Terminology in the Legitimating of the Tokugawa System: A Study of *Bakufu* and *Shōgun*," *Journal of Asian history* 34.2 (2000): 135–48.

[103] Harootunian, "Function of China," p. 16.

[104] Nakai, "Naturalization of Confucianism," p. 178, which records the opposite interpretation of the same passage by Ogyū Sōrai: "Even with their rulers, the barbarians of the East and North cannot match the Chinese states lacking them."

The initiative of Japanese Confucianists to invert the Sinocentrism implied in *Hua–Yi* discourse was further developed by thinkers in the *kokugaku* (National learning) school who decried the distortions of "Chinese" words and "Chinese spirit" (*Karagokoro*) as "trickery" that was contrary to wisdom based on "a pure heart" and the "pure spirit" of the "divine country," Japan.[105] Motoori Norinaga (1730–1801) wrote:

> Comparing the theories in Chinese writings and the ancient traditions of our country, one finds that the former appear quite reasonable and true, whereas the latter sound insignificant and shallow . . . all the scholars . . . have been captivated by Chinese theories . . . [But] it is very arrogant to believe that all things in the world . . . can be explained by one's theory. This is a false mental attitude in those who do not realize the limitation of man's intelligence and the inscrutability of the real principle.[106]

Norinaga's poems indicate that he believed true comprehension of the "Way of the Kami" required stripping away the "veil of Chinese doctrine" in order to "behold the clear mirrors," i.e. the *Kojiki*.[107] In order to present the *Kojiki* as "a transparent transcription of the oral transmissions of the Divine Age," he carefully rendered the *kanbun* (written in Chinese characters) text into *kana* (Japanese syllabary).[108]

The process of bringing China down to size was also encouraged by Japan's exposure to European traders and missionaries, which transformed Japanese conceptions of the world outside their shores.[109] The enhanced self-confidence of Japanese thinkers underpinned the discourse of *shinkoku* 神國, the notion that Japan was unique because it was the "land of the gods."

Shinkoku *discourse*

Kitabatake Chikafusa (1293–1354) is often credited as the first to clearly enunciate the shinkoku theory in the opening lines of his Record of the Orthodox Transmission of Gods and Sovereigns (神皇正統記 *Jinnō shōtōki*):

---

[105] Harootunian, "Function of China," pp. 17–25.
[106] Introduction to *Kojiki den*, quotation from Shigeru Matsumoto, *Motoori Norinaga, 1730–1801* (Cambridge, MA: Harvard University Press, 1970), p. 79.
[107] Matsumoto, *Motoori Norinaga*, pp. 80, 81.
[108] Susan L. Burns, *Before the Nation: Kokugaku and the Imagining of Community in Early Modern Japan* (Durham: Duke University Press, 2003), p. 76.
[109] Ronald P. Toby, "Three Realms/Myriad Countries: An 'Ethnography' of Other and the Re-bounding of Japan, 1550–1750," in *Constructing Nationhood in Modern East Asia*, ed. Kai-wing Chow, Kevin M. Doak, and Poshek Fu (Ann Arbor: University of Michigan Press, 2001), pp. 15–45.

Great Japan is the country of the gods. The heavenly ancestor founded it and the sun goddess bequeathed it to her descendants to rule eternally. Only in our country is this true; there are no similar examples in other countries. This is why our country is called the country of the gods (*shinkoku*).[110]

Kitabatake's *shinkoku* (*kami no kuni*, in alternative Japanese reading) has to be read within the context of his time. The author, descended from a collateral branch of the imperial house, served emperor Godaigo (r. 1318–39) before taking Buddhist vows. A supporter of the southern court, Chikafusa wrote the *Jinnō shōtōki* as a defense of Japan's superior claim to legitimacy. The work's assertions of an immutable social order based on the imperial house contrasted strikingly with the political instability of the 1330s, when two rival courts vied for legitimacy.[111]

The *shinkoku* of *Jinnō shōtōki* departed significantly from earlier usage. *Shinkoku* first appears in the early eighth-century *Nihon shoki*, and the term is repeated in ninth-century prayers for protecting the country, in an era when the country (*kuni*) was still "a patchwork of ... concrete territories," situated within a Buddhist cosmology, and the *kami* were conceived of not simply as local deities but as "manifestations of buddhas and bodhisattvas."[112] Unlike this cosmological vision, in which Japan, an "insignificant country," was situated at the periphery of the Three Realms, the discourse of *shinkoku* in the late thirteenth and early fourteenth century put Japan at the center.

Responding to a Mongol demand for submission, Sugawara Naganari wrote that since the imperial line was descended in an unbroken line from "Amaterasu Ōmikami, Tenshōkō, Japan had an indissoluble bond with the gods," which was the reason it was called "the land of the gods"

---

[110] Kitabatake Chikafusa, *Jinnō shōtōki*, ed. Iwasa Masashi et al., vol. LXXXVII, *Nihon koten bungaku taikei* (Tokyo: Iwanami shoten, 1966), p. 41. I have departed at some points from the English translation of H. Paul Varley: Kitabatake Chikafusa, trans. H. Paul Varley, *A Chronicle of Gods and Sovereigns: "Jinnō Shōtōki" of Kitabatake Chikafusa* (New York: Columbia University Press, 1980), p. 49, to underline the conceptual links between this text and others that will be discussed below.

[111] See Varley, *Chronicle of Gods and Sovereigns*, "Introduction," pp. 1–41.

[112] Fabio Rambelli, "Religion, Ideology of Domination, and Nationalism: Kuroda Toshio on the Discourse of *Shinkoku*," *Japanese Journal of Religious Studies* 23.3/4 (1996): 393–94, 395; Toshio Kuroda, trans. Fabio Rambelli, "The Discourse on the 'Land of Kami' (*Shinkoku*) in Medieval Japan: National Consciousness and International Awareness," *Japanese Journal of Religious Studies* 23.3/4 (1996): 353–85, argues that even Kitabatake Chikafusa, whose work Varley characterizes as "Shinto," was actually writing from a culture infused with Buddhist doctrine. See Tarō Sakamoto, *The Six National Histories of Japan*, trans. John S. Brownlee (Vancouver and Tokyo: UBC and University of Tokyo Press, 1991), chapter 2 on *Nihon shoki*.

(*shinkoku*).[113] Japanese writers credited the failure of the two Mongol invasions of 1274 and 1281 to the *kamikaze* (divine winds), sent by Amaterasu and Hachiman.

Kitabatake's vision of Japan as *shinkoku* suffused new schools of Shinto, including Watarai or Ise Shinto, and eventually in the late fifteenth century by Yoshida Shinto.[114] Yoshida Kanetomo (1435–1511), the founder of the dominant school of Shinto during the Edo period, inverted the medieval cosmology, which had incorporated native deities into the Buddhist pantheon: Kanetomo argued instead that *kami* were the original form of the Buddha.

Japan produced the seed, China produced the branches and leaves, India produced the flowers and fruit ... Buddhism and Confucianism are only secondary products of Shintō ... Buddhism came east only to reveal clearly that our nation is the trunk and the roots of these three nations.[115]

The understanding of *shinkoku* developed from Yoshida Kanetomo is the foundation for the views expressed in the 1587 pronouncement of Hideyoshi (later echoed by Tokugawa Ieyasu) when expelling the Jesuit missionaries from Japan: "Since Japan is the land of the gods, it is manifestly improper that the base doctrines of the lands of the Christians be propagated [here]."[116] In letters to the Portuguese viceroy to the Indies (1591) and to the Spanish governor-general to the Philippines (1597), Hideyoshi asserted the equivalence of Buddhism (for India), Confucianism (for China) and Shinto: all are manifestations of the *kami* – and, by extension, none is superior to the others.[117] In 1593, Hideyoshi directed negotiators to

---

[113] The original text is found in *Honchō monjū* (Collected writings of the state), comp. by the Mito Tokugawa, 30: 399–400 in *Shintei zōhō Kokushi taikei*, ed. Kuroita Katsumi (Tokyo: Yoshikawa kōbunkan, 1966). For an account of the Mongol invasion attempts, see Sansom, *History of Japan*, III: 438–50.

[114] Bernhard Scheid, "Land of the *Kami* and Way of the *Kami* in Yoshida Shintō," in *Religion and National Identity in the Japanese Context*, ed. Klaus Antoni, Hiroshi Kubota, Johann Nawrocki, and Michael Wachutka (Münster: Lit, 2002), 193–214; Martin Repp, "Hachiman – Protecting *Kami* of the Japanese Nation," pp. 169–92 in the same volume.

[115] Quotation from Scheid, "Land of the *Kami*," p. 201. See also Takagi, "Hideyoshi's and Ieyasu's Views," pp. 72–81. Maeda, "Imperial Authority and Local Shrines," chapter 1 discusses Yoshida Kanetomo's contributions to the political ascendancy of his house and argues against Kuroda Toshio that the emergence of Yoshida Shinto marks the date when an independent Shinto religious system appeared in Japan. See Breen and Teeuwen, "Introduction," pp. 3–8 for comments on broader interpretations of the history of Shinto.

[116] Quoted from Toby, *State and Diplomacy*, p. 216; a slightly different translation is provided by Asao, "Sixteenth-Century Unification," p. 74.

[117] Etsuko Hae-Jin Kang, *Diplomacy and Ideology*, p. 97; interpretation from Takagi, "Hideyoshi's and Ieyasu's Views," p. 73; see Fujita, "Kinsei Nihon ni okeru jiminzoku."

communicate to the Ming that Japan was the country of the gods and that these gods had provided him with "a special mandate."[118]

Shinkoku ideas were not simply expressed for external consumption but popularized through Chikamatsu's *Honchō Sangoku shi* 本朝三國誌 (Japan's Three Kingdoms History) and Ki no Kaion's *Jingū kōgō sankanzeme* 神功皇後三韓責.[119] The two plays reflect the *Nihon shoki's* account of how Empress Jingū crossed the sea to conquer the Korean Three Kingdoms. According to the Hachiman shrines, which recorded the legend in scrolls painted in the late fourteenth century, the empress's victory (strong winds and waves wafted her ship swiftly to Silla; the awestruck king quickly surrendered, to be followed by the rulers of Koguryŏ and Paekche) was due to the power of the deity Hachiman. Empress Jingū was invoked again to explain the failed Mongol invasions. As the *Hachiman gudōkin* 八幡愚童訓 put it,

Although Japan is a small and inferior country, it is a divine country of prestige and wisdom. At the time of Empress Jingū's conquest, the Ko[gu]ryŏ king swore that his people should become dogs for Japan and protect Japan. The Mongols are the descendants of these dogs, whereas the Japanese are the descendants of the gods. The distinction between the high and low is clear and is separated as much as heaven and earth are. How can the gods and the beasts be at an equal level?[120]

In 1592, as Hideyoshi prepared to invade Korea, he had three scrolls depicting Empress Jingū's conquest brought to him from a shrine-temple located on the island in Hakata Bay reputed to be the site from which the empress launched her Korean expedition (it was, not coincidentally, the site of a 1281 battle with the Mongol invaders). Hideyoshi seems to have taken the scrolls as an omen predicting his imminent triumph.[121]

Chikamatsu's most popular work, *The Battles of Coxinga* (*Kokusenya kassen* 國性爺合戰), first performed in 1715, drew on popular ideas about the differences between Japanese, Chinese, and the "Tartars" (Mongols, in the play, but the term was also applied to the Manchus): China has given the world rites and music; India, Buddhism; and Japan, "the way of the eternal gods enjoining honesty." By contrast, "there is

[118] Asao, "Sixteenth-Century Unification," p. 282; see a different rendering in Kang, *Diplomacy and Ideology*, p. 97. The deification of Tokugawa Ieyasu continues this trend: see Sonehara, "Tokugawa Ieyasu nenki kōji."

[119] Chikamatsu's play can be found in *Chikamatsu chosaku zenshū*; Ki no Kaion's 紀海音 (1663–1742) play is held in the Waseda University Library; my thanks to Hiroyuki Good for this information.

[120] Quoted from Haruko Wakabayashi, "The Mongol Invasions and the Making of the Iconography of Foreign Enemies: The Case of *Shikaumi jinja engi*," in *Tools of Culture*, ed. Goble, Robinson, and Wakabayashi, pp. 125–26.

[121] Wakabayashi, "Mongol Invasions," p. 105.

neither a Way nor laws" in Tartary; the "northern barbarians are no different from beasts, and their country is therefore commonly spoken of as a beast-land."[122]

Coxinga, the hero Watōnai, is the son of a banished Grand Tutor. When he goes to China to help Ming repel the Manchu invaders, his Japanese mother reminds him that he was born in *shinkoku* and "the gods dwell in your body." With the aid of an amulet from the Ise shrine, Watōnai confronts a tiger. After he easily subdues the soldiers of a villainous Ming minister, he tells them, "You who despise the Japanese for coming from a small country – have you learned now the meaning of Japanese prowess, before which even tigers tremble?"[123]

Intellectuals responded to the challenge of explaining how the small country, Japan, could match or outdo China in several different ways. Some saw the ocean between themselves and the continent as the reason why Japan need not fear invasion. Others compared Japan's high population density favorably to China's sparsely populated north. For Yamaga Sokō (1622–85), the very size of China was a disadvantage, because it increased the difficulty of defending the territory from invasion while also raising the cost of internal administration. A debate between Motoori Norinaga and Ueda Akinari used metaphors to argue that larger was not necessarily better: a big rock was inferior to a small precious jade, oxen and horses could not match human beings.[124]

Reminders of Japan's *shinkoku* self-image also affected the ships carrying the 1719 Korean embassy to Japan. They were denied shelter on Ōshima during a storm because the island's shrine was dedicated to a goddess descended from Amaterasu. This shrine, part of a nation-wide network of Munakata shrines, was "too sacred to be defiled by foreigners."[125] Such interpolations must have aggravated the hostile sentiments nursed by Korean embassies who were forced to visit the "Mound of Ears" collected during the Japanese invasion of their country because the site represented "the glory of *shinkoku*."[126]

---

[122] "The Battles of Coxinga," pp. 19, 8–99 in Chikamatsu Monzaemon, trans. Donald Keene, *Major Plays of Chikamatsu* (New York: Columbia University Press, 1990). Keene points out that the hero's name 和唐内 (literally, between Japan and China) shows his mixed nature and allegiances.
[123] *Ibid.*, p. 227.   [124] Fujita, "Kinsei Nihon ni okeru jiminzoku," pp. 110–11.
[125] Hur, "Korean Officials in the Land of Kami," p. 89.
[126] *Ibid.*, pp. 90–91. Hur notes that the name of the mound, Mimitsuka ("mound of ears") was a misnomer of Hanatsuka ("mound of noses"). He also cites a text of 1659, which states that both ears and noses were interred in front of the Daibutsu Hall on Higashiyama.

Hwa–Yi discourse in Korea

Korean officials adopted *Pŏn* (蕃, 藩, C. *fan*), another term for "barbarian" that appeared in Chinese discussions of policies toward frontier tribes. Ch'u Myŏngyŏp's study of Korean documents dating from the eleventh through twelfth centuries evokes the evolving geopolitical situation on Korean frontiers that dictated how the terms "Northern barbarian" (*Puk Pŏn* 北蕃), "Eastern" and "Western barbarian" 東, 西 蕃 appeared in court deliberations to denote various tribal peoples in northeast Asia. The controversial *Ten Injunctions* of the Koryŏ founder, T'aejo (r. 918–43) proclaimed Khitan to be "a nation of savage beasts" 契丹是禽獸之國, whose "dress and institutions should never be copied."[127] During periods of heightened tension, these terms with the suffix *chŏk* (賊, C. *zei*, "bandit") referred to the Khitan Liao and Jurchen Jin who threatened Koryŏ security.[128]

Korean historians of the Chosŏn dynasty have noted that the court's attitude toward the Qing was rooted in its own interactions with the progenitors of the Manchus. Especially in P'yŏng'an province, assimilated Jurchen were part of the local society.[129] During the fifteenth century the government successfully brought the Jurchen tribes under bureaucratic control by alternating inducements (described in Chapter 1) with coercive force.[130]

Contemporary government documents also show that alternative views denying the possibility of culturally incorporating Jurchen appeared from this period onward. Officials wrote that as "savages" (*yain*) the Jurchen were animals lacking the capacity to be transformed, i.e. civilized. The *sillok* entries use the characters for "wolf" (狼, K. *nang*, C. *lang*) and "panther" (豹, K. *p'yo*, C. *bao*) as epithets designating the Jurchen.[131]

[127] Peter Yun, "Koryŏ–Khitan Relations and Khitan Cultural Influence," p. 69. The controversy over whether this document dates from the ninth or early eleventh centuries does not affect the cultural judgment it expressed.

[128] Ch'u Myŏngyŏp, "Koryŏ chŏn'gi 'Pŏn' (蕃) insik kwa 'Tong-Sŏbŏn ŭi hyŏngsŏng" (The consciousness of 'Pŏn' in early Koryŏ and the formation of the eastern and western barbarians), *Yŏk'sa wa hyŏnsil* 43 (1999): 14–46.

[129] Karlsson, "A Hermit Nation," analyzes the ways in which natives of P'yŏng'an might have chosen to represent themselves as Manchu in the Hong Kŏngnae rebellion of 1811–12.

[130] Ha Ubong, "Chosŏn chŏn'gi taeŭi kwan'gye e nat'anan cha'a insik kwa t'aja insik" (Self-perception and the perception of others appearing in foreign relations in early Chosŏn), *Han'guksa yŏn'gu* 123 (2003): 247–70. See also Morris Rossabi, *The Jurchens in the Yüan and Ming*, Cornell University East Asia Papers Number 27 (Ithaca: Cornell University China–Japan Program, 1982).

[131] The Chosŏn-era derogatory remarks about Jurchen contrast strongly with one recent scholarly attempt to argue that the Manchus considered themselves to be descendants of "the advanced civilizations of Baekje and Silla," because they, like Koreans, were "Eastern Yi": see Song Jhune Hyueck, "Eastern Barbarian Consciousness in *Research*

The Japanese invasion and the two Jurchen/Manchu assaults on the peninsula hardened Chosŏn attitudes. A substantial segment of the Chosŏn bureaucracy drew on this earlier history of relations to denounce the Jianzhou Jurchen led by Nurhaci as "dogs and pigs" or "dogs and sheep"; in documents of the early seventeenth century, the character for "slave"(奴) was regularly used to refer to the Jurchen.

Elsewhere (see Chapter 4), we have discussed the intensification of anti-Qing rhetoric after Chosŏn's subjugation in 1637. Many Korean specialists have described the development of the idea that by virtue of their origins outside the Central Plain, Manchus could never be legitimate Sons of Heaven.[132] The Neo-Confucian, Song Siyŏl (1607–89), a dominant figure in the court of Hyojong (r. 1649–59), was committed to two inherently contradictory views: first, that the potential for moral transformation had been realized in Chosŏn Korea, and second, that the Qing remained "barbarians," who must be driven out of the civilized core region.[133]

Song's plans for a northern expedition against the Manchus were thwarted by Hyojong's untimely death, but the idea did not wholly disappear. A century later, a work entitled *Kija p'alchoji* 箕子八條志 presented proposals for the governmental reforms that would facilitate a northern expedition. Yamauchi Kōichi points to passages in *Kija p'alchoji* that reiterate the idea of Chosŏn as the new civilized center of the world order: "the Rong and Di have created chaos in China, but Chosŏn alone has preserved culture," "the true Ming has been restored here" 戎狄亂華, 而朝鮮獨保文物衣冠: 真明復起於此.[134]

By the late eighteenth century, awareness of the world outside East Asia was increasing. Envoys who travelled to Peking witnessed its prosperity during the Qianlong reign, and some suggested that Chosŏn could learn from the Qing. Sŏng Daejung (1732–1812) praised China and attributed its achievements to the Manchu ability to incorporate European knowledge and technology with the products of Chinese civilization. Even if the barbarian Qing controlled China, Chosŏn could still acquire valuable

on Manchu Origins," *The Review of Korean Studies* 12.3 (2009): 163–75. Of course, Korean officials used similar epithets for the Japanese.

[132] Kye Sŭngbŏm, "Chosŏn hugi Chunghwaron," 63–64; Yamauchi Kōichi, *Chōsen kara mita Ka-I shisō* (Civilized–barbarian thought from the Korean perspective) (Tokyo: Yamakawa shuppansha, 2003), pp. 58–74.

[133] Haboush, "Constructing the Center," pp. 78–9; Yamauchi, *Chōsen kara mita*, p. 65. By stressing Chosŏn's moral transformation, Song accepted the universalist message of Confucianism, but he rejected Manchu claims to the same possibility.

[134] Yamauchi Kōichi, "Chōsen wo motte Tenka ni ō tarashimu – Gakushūin daigaku zō [Kishi hasshū shi] ni miru zaiya Nōron chishikijin no yume" (The dream of Korean Noron intellectuals on ruling all under heaven, using the *Kija p'alchoji* held in the Gakushūin University collection), *Tōyō gakuhō* 84.3 (2002): 4.

knowledge there.[135] Knowledge of worlds outside Asia, however, had permanently altered the perceptions of elites. China was no longer the sole center. Hong Daeyŏn (1731–83), a Sirhak (Statecraft) scholar, wrote that "China thinks it is the center and Europe the periphery, but Europeans consider Europe to be the center and China the periphery. The truth is that heaven above and earth below are the same everywhere. There is no center and no periphery."[136]

Manchu perspectives

As noted previously, the Jurchen/Manchu regime had particularly close links with both the Ming and the Chosŏn during the period 1616–37. The heightened level of state-to-state contact is reflected in shifts in the Manchu terms used to refer to these states. In the texts of Nurhaci's time, the Ming dynasty was *nikan gurun* (literally, Chinese country/tribe), and the Chosŏn, *solgo/solho gurun* (Korean country/tribe). In the 1630s, new terms that were transliterations of Chinese pronunciations (*daiming gurun, coohiyan gurun*) suggest that a process of accommodation was taking place. Hongtaiji used *solho* and *nikan* in his speech to the troops on the eve of his second invasion of Korea, but in his proclamation to Chosŏn officials and people explaining the reasons for the military campaign, he switched to *daiming gurun* and *coohiyan gurun*.[137] Manchu references to the Ming as the "southern dynasty" in other communications with Chosŏn implied that it no longer accepted the Sinocentric world order.

The pronouncements by Nurhaci and Hongtaiji reveal much about the basis for Qing claims on the Mandate of Heaven. To representations that the Later Jin were "rebels" against their legitimate overlord, Hongtaiji argued that Manchu military victory proved that Heaven had abandoned the Ming and bestowed its favor on him.[138] The Ming emperor, as Nurhaci pointed out in 1621, "does not rule fairly" and "allows the eunuchs to take property . . . causing those with property who are upright and honest to suffer." That is why Heaven has turned against him.[139] Hongtaiji, writing to the Ming general in charge of Liaodong in 1629,

---

[135] Yamauchi, *Chōsen kara mita*, p. 71–3.   [136] *Ibid.*, p. 74.

[137] See Kanda, *Manbun rōtō*, VII: 1471–73, 1473–76. On the historical evolution of the term *nikan*, see Crossley, *Translucent Mirror*, pp. 90–99.

[138] Mark Elliott, "Whose Empire Shall It Be? Manchu Figurations of Historical Process in the Early Seventeenth Century," in *Time, Temporality, and Imperial Transition*, ed. Lynn A. Struve (Honolulu: University of Hawai'i Press, 2005), pp. 31–72.

[139] *Ibid.*, p. 39.

reiterated, "*Tianxia* is not one person's realm . . . [but] . . . belongs to all people. To whomsoever Heaven gives it, that person must take it."[140]

During the conquest period (1644–83), Manchu/Qing proclamations tended to emphasize the universalist Confucian message that Heaven did not bestow the Mandate on the basis of ethnic origin but on the basis of the ruler's virtue. Even though the rulers paid little attention to censorship – with the exception of the period 1661–69, which was dominated by the conservative regency of Manchu banner officials led by Oboi – experience with prior regimes made educated elites wary of writing histories of Ming policy in the northeast which would have to discuss the origins and development of the Jurchen/Manchu/Qing state.[141] Among other "delicate" topics were issues such as: should Ming histories include sections on the Southern Ming regimes (i.e., those who had attempted to claim the succession after the suicide of the Chongzhen emperor)? Could calendrical references to Southern Ming year names be included? How should historians attempt to explain the demise of the Ming dynasty?

The exception to the lax censorship of the pre-1683 period was the 1661–62 literary "inquisition," which focused on a Zhejiang merchant named Zhuang Tinglong who had commissioned a revision and publication of a private history of the Ming, which used the (prohibited) personal names of Manchu rulers (a Chinese convention which the Qing adopted) and Ming calendrical dates for events occurring after the Manchu entry into Peking in 1644. In response to what they regarded as the Shunzhi emperor's excessive accommodation of his Han subjects, Oboi and the other regents took a hard line on the core of anti-Manchu literati resistance situated in the cultural heartland of Jiangsu/Zhejiang, especially when they discovered bribery and attempts at a cover-up which implicated local "southern, Han Chinese, Qing officials."[142] In the course of its inquiry, the court executed over seventy persons who had participated in preparing the history, confiscated their estates and enslaved their families, and ordered the printing blocks and extant copies of the work destroyed.[143]

---

[140] Letter to Yuan Chonghuan, translated by Elliott, "Whose Empire," p. 40.

[141] Struve, *Ming–Qing Conflict*, chapter 2, pp. 25–47, presents a detailed and nuanced exposition of the political climate confronting early Qing writers. As an example of the Shunzhi emperor's attempts to court Chinese literati, she cites the case of Gu Yingtai, accused by a censor of "disrespect" toward the Qing in his compilation, *Minshi jishi benmo*, who nonetheless was cordially received by the emperor (p. 31).

[142] On the political background, see Robert B. Oxnam, *Ruling from Horseback: Manchu Politics in the Oboi Regency, 1661–1669* (Chicago: University of Chicago Press, 1975); on the Zhuang Tinglong case, see pp. 108–11.

[143] Struve, *Ming–Qing Conflict*, pp. 31–32; Lawrence D. Kessler, *K'ang-hsi and the Consolidation of Ch'ing Rule, 1661–1684* (Chicago: University of Chicago Press, 1976), pp. 31–33.

In keeping with his desire to win the loyalty of the Han Chinese literati, in 1679 the Kangxi emperor revived the Ming History project initiated by his father.[144] Later, when he became embroiled in a bitter struggle over selecting an heir, he shifted his priorities, and decisively suppressed popular movements that were linked to Ming loyalists. Ironically, the project designed to "close the book" on the fallen dynasty, compilation of the official Ming History, again brought the "delicate questions" of interpretation (see above) to the fore, and subjected them to the imperial gaze. When called upon to make a judgment call, the Yongzheng emperor responded:[145]

It is imperative that the Ming History be finished, that general agreements be found, that right and wrong be clarified, and that people's minds and hearts [thereby] be won ... Every day I manage ten thousand critical affairs with limited energy. *I* certainly cannot read every single item in [the Ming History] drafts and facilely make [the necessary judgements] ... The truths and falsities of Ming History are self-illuminating. You ministers must jointly come to a solid recognition of them.

The Ming History was finally completed in 1736, in the first year of a new reign. Unlike his father and grandfather, Hongli, the Qianlong emperor (r. 1735–96), inherited a throne that was much more confident of its legitimacy. He was quick to proscribe books that described the ancestors of the Manchus, the pre-1644 history of the Qing state, and conquest dynasties such as the Jin (whom the Manchus claimed as forebears) and Yuan.[146] Although scholars remember the "Literary Inquisition" of 1772–1793, a byproduct of his desire to mark his reign with the compilation of the Complete Library of the Four Treasuries (*Siku quanshu*), Pamela Crossley and others have focused instead on the Qianlong emperor's response to the Zeng Jing case, which confronted the question of how people of different ethnic origins could become "transformed."[147]

Zeng Jing (1679–1736) was a failed scholar living in Hunan province who became convinced of the personal iniquities of Yinzhen, the

---

[144] Franke, *Introduction to Sources of Ming History*, 2.1.9, pp. 48–49.

[145] Quoted from Struve, *Ming–Qing Conflict*, p. 40.

[146] Banning books with anti-Manchu content was only part of a larger project of state censorship: see Okamoto Sae, *Shindai kinsho no kenkyū* (Research on Qing banned books) (Tokyo: University of Tokyo Press, 1996), who estimates that approximately 150,000 titles were proscribed during the Qing dynasty.

[147] On the literary inquisition, see R. Kent Guy, *The Emperor's Four Treasures: Scholars and the State in the Late Ch'ien-lung Era* (Cambridge, MA: Harvard University Asia Center, 1987); Crossley, *Translucent Mirror*, pp. 253–62. On the Zeng Jing case, see Jonathan D. Spence, *Treason by the Book* (New York: Viking Penguin, 2001) and Pei Huang, *Autocracy at Work: A Study of the Yung-cheng Period, 1723–1735* (Bloomington: Indiana University Press, 1974), pp. 215–20.

Yongzheng emperor (he believed that the emperor had killed his father and brothers), which justified his attempts to overthrow the Manchu ruling house.[148] In this he was influenced by the writings of Lü Liuliang (1626–83), a scholar who had taken the lower-level exams before electing to remain faithful to the fallen Ming dynasty.[149] Lü urged scholars not to serve the Qing because of its "barbaric origin."[150] Zeng echoed these ideas when he wrote that the loss of virtue in late Ming rulership allowed the "barbarians" to take advantage of weakness to usurp "our precious throne." "The barbarians are a different species from us, like animals; it is the Chinese who should stay in this land, and the barbarians who should be driven out."[151]

Zeng's ideas came to the attention of higher authorities in 1728 when he wrote to the governor-general of Shaanxi, Yue Zhongqi, informing him of his plans and inviting him to lead the uprising. Zeng and his fellow plotters were arrested and interrogated; Lü's writings were searched out and destroyed, his corpse was posthumously mutilated, his family enslaved, and his followers punished. Zeng, however, was freed and allowed to return to his native place in 1730, as proof of the emperor's magnanimity, living proof that "the rumors about the emperor's character and conduct had been invented by unscrupulous persons."[152] The Yongzheng emperor had Zeng Jing's testimony and his own thoughts on the subject compiled and published under the title *Dayi juemi lu* (大義覺密線, A record of how true virtue led to an awakening from delusion).[153] The emperor intended that his compilation should circulate widely among bureaucrats and local elites.

---

[148] The accusations that the emperor had killed his father and brothers were uncomfortably close to the truth. For an example of the continuing scholarly speculation surrounding the Kangxi emperor's deathbed will, see Jiang Xiangshun, "Kangxi di wannian lichu zhi mi" (On the puzzle of the succession during the late Kangxi reign), *Manzu yanjiu* 1 (1995: 40–45). On the succession struggle, see Silas H. L. Wu, *Passage to Power: K'ang-hsi and His Heir Apparent, 1661–1722* (Cambridge, MA: Harvard University Press, 1979). That Zeng, living in central China, became aware of the Yongzheng emperor's actions against his brothers in 1728, within a few years of Yinzhen's accession, suggests a very broad circulation of the political information network.

[149] See Lü's biography in Hummel, *Eminent Chinese*, I: 551–52 and Zeng Jing's biography, II: 747–49; also Thomas S. Fisher, "Accommodation and Loyalism: The Life of Lü Liuliang (1629–1683)," *Papers on Far Eastern History* 15 (1977): 97–104; 16 (1977): 107–45; 18 (1978): 1–42.

[150] Pei Huang, *Autocracy at Work*, p. 217.

[151] Translation from Spence, *Treason by the Book*, p. 7.

[152] Hummel, *Eminent Chinese*, II: 749.

[153] I take the translation of the title from Spence, *Treason by the Book*. For a note on the varied fortunes of this work, which survived the Qianlong emperor's efforts to collect and destroy all copies, see his pp. 250–51. Crossley, *Translucent Mirror*, pp. 253–61, translates the title as "Great Righteousness Resolving Confusion," and Pei Huang, *Autocracy at Work*, p. 499, "A record of great tenor for the deluded."

He sent copies of the work to high officials in the central government, and ordered provincial governors-general and governors to print copies for distribution to educational officials, local officials, and local schools.[154]

Dayi juemi lu presents the Yongzheng emperor's response to both the personal calumnies challenging the legitimacy of his succession and anti-Manchu sentiments behind attempts to expel the Qing from Ming territories. In this discussion, we will focus only on the latter issue. What were the arguments summoned by the emperor to justify Qing rule?

Dayi juemi lu begins with an edict the emperor issued on November 2, 1729:[155]

From ancient times, of rulers who have received "all under Heaven," there are none who did not cherish and protect the people and bestow favor upon all within the four seas ... having received Heaven's Mandate, to be the ruler of the ministers and peoples within and without, who ought to be soothed and cherished, how could we look with particularity on the Chinese [*Hua*] and the *Yi*?

The Yongzheng emperor's arguments rested on the idea that Heaven did not discriminate between *Hua* and *Yi* in conferring the Mandate. In a rhetorical flourish echoing his ancestor Hongtaiji (and following an argument first voiced in the fourth century),[156] he cited the historical examples of the mythical ruler Shun and King Wen of Zhou. Both men came from the periphery of the Central Plain, one from the far west and the other from the far east, yet both received the Mandate because of their virtue (舜為東夷之人，文王為西夷之人，曾何損與聖德乎?).[157] Heaven does not discriminate, and in turn the Son of Heaven is obliged likewise to bestow his nurturance upon all under Heaven, without regard to birth. The Manchus had entered China Proper not as rebels but as saviors, to rid Peking of the rebel Li Zicheng. They had brought order and peace to a society in turmoil. Not only that, but they had expanded the territorial expanse of "all under Heaven." These were surely signs of Heaven's favor.

The emperor's edict drew upon Confucian frameworks based on the universalizing potential for moral transformation to refute Zeng Jing's

---

[154] Spence, *Treason by the Book*, chapter 10. Crossley says (*Translucent Mirror*, p. 254) that *Dayi juemi lu* "was clearly intended to become study material for the examination system."

[155] *Da Qing shilu, Shizong Xian huangdi shilu*, Yongzheng 7/9/12= November 2, 1729, II: 147–52 in the Beijing reprint edition of 1986. The edict, in edited form, appears in (Qing) Yongzheng di, *Dayi juemi lu*, reproduced in vols. 351–52 of *Jindai Zhongguo shiliao congkan*, comp. Shen Yunlong (Taipei: Wenhai chubanshe, 1966).

[156] The emperor echoed the words of Liu Yuan of the Han Zhao state, presented at the beginning of this chapter.

[157] Quotation from (Qing) Yongzheng di, *Dayi juemi lu*, 351: 4–5.

writings. Elsewhere in *Dayi juemi lu*, the emperor reinforces this principle: if "the world is one family, and all things have a single origin," there should be no "distinction between the Chinese and the barbarians." No distinction did not mean the erasure of identities. The emperor's reference to *Hua* and *Yi*, even if they are now "one family" 華夷一家, reflected fundamental political categories within the Qing empire. *Yi* could not be erased, because their northeast origins were a fundamental element in the self-identity of the ruling house.[158]

Retention of this memory of origins became a key policy under the Qianlong emperor. In *A Translucent Mirror*, Pamela Crossley argues that for Hongli, "cultural identity was absolute, the Aisin Gioro lineage represented the apex of the autochthonous civilization of the Northeast," and the Qing "ruled China because of their unique and inherent favor by heaven." Within weeks of ascending the throne, Hongli reversed the Yongzheng decision on Zeng Jing, arresting and condemning him to death by slicing. He also recalled all copies of *Dayi juemi lu*, and ordered them destroyed.

Conclusion

The Manchu conquest strengthened Japan's move toward articulating a separate vision of a Japan-centered world order which focused on Japan's identity as a divine country. Long acquaintance with the Jurchen prompted Chosŏn intellectuals to promote a vision of themselves as the true successors of the civilized center. And in China itself, the Qing rulers responded to the Ming loyalists by asserting that Heaven chose a ruling house on the basis of virtue, not ethnicity.

Lydia Liu's repudiation of the pejorative connotations of the Chinese term *Yi* in the case of Anglo-Chinese negotiations over the Treaty of Tianjin does not apply to the cultural exchanges presented here. In this chapter, we have seen how elites in China, Korea, and Japan applied the concept of "civilized–barbarian" to talk about internal and external "others." Seventeenth and eighteenth century intellectuals used the *Hua–Yi* binome to construct a world order which put their own country at the apex of an idealized world order. Japan asserted its unique heritage as "the land of the gods" and unbroken rule by the Yamato imperial line to claim superiority over a China that had experienced conquest at many points in its history. Japanese and Koreans cited the *Yi* origins of the

---

[158] See Crossley, *Translucent Mirror*, for the study of the evolving imperial ideology of the Qing.

Manchus to reject Qing claims to preeminent status in a Qing-centric world order.

The issue of whether one's identity was fixed by birth or by education also had special political relevance within China, given the long history of non-Han regimes in the Central Plain. If education could triumph over heredity, the Confucian order could survive conquest regimes, since most of these regimes at least rhetorically embraced Confucian principles.[159] Yet some Ming loyalists insisted on raising obstacles to the possibility of Confucian transformation. For Wang Fuzhi, transformation was not impossible, but would be a gradual process that would end up destroying the integrity of the barbarian's culture. *Hua* and *Yi* were better off when each clung to its own locality. Neither group should seek territorial expansion. How, then, was the Ming–Qing transition to be explained? Wang fell back on the Confucian trope that the Ming emperors had fallen from virtue. But he did not have a good answer to the question, why did Heaven remove the Mandate from the Ming, and allow barbarians to conquer China?

The early rulers of the Jurchen/Manchu state rehearsed a number of responses to this question, none of which repudiated their northeast origins. In 1637, Hongtaiji responded to the Korean challenge by declaring that "A man, if Heaven favors him, can become emperor; if Heaven faults him, he is a commoner."[160] Proclaiming that victory on the battlefield was proof of Heaven's favor, Hongtaiji invited the Koreans to come out from the walled city to fight, then everyone would be able to witness just whom Heaven favored. Hongtaiji denied that his *Yi* identity was an obstacle to attaining the Chinese emperorship. A century later, when confronted by Zeng Jing, the Yongzheng emperor's justification of rule made no reference to military prowess, but rather to the Qing accomplishment of bringing the *Hua* and *Yi* together into "one family." The Qianlong emperor resolved the issue by reiterating both his *Yi* origins and the universality of the Heavenly Mandate.

This chapter's analysis studied the *Hua–Yi* rhetoric propounded by three northeast Asian peoples. We have already observed that the Manchus retained a strong sense of their origins. Korean intellectuals insisted that the *Yi* origins of the Manchus precluded any possibility that they could be "Sons of Heaven," even as in moments of candor they acknowledged that by their own standard they were also barred from becoming the "sŏ Hwa" that they claimed to be. Even though

---

[159] This analysis should not stop at the level of contemporary national units: see Gregory Smits, *Visions of Ryukyu: Identity and Ideology in Early-Modern Thought and Politics* (Honolulu: University of Hawai'i Press, 1999).
[160] Text in Kawachi 2010, p. 5.

Japanese elites freed themselves from the *Hua–Yi* framework to instead assert their superiority to China, their statements reveal an intense awareness that others viewed them as the culturally backward inhabitants of a "small country." When the *Luochong lu* was reproduced in Japan, the illustration accompanying the description of Japanese, that of a pot-bellied half-naked loincloth-clad man shouldering a sword, was replaced by a more decorous one depicting warriors and officials in *hakama* (official dress).[161]

The innate contradiction in the *Hua–Yi* discourse was irresolvable. Chinese thinkers might denigrate the lower culture of the barbarians but they could never wholly repudiate the possibilities of Confucian transformation which formed such an important core of the doctrine. Northeast Asians might resent the condescension implied in Chinese writings about the *Dong Yi*, but they also seized upon the universalist messages of the Confucian canon to stake their own claims to being civilized. These internal discourses continued until the late nineteenth century, when East Asian intellectuals turned to confront new Eurocentric ideologies that moved their world from center-stage to periphery.

---

[161] He, "Book and the Barbarian," fig. 3, p. 80 and fig. 9, p. 85, also p. 77.

Conclusion

What would Chinese history look like if it were written from the perspective of the periphery and not the core? De-centering China entails focusing on interaction between the borderlands and the Central Plain as the dynamic engine behind the long-term development of China's imperial formation, and considering the long periods when China was divided or ruled by non-Han peoples, generally from its northern or northeastern frontiers, rather than concentrating attention on periods of unified rule. De-centering China also requires us to study texts produced by borderland peoples, and to contemplate events in which the Chinese heartland was encompassed in historical movements of regional or global dimensions.

Why de-center China? Orthodox historians neglect the story of how peoples from the borderlands interacted, formed states, and challenged Central Plain regimes. To justify this oversight, they rely on the traditional generalization that the horse-riding nomads had to dismount in order to rule, i.e. that they had to learn Chinese ways in order to govern the Central Plain. Despite scholarship that shows northeast regimes rather quickly developed bureaucratic modes of governance and political rhetoric through long contact with Chinese states, the notion that frontiersmen might conquer China, but would then find themselves enveloped by Chinese culture, persists. The traditional framework of dynastic cycles, along with officially commissioned dynastic histories that perpetuate this idealized and distorted vision of a unified China that exaggerates continuity, downplays the distinctiveness of each ruling house, and thus its special historical contribution.

The gap between image and reality is especially significant with regard to the many centuries when non-Han rulers – including the Tang, Yuan, and Qing – governed the Chinese heartland. For example, although the Tang era has been described as a "golden age" of Chinese history, its frontier origins played virtually no role in analyses of its historical contributions outside the military sphere.[1] Recent scholarship, however, has not only emphasized the nomadic origins of the Tuoba Xianbei ancestors of the Tang imperial house, but presented Tang relations with its northern neighbors within a broader Eurasian context.[2]

Nonetheless, the re-examination of conquest rule suffers from the persistent tendency to organize all regimes into a unilinear history. John Langlois describes the Mongol success in citing canonical passages to justify its dynastic rule over China, but admits that "identifying areas of enduring Mongol impact on Chinese civilization is extremely difficult."[3] Despite a spate of recent scholarship, understanding the full significance of Qing rule is precluded by simply viewing it as the last of the dynasties. Only by looking at Qing as the last in a line of northeast Asian conquerors can one begin to appreciate the innovations and advances made by its unique imperial formation.

The major challenges to Central Plain states came in ancient times from the western and northern frontiers. This study highlights northeast Asia as a major factor in China's subsequent history. With the exception of the Ming, north or northeast Asian regimes have ruled North China for over two-thirds of the millennium ending in 2000.[4] The Qing incorporated China Proper into a multi-ethnic empire. The contemporary capital, Beijing, bears the marks of their presence in the names of its streets, the architecture of its palaces, and the Tibetan Buddhist temples that remain as artifacts of Qing imperial patronage, but many walking its streets read only the Chinese writing and ignore the rest. Qing rule, too, bore the marks of its northeast origins.

In addition to highlighting the oversights and distortions of Chinese histories that ignore the distinctive contribution of the Qing rulers, this

---

[1] See Jonathan Karam Skaff, "Tang Military Culture and Its Inner Asian Influences," in *Military Culture in Imperial China*, ed. Nicola DiCosmo (Cambridge, MA: Harvard University Press, 2009), pp. 165–91.

[2] Sanping Chen, *Multicultural China in the Early Middle Ages* (Philadelphia: University of Pennsylvania Press, 2012), provides linguistic evidence of the nomadic origins of the Tang rulers. Zhenping Wang, *Tang China in Multi-Polar Asia: A History of Diplomacy and War* (Honolulu: University of Hawai'i Press, 2013), delineates the fluid multi-polar geopolitical context of Tang foreign policy. In *Sui-Tang China and Its Turko-Mongol Neighbors*, Jonathan Skaff extends his analysis to argue that Tang and neighboring nomadic regimes participated in a political culture that extended across "Eastern Eurasia" (including Japan, Korea, Manchuria, Mongolia).

[3] Langlois, "Introduction," to *China Under Mongol Rule*, p. 12.

[4] In *Martial Spectacles of the Ming Court* (Cambridge, MA: Harvard University Asia Center, 2013), David M. Robinson attempts to transcend the dynastic framework by stressing historical continuities in imperial sponsorship of hunts, archery contests, and other martial activities between Yuan and early Ming, asking (p. 372), whether both the Ming and Qing were "heirs to a rich set of practices that drew on precedents from not only the Central Plains but also Turkic, Mongol, and Tungut (sic) traditions."

study recasts China's interrelations with Japan and Korea into a northeast Asian perspective. Part I of this book documents the importance of northeast Asia as a frontier for the Central Plain states. Geographical contiguity and close economic, political and cultural interactions from at least the fourth century BCE onward justify considering states in the Korean peninsula and the Japanese archipelago as part of China's northeast frontier. Japan and Korea were not bystanders but players in a geopolitical arena that stretched from the steppe eastward to Japan. The political reverberations of events taking place in north and northeast Asia affected them too.

Putting Korea and Japan into a northeast Asian regional context tightens their relationship to Chinese regimes while discarding the view, implicit in orthodox histories and the modern notion of "East Asia," that Japan and Korea were subordinate actors within a Chinese world order. Our examination of historical events from the 1590s through the 1630s shows that Japan, Korea, and China operated within a shared geopolitical arena in which each country's actions stimulated responses from the others. Hideyoshi's invasion spurred the Ming Wanli emperor to send troops to the Korean peninsula to aid the Chosŏn regime. The success of this intervention put extra pressure on the Korean court to follow a pro-Ming policy just as other external factors – the expansion of Jianzhou Jurchen power, and the flurry of border uprisings confronting Ming in the last decades of the late sixteenth century – turned a rhetorical obligation (of a subordinate state in the tribute system) into a Ming demand for military support. Reluctantly forced to take sides, the Korean king joined the Ming effort to check the rising northeastern power of the Jianzhou Jurchen. The devastating defeat of the Ming–Chosŏn forces at the battle of Sarhū was a milestone in advancing the Jurchen toward the "great enterprise" of overthrowing the Ming that they finally achieved twenty-five years later.

What national histories present in narrow, constricted terms, a larger view can identify as interrelated. The national histories variously present the events of 1592–1637 as a rash adventure, the prelude to the Tokugawa shogunate, or as the relatively minor narrative of the rise of the Manchu/Qing regime before it burst into China's national history by entering China Proper in 1644, after the death by suicide of the last Ming emperor in Peking. For Chosŏn, the same events represent a national humiliation and tragedy: more than at any point previously (but presaging the twentieth century), Korea's strategic location rendered it vulnerable to invasion and subjugation. Looking at these events in a regional and global context allows us to understand their interconnectedness.

This enlarged historical vision extends beyond China, Japan, and Korea. The sixteenth-century arrival of European missionaries and traders in Asian waters intensified cultural contacts and stimulated dynamic political and cultural changes that many have hailed as "early modern." Integration into world markets encompassed a wide range of activities, from the importation of European weapons to the introduction of new concepts of territoriality, embodied in the European cartography brought to Asia by the Jesuits. Just as the adoption of European muskets aided Japan's unification, and the rising demand for saltpeter and other raw materials drove daimyo into trade with Southeast Asia, so Hideyoshi's growing awareness of Spanish colonization in the Philippines and European activities in Asian waters encouraged him to dream of conquering the Ming. Meanwhile, Jesuits at the Ming court introduced calculus, European astronomy, and new visual conceptions of the world to Chinese and Manchu elites, while Portuguese gunners in Macao stimulated Chinese adaptations of European guns and a rash of new military handbooks.

The illegal but flourishing maritime trade of the sixteenth century forced the Ming to abandon the tribute system as a vehicle for controlling foreign trade. Constrained by its own policies, the Ming failed to tap into the wealth generated by maritime commerce, whose main beneficiaries were coastal entrepreneurs and "pirates," shipping magnates like Zheng Chenggong, who were familiar to European traders, even if barely recognized by Ming authorities.

The lure of European maritime trade transcended the coastal ports of Asia and penetrated inland. In their northeast homeland, the Jurchen, like their Mongol neighbors, became keenly appreciative of the revenues to be reaped from selling sable furs and ginseng to maritime traders.

Wielding skills acquired during their long apprenticeship as officials in the Ming border commandery system, the Jianzhou Jurchen used marriage alliances and coercion to unify other Jurchen and Mongol tribes in the northeast. Although it was not the primary cause of the Manchu conquest, European trade played a significant role in funding the early stages of Jurchen expansion.

European influence continued to be important into the seventeenth and eighteenth centuries. Much has been written of the Dutch and English East India Companies' activities in Nagasaki and Canton, but this study focuses on the Russian presence looming over north and northeast Asia that commanded the close attention of both the Qing and Tokugawa authorities. Russian settlement in Siberia prompted Qing military responses.[5] At the same time, Russia's strategic role vis-à-vis the nomadic tribes of Central Asia led the Qing to adopt the position of petitioner in St. Petersburg. Russian exploration and mapping spurred Qing and Japanese exploration of north Asia and the north Pacific, for both commercial and geopolitical motives.

Cartography, which informed rulers about the new territories lying at the fringes of their empires, had a tremendous political and intellectual impact when it was applied to the interior. In the style of other early modern states, the Qing geographies collected vital economic and demographic information about Qing subjects that strengthened state administration. Maps provided visual challenges to a theoretically Sinocentric world order: Matteo Ricci's *mappa mundi* depicted China on the fringes of the world. Long before the nineteenth century, elites in these countries mused on the significance of a world order which was not centered on China.

Cultural negotiations between China and northeast Asia have a long history. Early states in Japan and Korea adopted Chinese legal codes and ritual forms that were ill-suited to their indigenous cultures. The institutions, in particular state rituals, that developed from these beginnings were distinctive, reflecting the complicated negotiations necessary to accommodate indigenous legacies and sensibilities. The Japanese elite cases of self-deification sprang from Shinto/Buddhist theological roots and responded to the warrior ethos of the Edo period. They bore no resemblance to the cults formed around outstanding individuals in China. While drawing on the cultural capital embodied in Chinese-style state rites, the actual rituals performed in Japan and China served as vehicles for asserting each country's individuality. Chosŏn's use of sacrifices to the former Ming emperors to express anti-Qing sentiments exemplifies the flexibility of ritual forms to accommodate a wide range of political agendas. In the seventeenth and early eighteenth centuries, Japanese and Korean elites found justifications for a world order that denied Sinocentric pretensions, even as the Qing reconceived the empire in terms of universal monarchy, and performed shamanic, Tibetan Buddhist, and Confucian rituals that catered to selected segments of its subject populations.

Japanese and Korean indigenous kinship systems slowed the implementation of legal codes predicated on the Chinese kinship system. Patrilineality, a hallmark of Chinese society, was alien to ancient Korea and Japan. Systems in which descent was marked through both sets of

[5] See Mancall, *Russia and China*. On the geopolitics of Sino-Russian relations in this period, see Perdue, *China Marches West*, pp. 161–73.

parents, a monopoly on rule by sacred descent groups which encouraged endogamous marriage across generational lines, and the occasional appearance of female rulers were the hallmarks of ancient Japanese and Korean rulership that separated the kinship practices of these northeast Asian societies from the customs of the Central Plain.

The adoption of a Chinese-style legal code began a gradual process of social change that culminated in the appearance of patrilineal kinship organization in both Japan and Korea. Yet each country's kinship system remained distinctive. In Japan, commoner households and even the shoguns adopted patrilineality, yet rejected partible inheritance in favor of unigeniture. Japanese raised the household to an abstract ideal, which justified meritocratic adoption in place of blood-based succession. Korea's *yangban* families embraced patrilineality, but rejected the Chinese practice of recognizing all sons in favor of limiting *yangban* status to sons of the wife. Wives of *yangban* were required to show *yangban* descent on both the maternal and the paternal side. The Korean vision of patrilineality was thus far narrower than the Chinese norm.

Patrilineality, while central to Chinese ideology, did not affect imperial family dynamics in either Japan or Korea. Japanese imperial succession continued along traditional lines, with emperors determining their successors through abdication. Korean royal succession also continued older traditions, different enough from the Chinese model to mystify Ming officials who could not understand the reason for sudden "abdications" (in the case of coups d'état) and the choice of heirs from relatively distant collateral lines. Even the Qing emperors, who consciously modeled their practices on Chinese precedents, eventually adopted succession principles, which synthesized elements from northeast traditions and the Central Plain. Eschewing the Chinese eldest-son principle, emperors chose heirs from amongst all their sons. Instead of following the Ming practice of designating an infant Crown Prince and dispatching all other sons to fiefs outside the capital, Qing emperors kept all sons in the capital, and assigned them diplomatic, ritual, military, and administrative duties, with the idea that the ablest son should succeed to the throne. In the emphasis on merit instead of birth order we see the northeast influence shaping imperial policy.

The adoption of the Chinese binome for "civilized" and "barbarian" demonstrates the complexity of cultural appropriation and the assertion of distinctive self-identities within Japan, Korea, and China. These terms first appear in early China, where they denote groups distinguishable from the *Hua* and Xia by different spoken languages and cultures, in a context in which ethnic boundaries appear to have been low, permitting intermarriage and integration of some non-Hua/Xia individuals into elite strata in Central Plain society. The designation *Yi* and its cognates, the *Rong, Di,* and *Man,* may initially have simply referred to persons belonging to recognizably "other" groups, but over time, and certainly by the sixteenth century, many Chinese intellectuals agreed that the cultural and other differences they perceived barred outsiders from behaving in ways that educated Chinese regarded as "civilized."

Seventeenth-century Ming loyalists and xenophobes denied the possibility of a civilizing process even as the Manchu conquest elite took up Confucianism, reinstalled a Confucian-based civil service examination system, and, as we have seen, used Confucian rhetoric to proclaim and uphold their legitimacy. We can interpret the hardening of the *Hua–Yi* boundary as a sign of the early modern era, when the enhanced circulation of knowledge through books, maps, and the increase in global contact led elites in various societies to become more keenly aware of the larger world and hence to draw boundaries between themselves and others. Japanese and Korean elites adopted the same Chinese binome to draw their own boundaries and create worlds which challenged Qing hegemony. Their use of this vocabulary to attack the Manchus, who shared their northeast Asian origins, underlines the historical irony of this cultural diffusion.

Their northeast origins provided early Qing rulers with a cultural repertoire that was crucial to the success of their alliance with Mongols and their incorporation of the Inner Asian periphery into the empire.[6] Like earlier conquest regimes, the Manchus differentiated between a multi-ethnic conquest elite, consisting of banner nobles, Mongol tribal leaders, Tibetan Buddhist prelates and Uighur begs, and the subjugated population of the former Ming territory. Like earlier conquest states, they separated the administration of China Proper (the former Ming territory) from the Inner Asian periphery. China Proper was governed by officials and civil servants recruited through the examination system, Inner Asia (the "outer" realm), by bannermen and members of the conquest elite.

Qing governance protected the interests of the ruling house by assigning members of the conquest elite to key positions in the civil administration and in the Inner Asian periphery. The Court of Colonial Affairs (Lifanyuan), not the Board of Rites, handled relations with Tibetan prelates. During the Qianlong reign, the primary responsibility for relations

---

[6] Evelyn S. Rawski, "Reenvisioning the Qing: The Significance of the Qing Period in Chinese History," *Journal of Asian Studies* 55.4 (1996): 829–50. For an analysis that adopts the Mongol perspective, see Johan Elverskog, *Our Great Qing: The Mongols, Buddhism and the State in Late Imperial China* (Honolulu: University of Hawai'i Press, 2006).

with Tibet was given to the Sutra Recitation Office, housed in the Zhongzhengdian in the Forbidden City.[7] Indirect rule through traditional elites of the Inner Asian frontiers maintained continuity while bannermen appointed through the Lifanyuan added a new layer of administrative scrutiny and accountability.

Drawing on its northeast heritage, the Qing not only created the largest empire in Chinese history which was the direct forerunner of the contemporary Chinese nation, but also contributed in other significant ways to what today's Chinese regard as the "Hua" or Central Plain tradition.[8] Within its own borders, the early Qing state increased government revenues, expanded the size of the empire through military campaigns against the nomads, and strengthened the emperor's personal control of the administration through a number of institutional innovations.[9] Their experience in the northeast gave them a keen appreciation of foreign trade "as key to the wealth and power of a state," and their early economic policy featured the opening up of private maritime trade, the establishment of maritime customs, and recognition of a world order lying beyond their shores.[10] The economic, political, and cultural changes that occurred during the first two centuries of Qing rule created a new stable multi-ethnic empire. Many of these changes paralleled developments in other states across Eurasia during the early modern period.

In China Proper, Qing emperors refined and strengthened the system of territorial administration by systematizing appointments, creating special offices to meet the perceived needs of specific regions, and injecting incentives for performance into the personnel system. These administrative reforms strengthened the province as an administrative unit under the central government.[11] The Qing also added an extra layer of

[7] Rawski, *The Last Emperors*, p. 258.
[8] See Mark C. Elliott, "*Hushuo*: The Northern Other and the Naming of the Han Chinese," in *Critical Han Studies: The History, Representation, and Identity of China's Majority*, ed. Thomas S. Mullaney, James Leibold, Stéphane Gros, and Eric Vanden Bussche (Berkeley: University of California Press, 2012), pp. 173–90. Elliott argues that the use of the term "Han" as a "kind of ethnic supersign" evolved historically from the "persistent occupation" of the Central Plain by "Northern Others," with the Qing contributing to this evolution.
[9] Evelyn S. Rawski, "The Qing Formation and the Early-Modern Period," in *The Qing Formation in World-Historical Time*, ed. Lynn A. Struve (Honolulu: University of Hawai'i Press, 2004), pp. 207–41.
[10] Gang Zhao, *Qing Opening to the Ocean*, p. 77.
[11] R. Kent Guy, *Qing Governors and Their Provinces: The Evolution of Territorial Administration in China, 1644–1796* (Seattle: University of Washington Press, 2010), details the concrete ways in which the Qing improved on Ming provincial administration. See Yingcong Dai, *The Sichuan Frontier and Tibet: Imperial Strategy in the Early Qing* (Seattle: University of Washington Press, 2009) for an excellent case study of

personnel in the form of dual appointments at the head of the central ministries and the provinces. This "dyarchy" of a Han and a bannerman president of the five boards and a bannerman and Han governor-general/ governor heading provincial administration was part of the "checks and balances" system which foreigners noted with admiration and copied in the nineteenth century.

Reversing the weakening of imperial prerogative that had occurred during the late Ming, early Qing emperors successfully centralized power in their own hands. The Qing established strict controls over eunuchs, whose dominant administrative role contributed to the waning of Ming rule. The new regime assigned bondservants, members of the conquest elite who were registered in the upper three (imperial) banners, to supervise eunuchs. To manage palace affairs, the Qing elevated the Imperial Household Department, which became an important agency whose profit-making activities frequently escaped bureaucratic scrutiny.[12] The palace memorial, introduced to skirt the normal bureaucratic channels that often impeded the flow of information from localities to the emperor, successfully sorted out urgent (and confidential) communications from routine reports, and channeled official documentation through the emperor's hands. Similarly, fiscal reforms reversed the Ming practice of providing central government ministries with earmarked revenue sources, centralized tax collection, and tightened the center's control over public revenues.[13]

Qing rulers bypassed bureaucratic channels to create inner court agencies that they staffed with their own appointees. The term "inner court" denoted first a physical space in the imperial palace which was closed off from the "outer court" where civil servants normally assembled. The inner court became the site for conducting state affairs from the late seventeenth century onward. With the exception of Han-Chinese officials who were appointed to the Southern Study in the inner court, admission to this part of the palace was closed to all but imperial kinsmen, imperial guards, and specially favored individuals. The emperor would summon his close associates, form ad hoc committees to deliberate on military strategy and other state matters, and thus bypass the constraints imposed on the imperial prerogative by the bureaucracy of the outer court.

administrative innovation that was driven by military campaigns. Sichuan was transformed from a geopolitical backwater to a major strategic region during the late seventeenth and early eighteenth centuries as Qing attention focused on Tibet.

[12] See Preston M. Torbert, *The Ch'ing Imperial Household Department: A Study of Its Organization and Principal Functions, 1662–1796* (Cambridge, MA: Council on East Asian Studies, Harvard University, 1977).

[13] Rawski, "Qing Formation," pp. 211–15.

The major policy-making body during the early Qing was the Deliberative Council of Princes and High Officials, composed of the conquest elite. Military campaigns in the 1720s prompted the Yongzheng emperor to create new inner court agencies, staffed by his favorites, that later evolved into the Grand Council. This inner core of Manchu advisers persisted into the early twentieth century.

These innovations – maintaining a politically separate conquest elite, introducing dyarchy at the top of the central and provincial administration of China Proper, and governing the periphery with a more flexible blend of indirect rule and bureaucratic surveillance – were Qing achievements that reshaped the institutions of imperial rule in directions that bore the distinctive imprint of the dynasty's ethnic identity and strategic experience.

Early emperors often deployed tools taken from the northeast tradition. The banner system, which originated from Mongol institutions, was key to Qing success in expanding the empire to its largest territorial extent. Northeast traditions also informed the segmentation of policies to accommodate the diverse groups occupying strategic regions, and the willingness to compartmentalize cultural policies while openly proclaiming a multi-cultural stance through imperial patronage of the arts, religious establishments, and scholarly compilations and publication. Ideological flexibility allowed emperors to adopt cartographic, military, and other techniques of rulership from European Jesuits, which advanced state capacities to govern the empire. The Qing ability to encompass frontier peoples on the Inner Asian periphery was a product of their innate understanding of Mongol culture. Finally, like Korea and Japan, the ruling house adopted policies that consciously distinguished and preserved a separate northeast identity among its people. In all these ways, their northeast frontier origins enabled the Qing to synthesize institutional and intellectual elements from many different sources to create strong rule.

A history of China written from the perspective of the northeast periphery resonates with contemporary issues linked with ongoing scholarly debates concerning the role of minority nationalities in Chinese history. Recent attempts to incorporate Koguryŏ/Gaogouli history into the Chinese nation (see the Epilogue) have stimulated a spirited dialogue with North and South Korea over "ownership" of a state that they all claim as one of their own. In this historically anachronistic debate, history is entangled with contemporary geopolitics. The current players (including Russia and Japan) are, surprisingly, exactly the same multi-state configuration that we found in the sixteenth century. Northeast Asia continues to be a major factor in the geopolitical calculations of China's rulers.

Epilogue: drawing boundaries in northeast Asia

By shaping contemporary academic and popular understanding of China's historical relations with northeast Asia, the national histories of the twentieth century continue to affect China's relations with Korea and Japan.[1] This chapter begins with a survey of the introduction into Asia of a European model of "scientific history," its subordination to the demands of nation-building, and the interstate quarrels that the new national history provoked. Throughout the twentieth century, national history remained the dominant framework within which history was written and taught. The new history served the political need to legitimate and explain "the nation-state in its present expanding form."[2] In Asia as in Europe, historians served the nation not only in inculcating nationalism – developing loyalty to the state as the citizens' preeminent obligation and primary identity – but in fulfilling the government's need for specialized language and regional knowledge in articulating and legitimating the foreign policy agenda. Inverting the sequence that prevailed in the pre-modern era, new knowledge appeared first in Japan, then several decades later in China, and finally after 1945 in Korea.

The new national histories and Japan's imperial expansion raised issues of historical "ownership" of northeast Asia. As Japanese scholars created a history that extended beyond contemporary boundaries, Korean and Chinese historians responded with their own counter narratives. Despite the changing geopolitics of the post-1945 period, the nationalist-inspired controversies have persisted and continue to create political tensions.

---

[1] Although a number of disputes concerning Japanese war guilt, the "ownership" of islands (Diaoyutai/Senkaku, Tokto/Takashima) and naming of coastal waters (East Sea/Japan Sea) currently roil the interstate relations of the two Koreas, Japan, and China, this epilogue will focus on the Gaogouli/Koguryŏ controversy.

[2] Remco E. Breuker, "Contested Objectivities: Ikeuchi Hiroshi, Kim Sanggi and the Tradition of Oriental History (*Tōyōshigaku*) in Japan and Korea," *East Asian History* 29 (2005): 72; Prasenjit Duara, *Rescuing History from the Nation: Questioning Narratives of Modern China* (Chicago: University of Chicago Press, 1995), on the "linear, evolutionary" model of the history of the nation that was produced.

The fall-out in 2004 from conflicting claims for international recognition of the northeast Asian kingdom of Gaogouli/Koguryŏ illustrates the ways in which national history caused international wrangles with neighboring states. The Chinese–Korean struggle over historical ownership of Gaogouli/Koguryŏ, a northeast Asian state that existed in ancient times (first century BCE – 668 CE) serves as a good example of the repercussions surrounding the PRC leadership's moves to shore up its control over territories that were acquired by the Qing empire, but it also introduces us to the broader ongoing debate among scholars on how concepts of the nation could be applied to antiquity, an issue of particular relevance to China's multi-ethnic citizenry and germane to a fundamental issue, the role of China's minority nationalities in the writing of national history.

From universal to people's history

During the late nineteenth and early twentieth centuries, history in China, Korea, and Japan, once conceptualized in universal terms, became "national history" (國史C. *guoshi*, K. *guksa*, J. *kokushi*). The dominant Chinese historical model, based on Confucian values, was displaced by a new framework which first appeared in Germany in the second half of the nineteenth century.[3] This new history was empirical, and its methodology emphasized rigorous analysis and evaluation of primary sources.[4]

Ludwig Riess (1861–1928), a student of Leopold van Ranke, founded the new discipline of Western-inspired history and produced a cohort of scientific historians during his stint at the recently established Tokyo University (Tōdai) in 1887 (he taught there until 1902). In China, adoption of the new historical model had to wait until 1905, when the traditional educational curriculum was abolished. Even then, the political instability that followed the Revolution of 1911 slowed the pace of academic change.

Perhaps more clearly than in Japan, Chinese intellectuals saw Western-style history as a tool for nation-building. In his *New Historiography* (*Xin shixue*, 1902), Liang Qichao attacked the dynastic historiographical tradition as having merely legitimized and perpetuated imperial rule. He explicitly cited Japan as a model for history that would support the new nation-state.[5] Writing in 1905, Zhang Taiyan and the founders of the *National Essence Journal* (*Guocui xuebao*) also proposed that history

---

[3] Georg G. Iggers and Q. Edward Wang, with contributions from Supriya Mukherjee, *A Global History of Modern Historiography* (New York: Pearson Longman, 2008), chapter 3.
[4] *Ibid.*, pp. 121–28.   [5] *Ibid.*, pp. 209–10.

should focus not on rulers but on "people's history," *minshi*, to "make history writing useful for the nationalist cause."[6]

The first concrete steps to introduce "scientific history" into Chinese universities occurred in the 1910s. Hu Shi (1891–1962), a disciple of John Dewey, returned from Columbia University to propagate the scientific method as part of the New Culture movement. Gu Jiegang (1893–1980) used this method to challenge the authenticity of the ancient canonical texts. He Bingsong introduced the work of American historians to Chinese academics through his translations, while Yao Congwu, who studied in Germany under Otto Franke (1836–1946) and Erich Haenisch (1880–1966) brought European sinology to China. These historians attempted to selectively re-evaluate cultural traditions in order to create a new national narrative. Hu and his students hoped that the new history they produced would bring about a Chinese "Renaissance."[7] The political disorder within China resulting from battles among regional military coalitions and the onset of the second Sino-Japanese War in 1937, however, postponed a full institutionalization of national history until after 1945.

Korea's reception of new historical models was still more tortuous. In order to create a new Korean identity, intellectuals had to first "decenter" the Middle Kingdom, replacing Confucianism with Social Darwinism and the concept of the modern nation-state, now rooted in a distinctive *ethnos* (*minjok*).[8] During its last decades, the Chosŏn government did take steps toward breaking with traditional cultural institutions, but its efforts were stymied by larger political events.[9]

Koreans found themselves caught between an expansive Japan that offered a model for Westernization and a China that attempted to preserve its traditional tributary privileges even as it adapted its tactics to the new diplomatic framework introduced by its own westernizing

[6] *Ibid.*, p. 211.

[7] Q. Edward Wang, *Inventing China Through History: The May Fourth Approach to Historiography* (Albany: SUNY Press, 2001). But the existence of the evidentiary school within Confucianism, which took similar stances towards authenticating texts, may have aided acceptance of the Rankean model of history: see Breuker, "Contested Objectivities," p. 78.

[8] Andre Schmid, "Decentering the 'Middle Kingdom': The Problem of China in Korean Nationalist Thought, 1895–1910," in *Nation Work: Asian Elites and National Identities*, ed. Timothy Brook and Andre Schmid (Ann Arbor: University of Michigan Press, 2000), p. 84; Henry H. Em, "Minjok as a Modern and Democratic Construct: Sin Ch'aeho's Historiography," in *Colonial Modernity in Korea*, ed. Gi-Wook Sin and Michael Robinson (Cambridge, MA: Harvard University Asia Center, 1999), pp. 336–61.

[9] Breuker, "Contested Objectivities," p. 79 notes that the government followed Japanese precedent in creating a new Bureau for the Compilation of History in 1891, but as in the Japanese case, producing textbooks that incorporated the new historical outlook proved more difficult.

reforms.[10] After Japanese gunboat diplomacy led to the opening of Korean treaty ports through the Treaty of Kanghwa (1976), Korea became a zone where Russia, Japan, and China each attempted to manipulate internal political divisions to favor its own national interests. The struggle over Korea was eventually decided by Japan's victories over the Qing in the Sino-Japanese War (1894–95) and over Russia in the Russo-Japanese War (1904–5). Even as Korean intellectuals read Japanese history texts for information on the new historiography, they tried to resist Japanese attempts to take over Korea. After Korea was annexed by Japan in 1910, its status as a Japanese colony left little space for professional historians who wished to assert Korean nationalism.

Almost immediately after its adoption, proponents of "scientific history" faced political pressures to smooth out historical incongruities and contradictions that hindered construction of unilinear national narratives. The first dispute arose in Japan, where two Tōdai history professors, Hoshino Hisashi and Kume Kunitake, became embroiled in controversies concerning Shinto myths about the divine origins of Japan and the imperial house. In 1890, Hoshino was publicly attacked after he published an article in *Shigaku zasshi* suggesting a Korean origin for one of the deities cited in the *Nihon shoki*'s description of the Age of the Gods. Kume added more fuel to the fire with an 1891 article that stated his view that Shinto "was nothing more than ancient nature worship," an "ancient custom of Heaven worship."[11] In making these points, Kume ignored the increasing importance of these myths in the creation of the emperor ideology, *tennōsei*, which dominated the late Meiji period. His article sparked intense public discussion and debate, much of it highly critical of a Tōdai professor who had forsaken his responsibility as "a teacher of the nation."[12] Kume was forced to publish a retraction and to resign his post in March 1892.

Government officials wanted the new history to create a seamless narrative that traced the history of the nation from antiquity to the present. In 1911 there was a public uproar over an elementary history textbook which factually reported the period of divided imperial rule in Japan from 1333 to 1392. Its account contradicted the government

---

[10] See Kirk W. Larsen, *Tradition, Treaties, and Trade: Qing Imperialism and Chosŏn Korea, 1850–1910* (Cambridge, MA: Harvard University Asia Center, 2008), which argues that Qing officials like Li Hongzhang used the new "technologies" used by Western imperialists – treaties, international law, gunboats, and the telegraph in its attempts to retain its privileges in Korea.

[11] John S. Brownlee, *Japanese Historians and the National Myths, 1600–1945: The Age of the Gods and Emperor Jinmu* (Vancouver: University of British Columbia Press, 1997), pp. 95–98.

[12] Miyaji Itsuo, quoted in *Japanese Historians*, p. 99.

position as stated in the official history *Dai Nihon shi,* which stressed the unbroken continuity of the imperial house and favored the legitimacy of the Southern Court of Emperor Go-Daigo rather than the Northern line which eventually triumphed.[13] The "leading professional historians" of the day were subjected to withering attack and told that as civil servants employed in the imperial university they had to subsume their own research findings to state policy.[14]

Japanese research, teaching, and writing of the history of other Asian states reflected the nation state's geopolitical priorities. As the academic curriculum was reorganized, "Oriental history" came to include the study of Korea, Manchuria, Mongolia, the Western regions (Central Asia) and China, areas which were of increasing interest to Japanese officials and decision-makers. Writers no longer portrayed China as an admired source of culture and civilization, but as a corrupt, weak, and backward society, which needed Japanese aid in order to modernize.[15]

Tracing the nation to antiquity

Archaeology supported the Japanese search for cultural origins as they turned their attention to northeast Asia. In the second half of the nineteenth century, archaeology first provided material evidence of Jōmon culture, dating back to *c.* 7500 BCE. New digs in the 1920s revealed that Jōmon had been supplanted by a rice-growing culture that was believed to be the direct ancestor of the historic Japanese. Further excavation, spurred by debates concerning the origins and evolution of Yayoi culture in the Japanese islands, unearthed hundreds of Yayoi sites in Kyushu, but the diverse array of local cultures displayed hindered the creation of a coherent unilinear narrative. There was agreement, however, that Yayoi man came from the continent, and many Japanese scholars searched for Yayoi origins in China's northeastern provinces.[16]

---

[13] Brownlee, *Japanese Historians,* p. 119, points out that the Meiji emperor himself was a descendant of the Northern line.

[14] Iggers and Wang, *Global History,* p. 217; Brownlee, *Japanese Historians,* chapter 10. On the 1939–42 trial of Tsuda Sōkichi for *lèse majesté,* see Joël Joos, "A Stinking Tradition: Tsuda Sōkichi's View of China," *East Asian History* 28 (2004): 1–26.

[15] Joshua A. Fogel, *Politics and Sinology: The Case of Naitō Kōnan (1866–1934)* (Cambridge, MA: Council on East Asian Studies, Harvard University, 1984).

[16] On paradigm shifts in Chinese archaeology, see Lothar von Falkenhausen, "The Regionalist Paradigm in Chinese Archaeology," in *Nationalism, Politics, and the Practice of Archaeology,* ed. Philip L. Kohl and Clare Fawcett (Cambridge: Cambridge University Press, 1995), pp. 198–217. The early history of Japanese archaeology is described in Mark J. Hudson, *Ruins of Identity: Ethnogenesis in the Japanese Islands* (Honolulu: University of Hawai'i Press, 1999), chapter 2; Clare Fawcett, "Archaeology and Japanese Identity," in *Multicultural Japan: Paleolithic to Postmodern,* ed. Donald Denoon, Mark Hudson,

History writing in Korea under Japanese colonial rule developed in several directions.[17] Looking to northeast Asia, Sin Ch'aeho (1880–1936) was a nationalist who asserted that Korea must divorce itself from China in order to find "the spirit of the people." Rejecting a widely held theory that identified a Chinese ancestor, Kija (C. Jizi) as the progenitor of the Korean people, he proposed that the *minjok* (people of the nation, i.e. Koreans) began with Tan'gun, the mythical progenitor of the Korean people.[18] His history of the Korean people placed them far beyond the Yalu and Tumen Rivers that marked the modern borders of the Korean state.[19] It included Puyŏ, Koguryŏ, and Parhae, states whose inhabitants, like those of Silla and Paekche, were also descended from Tan'gun. As elaborated in Kim Kyohŏn's *History of the Divine Tan'gun's People* (*Sindan minsa*), the *minjok*'s northern branch could be traced in a continuous line from Koguryŏ to Parhae, then through the Liao, Jin, and down to the Manchu Qing.[20] Genealogically based *minjok* history produced a version that saw the Qing and Chosŏn as two branches of the same extended lineage whose focal ancestor was Tan'gun.

Sin's vision of a Korean national history promoted a northeast Asian identity which would later come into conflict with Chinese historiography. In the Republican era (1927–49), however, the writers of China's national history were primarily intent on pushing the boundaries of the nation backward into ancient times. Archaeology came to be regarded "as a branch of history."[21] Its leader was Fu Sinian (1896–1950), who after

---

Gavan McCormack, and Tessa Morris-Suzuki (Cambridge: Cambridge University Press, 1996), pp. 60–77; and Clare Fawcett, "Nationalism and Postwar Japanese Archaeology," in *Nationalism, Politics, and the Practice of Archaeology*, ed. Philip L. Kohl and Clare Fawcett (Cambridge: Cambridge University Press, 1995), pp. 232–46. For a survey of recent work, see Kidder, *Himiko and Japan's Elusive Chiefdom*.

[17] See Henry H. Em, *The Great Enterprise: Sovereignty and Historiography in Modern Korea* (Durham: Duke University Press, 2013), chapters 3 and 4 on history writing in the colonial era.

[18] See Michael E. Robinson, "National Identity and the Thought of Sin Ch'aeho: Sadaejuŭi and Chuch'e in History and Politics," *Journal of Korean Studies* 5 (1984): 121–42, and his *Cultural Nationalism in Colonial Korea, 1920–1925* (Seattle: University of Washington Press, 1988), pp. 34, 80. Robinson remarks on the parallels between the Sinocentrism of traditional elites and the European centrism of the early twentieth-century cultural nationalists, p. 161. Andre Schmid, "Rediscovering Manchuria: Sin Ch'aeho and the Politics of Territorial History in Korea," *Journal of Asian Studies* 56.1 (1997): 28–30 notes that Sin was out of the mainstream; most of his colleagues defined Korea as a peninsular nation. See Jae-hoon Shim, "A New Understanding of Kija Chosŏn as a Historical Anachronism," *Harvard Journal of Asiatic Studies* 62.2 (2002): 271–305.

[19] Andre Schmid, *Korea Between Empires, 1895–1919* (New York: Columbia University Press, 2002), p. 190.

[20] *Ibid.*, p. 196.

[21] Quote from Sarah M. Nelson, "The Politics of Ethnicity in Prehistoric Korea," in *Nationalism, Politics, and the Practice of Archaeology*, ed. Kohl and Fawcett, p. 218.

almost seven years studying in London and Berlin, established what became the Institute of History and Philology (Lishi yuyan yanjiusuo) in Academia Sinica. Fu became professor of history at Peking University (Beida) in 1930, and conducted the excavations at Anyang that confirmed the historical existence of the Shang dynasty.[22]

Chinese scholars reacted against the territorial claims over northeast Asia made in new Japanese and Korean national histories. In *Dongbei shigang* (Outline history of the Northeast, 1932), challenging Japanese assertions of their ancient affinity with Manchuria, Fu Sinian argued that commonalities in language and culture made the *minzu* (ethnic group) of South Manchuria identical to the *minzu* of North China. Chinese scholars also took sides over the Korean claims to the history of northeast Asia. Lü Simian, author of *Zhongguo minzu shi* (History of China's ethnic groups, 1933), included the Maek, a people expelled from present-day Hebei and Liaoning provinces by the expansion of the state of Yan (third century BCE), as the progenitors of modern Koreans, imputing a Chinese origin to the Korean people. Jin Yufu, in *Dongbei tongshi* (General history of the Northeast, 1941), anticipated the late twentieth-century writers in asserting that Old Choson was a Han (Chinese) regime and that Gaogouli was a part of ancient China.[23] The same period also saw the publication of *Zhongguo bianjiang* (China's frontier) by Hua Qiyun, and the formation of the Yugong Society, organized to "study the history of Chinese geographical transformation and ethnic experience."[24]

National history in the postwar period

Japan's defeat in 1945 marked the end of one era and the beginning of another in northeast Asian geopolitics. The Chinese civil war ended with the Chinese Communist Party establishing the People's Republic of

---

[22] See Clayton Brown, "Making the Majority: Defining Han Identity in Chinese Ethnology and Archaeology," PhD thesis, University of Pittsburgh, 2008, for a study of the founders of the disciplines of archaeology and ethnology. A. F. P. Hulsewé, writing in the 1960s, observed the tendency of modern Communist Chinese studies in ancient history "to grow more and more nationalistic"; see his "Chinese Communist Treatment of the Origins and the Foundation of the Chinese Empire," in *History in Communist China*, ed. Albert Feuerwerker (Cambridge, MA: MIT Press, 1968), p. 122.

[23] Mark Byington, "The Creation of an Ancient Minority Nationality: Koguryŏ in Chinese Historiography," in *Embracing the Other: The Interaction of Korean and Foreign Cultures, Proceedings of the First World Congress of Korean Studies, 2002*, vol. I. Sponsored by the Academy of Korean Studies, International Society for Korean Studies, Association for Korean Studies in Europe, and Korean Studies Association of Australasia (Songnam: Academy of Korean Studies, 2002), pp. 1426–33.

[24] Ma Dazheng and Patrick Fuliang Shan, "Frontier History in China: A Scholarly Dialogue Across the Pacific Ocean," *The Chinese Historical Review* 19.1 (2012): 71.

China. The Korean peninsula split between a South Korean state supported by the United States, and a Democratic People's Republic of Korea, dominated first by the Soviet Union and subsequently by the PRC. During the Cold War (1947–1991), the US security umbrella shielded Japan, Taiwan, and South Korea while confronting a China that attempted to "march toward socialism" under the leadership of Mao Zedong (1893–1976). In the 1980s, even before the end of the Cold War, however, China's leaders launched a spectacular change of course toward "market socialism" that has made China a major economic power of the twenty-first century. These developments have influenced the writing of national history. Conversely, Chinese nationalism has spurred international disputes, including those focused on recent events such as the attacks on Japan for whitewashing Japanese imperialism and wartime atrocities in its history textbooks. Here we turn instead to examine the Sino-Korean quarrel over historical "ownership" of the ancient kingdom of Koguryŏ/Gaogouli which flared in 2004 and again in 2006.

Koguryŏ/Gaogouli: whose ancestors?

Rewriting Korean history

Japan's 1945 surrender liberated Korea from Japanese colonial rule, and allowed Korean historians to renew Sin Ch'aeho's pursuit of a history of the *minjok*. This new history traced Korean settlement deep into northeast Asia.[25] North and South Korea jockeyed for ownership of cultural symbols that would highlight their respective territories. Whereas South Korean scholars pushed Korean origins back to the purported time of Tan'gun, the founder of Old Chosŏn,[26] North Korea sought the embodiment of the Korean *minjok* in the "first king of Koguryŏ," Tongmyŏng, perhaps because its capital, P'yŏngyang, had been the Koguryŏ capital after 427 CE. North Korea's interest in Koguryŏ and its successor state, Parhae, contrasts with the South Korean emphasis on Silla, whose capital was located in present-day Seoul. In October 1993, the North Koreans announced the discovery of the tomb of Tan'gun at a site near

---

[25] Hyung-Il Pai, *Constructing "Korean" Origins: A Critical Review of Archaeology, Historiography, and Racial Myth in Korean State-Formation Theories* (Cambridge, MA: Harvard University Asia Center, 2000), chapter 1; Pai notes that many of these theories have not been substantiated by the archaeological evidence.

[26] Tan'gun's historical existence is said to be supported by archaeological evidence that locate his state far west of the Korean peninsula and date it to the second century BCE. See Shim, "New Understanding," for a critical appraisal of theories identifying Old Chosŏn as the first Korean state.

P'yŏngyang. The new cult, which highlighted "a five-thousand year continuity centred on P'yŏngyang," led Kim Il-Sung to propose a Koryŏ Federation in which all of Tan'gun's descendants, i.e. all Koreans, might be reunited.[27]

Koguryŏ was also at the center of disputes between scholars in Japan and Korea concerning the authenticity of a stele, which was the primary evidence of a Japanese colony in the peninsula during ancient times. The Kwanggaet'o (Gwanggaeto) stele, discovered in 1883, was dedicated to the king of Koguryŏ who reigned 391–413 CE. According to Japanese scholars, the stele, situated along the Yalu River in present-day Ji'an, Jilin province, dates to 414 CE, after the king's death. An inscription on the stele recounts Kwanggaet'o's military triumphs, among them victories of the soldiers of "Wa," or the early Yamato state. Hence, the stele seemed to document a Japanese presence in southeastern Korea in the fourth century, about 400 years before the first Japanese histories.[28]

The Kwanggaet'o stele was the subject of intense controversy throughout the twentieth century. The inscription was in bad condition, with portions that were illegible. As early as the second and third decades of the twentieth century, scholars in Japan questioned the accuracy of the rubbings of the inscription that were in circulation. Later, some Korean scholars accused the Japanese army of falsifying the text to justify their imperialist expansion. Still others challenged interpretations of key passages of the text, arguing for alternative readings of both the dates and the enemy that the king confronted in battle. Chinese scholars joined in the debate in the post-Mao period, as they incorporated Koguryŏ into the Chinese national history.[29] As North Korean archaeologists pushed the territorial boundaries of Old Chosŏn west of the Liao River into present-day Liaoning province, and emphasized the historical importance of Koguryŏ in northeast Asian and

---

[27] John Jorganson, "Tan'gun and the Legitimation of a Threatened Dynasty: North Korea's Rediscovery of Tan'gun," *Korea Observer* 27.2 (1996): 275.

[28] See Pai, *Constructing "Korean" Origins*, pp. 26–27 for the historical impact of the Kwanggaet'o stele.

[29] Pankaj N. Mohan, "Rescuing a Stone from Nationalism: A Fresh Perspective on the King Kwanggaet'o Stele of Koguryŏ," *Journal of Inner and East Asian Studies* 1 (2004): 91–115. For a detailed account of the textual controversies, see Yukio Takeda, "Studies on the King Kwanggaito Inscription and Their Basis," *The Memoirs of the Toyo Bunko* 47 (1989): 57–89. For a discussion of the Japanese scholarship on this subject in the postwar period, see Farris, *Sacred Texts and Buried Treasures*, chapter 2. See Piggott, *The Emergence of Japanese Kingship*, p. 41, and Kidder, *Himiko and Japan's Elusive Chiefdom*, p. 58 for recent scholarly appraisals of Japan's continental connections in the fourth and fifth centuries.

Korean history, Chinese historians registered opposition.[30] The dispute peaked in 2003–4, when North Korea and the PRC clashed over competing applications claiming Koguryŏ as a World Heritage Site.

World heritage sites

The dispute between the two Koreas and the PRC over "ownership" of Koguryŏ began in 2001, when North Korea applied to UNESCO to accept a Koguryŏ tomb complex in P'yŏng'an and Hwanghae provinces as a World Heritage site. North Korea's application was supported by South Korea and Japan, but opposed by the People's Republic of China. The North Korean application was rejected at the World Heritage general assembly sessions in 2003.[31] The following year, the PRC submitted its own Koguryŏ sites for World Heritage recognition. On July 1, 2004, at its Suzhou meeting, the World Heritage Committee approved both the North Korean application and an application by China to designate Koguryŏ capital cities and tombs located in Liaoning and Jilin provinces as World Heritage Sites, recommending that both countries "consider the possibility of a future joint, transboundary nomination of the Koguryŏ culture."[32]

The two countries argued for World Heritage status in slightly different terms. The North Korean application for burial sites beginning with the "Tomb of King Tongmyong" (first Koguryŏ king) hailed the murals on the walls of its Koguryŏ tombs as "masterpieces," and praised the "ingenious engineering solutions" of tomb construction, concluding that the tomb complex was "an important example of burial typology." Moreover, the special burial customs of Koguryŏ influenced "other cultures in the region, including Japan."[33] China's application for the "Capital Cities and Tombs of the Ancient Koguryŏ Kingdom, China"

---

[30] Ki-dong Lee, "Ancient Korean Historical Research in North Korea: Its Progress and Problems," *Korea Journal* 32.2 (1992): 22–41.

[31] See "China and Korea: A Shared Heritage," *China Heritage Quarterly*, No. 11 (2007), www.chinaheritagequarterly.org/editorial.php?issu ..., a website maintained by the Research School of Pacific and Asian Studies, The Australian National University. In general, obtaining recognition of a World Heritage site requires that the nominating country demonstrate its efforts to preserve the site, and North Korea had only joined the World Heritage convention in 1999.

[32] See 28COM 14B.25, "Nominations of Cultural Properties to the World Heritage List (Capital Cities and Tombs of the Ancient Koguryŏ Kingdom) and 28 COM 14B.33, "Nominations of Cultural Properties to the World Heritage List (Complex of Koguryŏ Tombs)," in "Decisions Adopted at the 28th Session of the World Heritage Committee (Suzhou, 2004)," on the World Heritage website, http://whc.unesco.org. The web address of the document is whc.unesco.org/archives/2004/whc04–28com-26e.pdf.

[33] *Ibid.*, 28COM 14B.33.

cited the Koguryŏ capitals as early and influential examples of mountain cities, noting that "the tombs, particularly the important stele and a long inscription in one of the tombs, show the impact of Chinese culture on the Koguryŏ (who did not develop their own writing)." Moreover, the tomb paintings "are also an example of strong impact from other cultures."[34]

China's application to UNESCO was part of a cultural offensive to gain international recognition of the high achievements of Chinese civilization. In an article in *People's Daily* in spring 2004, Wang Damin, an official in the State Administration of Cultural Heritage, announced the agency's efforts to obtain UNESCO recognition for two other sites in China's northeast provinces: the Qing imperial palace in Mukden (Shenyang), and the Qing imperial mausolea in Shenyang. The goal was to place more Chinese historical sites on the World Heritage list in future years.[35] *China Daily*, announcing the success of the Chinese application, noted that these approvals brought China's total of world heritage entries up to 30.[36] At the same time, the PRC initiative was part of a larger national effort to affirm China's symbolic ownership of Northeast Asia's historic past, known as the Northeast Regional Project.

China's Northeast Regional Project

The Northeast Regional Project is the abbreviated name of the "Sequential research project on northeast borderland history and current conditions" (*Dongbei bianjiang lishi yu xianzhuang xilie yanjiu gongcheng*), which was formally launched in February 2002 by the Chinese Academy of Social Sciences and research units in the three northeastern provinces of Heilongjiang, Jilin, and Liaoning. The mission of the participants was "to summarize the fruits of past research, accumulate excellent and penetrating research on doubtful points in the history of the northeast borderlands, on contemporary hot issues and difficult theoretical issues, to raise the whole level of research in a relatively big way, and on this foundation, to form sequential and

---

[34] *Ibid.*, 28 COM 14B.25.
[35] "China to put forward 3 historical sites for UNESCO heritage list," www.chinaview.cn 2004–05-12 10.52:53.
[36] "Koguryŏ sites put onto heritage list," *China Daily*, July 2, 2004, p. 1. As of September 18, 2013, the UNESCO World Heritage List, posted online, lists forty-five World Heritage sites for the PRC; ten of these are natural heritage sites, and three are both natural and cultural heritage sites (Taishan, for example). For comparison, as of September 18, 2013 North Korea has two World Heritage Sites, South Korea has nine, and Japan has seventeen (http://whc.unesco.org/).

authoritative research achievements."[37] The project's five-year plan for research had a total budget of 15 million RMB, one-third to be supplied by the participating units and two-thirds by the central government. A group of specialists were appointed to a special eighteen-man committee, which would oversee the organization of the scholarly work.

In accordance with the project's five-year plan, guidelines on priority research topics were announced in March and April of 2002, 2003, and 2004, and in each of those years researchers met to report on their findings. The 2002 plan listed research, translation, and archival work on all periods, from ancient times to the present. Priority topics included the historical origins of various ethnicities, the historical relationships of state entities established by various ethnic groups with Chinese states, Old Chosŏn, Gaogouli, and Bohai (Parhae in Korean), China's historical relations with Korea and Russia, and the dynastic tributary system. According to one [Korean] author, a total of twenty-seven books were published from 2002 to December 2004, ranging from regional histories of the northeast to specific histories of early northeastern states. In addition, fourteen books were translated into Chinese and four collections of archival materials from the First Historical Archives, the Heilongjiang Provincial Archives, the Jilin Provincial Archives, and the Liaoning Provincial Archives appeared in the same period.[38]

The Northeast Regional Project was a first-priority item (*ji zhongda keti zhi yi*) for the Chinese Academy of Social Sciences.[39] It followed on an earlier effort to articulate the historical grounds for PRC policy concerning its political boundaries, particularly those inhabited by non-Han ethnic groups, through its Center for the Study of China's Borderland History and Geography (Zhongguo bianjiang shidi yanjiu zhongxin, hereafter Borderland History Center), which was established in 1983.[40] As China's leaders entered the reform era, they turned their attention to tightening the boundaries between themselves and their neighbors and promoting "patriotic education"

---

[37] Li Guoqiang, "'Dongbei gongcheng' yu Zhongguo dongbeishi de yanjiu" (The Northeast Research Project and the study of northeast China's history). *Zhongguo bianjiang shidi yanjiu* 14.4 (2004): 1.

[38] Yun Hwit'ak, "Hyŏndae Chungguk ŭi pyŏnyŏng, minjok insik kwa [tongbuk kongjŏng]" (Contemporary China's perception of the border, ethnic peoples, and the 'Northeast Project'), *Yŏksa pip'yŏng* 65 (2003): 184–205.

[39] *Ibid.*, p. 3.

[40] "Relie zhuhe Zhongguo bianjiang shidi yanjiu zhongxin chengli ershi zhou nian" (Warmly congratulate the Center for the Study of China's Borderland History and Geography's twentieth anniversary), *Zhongguo bianjiang shidi yanjiu* 13.3 (2003): 1.

(*aiguozhuyi jiaoyu*).[41] The government's infusion of new resources into borderland research was closely linked to contemporary Chinese reality, responding to "China's rapid development and sudden changes in the world situation."[42]

The new Center not only directed the research work of its own staff but also coordinated the projects undertaken by scholars in other units, in accordance with the Seventh Five-Year Plan, issued in 1986, which identified modern borderland studies as a "key target" (*zhongdian xiangmu zhi yi*).[43] Its journal, which began publication in 1989, presented a mixture of policy statements, empirical history, book reviews, and annual bibliographies of new secondary literature on borderland history and geography.[44] A 1992 essay hailing the revival of research on China's borderlands also cited Jiang Zemin's 1990 call for strengthening China's modern and contemporary history education; research on modern history and on modern borderlands had to "appropriately respond to the needs of the state and society in the new era."[45]

From its inception, *Zhongguo bianjiang shidi yanjiu* (China's Borderland History and Geography Studies) published articles on the northeast[46] and

---

[41] Lin Ganquan, "Zhongguo bianjiang shidi yanjiu yu aiguozhuyi jiaoyu" (China's borderland research and patriotic education), *Zhongguo bianjiang shidi yanjiu* 1992.2: 1. For other aspects of patriotic education, see Zheng Wang, *Never Forget National Humiliation: Historical Memory in Chinese Politics and Foreign Relations* (New York: Columbia University Press, 2012).

[42] Deputy Director of the Center for the Study of China's Borderland History and Geography Ma Dazheng, "Dangdai Zhongguo bianjiang yanjiuzhe de lishi shiming" (The historical mission of contemporary researchers of China's borderlands), *Zhongguo bianjiang shidi yanjiu* 1992.2: 10. See Patrick Fuliang Shan's interview of Ma Dazheng in Ma and Shan, "Frontier History in China."

[43] Wang Qingcheng, Director of the Modern History Institute, CASS, "Zhongguo jindaishi he bianjiang yanjiu" (Research on China's modern history and the borderlands), *Zhongguo bianjiang shidi yanjiu* 1992.2: 7–8.

[44] *Zhongguo bianjiang shidi yanjiu* is available on the China Academic Journals Full-Text Database: http://china.eastview.com/.

[45] *Ibid.*

[46] Ma Dazheng, "Zhongguo xuezhe Gaogouli lishi yanjiu de bainian licheng" (A century of research by Chinese scholars on Gaogouli history), *Zhongguo bianjiang shidi yanjiu* 10.1 (2000): 93–102; Ma Dazheng, "Jindai dongbeiYa guoji guanxi shi yanjiu de xin jinzhan – du Jiang Longfan zhu [Jindai Zhong Chao Ri sanguo dui Jiandao Chaoxian ren zhengce yanjiu]" (New development in the study of the international relations in northeast Asia – a review of Jiang Longfan's [*Chinese, Korean, and Japanese policies regarding the Koreans on Jiandao Island in the Modern Era*]), *Zhongguo bianjiang shidi yanjiu* 10.4 (2000): 111–16; Liu Housheng, "Jidai jiaqiang dongbei bianjiang shi de yanjiu" (Earnestly await the strengthening of research on the northeast borderland history), *Zhongguo bianjiang shidi yanjiu* 2000.1: 20–22; Li Zhiting, "Dongbei difang shi yanjiu de huigu yu zhanwang" (Looking backward and forward in studies on northeast China's local history), *Zhongguo bianjiang shidi yanjiu* 11.4 (2001): 1–10; Cheng Nina, "Dongbei gushi fenqi tanze" (On the periodization of the ancient history of the northeast), *Zhongguo bianjiang shidi yanjiu* 14.2 (2002): 1–7.

surveys of prior research on northern borderlands, which had achieved a "high tide" during the 1930s and 1940s, at the time of the struggle against Japanese invasion.[47] Two incidents appear to have sharpened PRC anxieties about the Korean border. After the 1992 normalization of relations, many South Koreans toured the Koguryŏ archaeological sites, and Korean scholars obtained "privileged access" to Koguryŏ artifacts and sites. Their vocal identification of these sites as "Korean" seems to have aroused Chinese concern. In 1993, at an international conference on Koguryŏ, the North Korean scholar Pak Sihyŏng and others criticized the Chinese claim that Koguryŏ was part of ancient Chinese history, arguing that "Koguryŏ had long been viewed by both Koreans and Chinese as a Korean state and people."[48] This criticism was strongly rebutted by the Chinese side.

As directly stated in an article in 2001, to "earnestly strengthen the study of northeast borderland history," the new research aimed to clarify the historical evolution of national boundaries, showing the world and Chinese citizens the land that had been lost to nineteenth-century Russian and twentieth-century Japanese imperialism, in order "to make the world understand that stage of China's bitter history" and arouse patriotism in China's youth. Despite China's close relationship with Korea, Chinese researchers needed to pay attention to recent claims by some South and North Korean writers that Gaogouli was their "native land" (*gutu*), and Changbaishan their "ancestral sacred mountain," with the expressed desire that the "northern territory" be returned to Korea.[49]

The Borderland History Center also co-organized conferences with Yanbian University's Center for the Study of Sino-Korean–Japanese Comparative Cultures (Zhong Chao Han Ri wenhua bijiao yanjiu zhongxin): the August 2003 "Conference on Gaogouli and Bohai Scholarly Issues," held at Yanji, attracted twenty-five participants from Beijing, Henan, and the three northeast provinces, while the August 2004 "Conference on Gaogouli Scholarly Issues" brought fifty participants from Beijing and the northeast.[50]

---

[47] Li Zhiting, "Dongbei difang shi yanjiu"; Wei Qingfeng, "Jindai Zhongguo bianjiang yanjiu de dierci gaochao yu guofang zhanlüe" (The second high tide and national defense strategy in modern China's study of borderlands), *Zhongguo bianjiang shidi yanjiu* 1996.3: 101–12.

[48] Byington, "Creation of an Ancient Minority," p. 1436.

[49] Liu Housheng, "Jidai jiaqiang dongbei bianjiang shi de yanjiu"; Du Yonghao and Wang Yulang, "Dui dongbeiYa minzu yu lishi wenti yanjiu de lilun sikao" (Theoretical deliberations on historical research issues concerning Northeast Asian peoples), *Zhongguo bianjiang shidi yanjiu* 13.3 (2003): 39.

[50] Long Mu, "'Gaogouli, Bohai wenti xueshu yantao hui' jiyao" (Summary of the conference on Gaogouli and Bohai scholarly issues), *Zhongguo bianjiang shidi yanjiu* 13.3 (2003): 114; Yu Fengchun, "Gaogouli lishi wenti xueshu yantao hui shuping" (Review of the conference on scholarly issues in Gaogouli history), *Zhongguo bianjiang shidi yanjiu* 14.4 (2004): 141–43.

Of course, not all PRC scholars sided with the nationalist revision of ancient history. There was widespread recognition of the Korean element, especially after the political capital of Koguryŏ moved in 427 CE to P'yŏngyang.[51] Chinese historians were divided between those who incorporated Gaogouli history into Chinese history and those who advocated recognizing that Gaogouli was part of Korean as well as Chinese history. Ma Dazheng, a leading participant in the Koguryŏ/Gaogouli debates, appealed for calm in *China Daily* (June 2003), warning against "politicization of studies" and expressing the hope that international scholarly exchanges would "seek common ground, while reserving differences with mutual respect."[52]

During the "high tide" of Gaogouli historical research which began in 1993 and extended into 2004,[53] Chinese articles rebutted three major points in the Korean claims: Gaogouli was not an ancient Korean kingdom, but was born and nurtured in China's territory and within China's multi-ethnic culture. It entered into a lord–vassal relationship with successive Chinese dynasties, from the Han to the Tang.[54] Even after its capital was moved to P'yŏngyang, Gaogouli remained part of China and cannot be considered to be part of Korean history.[55] Finally, to interpret the Sui and Tang military campaigns against Gaogouli as Gaogouli's resistance struggle against Chinese invaders was misguided. Tang actually introduced almost two centuries of peace and political stability in the northeast by annihilating Gaogouli.[56] As for the

[51] See the discussion of archaeologist Wang Mianhou's position in "China and Korea: A Shared Heritage," *China Heritage Quarterly* No. 11 (September 2007), on the Australian National University website, www.chinaheritagequarterly.org/. The Chinese and Korean historiographical positions are laid out in Yonson Ahn, "The Korea–China Textbook War – What's It All About?" The article was first posted at *Japan Focus* on February 9, 2006 (www.japanfocus.org) and posted on the History News network, George Mason University on March 6, 2006.

[52] "Gaogouli role in Chinese history traded: Researcher warns against politicization of studies," *China Daily*, June 24, 2003, p. 5. An interesting appraisal from the Korean side, which cites this controversy as stimulating popular interest in Koguryŏ in South Korea, is "Goguryeo's Popularity? Blame it on the Chinese," *JoongAng Daily*, July 13, 2006, p. 8.

[53] Byington, "Creation of an Ancient Minority," p. 1436.

[54] See Li Dalong, "Cong Gaogouli xian dao Andong duhufu – Gaogouli he lidai zhongyang wangchao guanxi shulun" (From Gaogouli country to Andong protectorate – the relations between Gaogouli and successive central dynasties), *Minzu yanjiu* 1998.4: 74–85, which aims to refute the incorrect scholarship that sets up Gaogouli as an independent state.

[55] For a Korean scholar's refutation, see Kim Jung Bae, "A Critique of the Chinese Theory of 'One History Shared by Two States' (一史兩用論) As Applied to Koguryŏ History," *Journal of Inner and East Asian Studies* 3.1 (2006): 5–26.

[56] See Zhang Bibo, "Yige yanjiu xin jieduan de biaozhi – Ping [Gudai Zhongguo Gaogouli lishi conglun]" (A symbol of a new phase of research – reviewing *Collected Essays on Ancient China's Gaogouli History*), *Zhongguo bianjiang shidi yanjiu* 12.2 (2002): 96–99; and his "Gaogouli yanjiu zhong de wuqu" (Errors in Gaogouli research), *Zhongguo bianjiang shidi yanjiu* 1999.3: 34–41. Also Li Deshan, "Tangchao dui Gaogouli zhengce

successor state of Bohai, it was also linked to the Central Plain regimes as well as to contiguous states in northeast Asia.[57] The Education Ministry published new textbooks incorporating these points for use in colleges and universities.[58]

In 2003 and 2004, as UNESCO reviewed the World Heritage Site application by North Korea for its Koguryŏ site and the PRC application, the number of articles on Gaogouli increased. Li Deshan argued that Chinese scholars should recognize the Korean cultural elements but pointed to the "unquestioned historical fact" that Gaogouli had submitted to a Central Plain dynasty, and was hence part of Chinese history. More broadly, "The Gaogouli peoples were nurtured ... and became great within China's borders" and were fostered by "Zhonghua wenhua" – not Han culture, but the composite "Chinese" culture made up of the multi-ethnic mix of various peoples within China's borders.[59] Gaogouli had been a tributary vassal of the Han dynasty, was established on land that was within the Han administrative system, therefore it was a "separatist" (*geju*) regime on Chinese soil.[60] Although Chinese academics were not unified on the issue of whether Gaogouli might not legitimately also be considered to be part of Korean history, they cited historical fact and international law to

de xingcheng, shanbian ji qi yuanyin" (The formation, evolution and causes of Tang policy towards Gaogouli), *Zhongguo bianjiang shidi yanjiu* 14.4 (2004): 23–29, and Ma Yihong, "Cong Tang muzhi kan ru Tang Gaogouli yimin guishu yizhi de bianhua" (Change in the awareness of Gaogouli remnants submitting to Tang, seen from Tang grave inscriptions), *Beifang wenwu* 2006.1: 29–37.

[57] Teng Hongyan, "Bohai zhi Riben liwu tanzhe," (Inquiry into the gifts presented by Bohai to Japan), *Zhongguo bianjiang shidi yanjiu* 16.2 (2006): 69–76. Also Wang Chengguo, "Bohai shi yanjiu de yizuo fengpei: Ping Wang Chengli xiansheng yizhu *Zhongguo dongbei de Bohaiguo yu DongbeiYa*" (A monument in Bohai historical studies: reviewing Prof. Wang Chengli's posthumous *China's northeast Bohai kingdom and Northeast Asia*), *Beifang wenwu* 2002.1: 91–93.

[58] The Preface in Cheng Nina, ed., *Dongbei shi* (Northeast history) (Changchun: Jilin daxue chubanshe, 2001), p. 1, notes that this was part of the Education Ministry's project to reform the content and curriculum of higher education in the twenty-first century. Chapter 2.3 and chapter 3 treat Gaogouli, the Sui and Tang campaigns against the state, and the establishment of Bohai after the destruction of Gaogouli.

[59] Li Deshan, "Dangqian Gaogouli shi yanjiu zhong de jige wenti" (Some issues in prior studies of Gaogouli history), *Zhongguo bianjiang shi di yanjiu* 13.2 (2003): 66. In his article, Li specifically rebuts statements made by the North Korean author Kim Tŭk-hwang in the preface to his 1995 work, *Paektusan and the Northern Borders*.

[60] Miao Wei, "Cong Jin Fushi [Kim Pu-sik] de Gaogouli guan kan Gaogouli zhengquan de xingzhi ji qi lishi guishu" (Viewing the nature of Gaogouli political authority and its historical submission from Kim Pu-sik's Gaogouli perspective), *Zhongguo bianjiang shidi yanjiu* 14.4 (2004): 76–82; Li Shuying and Nie Tiehua, "Liang Han shiqi Gaogouli de fengguo diwei" (Gaogouli's subordinate status in the two Han dynasties), *Zhongguo bianjiang shidi yanjiu* 14.4 (2004): 62–68. See also Jiang Weigong, "Nanchao yu beichao dui Gaogouli zhengce de bijiao yanjiu" (Comparative study of the southern dynasty and northern dynasty's policies toward Gaogouli), *Zhongguo bianjiang shidi yanjiu* 14.4 (2004): 14–22.

attack the (Korean) thesis that the land where their ancestors had lived was Korean territory; they also rejected the notion that the ethnic origins of the ruling class determined the identity of the regime, as well as the idea that the ethnic ancestry of contemporary peoples determined the rightful claimant of national territory.[61] The Gaogouli people's spoken language may have approximated Japanese, but they also spoke Chinese. They used Chinese characters as phonetic markers for their own language, but also wrote Chinese texts – i.e. they were part of Chinese culture.[62]

Korea's response

News of the PRC's success at winning World Heritage recognition for its Gaogouli tombs and city ruins, coupled with Chinese press releases describing Gaogouli as a "subordinate state that fell under the jurisdiction of the Chinese dynasties and was under the great influence of China's politics, culture and other areas" aroused intense emotion in South Korea, where protestors dressed in Koguryŏ garb picketed the Chinese Embassy in Seoul. Official relations between the PRC and South Korea, begun in 1992, were strained over this matter. Earlier in 2004, the Chinese Foreign Ministry deleted references to Koguryŏ from the Korean history section on its web site, so the World Heritage affair exacerbated Korean suspicions that China intended to remove any challenges to its incorporation of Koguryŏ into Chinese national history. A diplomatic "understanding" was hastily negotiated in an effort to ease tensions, but the underlying issues were not so easily resolved.[63]

Shortly after the UNESCO announcement, *The Korea Times* (*Han'guk ilbo*) ran a series of three articles by Choi (Ch'oe) Kwang-shik, a professor at Korea University, who traced China's "distortion of history" back to its establishment of the Northeast Asia Project in 2002. According to Choi, the motivation was Chinese concern over North Korean migration into the northeast provinces and a 2001 South Korean law dealing with ethnic Koreans residing in China.[64] He ascribed the Chinese actions to a shift in

[61] Jiao Runming, "Guanyu lishi jiangyu guishu ruogan lilun wenti de yanjiu" (Research on some theoretical issues about the ascription of historical territory), *Zhongguo bianjiang shidi yanjiu* 13.2 (2003): 1–12.

[62] Xu Deyuan, "Gaogoulizu yuyan weishilu" (A primary study of the Gaogouli people's language), *Zhongguo bianjiang shidi yanjiu* 15.1 (2005): 78–94.

[63] "China Fears Once and Future Kingdom," *New York Times*, August 25, 2004, A3. Also Bruce Klingner, "China Shock for South Korea," *Asia Times*, September 11, 2004 (http://www.atimes/Korea/).

[64] Choi Kwang-shik, "What is Behind China's Attempt to Distort the Past?" *The Korea Times*, August 24, 2004 (http://times.hankooki.com/).

policy dating back to the 1980s, when China began to pay much more attention to consolidating its control over the peoples living along its borders. China's challenge to North Korea over Koguryŏ could be interpreted either as "a proactive measure to deal with a potential border dispute that could arise if South and North Korea were to be unified," or as "a preemptive act in preparation for possible power changes in North Korea." Finally, "China might wish to prevent any confusion of identity that ethnic Koreans in China might feel due to a future unification of the Koreas."[65]

In a second article, Choi raised objections to the Chinese argument.[66] Koguryŏ's people were closely related both to the inhabitants of Paekche, another Korean state, and to the subjects of Parhae, a state established in the late seventh century. Chinese records of Koguryŏ's conflicts with Sui and Tang did not confirm the Chinese claim to overlordship, but rather showed that Koguryŏ behaved like an "independent state" with respect to the Chinese central power. Koguryŏ's independence was expressed through state rituals and in the titles adopted by its rulers, both of which were incompatible with the Chinese regulations governing vassal states.

In a final article, Choi declared that "The problem of Koguryŏ's history is not one for South or North Korea, but one for all Korean people." South Korea should lend technical support to North Korea and in the short term, establish a website that would inform the rest of the world about China's distortion of history. International academic meetings, with proceedings to be published in English, should propagate the correct information not only about Koguryŏ, but also Parhae and Old Chosŏn. Choi suggested that Korea create "an institute like China's state-run China (sic) Academy of Social Sciences." The Koguryŏ Research Foundation, which the South Korean government created on March 1, 2004, should "work with the government and academia" to collect information, create bibliographies of materials from the Koreas, China, and Japan, and publish collections of historical sources. Choi concluded:

The misrepresentation of history by the Northeast Asia Project is in many ways a more serious issue than the distortions attempted by the Japanese with their textbooks . . . because while the Japanese problem concerns only "new textbooks," it is the Chinese government that is behind the Koguryŏ distortions. If left alone, the history of not only Koguryŏ but also of Palhae and Old Chosŏn could be

---

[65] *Ibid.*

[66] Choi Kwang-shik, "Records Contradict China's Claims Over Koguryŏ," *The Korea Times*, August 25, 2004 (http://times.hankooki.com).

distorted as well, leaving Korea with only 2,000 years of history. It is important for the Korean people to take an interest in Korea's culture and history as well as these problems.[67]

Even before Choi's articles appeared, the Koguryŏ Research Foundation attempted to act as a political pressure group, with one of its researchers proposing that the South Korean government urge private investors to reduce their business in China unless Beijing dropped its claims over Koguryŏ. In addition, Korean students should be "encouraged to boycott China in favor of other study destinations." Others, however, warned that boycotts would not work; the foundation should stick to scholarly activities.[68] Although an official of the South Korean Foreign Ministry claimed in August 2004 that diplomats had agreed that neither China nor South Korea would support "government-level, central or provincial, attempts to distort the history of Koguryŏ," in reality both states continued to fund academic bodies that represented their very divergent historical positions.[69]

According to its website, the Koguryŏ Research Foundation was "an academic foundation, sponsoring research in ancient Korean and East Asian history. By supporting research projects on this period, often little-understood and clouded with misconceptions, we aspire to restore historical truths of Korea and its surrounding regions, thus contributing to the body of historical knowledge of this important era."[70] The foundation offered Visiting International Scholar Research Fellowships and sponsored an academic journal, *Journal of Inner and East Asian Studies*, "a bi-annual and peer-reviewed international journal featuring original scholarship on the history, religion, literature, language, folklore, archaeology, and related studies of [the] Inner and East Asian region."[71] Articles appeared in English, and the journal listed an editorial board including scholars at institutions in Mongolia, Russia, Australia, Germany, and the United States.

The South Korean academic response to China's World Heritage application for Koguryŏ came quickly. In 2004, *Han'guk kodaesa yŏn'gu* published seven articles in a "special edition" entitled "The erroneous

---

[67] Choi Kwang-shik, "Two Koreas Should Join Forces to Rectify China's Folly," *The Korea Times*, August 26, 2004 (http://times.hankooki.com/).

[68] Reuben Staines, "Researcher Proposes Economic Pressure on China Over Koguryŏ," *The Korea Times*, August 20, 2004 (http://times.hankooki.com/).

[69] Klinger, "China Shock," reports the Foreign Ministry official's statement but also notes that others argued that there was no such clause in the understanding arrived at by diplomats.

[70] http://www.pkuef.org/.

[71] "Editorial," *Journal of Inner and East Asian Studies* 1 (2004): 1–2.

distortions of China's Koguryŏ history and a plan to respond."[72] The authors pointed to the contemporary political motivation for the PRC position, which had previously acknowledged Koguryŏ as part of Korean history. The seventy years of conflict between Koguryŏ and Sui and Tang could not, they argued, fit comfortably into the tributary model. Rather than assimilating, many of the Koguryŏ subjects who later founded the state of Parhae retained a strong sense of their Koguryŏ identity, and could not simply be labeled as Chinese. Moreover, Korean and Chinese histories of Koryŏ, which ruled the Korean peninsula from 918–1392, explicitly state that it was the successor to Koguryŏ.[73] The Koguryŏ controversy stirred up academic interest in Korean identity in different historical periods. *Han'guksa yŏn'gu* in 2005 devoted space to essays exploring Korean territories and perceptions of territory in different time periods.[74]

China's Northeast Regional Project occupied a central place in many essays which described the institutional structure in which the project was embedded, surveyed the arguments mounted in *Zhongguo bianjiang shidi yanjiu*, and compared them (generally unfavorably) to the scholarship produced in South Korea.[75] Many authors commented on the underlying issues. One traced the historical evolution of the concept of *Zhonghua minzu* (literally, Chinese people) from the late Qing writings of Liang Qichao on through Sun Yat-sen, the Guomindang and into the post-1949

---

[72] *Han'guk kodaesa yŏn'gu*, 33 (2004): 5–141.

[73] John B. Duncan, "Historical Memories of Koguryŏ in Koryŏ and Chosŏn Korea," *Journal of Inner and Asian Studies* 1 (2004): 119–36.

[74] *Han'guksa yŏn'gu*, 129 (2005). See also Yi Sung'ŭn, "Koguryŏ yŏksa, kwayŏn nugu ŭi yŏksain ka?" (Truly, whose history is Koguryŏ history?), *Yŏksa pip'yŏng* 70 (2005): 197–220. Yi Hŭi-jin, "Koguryŏ ŭi tae Chung insingnon e taehan pip'anjŏk koch'al" (A critical examination of the Chinese discourse on Koguryŏ), *Yŏksa hakpo* 190 (2006): 277–300. See also Pak Sŏnyŏng, "Chŏngch'e-sŏng (Identity) ke'im sidae ŭi Chungguk kwa'ŭi yŏksa chŏnjaeng – tongbuk p'ŭrojekt'ŭ rŭl t'onghae pon 'tongbuk' ŭi ŭimi" (China's historical battle in the era of the identity game – the significance of "northeast" based on the Northeast Project), *Yŏksa hakpo* 182 (2004): 295–330.

[75] Yo Hogyu, "Chungguk ŭi tongbuk kongjŏng kwa Koguryŏ sa insik ch'egye ŭi pyŏnhwa" (China's northeast regional project and the changes in organized knowledge of Koguryŏ history), *Han'guksa yŏn'gu* 126 (2004): 277–315; Cho Sŏng-ŭl, "Hyŏndae Chungguk eso ŭi Hanguk sa yŏn'gu – kaesŏlsŏ ŭi sidae kubun ŭl chungsim ŭro" (Study of Korean history in contemporary China – focusing on the periodization in surveys), *Kyŏnggi sahak* 8 (2004): 529–53; Ch'oe Kwang-sik, "[Tongbuk kongjŏng] ŭi paegyŏng naeyong mit tae'ŭng pang'an – Koguryŏsa yŏn'gu tonghyang kwa munje chŏm ŭl chungsim ŭro" (The northeast regional project's background content and a plan for response: focusing on the trends and issues in Koguryŏ history), *Han'guk kodaesa yŏn'gu* 33 (2004): 5–21; Chŏng Tu-hŭi, "Chungguk ŭi tongbuk kongjŏngŭro chegidoen Hanguk sahakkye ŭi myŏt kaji munje" (Several issues in the Korean scholarly world raised by China's northeast project), *Yŏksa hakpo* 183 (2004): 457–76; Kim Nam-ch'ŏl, "Yŏksa kyoyuk eso ŭi [tongbuk kongjŏng] kwa minjokchuŭi" (Ethnic ideology and the northeast regional project in history education), *Yŏksa kyoyuk* 95 (2005): 89–115.

period.[76] The UNESCO application was seen as part of a much broader effort, which began in the reform era, to "sinify" the histories of the minority peoples who inhabited the borderlands in historical times. Another scholar, Kwŏn Chungdal, noted that Chinese scholars had two models of Chinese identity. The first limited the term to the Hua and Xia people of ancient times, but the second incorporated other peoples who became "Chinese" through cultural assimilation. Both models could serve the interests of Chinese nationalism. The first aimed at presenting a core identity, while the second was posited on the expansive properties of Chinese culture.[77]

From the Korean perspective, the PRC policy stance raised new questions about why Mao Zedong decided to enter the Korean War on the side of North Korea. Assuming that the decision reflected China's view of North Korea as a buffer zone, how would this viewpoint affect the map after a reunification of the two Koreas? Would China impinge on Korean sovereignty?[78]

Despite its publicly stated academic focus, the Koguryŏ Research Foundation's activities and reports were apparently regarded as threatening the delicate balance of foreign relations and business with China. In 2003, the PRC had displaced the United States as South Korea's largest trading partner. From 2004, political commentators noted that both South Korea and the PRC had an economic interest in calming the Korean public's anger over the incorporation of Koguryŏ into Chinese history.[79] A 2005 issue of *Yŏksa wa hyŏnsil* (Quarterly Review of Korean History) devoted a special section to articles exploring different aspects of the Koguryŏ dispute.[80] In August 2006, the South Korean government abandoned its support of the Koguryŏ Research Foundation while simultaneously funding a new body, the Northeast Asia History Foundation. Kim Jeong-bae, who headed the former institution, complained that "The Koguryŏ history materials we prepared could not be distributed to students because of objections by the Foreign Ministry, and the education minister and vice minister declined to listen to our stories about the

---

[76] Pak Changbae, "Hyŏndae Chungguk hakkye ŭi Koguryŏsa yŏn'gu saŏp ŭi tŭngjang paekyŏng" (The emergent backdrop to the Koguryŏ history research enterprise in contemporary Chinese scholarly circles), *Yŏksa wa hyŏnsil* 55 (2005): 140–49. Also see Yi Sŏnggyu, "Chunghwa cheguk ŭi p'aengch'ang kwa ch'ukso: kŭ i nyŏm kwa silje" (The expansion and contraction of the Chinese empire: its ideal and reality), *Yŏksa hakpo* 186 (2005): 87–133.

[77] Kwŏn Chungdal, "Chungguk ŭi hwaktae wa Hanjok kwan" (The expansion of China and views of the Han people), *Han'guk sahaksa hakpo* 10 (2004): 147–62.

[78] Pak Changbae, "Hyŏndae Chungguk hakkye."   [79] Klinger, "China Shock."

[80] The six articles ranged from re-examinations of the Kwanggaet'o stele inscription to a study of the treatment of Koguryŏ and Parhae in Korean history textbooks throughout the twentieth century: *Yŏksa wa hyŏnsil* 55 (2005).

foundation's projects for even five or 10 minutes."[81] In short, as a former Seoul National University professor said, the South Korean government was "trying to sweep the matter under the carpet for fear of stirring conflict with China."[82]

Established in September 28, 2006, the Northeast Asia History Foundation was intended as the Korean counterpart to China's Northeast Asia project, with expanded responsibilities to present the South Korean position on issues roiling relations with Japan as well as the PRC. Its activities were four-fold: (1) research, (2) strategy policy development, (3) international exchange and cooperation, and (4) publicity and education/translation and publication. In the area of research, it would "examine disputed issues in modern and contemporary East Asian history," study "Northeast Asian history, including the history of Korea–Japan relations and the history of Koguryŏ," study "agreements signed between Korea and Japan throughout history," and "conduct research on ways to strengthen Korea's dominium of Dokdo" (Takeshima in Japanese). In the strategy/policy development arena the foundation aimed to develop "strategies based on an analysis of historical issues between Korea and Japan and Korea and China, and Japan's political shift toward the right." The foundation also sought to expand its academic networks abroad, and disseminate "important documents regarding Korea's history, territory and territorial waters" in translation.[83]

Chinese identity in flux

The Koreans who interpreted the World Heritage controversy as a symptom of Chinese debates over identity issues were correct. Articles in *Zhongguo bianjiang shidi yanjiu* considered fundamental issues of national identity, such as: What is China? What is the proper relationship between the contemporary nation-state and earlier historical regimes? Since the PRC is a multi-ethnic state, should the history of its fifty-five minority nationalities be part of Chinese history, or is Chinese history primarily the history of the Han majority? Whereas pre-1949 history writing favored the latter position, in the 1990s authors began with the statement that

[81] "Seoul Smiles at China's Daylight Robbery," *Digital Chosun ilbo* (English Edition), October 31, 2006 (http://english.chosun.com/).

[82] *Ibid.* The Chinese press reported demonstrations by Koreans in front of the Chinese embassy on September 7, 2006 protesting the PRC's attempts to incorporate Koguryŏ into Chinese history; see "South Koreans resist Beijing's revision of Gaogouli history, rip up the Chinese flag," September 8, 2006, www.wenxuecity.com.

[83] Northeast Asian History Foundation website, http://www.historyfoundation.or.kr/, under "Key Programs."

the PRC society represents a "fusion" (*ronghe*) of its nationalities and not sinicization, or, as the distinguished anthropologist Fei Xiaotong phrased it, "The Chinese people are diverse but unified" (*duoyuan yiti*).[84]

Scholars addressing these questions of identity analyzed key terms such as *guo* (kingdom, state), *Zhongguo* (China), *jiangyu* (territory), and *minzu* (ethnic group), found in historical documents, and surveyed scholarly interpretations in Chinese and foreign publications in attempts to clarify definitions of China's historical territory.[85] They analyzed the concept of *zhengtong*, used in premodern China to selectively organize the dynasties into an orthodox succession, and compared the merits of this approach to a "legal genealogy" which would give a more central role to the minority nationalities.

In a 2006 review of *The Chinese World Order*, a conference volume edited by John King Fairbank in 1968, Xu Jianying highlighted the Sinocentric model's usefulness for current studies of China's historical relations with its neighbors along its frontiers. Rather than denouncing Western imperialism, Xu commented that one positive consequence of the unequal treaties forced on the Qing dynasty during the nineteenth century was the introduction of the concept of a state with clearly demarcated borders that is defined not by culture but by its territory.[86]

---

[84] Fei Xiaotong, *Zhonghua minzu duoyuan yiti geju* (China's nationalities, diverse but unified), rev. edn. (Beijing: Zhongyang minzu daxue chubanshe, 1999). Articles discussing the historical origins of the term *minzu* include Ruan Xihu, "'Minzu' yici zai Yingwen zhong ruhe biaoshu" (How *minzu* is expressed in English), *Shijie minzu* 2001.6:78; Hao Rui (Stevan Harrell), trans. Yang Zhiming, "Lun yixie renleixue zhuanmen shuyu de lishi he fanyi" (The history of specialized anthropological terms and their translation), *Shijie minzu* 2001.4: 65–72; and Huang Xingtao, "'Minzu' yici jiujing heshi zai Zhongwenli chuxian?" (When did the term *minzu* appear in Chinese), *Zhejiang xuekan* 1 (2002): 168–70. These authors agree that *minzu* as understood today was imported from the West via Japan in the late nineteenth century; for arguments asserting its native origins see Ru Ying, "Hanyu 'minzu' yici zai wo guo de zuizao chuxian" (The first appearance of the phrase minzu in Chinese), *Shijie minzu* 2001.6: 1, and Hao Shiyuan, "Zhongwen 'minzu' yici yuanliu kaobian" (Investigation of the origin of the phrase 'minzu' into Chinese), *Minzu yanjiu* 2004.6: 60–69.

[85] Citations of Western scholarship on China are to be found in Zhang Shiming and Gong Shengquan, "Zhengtong de jiegou yu fatong de chongjian: dui Qingdai bianjiang minzu wenti yanjiu de lixing sikao" (On the concept of orthodox succession and the reconstruction of a legal genealogy: study of issues concerning the Qing border peoples), *Zhongguo bianjiang shidi yanjiu* 11.4 (2001): 32–45 and Du and Wang, "Dui dongbeiYa minzu."

[86] Xu Jianying, "'Zhongguo shijie zhixu' guan zhi yingxiang ji qi yu Zhongguo gudai bianjiang yanjiu – Fei Zhengqing [Zhongguo shijie zhixu: Zhongguo chuantong de duiwai guanxi] du hou" (The influence of the view of China's world order and research on China's traditional ancient frontiers: after reading J. K. Fairbank's *The Chinese World Order: Traditional China's Foreign Relations*), *Zhongguo bianjiang shidi yanjiu* 16.1 (2006): 35–46.

Another group of articles debated the evolving meaning of terms like *Zhongguo* (literally, the "Middle Kingdom," i.e. China). *Zhongguo* was never part of the formal name of a Chinese state until the twentieth century. When first found in texts dating from the Zhou, it designated a central state or regime, even a capital city. Slightly later, *Zhongguo* referred to the Hua and Xia people (progenitors of today's Han Chinese), distinguishing them from other peoples (*si Yi*). From 221 BCE to the Tang dynasty (618–907 CE), *Zhongguo* generally denoted the Central Plain (*zhongyuan*), which was the "homeland" of the Hua and Xia. From Song to Ming, the establishment of non-Han regimes in north China stimulated the emergence of the concept of *zhengtong*, which constituted a new political genealogy of legitimate regimes, transcending individual dynasties.[87] The *zhengtong* logic masked the "foreignness" of the conquest dynasties, even in their pre-dynastic phases.[88]

According to Yang Jianxin, the literati of the tenth to fourteenth centuries determined that although the non-Han regimes occupying the central plain could be *Zhongguo*, they could not be recognized as *zhengtong* (legitimate). In short, rulers who were not descended from the Hua and Xia could not enter the orthodox political succession. The Manchus, who founded the Qing dynasty, succeeded in expanding the meaning of *Zhongguo* to encompass the territories of the Qing empire, thus creating the foundation for the modern concept.[89] Of course, the Qing was also incorporated into the *zhengtong*.

Another group of articles compared two key Chinese terms for "territory" found in ancient texts, *jiangyu* 疆域 and *pantu* 盤土, to the modern territorially-based concept of the nation-state. *Pantu* originally referred to a map which was used as the basis for taxation and household registration; hence, it denotes the sphere of direct dynastic control. *Jiangyu* includes the area covered by *pantu* but also includes territories

---

[87] Bi Aonan, "Lishiyu jing zhong de wangchao Zhongguo jiangyu gainian bianzhe – yi tianxia, sihai, zhongguo, jiangyu, pantu wei li" (Analyzing the traditional concept of China's territory in historical context: the examples of *tianxia, sihai, zhongguo, jiangyu, and pantu*), *Zhongguo bianjiang shidi yanjiu* 16.2 (2006): 9–16.

[88] David M. Farquhar, "Chinese Communist Assessments of a Foreign Conquest Dynasty," in *History in Communist China*, ed. Albert Feuerwerker (Cambridge, MA: MIT Press, 1968), p. 188.

[89] Yang Jianxin, "'Zhongguo' yici he Zhongguo jiangyu xingcheng zai tantao" (A restudy of the word 'China' and the formation of China's territory). *Zhongguo bianjiang shidi yanjiu* 16.2 (2006): 1–6. Yang argues that the distinction between Hua and Yi (Han and non-Han) faded in Qing times as did the territorial distinction between *nei* (China Proper) and *wai* (the non-Han periphery), but this argument is contradicted by the administrative differentiation of the two regions during the Qing. Also Cheng Chongde. "Lun Qingchao jiangyu xingcheng yu lidai jiangyu de guanxi" (On the formation of Qing borderlands and their relationship to historical borderlands), *Zhongguo bianjiang shidi yanjiu* 15.1 (2005): 1–10.

which may render tribute to the regime, i.e. vassal states. Using *jiangyu* to denote China's territory in earlier historical epochs, therefore, claims a retroactive sovereignty over borderlands that were formerly ruled by minority nationalities who participated in tributary relations with a *Zhongguo* regime. The expansion of territorial sovereignty involved raised a new question: will China claim all territories whose past rulers sent tribute embassies to earlier dynasties?

Considerations such as these spurred the particular definition presented by Zhao Yongchun, a historian at Jilin University:[90]

I believe that China's historical territory ought to use the peoples included in today's Chinese territory as the starting point to mold the history and territory of China's various nationalities (*minzu*); all of the nationalities that today live on Chinese territory and those who are extinct but who historically lived in today's territory are part of the Chinese people (*Zhonghua minzu*).

Because the historical concept of *Zhongguo* varied in different periods and was different from the modern concept, evocations of former *Zhongguos* cannot be used to define the territory that should be China's. Unlike Yang Jianxin, Zhao does not adopt the distinction between *Zhongguo/zhengtong* as a non-Han/Han binary, but cites regimes founded by Han that were not recognized as *Zhongguo*, and non-Han regimes that were called *Zhongguo*.[91]

At the same time, Zhao assigns primacy to the Han role in the historical process: the Han nationality and the regimes occupying the Central Plain were at the core of "historical China." Over the long-term, by gradually extending their cultural influence to their neighbors, the Central Plain regimes transformed formerly peripheral regions into administrative regions that they directly controlled. In other words, the interior (*neidi*) expanded outward. Zhao's exposition of this process (which he does not call sinicization) is nevertheless familiar to Western historians, being based on the acceptance by other *minzu* of Chinese writing, Confucian culture, and other customs, accompanied by the idea that those adopting the norms of the Central Plain transformed themselves into "Hua or Xia." We are back to Fairbank's Sinocentric model.[92]

[90] Zhao Yongchun, "Guanyu Zhongguo lishishang jiangyu wenti de jidian renshi" (Several viewpoints on the issue of China's historical territory), *Zhongguo bianjiang shidi yanjiu* (China's borderland history and geography studies) 12.3 (2002): 1–9. Quotation is from p. 1.
[91] *Ibid.*, pp. 2–3.
[92] *Ibid.*, pp. 7–9. Zhao and several other authors quote the historical phrase, "Hua and Rong are one people." Zhang Bibo, "Gaogouli lishi kaogu yanjiu de xin chengjiu – ping Wang Jinhou de [Gaogouli gucheng yanjiu]" (New results in the study of Gaogouli historical archaeology – a review of Wang Jinhou's [Study of the ancient city of Gaogouli],

Responding to the question, "What is China?" most scholars writing in *Zhongguo bianjiang shidi yanjiu* agreed that any definition must include the fifty-five minority nationalities legally recognized in the PRC as well as the Han majority. Chinese history should also incorporate peoples who appear in historical eras but have no living descendants. This includes the Gaogouli people, "annihilated" during the Tang dynasty, who resided in what is today Chinese territory.[93] What about minorities in the PRC, whose kinsmen also live in contiguous states, such as the Koreans and the Russians? Zhao's answer was that the history that China should claim dates back only to the time of a group's entry into Chinese territory. Their prior history and other lands, outside current borders, in which they may have resided, "cannot be considered to be Chinese history or territory." Cheng Chongde, a professor in the Qing History Institute, People's University, cautioned that the territory of the Yuan dynasty which lay in Central Asia and Europe "cannot be reckoned as Chinese (national) territory" because the Mongol occupation was "temporary." In short, the PRC has no grounds for challenging the sovereignty of Russia or the two Koreas.[94]

Conclusion

On one level, the Gaogouli/ Koguryŏ controversy reflects contemporary stresses of state-to-state relations in East Asia that arise from recent changes in China's policies. China's expanding economic links with South Korea and Japan and its growing prominence in world affairs affect its neighbors, who worry about China's future actions with respect to pending or potential territorial disputes.

South Koreans especially have voiced their fear that China may be preparing to redefine its traditional borders should North Korea dissolve

---

Zhongguo bianjiang shidi yanjiu 13.4 (2003): 89–92 underlines the heavy Chinese cultural presence in the architecture, building methods and materials found in the excavations.

[93] For example, Fu Langyun, "Zhongguo dongbei yu gudai dongbei Yi," (China's northeast and the northeast Yi of ancient times), *Zhongguo bianjiang shidi yanjiu* 1992.2: 87–88, 114, traces the evolution of various non-Han groups in the northeast.

[94] Cheng Chongde, "Lun Qingchao jiangyu xingcheng," p. 10. Du Yonghao and Wang Yulang, "Dui DongbeiYa minzu," p. 44, state that "Gaogouli was one of China's ancient peoples (*minzu*) but also the source of the formation of the Korean people"; but this view was disputed by some scholars: see Zhang Bibo, "Guanyu lishi shang minzu guishu yu jiangyu wenti de zai sikao – jianping 'yishi liang yong' shiguan" (A reexamination of the historical submission of peoples and the issue of national territory – a critique of the historical 'one history two uses' view), *Zhongguo bianjiang shidi yanjiu* 10.2 (2000): 1–9.

or should there be a reunification of the two Koreas.[95] Articles published by both sides show that border disputes are by no means resolved.[96] One author, citing Mao Zedong, argued that Mao saw Korea and other neighboring states as "vassal countries," a "territory in which military force can be used."[97] Chinese moves to incorporate Kija Chosŏn and Koguryŏ into Chinese history might foreshadow a Chinese claim on the current territory of North Korea.[98]

What made the Koguryŏ/Gaogouli controversy so explosive in 2004 was the fact that PRC historians had adhered to a rather less confrontational position before the 1980s. Even though a 1960 joint archaeological project with North Korea had raised the same issues of historical ownership, Chinese publications in the Maoist period showed little interest in exploring Koguryŏ/Gaogouli's place in Chinese history. The reform era's new focus on clarifying issues of Chinese identity and consolidating China's current borders followed the turn away from class struggle to nationalism as the major national motif that accompanied the post-Mao reforms.

The Koguryŏ/Gaogouli brouhaha is an example of the polemical potential of historical studies of Northeast Asia. The foundations for the current "history war" were laid in the national histories of the early twentieth century outlined above. They could be found in the nationalist archaeologies which attempted to trace the nation-state back to the earliest origins, and ended in projecting current geopolitical rivalries backward in time.[99] The international quarrel about the identity of

---

[95] Alexander Y. Mansourov, "Will Flowers Bloom Without Fragrance? Korean–Chinese Relations," *Harvard Asia Quarterly* 10.2 (2006): 46–58; Yun Hwit'ak, "Hyŏndae Chungguk ŭi pyŏnyŏng."

[96] As examples, see Sun Chunri, "Qing mo Zhong Chao Ri 'Jiandao wenti' jiaoshe zhi yuanwei" (The whole story of negotiations between China, Korea and Japan on the 'Jiandao issue' in late Qing), *Zhongguo bianjiang shidi yanjiu* 12.4 (2002): 48–58; Jian Wen, "Lun Mingdai dui dongjiang diqu de guanxia wenti – jian jiu 'bei Jiandao' yanjiu bo Hanguo xuezhe" (On the issue of Ming administration over the eastern frontier – a refutation of Korean scholars' research on northern Jiandao), in *Zhong Han guanxishi yanjiu lunwenji*, ed. Diao Shuren and Yi Xingguo (Changchun: Wenshi chubanshe, 1995), pp. 191–99; and Pak Sŏnyŏng, "Chunghwa min'guk naejŏngbu chidoropon Paektusan chŏnggyebi – Chunghwa min'guk Chungyang yŏn'guwŏn esŏ saeropke palguhan Kando charyo" (Maps made by the Republic of China's Interior Ministry of the Paektusan stele – maps in the Academia Sinica, ROC, on the Kando problem), *Tongyang sahak yŏn'gu* 105 (2008): 295–313.

[97] Pak Changbae, "Hyŏndae Chungguk hakkye," pp. 157, 159.   [98] *Ibid.*, p. 160.

[99] For analysis of the influence of Japanese colonial archaeology on post-45 Korea, see Pai, *Constructing "Korean" Origins*. On the nationalist implications of the founding of Chinese archaeology, see Brown, "Making the Majority," also von Falkenhausen, "The Regionalist Paradigm in Chinese Archaeology." For a survey of Japanese archaeological shifts in the late nineteenth and twentieth centuries, see Hudson, *Ruins of Identity*.

Gaogouli both underlines the contemporary relevance of history and demonstrates the need for a critical analysis of historical narratives embedded in the framework of the nation-state.[100] Many of the scholars participating in the debate have traced the Chinese and Korean claims back to the early twentieth-century writings of Liang Qichao on the Chinese side, and of Sin Ch'aeho and Pak Ŭnsik in Korea.[101]

The controversy has not ended. The "history wars" between the Koreas and the PRC erupted again in 2006 over China's decision to nominate Changbaishan/Paekdusan, a mountain sacred to both Manchus and Koreans, for World Heritage site status.[102] According to a 1962 treaty, the mountain straddles the Sino-Korean border, and until recently, there were hotels run by North and South Koreans located on the Chinese side to accommodate tourists. In 2005, however, the Jilin Provincial Government, which has jurisdiction over Changbaishan, created the "Committee for Protection, Development and Management of Mount Changbai" to oversee development of the region for tourism but also as part of its overall effort to stress its Chinese identity (Manchus are one of China's minority nationalities, which makes the site "Chinese" according to PRC policy).

The PRC actions set off another backlash in the two Koreas. Koreans revere Paekdusan as "the ancestral mountain;" it was also the birthplace of Kim Il-Sung, the founding leader of North Korea. Nationalists in both North and South Korea feared an eventual incorporation of the entire mountain into Chinese territory. During the 2007 Asian Winter Games in Changchun, South Korean athletes on the medal podium held up signs in Korean which said, "Paekdusan is our territory," leading to charges and countercharges on the internet and some street demonstrations by South Koreans in front of the Chinese embassy. Invariably, the Korean protests referred back to the Koguryŏ/Gaogouli controversy.

This study of China's historical relations with northeast Asia raises fundamental questions about how Chinese interpret their history, questions which, as we have shown, directly affect contemporary interstate relations but, more importantly, how Chinese see themselves. The PRC

---

[100] One of many Korean critiques of the Chinese publications is Pak Changbae, "Hyŏndae Chungguk hakkye." For statements of the Chinese position, see the many articles in *Zhongguo bianjiang shidi yanjiu*, a journal published by the Center for Borderland History and Geography Studies, Chinese Academy of Social Sciences.

[101] Sin Chubaek, "Hanguk kŭnhyŏndaesa eso Koguryŏ wa Parhae e kwanhan insik – yŏksa kyokwasŏ rŭl chungsim ŭro" (The contemporary perception of Koguryŏ and Parhae, focusing on history textbooks), *Yŏksa kwa hyŏnsil* 55 (2005): 106–10.

[102] "China and Korea: A Shared Heritage"; Yonson Ahn, "China and the Two Koreas Clash Over Mount Paekdu/Changbai: Memory Wars Threaten Regional Accommodation," Article 885 on *Japan Focus*, http://japan.focus.org/

search for a Chinese identity that can command the loyalty of all of its minorities, especially those residing along the frontiers, has recently caused PRC scholars to re-evaluate Chinese historiography. The goal of writing a history that acknowledges the contributions of its many diverse nationalities wars with earlier, still powerful drives to counter China's history of political atomization and its periodic subjugation at the hands of northern and northeastern tribes with a Han-centered narrative. Yet, as this book has shown, northeast Asian peoples played a central role in creating the political and cultural institutions that we call "Chinese." Moreover, the relations between the many groups who have occupied the Central Plain fluctuated and evolved over time. Future research analyzing the nature of the post-Han regimes in north China will help further our understanding of the components that made the northeast frontier a "dynamic center" for Chinese history.

Bibliography

PRIMARY SOURCES

Arai Hakuseki 新井白石. *Arai Hakuseki zenshū* 新井白石全集 (Complete works of Arai Hakuseki). 6 vols. Tokyo: Naigai insatsu, 1907.

Chaoxian [Lichao shilu] zhong de Nüzhen shiliao xuanbian 朝鮮[李朝實錄]中的女真史料的選編 (Jurchen historical materials from the Korean *Yichao shilu*). Ed. Wang Zhonghan 王鍾翰. Shenyang: Liaoning daxue lishixi, 1979.

Chaoxian [Lichao shilu] zhong de Zhongguo shiliao 朝鮮[李朝實錄] 中的中國史料 (Historical materials about China in the Korean *Yichao shilu*). Ed. Wu Han 吳晗. 12 vols. Beijing: Zhonghua shuju, 1980.

Chikamatsu Monzaemon. Trans. Donald Keene. *Major Plays of Chikamatsu*. New York: Columbia University Press, 1990.

Chongde sannian Manwen dang'an yibian 崇德三年滿文檔案譯編 (Translation of Manchu-language archives dated Chongde 3). Trans. and ed. Ji Yonghai 季永海 and Liu Jingxian 劉景憲. Shenyang: Liao Shen shushe, 1988.

Chŏnju Yi ssi taegwan 全州李氏大觀 (Overview of the Chŏnju Yi). Comp. Chŏnju Yi ssi taedong chongyagwŏn 全州李氏大同宗約院. 2 vols. Seoul: Chŏnju Yi ssi taedong chongyagwŏn, 2002.

Chosŏn wangjo sillok 朝鮮王朝實錄 (The veritable records of the Chosŏn dynasty). http://sillok.history.go.kr

Chu Hsi. *See* Zhu Xi.

Di Cosmo, Nicola and Dalizhabu Bao, trans. and ed. *Manchu–Mongol Relations on the Eve of Qing Conquest: A Documentary History*. Leiden: E. J. Brill, 2003.

Da Qing shilu 大清實錄 (The veritable records of the Qing dynasty). 1986 reprint entitled *Qing shilu* published by Zhonghua shuju, Beijing. 60 vols.

Guoli gugong bowuyuan 國立故宮博物院, comp. *Jiu Manzhou dang*. (Old Manchu-language archive). 10 vols. Taipei: National Palace Museum, 1969.

Han'guk sajŏn p'yŏnch'anhoe, comp. *Han'guk kojung sesa sajŏn* (Dictionary of matters in Korea during ancient and medieval times). Seoul: Kalam kihoek, 1995.

Hayashi Gahō 林鵞峯 and Hayashi Hōkō 林鳳岡, comps. *Ka'I hentai* 華夷變態 (Metamorphosis from civilized to barbarian). 3 vols. Tokyo: Toyo Bunko, 1958–59. In *Shintei zōhō Kokushi taikei* 新訂增補國史大系, vol. 30. Ed. Kuroita Katsumi 黒板勝美. Rev. edn. Tokyo: Yoshikawa kōbunkan, 1966.

Kaempfer, Engelbert. Trans. and annotated by Beatrice M. Bodart-Bailey. *Kaempfer's Japan: Tokugawa Culture Observed.* Honolulu: University of Hawai'i Press, 1999.

Kanda Nobuo 神田信夫 et al., trans. and ed. *Manbun rōtō* 滿文老檔 (Manchu archives). 7 vols. Tokyo: Toyo Bunko, 1955–63.

Kanda Nobuo et al., comp. *Naikokushientō Tensō shichi nen* 內國史院檔 天聰 七年 (Early Manchu archives of the Qing Historiography Academy for Tiancong 7, 1633/34). Tokyo: Toyo Bunko, Shindaishi kenkyū iinkai, 2003.

Kang Taegŏl 姜大杰 and Sŏ Inhan 徐仁漢, eds. *Imjin waeran saryo ch'ongsŏ: Yŏksa* 壬辰倭亂史料叢書: 歷史 (Collected historical materials on the 1592 Japanese invasion of Korea: History). 10 vols. Seoul: Kungnip Chinju pangmulgwan, 2002.

Kawachi 2010. Kawachi Yoshihiro 河內良弘, trans. and ed. *Chūgoku daiichi rekishitōankansō Naikokushien Manbun tōan yakuchū: Sūtoku ni, san nenbun* 中國第一歷史檔案館藏 內國史院滿文檔案譯註: 崇德二, 三年分 (Translation and annotation of Manchu-language archives in the Qing Historiography Academy, the second and third years of the Chongde reign, 1637, 1638). Kyoto: Shōkōdō, 2010.

Kitabatake Chikafusa 北畠親房. *Jinnō shōtoki; Masukagami* 神皇正統記; 增鏡 (Record of the orthodox transmission of gods and sovereigns; expanded mirror). Ed. Iwasa Masashi 岩佐正 et al. vol. LXXXVII, *Nihon koten bungaku taikei* 日本古典文學大系. Tokyo: Iwanami shoten, 1966.

Kitabatake Chikafusa. Trans. H. Paul Varley. *A Chronicle of Gods and Sovereigns: "Jinnō Shōtoki" of Kitabatake Chikafusa.* New York: Columbia University Press, 1980.

Kukjo oryeŭi 國朝五禮儀 (The dynastic five rites). Completed in 1474. Reprint edn. Seoul: Munchang munhwasa, 1994.

Kungnip Chinju pangmulgwan 國立晉州博物館, ed. *Imjin waeran saryo ch'ongsŏ: Munhak* 壬辰倭亂史料叢書: 文學 (Collected historical materials on the Japanese invasion of Korea: Literature). 10 vols. Seoul: Kungnip Chinju pangmulgwan, 2000.

Li Guangtao 李光濤, comp. *Wanli ershisannian feng Riben guowang Fengchen Xiuji kao* 萬曆二十三年奉日本國王豐臣秀吉考 (On the investiture of the Japanese king Toyotomi Hideyoshi in Wanli 23). Taipei: Institute of History and Philology, Academia Sinica, 1967.

Chaoxian renzhen wohuo shiliao 朝鮮壬辰倭禍史料 (Historical materials on the Japanese invasion of Chosŏn). 5 vols. Taipei: Institute of History and Philology, Academia Sinica, 1970.

Ji Ming ji Chaoxian zhi Dingmao lǔhuo yu Bingzi lǔhuo 記明記朝鮮之丁卯盧禍 與丙子盧禍 (Ming and Chosŏn records on the 1627 and 1636 invasions of Chosŏn). Taipei: Institute of History and Philology, Academia Sinica, 1972.

Li Guangtao and Li Xuezhi 李學智, comps. *Ming Qing dang'an cun zhen xuanji* 明清當安存真選輯 (Selected materials from the Ming–Qing Archives: Documents of the late Ming dynasty and early Qing dynasty, photographically reproduced). Vol. II. Taipei: Institute of History and Philology, Academia Sinica, 1973.

Manwen laodang 滿文老檔 (Old Manchu-language archives). Comp. Zhongguo diyi lishi dang'an guan, Zhongguo shehui kexueyuan, Lishi yanjiu suo. 2 vols. Beijing: Zhonghua shuju, 1990.

Mindai Man Mō shiryō: Richō jitsuroku shō 明代滿蒙史料: 李朝實錄抄 (Historical materials excerpted from the Yi Dynasty Veritable Records pertaining to Manchu and Mongolian matters during the Ming). Comp. Tokyo Daigaku, Bungaku Bu. 15 vols. Tokyo: Tokyo Daigaku Bungaku Bu, 1949–59.

Ming Xizong shilu 明熹宗實錄 (Veritable records of Xizong, the Tianqi reign). Collated by Huang Zhangjian 黄彰健. Nan'gang: Institute of History and Philology, Academia Sinica, 1966.

MSLC. See Wang Qiju, comp. *Ming shilu: Lingguo Chaoxian pian ziliao.*

Naikokushientō: Tensō hachinen 內國史院檔: 天聰8年 (The Neiguoshiyuan archives: Tiancong 8 (1634). Comp. Kusunoki Yoshimichi 楠木賢道 et al. Tokyo: Seminar on Manchu History, Toyo Bunko, 2009.

Naikokushientō: Tensō shichinen 內國史院檔: 天聰7 年 (The early Manchu archives of the Qing historiography academy, Tiancong 7 (1633/34). Comp. Kanda Nobuo 神田信夫 et al. Tokyo: Seminar on Manchu History, Toyo Bunko, 2003.

Nishikawa Joken 西川如見 (Kyūrinsai 求林齋). *Ka-I tsūshō kō* 華夷通商考 (On Japan–China trade). Reprint of 1708 edn. In *Nihon keizai taiten* 日本経済大典 (Encyclopedia of Japanese economy), IV: 275384. Ed. Takimoto Seiichi 滝本誠一. Tokyo: Yoshikawa kōbunkan, 1928–30.

Northeast Asian History Foundation website. http.historyfoundation.or.kr/.

Pak Chiwŏn. Trans. Yang Hi Choe-Wall. *The Jehol Diary: Yŏrha ilgi of Pak Chi-wŏn, 1737–1805.* Leiden: E. J. Brill, 2010.

Pan Zhe 潘喆, Li Hongbin 李鴻彬, and Sun Fangming 孫方明, eds. *Qing ruguan qian shiliao xuanji* 清入關前史料選輯 (Selected historical materials from the pre-1644 period). Vol. I. Beijing: Renmin daxue chubanshe, 1985.

Qing chu Neiguoshiyuan Manwen dang'an yibian 清初內國史院滿文檔案譯編 (Chinese translation of early Manchu archives in the Nei Guoshiyuan). Comp. Zhongguo Diyi lishi dang'an guan. 3 vols. Beijing: Guangming ribao chubanshe, 1989.

(Qing) Yongzheng di [清]雍正帝. *Dayi juemi lu* 大義覺迷錄 (A record of how true virtue led to an awakening from delusion). Reproduced in *Jindai Zhongguo shiliao congkan* 近代中國史料叢刊, vols. 351–2. Comp. Shen Yunlong 沈雲龍. Taipei: Wenhai chubanshe, 1966.

T'aejo sillok. Trans. and annotated by Byonghon Choi. *The Annals of King T'aejo, Founder of Korea's Chosŏn Dynasty.* Cambridge, MA: Harvard University Press, 2014.

Tan Qian 談遷, comp. *Guoque* 國榷 (Evaluations of the work of our dynasty). 6 vols. Beijing: Guji chubanshe, 1958.

Tokugawa shoka keifu 德川諸家系譜 (Genealogy of the Tokugawa shogunal house). Comp. Saiki Kazuma 斎木一馬. Rev. Iwasawa Toshihiko 岩沢愿彦. 4 vols. Tokyo: Zokugunsho ruijū kanseikai, 1970–84.

Tokyo daigaku shiryō hensanjo, comp. *Dai Nihon kinsei shiryō: Tō tsūji kaisho nichiroku* 大日本近世史料: 唐通事會所日錄. 7 vols. Tokyo: Tokyo University Press, 1955–68.

Toyo Bunko Tōhoku Ajia kenkyūshitsu 東洋文庫東北アジア研究室 (Northeast Asia Research Center, Toyo Bunko). Comp. *Naikokushientō Tensō gonen* 內國史院檔 天聰五年 (Archival Manchu-language records from the Imperial Historiography office for Tiancong 5, 1631). 3 vols. Tokyo: Toyo Bunko, 2003.

Tsūkō ichiran 通航一覽 (Maritime exchanges). Comp. Hayashi Fukusai 林復齋 et al. 8 vols. Tokyo: Kokusho kankōkai, 1912–13.

Wang Qiju 王其榘, comp. *Ming shilu: Lingguo Chaoxian pian ziliao* 明實錄: 領國朝鮮篇資料 (The Ming Veritable Records: Materials on our neighbor Korea). Beijing: Zhongguo bianjiang shidi yanjiu zhongxin, 1983. Referred to in the text and notes as MSLC.

Qing shilu: Lingguo Chaoxian pian ziliao 清實錄: 領國朝鮮篇資料 (The Qing Veritable Records: Materials on our neighbor Korea). Beijing: Zhongguo shehui kexue yuan, Zhongguo bianjiang shidi yanjiu zhongxin, 1987.

World Heritage Centre (UNESCO) website. http://whc.unesco.org.

Wu Fengpei 吳豐培 et al., comp. *Renchen zhi yi shiliao huiji* 壬晨之役史料匯輯 (Collected historical materials on the Japanese invasion). 2 vols. Beijing: Quanguo tushuguan wenxian suowei fuzhi zhongxin chubanshe, 1990.

Yi Sunsin 李舜臣. *Nanjung ilgi* 亂中日記 (Diary in the midst of the war). Trans. and annotated by Kitajima Manji as *Jinshin waran no kiroku* 壬辰倭亂の記録 (Records of the Japanese invasion of Korea). 3 vols. Tokyo: Heibonsha, 2000.

Yuan Chonghuan 袁崇煥. *Yuan Chonghuan ziliao jilu* 袁崇煥資料集錄 (Collected materials of Yuan Chonghuan). Ed. Yan Chongnian 閻崇年 and Yu Sanle 余三樂. 2 vols. Nanning: Guangxi minzu chubansha, 1984.

Zhu Xi. Trans. and annotated by Patricia Buckley Ebrey. *Chu Hsi's Family Rituals: A Twelfth-Century Chinese Manual for the Performance of Cappings, Weddings, Funerals, and Ancestral Rites*. Princeton: Princeton University Press, 1991.

SECONDARY LITERATURE

Abé, Takao. "The Seventeenth Century Jesuit Missionary Reports on Hokkaido." *Journal of Asian History* 39.2 (2005): 111–28.

Abe, Yoshio. "Development of Neo-Confucianism in Japan, Korea, and China: A Comparative Study." *Acta Asiatica* 19 (1970): 16–39.

Adachi Keiji 足立啓二. "Higashi Ajia ni okeru senka no ryūtsū" 東アジアにおける錢貨の流通 (The circulation of coins in East Asia). In *Ajia no naka no Nihon shi* アジアのなかの日本史 (Japanese history in Asian context), vol. III: *Kaijō no michi* 海上の道 (Maritime routes), pp. 89–114. Ed. Arano Yasunori 荒野泰典, Ishii Masatoshi 石井正敏, and Murai Shōsuke 村井章介. Tokyo: University of Tokyo Press, 1992.

Adams, Edward B. *Palaces of Seoul: Yi Dynasty Palaces in Korea's Capital City*. Seoul: Taewon Publishing Company, 1972.

Ahn, Yonson. "The Korea–China Textbook War – What's It All About?" First posted at *Japan Focus*, February 9, 2006 and posted March 6, 2006 on the History News network, George Mason University. hnn.us/article/21617.

"China and the Two Koreas Clash Over Mount Paekdu/Changbai: Memory Wars Threaten Regional Accommodation." Posted at *Japan Focus*, July 27, 2007. www.japanfocus.org/-Yonson-Ahn/2483.

Aihara, Ryōichi. "Ignacio Moreira's Cartographical Activities in Japan (1590–2), with Special Reference to Hessel Gerritsz's Hemispheric World Map." *Memoirs of the Research Department of the Toyo Bunko* 34 (1976): 209–42.

Allen, Sarah. "Drought, Human Sacrifice and the Mandate of Heaven in a Lost Text from the *Shang Shu*." *Bulletin, School of Oriental and African Studies, London University* 47 (1984): 523–39.

Amino, Yoshihiko. Trans. Gavan McCormack. "Deconstructing 'Japan.'" *East Asian History* 3 (1992): 121–42.

Amino, Yoshihiko. Trans. Alan S. Christy. *Rethinking Japanese History*. Ann Arbor: Center for Japanese Studies, 2012.

Andrade, Tonio. *How Taiwan Became Chinese: Dutch, Spanish, and Han Colonization in the Seventeenth Century*. New York: Columbia University Press, 2008.

Lost Colony: The Untold Story of China's First Great Victory over the West. Princeton: Princeton University Press, 2011.

Arano Yasunori 荒野泰典. "Nihongata Ka-I chitsujo no keisei" 日本型華夷秩序の形成 (The formation of a Japanese-style civilized/barbarian order). In *Nihon no shakaishi 1: Rettō naigai no kōtsū to kokka* 日本の社会史 1：列島内外の交通と国家 (A social history of Japan 1: The state and transport within and without the archipelago), pp. 183–226. Ed. Amino Yoshihiko 網野善彦 et al. Tokyo: Iwanami shoten, 1987.

Kinsei Nihon to Higashi Ajia 近世日本と東アジア (Early modern Japan and Asia). Tokyo: Tokyo University Press, 1988.

"Kaikin to sakoku" 海禁と鎖國 (The maritime prohibition and the closure of the country). In *Ajia no naka no Nihon shi* アジアのなかの日本史 (Japanese history from inside Asia), vol. II: *Gaikō to sensō* 外交と戦争 (Foreign relations and war), pp. 191–222. Ed. Arano Yasunori, Ishii Masatoshi 石井正敏, and Murai Shōsuke 村井章介. Tokyo: University of Tokyo Press, 1992.

"Edo bakufu to Higashi Ajia – aru josei no tegami kara, jō ni kaete" 江戸幕府と東アジア：ある女性の手紙から序にかえて (The Edo shogunate and East Asia from a woman's letter, in place of a preface) in *Edo bakufu to Higashi Ajia* 江戸幕府と東アジア (The Edo shogunate and East Asia), pp. 7–181. Ed. Arano Yasunori. Tokyo: Yoshikawa kōbunkan, 2003.

Asao, Naohiro. "The Sixteenth-Century Unification." In *The Cambridge History of Japan*, vol. IV: *Early Modern Japan*, pp. 40–95. Ed. John Whitney Hall. Cambridge: Cambridge University Press, 1991.

Atwell, William. "Another Look at Silver Imports into China, ca. 1635–1644." *Journal of World History* 16.4 (2005): 467–89.

Atwood, Christopher P. *Encyclopedia of Mongolia and the Mongol Empire*. New York: Facts on File, 2004.

Ba Zhaoxiang 巴兆祥. "17–19 shiji zhongye Zhong Ri shuji jiaoliu shi de jingjixue fenzhe: yi difangzhi wei li" 17–19世紀中葉中日書籍交流史的經濟學分析: 以地方志為例 (An economic analysis of the history of Sino-Japanese book exchange from the seventeenth to the middle of the nineteenth century: a case study of Chinese local gazetteers). *Qingshi yanjiu* 2 (2008): 37–48.

Bai Xinliang 白新良. "Saerhu zhi zhan yu Chaoxian chubing"薩爾湖之戰與朝鮮
出兵 (The battle of Sarhu and the Chosŏn dispatch of troops). *Qingshi yanjiu*
3 (1997): 9–15.

Baranovitch, Nimrod. "Others No More: The Changing Representation of
Non-Han Peoples in Chinese History Textbooks, 1951–2003." *Journal of
Asian Studies* 69.1 (2010): 85–122.

Barfield, Thomas J. *The Perilous Frontier: Nomadic Empires and China*. Oxford:
Blackwell, 1989.

Barnes, Gina L. *The Rise of Civilization in East Asia: The Archeology of China, Korea
and Japan*. London: Thames and Hudson, 1999.

  State Formation in Korea: Historical and Archaeological Perspectives. Richmond:
Curzon, 2001.

Barrett, Tim. "Shinto and Taoism in Early Japan." In *Shinto in History: Ways of
the Kami*, pp. 13–31. Ed. John Breen and Mark Teeuwen. Honolulu:
University of Hawai'i Press, 2000.

Bassin, Mark. "Expansion and Colonialism on the Eastern Frontier: Views of
Siberia and the Far East in Pre-Petrine Russia." *Journal of Historical
Geography* 14.1 (1988): 3–21.

Batten, Bruce L. *To the Ends of Japan: Premodern Frontiers, Boundaries, and
Interactions*. Honolulu: University of Hawai'i Press, 2003.

  Gateway to Japan: Hakata in War and Peace, 500–1300. Honolulu: University of
Hawai'i Press, 2006.

Beckwith, Christopher J. *Empires of the Silk Road: A History of Central Eurasia from
the Bronze Age to the Present*. Princeton: Princeton University Press, 2009.

Bejarano, Shalmit. "Picturing Rice Agriculture and Silk Production:
Appropriation and Ideology in Early Modern Japanese Painting." PhD
thesis, University of Pittsburgh, 2010.

Bentley, John R. "The Birth and Flowering of Japanese Historiography from
Chronicles to Tales to Historical Interpretation." In *The Oxford History of
Historical Writing*, vol. II: *400–1400*, pp. 58–79. Ed. Sarah Foot and Chase
F. Robinson. Oxford: Oxford University Press, 2012.

Berger, Patricia. *Empire of Emptiness: Buddhist Art and Political Authority in Qing
China*. Honolulu: University of Hawai'i Press, 2003.

Bergholz, Fred W. *The Partition of the Steppe: The Struggle of the Russians, Manchus,
and the Zunghar Mongols for Empire in Central Asia, 1619–1758: A Study in
Power Politics*. New York: Peter Lang, 1993.

Berry, Mary Elizabeth. *The Culture of Civil War in Kyoto*. Berkeley: University of
California Press, 1994.

  Japan in Print: Information and Nation in the Early Modern Period. Berkeley:
University of California Press, 2006.

Best, Jonathan. *A History of the Early Korean Kingdom of Paekche, together with an
Annotated Translation of The Paekche Annals of the Samguk Sagi*. Cambridge,
MA: Harvard University Asia Center, 2006.

Bi Aonan 毕奥南. "Lishiyu jing zhong de wangchao Zhongguo jiangyu gainian
bianzhe – yi tianxia, sihai, zhongguo, jiangyu, pantu wei li" 历史语境中的王
朝中国疆域概念辨折 – 以天下, 四海, 中國, 疆域, 盤土 为例 (Analyzing the
traditional concept of China's territory in historical context: the examples of

tianxia, sihai, zhongguo, jiangyu, and pantu). Zhongguo bianjiang shidi yanjiu 16.2 (2006): 9–16.

Bitō, Masahide. "Thought and Religion: 1550–1700." In *The Cambridge History of Japan*, vol. IV: *Early Modern Japan*, pp. 373–424. Ed. John Whitney Hall. Cambridge: Cambridge University Press, 1991.

Bodart-Bailey, Beatrice M. *The Dog Shogun: The Personality and Policies of Tokugawa Tsunayoshi.* Honolulu: University of Hawai'i Press, 2006.

Boot, W. J. "The Death of a Shogun: Deification in Early Modern Japan." In *Shinto in History: Ways of the Kami*, pp. 144–66. Ed. John Breen and Mark Teeuwen. Honolulu: University of Hawai'i Press, 2000.

Borgen, Robert. "Jōjin's Travels from Center to Center (with Some Periphery in Between). In *Heian Japan: Centers and Peripheries*, pp. 384–413. Ed. Mikael Adolphson, Edward Kamens, and Stacie Matsumoto. Honolulu: University of Hawai'i Press, 2006.

"Jōjin's Discoveries in Song China." In *Tools of Culture: Japan's Cultural, Intellectual, Medical, and Technological Contacts in East Asia, 1000s–1500s*, pp. 25–47. Ed. Andrew Edmund Goble, Kenneth R. Robinson, and Haruko Wakabayashi. Ann Arbor: Association for Asian Studies, 2009.

Breen, John and Mark Teeuwen. "Introduction: Shinto Past and Present." In *Shinto in History: Ways of the Kami*, pp. 1–12. Ed. John Breen and Mark Teeuwen. Honolulu: University of Hawai'i Press, 2000.

Breuker, Remco E. "Koryŏ as an Independent Realm: The Emperor's Clothes?" *Korean Studies* 27 (2003): 48–84.

"Contested Objectivities: Ikeuchi Hiroshi, Kim Sanggi and the Tradition of Oriental History (*Tōyōshigaku*) in Japan and Korea." *East Asian History* 29 (2005): 69–106.

"Forging the Truth: Creative Deception and National Identity in Medieval Korea." *East Asian History* 35 (2008): 1–73.

Establishing a Pluralist Society in Medieval Korea, 918–1170: History, Ideology, and Identity in the Koryŏ Dynasty. Leiden: E. J. Brill, 2010.

"Within or Without? Ambiguity of Borders and Koryŏ Koreans' Travels during the Liao, Jin, Song and Yuan." *East Asian History* 38 (2014): 47–61.

Brown, Clayton. "Making the Majority: Defining Han Identity in Chinese Ethnology and Archaeology." PhD thesis, University of Pittsburgh, 2008.

Brown, Delmer M. "Introduction." In *The Cambridge History of Japan*, vol. I: *Ancient Japan*, pp. 1–47. Ed. Delmer M. Brown. Cambridge: Cambridge University Press, 1993.

Brownlee, John S. *Japanese Historians and the National Myths, 1600–1945: The Age of the Gods and Emperor Jinmu.* Vancouver: University of British Columbia Press, 1997.

Burns, Susan L. *Before the Nation: Kokugaku and the Imagining of Community in Early Modern Japan.* Durham: Duke University Press, 2003.

Butler, Kenneth D. "Woman of Power Behind the Kamakura Bakufu: Hōjō Masako." In *Great Historical Figures of Japan*, pp. 91–101. Ed. Hyōe Murakami. Tokyo: Japan Culture Institute, 1978.

Butler, Lee. *Emperor and Aristocracy in Japan, 1467–1680: Resilience and Renewal.* Cambridge, MA: Harvard University Asia Center, 2002.

Byington, Mark. "The Creation of an Ancient Minority Nationality: Koguryŏ in Chinese Historiography." In *Embracing the Other: The Interaction of Korean and Foreign Cultures, Proceedings of the First World Congress of Korean Studies, 2002*, I: 1426–42. Sponsored by the Academy of Korean Studies, International Society for Korean Studies, Association for Korean Studies in Europe, and Korean Studies Association of Australasia. Songnam: The Academy of Korean Studies, 2002.

———. "A History of the Puyŏ State, Its People, and Its Legacy." PhD thesis, East Asian Languages and Civilizations, Harvard University, May 2003.

Carioti, Patrizia. "The Zhengs' Maritime Power in the International Context of the 17th Century Far Eastern Seas: The Rise of a 'Centralised Piratical Organisation' and Its Gradual Development into an Informal 'State.'" *Ming Qing yanjiu* (1996): 29–67.

———. *Cina e Giappone sui mari nei secoli XVI e XVII*. Naples: Edizioni Scientifiche Italiane, 2006.

Chan, Hok-lam. "The Chien-wen, Yung-lo, Hung-hsi, and Hsüan-te Reigns, 1399–1435." In *The Cambridge History of China*, vol. VII, part1: *The Ming Dynasty, 1368–1644*, pp. 182–304. Ed. Frederick W. Mote and Denis Twitchett. Cambridge: Cambridge University Press, 1988.

Chang, Chu-kun. "Some Correlations between the Ancient Religions of Japan and Korea." In *Shamanism: The Spirit World of Korea*, pp. 52–59. Ed. Richard W. I. Guisso and Chai-shin Yu. Berkeley: Asian Humanities Press, 1988.

Chang, Kang-i Sun. "Women's Poetic Witnessing: Late Ming and Late Qing Examples." *In Dynastic Crisis and Cultural Innovation: From the Late Ming to the Late Qing and Beyond*, pp. 504–22. Ed. David Der-wei Wang and Shang Wei. Cambridge, MA: Harvard University Press, 2005.

Chang, K. C. *Art, Myth, and Ritual: The Path to Political Authority in Ancient China*. Cambridge, MA: Harvard University Press, 1983.

Chase, Kenneth W. "Mongol Intentions towards Japan in 1266: Evidence from a Mongol Letter to the Sung." *Sino-Japanese Studies* 9.2 (1997): 13–28.

———. *Firearms: A Global History to 1700*. Cambridge: Cambridge University Press, 2003.

Chen, Chieh-hsien (Chen Jiexian). "The Value of the Chiu Man-chou Tang (The Early Manchu Archives)." In his *Manchu Archival Materials*. Taipei: Linking Publishing, 1988.

Chen Jiexian 陳捷先. "Lue lun Tiancongnian jian HouJin yu Chaoxian de guanxi" 略論天聰年間後金與朝鮮的關係 (Establishing relations between the Later Jin and Chosŏn in the Tiancong years). In *Zhong Chao guanxi shi yanjiu lunwenji* 中朝關係史研究論文集 (Collected writings on the history of Sino-Korean relations), pp. 299–321. Ed. Diao Shuren 刁書仁 and Yi Xingguo 衣興國. Changchun: Jilin wenshi chubanshe, 1995.

Ch'en, Kenneth. *Buddhism in China: A Historical Survey*. Princeton: Princeton University Press, 1964.

Chen Liankai 陳連開. "Zhongguo, Hua-Yi, Fan-Han, Zhonghua, Zhonghua minzu" 中國, 華夷, 藩漢, 中華, 中華民族 (Studying terms such as Zhongguo, Hua–Yi, Fan-Han, Zhonghua, and Zhonghua minzu). In *Zhonghua minzu duoyuan yiti geju* 中華民族多元一體格局 (China's nationalities, diverse but unified), pp. 211–53. Ed. Fei Xiaotong 費孝通. Rev. edn. Beijing: Zhongyang minzu da xue chubanshe, 1999.

Chen Long 陳龍 and Shim Jaegwŏn 沈載權, "Chaoxian yu Ming Qing biaojian waijiao wenti yanjiu" 朝鮮與明清表箋外交問題研究 (Research on the documentary form for diplomatic exchange between Chosŏn and Ming–Qing). *Zhongguo bianjiang shidi yanjiu* 20.1 (2010): 61–68.

Chen, Sanping. *Multicultural China in the Early Middle Ages*. Philadelphia: University of Pennsylvania Press, 2012.

Cheng Chongde 成崇德. "Lun Qingchao jiangyu xingcheng yu lidai jiangyu de guanxi" 論清朝疆域形成與歷代疆域的關係 (On the formation of Qing borderlands and their relationship to historical borderlands). *Zhongguo bianjiang shidi yanjiu* 15.1 (2005): 1–10.

Cheng Nina 程妮哪. "Dongbei gushi fenqi tanze" 東北古史分期攤蹟 (Periodization of the ancient history of the northeast). *Zhongguo bianjiang shidi yanjiu* 14.2 (2002): 1–7.

Cheng Nina, ed. *Dongbei shi* 東北史 (Northeast history). In the "Gaodeng jiaoyu mianxiang ershiyi shiji kecheng jiaocai" 高等教育面向21世紀課程教材 (Higher Education Textbook Series for the Twenty-first Century). Changchun: Jilin daxue chubanshe, 2001.

Chi Tuhwan 池斗煥. *Chosŏn chŏn'gi ŭirye yŏn'gu – sŏngnihak chŏngt'ongnon ŭl chungsim ŭro* 鮮賢前期 儀禮研究 – 性理學 正統論을 中心으로 – (A study of early Chosŏn ritual: focusing on orthodox neo-Confucianism). Seoul: Seoul University Press, 1994.

Chikusa, Tatsuo. "Succession to Ancestral Sacrifices and Adoption of Heirs to the Sacrifices: As Seen from an Inquiry into Customary Institutions in Manchuria." In *Chinese Family Law and Social Change in Historical and Comparative Perspective*, pp. 151–75. Ed. David C. Buxbaum. Seattle: University of Washington Press, 1978.

"China and Korea: A Shared Heritage." *China Heritage Quarterly*, No. 11 (2007). http://www.chinaheritagequarterly.org/editorial/php?issu.

"China Fears Once and Future Kingdom." *New York Times*, August 25, 2004, A3.

"China to put forward 3 historical sites for UNESCO heritage list." www.chinaview.cn 2004–05–12 10.52:53.

Cho Sŏng'ŭl. "Hyondae Chungguk eso ŭi Han'guksa yŏn'gu – kaesŏlsŏ ŭi sidae kubun ŭl chungsim ŭro" (Study of Korean history in contemporary China – focusing on the periodization in surveys). *Kyŏnggi sahak* 8 (2004): 529–53.

Cho Wŏllae 趙湲來. *Saero'un kwanjŏm ŭi Imjin waeran sa yŏn'gu* 새 로 운 觀點 의 임진 왜 란 사 研究 (Research on the Japanese invasion from a new perspective). Seoul: Asea munhwa sa, 2005.

Ch'oe Chaebok 催載馥. "Chosŏn ch'ogi kuksang esŏ ŭi 49che sŏlhaeng kwa pyŏnhwa" 朝鮮初期國喪에서의49 齋설행과 변화 (The forty-nine days of abstinence and changes in state mourning in early Chosŏn). *Chosŏn sidaesa hakpo* 19 (2001): 5–28.

Ch'oe Hyŏsik 崔孝軾. "Myŏng ŭi Imjin waeran ch'amyŏ tonggi wa kŭ silje" 明의壬辰倭亂參與動機와그實際 (The Ming motivation to participate in the Injin waeran and the reality). *Paeksan hakpo* 53 (1999): 245–81.

Ch'oe Kwangsik. "[Tongbuk kongjŏng] ŭi paegyŏng naeyong mit tae'ŭng pang'an – Koguryŏ sa yŏn'gu tong'hyang kwa munje chŏm ŭl chungsim ŭro" (The northeast regional project's background content and a plan for response: focusing on the trends and issues in Koguryŏ history). *Han'guk kodaesa yŏn'gu* 33 (2004): 5–21.

Ch'oe Sŏnhye 崔先惠, "Chosŏn ch'ogi T'aejo, T'aejongdae ch'oje ŭi sihaeng kwa wang kwŏn kanghwa" 조선초기 태조, 태종대 醮祭의 시행과 왕권 강화 (The implementation of the *ch'o* ritual during the T'aejo and T'aejong reigns in early Chosŏn and the strengthening of the royal prerogative). *Han'guk sasang sahak* 17 (2001): 359–93.

Choi, Kwang-shik [Ch'oe Kwangsik]. "What is Behind China's Attempt to Distort the Past?" *The Korea Times*, August 24, 2004. http://times.hankooki.com/.

"Records Contradict China's Claims Over Koguryŏ." *The Korea Times*, August 25, 2004. http://times.hankooki.com/.

"Two Koreas Should Join Forces to Rectify China's Folly." *The Korea Times*, August 26, 2004. http://times.hankooki.com/.

Chŏng Tuhŭi 鄭杜熙. "Chungguk ŭi tongbuk kongjŏng ŭro chegidoen Han'guk sahakkye ŭi myŏt kaji munje" 中國의 東北工程으로 제기된 韓國史學界의 몇 가지 문제 (Several issues in the Korean scholarly world raised by China's northeast project). *Yŏksa hakpo* 183 (2004): 457–76.

Chŏng Tuhŭi and Yi Kyŏngsun, eds. *Imjin waeran, Tong Asia samguk chŏnjaeng* (A transnational history of the Japanese invasions, 1592–1598: the East Asian dimension). Seoul: Hyumŏnisŭt'ŭ, 2007.

Ch'u Myŏngyŏp 秋明燁."Koryŏ chŏn'gi 'Pŏn'蕃 insik kwa 'Tong-Sŏbŏn ŭi hyŏngsŏng" (The consciousness of 'Pŏn'(barbarian) in early Koryŏ and the formation of the eastern and western barbarians). *Yŏksa wa hyŏnsil* 43 (1999): 14–46.

"Koryŏ sigi [haedong] insik kwa [haedong ch'ŏnha]" (The consciousness of the terms *Haedong* [east of the sea] and *haedong ch'ŏnha* (all under heaven east of the sea) during the Koryŏ period). *Han'guksa yŏn'gu* 129 (2005): 29–57.

Chun, Hae-jong. "Sino-Korean Tributary Relations in the Ch'ing Period." In *The Chinese World Order*, pp. 90–111. Ed. John K. Fairbank. Cambridge, MA: Harvard University Press, 1968.

Chung, Chai-sik. "Chŏng Tojŏn: 'Architect' of Yi Dynasty Government and Ideology." In *The Rise of Neo-Confucianism in Korea*, pp. 59–88. Ed. William T. de Bary and JaHyun Kim Haboush. New York: Columbia University Press, 1985.

Clark, Donald N. "Sino-Korean Tributary Relations under the Ming." In *The Cambridge History of China*, vol. VIII, part 2: *The Ming Dynasty, 1368–1644*, pp. 272–300. Ed. Denis Twitchett and Frederick W. Mote. Cambridge: Cambridge University Press, 1998.

Clulow, Adam. "From Global Entrepôt to Early Modern Domain: Hirado, 1609–1641." *Monumenta Nipponica* 65.1 (2010): 1–35.

Coaldrake, William. *Architecture and Authority in Japan*. London: Routledge, 1996.

Collcutt, Martin. "'Nun-Shogun': Politics and Religion in the Life of Hōjō Masako (1157–1225)." In *Engendering Faith: Women and Buddhism in Premodern Japan*, pp. 165–87. Ed. Barbara Ruch. Ann Arbor: Center for Japanese Studies, University of Michigan, 2002.

"Lanxi Daolong (1213–1278) at Kenchōji: Chinese Contributions to the Making of Medieval Japanese Rinzai Zen." In *Tools of Culture: Japan's Cultural, Intellectual, Medical, and Technological Contacts in East Asia, 1000–1500s*, pp. 135–59. Ed Andrew E. Goble, Kenneth R. Robinson, and Haruko Wakabayashi. Ann Arbor: Association for Asian Studies, 2009.

Como, Michael. "Silla Immigrants and the Early Shōtoku Cult: Ritual and the Poetics of Power in Early Yamato." PhD thesis, Stanford University, 2000.

Weaving and Binding: Immigrant Gods and Female Immortals in Ancient Japan. Honolulu: University of Hawai'i Press, 2009.

Conlan, Thomas D. "Thicker than Blood: The Social and Political Significance of Wet Nurses in Japan, 950–1330." *Harvard Journal of Asiatic Studies* 65.1 (2005): 159–205.

Crossley, Pamela K. "*Manzhou yuanliu kao* and the Formalization of the Manchu Heritage." *Journal of Asian Studies* 46.4 (1987): 761–90.

The Manchus. Oxford: Blackwell Publishers, 1997.

A Translucent Mirror: History and Identity in Qing Imperial Ideology. Berkeley: University of California Press, 1999.

Crossley, Pamela Kyle and Evelyn S. Rawski. "A Profile of the Manchu Language in Ch'ing History." *Harvard Journal of Asiatic Studies* 58.1 (1993): 63–102.

Dai, Yingcong. *The Sichuan Frontier and Tibet: Imperial Strategy in the Early Qing*. Seattle: University of Washington Press, 2009.

de Bary, William T. "Introduction." In *The Rise of Neo-Confucianism in Korea*, pp. 1–53. Ed. William T. de Bary and JaHyun Kim Haboush. New York: Columbia University Press, 1985.

De Heer, Philip. "Three Embassies to Seoul: Sino-Korean Relations in the Fifteenth Century." In *Conflict and Accommodation in Early Modern East Asia: Essays in Honour of Erik Zürcher*, pp. 240–58. Ed. Leonard Blussé and Harriet T. Zurndorfer. Leiden: E. J. Brill, 1993.

Deuchler, Martina. "'Heaven Does Not Discriminate': A Study of Secondary Sons in Chosŏn Korea." *Journal of Korean Studies* 6 (1988–89): 121–63.

The Confucian Transformation of Korea: A Study of Society and Ideology. Cambridge, MA: Council on East Asian Studies, Harvard University, 1992.

"Despoilers of the Way – Insulters of the Sages: Controversies over the Classics in Seventeenth-Century Korea." In *Culture and the State in Late Chosŏn Korea*, pp. 91–133. Ed. JaHyun Kim Haboush and Martina Deuchler. Cambridge, MA: Harvard University Asia Center, 1999.

"The Practice of Confucianism: Ritual and Order in Choson Dynasty Korea." In *Rethinking Confucianism: Past and Present in China, Japan, Korea, and Vietnam*, pp. 292–334. Ed. Benjamin A. Elman, John B. Duncan, and Herman Ooms. Los Angeles: Asia Institute, UCLA, 2002.

Di Cosmo, Nicola. "Qing Colonial Administration in Inner Asia." *International History Review* 20.2 (1998): 287–309.

"European Technology and Manchu Power: Reflections on the 'Military Revolution' in Seventeenth-Century China." In *Making Sense of Global History: The Nineteenth International Congress of the Historical Sciences, Oslo 2000, Commemorative Volume*, pp. 119–39. Ed. Sølvi Sogner. Oslo: Universitetsforlaget, 2001.

"Did Guns Matter? Firearms and the Qing Formation." In *The Qing Formation in World Historical Time*, pp. 121–66. Ed. Lynn Struve. Cambridge, MA: Harvard University Asia Center, 2004.

Di Cosmo, Nicola and Dalizhabu Bao. "Introduction: A Brief Survey of Manchu–Mongol Relations Before the Qing Conquest." In *Manchu–Mongol Relations on the Eve of Qing Conquest: A Documentary History*, pp. 1–14. Ed. Nicola Di Cosmo and Dalizhabu Bao. Leiden: Brill, 2003.

Dictionary of Ming Biography. Ed. L. Carrington Goodrich and Chaoying Fang. 2 vols. New York: Columbia University Press, 1976.

Di Yongjun 邱永君. "'Minzu' yici jian yu Nan Qi shu" 民族 一詞 見于'南齐书' (The term 'minzu' appears in the *Nan Qi shu*). *Minzu yanjiu* 3 (2004): 98–99.

Diao Shuren 刁書仁. "Lun Saerhu zhi zhan qianhou Hou Jin yu Chaoxian de guanxi" 論薩爾湖之戰前後後金與朝鮮的關係 (Relations between the Later Jin and Korea before and after the Battle of Sarhū). *Qingshi yanjiu* 4 (2001): 43–50.

"Lun Ming qianqi Woduoli Nüzhen yu Ming, Chaoxian de guanxi" 論 明 前 期 斡朵里 女貞 與 明, 朝鮮 的 關係 (On the Woduoli Jurchen and Ming-Chosŏn relations in early Ming). *Zhongguo bianjiang shidi yanjiu* 12.1 (2002): 44–54.

"Kangxi nianjian Mukedeng chabian dingjie kaobian" 康熙年間穆克登查編定 界考辨 (Analyzing Mukedeng's frontier survey and fixing of the border in the Kangxi period). *Zhongguo bianjiang shidi yanjiu* 13.3 (2003): 45–56.

Don, Ju Bo. "Problems Concerning the Basic Historical Documents Related to the Samhan." In *Early Korea*, vol. II: *The Samhan Period in Korean History*, pp. 95–122. Ed. Mark E. Byington. Cambridge, MA: Korea Institute, Harvard University, 2011.

Dow, Tsung-i. "The Confucian Concept of a Nation and Its Historical Practice." *Asian Profile* 10.4 (1982): 347–61.

Dreyer, Edward L. "Military Origins of Ming China." In *The Cambridge History of China*, vol. VII, part 1: *The Ming Dynasty, 1368–1644*, pp. 58–106. Ed. Frederick W. Mote and Denis Twitchett. Cambridge: Cambridge University Press, 1988.

Du Yonghao 都永浩 and Wang Yulang 王禹浪. "Dui dongbeiYa minzu yu lishi wenti yanjiu de lilun sikao" 對東北亞民族與歷史問題研究的理論思考 (Theoretical deliberations on historical research issues concerning Northeast Asian peoples). *Zhongguo bianjiang shidi yanjiu* 13.3 (2003): 39–44.

Duara, Prasenjit. "Superscribing Symbols: The Myth of Guandi, Chinese God of War." *Journal of Asian Studies* 47.4 (1988): 778–95.

Rescuing History from the Nation: Questioning Narratives of Modern China. Chicago: University of Chicago Press, 1995.

Duncan, John B. "The Formation of the Central Aristocracy in Early Koryŏ." *Korean Studies* 12 (1988): 39–58.

"The Social Background of the Founding of the Chosŏn Dynasty: Change or Continuity?" *Journal of Korean Studies* 6 (1988–89): 66–75.

The Origins of the Chosŏn Dynasty. Seattle: University of Washington Press, 2000.

"Historical Memories of Koguryŏ in Koryŏ and Chosŏn Korea." *Journal of Inner and East Asian Studies* 1 (2004): 119–36.

Dunnell, Ruth W. "The Hsi Hsia." In *The Cambridge History of China*, vol. VI: *Alien Regimes and Border States, 907–1368*, pp. 154–214. Ed. Herbert Franke and Denis Twitchett. Cambridge: Cambridge University Press, 1994.

The Great State of White and High: Buddhism and State Formation in Eleventh-Century Xia. Honolulu: University of Hawai'i Press, 1996.

Ebrey, Patricia B. "Types of Lineages in Ch'ing China: A Reexamination of the Chang Lineage of T'ung-ch'eng." *Ch'ing-shih wen-t'i* 4.9 (1983): 1–20.

"The Early Stages in the Development of Descent Group Organization." In *Kinship Organization in Late Imperial China, 1000–1940*, pp. 16–61. Ed. Patricia Buckley Ebrey and James L. Watson. Berkeley: University of California Press, 1986.

Confucianism and Family Rituals in Imperial China: A Social History of Writing about Rites. Princeton: Princeton University Press, 1991.

Ebrey, Patricia Buckley and James L. Watson. "Introduction." In *Kinship Organization in Late Imperial China, 1000–1940*, pp. 1–15. Ed. Patricia Buckley Ebrey and James L. Watson. Berkeley: University of California Press, 1986.

Edwards, Walter. "In Pursuit of Himiko: Postwar Archaeology and the Location of Yamatai." *Monumenta Nipponica* 51.1 (1996): 53–79.

Elisonas, Jurgis. "The Inseparable Trinity: Japan's Relations with China and Korea." In *The Cambridge History of Japan*, vol. IV: *Early Modern Japan*, pp. 235–300. Ed. John Whitney Hall. Cambridge: Cambridge University Press, 1991.

Elliott, Mark C. "Whose Empire Shall It Be? Manchu Figurations of Historical Process in the Early Seventeenth Century." In *Time, Temporality, and Imperial Transition: East Asia from Ming to Qing*, pp. 31–72. Ed. Lynn A. Struve. Honolulu: University of Hawai'i Press, 2005.

"Manshūgo bunsho shiryō to atarashii Shinchōshi" 滿州語文書資料と新しい清朝史 (Manchu language archives and the new Qing history). In *Shinchōshi kenkyū no aratanaru chihei – fuildo to bunko wo otte* 清朝史研究の新たなる地坪 ― フィールドと文庫を追って (New perspectives in Qing history: in pursuit of fieldwork and texts), pp. 124–39. Ed. Hosoya Yoshio 細谷良夫. Tokyo: Yamakawa shuppansha, 2008.

"*Hushuo:* The Northern Other and the Naming of the Han Chinese." In *Critical Han Studies: The History, Representation, and Identity of China's Majority*, pp. 173–90. Ed. Thomas S. Mullaney, James Leibold, Stéphane Gros, and Eric Vanden Bussche. Berkeley: University of California Press, 2012.

Ellwood, Robert S. *The Feast of Kingship: Accession Ceremonies in Ancient Japan.* Tokyo: Sophia University, 1973.

Elman, Benjamin A. "Geographical Research in the Ming–Ch'ing Period." *Monumenta Serica* 35 (1981–83): 1–18.

Classicism, Politics, and Kinship: The Ch'ang-chou School of New Text Confucianism in Late Imperial China. Berkeley: University of California Press, 1990.

"Jesuit *Scientia* and Natural Studies in Late Imperial China, 1600–1800." *Journal of Early Modern History* 6.3 (2002): 209–31.

"The Search for Evidence from China: Qing Learning and Kōshūgaku in Tokugawa Japan." In *Sagacious Monks and Bloodthirsty Warriors: Chinese Views of Japan in the Ming–Qing Period*, pp. 158–82. Ed. Joshua A. Fogel. Norwalk: Eastbridge, 2002.

Elverskog, Johan. *Our Great Qing: The Mongols, Buddhism and the State in Late Imperial China.* Honolulu: University of Hawai'i Press, 2006.

Em, Henry H. "Minjok as a Modern and Democratic Construct: Sin Ch'aeho's Historiography." In *Colonial Modernity in Korea*, pp. 336–61. Ed. Gi-Wook Shin and Michael Robinson. Cambridge, MA: Harvard University Asia Center, 1999.

The Great Enterprise: Sovereignty and Historiography in Modern Korea. Durham: Duke University Press, 2013.

Emori Susumu 榎森進. *Hokkaidō kinseishi no kenkyū – Bakuhan taisei to Ezochi* 北海道近世史の研究–幕藩体制と蝦夷地 (The early modern history of Hokkaidō – the bakuhan system and Ezochi). Sapporo: Hokkaidō shuppan kikaku sentā, 1982.

"Jūsan-jūkyū seiki no Nihon ni okeru Hoppō chiiki no kyōkai ninshiki" 13–19 世紀の日本における北方地域の境界認識 (Perceptions of northern boundaries in thirteenth to nineteenth century Japan). *Rekishigaku kenkyū* 613 (1990): 2–16.

"Jūsan – jūshichi seiki no Ainu minzoku to shūhen shokoku, shominzoku" 十三 – 十七世紀のアイヌ民族と周邊諸國, 諸民族 (The Ainu people from the thirteenth to seventeenth centuries and the states and peoples on their periphery). In *Chūsei shi kōza* 中世史講座 (Lectures on medieval history) 11: *Chūsei ni okeru chiiki, minzoku no kōryū* 中世における地域, 民族の交流 (Regional and ethnic exchanges in the middle ages), pp. 344–81. Ed. Kimura Shōsaburō 木村尚三郎. Tokyo: Gakusha, 1996,

Fairbank, John K. "A Preliminary Framework." In *The Chinese World Order: Traditional China's Foreign Relations*, pp. 5–11. Ed. John K. Fairbank. Cambridge, MA: Houghton Mifflin, 1968.

Fairbank, John K. and S. Y. Teng. "On the Ch'ing tributary system." *Harvard Journal of Asiatic Studies* 6.2 (1941): 135–246.

Fairbank, John K. and Ssū-yu Teng. *Ch'ing Administration: Three Studies.* Cambridge, MA: Harvard University Press, 1960.

Fang Weigui 方維規. "Lun jindai sixiang shi shang de 'minzu,' 'Nation' yu Zhongguo" 論近代 思想史 上的 '民族' ('Nation'), 與 中國 ('Minzu,' 'Nation,' and China in modern intellectual history). Xianggang *Ershiyi shiji* 70 (2002): 33–43.

Farmer, Edward L. *Early Ming Government: The Evolution of Dual Capitals.* Cambridge, MA: East Asian Research Center, Harvard University, 1976.

Farquhar, David M. "Chinese Communist Assessments of a Foreign Conquest Dynasty." In *History in Communist China*, pp. 175–88. Ed. Albert Feuerwerker. Cambridge, MA: MIT Press, 1968.

"Emperor as Bodhisattva in the Governance of the Qing Empire." *Harvard Journal of Asiatic Studies* 38 (1978): 5–34.

Farris, William Wayne. *Sacred Texts and Buried Treasures: Issues in the Historical Archaeology of Ancient Japan*. Honolulu: University of Hawai'i Press, 1998.

Fawcett, Clare. "Nationalism and Postwar Japanese Archaeology." In *Nationalism, Politics, and the Practice of Archaeology*, pp. 232–46. Ed. Philip L. Kohl and Clare Fawcett. Cambridge: Cambridge University Press, 1995.

"Archaeology and Japanese Identity." In *Multicultural Japan: Paleolithic to Postmodern*, pp. 60–77. Ed. Donald Denoon, Mark Hudson, Gavan McCormack, and Tessa Morris-Suzuki. Cambridge: Cambridge University Press, 1996.

Fei Xiaotong 費孝通. Ed. *Zhonghua minzu duoyuan yiti geju (xiu ding ben)* 中華民族多元一體格局 (China's nationalities, diverse but unified). Rev. edn. Beijing: Zhongyang minzu daxue chubanshe, 1999.

Ferejohn, John A. and Frances McCall Rosenbluth, eds. *War and State Building in Medieval Japan*. Stanford: Stanford University Press, 2010.

Fisher, Thomas S. "Accommodation and Loyalism: The Life of Lü Liu-liang (1629–1683)." *Papers on Far Eastern History* 15 (1977): 97–104; 16 (1977): 107–45; 18 (1978): 1–42.

Fiskesjö, Magnus. "On the 'Raw' and the 'Cooked' Barbarians of Imperial China." *Inner Asia* 1 (1999): 139–68.

Flynn, Dennis O. and Arturo Giraldez. "China and the Manila Galleons." In *Japanese Industrialization and the Asian Economy*, pp. 71–90. Ed. A. J. H. Latham and Heita Kawakatsu. London: Routledge, 1994.

"Arbitrage, China, and World Trade in the Early Modern Period." *Journal of the Economic and Social History of the Orient* 38.4 (1995): 429–48.

Flynn, Dennis O. and Marie A. Lee. "East Asian Trade Before/After 1590s Occupation of Korea: Modeling Imports and Exports in Global Context." *Asian Review of World Histories* 1.1 (2013): 117–49.

Fogel, Joshua A. *Politics and Sinology: The Case of Naitō Konan (1866–1934)*. Cambridge, MA: Council on East Asian Studies, Harvard University, 1984.

"On Japanese Expressions for 'China'." *Sino-Japanese Studies* 2.1 (1989): 5–16.

"Chinese Understanding of the Japanese Language from Ming to Qing." In *Sagacious Monks and Bloodthirsty Warriors: Chinese Views of Japan in the Ming-Qing Period*, pp. 63–87. Ed. Joshua A. Fogel. Norwalk: Eastbridge, 2002.

Franke, Herbert. *From Tribal Chieftain to Universal Emperor and God: The Legitimation of the Yuan Dynasty*. Munich: Verlag der Bayerischen Akademie der Wissenschaften, 1978.

"The Chin Dynasty." In *The Cambridge History of China*, vol. VI: *Alien Regimes and Border States, 907–1368*, pp. 215–320. Ed. Herbert Franke and Denis Twitchett. Cambridge: Cambridge University Press, 1994.

Franke, Herbert and Denis Twitchett. "Introduction." In *The Cambridge History of China*, vol. VI: *Alien Regimes and Border States, 907–1368*, pp. 1–42. Ed. Herbert Franke and Denis Twitchett. Cambridge: Cambridge University Press, 1994.

Franke, Wolfgang. *An Introduction to the Sources of Ming History*. Kuala Lumpur: University of Malaya Press, 1968.

Fu Langyun 傅朗云. "Zhongguo dongbei yu gudai dongbei Yi" 中國東北與古代
　　東北夷 (China's northeast and the northeast Yi of ancient times). *Zhongguo
　　bianjiang shidi yanjiu* 2 (1992): 87–88, 114.

Fujita Satoru 藤田覚. "Ezochi dai-ichiji jōchi no seiji katei" 蝦夷地第一次上知の
　　政治過程 (The political process of the first knowledge of Ezochi). In *Nihon
　　zenkindai no kokka to taigai kankei* 日本前近代の國家と對外關係 (Japan's
　　premodern state and foreign relations), pp. 605–35. Ed. Tanaka Takeo 田中
　　健夫. Tokyo: Yoshikawa kōbunkan, 1987.

Fujita Yūji 藤田雄二. "Kinsei Nihon ni okeru jinminzoku chūshinteki shikō –
　　'senmin' ishiki to shite no Nihon chūshin shugi" 近世日本における自民族
　　中心的思考 –「選民」意識としての日本中心主義 (An analysis of the core
　　of ethnocentrism in Japan: the concept of a "chosen people" and Japan-
　　centered ideology). *Shisō* 832 (1993): 106–29.

Funakoshi Akio 船越昭. *Sakoku Nihon ni kita [Kōkizu] no chirigaku shiteki
　　kenkyū* 鎖国日本にきた「康熙圖」の地理学史的研究 (Research on the
　　geographical history of the Kangxi map which entered Japan in the era of
　　seclusion). Tokyo: Hōsei daigaku shuppankyoku, 1986.

"Gaogouli role in Chinese history traded: Researcher warns against politicization
　　of studies." *China Daily*, June 24, 2003, p. 5.

Geiss, James. "The Leopard Quarter During the Cheng-te Reign." *Ming Studies*
　　24 (1987): 1–38.

"The Cheng-te Reign, 1506–1521." In *The Cambridge History of China*,
　　vol. VII, part 1: *The Ming Dynasty, 1368–1644*, pp. 403–39. Ed. Frederick
　　W. Mote and Denis Twitchett. Cambridge: Cambridge University Press,
　　1988.

"The Chia-ching Reign, 1522–1566." In *The Cambridge History of China*, vol. VII,
　　part 1: *The Ming Dynasty, 1368–1644*, pp. 440–510. Ed. Frederick W. Mote
　　and Denis Twitchett. Cambridge: Cambridge University Press, 1988.

Goble, Andrew E. *Kenmu: Go-Daigo's Revolution*. Cambridge, MA: Council on
　　East Asian Studies, Harvard University, 1996.

"Kajiwara Shōzen (1265–1337) and the Medical Silk Road: Chinese and
　　Arabic Influences on Early Medieval Japanese Medicine." In *Tools of
　　Culture: Japan's Cultural, Intellectual, Medical, and Technological Contacts in
　　East Asia, 1000–1500s*, pp. 231–57. Ed. Andrew E. Goble, Kenneth
　　R. Robinson, and Haruko Wakabayashi. Ann Arbor: Association for Asian
　　Studies, 2009.

Goble, Andrew E., Kenneth R. Robinson, and Haruko Wakabayashi.
　　"Introduction." In *Tools of Culture: Japan's Cultural, Intellectual, Medical,
　　and Technological Contacts in East Asia, 1000–1500s*, pp. 1–17. Eds. Andrew
　　E. Goble, Kenneth R. Robinson, and Haruko Wakabayashi. Ann Arbor:
　　Association for Asian Studies, 2009.

"Goguryeo's Popularity? Blame it on the Chinese." *JoongAng Daily*, July 13,
　　2006, p. 8.

Goldstone, Jack A. *Revolution and Rebellion in the Early Modern World*. Berkeley:
　　University of California Press, 1991.

"The Problem of the 'Early Modern' World." *Journal of the Economic and Social
　　History of the Orient* 41.3 (1998): 249–81.

"Neither Late Imperial nor Early Modern: Efflorescences and the Qing Formation in World History." In *The Qing Formation in World-Historical Time*, pp. 242–302. Ed. Lynn A. Struve. Cambridge, MA: Harvard University Asia Center, 2004.

Goodrich, L. Carrington and Chao-ying Fang, eds. *Dictionary of Ming Biography: 1368–1644*. 2 vols. New York: Columbia University Press, 1976.

Granet, Marcel. Trans. Maurice Freedman. *The Religion of the Chinese People*. Oxford: Blackwell, 1975.

Grapard, Allan G. *The Protocol of the Gods: A Study of the Kasuga Cult in Japanese History*. Berkeley: University of California Press, 1992.

"Of Emperors and Foxy Ladies." *Cahiers d'Extrême-Asie* 13 (2002–3): 127–49.

Grayson, J. H. "Some Structural Patterns of the Royal Families of Ancient Korea." *Korea Journal* 16.6 (1976): 27–32.

Guan Jialu 關嘉錄 and Tong Yonggong 佟永功, "Zhongguo Manwen jiqi wenxian zhengli yanjiu" 中國滿文及其文獻整理研究 (On the organization of China's Manchu-language texts and their contribution). *Qingshi yanjiu* 4 (1991): 29–36.

Gunder Frank, Andre. *ReOrient: Global Economy in the Asian Age*. Berkeley: University of California Press, 1998.

Guo Songyi 郭松義. "Lun Ming Qing shiqi de Guan Yu chongbai" 論明清時期的關羽崇拜 (On the worship of Guan Yu in Ming and Qing times). *Zhongguo shi yanjiu* 3 (1990): 127–39.

Guo Yunjing. "Views of Japan and Policies Toward Japan in the Early Qing." In *Sagacious Monks and Bloodthirsty Warriors: Chinese Views of Japan in the Ming–Qing Period*, pp. 88–108. Ed. Joshua A. Fogel. Norwalk: Eastbridge, 2002.

Guy, R. Kent. *The Emperor's Four Treasures: Scholars and the State in the Late Ch'ien-lung Era*. Cambridge, MA: Harvard University Asia Center, 1987.

Qing Governors and Their Provinces: The Evolution of Territorial Administration in China, 1644–1796. Seattle: University of Washington Press, 2010.

Ha Ubong. "Chosŏn chŏn'gi taeŭi kwan'gye e nat'anan cha'a insik kwa t'aja insik" (Self-perception and the perception of others appearing in foreign relations in early Chosŏn). *Han'guksa yŏn'gu* 123 (2003): 247–70.

Haboush, JaHyun Kim. "The Education of the Yi Crown Prince: A Study in Confucian Pedagogy." In *The Rise of Neo-Confucianism in Korea*, pp. 161–222. Ed. William T. de Bary and JaHyun Kim Haboush. New York: Columbia University Press, 1985.

A Heritage of Kings: One Man's Monarchy in the Confucian World. New York: Columbia University Press, 1988.

"Constructing the Center: The Ritual Controversy and the Search for a New Identity in Seventeenth-Century Korea." In *Culture and the State in Late Chosŏn Korea*, pp. 46–90. Ed. JaHyun Kim Haboush and Martina Deuchler. Cambridge, MA: Harvard University Asia Center, 1999.

The Confucian Kingship in Korea: Yŏngjo and the Politics of Sagacity. New York: Columbia University Press, 2001.

"Contesting Chinese Time, Nationalizing Temporal Space: Temporal Inscription in Late Chosŏn Korea." In *Time, Temporality, and Imperial*

Transition: East Asia from Ming to Qing, pp. 115–41. Ed. Lynn Stuve. Honolulu: University of Hawai'i Press, 2006.

"Yun Hyu and the Search for Dominance: A Seventeenth-Century Korean Reading of the *Offices of Zhou* and the *Rituals of Zhou.*" In *Statecraft and Classical Learning: The* Rituals of Zhou *in East Asian History,* pp. 309–29. Ed. Benjamin A. Elman and Martin Kern. Leiden: E. J. Brill, 2010.

Haboush, JaHyun Kim, ed. *Epistolary Korea: Letters in the Communicative Space of the Chosŏn, 1392–1910.* New York: Columbia University Press, 2009.

Habu, Junko and Clare Fawcett. "Jomon Archaeology and the Representation of Japanese Origins." *Antiquity* 73 (1999): 587–93.

Hall, John. "Notes on the Early Ch'ing Copper Trade with Japan." *Harvard Journal of Asiatic Studies,* 12.3/4 (1949): 444–61.

"Introduction." In *The Cambridge History of Japan,* vol. IV: *Early Modern Japan,* pp. 1–39. Ed. John W. Hall. New York: Cambridge University Press, 1991.

"The *Bakuhan* System." In *The Cambridge History of Japan,* vol. IV: *Early Modern Japan,* pp. 130–82. Ed. John W. Hall. New York: Cambridge University Press, 1991.

Hamashita Takeshi 浜下武志. "Chūgoku no gin kyūshūryoku to chōkō bōeki kankei" 中國の銀吸收力と朝貢貿易關係 (The absorptive power of China for silver and tributary trade relations). In *Ajia kōekiken to Nihon kōgyoka* アジア交易圏と日本工業化 (The Asian exchange realm and Japanese industrialization), pp. 22–50. Ed. Hamashita Takeshi and Kawakatsu Heita 川勝平太. Tokyo: Libro, 1991.

"The Tribute Trade System and Modern Asia." In *Japanese Industrialization and the Asian Economy,* pp. 91–107. Ed. A. J. H. Latham and Heita Kawakatsu. London: Routledge, 1994.

Han Ch'unsun 韓春順. "Sŏngjong ch'ogi Chŏnghŭi wanghu (Sejo bi) ŭi chŏngch'i chŏngdan kwa hunch'ŏk chŏngch'i (Dowager Queen Chŏnghŭi's political decisions and affinal politics in the early Sŏngjong reign). *Chosŏn sidaesa hakpo* 22 (2002): 29–74.

Han Chunghŭi 韓忠熙. "Chosŏn Sejodae (1455–1468) ŭi naejongch'in e taehayŏ" 朝鮮世祖代 (1455–1468)의內宗親에 대하여 (On the royal kinsmen in the Chosŏn Sejo reign, 1455–1468). *Kyŏngbuk sahak* 21 (1998): 913–944.

Chosŏn ch'ogi kwanjik kwa chŏngch'i (Bureaucratic offices and politics in early Chosŏn). Seoul: Kyemyŏng taehakgyo ch'ulpanbu, 2008.

Han Hyŏngju 韓享周. "Chosŏn Sejodae ŭi chech'ŏn ye e taehan yŏn'gu – T'ae, Sejongdae chech'ŏn ye wa ŭi pigyo – kŏmt'o rŭl chungsim ŭro" (Research on the sacrifice to heaven during the Sejo reign, focusing on an examination and comparison with the sacrifice to heaven ritual in the T'aejo and Sejong reigns). *Chindan hakpo* 81 (1996): 107–33.

Chosŏn ch'ogi kukka cherye yŏn'gu 朝鮮初期國家祭禮研究 (Research on state rituals in early Chosŏn). Seoul: Ilchogak, 2002.

Han, Kyung Koo. "The Archaeology of the Ethnically Homogeneous Nation-State and Multi-Culturalism in Korea." *Korea Journal* 47.4 (2007): 8–31.

Han Myŏnggi 韓明基. *Imjin waeran kwa Han-Chung kwan'gye* 壬辰倭亂 과 韓中關係 (The Japanese invasion of Korea and Korean–China relations). Seoul: Yŏksa Pip'yŏngsa, 1999.

Kwanghaegun: t'agwŏrhan oegyo chŏngch'aek ŭl p'yŏlch'in kunju (Kwanghaegun: the king with an excellent foreign policy). Seoul: Yŏksa Pip'yŏngsa, 2000.

"Injo panjŏng ihu chaejo Pug'in e taehan sogo" 仁祖反正이후在朝北人에 대한 小考 (Inquiry into the northerners at court after the Injo coup d'etat). In *Ch'oe Sŭnghŭi kyosu kinyŏm nonmunjip, Chosŏn ŭi chŏngch'i wa sahoe*, pp. 279–96. Ed. Ch'oe Sŭnghŭi kyosu kinyŏm nonmunjiphoe. Seoul: Chimmundang, 2002.

"Sipch'il, p'al segi Han-Chung kwan'gye wa Injo panjŏng – Chosŏn hugi ŭi 'Injo panjŏng pyŏnmu' munje" 17, 18 世紀韓中關係와 仁祖反正 – 조선후기의 [仁祖反正辨誣] 문제 (Sino-Korean relations in the seventeenth and eighteenth centuries and the Injo coup – the issue of the 'Injo coup controversy' in late Chosŏn). *Han'guksa hakpo* 13 (2002): 9–41.

"Chosŏn kwan'gye (Myŏng-Ch'ŏng kwan'gye) ŭi ch'u' i" (A shift in Chosŏn–Qing relations). In *Chosŏn chunggi chŏngch'i wa chŏngch'aek, Injo – Hyŏnjong sigi* (Politics and Policy in the middle Chosŏn period, from Injo to Hyŏnjong), pp. 259–304. Comp. Han'guk yŏksa yŏn'guhoe, 17 segi chŏngch'isa yŏn'guban. Seoul: Arknet, 2003.

"Pyŏngja horan p'aejŏn ŭi chŏngch'ijŏk p'ajang – Ch'ŏng ŭi Chosŏn ap'pak kwa Injo ŭi tae'ŭng ŭl chungsim ŭro – " 丙子胡亂패전의정치적 파장 – 청의조선압박과 仁祖의 대응을 중심으로 (The second Manchu invasion surrender's political effects: focusing on the Qing pressure on Chosŏn and Injo's response). *Tongbong hakji* 119 (2003): 53–93.

Han Ugŭn 韓우근. "Chosŏn wangjo ch'ogi e issŏsŏ ŭi Yugyo inyŏm ŭi silch'ŏn kwa sin'ang, chonggyo chesa munje rŭl chungsim ŭro" 朝鮮王朝初期에있어서의儒教理念의實踐과信仰, 宗教祀祭問題를中心으로 (The implementation of Confucian concepts, beliefs and religion in the early Chosŏn – focusing on ritual issues). *Han'guk saron* 3 (1976): 147–228.

"Policies Toward Buddhism in Late Koryŏ and Early Chosŏn." In *Buddhism in the Early Chosŏn: Suppression and Transformation*, pp. 1–58. Ed. Lewis R. Lancaster and Chai-shin Yu. Berkeley: University of California Institute of East Asian Studies, 1996.

Han, Young-woo. "Kija Worship in the Koryŏ and Early Yi Dynasties: A Cultural Symbol in the Relationship Between Korea and China." In *The Rise of Neo-Confucianism in Korea*, pp. 349–74. Ed. William T. de Bary and JaHyun Kim Haboush. New York: Columbia University Press, 1985.

Han, Young-woo. Trans. Byonghyon Choi. "The Historical Development of Korean Cartography." In *The Artistry of Early Korean Cartography*, pp. 3–90. Ed. Young-woo Han, Hwi-Joon Ahn, and Bae Woo Sung. Larkspur, CA: Tamal Vista Publications, 1999.

Han'guk kodaesa yŏn'gu 韓國古代史研究 (Research on ancient Korean history). 33 (2004). "T'ŭkchip: Chungguk ŭi Koguryŏsa waegok ŭi silt'ae wa taech'ŏ pang'an" (Special edition: The erroneous distortions of China's Koguryŏ history and a plan to respond).

Han'guk sa yŏn'gu 韓國史研究 (Research on Korean history). 129 (2005). "T'ŭkchip: Han'guk ŭi yŏngt'o wa yŏngt'o ŭisik" (Korea's territory and territorial consciousness).

Hanley, Susan B. "Family and Fertility in Four Tokugawa Villages." In *Family and Population in East Asian History*, pp. 196–228. Ed. Susan B. Hanley and Arthur P. Wolf. Stanford: Stanford University Press, 1985.

Hanley, Susan B. and Kozo Yamamura. *Economic and Demographic Change in Preindustrial Japan, 1600–1868*. Princeton: Princeton University Press, 1977.

Hao Qingyun 郝慶雲. "Sushen – Nüzhen zuxi lishi yange yu fenbu diyu yanjiu yu Zhongguo bianjiangxue de jianshe" 蕭慎 – 女偵族系歷史沿革與分布地域研究與中國邊疆學的建設 (Sushen: the historical evolution of the Jurchen people, the study of their regional distribution, and the establishment of the study of Chinese borderlands). *Manzu yanjiu* 2 (2010): 11–14.

Hao Rui 郝瑞 (Stevan Harrell). Trans. Yang Zhiming 楊志明. "Lun yixie renleixue zhuanmen shuyu de lishi he fanyi" 論一些人類學專門術語的歷史和翻譯 (On the history and translation of many specialized terms in anthropology). *Shijie minzu* 4 (2001): 65–72.

Hao Shiyuan 郝時遠. "Zhongwen 'minzu' yi ci yuanliu kaobian" 中文 '民族' 一詞源流考辨 (Investigation of the origin of the phrase 'minzu' in Chinese). *Minzu yanjiu* 6 (2004): 60–69.

Hardacre, Helen. *Shinto and the State, 1868–1988*. Princeton: Princeton University Press, 1989.

Harootunian, Harry D. "The Function of China in Tokugawa Thought." In *The Chinese and the Japanese: Essays in Political and Cultural Interactions*, pp. 9–36. Ed. Akira Iriye. Princeton: Princeton University Press, 1980.

Hartman, Charles. "Chinese Historiography in the Age of Maturity, 960–1368." In *The Oxford History of Historical Writing*, vol. II: *400–1400*, pp. 37–57. Ed. Sarah Foot and Chase F. Robinson. Oxford: Oxford University Press, 2012.

Hartman, Charles, and Anthony DeBlasi. "The Growth of Historical Method in Tang China." In *The Oxford History of Historical Writing*, vol. II: *400–1400*, pp. 17–36. Ed. Sarah Foot and Chase F. Robinson. Oxford: Oxford University Press, 2012.

Hawley, Samuel. *The Imjin War: Japan's Sixteenth-Century Invasion of Korea and Attempt to Conquer China*. Seoul: Royal Asiatic Society, Korea Branch and Berkeley: Institute of East Asian Studies, University of California, 2005.

Hayami, Akira. "The Myth of Primogeniture and Impartible Inheritance in Tokugawa Japan." *Journal of Family History* 8 (1983): 3–29.

He, Yuming. "The Book and the Barbarian in Ming China and Beyond: The *Luo chong lu*, or "Record of Naked Creatures." *Asia Major* 24.1 (2011): 43–85.

Home and the World: Editing the "Glorious Ming" in Woodblock-Printed Books of the Sixteenth and Seventeenth Centuries. Cambridge, MA: Harvard University Asia Center, 2013.

Heer, Philip de. *The Caretaker Emperor: Aspects of the Imperial Institution in Fifteenth-Century China as Reflected in the Political History of the Reign of Chu Ch'i-yü*. Leiden: E. J. Brill, 1986.

Hellyer, Robert L. *Defining Engagement: Japan and Global Contexts, 1640–1868*. Cambridge, MA: Harvard University Asia Center, 2009.

Hess, Laura E. "Qing Reactions to the Reimportation of Confucian Canonical Works from Tokugawa Japan." In *Sagacious Monks and Bloodthirsty Warriors:*

Chinese Views of Japan in the Ming–Qing Period, pp. 126–57. Ed. Joshua A. Fogel. Norwalk: Eastbridge, 2002.

Hinsch, Bert. "Myth and the Construction of Foreign Ethnic Identity in Early and Medieval China." *Asian Ethnicity* 5.1 (2004): 84–103.

Hiraki Makoto 平木實. "Chōsen kōki ni okeru Enkudan saishi ni tsuite (2)" 朝鮮後期における圓丘壇祭祀について (2) (The Altar to Heaven sacrifice in late Chosŏn, 2). *Chōsen gakuhō* 176/77 (2000): 283–310.

Hiraishi Naoki 平石直昭. "Tokugawa shisō shi ni okeru [ten] to [onigami]" 德川思想史に置ける「天」と [鬼神] ("Heaven" and "demons" in Tokugawa thought). In *Ajia kara kangaeru 7: Sekaizō no keisei* アジアからかんがえる 7: 世界像の形成 (From the perspective of Asia, vol. VII: The formation of world images), pp. 243–86. Ed. Mizoguchi Yūzō 溝口雄三 et al. Tokyo: Tokyo University Press, 1994.

Hirano, Kunio 平野邦雄。. "The Yamato State and Korea in the Fourth and Fifth Centuries." *Acta Asiatica* 31 (1977): 51–77.

Kikajin to kodai kokka 帰化人と古代国家 (Immigrants and the ancient state). Tokyo: Yoshikawa kōbunkan, 1993.

Hŏ Ch'iŭn 許芝銀. "Kŭnse ch'yosyu (Choshu) Sach'ŭma (Satsuma) ŭi Chosŏn'ŏ tongsa wa Chosŏn chŏngbo sujip" 근세쵸슈 (長州), 사츠마 (薩摩)의 朝鮮語通詞와조선정보수집 (The Korean interpreters of Choshu and Satsuma and information gathering about Chosŏn). *Tongyang sahak yŏn'gu* 109 (2009): 311–58.

Ho, Chuimei. "The Ceramic Trade in Asia, 1602–82." In *Japanese Industrialization and the Asian Economy*, pp. 35–70. Ed. A. J. H. Latham and Heita Kawakatsu. London: Routledge, 1994.

Hŏ, Hŭng-sik. "Buddhism and Koryŏ Society." In *Buddhism in Koryŏ: A Royal Religion*, pp. 1–33. Ed. Lewis R. Lancaster et al. Berkeley: University of California Institute of East Asian Studies, 1996.

Hŏ T'aegu 許泰玖. "Pyŏngja horan kanghwa hyŏpsang ŭi ch'u'i wa Chosŏn ŭi tae'ŭng" 병자호란講和 협상의 추이 와 조선의 대응 (Changes in the peace negotiations during the 1636–37 Manchu invasion and the response of Chosŏn), *Chosŏn sidaesa hakpo* 52 (2010): 51–88.

Holcombe, Charles. "Re-Imagining China: The Chinese Identity Crisis at the Start of the Southern Dynasties Period." *Journal of the American Oriental Society* 115.1 (1995): 1–14.

The Genesis of East Asia, 221 BC–AD 907. Honolulu: University of Hawai'i Press, 2001.

Holmgren, Jennifer. "Imperial Marriage in the Native Chinese and Non-Han State, Han to Ming." In *Marriage and Inequality in Chinese Society*, pp. 58–96. Ed. Rubie S. Watson and Patricia Buckley Ebrey. Berkeley: University of California Press, 1991.

Holtom, D. C. *The Japanese Enthronement Ceremonies*. Tokyo: Sophia University, 1972.

Hou, Jen-chih. "Frontier Horse Markets in the Ming Dynasty." In *Chinese Social History: Translations of Selected Studies*, pp. 299–332. Comp. E-tu Zen Sun and John De Francis. Reprint of 1966 edn. Taipei: Rainbow Bridge Book Co., 1972.

Howell, David. "Territoriality and Collective Identity in Tokugawa Japan." *Daedalus* 127.3 (1998): 105–32.

Geographies of Identity in Nineteenth-Century Japan. Berkeley: University of California Press, 2005.

Hsiao, Kung-chuan. Trans. F. W. Mote. *A History of Chinese Political Thought*, vol. I: *From the Beginnings to the Sixth Century AD*. Princeton: Princeton University Press, 1978.

Hsu, Cho-yun. Trans. Timothy D. Baker, Jr. and Michael S. Duke. *China: A New Cultural History*. New York: Columbia University Press, 2012.

Hu, Axiang. "The Population Migration and Its Influence in the Period of the Eastern Jin, the Sixteen States, and the Northern and Southern Dynasties." *Frontiers of History in China* 8.4 (2010): 576–615.

Huang, Pei. *Autocracy at Work: A Study of the Yung-cheng Period, 1723–1735*. Bloomington: Indiana University Press, 1974.

Huang, Ray. *Taxation and Governmental Finance in Sixteenth-Century Ming China*. Cambridge: Cambridge University Press, 1974.

1587: A Year of No Significance. New Haven: Yale University Press, 1981.

"The Lung-ch'ing and Wan-li Reigns, 1567–1620." In *The Cambridge History of China*, vol. VII, Part 1: *The Ming Dynasty, 1368–1644*, pp. 511–84. Ed. Frederick W. Mote and Denis Twitchett. Cambridge: Cambridge University Press, 1988.

Huang Xingtao 黄興濤. "'Minzu' yici jiujing heshi zai Zhongwenli chuxian" "民族" 一詞 究竟 何時 在 中文里 出現 (When did the term "minzu" appear in Chinese). *Zhejiang xuekan* 1 (2002): 168–70.

Huang, Yi-long. Trans. Peter Engelfriet. "Sun Yuanhua (1581–1632): A Christian Convert Who Put Xu Guangqi's Military Reform Policy into Practice." In *Statecraft and Intellectual Renewal in Late Ming China: The Cross-Cultural Synthesis of Xu Guangqi (1562–1633)*, pp. 225–59. Ed. Catherine Jami, Peter Engelfriet, and Gregory Blue. Leiden: E. J. Brill, 2001.

Hudson, Mark J. *Ruins of Identity: Ethnogenesis in the Japanese Islands*. Honolulu: University of Hawai'i Press, 1999.

Hulsewé, A. F. P. "Chinese Communist Treatment of the Origins and the Foundation of the Chinese Empire." In *History in Communist China*, pp. 96–123. Ed. Albert Feuerwerker. Cambridge, MA: MIT Press, 1968.

Hummel, Arthur W. Ed. *Eminent Chinese of the Ch'ing Period (1644–1912)*. 2 vols. Washington, DC: US Government Printing Office, 1943.

Hur, Nam-lin. "A Korean Envoy Encounters Tokugawa Japan: Sin Yu-han and the Korean Embassy of 1719." In *Korea Between Tradition and Modernity: Selected Papers from the Fourth Pacific and Asian Conference on Korean Studies*, pp. 147–57. Ed. Chang Yun-Shik, Donald L. Baker, Hur Nam-lin, and Ross King. Vancouver: Institute of Asian Research, University of British Columbia, 2000.

"Korean Officials in the Land of the Kami: Diplomacy and the Prestige Economy, 1607–1811." *In Embracing the Other: The Interaction of Korean and Foreign Cultures, Proceedings of the First World Congress of Korean Studies, 2002*, 1: 82–93. Sponsored by the Academy of Korean Studies, International Society for Korean Studies, Association for Korean Studies in Europe, and

Korean Studies Association of Australasia. Songnam: Academy of Korean Studies, 2002.

Hurst, G. Cameron III. "The Development of the *Insei*: A Problem in Japanese History and Historiography." In *Medieval Japan: Essays in Institutional History*, pp. 60–90. Ed. John W. Hall and Jeffrey P. Mass. New Haven: Yale University Press, 1974.

"The Structure of the Heian Court: Some Thoughts on the Nature of 'Familial Authority' in Heian Japan." In *Medieval Japan: Essays in Institutional History*, pp. 39–59. Ed. John W. Hall and Jeffrey P. Mass. New Haven: Yale University Press, 1974.

Insei: Abdicated Sovereigns in the Politics of Late Heian Japan, 1086–1185. New York: Columbia University Press, 1976.

"The Koobu Polity: Court–Bakufu Relations in Kamakura Japan." In *Court and Bakufu in Japan: Essays in Kamakura History*, pp. 3–28. Ed. Jeffrey P. Mass. New Haven: Yale University Press, 1982.

"Insei." In *The Cambridge History of Japan*, vol. II: *Heian Japan*, pp. 576–643. Ed. Donald H. Shively and William H. McCullough. New York: Cambridge University Press, 1999.

Hwang, Kyung Moon. *A History of Korea*. New York: Palgrave Macmillan, 2010.

Hwang Wŏn'gu 黃元九. "Ch'ŏngdae ch'iljong sŏ sojae Chosŏn kisa ŭi pyŏnjŏng" 清代七種書所載 朝鮮記事 의 辨正 (Corrections of Chosŏn affairs recorded in seven Qing books). *Tongbang hakji* 30 (1982): 265–73.

Hymes, Robert P. "Marriage, Descent Groups, and the Localist Strategy in Sung and Yuan Fu-chou." In *Kinship Organization in Late Imperial China, 1000–1940*, pp. 95–136. Ed. Patricia Buckley Ebrey and James L. Watson. Berkeley: University of California Press, 1986.

Hyueck, Song Jhune. "Eastern Barbarian Consciousness in *Research on Manchu Origins*." *The Review of Korean Studies* 12.3 (2009): 163–75.

Iggers, Georg G. and Q. Edward Wang, with contributions from Supriya Mukherjee. *A Global History of Modern Historiography*. New York: Pearson Longman, 2008.

Ikegami, Eiko. *Bonds of Civility: Aesthetic Networks and the Political Origins of Japanese Culture*. Cambridge: Cambridge University Press, 2005.

Im Chung'ung. *Chosŏn wangjo wangbi yŏlchŏn* (Biographies of Chosŏn queens). Seoul: Sŏkch'ŏn midiŏ, 2002.

Im Hyeryŏn. "Sunjo ch'oban Chŏngsun wanghu ŭi suryom ch'ŏngjŏng kwa ch'ŏngguk pyŏnhwa" 純祖初半真純王后의 垂簾聽政과政局變化 (The female regency of Queen Chŏngsun during the first half of the Sunjo reign and political change). *Chosŏn sidaesa hakpo* 15 (2000): 153–79.

Im Minhyŏk 任敏赫. "Chosŏn sidae ŭi myoho wa sadae ŭisik" (Temple names and the consciousness of "serving the great" during the Chosŏn period). *Chosŏn sidaesa hakpo* 19 (2001): 147–68.

Imamura, Keiji. *Prehistoric Japan: New Perspectives on Insular East Asia*. Honolulu: University of Hawai'i Press, 1996.

Imatani, Akira, Trans. Kozo Yamamura. "Not for Lack of Will or Wile: Yoshimitsu's Failure to Supplant the Imperial Lineage." *Journal of Japanese Studies* 18.1 (1992): 45–78.

Institute of Geography, USSR Academy of Sciences. *The Physical Geography of China*. 2 vols. New York: Frederick A. Praeger, 1969.

Ishii, Susumu. Trans. Jeffrey P. Mass and Hitomi Tonomura. "The Decline of the Kamakura Bakufu." In *Warrior Rule in Japan*, pp. 44–90. Ed. Marius B. Jansen. Cambridge: Cambridge University Press, 1995.

Itō, Kōji. "Japan and Ryukyu during the Fifteenth and Sixteenth Centuries." *Acta Asiatica* 95 (2008): 79–99.

Iwai Shigeki 岩井茂樹. "Jūroku, jūshichi seiki no Chūgoku henkyō shakai" 十六、十七世紀の中国邊境社會 (Chinese frontier society in the sixteenth and seventeenth centuries). In *Minmatsu Shinsho no shakai to bunka* 明末清初の社会と文化 (Chinese society and culture in late Ming and early Qing), pp. 625–59. Ed. Ono Kazuko 小野和子. Kyoto: Kyoto daigaku Jinbun kagaku kenkyūjo, 1996.

"Jūroku seiki Chūgoku ni okeru bōeki chitsujō no mosaku – goshi no genjitsu to sono ninshiki" 十六世紀中國における貿易秩序の模索 – 互市の現實とその認識 (The pattern of the trading order in sixteenth-century China – the realization of mutual trade marts and their acknowledgement). In *Chūgoku kinsei shakai no chitsujo keisei* 中國近世社會の秩序形成 (The social formation of early modern China), pp. 97–142. Ed. Iwai Shigeki. Kyoto: Kyoto University Press, 2004.

"China's Frontier Society in the Sixteenth and Seventeenth Centuries." *Acta Asiatica* 88 (2005): 1–20.

Jami, Catherine. "Imperial Control and Western Learning: The Kangxi Emperor's Performance." *Late Imperial China* 23.1 (2002): 28–49.

Jansen, Marius B. *The Making of Modern Japan*. Cambridge, MA: Belknap Press, 2000.

Jian Wen 建文. "Lun Mingdai dui dongjiang diqu de guanxia wenti – jian jiu 'beijiandao' yanjiu bo Hanguo xuezhe" 論明代對東疆地區的管轄問題 – 兼就'北間島'研究駁韓國學者 (On the issue of Ming administration over the eastern frontier district – a refutation of the Korean scholars' research on "Northern Jiandao"). In *Zhong Chao guanxi shi yanjiu lunwenji* 中朝關係史論文集 (Collected writings on the history of Sino-Korean relations), pp. 200–15. Ed. Diao Shuren 刁書仁 and Yi Xingguo 衣興國. Changchun: Jilin wenshi chubanshe, 1995.

Jiang Shoupeng 姜守鵬. "Liaodong zhanzheng shiqi Mingchao yu Chaoxian guanxi de bianhua" 遼東戰爭時期明朝與朝鮮關係的變化 (Changes in the relations between Ming and Chosŏn during the period of fighting in Liaodong). In *Zhong Chao guanxi shi yanjiu lunwenji* 中朝關係史研究論文集 (Collected writings on the history of Sino-Korean relations), pp. 191–99. Ed. Diao Shuren 刁書仁 and Yi Xingguo 衣興國. Changchun: Jilin wenshi chubanshe, 1995.

Jiang Weigong 姜維公 "Nanchao yu beichao dui Gaogouli zhengce de bijiao yanjiu" 南朝與北朝對高句麗政策的比較研究 (Comparative study of the southern dynasty and northern dynasty's policies toward Gaogouli). *Zhongguo bianjiang shidi yanjiu* 14.4 (2004): 14–22.

Jiang Xiangshun 姜像順. "Kangxi di wannian lichu zhi mi" 康熙帝晚年立儲之謎 (On the puzzle of the succession during the late Kangxi reign). *Manzu yanjiu* 滿族研究1 (1995): 40–45.

Jiang, Yonglin. *The Mandate of Heaven and The Great Ming Code*. Seattle: University of Washington Press, 2011.

Jiao Runming 焦潤明. "Guanyu lishi jiangyu guishu ruogan lilun wenti de yanjiu" 關于 歷史 疆域 歸屬 若干 理論 問題 的 研究 (Research on some theoretical issues on the ascription of historical territory). *Zhongguo bianjiang shidi yanjiu* 13.2 (2003): 1–12.

Johnson, David G. *The Medieval Chinese Oligarchy*. Boulder: Westview Press, 1977.

"The City-God Cults in T'ang and Sung China." *Harvard Journal of Asiatic Studies* 45.2 (1985): 363–457.

Joos, Joël. "A Stinking Tradition: Tsuda Sōkichi's View of China." *East Asian History* 28 (2004): 1–26.

Jorganson, John. "Tan'gun and the Legitimization of a Threatened Dynasty: North Korea's Rediscovery of Tan'gun." *Korea Observer* 27.2 (1996): 273–306.

Kaiho Mineo 海保嶺夫. *Kinsei Ezochi seiritsu shi no kenkyū* 近世蝦夷地成立史の研究 (Research on the early modern establishment of Ezochi). Tokyo: San'ichi shobō, 1984.

Kamikawa, Michio. "Accession Rituals and Buddhism in Medieval Japan." *Japanese Journal of Religious Studies* 17.3/4 (1990): 243–80.

Kamiya, Nobuyuki. "Japanese Control of Ezochi and the Role of Northern Koryŏ." *Acta Asiatica* 67 (1994): 49–68.

Kamiya Nobuyuki 紙屋敦之. "Nihon kinsei no tōitsu to Tattan" 日本近世の統一と韃靼 (The unification of early modern Japan and the Tartars). In *Nihon zenkindai no kokka to taigai kankei* 日本前近代の國家と對外關係 (Japan's early modern state and foreign relations), pp. 145–76. Ed. Tanaka Takeo 田中健夫. Tokyo: Yoshikawa kōbunkan, 1987.

Taikun gaikō to Higashi Ajia 大君外交と東アジア (Taikun diplomacy and East Asia). Tokyo: Yoshikawa kōbunkan, 1997.

Kanda, Nobuo. "Present State of Preservation of Manchu Literature." *Memoirs of the Research Department of the Toyo Bunko* No. 26 (1968): 63–95.

"From Man Wen Lao Tang to Chiu Man-chou Tang." *Memoirs of the Research Department of the Toyo Bunko* 38 (1980): 71–94.

"Japanese Studies in Ch'ing History, Particularly Those Based on Manchu Source Materials." *Acta Asiatica* 53 (1988): 83–113.

Kanda Nobuo 神田信夫. "Sanhan no ran to Chōsen" 三藩の亂と朝鮮 (The Sanfan rebellion and Chosŏn). In *Shinchōshi ronkō* 清朝史論考 (Essays on Qing history), pp. 260–79. Ed. Kanda Nobuo. Tokyo: Yamakawa shuppansha, 2005.

Kang, David C. *East Asia Before the West: Five Centuries of Trade and Tribute*. New York: Columbia University Press, 2010.

Kang, Etsuko Hae-jin. *Diplomacy and Ideology in Japanese–Korean Relations from the Fifteenth to the Eighteenth Century*. New York: St. Martin's Press, 1997.

Kang Hŭngsu 姜興秀. *Imjin waeran kwa Pyŏngja horan: Chosŏn oeran sahwa* 壬辰倭亂과 丙子胡亂: 朝鮮外亂史話 (The Japanese and Manchu invasions: on the history of foreign invasions in Chosŏn). Seoul: Munch'angdang, 1951.

Karlsson, Anders. "A Hermit Nation Not for Everyone: First-hand Contacts with Qing and Their Consequences in Late Chosŏn P'yŏngan Province." In *Embracing the Other: The Interaction of Korean and Foreign Cultures, Proceedings of the First World Congress of Korean Studies, 2002*, 3: 1289–1300. Sponsored by the Academy of Korean Studies, International Society for Korean Studies, Association for Korean Studies in Europe, and Korean Studies Association of Australasia. Songnam: Academy of Korean Studies, 2002.

Kasuya Ken'ichi 糟谷憲一. "Kindaiteki gaiko taisei no sōshutsu – Chōsen no ba'ai wo chūshin ni –" 近代的外交體制の創出 – 朝鮮の場合を中心に – (The creation of an early modern diplomatic system, focusing on the Chosŏn example). In *Ajia no naka no Nihonshi* アジアのなかの日本史 (Japanese history in Asia), vol. II: *Gaiko to sensō* 外交と戰爭 (Diplomacy and war), pp. 223–55. Ed. Arano Yasunori 荒野泰典, Ishii Masatoshi 石井正敏 and Murai Shōsuke 村井章介. Tokyo: University of Tokyo Press, 1992.

Kawachi Yoshihiro. *Mindai Joshinshi no kenkyū* 明代女眞史の研究 (Studies of Jurchen history during the Ming dynasty). Kyoto: Dōhōsha, 1992.

"Yi Manjū to Daikin" 李滿住と大金 (Li Manju and the Jin). In *Matsumura Jun sensei koki kinen Shindai shi ronsō* 松村潤先生古稀記念清代史論叢 (Collected articles on Qing history, Festschrift in honor of Professor Matsumura Jun's seventieth birthday), pp. 5–18. Ed. Matsumura Jun sensei koki kinen ronbunshū hensan iinkai. Tokyo: Kyūko shoin, 1994.

Kawakatsu, Heita. "The Emergence of a Market for Cotton Goods in East Asia in the Early Modern Period." In *Japanese Industrialization and the Asian Economy*, pp. 9–34. Ed. A. J. H. Latham and Heita Kawakatsu. London: Routledge, 1994.

Kawamura Hirotada 川村博忠. *Edo bakufu sen kuni-ezu no kenkyū* 江戸幕府撰國繪圖の研究 (Research on the domain maps compiled by the Tokugawa shogunate). Tokyo: Kojin shoin, 1984.

Kawazoe, Shōji. Trans. G. Cameron Hurst III. "Japan and East Asia." In *The Cambridge History of Japan*, vol. III: *Medieval Japan*, pp. 396–446. Ed. Kōzō Yamamura. Cambridge: Cambridge University Press, 1990.

Kertzer, David. *Ritual, Politics, and Power*. New Haven: Yale University Press, 1988.

Kessler, Lawrence D. *K'ang-hsi and the Consolidation of Ch'ing Rule, 1661–1684*. Chicago: University of Chicago Press, 1976.

Ketelaar, James E. *Of Heretics and Martyrs in Meiji Japan: Buddhism and its Persecution*. Princeton: Princeton University Press, 1990.

Kidder, J. Edward. *Himiko and Japan's Elusive Chiefdom of Yamatai: Archaeology, History, and Mythology*. Honolulu: University of Hawai'i Press, 2007.

Kikuchi Isao 菊池勇夫. *Ainu minzoku to Nihonjin: Higashi Ajia no naka no Ezochi* アイヌ民族と日本人：東アジアのなかの蝦夷地 (The Ainu people and Japanese: Ezochi within East Asia). Tokyo: Asahi shinbunsha, 1994.

Kikuchi, Toshihiko. "Continental Culture and Hokkaido." In *Windows on the Japanese Past: Studies in Archaeology and Prehistory*, pp. 149–62. Ed. Richard J. Pearson et al. Ann Arbor: Center for Japanese Studies, 1986.

Kikuchi Toshihiko 菊池俊彦. "Hoppō sekai to Roshia no shinshutsu" 北方世界とロシアの進出 (The Russian advance and the northern world). In *Iwanami kōza sekai rekishi* 岩波講座世界歴史 (Iwanami series of lectures on world history), vol. XIII: *Higashi Ajia, Tōnan Ajia dentō shakai no keisei, 16–18 seiki* 東アジア，東南アジア傳統社會の形成，16–18 世紀 (The formation of traditional societies in East and Southeast Asia, 16–18th centuries), pp. 121–48. Ed. Kishimoto Mio et al. Tokyo: Iwanami, 1998.

Kim Ch'ŏl'ung 金澈雄. "Chosŏn ch'o ŭi Togyo wa ch'orye" 조선초의道教와醮祭 (Early Chosŏn Daoism and the ch'o rite). *Han'guk sasang sahak* 15 (2000): 359–93.

"Koryŏ kukka chesa ŭi cheje wa kŭ t'ŭkching" 고려國家祭祀의 體制와그특징 (The organization and characteristics of the Koryŏ state rituals). *Han'guksa yŏn'gu* 118 (2003): 135–60.

Kim, Gi-bong. "The Korean Conception of History: Shin Ch'aeho's Nationalistic Historiography." In *The Many Faces of Clio: Cross-Cultural Approaches to Historiography*, pp. 247–61. Ed. Q. Edward Wang and Franz L. Fillafer. New York: Berghahn Books, 2007.

Kim Haeyŏng 金海榮. *Chosŏn ch'ogi chesa chŏllye yŏn'gu* 朝鮮初期祭祀典禮研究 (Research on sacrificial rituals in the early Chosŏn period). Seoul: Chimmundang, 2003.

Kim Han'gyu. *Han-Chung kwan'gye sa* 韓中關係史 (The history of Korean–Chinese relations). Seoul: Arche, 1999.

Kim, Jongmyung. "Buddhist Rituals in Medieval Korea (918–1392)." PhD thesis, University of California at Los Angeles, 1994.

Kim, Jung Bae. "Á Critique of the Chinese Theory of 'One History Shared by Two States' (一史兩用論) As Applied to Koguryŏ History." *Journal of Inner and East Asian Studies* 3.1 (2006): 5–26.

Kim Kujin 金九鎮. "Chosŏn ch'ogi e Han minjok ŭro tonghwa toen t'och'ak Yŏjin" (The Koreanization of the aboriginal Jurchen in early Chosŏn). *Paeksan hakpo* 58 (2001): 139–80.

Kim Kyŏngnok 金景錄. "Chosŏn ch'ogi tae Myŏng oegyo wa oegyo chŏlch'a" 朝鮮初期對明外交와外交節次 (Early Chosŏn foreign relations and diplomatic procedures with respect to Ming). *Han'guk saron* 44 (2000): 1–44.

"Chosŏn ch'ogi chonggye pyŏnmu ŭi chŏn'gae yangsang kwa tae Myŏng kwan'gye" 朝鮮初期宗系辨誣의展開樣相과對明關係 (The development of the *chŏnggye pyŏnmu* and relations with Ming in early Chosŏn). *Kuk'sagwan nonch'ong* 國史館論叢 108 (2006): 147–83.

Kim Namch'ŏl 金難哲. "Yŏksa kyoyuk eso ŭi [tongbuk kongjŏng] kwa minjokchuŭi" (Ethnic ideology and the northeast regional project in history education). *Yŏksa kyoyuk* 95 (2005): 89–115.

Kim Pŏm 金範. *Sahwa wa panjŏng ŭi sidae* (Eras of literari purges and coups d'états). Seoul: Yŏksa Pip'yŏngsa, 2007.

Kim, Sang-hyun. "Buddhism and the State in Middle and Late Silla." In *State and Society in Middle and Late Silla*, pp. 95–137. Ed. Richard D. McBride II. Cambridge, MA: Harvard University Korea Institute, 2010.

Kim, Seonmin. "Borders and Crossings: Trade, Diplomacy and Ginseng Between Qing China and Choson Korea." PhD thesis, Duke University, 2006.

"Ginseng and Border Trespassing Between Qing China and Chosŏn Korea." *Late Imperial China* 28.1 (2007): 33–61.

"Insam kwa kang'yŏk – Hu Kŭm-Ch'ŏng ŭi kang'yŏk insik kwa taeoe kwan'gye ŭi pyŏnhwa –." (Ginseng and the borderland – changes in Later Jin/Qing borderland consciousness and foreign relations). *Myŏng-Ch'ŏngsa yŏn'gu* (Ming–Qing historical studies) 30 (2008): 227–57.

"Myŏngmal Yodong pyŏngyŏng chiyŏk ŭl tullŏssan Myŏng/Hu Kŭm/Chosŏn ŭi samgak kwan'gye"(Triangular relations between Ming, Later Jin, and Chosŏn surrounding the late Ming Liaodong borderland). *Chungguksa yŏn'gu* 55 (2008): 207–45.

Kim Seyŏng 金世英. "Chosŏn Hyojongjo pukpŏllon yon'gu" 朝鮮孝宗朝北伐論 研究 (Research on discussions of a northern expedition in the Choson Hyojong reign). *Paeksan hakpo* 51 (1998): 121–53.

Kim Sihwang. "Ku-I wa Tong-I" (The nine I and the eastern I). *Tongbang hanmunhak* 17.1 (1990): 71–90.

Kim Songhŭi 金松姬. "Chosŏn ch'ogi tae Myŏng oegyo e taehan il yŏn'gu – tae Myŏng sasin kwa Myŏng sasin yŏngjŏpgwan ŭi sŏngkyŏk ŭl chungsim ŭro" 조선 초기 對明外交에 대한 一研究 – 對明使臣과 明使臣 迎接官의 성격을 중심으로 – (Research on relations with Ming in early Chosŏn – focusing on the Ming embassy and the characteristics of the office to welcome Ming emissaries). *Sahak yŏn'gu* 55–56 (1998): 205–26.

Kim Sŏnghwan. "Koryŏ chŏn, chunggi ŭi Tan'gun ihae" 高麗前中期의 檀君理解 (Explaining the Tan'gun of early and mid-Koryŏ). *Paeksan hakpo* 57 (2000): 229–63.

Kim Ton 金燉. *Chosŏn chŏngi kunsin kwŏnnyŏk kwan'gye yŏn'gu* 朝賢前期君臣權 力關係研究 (Research on ruler-servant authority relations in early Chosŏn). Seoul: Seoul taehakgyo ch'ulpanbu, 1997.

"Sejodae 'Tanjong pongnip undong' kwa wangwi sŭnggye munje" 世祖代 [端 宗復立運動] 과 왕위승계 문제 (The movement to restore Tanjong in the Sejo reign and succession issues). *Yŏksa kyoyuk* 98 (2006): 205–35.

Kim Ugi 金宇基. "Chosŏn Myŏngjongdae ŭi chŏngch'i sillyŏ wa chŏngguk tonghyang –ch'ŏksin sillyŏ rŭl chungsim ŭro –" (Political power and political trends in the Chosŏn Myŏngjong reign – focusing on the power of affinal officials). *Chosŏnsa yŏn'gu* 2 (1993): 1–64.

Chosŏn chunggi ch'ŏksin chŏngch'i yŏn'gu (Research on affinal governance in the mid– Chosŏn period). Seoul: Chimmundang, 2001.

"Chosŏn Sŏngjongdae Chŏnghŭi wanghu ŭi suryŏm chŏngjŏng" (The regency of Queen Chŏnghŭi during the Sŏngjong reign in the Chosŏn dynasty). *Chosŏnsa yŏn'gu* 10 (2001): 169–212.

Kim-Renaud, Young-Key. Ed. *The Korean Alphabet: Its History and Structure.* Honolulu: University of Hawai'i Press, 1997.

Kishi Toshihiko 貴志俊彥, Arano Yasunori 荒野泰典, and Kokaze Hidemasa 小 風秀雄. Eds. *Higashi Ajia no jidaisei* 東アジアの時代性 (Periodization in East Asia). Hiroshima: Keisui sha, 2005.

Kishimoto Mio 岸本美緒. "Shinchō to Yūrasia" 清朝とユーラシア (The Qing and Eurasia), in *Kōza sekaishi*, vol. II: *Kinsei e no michi: Henyō to masatsu* 講座 世界史, vol. II: 近世への道：變容と摩擦 (Lecture series on world history, II: The road to modernity: Change and conflict), pp. 11–42. Ed. Rekishigaku kenkyūkai. Tokyo: Tokyo University Press, 1995.

Kishimoto, Mio. "The Ch'ing Dynasty and the East Asian World." *Acta Asiatica* 88 (2005): 87–109.

Kishimoto Mio and Miyajima Hiroshi 宮島博史. *Min Shin to Richō no jidai* 明清と 李朝の時代. (Sekai no rekishi 世界の歴史, 12). Tokyo: Chūo kōronsha, 1998.

Kitajima Manji 北島万次. "Jinshin Waranki no Chōsen to Min" 壬辰倭亂期の朝 鮮と明 (Chosŏn and Ming in the Japanese invasion period). In *Ajia no naka no Nihonshi* アジアのなかの日本史 (Japanese history in Asian context), vol. II: *Gaikō to sensō* 外交と戰爭 (Diplomacy and war), pp. 127–60. Ed. Arano Yasunori 荒野泰典, Ishii Masatoshi 石井正敏, and Murai Shōsuke 村 井章介. Tokyo: University of Tokyo Press, 1992.

Toyotomi Hideyoshi no Chōsen shinryaku 豊臣秀吉の朝鮮侵略 (Toyotomi Hideyoshi's Korean invasions). Tokyo: Yoshikawa Hirobunkan, 1995.

"Min no Chōsen satsuhō to kōeki kankei" 明の朝鮮冊封と交易關係 (The Ming investiture of Chosŏn and trade relations). In *Chūsei shi kōza* 中世史講座 (Lectures on medieval history) 11: *Chūsei ni okeru chiiki, minzoku no kōryū* 中 世における地域, 民族の交流 (Regional and ethnic exchanges in the middle ages), pp. 152–87. Ed. Kimura Shōsaburō 木村尚三郎. Tokyo: Gakusha, 1996.

Klein, Peter W. "The China Seas and the World Economy Between the Sixteenth and Nineteenth Centuries: The Changing Structures of Trade." In *Interactions in the World Economy: Perspectives from International Economic History*, pp. 61–89. Ed. Carl-Ludwig Holtfrerich. New York: New York University Press, 1989.

Klinger, Bruce. "China Shock for South Korea." *Asia Times*, September 11, 2004, http://www.atimes/Korea/.

"Koguryŏ sites put onto heritage list." *China Daily*, July 2, 2004, p. 1.

Koguryŏ Research Foundation website. http://www.pkuef.org

Kojima Yoshitaka 小嶋芳孝. "Kōkurei, Botsukai to no kōryu" 高句麗, 渤海と の交流 (The exchanges with Koguryŏ and Parhae). In *Nihonkai to hokkoku bunka: Umi to rettō bunka* 日本海と北国文化：海と列島文化 (The Japan sea and northern culture: The maritime and archipelago culture), I: 195–230. Ed. Amino Yoshihiko 網野善彦 et al. Tokyo: Shūgakkan, 1990.

Koo, Han Kyung. "The Archaeology of the Ethnically Homogeneous Nation-State and Multiculturalism in Korea." *Korea Journal* 47.4 (2007): 8–31.

Kornicki, Peter. *The Book in Japan: A Cultural History from the Beginnings to the Nineteenth Century*. Honolulu: University of Hawai'i Press, 2001.

Ku Pŏmjin. "Ch'ŏng ŭi Chosŏn sahaeng insŏn kwa [Tae Ch'ŏng cheguk ch'eje]" 淸의 朝鮮使行 人選 과 '大淸帝國體制' (On personnel appointments of Qing imperial envoys to Chosŏn and the Great Qing imperial system). *Inmun nonch'ong* 59 (2008): 179–228.

Kuba Takashi 久芳崇. "Jūroku seiki matsu, Nihonshiki teppō no Minchō e no dempa – Manreki Chōsen no eki kara Banshū Yō Ōryū no ran e" 十六世紀末日本式鐵砲の明朝への傳播 – 萬曆朝鮮の役から播州楊應龍の亂へ (On the spreading of Japanese type muskets to the Ming in the late sixteenth century – from the Wanli Chosŏn campaign to the Bozhou Yang Yinglong rebellion). *Tōyōgakuhō* 84.1 (2002): 33–54.

"Chōsen no eki ni okeru Nihon heihoryo – Minchō ni okeru renkō to shochi" 朝鮮の役における日本兵捕虜 – 明朝における連行と處置 (Japanese prisoners of war in the Korea campaign: their treatment at the hands of the Ming). *Tōhōgaku* 105 (2003): 106–20.

Kurachi Katsunao 倉地克直. *Kinsei Nihonjin wa Chōsen wo dō mite itaka – [sakoku] no naka no [ijin] tachi* 近世日本人は朝鮮をどうみていたか – [鎖国] のなかの「異人」たち (How did early modern Japanese view Koreans – foreigners in the secluded country). Tokyo: Kadokawa shoten, 2001.

Kuroda, Akinobu. "Copper Coins Chosen and Silver Differentiated: Another Aspect of the 'Silver Century' in East Asia." *Acta Asiatica* 88 (2005): 65–86.

Kuroda, Toshio. Trans. James C. Dobbins and Suzanne Gay. "Shinto in the History of Japanese Religion." *Journal of Japanese Studies* 7.1 (1988): 1–21.

Trans. Fabio Rambelli. "The Discourse on the 'Land of Kami' in Medieval Japan: National Consciousness and International Awareness." *Japanese Journal of Religious Studies* 23.3/4 (1996): 353–85.

Kurozumi, Makoto. Trans. David Lurie. "*Kangaku*: Writing and Institutional Authority." In *Inventing the Classics: Modernity, National Identity, and Japanese Literature*, pp. 201–19. Ed. Haruo Shirane and Tomi Suzuki. Stanford: Stanford University Press, 2000.

Kushner, Barak. "Nationality and Nostalgia: The Manipulation of Memory in Japan, Taiwan, and China since 1990." *The International History Review* 29.4 (2007): 793–820.

Kuwano Eiji 桑野栄治. "Chōsen han [Shōtoku daiMin kaiten] no seiritsu to sono genson – Chōsen zenki taiMin gaikō kōshō to sono kanren kara" 朝鮮版 [正徳大明會典] の成立とその現存—朝鮮前期對明外交交渉とその関連から (The establishment of a Chosŏn edition of the *Zhengde da Ming huidian* and its current whereabouts – relating to foreign negotiations with Ming in early Chosŏn). *Chōsen bunka kenkyū* 5 (1998): 1–25.

"Chōsen Chūsō nijūnendai no taiMin gaikō kōshō" 朝鮮中宗20年代の對明外交交渉 (Chosŏn's diplomatic negotiations with the Ming in the third decade of the Chungjong reign). *Tōyōshi kenkyū* 67.3 (2008): 72–101.

"Chōsen Chūsōdai ni okeru sōkei benbu mondai no sainen" 朝鮮中宗代における宗系辨武問題の再燃 (The recurrence of "clarifying the royal lineage" during the Chungjong reign in Chosŏn Korea). *Kurume daigaku bungakubu kiyō, Kokusai bunka gakkai hen* 25 (2008): 51–78.

Kwŏn Chungdal. "Chungguk ŭi hwaktae wa Hanjok kwan" 중국의 확대와 漢族觀 (The expansion of China and views of the Han people). *Han'guk sahaksa hakpo* 10 (2004): 147–62.

Kwŏn, Oh Young. "The Influence of Recent Archaeological Discoveries on the Research of Paekche History." *Early Korea*, vol. I: *Reconsidering Early Korean*

History Through Archaeology, pp. 65–112. Ed. Mark E. Byington. Cambridge, MA: Korea Institute, Harvard University, 2008.

Kye, Seung B. "The Posthumous Image and Role of Ming Taizu in Korean Politics." *Ming Studies* 50 (2004): 104–30.

"In the Shadow of the Father: Court Opposition and the Reign of King Kwanghae in Early Seventeenth-Century Chosŏn Korea." PhD thesis, University of Washington, 2006.

Kye Sŭngbŏm 桂勝範. "Chosŏn kamhoron munje rŭl t'onghae pon Kwanghaegundae oegyo nosŏn nonjaeng" (A Ming proposal for superintendence of Chosŏn: disputes over foreign policy in the Kwanghaegun era). *Chosŏn sidaesa hakpo* 34 (2005): 5–33.

"P'apyŏng nonŭi rŭl t'onghae pon Chosŏn chŏn'gi tae Myŏnggwan ŭi pyŏnhwa" (A change in the Chosŏn view of Ming China: Court debates on Ming requests for Korean troops in early Chosŏn). *Taedong munhwa yŏn'gu* 53 (2006): 309–46.

"Imjin waeran Nurŭhach'i: Tong Asia ŭi saeroun p'aeja, Nurŭhach'i sigak esŏ pon chŏnjaeng" (The Japanese invasion and Nurhaci: the new winner in East Asia, the battle from Nurhaci's perspective). In *Imjin waeran: Tong Asia samguk chŏnjaeng* (The Japanese invasion of Korea: a three-country East Asian war), pp. 355–84. Ed. Chŏng Tuhŭi and Yi Kyŏngsun. Seoul: Humanities Press, 2007.

"Kwanghaegundae maryŏp (1621–1622) oegyo nosŏn nonjaeng ŭi silje wa kŭ sŏnggyŏk" (The reality and nature of the foreign policy dispute in 1621–1622). *Yŏksa hakpo* 193 (2007): 1–37.

"Chosŏn hugi Chunghwaron ŭi imyŏn kwa kŭ yusan – Myŏng, Ch'ŏng kwallyŏn hoch'ing ŭi pyŏnhwa rŭl chungsim ŭro" (On the inner face and legacy of the late Chosŏn discourse on civilized center – focusing on the changes in the naming of the connection with Ming and Qing). *Han'guk sahaksa hakpo* 19 (2009): 39–81.

Chosŏn sidae haeoe p'abyŏng kwa Han-Chung kwan'gye (Foreign dispatch of troops in the Chosŏn period and Korean–Chinese relations). Seoul: P'urŭn yŏksa, 2009.

"Chosŏn hugi Taebodan ch'inhaeng hyŏnhwang kwa kŭ chŏngch'i'i, munhwajŏk hamŭi"(The royal sacrifices at the Taebodan in late Chosŏn and their political and cultural aspects). *Yŏksa wa hyŏnsil* 75 (2010): 165–200.

Lancaster, Lewis R. "Introduction." In *Buddhism in Koryŏ: A Royal Religion*, pp. ix–xvi. Ed. Lewis R. Lancaster, Kikun Suh, and Chai-shin Yu. Berkeley: University of California Institute of East Asian Studies, 1996.

Langlois, John D. Jr. "Introduction." In *China Under Mongol Rule*, pp. 3–21. Ed. John D. Langlois, Jr. Princeton: Princeton University Press, 1981.

"The Hung-wu Reign, 1368–1398." In *The Cambridge History of China*, vol. VII, part 1: *The Ming Dynasty, 1368–1644*, pp. 107–81. Ed. Frederick W. Mote and Denis Twitchett. Cambridge: Cambridge University Press, 1988.

Lankov, Andrei. "The Legacy of Long-Gone States: China, Korea and the Koguryo War." Revision of an article that appeared in the *Asia Times*, September 16, 2006 www.atimes.com/atimes/Korea/HI16Dg01.html

Larsen, Kirk W. *Tradition, Treaties, and Trade: Qing Imperialism and Chosŏn Korea, 1850–1910*. Cambridge, MA: Harvard University Asia Center, 2008.

Lary, Diana. "Introduction." In *The Chinese State at the Borders*, pp. 1–10. Ed. Diana Lary. Vancouver: University of British Columbia Press, 2007.

Lattimore, Owen. *Inner Asian Frontiers of China*. Reprint of 1940 edn. Hong Kong: Oxford University Press, 1988.

Lebra, Takie Sugiyama. *Above the Clouds: Status Culture of the Modern Japanese Nobility*. Berkeley: University of California Press, 1993.

Ledyard, Gari. "Confucianism and War: The Korean Security Crisis of 1598." *Journal of Korean Studies* 6 (1988–89): 81–119.

"Cartography in Korea." In *The History of Cartography*, vol. II, book 2: *Cartography in the Traditional East and Southeast Asian Societies*, pp. 235–345. Ed. J. B. Hartley and David Woodward. Chicago: University of Chicago Press, 1994.

Lee, Chul-sung. "Re-evaluation of the Chosŏn Dynasty's Trade Relationship with the Ch'ing Dynasty." *International Journal of Korean History* 3 (2002): 95–122.

Lee, Ki-baik. Trans. Edward W. Wagner with Edward J. Shultz. *A New History of Korea*. Cambridge, MA: Harvard University Press, 1984.

Lee, Ki-dong. "Ancient Korean Historical Research in North Korea: Its Progress and Problems." *Korea Journal* 32.2 (1992): 22–41.

Levine, Ari Daniel. "Che-tsung's Reign (1085–1100) and the Age of Faction." In *The Cambridge History of China*, vol. V, part 1: *The Sung Dynasty and Its Precursors, 907–1279*, pp. 484–531. Ed. Denis Twitchett and Paul Jakov Smith. Cambridge: Cambridge University Press, 2009.

"The Reigns of Hui-tsung and Ch'in-tsung." In *The Cambridge History of China*, vol. V, part 1, *The Sung Dynasty and Its Precursors, 907–1279*, pp. 616–14. Ed. Denis Twitchett and Paul Jakov Smith. Cambridge: Cambridge University Press, 2009.

Lewis, James B. "Late Chosŏn-Era Korean Interaction with Japanese in Pusan: Defining Boundaries." In *Embracing the Other: The Interaction of Korean and Foreign Culture, Proceedings of the First World Congress of Korean Studies, 2002*, III: 1275–88. Sponsored by the Academy of Korean Studies, International Society for Korean Studies, Association for Korean Studies in Europe, and Korean Studies Association of Australasia. Songnam: Korean Academy, 2002.

Frontier Contact between Chosŏn Korea and Tokugawa Japan. London: Routledge Curzon, 2003.

Lewis, Mark Edward. "The *Feng* and *Shan* Sacrifices of Emperor Wu of the Han." In *State and Court Ritual in China*, pp. 50–80. Ed. Joseph P. McDermott. Cambridge: Cambridge University Press, 1999.

China Between Empires: The Northern and Southern Dynasties. Cambridge, MA: Belknap Press, 2009.

Lewis, Martin W., and Kären E. Wigen. *The Myth of Continents: A Critique of MetaGeography*. Berkeley: University of California Press, 1997.

Li Dalong 李大龍. "Cong Gaogouli xian dao Andong duhufu – Gaogouli he lidai zhongyang wangchao guanxi shulun" 從高句麗縣到安東都護府 – 高句麗和

歷代中央王朝關係述論 (From Gaogouli county to Andong protectorate – the relations between Gaogouli and successive central dynasties). *Minzu yanjiu* 1998.4: 74–85.

"Chuantong Yi Xia guan yu Zhongguo jiangcheng de xingcheng – Zhongguo jiangcheng xingcheng lilun tantao zhi yi" 傳統夷夏觀與中國疆城的形成 – 中國疆城形成理論探討之一 (The formation of Chinese territory and the traditional concept of the Yi and Xia – an exploration of Chinese territorial theory). *Zhongguo bianjiang shidi yanjiu* 14.1 (2004): 1–14.

Li Deshan 李德山. "Dangqian Gaogouli shi yanjiu zhong de jige wenti" 當前高句麗史研究中的幾個問題 (Some issues in prior studies of Gaogouli history). *Zhongguo bianjiang shidi yanjiu* 13.2 (2003): 66–71.

"Tangchao dui Gaogouli zhengce de xingcheng, shanbian ji qi yuanyin" 唐朝對高句麗政策的形成, 嬗變及其原因 (The shaping, evolution and cause of Tang policy towards Gaogouli). *Zhongguo bianjiang shidi yanjiu* 14.4 (2004): 23–29.

Li, Gertraude Roth. "The Manchu–Chinese Relationship, 1618–1636." In *From Ming to Ch'ing: Conquest, Region, and Continuity in Seventeenth-Century China*, pp. 1–38. Ed. Jonathan D. Spence and John E. Wills, Jr. New Haven: Yale University Press, 1979.

Li Guoqiang 李國強. "'Dongbei gongcheng' yu Zhongguo dongbeishi de yanjiu" '東北工程' 與中國東北史的研究 (The Northeast Research Project and the study of northeast China's history). *Zhongguo bianjiang shidi yanjiu* 14.4 (2004): 1–6.

Li Huizhu 李慧竹. "Handai yiqian Shandong yu Chaoxian bandao nanbu de jiaowang" 漢代以前山東與朝鮮半島南部的交往 (Contacts between Shandong and the southern Korean peninsula before the Han). *Beifang wenwu* 1 (2004): 16–24.

Li Jiancai 李健才. *Mingdai dongbei* 明代東北 (The northeast during the Ming). Shenyang: Liaoning renmin chubanshe, 1986.

Li Shanhong 李善洪. "Hou Jin Chaoxian [Ding mao zhi yi] yuanyin qianzhe" 後金朝鮮 '丁卯之役' 原因淺折 (A preliminary analysis of the causes of the 1627 invasion of Chosŏn by the Later Jin). In *Zhong Han guanxishi lunwenji* 中朝關係史研究論文集 (Collected essays on the history of Sino-Korean relations), pp. 322–28. Ed. Diao Shuren 刁書仁 and Yi Xingguo 衣興國. Changchun: Jilin wenshi chubanshe, 1995.

Li Shuying 李淑英 and Nie Tiehua 聶鐵華. "Liang Han shiqi Gaogouli de fengguo diwei" 兩漢時期高句麗的封國地位 (Gaogouli's vassal state status in the two Han dynasties). *Zhongguo bianjiang shidi yanjiu* 14.4 (2004): 62–68.

Li, Thomas Shiyu and Susan Naquin. "The Baoming Temple: Religion and the Throne in Ming and Qing China." *Harvard Journal of Asiatic Studies* 48 (1988): 131–88.

Li Zhiting 李治亭. "Hou Jin (Qing) yu Lishi Chaoxian zhanzheng shulue" 後金 (清) 與李氏朝鮮戰爭述略 (The Later Jin (Qing) and war with Yi Korea). In *Zhong Chao guanxi shi yanjiu lunwenji* 中朝關係史研究論文集 (Collected writings on the history of Sino-Korean relations), pp. 258–73. Ed. Diao Shuren 刁書仁 and Yi Xingguo 衣興國. Changchun: Jilin wenshi chubanshe, 1995.

"Dongbei difangshi yanjiu de huigu yu zhanwang" 東北地方史研究的回顧與展望 (On the past and future of research on northeast local history). *Zhongguo bianjiang shidi yanjiu* 11.4 (2001): 1–10.

Lidin, Olof G. *Tanegashima: The Arrival of Europe in Japan.* Copenhagen: Nordic Institute of Asian Studies, 2002.

Lieberman, Victor. "Transcending East–West Dichotomies: State and Culture Formation in Six Ostensibly Disparate Areas." *Modern Asian Studies* 31.3 (1997): 463–546.

Strange Parallels: Southeast Asia in Global Context, c. 800–1830. 2 vols. Cambridge: Cambridge University Press, 2003, 2009.

"What *Strange Parallels* Sought to Accomplish." *Journal of Asian Studies* 70.4 (2011): 931–38.

Lieberman, Victor, ed. *Beyond Binary Histories: Re-Imagining Eurasia to c. 1830.* Ann Arbor: University of Michigan Press, 1997.

Lin Ganquan 林甘泉. "Zhongguo bianjiang shidi yanjiu yu aiguozhuyi jiaoyu" 中國邊疆史地研究與愛國主義教育 (Research on China's borderland history and patriotism education). *Zhongguo bianjiang shidi yanjiu* 1992.2: 1–2.

Lin, Man-houng. "The Shift from East Asia to the World: The Role of Maritime Silver in China's Economy in the Seventeenth to Late Eighteenth Centuries." In *Maritime China in Transition, 1750–1850*, pp. 77–96. Ed. Wang Gungwu and Ng Chin-keong. Wiesbaden: Harrassowitz, 2004.

Liu Housheng 劉厚生. *Jiu Manzhoudang yanjiu* 舊滿洲檔研究 (Research on the old Manchu archives). Changchun: Jilin wenshi chubanshe, 1993.

"Changbaishan yu Manzu de zuxian chongbai" 長白山與滿族的祖先崇拜 (Changbaishan and Manchu ancestor worship). *Qingshi yanjiu* 3 (1996): 93–96.

"Jidai jiaqiang dongbei bianjiang shi de yanjiu" 亟待加強東北邊疆史的研究 (Earnestly strengthen the study of northeast borderland history). *Zhongguo bianjiang shidi yanjiu* 10.1 (2001): 20–22.

Liu Jiaju 劉家駒. *Qingdai chuqi de Zhong Han guanxi* 清代初期的中韓關係 (Sino-Korean relations in early Qing). Taipei: Wenshizhe chubanshe, 1986.

Liu, Lydia H. *The Clash of Empires: The Invention of China in Modern World Making.* Cambridge: Harvard University Press, 2004.

Liu Wei 刘為. "Qingdai Zhong Chao zongfan guanxi xia de tongshi wanglai" 清代中朝宗藩關係下的通使往來 (Diplomatic missions under the Sino-Korean tributary relationship during the Qing). *Zhongguo bianjiang shidi yanjiu* 10.3 (2000): 25–36.

"Chaoxian fu Qingchao shituan de wenhua jiaoliu huodong" 朝鮮赴清朝使團的文化交流活動 (Cultural exchanges of the Chosŏn emissaries to the Qing court). *Zhongguo bianjiang shidi yanjiu* 10.3 (2001): 74–82.

"Qingdai Chaoxian shituan maoyi zhidu shulüe – ZhongChao chaogong maoyi yanjiu zhi yi" 清代朝鮮使團貿易制度述略 – 中朝朝貢貿易研究之一 (A brief description of the trading system of Korean emissaries during the Qing dynasty – part of research on Sino-Korean tributary trade). *Zhongguo bianjiang shidi yanjiu* 12.1 (2002): 36–47.

Qingdai Zhong Chao shizhe wanglai yanjiu 清代中朝使者往來研究 (Sino-Korean diplomatic exchanges during the Qing dynasty). Harbin: Heilongjiang jiaoyu chubanshe, 2002.

"Shilun shezheng wang Duoergun de Chaoxian zhengce" 試論攝政王多爾袞的朝鮮政策 (On the Chosŏn policy of Regent Prince Dorgon). *Zhongguo bianjiang shidi yanjiu* 15.3 (2005): 91–102.

Long Mu 龍木. "'Gaogouli, Bohai wenti xueshu yanjiu hui' jiyao" '高句麗, 渤海問題 學術研究會' 紀要 (Summary of the "Conference on scholarly research issues concerning Gaogouli and Bohai). *Zhongguo bianjiang shidi yanjiu* 13.3 (2003): 114.

Lorge, Peter. *War, Politics, and Society in Early Modern China, 900–1795.* New York: Routledge, 2005.

The Asian Military Revolution: From Gunpowder to the Bomb. Cambridge: Cambridge University Press, 2008.

Lurie, David B. *Realms of Literacy: Early Japan and the History of Writing.* Cambridge, MA: Harvard University Asia Center, 2011.

Ma Dazheng 馬大正. "Dangdai Zhongguo bianjiang yanjiuzhe de lishi shiming" 當代中國邊疆研究者的歷史使命 (The historical mission of contemporary researchers of China's borderlands). *Zhongguo bianjiang shidi yanjiu* 2 (1992): 13–14.

"Jindai dongbeiYa guoji guanxi shi yanjiu de xin jinzhan – du Jiang Longfan zhu [Jindai Zhong Han Ri sanguo dui Jiandao Chaoxianren zhengce yanjiu]" 近代 東北亞 國際關係史研究的新進展 – 讀姜龍范著 [近代中韓日三國對間島朝鮮人政策研究] (New advances in research on northeast Asian international relations – a review of Jiang Longfan's *Chinese, Korean and Japanese Policies concerning Koreans on Jiandao Island in the Modern Era). Zhongguo bianjiang shidi yanjiu* 10.4 (2000): 111–16.

"Zhongguo xuezhe Gaogouli lishi yanjiu de bainian licheng" 中國學者高句麗歷史研究的百年歷程 (A century of research on Gaogouli history by Chinese scholars). *Zhongguo bianjiang shidi yanjiu* 10.1 (2000): 93–102.

Ma, Dazheng and Patrick Fuliang Shan. "Frontier History in China: A Scholarly Dialogue Across the Pacific Ocean." *The Chinese Historical Review* 19.1 (2012): 65–78.

Ma Yihong 馬一虹. "Cong Tang muzhi kan ru Tang Gaogouli yimin guishu yishi de bianhua" 從唐墓志看入唐高句麗遺民歸屬意識的變化 (Change in the awareness of Gaogouli remnants submitting to Tang, seen from Tang grave inscriptions). *Beifang wenwu* 2006.1: 29–37.

Maeda, Hitomi. "Imperial Authority and Local Shrines: The Yoshida House and the Creation of a Countrywide Shinto Institution in Early Modern Japan." PhD thesis, Harvard University, 2003.

Maehira Fusaaki 真栄平房明. "Min Shin dōranki ni okeru Ryūkyū bōeki no ichi kōsatsu – Kōki Keigasen no haken wo chūshin ni – " 明清動亂期における琉球貿易の一考察 – 康熙慶賀船の派遣を中心に – (A study of Ryukyuan trade during the Ming–Qing disorders – focusing on the dispatch of a ship to congratulate Kangxi). *Kyūshū shigaku* 80 (1984): 1–27.

"Taigai kankei ni okeru Kakyō to kokka – Ryūkyū no Minjin sanjuroku shō wo megutte" 對外關係における華僑と國家 – 琉球の閩人三十六姓をめぐって – (The Overseas Chinese merchants and the state in foreign relations – the 36 Fujianese surnames in the Ryukyus). In *Ajia no naka no Nihonshi* (Japanese history in Asian context), vol. III: *Kaijō no michi* 海上の道 (Maritime routes), pp. 245–64. Ed. Arano Yasunori 荒野泰典, Ishii Masatoshi 石井正敏, and Murai Shōsuke 村井章介. Tokyo: University of Tokyo Press, 1992.

Maier, Lothar. "Gerhard Friedrich Müller's Memoranda on Russian Relations with China and the Reconquest of the Amur." *The Slavonic and East European Review* 59.2 (1981): 219–40.

Mair, Victor. "The Northwestern Peoples and the Recurrent Origins of the 'Chinese' State." In *The Teleology of the Modern Nation-State: Japan and China*, pp. 46–84, 205–17. Ed. Joshua A. Fogel. Philadelphia: University of Pennsylvania Press, 2005.

Mancall, Mark. *Russia and China: Their Diplomatic Relations to 1728*. Cambridge, MA: Harvard University Press, 1971.

Mansourov, Alexander Y. "Will Flowers Bloom Without Fragrance? Korean–Chinese Relations." *Harvard Asia Quarterly* 10.2 (2006): 46–58.

Mason, David A. "The *Sam Hwangje Paehyang* (Sacrificial Ceremony for Three Emperors): Korea's Link to the Ming Dynasty." *Korea Journal* (Autumn 1991): 117–36.

Mass, Jeffrey P. "Patterns of Provincial Inheritance in Late Heian Japan." *Journal of Japanese Studies* 9.1 (1983): 67–95.

Lordship and Inheritance in Early Medieval Japan: A Study of the Kamakura Sōryō System. Stanford: Stanford University Press, 1989.

Antiquity and Anachronism in Japanese History. Stanford: Stanford University Press, 1992.

Matsui, Yōko 松井洋子. "Nagasaki Deshima to Karajin yashiki" 長崎出島と唐人屋敷 (Chinese residences in Deshima, Nagasaki). In *Edo bakufu to Higashi Ajia* 江戸幕府と東アジア (The Edo shogunate and East Asia), pp. 363–88. Ed. Arano Yasunori. Tokyo: Yoshikawa kōbunkan, 2003).

Matsumae, Takeshi. "Early kami worship." In *The Cambridge History of Japan*, vol. I: *Ancient Japan*, pp. 317–58. Ed. Delmer M. Brown. Cambridge: Cambridge University Press, 1993.

Matsumoto, Shigeru. *Motoori Norinaga, 1730–1801*. Cambridge, MA: Harvard University Press, 1970.

Matsumura Jun 松村潤. *Shin Taiso jitsuroku no kenkyū* 清太祖實錄の研究 (Research on the Qing veritable records for Nurhaci). Tokyo: Ajia bunken kenkyūkai, 2001.

Matsuura Shigeru 松浦茂. "Jūshichi seiki igo no Tōhoku Ajia ni okeru keizai kōryū" 一七世紀以降の東北アジアにおける經濟交流 (Economic exchange in northeast Asia from the seventeenth century onward). In *Matsumura Jun sensei koki kinen Shindai shi ronsō* 松村潤先生古稀記念清代史論叢 (Collected articles on Qing history, Festschrift in honor of Professor Matsumura Jun's seventieth birthday), pp. 35–67. Comp. Matsumura Jun sensei koki kinen iinkai. Tokyo: Kyūko shoin, 1994.

Shinchō no Amūru seisaku to shōsū minzoku 清朝のアムール政策と少數民族 (Qing policy toward the Amur and the minority peoples). Kyoto: Kyoto University Press, 2006.

McBride, Richard D. II. "Introduction." In *State and Society in Middle and Late Silla*, pp. 3–30. Ed. Richard D. McBride II. Cambridge, MA: Korea Institute, Harvard University, 2010.

McCullough, William H. "Japanese Marriage Institutions in the Heian Period." *Harvard Journal of Asiatic Studies* 27 (1967): 103–67.

"The Capital and Its Society." In *The Cambridge History of Japan*, vol. II: *Heian Japan*, pp. 97–182. Ed. Donald H. Shively and William H. McCullough. Cambridge: Cambridge University Press, 1999.

McMorran, Ian. "The Patriot and the Partisans: Wang Fu-chih's Involvement in the Politics of the Yung-li Court." In *From Ming to Ch'ing: Conquest, Region, and Continuity in Seventeenth-century China*, pp. 133–66. Ed. Jonathan D. Spence and John E. Wills, Jr. New Haven: Yale University Press, 1979.

McMullen, James. "Tokugawa Intellectual History: State of the Field." *Early Modern Japan* 10.1 (2002): 22–85.

Meyer, Jeffrey F. *The Dragons of Tiananmen: Beijing as a Sacred City*. Columbia, SC: University of South Carolina Press, 1991.

Miao Wei 苗威. "Cong Jin Fushi (Kim Pu-sik) de Gaogouli guan kan Gaogouli zhengquan de xingzhi ji qi lishi guishu" 從金富軾的高句麗觀看高句麗政權的性質及其歷史歸屬 (Viewing the nature of Gaogouli political authority and its historical ownership from Kim Pu-shik's Gaogouli perspective). *Zhongguo bianjiang shidi yanjiu* 14.4 (2004): 76–82.

Min Tŏkki 閔德基. "Chosŏn sidae kyorin ŭi inyŏm kwa kukche sahoe ŭi kyorin" 조선 시대 交隣의理念과 국제 사회의 交隣 (The concept of *kyorin* in the Chosŏn period and *kyorin* in international society). *Minjok munhwa* 21 (1998): 28–55.

Misaki Yoshiaki 三崎良章. "Tōi kōi ko – sono setchi to [TōI] e no juyo" 東夷校尉考 – その設置と「東夷」への授與 (A study of the title "Commandant of the Eastern Barbarians": Its establishment and conferment on the Eastern barbarian). In *Nishijima Sadao hakase tsuitō ronbunshū, Higashi Ajia shi no tenkai to Nihon* 西島定生博士追悼論文集、東アジア史の展開と日本 (Studies on the development of East Asian history and Japan, in memory of Dr. Nishijima Sadao), pp. 227–41. Comp. Nishijima Sadao hakase tsuitō ronbunshū iiinkai. Tokyo: Yamakawa shuppansha, 2000.

Mitamura Taisuke 三田村泰助. "Shin Taiso jitsuroku no sanshū ni tsuite" 清太祖實錄の纂修について (On the compilation of the veritable records for Qing Taizu). *Tōhōgaku* 19 (1959): 1–12.

Mittag, Achim. "Scribe in the Wilderness: The Manchu Conquest and the Loyal-Hearted Historiographer's (*xinshi* 心史) Mission." *Oriens Extremus* 44 (2003/04): 27–41.

Mitter, Rana. "Old Ghosts, New Memories: China's Changing War History in the Era of Post-Mao Politics." In *Warfare in China Since 1600*, pp. 505–19. Ed. Kenneth Swope. London: Ashgate, 2005.

Miura, Kunio. "Orthodoxy and Heterodoxy in Seventeenth-Century Korea: Song Siyŏl and Yun Hyu." In *The Rise of Neo-Confucianism in Korea*, pp. 411–38. Ed. William Theodore de Bary and JaHyun Kim Haboush. New York: Columbia University Press, 1985.

Mizoguchi Yūzō 溝口雄三, Tominaga Ken'ichi 富永健一, Nakajima Mineo 中島嶺雄, and Hamashita Takeshi 浜下武志. Eds. *Kanji bunkaken no rekishi to mirai* 漢字文化圏の歴史と未来 (The history and future of the Chinese character culture sphere). Tokyo: Daishūkan shoten, 1992.

Mizuno, Norihito. "China in Tokugawa Foreign Relations: The Tokugawa Bakufu's Perception of and Attitudes toward Ming–Qing China." *Sino-Japanese Studies* 15 (2003): 108–44.

"Japan and Its East Asian Neighbors: Japan's Perception of China and Korea and the Making of Foreign Policy from the Seventeenth to the Nineteenth Century." PhD thesis, Ohio State University, 2004.

Mohan, Pankaj N. "Rescuing a Stone from Nationalism: A Fresh Perspective on the King Kwanggaet'o Stele of Koguryŏ." *Journal of Inner and East Asian Studies* 1 (2004): 91–115.

Mohr, Michel. "Invocation of the Sage: The Ritual to Glorify the Emperor." In *Zen Ritual: Studies of Zen Buddhist Theory in Practice*, pp. 205–22. Ed. Steven Heine and Dale S. Wright. Oxford: Oxford University Press, 2008.

Mote, Frederick. "The Ch'eng-hua and Hung-chih Reigns, 1465–1505." In *The Cambridge History of China*, vol. VII, part 1: *The Ming Dynasty, 1368–1644*, pp. 343–402. Ed. Frederick W. Mote and Denis Twitchett. Cambridge: Cambridge University Press, 1988.

Mullaney, Thomas S. "Critical Han Studies: Introduction and Prolegomenon." In *Critical Han Studies: The History, Representation, and Identity of China's Majority*, pp. 1–20. Ed. Thomas S. Mullaney, James Leibold, Stéphane Gros, and Eric Vanden Bussche. Berkeley: University of California Press, 2012.

Müller, Gotelind, ed. *Designing History in East Asian Textbooks: Identity Politics and Transnational Aspirations*. New York: Routledge, 2011.

Murai, Shōsuke. "The Boundaries of Medieval Japan." *Acta Asiatica* 81 (2001): 72–91.

Trans. and adapted by Haruko Wakabayashi. Poems translated by Andrew Edmund Goble. "Poetry in Chinese as a Diplomatic Art in Premodern East Asia." In *Tools of Culture: Japan's Cultural, Intellectual, Medical, and Technological Contacts in East Asia, 1000–1500s*, pp. 49–69. Ed. Andrew Edmund Goble, Kenneth R. Robinson, and Haruko Wakabayashi. Ann Arbor: Association for Asian Studies, 2009.

Murai Shōsuke 村井章介. "Wakō to wa dareka – juyon, jugo seiki no Chōsen hantō wo chūshin ni – " 倭冠とはだれか－十四, 十五 世紀の朝鮮半島を中心に (The identity of the Wakō – focusing on the Korean peninsula in the fourteenth and fifteenth centuries). *Tōhōgaku* 119 (2010): 1–21.

Na Hwira. "Kodae Han'guk ŭi syamanichŭmjŏk seg egwan kwa pulkyojŏk isang sege" (The ancient Korean shamanistic world view and the Buddhist ideal world). *Han'guk kodaesa yŏn'gu* 20 (2000): 197–249.

Nakai, Kate Wildman. "The Naturalization of Confucianism in Tokugawa Japan: The Problem of Sinocentrism." *Harvard Journal of Asiatic Studies* 40.1 (1980): 157–99.

Shogunal Politics: Arai Hakuseki and the Premises of Tokugawa Rule. Cambridge, MA: Council on East Asian Studies, Harvard University, 1988.

Nakajima Gakusho 中島樂章. "Jūroku seikimatsu no Kyūshu – Tōnan Ajia bōeki – Katō Kiyomasa no Luzon bōeki wo megutte" 十六世紀末の九州－東南アジア貿易－加藤清正のルソオン貿易をめぐって (Kyushu and the Southeast Asian trade in the sixteenth century: Examining Katō Kiyomasa's trade). *Shigaku zasshi* 118.8 (2009): 1–36.

Nakami Tatsuo 中見立夫. "Hokutō Ajia wa do no yō ni, toraerete kita ka?" (How did the term Hokutō Ajia come to be adopted?). *Hokutō Ajia kenkyū* 7 (2004): 43–56.

"Nihon teki [Tōyōgaku] no keisei to kōzu" 日本的「東洋學」の形成と構圖 (The shaping and design of a Japanese "Oriental Studies"). In *[Teikoku] Nihon no gakuji* [帝國] 日本の學知 (The academic knowledge of imperial Japan), pp. 14–54. Ed. Kishimoto Mio. Tokyo: Iwanami shoten, 2006.

"[Higashi Ajia] to [TōĀ] no aida – kinsendai Nihon ni okeru [Higashi Ajia] rikai" 「東アジア」と東亞の間 – 近現代日本における「東アジア」理解 (Between *higashi Ajia* and *TōA* – Understanding *higashi Ajia* in contemporary Japan). *Nihon daigaku tsūshin kyōiku bu, tsūshin kyōiku kenkyūjo, 2011 nen Kenkyū kiyō* #24 (2011): 25–44.

Nakane, Chie. *Japanese Society*. Berkeley: University of California Press, 1970.

Naoki, Kōjirō. Trans. Felicia G. Bock. "The Nara State." In *The Cambridge History of Japan*, vol. I: *Ancient Japan*, pp. 221–67. Ed. Delmer M. Brown. Cambridge: Cambridge University Press, 1993.

Naquin, Susan. *Peking: Temples and City Life, 1400–1900*. Berkeley: University of California Press, 2000.

Naumann, Nelly. "The State Cult of the Nara and Early Heian Periods." In *Shinto in History: Ways of the Kami*, pp. 47–67. Ed. John Breen and Mark Teeuwen. Honolulu: University of Hawai'i Press, 2000.

Needham, Joseph et al. *Science and Civilisation in China*, vol. V: *Chemistry and Chemical Technology*, part 7: *Military Technology; The Gunpowder Epic*. Cambridge: Cambridge University Press, 1986.

Nelson, Sarah M. "The Statuses of Women in Ko-Shilla: Evidence from Archaeology and Historic Documents." *Korea Journal* 31.2 (1991): 101–07.

"Gender Hierarchy and the Queens of Silla." In *Sex and Gender Hierarchies*, pp. 297–315. Ed. Barbara D. Miller. Cambridge: Cambridge University Press, 1993.

"Introduction." In *The Archaeology of Northeast China: Beyond the Great Wall*, pp. 1–18. Ed. Sarah M. Nelson. London: Routledge, 1995.

"The Politics of Ethnicity in Prehistoric Korea." In *Nationalism, Politics, and the Practice of Archaeology*, pp. 218–31. Eds. Philip L. Kohl and Clare Fawcett. Cambridge: Cambridge University Press, 1995.

"The Queens of Silla: Power and Connections to the Spirit World." In *Ancient Queens: Archaeological Explorations*, pp. 77–92. Ed. Sarah M. Nelson. Walnut Creek, CA: Altamira Press, 2003.

Ng, On-cho, and Q. Edward Wang. *Mirroring the Past: The Writing and Use of History in Imperial China*. Honolulu: University of Hawai'i Press, 2005.

Ng, Wai-ming. "Political Terminology in the Legitimating of the Tokugawa System: A Study of *Bakufu* and *Shōgun*." *Journal of Asian History* 34.2 (2000): 135–48.

"Overseas Chinese in the Japan–Southeast Asia Maritime Trade during the Tokugawa Period (1603–1868)." In *Maritime China in Transition, 1750–1850*, pp. 213–26. Ed. Wang Gungwu and Ng Chin-keong. Wiesbaden: Harrassowitz, 2004.

Northeast Asian History Foundation website. http://www.historyfoundation.or.kr/
Nosco, Peter. "Confucianism and Nativism in Tokugawa Japan." In *Meeting of Minds: Intellectual and Religious Interaction in East Asian Traditions of Thought: Essays in Honor of Wing-tsit Chan and William Theodore de Bary*, pp. 278–96. Ed. Irene Bloom and Joshua A. Fogel. New York: Columbia University Press, 1997.

Ōba, Osamu. Trans. Joshua A. Fogel. "Sino-Japanese Relations in the Edo Period." *Sino-Japanese Studies* 10.1 (1997): 33–55.

Trans. Joshua A. Fogel. *Books and Boats: Sino-Japanese Relations in the Seventeenth and Eighteenth Centuries*. Portland: MerwinAsia, 2012.

Oh, Chongnok. "Chosŏn sidae ŭi wang" (Kings of the Chosŏn period). *Yoksa pi p'yŏng* 54 (2001): 283–301.

Oh, Doo Hwan. "The Silver Trade and Silver Currency in Chosŏn Korea." *Acta Koreana* 7.1 (2004): 87–114.

Ōji Toshiaki 應地利明. *Echizu no sekaizō* 繪地圖の世界像 (World images of maps). Tokyo: Iwanami shoten, 1996.

Okamoto, Hiromichi. "Foreign Policy and Maritime Trade in the Early Ming Period: Focusing on the Ryukyu Kingdom." *Acta Asiatica* 95 (2008): 33–55.

Okamoto, Sae 岡本さえ. *Shindai kinsho no kenkyū* 清代禁書の研究 (Research on banned books). Tokyo: University of Tokyo Press, 1996.

Okazaki, Takashi. Trans. Janet M. Goodwin. "Japan and the Continent." In *The Cambridge History of Japan*, vol. I: *Ancient Japan*, pp. 269–316. Ed. Delmer M. Brown. Cambridge: Cambridge University Press, 1993.

Ooms, Herman. *Charismatic Bureaucrat: A Political Biography of Matsudaira Sadanobu, 1758–1829*. Chicago: University of Chicago Press, 1975.

Tokugawa Ideology: Early Constructs, 1570–1680. Princeton: Princeton University Press, 1985.

Imperial Politics and Symbolics in Ancient Japan: The Tenmu Dynasty, 650–800. Honolulu: University of Hawai'i Press, 2009.

Oyokawa Shōji 及川將基. "Ainu Moshiri, Ezochi to Higashi Ajia" アイヌモシリ, 蝦夷地と東アジア (The Ainu Moshiri, Ezochi, and East Asia). In *Higashi Ajia no jidaisei* 東アジアの時代性 (Periodization in East Asian history), pp. 127–42. Ed. Kishi Toshihiko 貴志俊彦 et al. Tokyo: Keisui sha, 2005.

Oxnam, Robert B. *Ruling from Horseback: Manchu Politics in the Oboi Regency, 1661–1669*. Chicago: University of Chicago Press, 1975.

Pai, Hyung-Il. "The Colonial Origins of Korea's Collected Past." *In Nationalism and the Construction of Korean Identity*, pp. 13–32. Ed. Hyung-Il Pai and Timothy R. Tangherini. Berkeley: Institute of East Asian Studies, 2000.

Constructing "Korean" Origins: A Critical Review of Archaeology, Historiography, and Racial Myth in Korean State-Formation Theories. Cambridge, MA: Harvard University Asia Center, 2000).

Paine, S. C. M. *Imperial Rivals: China, Russia, and Their Disputed Frontier*. Armonk: M. E. Sharpe, 1996.

Pak Ch'angbae. "Hyŏndae Chungguk hakkye ŭi Koguryŏsa yŏn'gu sa'ŏp ŭi tŭngjang paekyŏng" (The background of the rise of Koguryŏ history research in contemporary Chinese academic circles). *Yŏksa wa hyŏnsil* 55 (2005): 131–72.

Pak Kwangmyŏng 朴光明. "Tan'gun sin'ang ŭi ŏje wa onŭl – Tan'gunsa esŏ taejonggyoro" 단군 신앙의 어제와오늘 – 단군사 [檀君祠] 에서 대종교로 – (Tan'gun worship yesterday and today –on the main religion in the Tan'gun shrines). *Han'guksa simin kangjwa* 27 (2000): 59–79.

Pak Sŏnyŏng 朴宣泠. "Chŏngch'e-sŏng (Identity) ke'im sidae ŭi Chungguk kwa'ŭi yŏksa chŏnjaeng – tongbuk p'ŭrojekt'ŭ rŭl t'onghae pon 'tongbuk' ŭi ŭimi" (China's historical battle in the era of the identity game – the significance of 'northeast' based on the Northeast Project). *Yŏksa hakpo* 182 (2004): 295–330.

"Chunghwa minguk naejŏngbu chidoro pon Paektusan chŏnggyebi – Chunghwa minguk Chungyang yŏn'guwŏn esŏ saeropkye palgulhan kando charyo" (Maps made by the Republic of China's Interior Ministry of the Paektusan stele – Maps in the Academia Sinica, Republic of China on the Kando problem). *Tongyang sahak yŏn'gu* 105 (2008): 295–313.

Pak, Yangjin. "Contested Ethnicities and Ancient Homelands in Northeast Chinese Archaeology: The Case of Koguryo and Puyo Archaeology." *Antiquity* 73.281 (1999): 613–18.

Pak Yŏnggyu. *Han kwŏnŭro ingnŭn Chosŏn wangsil kyebo* (A condensed genealogy of the Chosŏn royal house). Seoul: Ŭngjin, 2008.

Palais, James B. "Confucianism and the Aristocratic/Bureaucratic Balance in Korea." *Harvard Journal of Asiatic Studies* 44.2 (1984):427–68.

Confucian Statecraft and Korean Institutions: Yu Hyŏngwŏn and the Late Chosŏn Dynasty. Seattle: University of Washington Press, 1996.

Pan, Yihong. *Son of Heaven and Heavenly Qaghan: Sui-Tang China and Its Neighbors*. Bellingham: Center for East Asian Studies, Western Washington University, 1997.

Pan, Yi-hong. "Integration of the Northern Ethnic Frontiers in Tang China." *The Chinese Historical Review* 19.1 (2012): 3–26.

Pan Yunhong 潘允洪. *Chosŏn sidae Pibyŏnsa yŏn'gu* 朝鮮時代備邊司研究 (Research on the Border Defence Council in Chosŏn). Seoul: Kyŏng'in munhwa sa, 2003.

Park, Cheun Soo. "Kaya and Silla in Archaeological Perspective." *Early Korea*, vol. I: *Reconsidering Early Korean History Through Archaeology*, pp. 113–53. Ed. Mark E. Byington. Cambridge, MA: Korea Institute, Harvard University, 2008.

Parker, Geoffrey. *The Military Revolution: Military Innovation and the Rise of the West, 1500–1800*. Cambridge: Cambridge University Press, 1988.

Pastreich, Emanuel. "Grappling with Chinese Writing as a Material Language: Ogyū Sorai's *Yakubunsentei.*" *Harvard Journal of Asiatic Studies* 61.1 (2001): 119–70.

The Observable Mundane: Vernacular Chinese and the Emergence of a Literary Discourse on Popular Narrative in Edo Japan. Seoul: Seoul National University Press, 2011.

Pearce, Scott, Audrey Spiro, and Patricia Ebrey. "Introduction." In *Culture and Power in the Reconstitution of the Chinese Realm, 200–600*, pp. 1–32. Ed. Scott Pearce, Audre Spiro, and Patricia Ebrey. Cambridge, MA: Harvard University Asia Center, 2001.

Perdue, Peter. "Military Mobilization in Seventeenth and Eighteenth-Century China, Russia, and Mongolia." *Modern Asian Studies* 30.4 (1996): 757–93.

"Boundaries, Maps, and Movement: Chinese, Russian, and Mongolian Empires in Early Modern Central Eurasia." *The International History Review* 20.2 (1998): 263–86.

China Marches West: The Qing Conquest of Central Eurasia. Cambridge, MA: Belknap Press, 2005.

"Embracing Victory, Effacing Defeat: Rewriting the Qing Frontier Campaigns." In *The Chinese State at the Borders*, pp. 105–25. Ed. Diana Lary. Vancouver: University of British Columbia Press, 2007.

Peterson, Mark A. *Korean Adoption and Inheritance: Case Studies in the Creation of a Classic Confucian Society*. Ithaca: East Asia Program, Cornell University, 1996.

Petrov, Leonid. "Turning Historians into Party Scholar-Bureaucrats: North Korean Historiography from 1955–58." *East Asian History* 31 (2006): 101–24.

Piggott, Joan R. *The Emergence of Japanese Kingship*. Stanford: Stanford University Press, 1997.

"Chieftain Pairs and CoRulers: Female Sovereignty in Early Japan." In *Women and Class in Japanese History*, pp. 17–52. Ed. Hitomi Tonomura, Anne Walthall, and Wakita Haruko. Ann Arbor: Center for Japanese Studies, University of Michigan, 1999.

Pines, Yuri. "Beasts or Humans: Pre-Imperial Origins of the 'Sino-Barbarian' Dichotomy." *In Mongols, Turks, and Others: Eurasian Nomads and the Sedentary World*, pp. 59–102. Ed. Reuven Amitai and Michal Biran. Leiden: E. J. Brill, 2005.

Pomeranz, Kenneth. "Water to Iron, Widows to Warlords: The Handan Rain Shrine in Modern Chinese History." *Late Imperial China* 12.1 (1991): 62–99.

Posonby-Fane, R. A. B. *The Imperial House of Japan*. Kyoto: Posonby Memorial Society, 1959.

Provine, Robert C. *Essays on Sino-Korean Musicology: Early Sources for Korean Ritual Music*. Seoul: Il Ji Sa, 1988.

Ptak, Roderich. "Sino-Japanese Maritime Trade, circa 1550: Merchants, Ports and Networks." In *China and the Asian Seas: Trade, Travel, and Visions of the Other (1400–1750)*, pp. 281–311. Ed. Roderich Ptak. Aldershot: Ashgate, 1998.

Pu Wencheng 蒲文成. "Zang zhuan Fojiao zhupai zai Qinghai de zaoqi zhuangbo ji qi gaizong" 藏傳佛教諸派在清海的早期轉播及其改宗 (The early propagation and reform of Tibetan Buddhist sects in Qinghai). *Xizang yanjiu* 2 (1990): 107–12, 125.

Qi Meiqin 祁美琴. "Dui Qingdai chaogong tizhi diwei de zai renshi" 對清代朝貢體制地位的再認識 (A re-examination of the status of the tributary system in the Qing). *Zhongguo bianjiang shidi yanjiu* 16.1 (2006): 47–55.

Qian Shoushan 千壽山. "Lun Chaoxian wangchao shiqi de bianjin zhengce he liumin fanyue" 論朝鮮王朝時期的邊禁政策和流民犯越 (On the border closure policy in the Chosŏn dynastic period and the incursions of the mobile population). *Beifang minzu* 2 (1999): 69–73.

Qiu, Jin. "History and State: Searching the Past in Light of the Present in the People's Republic of China." *Historiography East & West* 2.1 (2004): 1–44.

"The Politics of History and Historical Memory in China–Japan Relations." *Journal of Chinese Political Science* 11.1 (2006): 25–53.

Rambelli, Fabio. "Religion, Ideology of Domination, and Nationalism: Kuroda Toshio on the Discourse of *Shinkoku.*" *Japanese Journal of Religious Studies* 23.3/4 (1996): 387–426.

"The Emperor's New Robes: Processes of Resignification in Shingon Imperial Rituals." *Cahiers d'Extrême-Asie* 13 (2002–3): 427–53.

Ramsay, S. Robert. *The Languages of China*. Princeton: Princeton University Press, 1987.

Ravina, Mark. "State-building and Political Economy in Early-Modern Japan." *Journal of Asian Studies* 54.4 (1995): 997–1022.

Rawski, Evelyn S. "A Historian's Approach to Chinese Death Ritual." *In Death Ritual in Late Imperial and Modern China*, pp. 20–34. Ed. James L. Watson and Evelyn S. Rawski. Berkeley: University of California Press, 1988.

"Reenvisioning the Qing: The Significance of the Qing Period in Chinese History." *Journal of Asian Studies* 55.4 (1996): 829–50.

The Last Emperors: A Social History of Qing Imperial Institutions. Berkeley: University of California Press, 1998.

"The Qing Formation and the Early-Modern Period." In *The Qing Formation in World-Historical Time*, pp. 207–41. Ed. Lynn A. Struve. Honolulu: University of Hawai'i Press, 2004.

"Chinese Strategy and Security Issues in Historical Perspective." In *China's Rise in Historical Perspective*, pp. 63–87. Ed. Brantly Womack. Lanham: Rowman & Littlefield, 2010.

"War Letters: Hongtaiji and Injo during the Second Invasion of Korea." In *Political Strategies of Identity-Building in Non-Han Empires in China*, pp. 171–84. Ed. Francesca Fiaschetti and Julia Schneider. Wiesbaden: Otto Harrassowitz, 2014.

Reischauer, Edwin O. and John K. Fairbank. *East Asia: The Great Tradition*. Boston: Houghton Mifflin, 1958.

"Relie zhuhe Zhongguo bianjiang shidi yanjiu zhongxin chengli ershi zhou nian" 熱烈祝賀中國邊疆史地研究中心成立二十周年 (Warmly congratulate the Center for the Study of China's Borderland History and Geography's twentieth anniversary). *Zhongguo bianjiang shidi yanjiu* 13.3 (2003): 1.

Ren Xijun 任熙俊. "Changbaishan 'dingjiebei' shimo – jiankao Tumenjiang bianjie wenti" 長白山'定界碑'始末 – 兼考圖們江邊界問題 (On the boundary stone at Changbaishan – examining the issue of the Tumen River boundary). In *Zhong Chao guanxi shi yanjiu lunwenji* 中朝關係史研究論文集 (Collected writings on the history of Sino-Korean relations), pp. 234–52. Ed. Diao Shuren 刁書仁 and Yi Xingguo 衣興國. Changchun: Jilin wenshi chubanshe, 1995.

Repp, Martin. "Hachiman – Protecting *kami* of the Japanese Nation." In *Religion and National Identity in the Japanese Context*, pp. 169–92. Ed. Klaus Antoni, Hiroshi Kubota, Johann Nawrocki, and Michael Wachutka. Münster: Lit, 2002.

Rhee, Song Nai. "Secondary State Formation: The Case of Koguryŏ State." In *Pacific Northeast Asia in Prehistory: Hunter-Fisher-Gatherers, Farmers, and*

Sociopolitical Elites, pp. 191–96. Ed. C. Melvin Aikens and Song Nai Rhee. Pullman, WA: Washington State University Press, 1992.

Ri Seishi [Yi Sŏngsi] 李成市. *Higashi Ajia bunkaken no keisei* 東アジア文化圏の形成 (The formation of the East Asian cultural sphere). Tokyo: Yamakawa shuppansha, 2004.

Roberts, Luke S. *Performing the Great Peace: Political Space and Open Secrets in Tokugawa Japan*. Honolulu: University of Hawaiʻi Press, 2012.

Robinson, David M. "Korean Lobbying at the Ming Court: King Chungjong's Usurpation of 1506: A Research Note." *Ming Studies* 41 (1999): 37–53.

Empire's Twilight: Northeast Asia Under the Mongols. Cambridge: Harvard Asia Center, 2009.

Martial Spectacles of the Ming Court. Cambridge, MA: Harvard University Asia Center, 2013.

Robinson, Kenneth R. "From Raiders to Traders: Border Security and Border Control in Early Chosŏn, 1392–1450." *Korean Studies* 16 (1992): 94–115.

"The Tsushima Governor and Regulation of Japanese Access to Chosŏn in the Fifteenth and Sixteenth Centuries." *Korean Studies* 20 (1996): 23–50.

"The Jiubian and Ezogachishima Embassies to Chosŏn, 1478–1482." *Chōsenshi kenkyūkai ronbunshū* 35 (1997): 55–86.

"Chōsen ō-chō – jushoku Joshinjin no kankei to 'Chōsen'" 朝鮮王朝–受職女真人の関係と'朝鮮' (The Chosŏn dynasty – the relationship of Jurchen holding office and 'Chosŏn'). *Rekishi hyōron* 592 (1999): 29–42.

"The Imposter Branch of the Hatakeyama Family and Japanese–Chosŏn Korea Court Relations, 1455–1580s." *Asian Cultural Studies* 25 (1999): 67–87.

"Centering the King of Chosŏn: Aspects of Korean Maritime Diplomacy, 1392–1592." *Journal of Asian Studies* 59.1 (2000): 109–25.

"Treated as Treasures: The Circulation of Sutras in Maritime Northeast Asia from 1388 to the Mid-Sixteenth Century." *East Asian History* 21 (2001): 33–54.

"Shaping Interactions with Jurchens in the Early Chosŏn Period." In *Embracing the Other: The Interaction of Korean and Foreign Cultures, Proceedings of the First World Congress of Korean Studies, 2002*, I: 1443–50. Sponsored by the Academy of Korean Studies, International Society for Korean Studies, Association for Korean Studies in Europe, and Korean Studies Association of Australasia. Songnam: The Academy of Korean Studies, 2002.

"An Island's Place in History: Tsushima in Japan and in Chosŏn 1392–1592." *Korean Studies* 30 (2006): 38–64.

"Residence and Foreign Relations in the Peninsular Northeast during the Fifteenth and Sixteenth Centuries." In *The Northern Region of Korea: History, Identity and Culture*, pp. 18–36. Ed. Sun Joo Kim. Seattle: University of Washington Press, 2010.

Robinson, Michael E. "National Identity and the Thought of Sin Ch'aeho: Sadaejuŭi and Chuch'e in History and Politics." *Journal of Korean Studies* 5 (1984): 121–42.

Cultural Nationalism in Colonial Korea, 1920–1925. Seattle: University of Washington Press, 1988.

Rogers, Michael C. "Sung–Koryŏ Relations: Some Inhibiting Factors." *Oriens* 11.1–2 (1958): 194–202.

"Koryŏ's Military Dictatorship and Its Relations with Chin." *T'oung Pao* 47.1–2 (1959): 43–62.

"Sukchong of Koryŏ: His Accession and His Relations with Liao." *T'oung Pao* 47.1–2 (1959): 30–42.

"The Regularization of Koryŏ–Chin Relations (1116–1131)." *Central Asiatic Journal* 6.2 (1961): 51–84.

"National Consciousness in Medieval Korea: The Impact of Liao and Chin on Koryŏ." In *China Among Equals: The Middle Kingdom and Its Neighbors, 10th–14th Centuries*, pp. 151–72. Ed. Morris Rossabi. Berkeley: University of California Press, 1983.

Rosenfield, John M. "Introduction: Tōdai-ji in Japanese History and Art." In *The Great Eastern Temple: Treasures of Japanese Buddhist Art from Tōdai-ji*, pp. 17–31. Ed. Yutaka Mino et al. Bloomington: Art Institute of Chicago and Indiana University Press, 1986.

Rossabi, Morris. *China and Inner Asia from 1368 to the Present Day*. New York: Pica Press, 1975.

The Jurchens in the Yüan and Ming. Cornell University East Asia Papers, No. 27. Ithaca, New York: China–Japan Program, Cornell University, 1982.

Khubilai Khan: His Life and Times. Berkeley: University of California Press, 1988.

"The Ming and Inner Asia." In *The Cambridge History of China, 1368–1633*, vol. VIII, part 2: *The Ming Dynasty, 1368–1644*, pp. 258–71. Ed. Denis Twitchett and Frederick W. Mote. Cambridge: Cambridge University Press, 1998.

Roth, Gertraude. "The Manchu–Chinese Relationship, 1618–1636." In *From Ming to Ch'ing: Conquest, Region, and Continuity in Seventeenth-Century China*, pp. 1–38. Ed. Jonathan D. Spence and John E. Wills, Jr. New Haven: Yale University Press, 1979.

Ru Ying 茹瑩. "Hanyu 'minzu' yici zai wo guo de zuizao chuxian" 漢語 '民族' 一詞 在 我 國 的 最早 出現 (The first appearance of the phrase 'minzu' in Chinese). *Shijie minzu* 6 (2001): 1.

Ruan Xihu 阮西湖. "'Minzu' yici zai Yingwen zhong ruhe biaoshu" '民族' 一詞 在英文中如何表述 (How *minzu* is expressed in English). *Shijie minzu* 6 (2001): 78.

Rubinger, Richard. *Popular Literacy in Early Modern Japan*. Honolulu: University of Hawai'i Press, 2007.

Ryu Pojŏn 劉寶全. "Imjin waeran si pabyŏng ŭi silsang e taehan ilgo – kŭ tonggi wa sigi rŭl chungsim ŭro" 壬辰倭亂時派兵의實相에 대한 一考 – 그 動機와 時機를 中心으로 – (An investigation of the Ming dynasty's dispatch of troops in the Japanese invasion, focused on the motives and time). *Han'guksa hakpo* 14(2003): 151–84.

Saeki Kōji 佐伯弘次. "Kaizoku ron" 海賊論 (On pirates). In *Ajia no naka no Nihon shi* アジアのなかの日本史 (Japanese history in Asian context), vol. 3: *Kaijō no michi* 海上の道 (Maritime routes), pp. 35–61. Ed. Arano Yasunori 荒野泰典, Ishii Masatoshi 石井正敏, and Murai Shōsuke 村井章介. Tokyo: University of Tokyo Press, 1992.

Trans. Peter Shapinsky. "Chinese Trade Ceramics in Medieval Japan." In *Tools of Culture: Japan's Cultural, Intellectual, Medical, and Technological Contacts in East Asia, 1000–1500s*, pp. 163–82. Ed. Andrew E. Goble, Kenneth R. Robinson, and Haruko Wakabayashi. Ann Arbor: Association for Asian Studies, 2009.

Sakamaki, Shunzō. "Ryukyu and Southeast Asia." *Journal of Asian Studies* 23.3 (1964): 383–89.

Sakamoto, Tarō. Trans. John S. Brownlee. *The Six National Histories of Japan*. Vancouver and Tokyo: University of British Columbia Press and Tokyo University Press, 1991.

Sakayori Masashi 酒寄雅志. Tōhoku Ajia no dōkō to kodai Nihon – Botsukai no shiten kara:" 東アジアの動向と古代日本 – 渤海の視點から (Trends in northeast Asia and ancient Japan – the view from Parhae). In *Shinpan kodai no Nihon* 新版古代の日本, (New publication on ancient Japan), vol. II: *Ajia kara mita kodai Nihon* アジアから見た古代日本 (Ancient Japan in Asian perspective), pp. 295–318. Ed. Tsuboi Kiyotari 坪井清足 and Hirano Kunio 平野邦雄. Tokyo: Kadokawa shoten, 1992.

"Ka-I shisō no shosō" 華夷思想の諸相 (Aspects of civilized-barbarian thought). In *Ajia no naka no Nihonshi* アジアのなかの日本史 (Japanese history in Asian context), vol. V: *Jiishiki to sōgo rikai* 自意識と相互理解 (Reflection and Reciprocity), pp. 27–58. Ed. Arano Yasunori 荒野泰典, Ishii Masatoshi 石井正敏 and Murai Shōsuke 村井章介. Tokyo: University of Tokyo Press, 1993.

Trans. Han Kyuch'ŏl. "Ilbon kwa Parhae, Malgal ŭi kyoryu – Tonghae, Ohoch'ŭk'ŭ [Okhotsk] haeyŏkkwŏn kwa sŏn –" (Japan's exchanges with Parhae and Malgal – the East Sea Okhotsk maritime zone and ships). *Kuksakwŏn nonch'ong* 85 (1999): 263–77.

Sakuma Shigeo 佐久間重男. "Min Shin kara mita Higashi Ajia no Ka-I chitsujō" 明清からみた東アジアの華夷秩序 (The Civilized-Barbarian Order of East Asia as seen during the Ming and Qing). In his *Nichi Min kankeishi no kenkyū* 日明關係史の研究, pp. 349–73. Tokyo: Yoshikawa kōbunkan, 1992.

Sanjdorj, M. Trans. Urgunge Onon. *Manchu Colonial Rule in Northern Mongolia*. New York: St. Martin's Press, 1980.

Sansom, George B. *A History of Japan*. 3 vols. Stanford: Stanford University Press, 1958.

Sasse, Werner. "Trying to Figure Out How Kings Became Kings in Silla." In *Mélanges offerts à Li Ogg et Daniel Bouchez, Cahiers d'Études, Coréenes* No. 7, pp. 229–30. Paris: Centre d'Études Coréenes, 2001.

Sawa Miki 澤美香. "Tō'an shiryō kara mita [Kōyo zenranto] to Yoroppa gijutsu" 檔案史料から見た「皇輿全覽圖」とヨロッパ技術 (The *Huangyu quan lantu* and European technology, as seen from archival materials). *Shikan* 121 (1989): 53–64.

Scheid, Bernhard. "Land of the *Kami* and Way of the *Kami* in Yoshida Shintō." In *Religion and National Identity in the Japanese Context*, pp. 193–215. Ed. Klaus Antoni, Hiroshi Kubota, Johann Nawrocki, and Michael Wachutka. Münster: Lit, 2002.

Schmid, Andre. "Rediscovering Manchuria: Sin Ch'aeho and the Politics of Territorial History in Korea." *Journal of Asian Studies* 56.1 (1997): 26–46.

"Decentering the 'Middle Kingdom': The Problem of China in Korean Nationalist Thought, 1895–1910." In *Nation Work: Asian Elites and National Identities*, pp. 83–107. Ed. Timothy Brook and Andre Schmid. Ann Arbor: University of Michigan Press, 2000.

Korea Between Empires, 1895–1919. New York: Columbia University Press, 2002.

"Tributary Relations and the Qing–Chosŏn Frontier on Mount Paektu." In *The Chinese State at the Borders*, pp. 126–50. Ed. Diana Lary. Vancouver: University of British Columbia Press, 2007.

Schwartz, Benjamin I. *The World of Thought in Ancient China.* Cambridge, MA: Belknap Press, 1985.

Senda Minoru 千田稔. *Ise jingū – Higashi Ajia no Amaterasu* 伊勢神宮 – 東アジアのアマテラス (The Ise shrine: East Asia's Amaterasu). Tokyo: Chūōkōron shinsha, 2005.

"Seoul Smiles at China's Daylight Robbery." *Digital Chosun ilbo (English edition)*, October 31, 2006, http://english.chosun.com/.

Shepherd, John Robert. *Statecraft and Political Economy on the Taiwan Frontier, 1600–1800.* Stanford: Stanford University Press, 1993.

Shiba, Yoshinobu. "Ningpo and Its Hinterland." In *The City in Late Imperial China*, pp. 391–439. Ed. G. William Skinner. Palo Alto: Stanford University Press, 1977.

Shim, Jae-hoon. "A New Understanding of Kija Chosŏn as a Historical Anachronism." *Harvard Journal of Asiatic Studies* 62.2 (2002): 271–305.

Shima, Mutsuhiko. "In Quest of Social Recognition: A Retrospective View on the Development of Korean Lineage Organization." *Harvard Journal of Asiatic Studies* 50.1 (1990): 87–129.

Shin, Leo K. *The Making of the Chinese State: Ethnicity and Expansion on the Ming Borderlands.* Cambridge: Cambridge University Press, 2006.

Shin Tōkei 申東珪 (K. Sin Tonggyu). "Orandajin hōryūmin to Chōsen no Seiyōshiki buki no kaihatsu" オランダ人漂流民と朝鮮の西洋式武器の開発 (Dutch castaways and the development of Western weapons in Korea). *Shien* 史苑 61.1 (2000): 54–70.

Shively, Donald H. and William H. McCullough, "Introduction." In *The Cambridge History of Japan*, vol. II: *Heian Japan*, pp. 1–19. Ed. Donald H. Shively and William H. McCullough. Cambridge: Cambridge University Press, 1999.

Sin Chubaek. "Han'guk kŭnhyŏndaesa esŏ Koguryŏ wa Parhae e kwanhan insik – yŏksa kyokwasŏ rŭl chungsim uro" (The contemporary perception of Koguryŏ and Parhae, focusing on history textbooks). *Yŏksa wa hyŏnsil* 55 (2005): 101–30.

Sin Pyŏngju. "'Odaesanbon' Chosŏn wangjo sillok ŭi kanhaeng kwa pogwan" (The publication and custody of the Odaesan set of the Veritable Records of the Chosŏn Dynasty). *Yŏksa wa hyŏnsil* 61 (2006): 175–211.

Skaff, Jonathan Karam. "Tang Military Culture and Its Inner Asian Influences." In *Military Culture in Imperial China*, pp. 165–91. Ed. Nicola Di Cosmo. Cambridge, MA: Harvard University Press, 2009.

Sui-Tang China and Its Turko-Mongol Neighbors: Culture, Power, and Connections, 580–800. Oxford: Oxford University Press, 2012.

Smith, Paul Jakov. "Introduction: Problematizing the Song-Yuan-Ming Transition." In *The Song-Yuan-Ming Transition in Chinese History*, pp. 1–34. Ed. Paul Jakov Smith and Richard von Glahn. Cambridge, MA: Harvard University Asia Center, 2003.

Smith, Robert J. *Ancestor Worship in Contemporary Japan*. Stanford: Stanford University Press, 1974.

Smits, Gregory. *Visions of Ryukyu: Identity and Ideology in Early-Modern Thought and Politics*. Honolulu: University of Hawai'i Press, 1999.

Smits, Ivo. "China as Classic Text: Chinese Books and Twelfth-Century Japanese Collectors." In *Tools of Culture: Japan's Cultural, Intellectual, Medical, and Technological Contacts in East Asia, 1000–1500s*, pp. 185–210. Ed. Andrew Edmund Goble, Kenneth R. Robinson, and Haruko Wakabayashi. Ann Arbor: Association for Asian Studies, 2009.

Snyder-Reinke, Jeffrey. *Dry Spells: State Rainmaking and Local Governance in Late Imperial China*. Cambridge, MA: Harvard University Asia Center, 2009.

So, Kwan-wai. *Japanese Piracy in Ming China During the 16th Century*. Dearborn: Michigan State University Press, 1975.

Somers, Robert M. "The end of the T'ang." In *The Cambridge History of China*, vol. III, part 1: *Sui and T'ang China, 580–906*, pp. 682–789. Ed. Denis Twitchett. Cambridge: Cambridge University Press, 1979.

Son Sŭngch'ŏl 孫承喆. "Chosŏn t'ongsinsa wa 21 segi Han-Il kwan'gye" (The Chosŏn envoys and Korean-Japanese relations in the 21st century). In *Toedola pon Han-Il kwan'gyesa* (Revisiting the Korean–Japanese relationship), pp. 139–57. Ed. Han-Il munhwa kyoryu kigum. Seoul: Kyŏn'in munhwa sa, 2005.

Sonehara Satoshi 曾根原理. "Tokugawa Ieyasu nenki kōji ni arawareta shinkoku isshiki – Iemitsu ki wo taisō to shite" 德川家康年忌行事にあらわれた神國意識－家光期を對象として (The divine country consciousness revealed in commemorations of Tokugawa Iyeyasu's death day – focusing on the Iemitsu period). *Nihonshi kenkyū* 510 (2004): 92–119.

Song, Jhune Hyueck. "Eastern Barbarian Consciousness in *Research on Manchu Origins*." *The Review of Korean Studies* 12.3 (2009): 163–75.

Song, Ki-ho. "China's Attempt at 'Stealing' Parts of Ancient Korean History." *The Review of Korean Studies* 7 (2004): 93–122.

Song, Ki-joong. *The Study of Foreign Languages in the Chosŏn Dynasty (1392–1910)*. Seoul: Chimmundang, 2001.

Sonoda, Kōyū with Delmer M. Brown. "Early Buddha worship." In *The Cambridge History of Japan*, vol. I: *Ancient Japan*, pp. 359–414. Ed. Delmer M. Brown. Cambridge: Cambridge University Press, 1993.

Sørensen, Henrik H. "Lamaism in Korea during the Late Koryŏ Dynasty." *Korea Journal* 33.3 (1993): 67–81.

"South Koreans Resist Beijing's Revision of Gaogouli History, Rip Up the Chinese Flag." September 8, 2006, www.wenxuecity.com.

Souyri, Pierre François. Trans. Käthe Roth. *The World Turned Upside Down: Medieval Japanese Society.* New York: Columbia University Press, 2001.

Spence, Jonathan. *Treason by the Book.* New York: Viking Penguin, 2001.

Sperling, Elliot. "The Fifth Karma-pa and Some Aspects of the Relationship Between Tibet and the Early Ming." In *Tibetan Studies in Honour of Hugh Richardson,* pp. 280–89. Ed. Michael Aris and Aung San Suu Kyi. Warminster: Aris and Phillips, 1980.

"Early Ming Policy Toward Tibet: An Examination of the Proposition that the Early Ming Emperors Adopted a 'Divide and Rule' Policy toward Tibet." PhD thesis, Indiana University, 1983.

Staines, Reuben. "Researcher Proposes Economic Pressure on China Over Koguryŏ." *The Korea Times,* August 20, 2004. http://times.hankooki.com/.

Standen, Naomi. "(Re)Constructing the Frontiers of Tenth-Century China." In *Frontiers in Question: Eurasian Borderlands, 700–1700,* pp. 55–79. Ed. Daniel Power and Naomi Standen. New York: St. Martin's Press, 1999.

Unbounded Loyalty: Frontier Crossing in Liao China. Honolulu: University of Hawai'i Press, 2007.

Starn, Randoph. "Review Article: The Early Modern Muddle." *Journal of Early Modern History* 6.3 (2002): 296–307.

Steinhardt, Nancy Shatzman. *Liao Architecture.* Honolulu: University of Hawai'i Press, 1997.

Stephan, John H. *The Russian Far East: A History.* Stanford: Stanford University Press, 1994.

Struve, Lynn A. *The Ming–Qing Conflict, 1619–1683: A Historiography and Source Guide.* Ann Arbor: Association for Asian Studies, 1998.

Struve, Lynn A., ed. and trans. *Voices from the Ming–Qing Cataclysm: China in Tigers' Jaws.* New Haven: Yale University Press, 1993.

Sugiyama, Kiyohiko. "The Ch'ing Empire as a Manchu Khanate: The Structure of Rule under the Eight Banners." *Acta Asiatica* No. 88 (2005): 1–20.

"The Qing Empire in the Central Eurasian Context: Its Structure of Rule as Seen from the Eight Banner System." In *Comparative Imperiology,* pp. 87–108. Ed. Kimitaka Matsuzato. Sapporo: Slavic Research Center, Hokkaido University, 2009.

Sun Chunri 孫春日. "Qing mo Zhong Chao Ri 'Jiandao wenti' jiaoshe zhi yuanwei" 清末 中朝日 '間島問題' 交涉 之 原委 (The whole story of negotiations between China, Korea and Japan on the 'Jiandao issue' in late Qing). *Zhongguo bianjiang shidi yanjiu* 12.4 (2002): 48–58.

Sun, Laichen. "Military Technology Transfers from Ming China and the Emergence of Northern Mainland Southeast Asia (*c.* 1390–1527)." *Journal of Southeast Asian Studies* 34.3 (2003): 495–517.

Sun Wenliang 孫文良 and Li Zhiting 李治亭. *Tiancong han, Chongde di* 天聰汗, 崇德帝 (Biography of Hongtaiji). Changchun: Jilin wenshi chubanshe, 1993.

Sung, Bae Woo. Trans. Byonghyon Choi. "Worldviews and Early Cartography." In *The Artistry of Early Korean Cartography,* pp. 93–128. Ed. Young-woo Han, Hwi-Joon Ahn, and Bae Woo Sung. Larkspur, CA: Tamal Vista Publications, 1999.

Suzuki Nobuaki 鈴木信昭. "Richō Ninsoki o torimaku taigai kankei – tai Min, tai Shin, tai Nichi seisaku wo megutte" 李朝仁組期をとりまく對外關係－對明, 對清,對日政策をめぐって (Foreign relations surrounding the Injo reign in the Yi dynasty: Policy toward the Ming, Qing, and Japan). In *Zenkindai no Nihon to Higashi Ajia* 前近代の日本と東アジア (Premodern Japan and East Asia), pp. 421–50. Ed. Tanaka Takeo 田中健夫. Tokyo: Yoshikawa kōbunkan, 1995.

Swope, Kenneth M. "Deceit, Disguise, and Dependence: China, Japan, and the Future of the Tributary System, 1592–1596." *The International History Review* 24.4 (2002): 757–82.

"A Few Good Men: The Li Family and China's Northern Frontier in the Late Ming." *Ming Studies* 49 (2004): 34–81.

"Crouching Tigers, Secret Weapons: Military Technology Employed During the Sino-Japanese-Korean War, 1592–1598." *Journal of Military History* 69 (2005): 11–41.

"Beyond Turtleboats: Siege Accounts from Hideyoshi's Second Invasion of Korea, 1597–1598." *Sungkyun Journal of East Asian Studies* 6.2 (2006): 177–206.

A Dragon's Head and a Serpent's Tail: Ming China and the First Great East Asian War, 1592–1598. Norman: University of Oklahoma Press, 2009.

Symons, Van Jay. *Ch'ing Ginseng Management: Ch'ing Monopolies in Microcosm.* Tempe: Center for Asian Studies, Arizona State University, 1981.

Takagi, Shōsaku. "Hideyoshi's and Ieyasu's Views of Japan as a Land of the Gods and Its Antecedents: With Reference to the 'Writ for the Expulsion of Missionaries' of 1614." *Acta Asiatica* 87 (2004): 59–84.

"Introduction: Postwar Trends in the Study of Early Modern Japanese History." *Acta Asiatica* 87 (2004): iii–xvi.

Takahashi, Chikashi. "Inter-Asian Competition in the Fur Market in the Eighteenth and Nineteenth Centuries." In *Intra-Asian Trade and the World Market*, pp. 37–45. Ed. A. J. H. Latham and Heita Kawakatsu. London: Routledge, 2006.

Takeda, Yukio. "Studies on the King Kwanggaito Inscription and Their Basis." *The Memoirs of the Toyo Bunko* 47 (1989): 57–89.

Tamamuro, Fumio. "The Korean Embassy to Tokugawa Japan in 1748: Protocol and Reception by the Tokugawa Bakufu." In *Korea Between Tradition and Modernity: Selected Papers from the Fourth Pacific and Asian Conference on Korean Studies*, pp. 139–46. Ed. Chang Yun-shik, Donald L. Baker, Hur Nam-lin, and Ross King. Vancouver: University of British Columbia Press, 2000.

Tanaka Takeo with Robert Sakai. "Japan's Relations with Overseas Countries." In *Japan in the Muromachi Age*, pp. 159–81. Ed. John W. Hall and Takeshi Toyoda. Berkeley: University of California Press, 1977.

Tao Mian 陶勉. "Qing Han Zhongjiang maoyi shulüe" 清韓中江貿易述略 (A brief outline of the Qing trade at Chunggang in Korea). *Zhongguo bianjiang shidi yanjiu* 1997.1: 46–54.

Tashiro, Kazui. "Tsushima Han's Korean Trade, 1684–1710." *Acta Asiatica* 30 (1976): 85–105.

Trans. Susan Downing Videen. "Foreign Relations During the Edo Period: Sakoku Reexamined." *Journal of Japanese Studies* 8.2 (1982): 283–306.

"Exports of Japan's Silver to China via Korea and Changes in the Tokugawa Monetary System During the seventeenth and eighteenth Centuries." In *Precious Metals, Coinage and the Changes of Monetary Structures in Latin-America, Europe and Asia (Later Middle Ages-Early Modern Times)*, pp. 99–116. Ed. Eddy H. G. Van Cauwenburghe. Leuven: Leuven University Press, 1989.

Tashiro Kazui 田代和生. "Jūshichi seiki goki – jūhachi seiki Nihon gin no kaigai yushutsu – toku ni Tsushima, Chōsen ru-to o chūshin ni" 十七世紀後期 － 十八世紀日本銀の海外輸出 － 特に對馬，朝鮮ルートを中心に (The export of silver from Japan in the late seventeenth and eighteenth centuries, especially focusing on the Tsushima and Korea route). In *Atarashii Edo jidai shizō wo motomete – sono shakai keizai shiteki sekkin* 新らしい江戸時代史像を求めて－その社會經濟史的接近 (Pursuing the new historical image of the Edo period through its socio-economic history), pp. 47–68. Ed. Shakai keizai shigakkai. Tokyo: Tōyō keizai shinpōsha, 1977.

Taylor, Romeyn. "Official and Popular Religion and the Political Organization of Chinese Society in the Ming." In *Orthodoxy in Late Imperial China*, pp. 126–57. Ed. Kwang-ching Liu. Berkeley: University of California Press, 1990.

ten Grotenhuis, Elizabeth. *Japanese Mandalas: Representations of Sacred Geography*. Honolulu: University of Hawai'i Press, 1999.

Teng Hongyan 藤紅岩. "Bohai zhi Riben liwu tanzhe" 渤海致日本 禮物探折 (Inquiry into the gifts presented by Bohai to Japan). *Zhongguo bianjiang shidi yanjiu* 16.2 (2006): 69–76.

Teng Shaozhen 騰紹箴. "Shilun Ming yu Hou Jin zhanzheng de yuanyin ji qi xingzhi" 試論明與後金戰爭的原因及其性質 (On the causes and the nature of the war between Ming and Later Jin). *Minzu yanjiu* 1980 #5: 11–20.

Nuerhachi pingzhuan 怒爾哈赤評傳 (Biography of Nurhaci). Shenyang: Liaoning renmin chubanshe, 1985.

Toby, Ronald P. *State and Diplomacy in Early Modern Japan: Asia in the Development of the Tokugawa Bakufu*. Princeton: Princeton University Press, 1984.

"Contesting the Centre: International Sources of Japanese National Identity." *International History Review* 7.3 (1985): 347–63.

"Carnival of the Aliens: Korean Embassies in Edo-Period Art and Popular Culture." *Monumenta Nipponica* 41.4 (1986): 416–56.

"Three Realms/Myriad Countries: An 'Ethnography' of Other and the Re-bounding of Japan, 1550–1750." In *Constructing Nationhood in Modern East Asia*, pp. 15–45. Ed. Kai-wing Chow, Kevin M. Doak, and Poshek Fu. Ann Arbor: University of Michigan Press, 2001.

Tokutomi Iichirō 德富猪一郎 and Hiraizumi Kiyoshi 平泉澄. Ed. *Matsudaira Sadanobu jidai* 松平定信 時代. In their *Kinsei Nihon kokumin shi* 近世日本國民史 (History of the Japanese people in the early modern period). Tokyo: Kodansha, 1983.

Tonomura, Hitomi. "Women and Inheritance in Japan's Early Warrior Society." *Comparative Studies in Society and History* 32.3 (1990): 592–623.

Tonomura, Hitomi and Anne Walthall. "Introduction." In *Women and Class in Japanese History*, pp. 1–16. Ed. Hitomi Tonomura, Anne Walthall, and Wakita Haruko. Ann Arbor: Center for Japanese Studies, University of Michigan, 1999.

Torbert, Preston M. *The Ch'ing Imperial Household Department: A Study of Its Organization and Principal Functions, 1662–1796*. Cambridge, MA: Council on East Asian Studies, Harvard University, 1977.

Torii Yumiko 鳥井裕美子. "Kinsei Nihon no Ajia ninshiki" 近世日本のアジア認識 (Asian consciousness in early modern Japan). In *Ajia kara kangaeru* アジアから考える (From the Asian perspective), vol. I: *Kōsaku suru Ajia* 交錯するアジア (Asia in involvement), pp. 219–52. Ed. Mizoguchi Yūzō 溝口雄三 et al. Tokyo: Tokyo University Press, 1993.

Totman, Conrad. *Politics in the Tokugawa Bakufu, 1600–1843*. Berkeley: University of California Press, 1988.

Trekhsviatskyi, Anatole. "At the Far Edge of the Chinese Oikoumene: Mutual Relations of the Indigenous Population of Sakhalin with the Yuan and Ming Dynasties." *Journal of Asian History* 41.2 (2007): 131–55.

Tsuji, Tatsuya. "Politics in the Eighteenth Century." In *The Cambridge History of Japan*, vol. IV: *Early Modern Japan*, pp. 425–77. Ed. John Whitney Hall. Cambridge: Cambridge University Press, 1991.

Tsuruta, Kei. "The Establishment and Characteristic of the 'Tsushima Gate.'" *Acta Asiatica* 6.7 (1994): 30–48.

Twitchett, Denis and Howard Wechsler. "Kao-tsung (Reign 649–83) and the Empress Wu: The inheritor and the usurper." In *The Cambridge History of China*, vol. III, part 1: *Sui and T'ang China, 589–906*, pp. 242–89. Ed. Denis Twitchett and John K. Fairbank. Cambridge: Cambridge University Press, 1979.

Twitchett, Denis and Tilemann Grimm. "The Cheng-t'ung, Ching-t'ai, and T'ien-shun Reigns, 1436–1464." In *The Cambridge History of China*, vol. VII, part 1: *The Ming Dynasty, 1368–1644*, pp. 305–42. Ed. Frederick W. Mote and Denis Twitchett. Cambridge: Cambridge University Press, 1988.

Twitchett, Denis and Klaus-Peter Tietze. "The Liao." In *The Cambridge History of China*, vol. VI: *Alien Regimes and Border States, 907–1368*, pp. 43–153. Ed. Herbert Franke and Denis Twitchett. Cambridge: Cambridge University Press, 1994.

Udagawa Takehisa 宇田川武久. *Teppō no denrai: Heiki ga kataru kinsei no tanjō* 鐵砲の傳來: 兵器が說る近世の誕生 (The importation of guns: what weapons tell about the birth of the early modern). Tokyo: Chūō kōron, 1990.

Uezato Takashi 上里隆史. "Ko Ryūkyū, Naha no [Wajin] kyoryūchi to kan Shinakai sekai" 古琉球, 那霸の[倭人]居留地と環シナ海世界 (The Japanese settlement in Naha, old Ryukyu and the world of the China Sea). *Shigaku zasshi* 114.7 (2005): 1–33.

"The Formation of the Port City of Naha in Ryukyu and the World of Maritime Asia: From the Perspective of a Japanese Network." *Acta Asiatica* 95 (2008): 57–77.

Unno, Kazutaka. "Cartography in Japan." In *The History of Cartography*, vol. II, book 2: *Cartography in the Traditional East and Southeast Asian Societies*, pp. 346–477. Ed. J. B. Harley and David Woodward. Chicago: University of Chicago Press, 1994.

van Goethem, Ellen. *Nagaoka: Japan's Forgotten Capital*. Leiden: E. J. Brill, 2008.

Varley, Paul. *Imperial Restoration in Medieval Japan*. New York: Columbia University Press, 1971.

Von Falkenhausen, Lothar. "The Regionalist Paradigm in Chinese Archaeology." In *Nationalism, Politics and the Practice of Archaeology*, pp. 198–217. Ed. Philip L. Kohl and Clare Fawcett. Cambridge, MA: Cambridge University Press, 1995.

Von Glahn, Richard. *Fountain of Fortune: Money and Monetary Policy in China, Fourteenth to Seventeenth Centuries*. Berkeley: University of California Press, 1996.

"Myth and Reality of China's Seventeenth-Century Monetary Crisis." *Journal of Economic History* 56.2 (1996): 429–54.

"Money Use in China and Changing Patterns of Global Trade in Monetary Metals, 1500–1800." In *Global Connections and Monetary History 1400–1800*, pp. 187–205. Ed. Dennis O. Flynn, Arturo Giráldez, and Richard von Glahn. Burlington: Ashgate, 2003.

von Verschuer, Charlotte. Trans. Kristen Lee Hunter. *Across the Perilous Sea: Japanese Trade with China and Korea from the Seventh to the Sixteenth Centuries*. Ithaca: East Asia Center, Cornell University, 2006.

"Ashikaga Yoshimitsu's Foreign Policy, 1398 to 1408 AD: A Translation from *Zenrin Kokuhōki*, the Cambridge Manuscript." *Monumenta Nipponica* 62.3 (2007): 261–97.

Wada Masahiro 和田正. "Ri Seiryō kenryoku ni okeru zaiseiteki kiban" 李成梁權力における財政的基盤 (The fiscal foundation of Li Chengliang's authority), Parts 1–2. *Seinan gakuin daigaku bunri ronshū* 25.1 (1984): 99–142, 25.2 (1985): 93–140.

Wakabayashi, Bob Tadashi. "Rival States on a Loose Rein: The Neglected Tradition of Appeasement in Late Tokugawa Japan." In *The Ambivalence of Nationalism: Modern Japan Between East and West*, pp. 11–37. Ed. James W. White, Michio Umegaki, and Thomas R. H. Havens. Lanham: University Press of America, 1990.

"In Name Only: Imperial Sovereignty in Early Modern Japan." *Journal of Japanese Studies* 17.1 (1991): 25–57.

Wakabayashi, Haruko. "The Mongol Invasions and the Making of the Iconography of Foreign Enemies: the Case of *Shikaumi jinja engi*." In *Tools of Culture: Japan's Cultural, Intellectual, Medical, and Technological Contacts in East Asia, 1000–1500s*, pp. 105–33. Ed. Andrew Edmund Goble, Kenneth R. Robinson, and Haruko Wakabayashi. Ann Arbor: Association for Asian Studies, 2009.

Wakeman, Frederic Jr. "The Shun Interregnum of 1644." In *From Ming to Ch'ing: Conquest, Region and Continuity in Seventeenth-Century China*, pp. 39–87. Ed. Jonathan D. Spence and John E. Wills, Jr. New Haven: Yale University Press, 1979.

The Great Enterprise: The Manchu Reconstruction of Imperial Order in Seventeenth-Century China. 2 vols. Berkeley: University of California Press, 1985.

Wakita, Haruko. "Marriage and Property in Premodern Japan from the Perspective of Women's History." *Journal of Japanese Studies* 10.1 (1984): 73–99.

Wakita, Osamu. "The Emergence of the State in Sixteenth-Century Japan: From Oda to Tokugawa." *Journal of Japanese Studies* 8.2 (1982): 343–67.

Waley-Cohen, Joanna. "China and Western Technology in the Late Eighteenth Century." *American Historical Review* 98.5 (1993): 1525–44.

Walker, Brett L. "Reappraising the *Sakoku* Paradigm: The Ezo Trade and the Extension of Tokugawa Political Space into Hokkaidō." *Journal of Asian History* 30.2 (1996): 169–92.

The Conquest of Ainu Lands: Ecology and Culture in Japanese Expansion, 1590–1800. Berkeley: University of California Press, 2001.

Walraven, Boudewijn. "Reader's Etiquette, and Other Aspects of Book Culture in Chosŏn Korea." In *Books in Numbers: Conference Papers*, pp. 237–65. Ed. Wilt L. Idema. Cambridge, MA: Harvard-Yenching Library, 2007.

Wang, Baoping. "Chinese Scholars in Japan in the Late Qing: How They Lived and Whom They Knew." In *Sagacious Monks and Bloodthirsty Warriors: Chinese Views of Japan in the Ming–Qing Period*, pp. 185–99. Ed. Joshua A. Fogel. Norwalk: EastBridge, 2002,

Wang, Chengguo 王成國. "Bohai shi yanjiu de yizuo fengpei: Ping Wang Chengli xiansheng yizhu Zhongguo dongbei de Bohaiguo yu DongbeiYa" 渤海史研究的一座豐碑－　評王承禮先生遺著[中國東北的渤海國與東北亞 (A monument of Bohai historical studies: reviewing Prof. Wang Chengli's posthumous *China's northeast Bohai kingdom and Northeast Asia*). *Beifang wenwu* 1 (2002): 91–93.

Wang Chongshi 王崇時. "Zhongguo yi Tumen jiang wei dongduan bianjie de lishi wenti – bo Ridi xuyizhizao de 'Jiandao' miushuo" 中國以圖們江為東段邊界的歷史問題－駁日帝蓄意製造 的'間島' 謬說 (The historical issue of China's taking the Tumen River as its easternmost boundary – to refute the mistaken prefabricated notions of the Japanese imperialists on 'Jiandao'). In *Zhong Chao guanxi shi yanjiu lunwenji* 中朝關係史研究論文集 (Collected writings on the history of Sino-Korean relations), pp. 216–33. Ed. Diao Shuren 刁書仁 and Yi Xingguo 衣興國. Changchun: Jilin wenshi chubanshe, 1995.

Wang Dongfang 王冬芳. "Guanyu Mingdai Zhong Chao bianjie xingcheng de yanjiu" 關于 明代 中朝 邊界形成 的 研究 (Research on the formation of a Sino-Korean border in the Ming period). *Zhongguo bianjiang shidi yanjiu* 3 (1997): 54–62.

Wang Dongfang 王冬芳 and Ji Mingming 季明明. *Nüzhen – Manzu jianguo yanjiu* 女真 － 滿族建國研究 (Jurchen – the Manchu establishment of a state). Beijing: Xueyuan chubanshe, 2009.

Wang, Gungwu. "The Chinese Urge to Civilize: Reflections on Change." *Journal of Asian History* 18.1 (1984): 1–34.

Wang, Q. Edward. "History, Space, and Ethnicity: The Chinese Worldview." *Journal of World History* 10.2 (1999): 285–305.

Inventing China Through History: The May Fourth Approach to Historiography. Albany: State University of New York Press, 2001.

"Taiwan's Search for National History: A Trend in Historiography." *East Asian History* 24 (2002): 93–116.

Wang Qingcheng 王慶成. "Zhongguo jindaishi he bianjiang yanjiu" 中國近代史和邊疆研究 (Research on China's modern history and borderlands). *Zhongguo bianjiang shidi yanjiu* 2 (1992): 7–8.

Wang, Xiangyun. "Tibetan Buddhism at the Court of Qing: The Life and Work of lCang-skya Rol-pa'i-rdo-rje (1717–86)." PhD thesis, Harvard University, 1995.

"The Qing Court's Tibet Connection: Lcang skya Rol pa'i rdo rje and the Qianlong Emperor." *Harvard Journal of Asiatic Studies* 60.1 (2000): 125–63.

Wang, Yao. "The Cult of Mahakala and a Temple in Beijing." *Journal of Chinese Religions* 22 (1994): 117–26.

Wang, Yong. Trans. Laura E. Hess. "Realistic and Fantastic Images of 'Dwarf Pirates': The Evolution of Ming Dynasty Perceptions of the Japanese." In *Sagacious Monks and Bloodthirsty Warriors: Chinese Views of Japan in the Ming–Qing Period*, pp. 17–41. Ed. Joshua A. Fogel. Norwalk, CT: EastBridge, 2002.

Wang Zhaolan 王兆蘭. "Shiwu shiji sanshi niandai Chaoxian liangci ruqin Jianzhou" 十五 世紀三十年代朝鮮兩次入侵建州 (The two Chosŏn invasions of Jianzhou in the 1430s). In *Zhong Chao guanxi shi yanjiu lunwenji* 中朝關係史研究論文集 (Collected writings on the history of Sino-Korean relations), pp. 159–215. Ed. Diao Shuren 刁書仁 and Yi Xingguo 衣興國. Changchun: Jilin wenshi chubanshe, 1996.

Wang Zhen 王臻. *Chaoxian qianqi yu Ming Jianzhou Nüzhen guanxi yanjiu* 朝鮮前期與明建州女真關係研究 (Relations in early Chosŏn with the Ming Jianzhou Jurchen). Beijing: Zhongguo wenshi chubanshe, 2005.

Wang, Zheng. *Never Forget National Humiliation: Historical Memory in Chinese Politics and Foreign Relations.* New York: Columbia University Press, 2012.

Wang, Zhenping. "Speaking with a Forked Tongue: Diplomatic Correspondence Between China and Japan, 238–608 AD. " *Journal of the American Oriental Society* 114 (1994): 23–32.

Ambassadors from the Islands of Immortals: China–Japan Relations in the Han–Tang Period. Honolulu: University of Hawai'i Press, 2005.

Tang China in Multi-polar Asia: A History of Diplomacy and War. Honolulu: University of Hawai'i Press, 2013.

Watson, James L. "Introduction." In *Kinship Organization in Late Imperial China, 1000–1940*, pp. 1–15. Ed. Patricia Buckley Ebrey and James L. Watson. Berkeley: University of California Press, 1986,

Webb, Hershel. *The Japanese Imperial Institution in the Tokugawa Period.* New York: Columbia University Press, 1968.

Wechsler, Howard J. *Offerings of Jade and Silk: Ritual and Symbol in the Legitimation of the T'ang Dynasty.* New Haven: Yale University Press, 1985.

Wei Qingfeng 韋清風. "Jindai Zhongguo bianjiang yanjiu de dierci gaochao yu guofang zhanlüe" 近代中國邊疆研究的第二次高潮與國防戰略 (The second high tide and national defense strategy in modern China's study of borderlands). *Zhongguo bianjiang shidi yanjiu* 1996.3: 101–12.

Wilkinson, Endymion. *Chinese History: A New Manual.* Cambridge, MA: Harvard University Asia Center, 2012.

Wills, John E. Jr. "Maritime China from Wang Chih to Shih Lang: Themes in Peripheral History." In *From Ming to Ch'ing: Conquest, Region, and Continuity in Seventeenth-Century China,* pp. 201–38. Ed. Jonathan D. Spence and John E. Wills, Jr. New Haven: Yale University Press, 1979.

Woodside, Alexander. "The Centre and the Borderlands in Chinese Political Theory." In *The Chinese State at the Borders,* pp. 11–28. Ed. Diana Lary. Vancouver: University of British Columbia Press, 2007.

Woodworth, C. K. Review Article. "Ocean and Steppe: Early Modern World Empires." *Journal of Early Modern History* 11.6 (2007): 501–18.

Wright, Arthur F. *Buddhism in Chinese History.* Stanford: Stanford University Press, 1957.

"The Sui Dynasty (581–617)." In *The Cambridge History of China,* vol. III, Part 1: *Sui and T'ang China, 589–906,* pp. 75–77. Ed. Denis Twitchett. Cambridge: Cambridge University Press, 1979.

Wright, David C. "Parity, Pedigree, and Peace: Routine Sung Diplomatic Missives to the Liao." *Journal of Sung-Yuan Studies* 26 (1996): 55–85.

"The Northern Frontier." In *A Military History of China,* pp. 57–79. Ed. David A. Graff and Robin Higham. Lexington: University Press of Kentucky, 2012.

Wu Ling 吳玲 and Li Xiaokang 李曉航. "Cong Shandan maoyi de bianqian kan Qingdai dui dongbei diqu tongzhi de ruohua" 從山丹貿易的變遷看清代對東北地區統治的弱化 (The weakening of Qing control over the northeast localities from the perspective of the changes in the Shandan trade). *Beifang wenwu* 2007 #1: 91–98.

Wu, Silas H. L. *Passage to Power: K'ang-hsi and His Heir Apparent, 1661–1722.* Cambridge, MA: Harvard University Press, 1979.

Wylie, Turrell. "Reincarnation: A Political Innovation in Tibetan Buddhism." In *Proceedings of the Csoma de Kőrős Memorial Symposium Held at Mátrafüred, Hungary, September 1976,* pp. 579–86. Ed. Louis Ligeti. Budapest: Akádemiao Kiadó, 1978.

"Lama Tribute in the Ming Dynasty." In *Tibetan Studies in Honour of Hugh Richardson: Proceedings of the International Seminar on Tibetan Studies, Oxford, 1979,* pp. 335–40. Ed. Michael Aris and Aung San Suu Kyi. Warminster: Aris and Phillips, 1980.

Xie Zhaohua 謝肇華. "Pingzhe Chaoxian dui Jianzhouwei Nǚzhen de diyici yongbing" 評折朝鮮對建州衛女真的第一次用兵 (The first use of troops by Chosŏn against the Jianzhou Jurchen guard). *Zhongyang minzu daxue xuebao* 4 (2000): 54–58.

Xu Deyuan 徐德源. "Gaogoulizu yuyan weishilu" 高句麗族語言微識錄 (A primary study of the Gaogouli people's language). *Zhongguo bianjiang shidi yanjiu* 15.1 (2005): 78–94.

Xu Jianying 許建英. "'Zhongguo shijie zhixu' guan zhi yingxiang ji qi yu Zhongguo gudai bianjiang yanjiu – Fei Zhengqing [Zhongguo shijie zhixu: Zhongguo chuantong de duiwai guanxi] du hou" 中國世界秩序 觀之影響及其與中國古代邊疆研究–費正清[中國世界秩序:中國傳統的對外關係] 讀後 (The influence of the view of China's world order and research on China's traditional ancient frontiers: after reading J. K. Fairbank's *The Chinese World Order: Traditional China's Foreign Relations*). *Zhongguo bianjiang shidi yanjiu* 16.1 (2006): 35–46.

Xu, Jieshun. "Understanding the Snowball Theory of the Han Nationality." In *Critical Han Studies: The History, Representation, and Identity of China's Majority*, pp. 113–27. Ed. Thomas S. Mullaney, James Leibold, Stéphane Gros, and Eric Vanden Bussche. Berkeley: University of California Press, 2012.

Yamashita, Samuel Hideo. "Reading the New Tokugawa Intellectual Histories." *Journal of Japanese Studies* 22.1 (1996): 1–48.

Yamauchi Kōichi 山内弘一. *Chōsen kara mita Ka-I shisō* 朝鮮からみた華夷思想 (Civilized-barbarian thought as seen from Korea). Tokyo: Yamakawa shuppansha, 2003.

"Chōsen wo motte Tenka ni ō tarashimu – Gakushūin daigaku zō [Kishi hasshūshi] ni miru zaiya noron chishikijin no yume" 朝鮮を以て天下に王たらしむ－學習院大學臧[箕子八條志]にみる在野老倫知識人の夢 (Chosǒn as the legitimate successor to rule *Tianxia*: the dream of an out-of-office Noron intellectual as seen in *Kija p'aljoji* preserved in Gakushūin University). *Tōyōgakuhō* 84.3 (2002): 1–31.

Yan Chongnian 閻崇年. *Nuerhachi zhuan* 奴兒哈赤傳 (Biography of Nurhaci). Beijing: Beijing chubanshe, 1983.

Tianming han 天命汗 (Biography of Nurhaci). Changchun: Jilin wenshi chubanshe, 1993.

Yang Jianxin 楊建新. "'Zhongguo' yici he Zhongguo jiangyu xingcheng zai tantao" 中國一詞和中國疆域形成再探讨 (A restudy of the word "China" and the formation of China's territory). *Zhongguo bianjiang shidi yanjiu* 16.2 (2006):1–6.

Yang, Lien-sheng. "The Concept of 'Pao' as a Basis for Social Relations in China." In *Chinese Thought and Institutions*, pp. 291–309. Ed. John K. Fairbank. Chicago: University of Chicago Press, 1957.

Yang, Shao-yun. "Becoming *Zhongguo*, Becoming Han: Tracing and Reconceptualizing Ethnicity in Ancient North China, 6770 BC – AD 581." MA thesis, National University of Singapore, 2007.

Yang Zhaoquan 楊昭全 and Sun Yumei 孫玉梅. *Zhong Chao bianjie shi* 中朝邊界史 (History of the Sino-Korean border). Changchun: Jilin wenshi chubanshe, 1993.

Yao, Taochung. "Buddhism and Taoism under the Chin." In *China Under Jurchen Rule*, pp. 145–80. Ed. Hoyt Cleveland Tillman and Stephen H. West. Albany: State University of New York Press, 1995.

Yee, Cordell D. K. "Chinese Maps in Political Culture." In *The History of Cartography*, vol. II, book 2: *Cartography in the Traditional East and Southeast Asian Societies*, pp. 71–95. Ed. J. B. Hartley and David Woodward. Chicago: University of Chicago Press, 1994.

"Traditional Chinese Cartography and the Myth of Westernization." In *The History of Cartography*, vol. II, book 2: *Cartography in the Traditional East and Southeast Asian Societies*, pp. 170–202. Ed. J. B. Hartley and David Woodward. Chicago: University of Chicago Press, 1994.

Yeo, Ho-Kyu [Yŏ Hogyu]. "Arranging a Special Edition in Honor of the History of Goguryeo." *The Review of Korean Studies* 7.4 (2004): 3–10.

Yi Chaech'ŏl. *Chosŏn hugi Pibyŏnsa yŏn'gu* 朝鮮後期 備邊司研究 (Research on the Border Defence Council in Late Chosŏn). Seoul: Chimmundang, 2001.

Yi Hŭijin 李熙真. "Koguryŏ ŭi tae Chung insingnon e taehan pip'anjŏk koch'al" 고구려의對中認識論에 대한 비판적 고찰 (A critical examination of the Chinese discourse on Koguryŏ). *Yŏksa hakpo* 190 (2006): 277–300.

Yi Huili 易惠莉. "Qing Kangxi chao houqi zhengzhi yu Zhong Ri Changqi maoyi" 清康熙朝後期政治與中日長崎貿易 (On the politics of the late Kangxi reign and Sino-Japanese Nagasaki trade). *Shehui kexue* 2004 #1: 96–105.

Yi Hwa 李華. "Ch'ŏng ŭi Chungwŏn ipkwan chŏnhu Chosŏn'in ŭi wŏlkyŏng munje rŭl tullŏssan Cho-Ch'ŏng kyosŏp" 清의 中原入關전후 조선인 의 越境 문제를 둘러싼 朝清,교섭 (Chosŏn–Qing negotiations concerning the problem of Koreans crossing the border illegally around the time of the Qing entry into the Central Plain [1644]), *Han'guk hakpo* 112 (2003): 103–37.

Yi Hyŏnjin 李賢珍. "Chosŏn chŏngi Sorŭng pokwiron ŭi ch'u'i wa kŭ ŭimi" (Debates about the restoration of the Sorŭng in early Chosŏn and their significance). *Chosŏn sidaesa hakpo* 23 (2002): 49–83.

Yi Pŏmchik 李範稷. "Kukjo orye'ŭi ŭi songnip e taehan il koch'al" (An investigation of the establishment of the *Kukjo orye'ŭi*). *Yŏksa hakpo* 122 (1989): 1–27.

"Chosŏn hugi wangsil kujo yŏn'gu – Injodae rŭl chungsim ŭro" 朝鮮後期 王室 構造 研究 – 仁祖代 를 中心 으 로 (Research on the structure of the royal house in late Chosŏn – focusing on the Injo reign). *Kuksagwan nonch'ong* 80 (1998): 279–316.

Yi Sŏnggyu. "Chunghwa cheguk ŭi p'aengch'ang kwa ch'ukso: kŭ i'nyŏm kwa silje" (The expansion and contraction of the Chinese empire: its ideal and reality). *Yŏksa hakpo* 186 (2005): 87–133.

Yi Sung'ŭn. "Koguryŏ yŏksa, kwayŏn nugu ŭi yŏksa in ga?" (Truly, whose history is Koguryŏ history?), *Yŏksa pip'yŏng* 70 (2005): 197–220.

Yi Uk. "Chosŏn chŏngi Yugyo kukka ŭi sŏngnip kwa kukka chesa ŭi pyŏnhwa" (The establishment of a Confucian state in early Chosŏn and changes in the state sacrificial rites). *Han'guksa yŏn'gu* 118 (2002): 161–93.

Yi Wŏnjae 李院宰 and Kim Songhŭi 錦松姬. "Chosŏn ch'ogi ŭi Yugyojŏk kukka ŭirye e taehan yŏn'gu – Orye ŭi ŭiryegwan ŭl chungsim ŭro-" 조선초기의儒教 的國家儀禮에대한연구 – 五禮의儀禮官을중심으로 – (Research on Confucian state rites in early Chosŏn, focusing on the ritual officials of the "Five Rites"). *Han'guk sasang sahak* 10 (1998): 31–63.

Yi Wŏntaek 李元澤. "Sukchong ch'o ŭlmyo pokje nonjaeng ŭi sasangsajŏk ham'ŭi" 숙종 초 乙卯服制 논쟁의 사상사적 함의 (The intellectual historical content of the debates in the early Sukchong reign on the ŭlmyo dress code). *Han'guk sasang sahak* 14 (2000): 25–52.

Yi Yŏngch'un 李迎春. "Chosŏn hugi ŭi sajŏn ŭi chaepyŏn kwa kukka chesa" 朝鮮 後期 의祀典의再編과 國家祭祀 (The revision of the ritual code and state sacrifices in late Chosŏn). *Han'guksa yŏn'gu* 118 (2002): 195–219.

Chosŏn hugi wangwi kyesŭng yŏn'gu 朝鮮後期王位繼承研究 (Royal succession in the Late Chosŏn). Seoul: Chimmundang, 1998.

Yo Hogyu 余昊奎. "Chungguk ŭi tongbuk kongjŏng kwa Koguryŏsa insik ch'egye ŭi pyŏnhwa" 중국의 東北工程과 高句麗史인식체계의 변화 (China's northeast project and the changes in organized knowledge of Koguryŏ history). *Han'guksa yŏn'gu* 126 (2004): 277–315.

Yŏksa wa hyŏnsil (Quarterly review of Korean history) 55 (2005). "Kihoek: Han Chung yŏksa insik ŭi chŏpchŏm Koguryŏsa rŭl ŏttŏke pol kŏt'in ka" (Special section: Interface between Korean and Chinese understandings of history – how to understand the history of Koguryŏ).

Yonemoto, Marcia. "Maps and Metaphors of the 'Small Eastern Sea' of Tokugawa Japan (1603–1868)." *The Geographical Review* 89.2 (1999): 169–87.

Mapping Early Modern Japan: Space, Place and Culture in the Tokugawa Period (1603–1868). Berkeley: University of California Press, 2003.

Yonetani Hitoshi 米谷均. "Jūshichi seiki zenki Nitchō kankei ni okeru buki yūshutsu" 一七世紀前期日朝關係における武器輸出 (The exportation of weapons in Japanese-Korean relations in the first half of the seventeenth century). In *Jūshichi seiki no Nihon to Higashi Ajia* 十七世紀の日本と東アジア (Japan and East Asia in the seventeenth century), pp. 39–67. Ed. Fujita Satoru 藤田覚. Tokyo: Yamakawa shuppansha, 2000.

Yoshida, Kazuhiko "Revisioning Religion in Ancient Japan." *Japanese Journal of Religious Studies* 30.1–2 (2003): 1–26.

Yu Fengchun 于逢春. "Gaogouli lishi wenti xueshu yantaohui shuping" 高句麗歷史問題學術研討會述評 (A critique of the colloquium on issues in Koguryŏ history). *Zhongguo bianjiang shidi yanjiu* 14.4 (2004): 141–43.

Yu Kŭnho 柳根鎬. *Chosŏnjo taewi sasang ŭi hŭrŭm – Chunghwajŏk segyegwan ŭi hyŏngsŏng kwa punggoe* (The current of thought concerning the outside – The collapse and formation of the Chinese world view). Seoul: Sŏngsin yŏja taehakgyo ch'ulp'anbu, 2004.

Yun Hunpyo 音薰杓. "Chosŏn chŏngi pukpang kaech'ŏk kwa yŏngt'o ŭiŭi" 朝鮮前期北方開拓과 領土意義 (The opening up of the north in early Chosŏn and territorial consciousness). *Han'guksa yŏn'gu* 129 (2005): 61–93.

Yun Hwit'ak. "Hyŏndae Chungguk ŭi pyŏngyŏng, minjok insik kwa [tongbuk kongjŏng]" (Contemporary China's perception of the border, ethnic peoples, *and the 'Northeast Project'*). *Yŏksa pip'yŏng* 65 (2003): 184–205.

Yun, Peter. "Rethinking the Tribute System: Korean States and Northeast Asia Relations, 600–1600." PhD thesis, University of California at Los Angeles, 1998.

"Foreigners in Korea during the Period of Mongol Interference." In *Embracing the Other: The Interaction of Korean and Foreign Cultures. Proceedings of the First World Congress of Korean Studies*, 2002, III: 1221–28. Sponsored by the Academy of Korean Studies, International Society for Korean Studies, Association for Korean Studies in Europe, and Korean Studies Association of Australasia. Songnam: The Academy of Korean Studies, 2002.

"Koryŏ–Khitan Relations and Khitan Cultural Influence in the Eleventh and Twelfth Centuries." *Journal of Central Eurasian Studies* 3 (2012): 69–83.

Zatsepine, Victor. "The Amur: As River, as Border." In *The Chinese State at the Borders*, pp. 151–61. Ed. Diana Lary. Vancouver: University of British Columbia, 2007.

Zhang Bibo 張碧波. "Gaogouli yanjiu zhong de wuqu" 高句麗 研究中的誤區 (Errors in Gaogouli research). *Zhongguo bianjiang shidi yanjiu* 3 (1999): 34–41.

"Guanyu lishishang minzu guishu yu jiangyu wenti de zai sikao – jian ping [yi shi liang yong] shiguan" 關于 歷史上 民族 歸屬 與 疆域 問題 的 再 思考 – 兼評 [一史兩用] 史觀 (Rethinking the problems of historical nationality, identity and territory – a critique of the historical view of 'one history and double use'). *Zhongguo bianjiang shidi yanjiu* 10.2 (2000): 1–9.

"Yige yanjiu xin jieduan de biaozhi – ping 'Gudai Zhongguo Gaogouli lishi luncong'" 一個研究新階段的標志 – 評[古代中國高句麗 歷史 論叢] (A sign of a new research stage – critiquing *Collected writings on ancient Chinese Gaogouli history*). *Zhongguo bianjiang shidi yanjiu* 12.2 (2002): 96–99.

"Gaogouli lishi kaogu yanjiu de xin chengjiu – ping Wang Jinhou de [Gaogouli gucheng yanjiu] 高句麗歷史考古研究的新成就 – 評王錦厚的[高句麗古城研究] (New results in the study of Gaogouli historical archaeology – a review of Wang Jinhou's [Study of the ancient city of Gaogouli], *Zhongguo bianjiang shidi yanjiu* 13.4 (2003): 89–92.

Zhang Cunwu 張存武. "Qingdai Zhong-Han bianwu wenti tanyuan" 清代中韓邊務問題探源 (An inquiry into the causes of the Sino-Korean border issues during the Qing dynasty). *Zhongyang yanjiuyuan Jindai shi yanjiu suo jikan* 2 (1971): 463–503.

"Chaoxian dui Qing waijiao mimifei zhi yanjiu" 朝鮮對清外交秘密費之研究 (A study of the secret expenditures by Chosŏn in its diplomatic relations with Qing). *Zhongyang yanjiuyuan Jindai shi yanjiu suo jikan* 5 (1976): 409–46.

Zhang Deyu 張德玉. *Manzu fayuandi lishi yanjiu* 滿族發源地歷史研究 (Historical research on the Manchu homeland). Shenyang: Liaoning minzu chubanshe, 2001.

Zhang Shiming 張世明. "Qingdai zongfan guanxi de lishi faxue duowei xiushi fenxi" 清代宗藩關係的歷史法學多位秀視分析 (Suzerain–vassal state relations in the Qing period). *Qingshi yanjiu* 1 (2004): 21–38.

Zhang Shiming and Gong Shengquan 龔勝泉. "Zhengtong de jiegou yu fatong de chongjian: dui Qingdai bianjiang minzu wenti yanjiu de lixing sikao" 正統的解構與法統的重建: 對清代邊疆民族問題研究的理性思考 (On the concept of orthodox succession and the reconstruction of a legal genealogy: study of issues concerning the Qing border peoples). *Zhongguo bianjiang shidi yanjiu* 11.4 (2001): 32–45.

Zhang Weiguang 張維光. "Mingchao zhengfu zai Hehuang diqu de Zangzhuan Fojiao zhengce shulun" 明朝政府再河湟地區的藏傳佛教政策述論 (The Ming government policy on Tibetan Buddhism in the region where the Yellow River bends). *Qinghai shehui kexue* #2 (1989): 93–96.

Zhang Weiwei 張威威. "Han'guo dui 'Gaogouli shi' wenti pinglun zongshu" 韓國對 '高句麗史' 問題評論綜述 (Summary of the debate in Korea concerning "Gaogouli history"). *Guoji ziliao xinxi* (Beijing) 9 (2004): 27–31.

Zhao, Gang. "Reinventing China: Imperial Qing Ideology and the Rise of Modern Chinese National Identity in the Early Twentieth Century." *Modern China* 32.1 (2006): 3–30.

The Qing Opening to the Ocean: Chinese Maritime Policies, 1684–1757. Honolulu: University of Hawai'i Press, 2013.

Zhao Yongchun 趙永春. "Guanyu Zhongguo lishishang jiangyu wenti de jidian renshi" 關于中國歷史上疆域問題的幾點 認識 (Several viewpoints on the issue of China's historical territory). *Zhongguo bianjiang shidi yanjiu* 12.3 (2002): 1–9.

Zhou Yuanlian 周遠廉. "'Manwen laodang' yu Qingchao kaiguoshi yanjiu" [滿文老當]與清朝開國史研究 (The old Manchu archive and research on the founding of the Qing dynasty). In *Ming Qing dang'an yu lishi yanjiu, Zhongguo diyi lishi dang'anguan liushi zhounian jinian lunwenji* 明清檔案與歷史研究, 中國第一歷史檔案館六十周年紀念論文集 (Historical research in the Ming–Qing archives: collected writings on the sixtieth anniversary of the First Historical Archives), I: 322–41. Ed. Zhongguo diyi lishi dang'anguan. Beijing: Zhonghua shuju, 1988.

Zhu Yafei 朱亞非. "Lun Ming Qing shiqi Shandong bandao yu Chaoxian de jiaowang" 論明清時期山東半島與朝鮮的交往 (On exchanges between the Shandong peninsula and Chosŏn during the Ming and Qing). *Shandong shifan daxue xuebao (Renwen shehui kexue ban)* 49.5 (2004): 81–85.

Zito, Angela R. "Re-Presenting Sacrifice: Cosmology and the Editing of Texts." *Ch'ing-shih wen-t'i* 5.2 (1984): 47–78.

Of Body and Brush: Grand Sacrifice as Text/Performance in Eighteenth-Century China. Chicago: University of Chicago Press, 1997.

Index